THE ROMAN EASTERN FRONTIER
AND THE PERSIAN WARS

THE ROMAN EASTERN FRONTIER AND THE PERSIAN WARS

PART II   AD 363–630

A narrative sourcebook

Edited and compiled by
Geoffrey Greatrex
and Samuel N.C. Lieu

London and New York

First published 2002
by Routledge
2 Park Square, Milton Park, Abingdon, Oxon, OX14 4RN

Simultaneously published in the USA and Canada
by Routledge
270 Madison Ave, New York NY 10016

Routledge is an imprint of the Taylor & Francis Group

Transferred to Digital Printing 2008

© 2002 Geoffrey Greatrex and Samuel N.C. Lieu

Typeset in Garamond by Bookcraft Ltd, Stroud, Gloucestershire

British Library Cataloguing in Publication Data
A catalogue record for this book is available from the British Library

Library of Congress Cataloging in Publication Data
A catalog record has been requested

ISBN10: 0–415–14687–9 (hbk)
ISBN10: 0–415–46530–3 (pbk)

ISBN13: 978–0–415–14687–6 (hbk)
ISBN13: 978–0–415–46530–4 (pbk)

TO MARINA AND JUDITH

CONTENTS

MAPS

PREFACE

This book differs in several respects from its predecessor. Instead of offering merely a series of translated excerpts from ancient authors, we have attempted to fill the gaps between extracts, thus providing a history of the frontier and of Romano–Persian relations from 363 to 630. We have not sought to address broader issues, such as trading relations, or to analyse long-term developments (for instance) in diplomacy between the two powers. Discussion of these matters may be found elsewhere, and we may take the opportunity to refer the interested reader to a thematic sourcebook in German on the whole Sasanian period by E. Winter and B. Dignas (2001). We have consciously departed from the traditional sourcebook system of numbering the extracts in each chapter. Our intention is to encourage those using the sources here assembled to refer to the actual passage in the source itself, rather than simply to Greatrex and Lieu 9.2. We hope that this will lead to greater clarity for both students and researchers, and perhaps to more of an awareness of the actual sources themselves.

We believe that the passages translated here are of great importance to the subject. It does not follow from this that passages excluded from this book are not. Various criteria, such as relevance, the availability of an English translation and the reliability of the source in question, determined whether a given excerpt was included or not. Hence, just as in volume 1 few passages from Ammianus Marcellinus were presented, here the reader will not find much Procopius, Joshua the Stylite or Sebeos, because translations of all three are readily obtainable. We have not included any material by George of Pisidia, whose poems in honour of Heraclius are an important source for the early seventh century. Our decision in this was prompted partly by difficulties in how to interpret the information presented by George, and partly by the fact that an English translation of many of his poems is being prepared by Mary Whitby. Nonetheless we have tried to give references to all relevant sources, even when they are not quoted. By contrast, there are substantial excerpts from Zachariah of Mytilene and other lesser-known Syriac sources. Fairly long sections of Theophanes and the *Chronicon Paschale* have been included, particularly concerning the reign of Heraclius. Although excellent English translations of both are available, we considered them too important to omit.

The spelling of names is always problematic in a work of this nature. We have opted for conventional forms of names commonly referred to, e.g. Khusro, Shahrvaraz,

Heraclius, Bahram and the Tur Abdin. In the case of the name Khusro, used by both Armenian and Persian rulers, we have used the Armenian form Khosrov for Armenian rulers of this name. We thus refer to Arsaces rather than Arshak, but keep to the Armenian form of Musheł and others who do not feature in Latin or Greek sources. In less obvious cases we have tended simply to transliterate the name in question, occasionally correcting it where possible (e.g. rendering the Greek name Nakhoragan as the Persian title *nakhveragan*). We have avoided diacritics on the whole, and have omitted the Syriac letter *ain* in cases where a name is commonly used, e.g. Sabrisho for Sabrisho', Abdin for 'Abdin. In Chapter 16, upon the recommendation of Irfan Shahîd, we have tended to keep to the transliteration of Arabic place names adopted by *IGLS*. Anachronistic references to Greeks and Parthians have been retained; the former refers, of course to the Romans, the latter to the Persians. We have referred on occasion to 'volume 1', by which we mean Dodgeon and Lieu 1991. We have also tended to refer to the 'Transcaucasus' rather than 'Caucasia', although the latter term is probably now more common for the region south of the Caucasus mountains.

In translations, we have consistently referred to the 'king of Persia' and the 'Roman emperor'. In fact, the word used for both rulers is almost invariably the same; it is for the sake of convenience that we have translated them differently, so that references to 'king' and 'emperor' are instantly clear. We have also generally preferred to translate phrases such as 'king of the Romans' as 'Roman emperor' to avoid verbosity. The translations themselves aim to keep as close as possible to the original text, and may therefore appear somewhat inelegant; clarity, we hope, has not been sacrificed. We should point out too that we have considered the eastern frontier as running from the Transcaucasus in the north to Syria in the south. We have not sought to include material from the provinces of Palestine or Arabia on the whole, save when they became the scene of conflict between Romans and Persians.

In Syriac texts, we have translated 'Arbaye as Arabs, but have left Tayyaye as it stands: the latter is the more common term for Arabs, but we thought it best to preserve the distinction. We have distinguished throughout between Jafnids and Ghassanids: as several scholars have recently pointed out, the former were the descendants of Jafna who ruled (part of) the Ghassan tribe.[1] We have latinised the Greek terms *stratēgos* and *stratēlatēs* where it is possible to give the formal Roman office with certainty (e.g. *magister militum per Orientem*); if in doubt, however, we have left the Greek. We have referred consistently to the *catholicoi* of the Persian and Armenian Churches, although aware that these terms are anachronistic to some extent. They are, however, convenient and conventional.[2] We refer throughout to Monophysites and Nestorians for the sake of convenience, despite the unsatisfactory nature of these labels. Our system of bracketing also requires explanation:

( ) usually indicates an insertion by the translator to indicate that a word or phrase, though necessary to the English, is not present in the original text.

< > indicates an insertion by the editor of the text.

[ ] indicates a passage which the editor of the text considers was not present in the

original (and hence should be omitted) or, in the case of inscriptions, words or parts of words no longer surviving, but the restoration of which has been suggested.

The abbreviation AG, used in connection with chronicle entries, refers to a date according to the Seleucid era (starting on 1 October 312 BC). Access to the new edition of Malalas' *Chronicle* has proved difficult for us. We have used it for the passages translated, but elsewhere have had to content ourselves with giving book and chapter reference, together with the pages in the Bonn edition.

Many individuals have been of assistance to us in the preparation of this volume, often producing translations and answering questions at short notice. Among them we should like to thank Sebastian Brock, Richard Burgess, Ian Colvin, Jan van Ginkel, Marina Greatrex, Tim Greenwood, George Hewitt, Robert Hewsen, James Howard-Johnston, Robert Hoyland, Peter O'Brien, Stephen Rapp and Irfan Shahîd. Among them, we are particularly indebted to Jan van Ginkel, Marina Greatrex and Tim Greenwood, who provided us with numerous translations which appear here. Uncredited translations and revisions are by Geoffrey Greatrex. Engelbert Winter was kind enough to send us a draft of his forthcoming sourcebook, written in collaboration with Beate Dignas, on the East Roman frontier (from 224 to 630). We have tried to incorporate some references to this useful work, which offers a thematic approach rather than a narrative such as we have constructed. We are grateful also to the various graduate students who assisted in some of the translations for the project, in particular to Ken Donovan at Cardiff and John Holton at Dalhousie. John Holton was responsible for preparing the brief guide to the sources, which was then revised by the editors. We must also thank Corey and Stacey Owen and Marian Jago for the preparation of the index and Jane Anson for her diligent copy-editing.

It is a pleasure to acknowledge the support for the reseach behind this volume which has come from the Seven Pillars of Wisdom Trust and the Social Sciences and Humanities Research Council of Canada. The Hugh Last and Donald Atkinson Funds of the Society for the Promotion of Roman Studies also generously provided a grant to help cover the cost of preparing the maps. The maps themselves were drawn up by R. Hewsen, and we are grateful to him for the work involved.

There will be a website associated with this work, which will permit additional references and material to be supplied on a continuing basis.

Geoffrey Greatrex and S.N.C. Lieu
April 2001

ACKNOWLEDGEMENTS

The editors of this collection are grateful to the following publishers and authors for permission to republish copyright material:

The journal *Byzantion* for translations which first appeared there in 1999.

The journal *Revue des Études Byzantines* for a translation which appeared in *REB* 46 (1988).

The Calouste Gulbenkian Foundation for an extract from N. Adontz and N. Garsoïan, *Armenia in the Period of Justinian* (Lisbon, 1970).

Princeton University Press for three extracts from C. Pharr, *The Theodosian Code*, copyright © 1952 by Clyde Pharr (new edition 1980 by Roy Pharr).

The State University of New York Press and C.E. Bosworth for two passages from C.E. Bosworth, *The History of al-Tabari. Volume 5. The Sāsānids, the Byzantines, the Lakhmids, and Yemen* (1999).

The journal *Phoenix* for one translation by R.C. Blockley from *Phoenix* 39 (1985).

The University of California Press for a translation from O. Maenchen-Helfen, ed. M. Knight, *The World of the Huns* (1973).

Francis Cairns (Publications) Ltd and R.C. Blockley for translations by R.C. Blockley from Eunapius, Priscus, Malchus and Menander, taken from *The Fragmentary Classicising Historians of the Later Roman Empire*, vol.2 (1983) and *The History of Menander the Guardsman* (1985).

AMS Press for translations by E.W. Brooks and F.J. Hamilton of *The Syriac Chronicle known as that of Zachariah of Mytilene* (1899).

Byzantine and Modern Greek Studies and Frank Trombley for three translations by F.R. Trombley from *BMGS* 21 (1997).

Greek, Roman and Byzantine Studies for one translation by O.J. Schrier from *GRBS* 33 (1992).

Georgetown University Press for one translation by C. Toumanoff from *Studies in Christian Caucasian History* (1963).

Dumbarton Oaks for one translation from *DOP* 23–4 (1969–70) by Averil Cameron and one from *Nikephoros. Short History*, ed. and tr. C. Mango (1990).

The Australian Association of Byzantine studies, Brian Croke, Elizabeth Jeffreys and Roger Scott for translations from Malalas (1986) and Marcellinus *comes* (1995).

Michael and Mary Whitby for ten translations from *The History of Theophylact Simocatta* (Oxford, 1986).

The University of Pennsylvania Press for an extract from Maurice's *Stratēgikon: Handbook of Military Strategy*, translated by George T. Dennis, copyright © 1984 University of Pennsylvania Press, reprinted with permission.

The two extracts from S.P. Scott's translation of The Civil Law are reprinted by permission of Thomas Jefferson University.

The extract from Libanius, *Autobiography and Selected Letters* is reprinted by permission of the publishers and the Trustees of the Loeb Classical Library from Libanius: vol.479, translated by A.F. Norman, Cambridge, Mass.: Harvard University Press, 1992. The Loeb Classical Library ® is a registered trademark of the President and Fellows of Harvard College.

The extracts from Procopius are reprinted by permission of the publishers and the Trustees of the Loeb Classical Library from Procopius: vols. 048, 173, 290, 353, translated by H.B. Dewing, Cambridge, Mass.: Harvard University Press, 1914, 1928, 1935, 1940. The Loeb Classical Library ® is a registered trademark of the President and Fellows of Harvard College.

The extracts from Theophanes are © Cyril Mango and Roger Scott 1997. Reprinted from *The Chronicle of Theophanes Confessor: Byzantine and Near Eastern History AD 284–813*, translated with an Introduction and Commentary by Cyril Mango and Roger Scott, with the assistance of Geoffrey Greatrex (1997), by permission of Oxford University Press.

The extract from *Novel 28* is © David Braund 1994. Reprinted from *Georgia in Antiquity: A History of Colchis and Transcaucasian Iberia 550 BC–AD 562* by David Braund (1994) by permission of Oxford University Press.

Some entries in the glossary are based on the entries to be found in *The Chronicle of Theophanes Confessor: Byzantine and Near Eastern History AD 284–813*, translated with an Introduction and Commentary by Cyril Mango and Roger Scott, with the assistance of Geoffrey Greatrex (1997) and in G. Greatrex, *Rome and Persia at War, AD 502–532* (1998). We are grateful to both Oxford University Press and to Francis Cairns (Publications) Ltd for permission to use this material.

ABBREVIATIONS

Journal abbreviations not noted here follow the system used by *ODB*.

AAASH	*Acta Antiqua Academiae Scientiarum Hungaricae*
AASS	*Acta Sanctorum* (Paris 1863–1940)
AAES	*Publications of an American Archaeological Expedition to Syria in 1899–1900* (New York 1903–30)
AnTard	*Antiquité Tardive*
BICS	*Bulletin of the Institute of Classical Studies*
CHI	*The Cambridge History of Iran*, vol. 3, ed. E. Yarshater (Cambridge 1983)
CIL	*Corpus Inscriptionum Latinarum* (Berlin 1863–)
DRBE	*The Defence of the Roman and Byzantine East*, ed. P. Freeman and D. Kennedy, BAR International Series 297 (Oxford 1986)
EFRE	*The Eastern Frontier of the Roman Empire*, ed. D.H. French and C.S. Lightfoot, BAR International Series 553 (Oxford 1989)
EIr	*Encyclopaedia Iranica*, ed. E. Yarshater (London 1985–)
FCH	*The Fragmentary Classicising Historians of the Later Roman Empire*, 2 vols, R.C. Blockley (Liverpool 1981–3)
FHG	*Fragmenta Historicorum Graecorum*, ed. C. Müller, vols 4–5 (Paris 1851–70)
IGLS	*Inscriptions grecques et latines de la Syrie*, edd. L. Jalabert, P. Mouterde *et al.* (Paris 1929–)
LA	*Late Antiquity. A Guide to the Postclassical World*, ed. G.W. Bowersock, P. Brown and Oleg Grabar (Cambridge, Mass., 1999)
LRE	A.H.M. Jones *The Later Roman Empire, 284–602*, 3 vols (Oxford)
MGHAA	*Monumenta Germaniae Historica, Auctores Antiquissimi* (Berlin 1877–1919)
OCD[3]	*The Oxford Classical Dictionary*, third edition, edd. S. Hornblower and A. Spawforth (Oxford 1996)
ODB	*The Oxford Dictionary of Byzantium*, ed. A. Kazhdan, 3 vols (Oxford 1991)
PG	*Patrologia Graeca* (Paris 1857–)
PL	*Patrologia Latina* (Paris 1884–)

PLRE   *Prosopography of the Later Roman Empire*, ed. J. Martindale *et al.*, 3 vols
            (Cambridge 1971–92)
PO   *Patrologia Orientalis* (Paris 1903–)
PUAES   *Publications of the Princeton University Archaeological Expedition to Syria
            in 1904–5 and 1909* (Leiden 1907–49)
RBNE   *The Roman and Byzantine Near East*, ed. J.H. Humphrey, 2 vols
            (Portsmouth, RI, 1995–9)
SRA   *The Byzantine and Early Islamic Near East. States, Resources, Armies,*
            Studies in Late Antiquity and Early Islam, vol. 3, ed. A. Cameron
            (Princeton 1995)

EASTERN ROMAN EMPERORS (363–630)

Julian (361–3)

Jovian (363–4)

Valens (364–78)

Theodosius I (379–95)

Arcadius (395–408)

Theodosius II (408–50)

Marcian (450–7)

Leo I (457–74)

Leo II (474)

Zeno (474–5)

Basiliscus (475–6)

Zeno again (476–91)

Anastasius I (491–518)

Justin I (518–27)

Justinian I (527–65)

Justin II (565–78)

Tiberius II (578–82)

Maurice (582–602)

Phocas (602–10)

Heraclius (610–41)

PERSIAN KINGS (363–630)

Shapur II (309–79)

Ardashir II (379–83)

Shapur III (383–8)

Bahram IV (388–99)

Yazdgerd I (399–420)

Bahram V (420–38)

Yazdgerd II (438–57)

Hormizd III (457–9)

Peroz (459–84)

Balash (484–8)

Kavadh (488–96)

Zamasp (496–8)

Kavadh again (498–531)

Khusro I (531–79)

Hormizd IV (579–90)

Khusro II (590–628)

Kavadh II (628)

Ardashir III (628–30)

Khusro III (630)

Boran (630–1)

GLOSSARY

azats   An Armenian term literally meaning 'free', i.e. the nobility, and thus 'cavalry', supplied in the main by the nobles. Garsoïan 1989: 512–13.

a secretis   A high-ranking imperial secretary. *ODB* 204.

catholicos   The term in Greek for the head of the Persian, Armenian or other Transcaucasian churches. *ODB* 1116.

centenarion, pl. *centenaria*   A unit of weight (100 Roman lbs), often applied to gold coins. *ODB* 1121.

comes, pl. *comites*   A count, a term given to various imperial officials. *LRE* 104–5, *ODB* 484–5.

comes domesticorum   The official in charge of the corps of officer cadets, the *domestici et protectores. LRE* 372

comes excubitorum   The official in charge of the excubitors (on whom see below).

comes foederatorum   The official in charge of the 'federate' (allied) forces. *LRE* 665.

comes (sacrarum) largitionum   The count of the Sacred Largess, a high-ranking official in charge of finances. *LRE* 427–38, *ODB* 486.

comes Orientis   The count of the East. *LRE* 373–4.

comes rei militaris   A military count. *LRE* 105.

comitatenses   The Roman field army, more mobile than the *limitanei* (on whom see below). *LRE* 608–10, *ODB* 487.

dux, pl. *duces*   a duke or military commander attached to a particular province. *LRE* 609–10, *ODB* 659.

erist'avi, pl. *erist'avebi* (older *erist'avni*)   In feudal times in Georgia (Iberia) it signified the ruler/governor of a regional province or community. Also used to signify 'military leader, general' (equivalent to the Persian *sparapet*).

excubitor   A member of an elite corps of 300 Roman soldiers. *LRE* 658–9.

foederati, sing. *foederatus*   Technically, soldiers serving in the Roman army by the terms of a treaty (*foedus*), but in fact scarcely different from *comitatenses* by the sixth century. *LRE* 663–4, *ODB* 794.

hazarapet   Commander of a thousand/chancellor. An Armenian office, originally military in nature, but by late antiquity civilian. Garsoïan 1989: 531–2.

kanarang   The Persian military commander in charge of Abharshahr (the northeastern frontier of the Persian empire). Christensen 1944: 107 n.3.

limitanei   The 'frontier forces' of the Roman empire. *LRE* 608–10, *ODB* 1230.

magister militum   Master of soldiery, high-ranking military official. *LRE* 608–10, *ODB* 1266–7.

magister militum per Armeniam   The master of soldiery stationed on the north-eastern frontier. *LRE* 271.

magister militum per Orientem   The master of soldiery stationed on the eastern frontier.

magister militum praesentalis   A master of soldiery stationed in the capital. *LRE* 124–5.

magister officiorum   The master of offices, the head of the central civil administration of the empire. *LRE* 368–9, *ODB* 1267.

malkhaz   An Armenian title meaning prince or lord. The exact nature of the office is uncertain. Garsoïan 1989: 542.

mihran   The name of a Persian noble family, often misinterpreted by Roman sources as an office. Christensen 1944: 105 n.3.

marzban   The Persian title of a governor of a province. Christensen 1944: 136–7.

nakharar   The Armenian term for a noble. Garsoïan 1989: 549.

nakhveragan   A Persian title, often mistaken for a name in Greek sources (Nakhoragan), derived from the same root as *nakharar*. Christensen 1944: 21 and 452.

nomisma   pl. *nomismata*   The Greek term for the Latin *solidus* (see below).

numerus   A unit of (Roman) soldiers. *LRE* 659.

phylarch   A commander of auxiliaries (often Arab) allied to the empire. *LRE* 611, *ODB* 1672.

praetorian prefect   An important regional civil functionary. *LRE* 370–2, *ODB* 1710–11.

quaestor (sacri palatii)   High-ranking imperial official concerned with legal matters. *LRE* 387, *ODB* 1765–6.

Royal Gate (or Gate)   The headquarters of the Persian king, wherever he happens to be. See Peeters 1951a: 143 n.2.

scholae (palatinae), sing. *schola*   The corps of guards of the imperial palace. *LRE* 647–8, *ODB* 1851–2.

scriniarius   Member of an imperial department (or *scrinium*). *LRE* 449.

silentiarius   A member of the corps of Roman palace attendants. *LRE* 571–2, *ODB* III.1896

solidus, pl. *solidi*   A Roman unit of currency. There were 72 gold *solidi* to one (Roman) pound of gold. *ODB* 1924.

spahbadh   A Persian term for a general. Christensen 1944: 131.

sparapet   The Armenian term for commander-in-chief (which can refer to the *magister militum*). Garsoïan 1989: 560–1.

stade   A classical unit of measurement of distance. *ODB* 1373.

stratēgos   The traditional Greek word for a general, often a *magister militum. ODB* 1964.

stratēlatēs   Another Greek word for a general, often a *magister militum.*

tagma, pl. *tagmata*   A unit of soldiers (esp. a mobile unit), the Greek equivalent of a *numerus. ODB* 2007.

turmarch   Commander of a *turma* or military detachment, a term which came into use in the eighth century. *ODB* 2100.

NOTES ON THE SOURCES

(Sources which are quoted only once or twice are introduced in the notes.)

Agapius (died after 941)   Also known as Mahbub ibn Qustantin, bishop of Hierapolis in Euphratesia, author of a universal history in Arabic called *The Book of the Title*, from the Creation to his own day; the surviving portion records events down to 776. His work preserves fragments of the Greek Chronicle of Theophilus of Edessa (died 785) and uses earlier Syriac sources.

Agathias (c.532–c.580)   Greek historian, lawyer and poet. A native of Myrina in Asia Minor, he was the author of a continuation of Procopius' history, covering the years 552–8.

Ammianus Marcellinus (c.330–c.395)   Latin historian but of eastern origin. A native of Tyre or Sidon, he saw service on the eastern frontier on the staff of Ursicinus. The surviving portion of his history which covers the years 353–78 is an essential source of eyewitness information on the later Persian wars of Constantius II and the expedition of Julian.

(Anon.) *Life of John the Almsgiver* (*V. Ioh. Eleem.*)   An epitome of earlier biographies of John, the patriarch of Alexandria (610–619/20), by his contemporaries John Moschus and Sophronius.

Antiochus Strategius   A monk in Palestine and author of an eyewitness account of the Persian siege of Jerusalem in 614. The original Greek version of the work is lost, but Georgian and Arabic versions survive.

Augustine (354–430)   Bishop of Hippo Regia in Africa, Latin theologian. Author of the *Confessions* and the *City of God*, among many other works.

Barhebraeus (1225–86)   Western name of Gregory Abu'l-Faraj, a Syriac scholar and Monophysite bishop, who composed many works, including his *Chronicle* or *Chronography*, a universal history based on the *Chronicle* of Michael the Syrian; its secular history covers the period from Adam to the Mongol invasions, while its ecclesiastical history covers the period from Moses' brother Aaron to his own day.

Cedrenus, Georgius (twelfth century)   A Byzantine chronicler whose work, based on earlier chronicles, begins with the Creation and goes down to the year 1057.

Chronicon anonymum ad a.d. 819   A short annotated Syriac chronicle of important events and people from Christ to 819. Its author was a Monophysite, probably a monk from a monastery near Mardin. It was later drawn on extensively by the *Chronicon ad AD 846 pertinens*.

Chronicon anonymum ad a.d. 1234 pertinens   A universal Syriac history composed c.1240 by an anonymous Edessan author. It covers much of the same material as the *Chronicle* of Michael the Syrian while diverging in many details. It also preserves important passages of otherwise lost authors including John of Ephesus and Dionysius of Tel-Mahre.

Chronicle of Arbela   A Syriac work giving biographies of the bishops of Arbela (in Adiabene) up to the sixth century AD. The reliability of its first sections has been called into question.

Chronicle of Edessa (sixth century)   A Syriac chronicle (entitled *Histories of Events in Brief*), consisting of a list of important events and Church figures connected with the city of Edessa, covering the period from the second to the sixth centuries.

Chronicon Paschale (630s)   A Byzantine universal chronicle which covers the period from Adam to 629/30 from a Constantinopolitan perspective. The very last section of the work is lost. The chronicle preserves important information on Heraclius' final campaign against the Persians, based on the emperor's own despatches.

Claudian (c.370–404)   A Latin poet from Egypt, whose panegyrics and epigrams are a major source for the military and political history of the period 395–404.

Codex Justinianus   A predominantly Latin collection of imperial constitutions from the period of Hadrian to Justinian I, forming a part of the *Corpus Juris Civilis*. It was comissioned by Justinian as a categorised and internally consistent replacement of earlier codes including the *Codex Theodosianus*. It was first publicly introduced in 529, with an amended edition established in 534.

Codex Theodosianus   An official collection of imperial constitutions from AD 312 until 438 when the Code was published by Theodosius II.

Constantine VII Porphyrogenitus (905–59)   Emperor of the Macedonian dynasty (945–59), who compiled an encyclopaedic treatise on court ceremony entitled *De ceremoniis aulae byzantinae* (*On the ceremonies of the Byzantine court*).

Corippus (Flavius Cresconius Corippus) (died after 567)   A Latin poet and native of Africa, who celebrated the successes of the Roman general John Troglita in an epic poem, the *Iohannis*, and who later at Constantinople commemorated the accession of Justin II in four hexameter books in c.566.

Cyril of Scythopolis (c.525–59)   A monk and hagiographer who composed a number of biographies of Palestinian monks including Sabas, Abraham, Kyriakos, Theodosius, and Theognius; the biographies incorporate useful historical details.

Pseudo-Dionysius (of Tel-Mahre)   Unknown author of a late eighth-century universal chronicle in Syriac, also known as the Zuqnin chronicle, which records events from biblical times to 775 and incorporates important information from lost sources (including the entire work conventionally ascribed to Joshua the Stylite).

Ełishe (? sixth century)   Author of an Armenian History which describes the unsuccessful revolt of Vardan Mamikonian against Sasanian overlordship in 450/1.

Ephrem Syrus (c.306–73)   Syrian poet and theologian. Born in or near Nisibis, he was compelled to leave his native city because of the treaty of 363 which surrendered it to the Persians. He later settled in Edessa. His *Carmina Nisibena* and *Hymni contra Julianum* both include eyewitness material on the events they describe.

Epic Histories   An anonymous work written in Armenian in the 470s and based on local oral traditions. It relates in epic style the history of the later Arsacid dynasty as well as that of the Mamikonians and that of the house of Gregory the Illuminator.

Epitome de Caesaribus   Title given to an anonymous collection of biographies (in Latin) of emperors from Augustus to Theodosius. The work is sometimes wrongly associated with Aurelius Victor.

Eunapius (c.345–after 414)   Greek sophist, born near Sardis in Lydia, author of a continuation of the history of Dexippus from a pagan viewpoint covering the period AD 270–404.

Eustathius of Epiphania (died c.505)   Historian and author of a chronicle which now survives only in fragments. It probably covered the period from the fall of Troy to the Roman wars against Persia in 502–5, and was used as a source by Malalas and Evagrius.

Eustratius (died after 602)   A hagiographer and priest of Hagia Sophia in Constantinople. He wrote a biography of the Persian saint Golinduch, based on the work of Stephen of Hierapolis, as well as a panegyric of his teacher Eutychius.

Eutropius (late fourth century)   Latin historian who accompanied Julian on his Persian expedition. His epitome of Roman history, published in 369/70, begins with Romulus and finishes with the reign of Jovian.

Evagrius (c.536–c.594)   Greek lawyer and ecclesiastical historian. A native of Epiphania in Syria, he wrote a Church history, incorporating a considerable amount of information on secular matters, covering the period 431–594.

Festus (died 380)   Latin historian. He was *magister memoriae* when he published his brief summary (*Breviarium*) of Roman history in 369/70.

Firdausi (Abu 'l-Kasim) (940/1–1020)   Persian poet and author of the *Shāhnāma*, a vast epic of Persian history from the Creation to Sasanian times, which makes use of lost sources, some of which derive ultimately from the Sasanian royal annals.

George of Pisidia (died 631/4)   Church official at Constantinople and panegyrist of the Emperor Heraclius. Many of his epic poems recount the successes of Heraclius, which are attributed to divine favour. His style is often allusive and is difficult to use for historical purposes.

Gregory of Nazianzus (329/30–c.390)   Theologian and bishop of Constantinople (380–381) and of Nazianzus (382–84); author of numerous homilies and other works.

Gregory of Tours (c.540–593/4)   Bishop of Tours and author of the *Histories* in ten books. The work starts with Creation, but concentrates on the rising power of the Franks from the fifth century down to his own day.

Isaac of Antioch (fifth century)   Syriac writer and author of many poetical works, which are mostly mixed together with those of Isaac of Amida.

Jacob of Edessa (died 708)   Syriac scholar and bishop of Edessa. Author of a *Chronicle*, which continued that of Eusebius, taking it up to 692. Only fragments of this now survive, which can be supplemented by material from later works (derived from Jacob).

Jerome (Eusebius Hieronymus) (c.342–420)   Biblical scholar and theologian. Born near Aquileia, he spent much of his life in Bethlehem. He translated Eusebius' *Chronicle* into Latin and extended it up to 378.

John Chrysostom (c.340–407)   Bishop of Constantinople (398–404) and famous orator. Expelled from Constantinople for his criticism of the Empress Eudoxia, he died in exile at Cucusus in Armenia.

John Diakrinomenos (late fifth century)   Author of an ecclesiastical history from Theodosius I to Zeno, only fragments of which survive.

John of Biclar (died 621)   Bishop of Gerona in Spain. John was brought up in Constantinople, returning to Spain in c.576. His chronicle in Latin covers the period 567–90.

John of Ephesus (c.507–586/8)   Syriac historian and Monophysite leader in Constantinople during the reign of Justinian I, ordained bishop in 558. He wrote the *Lives of the Eastern Saints*, a collection of stories about 58 holy men and women of the Syriac-speaking world of his day, as well as a *Church History* with a Monophysite perspective, of which only about one-third survives, covering the period 571–86.

John of Epiphania (sixth/seventh century)   A relative of the Church historian Evagrius, a lawyer, and the author of a history which continued where Agathias had left off. Only one fragment survives.

John Lydus (the Lydian) (490–c.565)   Scholar, bureaucrat and writer who composed a treatise, *De Magistratibus* (*On the Magistracies*), a history and description of the Roman offices of state.

Jordanes (? died 552)   Former secretary of a Gothic leader. Author of a three-part history in Latin, one section of which, the *Romana*, offers a brief synopsis of Roman history from Romulus to 550/1.

Pseudo-Joshua the Stylite   Edessan priest and monk of unknown date, to whom a sixth-century *Chronicle of the Persian War* (entitled *The History of the Time of Troubles in Edessa, Amida, and all Mesopotamia*) is often attributed. The work is remarkably detailed and informative.

***K'art'lis C'xovreba* (Georgian Chronicles)**   An official collection of some Georgian historical works written between the eighth and fourteenth centuries, commissioned in the early eighteenth century by King Vakhtang VI. It includes a *History of the Kings of Iberia*, a *History of King Vakhtang Gorgasali* (*HVG*) and other works.

Khuzistan Chronicle (also known as the Guidi chronicle)   An anonymous work compiled in the 660s by a Nestorian author, probably in Khuzistan. It is valuable as a source written within the Persian kingdom not long after the events related.

Łazar (Łazar P'arpec'i) (second half of fifth century)   Author of a *History of Armenia*, containing an account of the Armenian revolt against Persia in 451, and of the career of Vahan Mamikonian in the aftermath of the Armenian defeat.

Leontius of Neapolis (seventh century)   Bishop and hagiographer who wrote a *Life* of St John Eleemon (John the Almsgiver), an important source on Egypt in the early seventh century.

Libanius (314–c.393)   Greek sophist and rhetor of Antioch. One of the most influential pagans of the fourth century; his speeches and letters provide a wealth of information on events in the East.

Malalas, Ioannes (c.490–c.575)   Rhetor and official at Antioch, who probably moved to Constantinople in the 540s. He wrote the first Byzantine universal chronicle, covering the period from Adam to AD 565. His work preserves many important notices on Antioch and the province of Syria.

Malchus of Philadelphia (fl. late fifth century)   A sophist at Constantinople who wrote a history called *Byzantiaka*, whose surviving fragments cover the period 473–480.

Marcellinus *Comes* (sixth century)   Latin author who wrote a chronicle at Constantinople which originally covered the period 379–518 (designed as a continuation of that of Jerome) to which he later added a sequel extending up to 534. A second supplement covering the period until 548 (where the manuscript breaks off) was added by a later, unknown author.

Maurice (c.539–602) Byzantine emperor (582–602) to whom is often attributed a work entitled the *Stratēgikon*, a Greek military treatise on cavalry warfare which includes a survey of various foreign peoples.

Menander Protector (Menander the Guardsman) (fl. late sixth century) Constantinopolitan historian and palace guardsman who wrote a history covering the period 558–582, which was designed as a continuation of Agathias, and survives today in seventy fragments.

Michael the Syrian (1126–99) Monophysite patriarch of Antioch and compiler of an important chronicle in Syriac from the Creation to 1194/5. His work makes use of many earlier sources, now lost (cf. *Chr. 1234*, above).

Moses Khorenats'i Name given to the author of a work of great importance on Armenian history, covering the period to 439, but of uncertain date.

Movsēs Daskhurants'i (or Kałankatuats'i) (? tenth century) Identified as the compiler of a tenth-century historical text focused upon successive kings, princes and Church leaders of Caucasian Albania. The work incorporates much earlier material from unidentified sources, in particular on the 620s.

Narratio de rebus Armeniae (c.700) A short Armenian text which survives only in Greek. Composed c.700, it concentrates primarily upon Armenian ecclesiastical history. Unusually for a surviving Armenian text, it is favourable towards the Council of Chalcedon.

Nicephorus I (c.750–828) Patriarch of Constantinople and historian. Author of a *Short History* (the *Historia Syntomos*) describing the events of 602–769 from an anti-Iconoclastic viewpoint.

Oracle of Baalbek An apocalyptic work, one of a series of supposed pronouncements of the Sibylline oracle. This 'oracle' was written in the opening years of the sixth century and provides an overview of earlier events, cast as a prophecy.

Orosius (fl. early fifth century) Spanish priest. In 417 he published, at the invitation of Augustine, a *Historia adversus Paganos* – i.e. an apologetic work designed to show how much better off the empire was since the birth of Christ.

Pacatus (late fourth century) Gallic orator and author of a panegyric of the Emperor Theodosius I which was delivered in the emperor's presence at Rome in summer 389.

Parastaseis Syntomoi Chronikai Anonymous work describing the monuments of Constantinople, possibly dating to the beginning of the eighth century.

Philostorgius (c.368–c.439) Greek ecclesiastical historian. His principal work, a history of the Church from the Arian viewpoint, has come down to us mainly in an epitome by Photius and in the historical sections of the *Artemii Passio*.

Priscus (c.410–c.474) Rhetorician and author of a history of the eastern Roman empire covering the period 434–74, which survives only in fragments.

Procopius (fl. sixth century) Greek historian of the reign of Justinian. A native of Caesarea (Palestine), he was military secretary to Belisarius and eyewitness to many of his campaigns.

Quodvultdeus (died c.453) Bishop of Carthage, correspondent of Augustine and probable author of the *Liber promissionum et praedictorum Dei* (the *Book of the promises and predictions of God*), completed in the mid-fifth century.

Rufinus (of Aquileia, c.345–410)   Latin author and translator who translated and abridged Eusebius' *Church History*, supplemented by two books detailing the period 324–395.

Sebeos (seventh century)   Traditionally identified as the author of an Armenian history which records Near Eastern history in the period 590–655, with brief updating notices down to 661. The work is a compilation put together by an unknown author interested in international affairs – Byzantine, Sasanian and Islamic.

Socrates (Scholasticus) (c.380–c.439)   Greek lawyer and ecclesiastical historian. He was the author of a continuation of the *Church History* of Eusebius which extends from 305 to 439.

Sozomen (fifth century)   Greek ecclesiastical historian and another continuator of Eusebius. His work, which covers the period 323–425, is heavily dependent on that of Socrates but contains valuable information on the history of Christianity in Armenia and the Sasanian Empire.

Stephen of Taron, also known as Asołik, 'singer' (eleventh century)   Armenian historian who wrote a *Universal History* around the year 1000.

Suda   A Greek encyclopaedic lexicon compiled about the end of the tenth century AD.

Synodicon Orientale   A work which contains the acts of the East Syrian Church (in late antiquity, the Church in Persia) from 410 to 775. The date at which the work was compiled is uncertain, but it preserves much useful documentation, including records of councils and letters.

Tabari, Abu Ja'far Muhammad b. Jarir al- (c.839–923).   Arab historian, whose principal work contains an important monograph on the history of the Sasanian dynasty in Persia, for which he used earlier, now lost, sources.

Themistius (c.317–c.388)   Greek philosopher and rhetor whose panegyrics found favour with every emperor from Constantius II to Theodosius I. His speeches are also important as sources for the history of his time.

Theodore Lector (Theodore Anagnostes) (died after 527)   Ecclesiastical historian from Constantinople, who wrote a *Church History* down to 527. It now survives in fragmentary form.

Theodoret (c.393–c.466)   Greek ecclesiastical historian. A native of Antioch, he later became the bishop of Cyrrhus. His *Church History* continues that of Eusebius down to 425 in a style rather different from that of Socrates and Sozomen.

Theophanes (Confessor)   A Byzantine monk who compiled a chronicle (in Greek) covering the years 284–814. His account of Heraclius' campaigns, often drawing on official reports and poems of George of Pisidia, is especially valuable.

Theophanes (of Byzantium) (late sixth century)   Author of a *Historika*, an account of the period 566–81, whose work survives in only a few fragments.

Theophylact Simocat(t)a (fl. first half of seventh century)   Greek rhetor, born in Egypt. He served in Constantinople as a court official during the reign of Heraclius. His *History* continues the work of Menander, covering the period 582–602 (and some earlier events), for which he drew on earlier sources (such as John of Epiphania).

V. Theod. Syk.   The *Life of Theodore of Sykeon* was composed by his disciple George, who went on to become *hegoumenos* (head) of the monastery at Sykeon.

Zachariah of Mytilene (c.465/6–after 536)   The *Church History* attributed to Zachariah was compiled in Amida c.569 and contains important information on secular events in the sixth century (as well as ecclesiastical history of the fifth and sixth centuries).

Zonaras, Ioannes (twelfth century)   Byzantine historian and canonist, author of a universal history (in Greek) down to 1118 which preserves fragments of many lost works.

Zosimus (late fifth/early sixth century)   Greek pagan historian and imperial bureaucrat, whose only surviving work, the *Historia Nova*, covers Roman history 180–410. The work contains much material drawn from the now lost *Histories* of Eunapius and Olympiodorus.

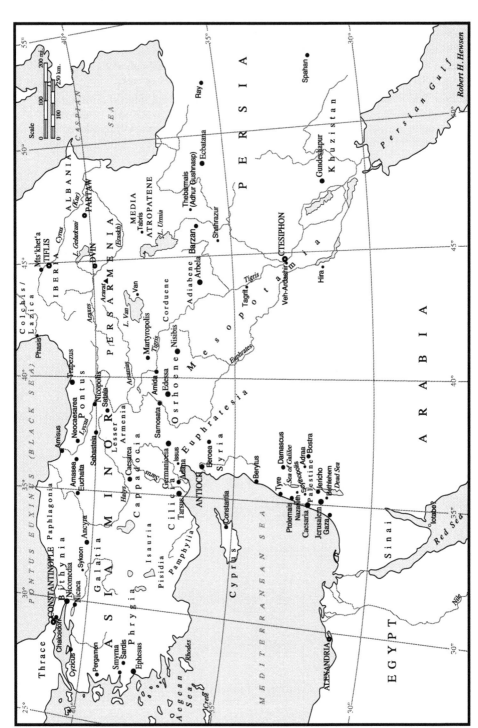

Map 1 The Near East in late antiquity

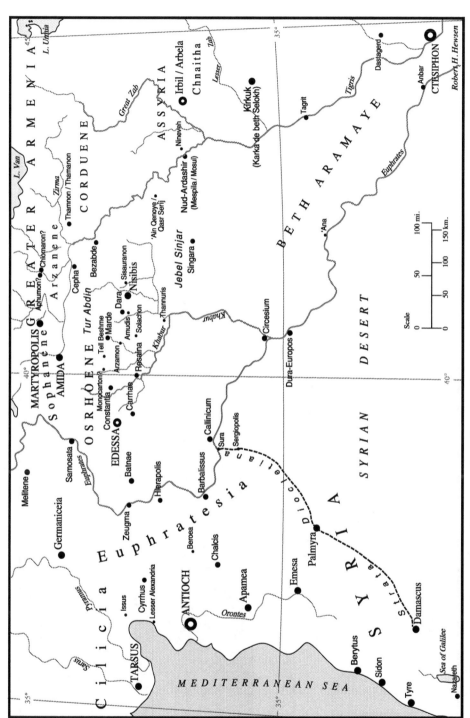

Map 2 The southern theatre of war (Mesopotamia and surrounding regions)

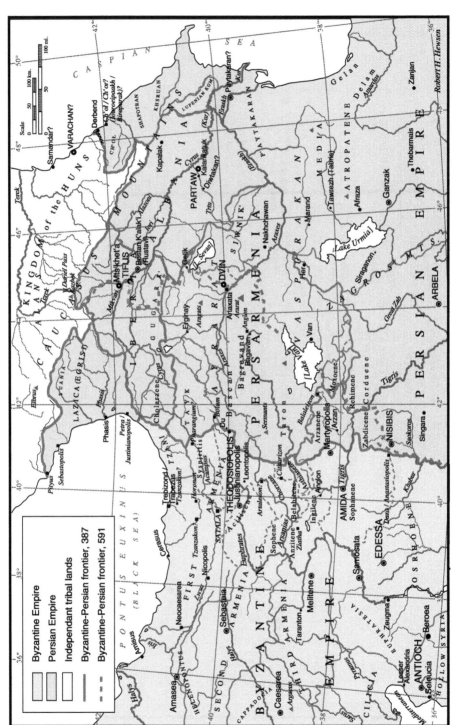

Map 3 The northern theatre of war (Armenia and surrounding regions)

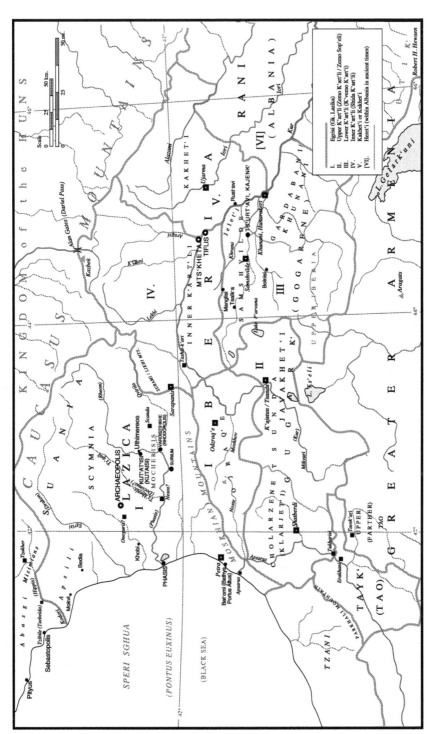

Map 4 The western Transcaucasus (Lazica and surrounding regions)

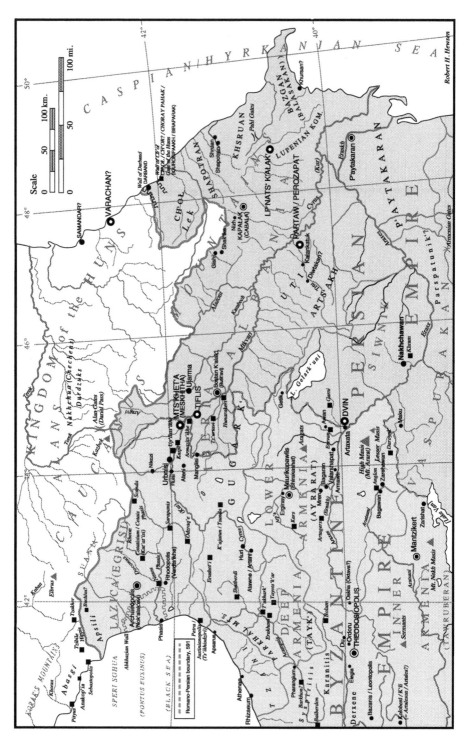

Map 5 The Transcaucasus

1

THE PEACE OF JOVIAN AND ITS AFTERMATH IN MESOPOTAMIA (363–99)

Peace terms agreed by Jovian during the return from Persia (363)

The Emperor Julian died from the wound he sustained in battle on 26 June 363. On the following day a relatively unknown commander by the name of Jovian was elevated to the throne. He continued the withdrawal from Persian territory, but, unable to cross the river Tigris, the army halted for four days at a place called Dura. There the Persians entered into negotiations with Jovian, who agreed to almost everything they demanded: the more time passed and supplies ran short, the less room for manoeuvre was available to him. Thus the new emperor surrendered several territories east of the Tigris to the Persians, as well as valuable frontier fortresses in eastern Mesopotamia, such as Nisibis; he also agreed not to lend assistance to the Armenian king Arsaces. Probably on 11 July the march back to Roman territory resumed; after enduring terrible privations, the remnants of the expeditionary force arrived back at Nisibis. See Chrysos 1976: 25–32, Blockley 1984: 31, 34–7, Gutmann 1991: 162–4, Winter and Dignas 2001: M18.[1]

The attitude of the sources to Jovian's peace ranges from utter condemnation to an acceptance that he accomplished all that was possible under the circumstances; Christian writers naturally shift the blame for the surrender of Roman territory onto Julian.[2]

(a) Sources hostile to the peace

Agath. IV.26.6–7: see volume 1.
Ammianus XXV.7.1–8.7: While these vain attempts were going on, king Shapur, both while at a distance, and also when he had drawn near, received from his scouts and from our deserters a true account of the gallant exploits of our men, of the disgraceful massacres of his own troops, and of the killing of his elephants, in numbers he did not recall (being lost before) during his reign. (And he heard) also that the Roman army, being hardened by its continual labours since the death of its glorious chief, did not now think so much, as they said,[3] of safety as of revenge, and (was resolved) to put an end to the distress of their current situation either by a complete victory or by a glorious death. (2) These many fearsome matters made him reflect, for he was aware by experience that our troops who were scattered in large numbers over

these provinces could be assembled by a simple password, and knowing also that his own men after their heavy losses were in a state of the greatest alarm; at the same time he also heard that we had left behind in Mesopotamia an army little inferior in numbers to that before him. (3) Above all (else), the thing which reduced his anxious mind to inactivity was the fact that 500 men had safely at one moment crossed that swollen river[4] by swimming, and having slain his guards, had emboldened the rest of their comrades to similar boldness. (4) In the meantime, as the violence of the stream prevented any bridges from being constructed, and as everything which could be eaten was consumed, we passed two days in great misery; and so the soldiery was raging, roused by starvation and anger, and was in a hurry to perish by the sword rather than by hunger, the most degrading death. (5) But the eternal power of the heavenly god was on our side and beyond our hopes the Persians made the first overtures, sending Surena[5] and another noble as ambassadors to establish peace; they themselves were in a state of despondency, as the Romans, having proved superior in almost every battle, weakened them daily. (6) But the conditions which they proposed were difficult and intricate, since they pretended that, out of regard for humanity, their most merciful monarch was willing to permit the remains of our army to return home, provided the Caesar, with his officers, would satisfy his demands.[6] (7) In reply, Arintheus was sent with the prefect Salutius; and while the proper terms were being discussed with great deliberation, four more days were spent in great suffering from want of provisions, more painful than any kind of torture. (8) And in this space of time, if before the ambassadors were sent, the emperor, making full use (of the opportunity), had retired slowly from the territories of the enemy, he would certainly have reached the forts of Corduene, a rich region belonging to us, only 100 miles from the spot where these transactions were being carried on.[7] (9) But Shapur obstinately demanded (to use his own language) the restoration of those territories which had been taken from him a short while ago by Maximian;[8] but as was seen in the process of the negotiation, he in reality required, as the price of our redemption, five provinces on the other side of the Tigris – Arzanene, Moxoene, Zabdicene, as well as Rehimene and Corduene, with fifteen fortresses and Nisibis and Singara, and Castra Maurorum,[9] an extremely well placed fort. (10) And though it would have been better to fight ten battles than to give up any of them, still a set of flatterers harassed our timid emperor with harping on the dreaded name of Procopius, and affirmed that if he (Procopius) returned with the fresh troops under his command when he heard of the death of Julian, he would easily bring about a revolution which no one would resist.[10] (11) Jovian, excessively[11] inflamed by the pernicious reiteration of these evil counsels, without further delay gave up everything that was demanded, (with this proviso), which he obtained with difficulty, that Nisibis and Singara should go over to Persian control without their inhabitants, and that the Roman garrisons in the forts to be surrendered should be permitted to retire to fortresses of our own. (12) To this another deadly and unfair condition was added, that after this treaty was concluded aid was not to be brought to Arsaces against the Persians, if he implored our aid, though he had always been our friend and trusty ally. And this was insisted on by Shapur for two reasons, in order that the man might be punished who had laid waste

Chiliocomum[12] at the emperor's command, and also that the opportunity might henceforth be given for invading Armenia without a check. In consequence of this it fell out subsequently that Arsaces was captured alive, and that amid different dissensions and disturbances, the Parthians laid violent hands on the greater portion of Armenia, where it borders on Media, and on the town of Artaxata. (13) Once this ignoble treaty had been made, in order that nothing might be done during the armistice, in contravention of its terms, some men of rank were given as hostages on each side: on ours, Nemota,[13] Victor and Bellovaedius, tribunes of distinguished legions: and on that of the enemy, one of their chief nobles named Bineses, and three other satraps of note. (14) So peace was made for thirty years, and ratified by solemn oaths; and we, returning by another line of march, avoiding the parts near the river because they were rugged and difficult, suffered severely for want of water and provisions.[14]

(8.1) The peace which had been granted on pretence of humanity was turned to the ruin of many who were so exhausted by want of food as to be at the last gasp, and who in consequence had set off in secret, and were carried away by the current of the river from not being able to swim; or, if able to overcome the force of the waves so far as to reach the bank, they were caught by the Saracens or the Persians, whom (as we said a little earlier) the Germans had driven out, and slain like cattle or sent off a distance to be sold as slaves. (2) But when the resounding trumpets openly gave the signal for crossing the river, it was with a terrible ardour that every individual hastened to rush into all kinds of danger, preferring himself to all his comrades, in the desire to avoid many dangers. Some tried to guide the beasts which were swimming about at random with paddles hurriedly put together; some, seated on bladders, and others, being driven by necessity to all kinds of expedients, sought to pass through the opposing waves by crossing them obliquely. (3) The emperor himself with a few others crossed over in the small boats, which we said were saved when the fleet was burnt, and then ordered the same vessels to go backwards and forwards until we were all brought across. And at length all of us, except such as were drowned, reached the opposite bank of the river, being saved amid our difficulties by the favour of the supreme deity.

(4) While fear of impending disasters oppressed us, we learnt from information brought in by our scouts that the Persians were throwing a bridge over the river beyond our sight, so that after peace was established and treaties (concluded), and the turmoils of war had been stilled, they might come upon our invalids as they proceeded carelessly onwards, and on the animals long exhausted with fatigue. But when they found their purpose discovered, they relinquished their base design. (5) Being now relieved from this suspicion, we hastened on by rapid marches, and approached Hatra, an ancient town in the middle of a desert, which had been long since abandoned, though at different times the warlike emperors, Trajan and Severus, had attacked it with a view to its destruction, but had been almost destroyed with their armies, which we have also related in our history of their exploits.[15] (6) And as we now learnt that over the vast plain before us for seventy miles in that arid region no water could be found but such as was brackish and fetid, and no kind of food but southernwood, wormwood, dracontium, and other bitter herbs, we filled the vessels which we had with sweet water, and after the camels and the rest of the beasts of burden had been

slain, other types of food, even harmful ones, were sought.[16] (7) For six days the army marched, until at last even grass, the last comfort of extreme necessity, could not be found; then Cassianus, *dux* of Mesopotamia, and the tribune Mauricius, who had been sent forward some time ago with this object, came to a Persian fort called Ur,[17] and brought some food from the supplies which the army under Procopius and Sebastian, by living sparingly, had managed to preserve. (tr. Yonge, revised)

Eunapius frg.29.1.3–6, 10–15: (...) Coming to Nisibis, a populous city, he (Jovian) stayed there for only two days, lavishly consuming all its resources and having neither a kindly word nor a good deed for the inhabitants. (...) When, as has been said, he became emperor of the Romans after Julian, ignoring everything else in his eagerness to enjoy the rank that had devolved upon him, he fled from Persia, hurried to reach the Roman provinces to display his (good) fortune, and handed over to the Persians the city of Nisibis, which had long been subject to the Romans.[18] (tr. Blockley, revised)

Festus, *Breviarium* 29: Jovian took over an army (which had proved) superior in battles, but which had been thrown into confusion by the sudden death of the emperor it had lost. When supplies were running short and the way back threatened to be rather long, the Persians held up the passage of the columns with frequent attacks, at one moment from the front, at another from the rear, as well as attacking the flanks of those in the middle; after some days had been spent (thus) such was the respect for the Roman name that it was from the Persians that the first mention of peace came; and the army, exhausted by starvation, was allowed to be led back. The conditions imposed – (something) which had never previously occurred – were costly to the Roman state, as Nisibis and part of Mesopotamia were handed over; Jovian, new to the throne, and greedier for power than glory, assented to them.

Libanius, *Or.*1.134 (I, 147.25–148.5): (...) We were sure that by these great afflictions[19] heaven (p.148) gave us a sign of some great disaster, and, as we prayed that our guess should not be right, the bitter news reached our ears that our great Julian was being carried in his coffin, that some nonentity held the throne, and that Armenia, and as much of the rest of the empire as they liked, was in Persian hands.[20] (tr. Norman)

Libanius, *Or.*18.277–8 (II, 357.8–358.4): (Libanius is complaining of the change in Roman policy once Jovian was on the throne) In the first place, they did not stand up to those whom previously they used to put to flight; secondly, ensnared by this word 'peace', for the enemy applied the same technique again, they all demanded its acceptance without demur, and the new emperor was the first to be taken in by it. The Mede found them hankering after peace and dillied and dallied with question and answer, accepting this point, deferring that, and exhausting their supplies with a string of parleys. (278) When they were in want of food and everything else, and they were begging for everything, and dire necessity encompassed them, at that moment (p.358) he (the Persian) presented his minimum terms, the cities, territories and provinces – the (very) walls (which guaranteed) the safety of the Romans. Our new emperor agreed and evacuated them all, and made no bones about it. (tr. Norman, revised)

(b) Sources which are balanced in their attitude to the peace

Artemii Passio 70: see volume 1.

Cedrenus I.539.16–21: see volume 1.

Chr. 724, 133.25–134.9: see volume 1.

Epic Histories IV.21: (describing the treaty of 363) (...) And he wrote in the treaty in the following way: 'I have granted you,' he (Jovian) said: 'the city of Ncbin (Nisibis), which is in Aruestan and Syrian Mesopotamia. And I am withdrawing from the middle country of Armenia. If you will be able to overcome and subject them, I shall not support them.' The king of the Greeks was then in a difficult situation, and (being) in an uncomfortable position, he in this manner sealed a deed of the words; and he gave (the agreement) to the king of Persia and so freed himself from him (...). (tr. Greenwood)

Eutropius, *Breviarium* X.17.1: After this, Jovian, who was then serving as a *domesticus*, was chosen to take over the empire by the general consensus of the army; he was known to the soldiers more by the reputation of his father than by his own merits. Since matters were already in a troubled state and the army suffering from a lack of supplies, and after he had been defeated in one battle, then another,[21] he made a peace with Shapur which was necessary indeed, but shameful; he was punished in regard to the frontier, and several parts of the Roman empire were handed over.

Josh. Styl. 7 (242.2–8): After the death of Julian in Persia, which took place in the year 674 (362/3), Jovinian (i.e. Jovian), who reigned over the Romans after him, valued peace more than anything; and for the sake of this he allowed the Persians to have authority over Nisibis for 120 years, after which they were to restore it to its masters.[22] (...) (tr. Wright, rev. M. Greatrex)

Orosius, *Hist.* VII.31.1–2: In the 1117th year after the foundation of Rome, Jovian was made the 37th emperor at a critical juncture of events. When, trapped by unfavourable terrain and surrounded by the enemy, he could find no opportunity for escape, he agreed a treaty with the Persian king Shapur, which, although some consider it unworthy, was nevertheless quite necessary; (2) and so, in order that he might rescue the Roman army safe and unharmed not only from the attack of the enemy, but also from the danger of the territory, he ceded the town of Nisibis and part of Upper Mesopotamia to the Persians.

Ps.-Dion. I, 180.4–8: He (Jovian) made peace between the two empires and ceded Nisibis to the Persians. The persecution came to an end in Persia because of the peace he made and all the churches were (re)opened. All the inhabitants of Nisibis went into exile to Amida in Mesopotamia and he constructed walls for them west of the city. (tr. Lieu, rev. Brock)

Rufinus, *HE* XI.1 (1001.10–1002.6): (...) In fact divine clemency immediately attended him (Jovian) against all (p.1002) hope, since they (the soldiers) were held (in a position) closed in on all sides by the enemy, and no means of escape was available. Suddenly they beheld spokesmen sent by the barbarians to seek peace, promising victuals and other necessities to the army, (which was) stricken by starvation, and repaying the boldness of our men with every kindness. But when peace was made for 29 years, he returned to Roman soil (...).

Socr. *HE* III.22.5–7 (218.11–18): The cry of all in unison therefore acknowledged that they were Christians; he (Jovian) accepted the throne, (6) suddenly taking over in a crisis, in Persian territory, with the soldiers perishing from hunger, and he brought the war to an end by a treaty. The treaty was shameful to Roman glory, but necessary in the situation. (7) For he received a fine in regard to the boundaries of the empire and handed over to the Persians Nisibis in Mesopotamia, <a very large and populous city>; he then departed from there.

Soz. *HE* VI.3.2 (239.17–20): Since matters were in a dangerous and confused state as a result of Julian's expedition[23] and the army suffering from a lack of provisions, he (Jovian) saw that it was necessary to come to terms and handed over to the Persians one of the (territories) previously tributary to the Romans.

Zonaras XIII.14.4–6 (217.3–13): He (Jovian) thus accepted the title of emperor, and made a treaty with the Persians which was not befitting to the Romans, but was made under compulsion. (5) He conceded two famous cities to them, Nisibis and Singara, and transferred the inhabitants of them elsewhere, by whom, in their grief, he was violently abused. (6) He abandoned to them (the Persians) many provinces and rights which had belonged to the Romans for a long time. When the hostages had been handed over by each side, the treaty was confirmed. The Romans then moved off, but endured a shortage of provisions, for they did not even have enough water. (tr. Dodgeon, revised)

Zos. III.31.1–2: Although the (Roman) army was in these circumstances, the Persians nonetheless entered negotiations about friendship and sent out Surena and others from those in power among them. Jovian received their words about peace and despatched Salutius the praetorian prefect and with him Arintheus. After talks between the two sides had taken place concerning this matter a treaty for thirty years was concluded. It was agreed that the Romans should cede the province of Zabdicene to the Persians, as well as Corduene, Rehimene and Zalene;[24] and in addition to these and in all these (regions, they were to hand over) the fortresses in them, fifteen in number, with their inhabitants, possessions, animals and all their equipment, while Nisibis should be handed over without its inhabitants. For it was determined that they would be resettled where the Romans decided. (2) The Persians also took most of Armenia, allowing the Romans to hold a small part of it. Once the treaty had been concluded on these terms and had been confirmed with contracts by both sides (the Persians) gave the Romans a free path for their return home; (for it was understood that the Romans) would not harm the lands of the Persians, and that they (in return) would not be the victims of Persian ambushes.[25]

(c) Sources favourable to the peace

Augustine, *De civ. dei* IV.29 (123.37–43): The army, deprived of it (food), and after even (Julian) himself had swiftly been slain by the wound (inflicted) by an enemy, was reduced to great scarcity. And no one would have escaped, for from all sides the enemy was attacking the soldiery, which was distressed by the death of the emperor, had not peace been agreed and the frontiers of the empire fixed in that place where they remain today; they were settled without such a great loss as Hadrian had conceded,[26] but rather by a compromise agreement.

Gregory Nazianzenus, Or.5.15: The one who immediately succeded to the throne after that man, and after that man was proclaimed in the camp itself – and the great danger absolutely required a leader – was a man outstanding, among other things, for his piety, and in appearance was truly worthy of supreme power. He was utterly unable to engage the Persians or to move forward, and yet he in no way lacked courage or zeal: the army had thrown up its hands and thrown away its hopes, but he sought to break up camp and he looked for any means by which he could safely accomplish this, since he had become the inheritor not of the empire, but of a defeat. Had not therefore the Persians, moderate in victory – for they have a law to know how to measure success – or through fear of one of the other things talked of,[27] come to terms, which were so unexpected and humane, nothing would have prevented not even a firebearer being left to the army, as they say.[28] To such an extent did the Persians have them (the Romans) in their grip, fighting on home territory and encouraged yet more by the events that had taken place; for it is sufficient to experience a piece of good luck to give hope for the future. But now, as I said, it was the task of one man to rescue the army and to leave the Romans their sinews: for they (the soldiers) were the sinews, even if they had fared badly more by the thoughtlessness of their general than by their own lack of courage. They (the Persians) came to an agreement on these terms, so disgraceful and unworthy of Roman might, to put it very shortly. If anyone would absolve that man (Julian) of responsibility for them, and blame this man (Jovian), I would say he is a senseless reckoner of the events which took place then. (...)

Jerome, Chron. a.364: see volume 1.

Joh. Chrys., De sancto Babylo 123.7–26: (...) Therefore when he (Julian) had fallen so shamefully, and the soldiers saw themselves in dire straits, they prostrated themselves at the feet of their enemies and gave oaths that they would withdraw from the safest place of all, which was like an impregnable wall for our inhabited world. (Because) they happened (to be dealing with) humane barbarians, they escaped in this way and returned – few out of many, and even they, after physical sufferings, in shame (at the terms) according to which they had been obliged by their oaths to withdraw from their ancestral possessions. It was possible to see a sight more pitiful than any capture in war. For those who lived in that city (Nisibis) were suffering at the hands of those from whom they expected to receive thanks because they had kept (safe) all those within as in a harbour, just like a breakwater, and because always, in place of everyone, they had been exposed to every danger. (Now) they were being transferred to another's country, giving up their houses and fields, dragged from their ancestral possessions – and they endured these things at the hands of their own people. Such were (the benefits) we had enjoyed from the noble emperor.[29]

Mal. 13.27 (258.73–259.93/335.1–336.5):[30] When Jovian went out with his army from the desert to the fertile Persian land, he considered anxiously how he might go out from Persian territory. Now the Persian king Sabburarsakios (Shapur) had not yet learnt of the emperor Julian's death and was filled with terror. Pleading and begging for peace, he sent from Persarmenia one of his nobles, named Surraeina (Surena), as an ambassador to the Roman emperor. The most sacred emperor Jovian welcomed him cordially and consented to receive (p.259) the peace embassy, saying that he too would send an ambassador to the Persian king. <Hearing this, Surena, the Persian ambassador,> asked the emperor Jovian to agree on a peace treaty there and then. Selecting one of his senators, the patrician Arintheus, he entrusted the whole affair to him. He agreed to abide by the terms approved or agreed by him, for the emperor was too proud to make a peace treaty with the Persian senator or ambassador; and he provided a truce in the war for three days during the peace negotiations. It was agreed (p.336) between the Roman patrician Arintheus and Surena, senator and ambassador of the Persians, that the Romans should cede to the Persians the entire province known as Mygdonia and its metropolis known as Nisibis, just the city with its walls alone, without the people who inhabited it. (tr. Jeffreys and Scott, revised)

Philostorgius, *HE* **VIII.1 (104.2–7):** On the next day after the apostate's (Julian's) death, the army appointed Jovian emperor. He – for there was no other way to safety, since the whole army had been reduced to one tenth (its orginal size) – made a treaty with the Persian for thirty years, giving up to him all claim to Nisibis and the fortresses which had been erected by the Romans as a barrier against the Persians as far as Armenia. (tr. Walford, revised)

Themistius, *Or.***5.66a (96.15–19):** That the Persians voted for you (Jovian) no less than the Romans they showed by throwing (down) their weapons when they heard about the public proclamation; and they who had felt confident against them (the Romans) soon afterwards grew more respectful.

Thdrt. *HE* **IV.2.2–3 (211.18–24):** (…) Immediately the God of all showed him (Jovian) his consideration and solved the problem which had arisen. For the Persian king, learning of his accession to the throne, sent envoys on an embassy about peace. He then despatched provisions to the soldiers and ordered that a market-place be set up for them in the desert. (3) When he had made a thirty-year treaty, he let the army go in good health.[31] (…)

Perhaps the most favourable version of all comes in the so-called *Julian Romance*, a work composed in Edessa probably in the late fourth century.[32]

Julian Romance, **220.17–24:** They (the leading Romans and Persians) received ideas from each other, and came from disputation to a decision. There was great dispute between them concerning what had been done illegally in the territory of the two sides. They considered the countries which Shapur had laid waste in the Roman territory in the days of the sons of Constantine, and the places which Julian had destroyed in the land of the Persians. There was less advantage on the side of the Romans than on that of the Persians;[33] and Nisibis was given to the Persians for a hundred years with all its land on its eastern side. That was done voluntarily and without compulsion.[34] (tr. Gollancz, rev. M. Greatrex)

Julian Romance, **224.22–225.2:** They (Jovian and Shapur) prepared a document on the frontier regarding Nisibis and the peace of the churches in Persia (to last for) a hundred years according to the contract which came from the kings. And Nisibis was surrendered to the Persians, devoid of its inhabitants, in the month of August in the year 674 (363), according to the chronology of the Greeks. Jovian was satisfied in his mind that, by making peace, he would be able by his skill to rescue his troops (from) the imprisonment in which they found themselves. He had not yet (p.225) set foot upon the territory of his kingdom when the news of the salvation of the churches was sped throughout all the lands of the Romans. (tr. Gollancz, rev. M. Greatrex)

Jovian himself took pains to cast his return from Persia in the best possible light. He despatched supporters to the west as soon as he could, in order to consolidate his position partly by representing the outcome of the expedition as a success (Ammianus XXV.8.8–12). This propaganda effort is reflected in the coins issued by Jovian, which proclaimed 'Victory of the Romans' and 'Victory of Augustus'; *solidi* issued at Thessalonica and Sirmium referred to the 'Safety of the State' and depicted the emperor holding the Christian *labarum* over a Persian prisoner.[35]

(d) The Persian tradition

Tabari, I, 843/62–3 (Nöldeke 62–3): While Jovinianus (Jovian) was quite willing to go to Shapur, none of his commanders favoured this intention. He, however, insisted and came to Shapur, with eighty of the most respected men in the camp and in the whole army, and wearing the crown. When Shapur heard that he was coming he went out to meet him. They both fell on the ground (in obeisance) before each other; then Shapur embraced him in gratitude for what he had done for him. He ate a meal with Shapur and was of good cheer. Shapur meanwhile, however, gave the Roman leaders and governors to understand that if they had made any other than Jovinianus to be emperor, they would all have perished in Persia; it was only because of his nomination that he did not let them feel his power. So through his efforts Jovinianus' position became very strong. Then he said: 'The Romans attacked our land, killed many people, chopped down date-palms and other trees in Sawad and devastated agriculture; now, they shall either pay us the full price for what they destroyed and laid waste, or give up the town Nisibis with its territory as compensation.' Jovinianus and his military leaders agreed to give Shapur compensation and yielded Nisibis to him. When the inhabitants of this town heard of it, they emigrated to other places in the Roman empire because they feared the reign of a king who was of a different religion.[36] When Shapur heard this, he had 12,000 people of good family from Istakhr, Ispahan and other regions of his lands sent to Nisibis and settled them there.[37] (tr. A. al-Issa and D. Dance)

Tabari's evidence may be supplemented by a rock relief at Taq-i Bustan which, it is argued, depicts the investiture of Shapur II, who triumphs over the Emperor Julian. See Trümpelmann 1975, Azarpay 1982: 184–7 (emphasising the role of Mithras, as god of boundary-lines, in punishing Julian), Nicholson 1983 and Schippmann 1990: 35. The famous Paris cameo, depicting a Sasanian king grasping the left arm of a Roman emperor, may also be relevant. Although the cameo is usually associated with Shapur I and Valerian (so, e.g. Fowden 1993: 23 plate 1), others have attributed it rather to Shapur II's defeat of Jovian. See von Gall 1990: 57–9.

The aftermath of the peace treaty

The surrender of Nisibis in July 363 was a dramatic event, as emerges from the following accounts, several by eyewitnesses. Many of the displaced inhabitants settled in Amida, which therefore grew considerably in size and required extensive refortification.[38]

Ammianus XXV.8.13–17; 9.1–6, 12: (Jovian sends out messengers to announce his accession and to report his peace treaty in a favourable light) (13) But Rumour (being always the most rapid bearer of bad news), outstripping these couriers, flew through the different provinces and nations, and above all others struck the citizens of Nisibis with bitter sorrow when they heard that their city was surrendered to Shapur, whose anger and enmity they dreaded from recollecting the losses he had regularly endured in his frequent attempts to take the place. (14) For it was clear that the whole eastern empire could have fallen under the power of Persia, if it had not been for the resistance which this city, with its admirable position and its mighty walls, had offered. But miserable as they now were, and although they were filled with a still greater fear of what was to come, they were supported by this slender hope, that, either from his own inclination or from being won over by their prayers, the emperor might consent to keep their city in its existing state, as the strongest bulwark of the East. (15) While different reports were flying about of what had taken place in the army, the scanty supplies which I have spoken of as having been brought were consumed, and necessity might have driven the men to (eat) the bodies of their own (dead), if the flesh of the animals slain had not lasted them a little longer; but the consequence of our destitute condition was that most of the arms and baggage were thrown away; for we were so worn out with this terrible famine that whenever a single bushel of corn was found – which seldom happened – it was sold for ten pieces of gold at the least. (16) Marching on from there, we came to Thilsaphata,[39] where Sebastian and Procopius, with the tribunes and chief officers of the legions which had been placed under their command for the protection of Mesopotamia, came to meet the emperor as the solemn occasion required, and being kindly received, accompanied us on our march. (17) After this, proceeding with all possible speed, we rejoiced when we saw Nisibis, where the emperor pitched a standing camp outside the walls; and being most earnestly entreated by the whole population to come to lodge in the palace according to the custom of his predecessors, he obstinately refused, being ashamed that an impregnable city should be surrendered to an enraged enemy while he was within its walls.

(9.1) The next day Bineses, one of the Persians of whom we have spoken as the most distinguished among them, hastening to execute the commission of his king, demanded the immediate performance of what had been promised; and by the permission of the Roman emperor he entered the city and raised the standard of his nation on the citadel, announcing to the citizens a miserable emigration from their native place. (2) Immediately they were all commanded to leave the place, weeping and stretching forth their hands in entreaty not to be compelled to depart, affirming that they by themselves, without either state provisions or soldiers, were sufficient to defend their own home in full confidence that Justice would be on their side while fighting for the place of their birth, as they had often found her to be before. Both nobles and common people joined in this supplication; but they spoke in vain as to the winds, the emperor fearing the crime of perjury, as he pretended, though fearing other things. (3) Then Sabinus, (a man) eminent among his fellow-citizens both for his fortune and birth, replied with great fluency that Constantius too was at one time defeated by the Persians in the terrible strife of fierce war, that in his flight he was led at last with a small body of comrades to the ungarded station of Hibita,[40] where he lived on a scanty and uncertain supply of bread which was brought him by an old woman from the country; and yet that to his last day he lost nothing; while Jovian, at the very beginning of his reign, was yielding up the wall of his provinces, by the protection of which barrier they had hitherto remained safe from the earliest ages. (4) But as nothing was accomplished, for the emperor persisted stubbornly in alleging the obligation of his oath, presently, when Jovian, who had for some time refused the crown which was offered to him, accepted it under a show of compulsion, an advocate named Silvanus, exclaimed boldly, 'May you, o emperor, be so crowned in the rest of your cities.' But Jovian was offended at his words, and ordered the whole body of citizens to leave the city within three days, complaining as they were at the existing state of affairs. (5) Accordingly, men were appointed to compel obedience to this order, with threats of death to everyone who delayed his departure; the walls were disturbed by mourning and lamentation, and in every quarter of the city the common sound from all was of wailing, matrons tearing their hair when about to be driven from their homes, in which they had been born and brought up, the mother who had lost her children, or the wife her husband, about to be driven far from the place of the spirits of their dead; the piteous crowds wept, embracing their doorways or thresholds. (6) Every road was crowded, each person escaping as he could. Many, too, took off with as much of their property as they thought they could carry, while casting aside abundant and costly furniture, for this they could not remove for lack of beasts of burden. (...) (12) Accordingly, when the citizens had been withdrawn, the city surrendered, and the tribune Constantius had been sent to deliver up to the Persian nobles the garrisoned forts and districts agreed upon, Procopius was sent forward with the remains of Julian, to bury them in the suburbs of Tarsus, according to his directions while alive. (tr. Yonge, revised)

Ephrem Syrus, *Hymni contra Iul.* II.22, 25 (80.9–14, 80.27–81.4): The Magian (Shapur II) who entered our place, kept it holy, to our shame, he neglected his temple of fire and honoured the sanctuary, he cast down the altars which were built through our laxity; he abolished the enclosures, to our shame, for he knew that from that one temple alone had gone out the mercy which had saved us from him three times.[41]

(25) That city (Nisibis) which was the head of the area between the rivers preserved the sack-cloth of the blessed one and was exalted. The tyrant by his blasphemy had abased it and it was humbled. Who has weighed its shame, how great it was! For the city which was the head of all that West they have made the last heels of all that East. (tr. J. Lieu)

Ephrem Syrus, *Hymni contra Iul.* III.1–2 (81.19–82.3): A fortuitous wonder! There met me near the city the corpse of that accursed one which passed by the wall;[42] the banner which was sent from the East wind the Magian took and fastened on the tower so that a flag might point out for spectators that the city was the slave of the lords of that banner. Response: Praise to him who clothed his corpse in shame. (2) I was amazed as to how it was that there met and were present the body and the standard, both at the same time. And I knew that it was a wonderful preparation of justice (p.82) that while the corpse of the fallen one was passing, there went up and was placed that fearsome banner so that it might proclaim that the injustice of his diviners had delivered that city. (tr. J. Lieu)

Mal. 13.27 (259.93–15/336.5–337.2): When this had been confirmed and the peace treaty committed to writing, the emperor Jovian took with him one of the satraps, a Persian named Junius, who was with the ambassador, to conduct him and his army safely from Persian territory, and to take over the province and its metropolis.

On reaching the city of Nisibis, the emperor Jovian would not enter it, but encamped outside the walls. But Junius, the Persian satrap, entered the city at the emperor's command, and set up a Persian standard on one of the towers, since the Roman emperor had ordered that all the citizens to the last man were to depart with all their possessions. Silvanus, a *comes* in rank and a magistrate of the city, came out and threw himself down before the emperor, beseeching him not to surrender the city to the Persians, but did not persuade him. For he said that he had taken an oath, and added that he did not wish to have a reputation among all people as a perjurer. Then, having built a walled city outside the wall of the city of Amida, <he connected this wall to the wall of the city of Amida and> called it the town of Nisibis, and made all the people from the (p.337) area of Mygdonia live there, including the magistrate Silvanus.[43] (tr. Jeffreys and Scott, revised)

Zos. III.33.1–34.2: Once peace had been concluded with the Persians in the way I have described, the Emperor Jovian returned with his army in safety; he encountered many rugged places and waterless regions and lost many of his forces in his journey through enemy country. He ordered Maurice, one of his tribunes, to bring food for the army from Nisibis and to meet him with this as far off (from Nisibis) as he could; others he sent off to Italy to announce the death of Julian and his own accession. (2) With difficulty and much distress he drew near to Nisibis, but not wishing to be in the city which had been handed over to the enemy, he set up camp in an open enclosure in front of the gate. On the next day he received crowns, along with supplications; and all those in the city entreated him not to abandon them and not to subject them to the experience of barbarian practices – they who had been brought up willingly under Roman laws for so many years. (3) (They pointed out that) it was disgraceful besides that while Constantius had taken on three Persian wars and had been beaten in all of them, he had retained hold of Nisibis and with much effort kept it safe, even when it was under siege and came into the gravest danger. Yet he, when no such exigency existed, (proposed) to hand over the city to the enemy and to show the Romans a day which they had never witnessed, (when they would be) obliged to allow such a great city and (its) territory to be bestowed on an enemy. (4) The emperor, hearing this, pointed to what had been agreed; (but) Sabinus, the leader of the city council, added another argument to those put forward by the people who had come in supplication.

(He asserted that) they had no need of any expenses for their war against the Persians, nor of any help from outside; they would be able to sustain the war which would engulf them with their own bodies and funds. And when they won, the city would again be subject to the Romans, fulfilling their requests in the same way as before. (5) But once the emperor had said that it was not possible to breach what had been agreed, men from the city frequently besought him not to deprive the Roman empire of such a frontier bastion. (34.1) Since they did not achieve anything else – the emperor withdrew in anger, while the Persians wanted to take possession of the provinces, the fortresses and the city according to the treaty – the inhabitants of the provinces and the fortresses, if they had been unable to flee secretly, gave themselves up to the Persians to treat them as they wished. The Nisibenes obtained a truce for their move and many, (in fact) almost all, emigrated to Amida, while a few settled in other cities.[44] (2) Everywhere was filled with wailing and lamentation, since it was believed that with Nisibis handed over to the Persians, every city lay exposed to their attacks. So great was the grief of the residents of Carrhae when news of Julian's death was brought that they stoned the one who reported the news, and erected a huge pile of stones on top of him. So great a change did the death of one man bring to public affairs.

Roman inability to upset the status quo (March 368)[45]

From the moment of his accession in 364, Valens was forced to deal with matters in western Asia Minor and the Balkans; hence Themistius, in a speech for the emperor Valens, plays up the undesirability of wars of revenge. See Turcan 1966: 882–3, Blockley 1992: 30, Vanderspoel 1995: 170–1, Greatrex 2000a: 36.

Themistius, *Or.*8.114c (172.11–18): So that I may pass over other matters, I declare that even this (point) alone is sufficient to warrant one prayer (of thanks), and its benefit reaches everyone: this is that Mesopotamia has not been recovered, the Scythians beyond (the river Danube) have not been punished, and the Germans have not rebuilt the cities which they sacked. For even if we gained the first (region), only the Syrians would notice; and if the other one, (only) the Thracians (would notice), or (if) the other one (again), (only) the Gauls, and (likewise only) the country adjacent to each victory (would notice).

Valens' arrival in Antioch (370)

Mal. 13.29–30 (261.39–48/338.8–19): He (Valentinian I) marched against the Persians, sending his brother Valens, whom he had made Caesar on 1st April; Valens did not fight but marched out and made a peace treaty, for he had full power as the representative of his brother. The Persians had come and sued for peace. (30) Thus, having arrived at Antioch in Syria with the greater part of the military forces on 10 November in the 14th indiction,[46] Valens lingered there to conclude the peace treaty with the

Persians. He negotiated a treaty for seven years, with the Persians suing for peace and ceding half of Nisibis.[47] (tr. Jeffreys and Scott, revised)

Zos. IV.13.1–2: While matters were in this state in the West, the Emperor Valens set out for the East against the Persians, something he had been intending from the outset (of his reign).[48] He advanced slowly, providing the help that was necessary for the cities which sent ambassadors and arranged everything else appropriately, readily bestowing on those with just requests what they sought. (2) Having arrived in Antioch, he made ready the (tools) of war with all caution and spent the winter in the palace there. In spring he departed for Hierapolis and from there led forward the troops against the Persians; and when winter arrived, he went back to Antioch. The war against the Persians was then prolonged and while the emperor was at Antioch, a case of a surprising nature arose, for this reason.[49]

Tensions in Mesopotamia (373)[50]

Only ten years after Julian's disastrous defeat – and despite the thirty years' peace signed by Jovian – the Romans were apparently making military preparations in the East.[51]

Themistius, *Or*.11.148d (224.11–16): We see the emperor (Valens) displaying judgement in these matters not only in private affairs, but also in public. For why did he agree to peace with the Scythians and withhold it from the Persians? For both barbarian tribes are hostile to the Roman empire, but the one is spirited and unintelligent, while the other is treacherous and deceitful.

The refortification of Amida (367/75)

CIL III.213 (= 6730): Under the emperors Valentinian, V[alens and] Gratian, preserved (by God), perpetual [leaders?] and *triumphators*, eternally Augusti, the city was built from its foundations by the direction of their piety.[52]

We may note here the likely construction of a fort at this time at Pagnik Oreni, usually identified with Roman Dascusa, to the north-east of Melitene, guarding a crossing of the Euphrates from Armenia. Whether it was built to defend against the Persians, as they sought to take over Armenia, or against Hunnic raids, is unclear. See Gregory 1997: I, 214, II, 46–8.

The rising of Mavia (c.376)

By the late fourth century the Arabs, or Saracens as they were now often known, were emerging as a significant force on the eastern frontier.[53] One instance of this importance is provided by the revolt of Mavia late in Valens' reign; it followed the death of the king of the tribe, probably that of the Tanukhids, and was only brought to a halt by diplomatic means. Queen Mavia was conciliated by the appointment of a bishop not tainted by the emperor's Arianism, and her daughter was married to a high-ranking commander in the East, Victor. But the rebellion had inflicted considerable damage on the eastern provinces, and the Roman inability to deal

with the situation was an ominous precedent for future relations with Arab tribesmen. See
Bowersock 1980: 477–95 (378), Sartre 1982a: 140–4 (c.376), Shahîd 1984: 140–69 (dating
the revolt to 375, 183–4), Graf 1989: 348–9, Gutmann 1991: 185–7 and Woods 1998:
330–1.[54]

Rufinus *HE* XI.6 (1010.12–1011.2): While Lucius was behaving with great arrogance and savagery,[55] Mavia, queen of the race of the Saracens, began to disturb the
towns and cities of the Palestinian and Arabian frontier in a fierce war, and at the same
time to lay waste the neighbouring provinces. And when she had worn down the
Roman army with frequent battles, and after she had slain many and turned the rest
(p.1011) to flight, she was asked for peace; she promised that she would not embrace
peace unless a certain monk, Moses by name, should be ordained bishop for her tribe.
Socr. *HE* IV.36.1–2 (270.25–271.3): When the emperor had left Antioch, the Saracens, who had previously been bound by treaty, then revolted, under the command of
Mavia, a woman, (p.271) whose husband had died. (2) Everything in the East was
therefore laid waste by the Saracens simultaneously. But some divine providence
restrained the (attacks) of the Saracens by the following means.[56]
Soz. *HE* VI.38.1–5 (297.12–298.4): Around this same time, following the death of
the Saracen king, the treaty with the Romans was dissolved; Mavia, the wife of this
man, gained control of the nation and laid waste the cities of Phoenice and Palestine,
as far even as Egypt, attacking those who inhabited the left side of the Nile as one sails
upstream, (in) the region called Arabia.[57] (2) It was not possible for the war to be
considered easy because it was undertaken by a woman, and they say that this fight
was (so) tough and hard to win for the Romans that the commander of the soldiers in
Phoenice and Palestine summoned the general (in charge) of all the cavalry and
infantry forces of the East. He laughed at the appeal and excluded from battle the man
who had summoned him.[58] (3) But when he had drawn up his forces in battle order to
face Mavia, who was leading her forces against (him), he was routed, and with difficulty rescued by the commander of the Palestinian and Phoenician soldiers. For when
he saw him (the general) in danger, he reckoned it foolish to remain outside the fray in
accordance with his order. Running forward, he engaged the barbarians and gave him
(the general) the opportunity of a safer flight, (4) while he himself conducted a gradual
withdrawal, firing off missiles in his flight, and he beat off the advancing enemy with
arrows. Many of those living there still now commemorate these events, and among
the Saracens they are (recounted) in odes.[59] (5) Because the war was becoming a
burden, it seemed necessary (to the Romans) to send an embassy to Mavia concerning
peace. (...)

Sozomen (*HE* VI.38.14–16) goes on to recount the baptism of another Arab leader, Zocomus,
'not long before the present reign'. He therefore, like Mavia, became a useful ally of the Romans.
Neither the date of his conversion nor the location of his tribe can be fixed with any certainty,
however. See Sartre 1982a: 144–6, Shahîd 1984: 188–9 on Zocomus, Isaac 1998a: 449.[60]

For further important developments in the East (in Armenia) under Valens, see Chapter 2
below.

The promotion of a frontier post

Resaina, a Roman veteran colony set up probably under Septimius Severus, and since the peace of Jovian not far from the frontier, was evidently upgraded by Theodosius I early in his reign. Theodosius also constructed walls for smaller places in Syria, such as Gindarus, 40 km northeast of Antioch, and Lytargon, also known as Litarba, nearly 50 km east of Antioch (Mal. 13.39 [345–6]).[61]

Chr. Ede. **35:** In the year 692 (380/1) Theodosius the Great built the city of Resaina in Osrhoene.
Mal. 13.38 (267.83–6/345.21–346.2): Theodosius made the village formerly known as Rophaeina (Resaina) into a city, which was renamed Theodosiopolis; from that point the village (p.346) received the status of a city during the consulship of Merobaudes and Saturninus (AD 383) up to the present day. (tr. Jeffreys and Scott, revised)

Roman–Persian negotiations (381–7)

By the start of 383, a marked improvement in relations between Rome and Persia had occurred, no doubt in part occasioned by the change of rulers in both states. See Greatrex 2000a: 41–4.[62]

Orosius, *Hist.* **VII.34.8:** In these days[63] the Persians, having slain the persecutor Julian and often defeated other emperors, and having just now put Valens to flight, spewed forth with coarse insults their satisfaction at their latest victory. They sent envoys back and forth to Constantinople to Theodosius, and asked for peace as suppliants; a treaty was then made, which the whole East has enjoyed in great calm up to now.
Themistius, *Or.*16.212d–213a (304.4–10):[64] If we have accomplished these things, then we may do more; just as we defeated the Scythians (Goths) without blood or tears, so we shall be reconciled with the Persians shortly, and thus we shall regain Armenia; so too we shall recover as much of Mesopotamia as belonged to others[65] and so we shall name many consuls for their good deeds and their good services.[66]

In 384 a Persian embassy arrived in Constantinople, its principal aim no doubt being to announce the accession of Shapur III (383–388). But it is clear that it was just part of a continuing process of negotiation, which was to result three years later in the partitioning of Armenia (see Chapter 2). From a Sasanian seal gem discovered in Pakistan it is supposed that the Persian ambassador of Shapur III was one Yazdān-Friy-Shābūhr. See Curiel and Gignoux 1975: 41–4, Stock 1978: 171–6 with Greatrex 2000a: 42.

Marc. com. a.384.1: Persian ambassadors came to Constantinople requesting peace from the Emperor Theodosius.[67] (tr. Croke)
Pacatus, *Pan. Lat.* II (XII) 22.4–5: (...) Persia itself, formerly a rival of our state and notorious for the deaths of many Roman leaders, seeks to excuse by obedience whatever harsh (actions) she has committed against our rulers. (5) At last that king (of Persia), having previously disdained to admit that he is a man, now admits fear and

pays reverence to you in those temples in which he (himself) is revered, (and) then by sending an embassy and by offering gems and silk, and in addition by providing triumphal animals for your chariots. Although in name (he is) still a federate, he is now, however, a tributary in his devotions.[68]

Peace with Persia agreed (387)

Epitome de Caesaribus 48.5 (174.30–1): He made peace also with the Persians, who had asked for it.[69]

The Hunnic invasion of the eastern provinces (395)

In 395, and again in 397 or 398, substantial numbers of Huns from the steppes crossed the Caucasus mountains and penetrated deep into the Roman east (and the western portions of the Sasanian empire). The Hunnic invaders, although eventually defeated by Eutropius, were able to wreak great havoc throughout the eastern provinces: the citizens there were unaccustomed to such lightning strikes, while many of the troops usually stationed in the east had been withdrawn by Theodosius to combat the western usurper Eugenius, who was defeated only in 394.[70] See Maenchen-Helfen 1973: 48–50, Thompson 1996: 31–2, Heather 1998: 501–2, Greatrex and Greatrex 1999: 65–73. Their most devastating incursion took place in 395; another was feared in 396, but failed to materialise. The impression made by the Huns is very clear from the following extracts; even if some are clearly derivative of one another, it is worthy of note that Joshua the Stylite, writing over one hundred years later, makes specific allusion to the episode.[71]

Chr. 724, 136.20–137.9: And in this year, the accursed people of the Huns came into the lands of the Romans and passed over Sophene, Armenia, Mesopotamia, Syria, Cappadocia, as far as Galatia; they took a great number of captives and turned back so that they might return to their (own) country. But they went down to the banks of the Euphrates and Tigris, in the province of the Persians, and reached the Persians' royal city; they did no damage there, but laid waste many villages by the Euphrates and Tigris, and killed (many) and took a great number of captives. But when the Huns heard that the Persians were marching against them, they prepared to flee, and (the Persians) pursued them and killed one of their detachments, and took back (p.137) from them all the spoils they had seized; and they freed male captives from them 18,000 in number, and led them to their cities Selok and Kaukaba, which are called Ardashir and Ctesiphon, where they were for many years. The Persian king assigned rations for them – bread, wine, date wine and oil. From these 18,000 there remained but a few (...) the first thousand; and the Persians let them go so that they might return to their (own) land. (tr. M. Greatrex)
Chr. Ede. 40: In the month of July that year (395), the Huns crossed over into the territory of the Romans. (tr. M. Greatrex)
Claudian, *In Rufinum* II.28–35: Others, brought by an unlooked-for pass across the Caspian Gates and the Armenian snows, fall upon the wealth of the East.[72] Now the pastures of Cappadocia and Argaeus, father of swift horses, are in smoke; now the deep Halys is reddened and the Cilician does not defend himself on his steep mountain. The

pleasant districts of Syria are laid waste and the enemy horse tramples the unwarlike (banks of) the Orontes, (more) accustomed to dances and a people rejoicing in songs.

Claudian, *In Eutropium* I.245–51: Across the Phasis are led Cappadocian mothers, and captive herds, led away from their ancestral quarters, drink the frosts of the Caucasus, exchanging the pastures of Argaeus for Scythian forests. Beyond the Cimmerian marshes, the Gates of the Tauri, the flower of Syrian (youth) is enslaved. The terrible barbarians cannot cope with their spoils; sated with booty, they turn to slaughter.[73]

Cyrillonas, ed. Bickell, 586–7 (verses 243–84): Every day stirrings, every day news, every hour torments, every (day) conflicts. Your will has drawn the East into captivity, and the wasted cities are uninhabited. The West is being struck, and behold, its cities hold peoples who do not know you. Dead are the merchants, the prayers have ceased, the women are widowed, the offerings have stopped. The North is distressed and full of wars. If you delay, my Lord, they will destroy me. If the Huns conquer me, my Lord, why have we taken refuge with the martyrs? If their swords kill my sons, why did we adopt your great cross? (p.587) If you will yield to them the cities, where will be the glory of your holy church? Not a year has passed since they came to destroy me and took my children prisoners, and lo, they are threatening to humiliate our land a second time. (tr. Maenchen-Helfen, rev. M. Greatrex)

***Euphemia*, §4, 46.2–8 (Syriac), cf. 150 (Greek):** In the year 707 (395/6) by the reckoning of the Greeks the Huns had come forth, and they took prisoners and laid waste the land and came as far as Edessa. And Addai, the *stratēlatēs* at that time, did not give permission <to the *foederati*> to go out against them because of treason in their midst, and for this cause the armies of the Romans came down and lived in Edessa for a time. (tr. Burkitt, rev. M. Greatrex)

Jerome, *Ep.*60.16: The East seemed to be free from these evils and merely dismayed at the reports; but lo, (I tell) you, in the year gone by,[74] the wolves not of Arabia but of the north, were unleashed from the furthest crags of the Caucasus, and overran so many provinces in a short time. How many monasteries were captured, how many rivers were stained with human blood! Antioch was besieged and other cities past which flow the Halys, Cydnus, Orontes and Euphrates. Hordes of captives were led off; Arabia, Phoenicia, Palestine and Egypt were seized by fear.[75] (...)

Philostorgius, *HE* XI.8 (138.3–8): But the eastern Huns crossed the river Tanais (Don), and pouring into the provinces of the East, broke through Greater Armenia into the district called Melitene. From there they attacked Euphratesia and penetrated as far as Coele Syria; and, overrunning Cilicia, they engaged in an incredible slaughter of people. (tr. Walford, revised)

Ps.-Dion. I, 187.17–188.14: In this year (706 [394/5]), the Huns entered the territory of the Romans and subdued all the lands of Syria[76] which are in the vicinity of the Cahja mountain,[77] that is Arzanene, and Martyropolis, and Amida and Anzitene and Samosata;[78] and after crossing the Euphrates, they cut the bridge behind them. And on all sides the Roman forces gathered against them and destroyed them; not one of them escaped. And at that time the people in the fortress of Ziatha were besieged.[79] When the terrible scourge of the Hunnic army reached the region of Amida, all the people of the country fled and entered the fortresses (p.188) which are by the river Tigris and by the Deba;[80] and they are called the fortress of Ziatha the great and the fortress of Ziatha the lesser, and the fortress of Eghil of Sennacherib the king of Assyria. That great fortress of Ziatha was situated between the Tigris and the Deba. The Deba flows past the wall from the west and the Tigris from the east, and they mix together to the south of the wall. (The place) is very rugged and inaccessible because it lies at a great height and has only one gate. But the Huns seized the gate of the wall and also the aqueducts which go down to the Tigris and the Deba; they stood on these and held them until the men who lay on the Cahja (mountain) perished; and at last those who were left handed over the fort. But the Huns, who are men without pity, slaughtered the whole populace with the edge of the sword and made the rest captive; and they set fire to the whole fort and it was never again inhabited.[81] (tr. M. Greatrex)

Socr. HE VI.1.5–7 (311.23–8): When therefore the Emperor Arcadius met the army outside the gates (of Constantinople) as was customary, the soldiers at that moment killed Rufinus, the emperor's prefect. (6) For Rufinus was suspected of aspiring to the sovereignty and had the reputation of having invited the Huns – the barbarian nation – into the Roman empire. (7) For at that time they were overrunning Armenia and certain parts of the East.

Soz. HE VIII.1.2 (347.10–13): Meanwhile the barbarian Huns were overrunning the Armenias and certain parts of the eastern provinces. It was said that Rufinus, the prefect of the East, secretly invited them to set the empire in confusion, since he was suspected in any case of wishing to seize the sovereignty.

Josh. Styl. 9 (243.2–8): What made these words[82] find credence was the devastation and depopulation which the Huns wrought in the Greek territory in the year 707 (395/6), in the days of the emperors Honorius and Arcadius, the sons of Theodosius the Great, when all Syria was delivered into their hands by the deception of the prefect Rufinus and the negligence[83] of the *stratēlatēs* Addai. (tr. Wright, rev. M. Greatrex)

The Roman counter-attack on the Huns

Despite the lack of evidence, it is clear that the eunuch Eutropius, for all the criticisms of Claudian, managed to defeat some Huns in 397 or 398. See Cameron 1970: 125 (placing the campaign in summer 398), Blockley 1992: 47 (preferring 397).[84]

Claudian, In Eutropium II.pr.55–6: You (Eutropius) will not now terrify the Armenians with javelins and bow, nor will you drive on your swift horse across the fields.
Claudian, In Eutropium I.252–4: He (Eutropius), however (for what will shame a weak slave? Or what could blush in his red face?), returns as a victor (…).

2

THE EVOLUTION OF THE
NORTH-EAST FRONTIER (363–99)

Roman–Persian negotiations concerning the
Caspian Gates from 363

This excerpt is of great importance to our understanding of Roman–Persian relations in the fifth century. While some regard it as proof of the existence of a treaty between the two sides, by which the Romans made annual payments to the Persians, others draw attention to how little it actually tells us. Of the two positions, the minimalist is preferable. As Blockley concludes, 'all that the passages of Lydus allow us to conclude is that the issue of the defence of the Caucasus might have emerged first during the third quarter of the fourth century; that it was discussed inconclusively until the reign of Anastasius; and that there was no agreement.' See Blockley 1985: 63–6, quotation from 66, Blockley 1992: 50–1, Luther 1997: 104–6.[1]

Joh. Lyd. *De Mag.* **III.52–53 (212.14–214.7):** (…) As long as the Romans controlled Artaxata and the regions even beyond, they were able, since they were on the spot, to resist them (the barbarians who might come through the Caspian Gates). But when they evacuated these and other regions under Jovian, the Persians were unable to defend both their own and the former Roman territory, and unbearable turmoil constantly gripped the Armenias subject to each state. Therefore, after the failure under Julian, talks were held between Salutius, who was then prefect, and the Persian grandees and later with Yazdgerd,[2] in order that, sharing the cost, both states should build a fortress on the aforementioned pass and bring help to the area in checking the barbarians who were overrunning it.[3] But since the Romans were embroiled in wars in the west and north, the Persians, insofar as they were more exposed to the barbarians' incursions, were compelled to build the fortress against them there, naming it Biraparakh[4] in their own language and establishing a garrison there. And the enemy was unable to effect an entrance. (53) For this reason the Persians attacked the Romans and spread little by little over Syria and Cappadocia, alleging that they had been wronged and had been deprived of the money for common (p.214) projects to the amount of the Roman contribution.[5] As a result, the first Sporacius was sent by Theodosius I to negotiate with the Persians. He, through the power of his money and his ability at speaking, almost persuaded the Persians to leave the Romans in peace and be their friends, since the Romans were so generous towards them.[6] And this affair dragged on until the reign of our Emperor Anastasius, being talked over, decreed about and, in short, having been prevaricated over. (…) (tr. Blockley, revised)

Wars in Armenia (363–87)

Once Jovian had agreed not to help the Armenian king Arsaces, Shapur took the opportunity to try to seize control of Armenia. The precise terms of the agreement of 363 concerning Armenia are unknown, and were clearly interpreted differently by Shapur and the Romans. The war soon took its toll on the kingdom, and Arsaces surrendered to Shapur in 368/9 (*Epic Histories*, IV.21–50). See Baynes 1955: 198–9.[7]

Ammianus XXVII.12.1–3: The king of Persia, the aged Shapur, who from the very commencement of his reign had been addicted to the love of plunder, after the death of the emperor Julian, and the disgraceful treaty of peace subsequently made, for a short time seemed with his people to be friendly to us; but presently he trampled underfoot the agreement which had been made under Jovian, and poured a body of troops into Armenia to annex that (country) to his own authority, as if the validity of the agreements had expired. (2) At first by various types of tricks he harassed (this) nation, rich in manpower, through slight expenditure, seeking to influence some of the nobles and satraps, and making sudden inroads into (the districts belonging to) others. (3) Then through careful enticements combined with perjury, he captured their king Arsaces, having invited him to a banquet, and ordered him to be conducted to a hidden back door. His eyes were put out, and he was loaded with silver chains, which among them is looked upon as a solace under punishment for men of rank, trifling though it be; then he removed him to a fortress called Agabana, where, after being tortured, he perished by the executioner's blade.[8] (tr. Yonge, revised)

Shapur was active on a broad front, intervening also in the Transcaucasus, where he ousted the Roman appointed king of Iberia, Sauromaces. Since the peace of 363 made no mention of Iberia, Shapur's actions were particularly provocative, as Ammianus makes clear. See Toumanoff 1963: 150 n.5, 460, Chrysos 1976: 45–8, Blockley 1984: 36–7, 48 n.61, Braund 1994: 260.[9]

Ammianus XXVII.12.4: After this (the capture of Arsaces), in order that his (Shapur's) perfidy might leave nothing unpolluted, having expelled Sauromaces, whom the authority of the Romans had made governor of Iberia, he conferred the government of that district on a man of the name of Aspacures, giving him a diadem to mark the insult offered to the decision of our emperors.[10] (tr. Yonge, revised)

With Arsaces disposed of, it remained for Shapur to eliminate the rest of the royal family, who had sought refuge in the fortress of Artogerassa. The Armenian tradition differs somewhat from the Roman: there is no reference to Cylaces and Arrabannus, nor to an initial defeat of the Persians. See Garsoïan 1989: 303–5.[11]

Ammianus XXVII.12.5–9: Having accomplished these (feats) with malicious enthusiasm, he committed the charge of Armenia to a eunuch named Cylaces and to

Arrabannus,[12] a couple of deserters whom he had received some time before (one of them, it was said, had been a prefect of that nation, and the other commander-in-chief); and he enjoined them to use every exertion to destroy Artogerassa, a town (made) strong by (its) walls and (its) garrison, in which were the treasures and the wife and son of Arsaces. (6) These generals commenced the siege as they were ordered. And as it is a fortress placed on a very rugged mountain height, it was inaccessible at that time, while the weather was cold and the ground covered with snow and frost; and so Cylaces being a eunuch, and, as such, suited to feminine flatteries, took Arrabannus with him and quickly approached the walls; having received a promise of safety, he and his companion were admitted into the city as he had asked. He advised the defenders and the queen in a threatening fashion to calm the passion of Shapur, the most unmerciful of all men, by a speedy surrender. (7) And after many arguments had been urged on both sides, the woman bewailing the cruel fortune of her husband, the men who had been most active in wishing to compel her to treachery, pitying her distress, changed their views; and conceiving a hope of higher preferment, they in secret conferences arranged that at an appointed hour of the night the gates should be suddenly thrown open, and a strong detachment should sally forth and fall upon the ramparts of the enemy's camp, (surprising it) with sudden slaughter; they promised that they would see to it that those undertaking these things would pass unnoticed. (8) Having ratified these matters with an oath, they left the town, and led the besiegers to acquiesce in inaction by representing that the besieged had required two days to deliberate on what course they ought to pursue. Then in the middle of the night, which was spent in sleep all the sounder on account of the greater freedom from danger, the gates of the city were thrown open, and a strong body of young men poured forth with great speed, creeping on with noiseless steps and drawn swords, and suddenly, when they entered the camp of the enemy, who feared nothing, they slew many men as they lay (there) without meeting any resistance. (9) This sudden treachery and the unexpected loss of the Persians gave grounds for a fierce quarrel between us and Shapur; and another cause for his anger was added, in that the Emperor Valens received Pap, the son of Arsaces, who at his mother's instigation had left the fortress with a small escort, and bade him stay at Neocaesarea, a most celebrated city of Pontus Polemoniacus, where he was treated with great liberality and high respect. Cylaces and Arrabannus, attracted by this humanity of Valens, sent envoys to him to ask for assistance, and to request that Pap might be given to them for their king.[13] (tr. Yonge, revised)

Epic Histories **IV.55**: Then Shapur king of Persia sent a certain two of his princes, one of whom was called Zik and the other Karēn,[14] with five million men against the country of Armenia, to go, undermine and destroy the country of Armenia. And they came and arrived at the land of Armenia. Then, when the queen of the country of Armenia Paranjem, the wife of Arsaces (Arshak) king of Armenia, saw that the forces of the Persian king had come and filled the countries of Armenia, she took with her some eleven thousand select armed, warlike *azats*, and together with these she rushed from the Persian forces and entered the fortress of Artagerk in the land of Arsharunik. Then the entire Persian army came up, installed itself around the fortress, kept watch, surrounded, and besieged it. Now those who were fortified inside trusted in the strength of the place, while the others entrenched and settled themselves outside around the valleys. And they were installed around the fortress for thirteen months but were unable to take the fortress because the site was extremely strong. They ravaged and devastated the whole land. They went out and plundered the whole land, and from the surrounding districts and countries led captive men and animals back to their fortified camp. They brought in supplies from elsewhere, consumed them, and besieged and guarded the fortress. (...) (tr. Greenwood)

Shapur's initial failure at Artogerassa and Roman support for Pap led to an escalation of hostilities, with the Romans drawn into playing an increasingly active role. Initially, however, they seem to have tried to keep their distance.[15]

Ammianus XXVII.12.10–13: However, for the moment assistance was refused them (Cylaces and Arrabannus); but Pap was conducted by the general Terentius back to Armenia, where he was to rule (that) nation in the meantime without any of the insignia (of royalty), which was a very wise regulation, in order that we might not be accused of breaking the treaty of peace. (11) When this arrangement became known, Shapur was enraged beyond all bounds, and collecting a vast army, entered Armenia and ravaged it by open pillaging.[16] Pap was terrified at his approach, as were also Cylaces and Arrabannus, and, as they saw no reinforcements (coming), they fled into the recesses of the lofty mountains which separate our frontiers from Lazica; there they hid in the depths of the woods and among the defiles of the hills for five months, eluding the various attempts of the king (to discover them). (12) And Shapur, when he saw that his efforts were being spent in vain while the winter stars were shining, burnt all the fruit trees, and all the fortified castles and camps of which he had become master by force or treachery. He also surrounded Artogerassa with the whole weight of his numerous forces, and, after battles of varying outcomes, when the defenders grew slack, he set fire to it (as it lay) exposed; and he carried off from there the captured wife of Arsaces and all his treasures.[17] (13) For these reasons the *comes* Arintheus was sent into these districts with an army, to aid the Armenians in case the Persians should attempt to harass them by (another) similar campaign.[18] (tr. Yonge, revised)

Epic Histories V.1: Then after all this Mushel, the son of Vasak,[19] collected the whole free contingent of the remaining men who had survived and travelled together with them to the king of the Greeks. He presented the request of the country of Armenia and all the instances of tribulation which had befallen them, and requested from the emperor Pap, son of Arsaces, as king over the country of Armenia. The great king of the Greeks made Pap the son of Arsaces king over the country of Armenia as he (Mushel) had sought from him, and the king of the Greeks gave them great support; they sent to the land of Armenia together with king Pap the *stratelat* named Tērent and a certain *comes* Adē with six million men.[20] (...) (tr. Greenwood)

The Roman intervention, even if not on the scale claimed by the *Epic Histories*, sufficed to persuade Shapur to continue the struggle by diplomatic, rather than military, means. The events narrated by Ammianus here fall probably in 370.[21]

Ammianus XXVII.12.14–18: At the same time, Shapur, who was extraordinarily cunning, being either humble or arrogant as best suited him, under pretence of an intended alliance sent secret messengers to Pap to reproach him for being neglectful of his own interests, since, under the guise of royal majesty, he was really the slave of Cylaces and Arrabannus. These two Pap hastily killed, having lured them (to him) with flattery; (and he then) sent the heads of the dead men to Shapur in proof of his obedience.[22] (15) When this calamity became generally known, Armenia would have been ruined without a blow, if the Persians had not been so alarmed at the approach of Arintheus that they forbore from invading it again. They contented themselves just with sending ambassadors to the emperor, demanding of him not to defend this same nation, in accordance with the agreement made between them and Jovian. (16) Their ambassadors were rejected, and Sauromaces, who, as we have said before, had been expelled from the kingdom of Iberia, was sent back with twelve legions under the command of Terentius; and when he was already close to the river Cyrus,[23] Aspacures entreated him that they might both reign as partners, being cousins, alleging that he could not withdraw nor cross over to the side of the Romans, because his son Ultra was still in the hands of the Persians as a hostage. (17) Once the emperor learnt this, in order to put an end to the difficulties arising out of this affair too through sensible planning, he assented to the division of Iberia, so that the Cyrus should divide it in the middle; Sauromaces was to retain the portion next to the Armenians and Lazi, and Aspacures to have the districts which border on Albania and Persia.[24] (18) Shapur, indignant at this, exclaimed that he was unworthily treated, because we had assisted Armenia contrary to the terms of the treaty, and (because) the embassy which he had sent to procure redress had been forgotten, and because it had been decided that the kingdom of Iberia be divided without his consent or knowledge; and so, as if the gates of friendship had been shut, he sought assistance among the neighbouring nations, and prepared his own army in order, with the return of fine weather, to overturn all the arrangements which the Romans had made with a view to their own interests.[25] (tr. Yonge, revised)

In the following year, 371, Roman troops became directly involved in the war. See Gutmann 1991: 176 and n.81, Seager 1996: 280.

Ammianus XXIX.1.1–4: At the conclusion of the winter, Shapur, king of the Persian peoples, being full of cruelty and arrogance from the confidence (engendered by) his former battles, having completed his army to its full number and greatly strengthened it, sent out a force of heavy cavalry, archers and mercenary troops to make an invasion of our territories. (2) Against this force the *comes* Trajan and Vadomarius,[26] the former king of the Alamanni, advanced with a mighty army, having been placed under orders from the emperor to see to it that they contain rather than harass the Persians. (3) When they arrived at Vagabanta,[27] a place well suited for the legions, they stood up to a fierce and rapid charge made upon them by the squadrons of the enemy, and reluctantly retreated with deliberate care so as not to be the first to slay any of the enemy soldiers, and not to be looked upon as guilty of having broken the treaty. At last, under the pressure of extreme necessity, they came to an engagement with the barbarians, and after having slain a great number of them, emerged the victors. (4) During the cessation of regular operations (which ensued) several light skirmishes were undertaken by both sides, which ended with different results; and after a truce was agreed by common consent, and the summer had been used up, the generals of the two sides departed, although they were still at odds (with one another). The king of Parthia, intending to pass the winter at Ctesiphon,[28] returned to his own home, and the Roman emperor went to Antioch; and while he tarried there, secure from foreign enemies, he very nearly perished through domestic treachery, as the series of events described (here) will show.[29] (tr. Yonge, revised)

Shapur's diplomacy continued nonetheless, and finally bore fruit. Pap had the patriarch Nerses executed, and then made unrealistic demands of the Romans. They in turn brought about the king's downfall and death, probably in 375 (*Epic Histories* V.24, *Vit. Ners.* 12 [p.36], Mos. Khoren. III.39). See Garsoïan 1967: 313 and n.56, Garsoïan 1989: 395.[30]

Ammianus XXX.1.1–5, 18–21: Amidst all these difficulties and disturbances which the treachery of the *dux* (Marcellinus) had provoked by the treacherous murder of the king of the Quadi, a terrible crime was committed in the East, where Pap, king of Armenia, was also murdered by secret plots. The original cause of this matter, brought about by wicked design, we have ascertained to be this. (2) Some clever men who often fed on public misfortunes heaped a number of accusations against this prince for acts which they imputed to him even though he had just become an adult, and maliciously exaggerated them to Valens. Among these men was the *dux* Terentius, a man who walked about dejectedly and always (appeared) somewhat sorrowful, and throughout his life was an unwearied sower of discord. (3) He, having formed an association with a few people of Pap's nation[31] whom a consciousness of their own crimes had filled with fear, was continually harping in his letters to the court on the deaths of Cylaces and Arrabannus, adding also that this same young king was full of haughtiness in all his conduct, and that he behaved with excessive cruelty to his subjects. (4) Therefore Pap was invited to court as if he were about to take part in a treaty, which, on account of existing circumstances, had to be made then; (he was treated) with the ceremony befitting a king, and then was detained at Tarsus in Cilicia, with a show of honour, without being able to procure permission to approach the emperor's camp or to learn why his arrival had been so urgent, since on this point everyone preserved a rigid silence. At last, however, by means of private information, he learnt that Terentius was endeavouring by letter to persuade the Roman sovereign to send at once another king to Armenia, in case, out of hatred to Pap, and in the expectation that he would return, his nation, which at present was friendly to us, should revolt to the Persians, who were most eager to reduce them under their power by either violence, fear, or flattery. (5) He (Pap), reflecting on this warning, foresaw that the threat of a grievous death hung over him. Now aware of the plot, he could not perceive any means of safety, save by a speedy departure, (and) by the advice of his most trusty friends he collected a body of 300 persons who had accompanied him from his own country. With horses selected for special speed, acting as men are wont to do (when faced by) great and uncertain fears, that is to say, with more boldness than prudence, late one afternoon he started boldly forth at the head of his escort, moving in wedge formation.

(*Pap successfully escapes from Roman territory*.) (18) In this manner (through further accusations against Pap) the baffling hatred which Valens had conceived against him (Pap) was increased; and plan after plan was laid to take his life, either by force or by stratagem; and orders to that effect were transmitted by secret letters to Trajan, who at that time was in Armenia, in command of the forces (there). (19) Trajan accordingly began to surround Pap with treacherous blandishments – at one time showing him some letters of Valens, showing his calm state of mind[32] – at another, partaking cheerfully of his entertainments. At last, when his deception was prepared, he invited him with great respect to supper. Pap, fearing no hostility, came, and was seated in the place of honour at the feast. (20) Exquisite delicacies were set before him, and the splendid palace resounded with the music of string and wind instruments. Presently, flushed with wine, the master of the feast himself left it for a moment, under pretence of some natural want, and immediately a ferocious and violent barbarian of the troop they call Scurrae was sent in, brandishing a drawn sword and glaring fiercely, to murder the youth, against whose escape ample precautions had been taken. (21) As soon as he saw him, the young king, who as it happened was leaning forwards beyond (his) couch, jumped up and drew his dagger to defend his life by every means in his power, but was stabbed in the breast, and fell like a disfigured victim (at the altar), being shamefully cut to pieces with repeated blows. (...) (tr. Yonge, revised)

Epic Histories V.32: And the king, Pap, changed his mind and turned his heart away from the king of the Greeks, and he wished to unite in love and make an agreement with the king of Persia. And so he began to make an alliance with the king of Persia and to send him envoys for the sake of an agreement. He also sent envoys to the king of the Greeks (to say): 'Caesarea, together with ten cities, belongs to me; now give them back. My ancestors also built Urha (Edessa). Now, if you do not wish to cause conflict, give it back; otherwise we will fight a great war.' But Musheł and all the Armenian princes urgently proposed to the king that he should not break the covenant with the kingdom of the Greeks. He, however, did not listen to them and openly manifested the hostility which he had towards the king of the Greeks. (...) (tr. Greenwood)[33]

In the wake of Pap's assassination, Valens became more willing to negotiate with Shapur, and a sequence of embassies passed back and forth between the two rulers. We follow the chronology of Blockley 1987: 227 n.22.

Ammianus XXX.2.1–5: These are the events (which took place) in Armenia that are worthy of note (i.e. the assassination of Pap); but Shapur, after the previous defeat which his troops had experienced, and having heard of the death of Pap, whom he had been earnestly labouring to win to his own alliance, was struck by great grief; and, as the activity of our army increased his apprehension, he paved the way for still greater (disasters) for himself. (2) He therefore sent Arraces as his ambassador to the emperor, to advise him that Armenia, as a perpetual cause of trouble, should be utterly destroyed;[34] or, if that plan was unsatisfactory, asking that an end might be put to the division of Iberia, that the garrison of the Roman sector might be withdrawn, and that Aspacures, whom he himself had made the sovereign of that nation, might be permitted to reign alone.[35] (3) To this proposal Valens replied with the view that he could not modify the resolutions which had been agreed to by common consent, but rather that he would maintain them by zealous care.[36] Towards the end of winter, a letter was received from the king in reply to this noble determination, (in which) he offered vain and presumptuous excuses. For in it Shapur affirmed that it was impossible for the seeds of discord to be radically extirpated unless those who had been witnesses of the peace which had been made with Julian were to become involved, some of whom he had heard were already dead.[37] (4) Afterwards the emperor gave greater attention to the matter, being now in a position to select his plans rather than respond,[38] (and) thinking that it would be beneficial to the state, ordered Victor, the *magister equitum*, and Urbicius, the *dux* of Mesopotamia, to march with all speed to the Persians, bearing a complete and plain answer (to the proposals of Shapur): namely that he, who boasted of being a just man, and one contented with his own, was acting wickedly in coveting Armenia, after a promise had been made to its inhabitants that they should be allowed to live according to their own laws.[39] And unless the garrisons of soldiers who had been assigned to Sauromaces as auxiliaries returned without hindrance at the beginning of the ensuing year, as had been agreed, Shapur would (have to) perform unwillingly the things which he had failed to do of his own accord. (5) And this embassy would in all respects have been a just and honourable one, if the ambassadors had not, contrary to their instructions, accepted some small districts in this same Armenia, which were offered to them.[40] After the ambassadors returned, Surena (second in power after the king) arrived, offering the same districts to the emperor which our ambassadors had rashly taken.[41] (6) He was received with liberality and magnificence, but dismissed without obtaining what he requested. And then great preparations were made for war, in order that, as soon as the severity of the winter was over, the emperor might invade Persia with three armies; and with this object he began with all speed to bargain for the services of some Scythian mercenaries.[42] (7) Then Shapur, having not obtained what his vain hopes had led him to reckon on, and being exasperated more than usual because he had learnt that our emperor was preparing an expedition, stifled his wrath, and gave Surena a commission to endeavour to recover by force of arms, if anyone should resist him, the territories which the *comes* Victor and Urbicius had accepted, and to do the most harm possible to those soldiers who had been detailed to aid Sauromaces. (8) His orders were at once carried out. Nor was it possible to prevent or resist their execution, because a new cause of alarm suddenly came upon the Roman state; as the entire nation of the Goths was boldly bursting into Thrace.[43] (...) (tr. Yonge, revised).

Before Valens' attention was forced back to the Balkans, he had appointed a new king for

Armenia, Varazdat. The king's chief general, Mushet, was keen to cooperate with his allies in the defence of the kingdom in the coming war.[44]

Epic Histories V.34: He (Mushet) also consulted with the Greek officers and through them with the emperor, (asserting) that they should build one city in every district of the land of Armenia: firstly (they should construct) cities, secondly they should establish strong fortifications and garrisons throughout the whole land of Armenia as far as the border of the land at Ganzak, which was on the Persian side and marked the frontier of Armenia. (They should also) enlist all the Armenian *azats* by means of imperial wages, and likewise the forces of the land of Armenia, so that every precaution should thus be taken against their enemies, the Persian forces. And the king of the Greeks gladly agreed to do this, so that the country might thus become strengthened in every way and unshakeable (in its loyalty) on his side, and that the king of Persia might not be able to usurp the country of Armenia.[45] (tr. Greenwood)

However, Varazdat subsequently executed Mushet, and was ousted from his throne by Manuel Mamikonean probably in 377; he therefore took refuge with the Romans. Manuel then turned to Shapur for help (*Epic Histories* V.37). See Gutmann 1991: 190, Redgate 1998: 137.

Epic Histories V.38: Then after this, the queen of Armenia, Zarmandukht, and the *sparapet* Manuel sent Garjoyl the *malkhaz* with many of the Armenian *nakharars* together with official letters, gifts, and presents to the king of Persia (to say) that they would assist him, serve him, submit to him faithfully, and give this country of Armenia to him. Garjoyl set out with his companions, arrived at the court of the Persian king, presented to him the official letters from the queen and the *sparapet* of Armenia, and transmitted to him the message of submission. When the king of Persia saw them, he received them with great joy, honoured them with great esteem, and lavished gifts upon Garjoyl. (tr. Greenwood)

The Persian king therefore despatched Surena with a force of 10,000 men to Armenia; he also sent crowns for Arsaces and Valarshak, the two sons of Zarmandukht and Pap. But a revolt soon broke out, led by Meruzhan. Manuel also turned against the Persians, and the Armenians succeeded in asserting their independence for a period of seven years.[46] Valens, before he left for Thrace early in 378, sought to come to an agreement with Shapur over Armenia; the outcome of his embassy, undertaken by Victor, is unknown.[47] Before his death, Manuel crowned Arsaces IV, son of Pap and Zarmandukht, as king, but he was unable to command the loyalty of all his countrymen. When Shapur's successor to the throne in 379, Ardashir II, nominated an alternative king for Armenia, the way lay open to the partitioning of the kingdom.[48]

The partition of Armenia (387)

General consensus now favours the date of 387 for the division of Armenia between the two great powers, but some continue to prefer 384. Direct contemporary references to the partition are non-existent, and so it is necessary to rely on later Armenian sources, supplemented by a different tradition preserved in the *Narratio de rebus Armeniae* and Procopius. See Blockley 1987:

230–4, viewing the partition as a loose arrangement (rather than a rigid division), Gutmann 1991: 229–32, Blockley 1992: 42–4, Garsoïan 1999: 45–6 and Greatrex 2000a.[49]

Epic Histories **VI.1:** Then, after the death of the commander of Armenia Manuel, nothing could sustain the kingship of Arsaces over the country. But many of the Armenian *nakharars* separated (from him) and went to the king of Persia; they delivered to him the country of Armenia, and requested from him an Arshakuni (Arsacid) king. And he agreed with great joy on his part to give (them) by his order (a king) from the same Armenian royal house of the Arsacids, and to appropriate for himself through him the country of Armenia. He then found a youth from the same house named Khosrov, placed the crown on his head, gave him his own sister Zruandukht as a wife, and placed under him all the forces in his power. He also gave his deputy Zik as a tutor to King Khosrov. And they went and arrived in the country of Armenia. And when King Arsaces saw them, he withdrew, abandoned the place, and went to the districts of the Greeks. And so (the king of the Greeks) was assisting Arsaces king of Armenia and the king of Persia, Khosrov.

Then the forces of the king of the Greeks came in assistance; King Arsaces (was) around the district of Ekełeats' (Acilisene), and the Persian army and King Khosrov were in the district of Ayrarat. Then envoys and messengers of the two kings – of the Greeks and of the Persians – went back and forth from one to the other. Consequently the king of the Greeks and the king of the Persians decided upon a mutual alliance with one another, and they reckoned that it would be good to divide the country of Armenia into two between themselves. 'For,' they said, 'this powerful and wealthy kingdom is situated between us. It will be good now that we shall be able to destroy and ruin this kingdom. First (we shall) divide it in two through these two Arsacid kings whom we have installed; then we shall attempt to eat away at them and impoverish them (and) drive them into submission so that they shall not be able to raise their head between us.'

They confirmed this plan and divided the country in two. The portion on the Persian side belonged to King Khosrov, and the portion on the Greek side belonged to King Arsaces. But many districts were eaten away and cut off from them here and there, and only a small part from both countries was left to the two kings.[50] But nevertheless, the two Armenian kings, Arsaces and Khosrov, (divided) between them the core districts of the Armenian kingdom[51] which remained to them on both sides; and the two Arsacid kings, having fixed boundaries between the two portions, established peace. And so the land of Armenia (was) in two parts (and) obeyed two kings, each part (being subject) to its own king. However, the portion of Khosrov was larger than that of Arsaces. And many districts were cut off from both. And the kingdom of Armenia was diminished, divided, and scattered.[52] And it declined from its greatness at that time and thereafter. (tr. Greenwood)

Narratio de rebus Armeniae, **10–12:** (10) And Arsaces the lord of Great Armenia was subject to him (Theodosius II). (11) But Khosrov the king of Armenia, who ruled in the land of the Armenians, was under the Persian king Shapur. (12) After four years Shapur expelled him from his kingship.[53]

Proc. *Aed.* III.1.8–15 offers a rather garbled account of events, based on a 'History of the Armenians' (1.6). The two kings between whom Armenia is divided are named Arsaces (in the west) and Tigranes (in the east); as in the *Narratio*, the division is said to have taken place during the reign of Theodosius II, and Procopius reports that the western portion of Armenia was only one fifth of the size of the eastern.[54]

The partition appears to have been stable, and over the years the boundary line became more defined. See Blockley 1992: 44–5. At some point after the split, the Romans installed a *comes* to succeed Arsaces, but considerable autonomy was left to the Armenians, both in Armenia Interior and in the Armenian satrapies (under five satraps) until the sixth century.[55] The Persians did not permanently remove the Armenian royal family from the throne until 428.[56] It is likely that Iberia too was partitioned, as it had been earlier, with the city of Tukharisi and Cholarzene in the west remaining under Roman control, and the rest of the kingdom under the Persian-nominated king. See Chrysos 1976: 48, following Toumanoff 1963: 461, Zuckerman 1991: 536–8 (noting contradictions in the sources), Braund 1994: 261, Redgate 1998: 137–8.[57]

On the Hunnic invasion of 395, which affected not only Armenia and Cappadocia, but also Syria and Mesopotamia, see Chapter 1.

3

THE MESOPOTAMIAN FRONTIER IN
THE FIFTH CENTURY

Roman anxieties over a new Persian king (399)

Yazdgerd I turned out to be one of the most amicable Sasanian rulers with whom the Romans had to contend. But at the opening of his reign in 399, there were fears that he might prove to be another Shapur II.[1]

Claudian, *In Eutropium* II.474–84: Among these rumblings another more sinister messenger flies in. (It announces that) Babylon, armed again and under a new king, is threatening; that the (hitherto) quiet Parthians, detesting slothful inactivity, are now seeking an end to the Roman peace. Rare among the Medes is the murder of kings, for a single retribution remains for the whole nation; and yet they calmly obey cruel masters. But what would the year of Eutropius not dare? It has overcome our faithful ally Shapur[2] and moved the Persians to kill their king, bringing them to the point of breaking their agreement. And in order that no quarter may be free from death, it has driven the torches of the Furies across the waters of the Tigris.

Marutha and the restoration of good relations between
the two powers (399)

That relations between the two powers flourished during Yazdgerd's reign was due to a great extent to the efforts of Marutha, who later became bishop of Martyropolis. He first visited the Persian court in 399, where he made a great impression on the Sasanian king. He was therefore permitted to take with him back to Roman territory the relics of the martyrs who had suffered during the persecutions of Shapur II's reign. With the backing of the emperor, the relics were placed in what was to become a new frontier city; the place was named 'The City of the Martyrs', i.e. Martyropolis. See Noret 1973: 86 (the Greek account), Marcus 1932: 63–4 (the earlier Armenian version), Fiey 1976: 41–3 (a later Arabic account) with Tisserant 1928: 144, Key Fowden 1999: 49–56. As is clear from the passage below, apparently going back to a contemporary account, the good relations fostered by Marutha soon bore fruit. See Greatrex and Greatrex 1999: 67–8.

Chr. 724, 137.9–22: But when the Persian king Yazdgerd was reigning, he again sent back 1330 of these captives to their (own) land; but around 800 captives stayed in

31

Persia, (while) all the others had died through a plague of dysentery[3] on account of the anxiety and distress which they had suffered from the cursed Huns. All these things the captives told us. Christians too and ascetics have related (these things); and junior clerics themselves have reported about the good deeds which the captives said were performed for them and about their gratitude towards the good and clement king Yazdgerd, a Christian and blessed man among kings. May his memory be blessed and his last days nobler than his first; (for) throughout his days he did good things for the needy and wretched. (tr. M. Greatrex)

Yazdgerd I's guardianship of Theodosius II (c.402)[4]

Such was the goodwill between the two courts at this point that the Emperor Arcadius was able to ensure the succession of his infant son Theodosius (II) in 408 by appointing the Persian king as some sort of guardian for him. Because war broke out once again twelve years later, contemporary historians preferred to omit the story; our first source for the episode is Procopius, and later writers add a few details. To Agathias, writing in the 570s, the episode seemed almost beyond belief, to such a point had Roman–Persian relations deteriorated. See Bardill and Greatrex 1996: 171–80 for an analysis of all the sources concerned.

Agath. IV.26.6–7 (157.5–13): In my opinion anyone who admires this is judging its good sense[5] from later events, not from the first impulse of the plan. How could it be a good thing to hand over one's dearest possessions to a stranger, a barbarian, the ruler of one's bitterest enemy, one whose good faith and sense of justice were untried, and, what is more, one who belonged to an alien and heathen faith? (7) And if we are to grant that no harm was done to the child, but that Theodosius' kingdom was most carefully safeguarded by his guardian, even while he was still a babe at the breast, we ought rather to praise Yazdgerd for his decency than Arcadius for the venture. (...) (tr. Cameron, revised)

Proc. Wars I.2.1–10 (7.17–9.7): When the Roman Emperor Arcadius was at the point of death in Byzantium,[6] having a male child, Theodosius, who was still unweaned, he felt grave fears both for him and for the government, not knowing how he should provide wisely for both. (2) For the consideration occurred to him that, if he provided a partner in government for Theodosius, he would in fact be destroying his own son by bringing forward against him a foe clothed in the regal power; (3) while if he set him alone over the empire, many would try to mount the throne, taking advantage, as they might be expected to do, of the isolation of the child. (p.8) These men would rise against the government, and, after destroying Theodosius, would make themselves tyrants without difficulty since the boy had no relative in Byzantium to be his guardian. (4) For Arcadius had no hope that the boy's uncle, Honorius, would succour him, since the situation in Italy was already troublesome.[7] (5) And the attitude of the Medes disturbed him no less, and he feared lest these barbarians should trample down the youthful emperor and do the Romans intolerable harm. (6) When Arcadius was confronted with this difficult situation, though he had not shown himself sagacious in other matters, he devised a plan which managed without trouble to preserve both his child and his throne, either as a result of conversation with certain of the learned men, such as are usually found in numbers with a sovereign, or from some divine inspiration which came to him. (7) For in drawing up the writings of his will, he proclaimed his son as successor to his sovereignty but designated as guardian over him Yazdgerd, the Persian king, enjoining upon him earnestly in his will to preserve the empire for Theodosius by all his power and foresight. (8) So Arcadius died, having thus arranged his private affairs as well as those of the empire. But Yazdgerd, the Persian king, when he saw this writing which was delivered to him, being even before a sovereign whose nobility of character had won for him the greatest renown, did then display a virtue at once amazing and remarkable. (9) For, loyally observing the behests of Arcadius, (p.9) he adopted and continued a policy of profound peace with the Romans the whole time, and thus preserved the empire for Theodosius. (10) Indeed, he straightaway despatched a letter to the Roman Senate, not declining the office of guardian of the Emperor Theodosius, and threatening war against any who should attempt to enter into a conspiracy against him. (tr. Dewing, revised)

Cedrenus I.586.3–7: And Arcadius died in his thirty-first year, having reigned for 26 years. And he ordained that the Persian king Yazdgerd look after his son Theodosius and accept an embassy (bearing) 1000 lbs of gold.[8]

Theoph. A.M. 5900 (80.8–24): Arcadius, perceiving that his son, the young Theodosius, was still very small and unprotected and fearing that someone would plot against him, proclaimed him emperor and by his will appointed the Persian king Yazdgerd his guardian. Yazdgerd, the Persian king, after accepting Arcadius' will, behaved with ungrudging peacefulness towards the Romans and preserved the empire for Theodosius. After despatching Antiochus,[9] a most remarkable and highly educated adviser and instructor, he wrote to the Roman senate as follows: 'Since Arcadius has died and has appointed me as his child's guardian,[10] I have sent a man who will take my place. Therefore let no one attempt a plot against the child so that I need not renew an implacable war against the Romans.' After Antiochus had come, he stayed with the emperor. Theodosius was educated wisely in Christian matters by his uncle Honorius and his sister Pulcheria. And there was peace between the Romans and the Persians, especially since Antiochus wrote many things on behalf of the Christians; and thus Christianity was spread in Persia, with the bishop of Mesopotamia, Marutha, acting as mediator. (tr. Mango and Scott, revised)

Soz. HE IX.4.1 (395.12–13): Then at any rate the Persians, having been stirred up for battle, concluded a one-hundred-year truce with the Romans.[11] (...)

Cooperation in regulating cross-border traffic (408/9)

The spirit of détente between the two sides is well illustrated by a law of 408/9, by which the two sides sought to confine cross-border trading to designated cities. See Synelli 1986: 89–94, Isaac 1992: 407, Lee 1993a: 62–4, Winter and Dignas 2001: 213–15.[12]

C.J. **IV.63.4:** Merchants subject to our government, as well as those (subject) to the king of the Persians, must not hold markets beyond the places agreed upon at the time of the treaty concluded with the above mentioned nation,[13] in order to prevent the secrets of either kingdom from being disclosed (which is improper). (1) Therefore no subject of our empire shall hereafter presume to travel for the purpose of buying or selling merchandise beyond Nisibis, Callinicum and Artaxata, nor think that he can exchange merchandise with a Persian anywhere beyond the above-mentioned cities. Because each party in the contract is aware of this, if one makes a contract under such circumstances, any merchandise which has been either sold or purchased beyond the said cities shall be confiscated by our sacred treasury, and, in addition to this merchandise, the price which was paid in cash or in kind shall be surrendered, and the offender sentenced to the penalty of perpetual exile. (2) Nor shall a fine of thirty pounds of gold be lacking for judges and their subordinates for every contract entered into beyond the above-mentioned limits; for through their borders travelled the Roman or Persian to forbidden places for the purpose of trade; (3) with the exception of those envoys of the Persians who have brought merchandise to be exchanged, to whom, for the sake of humanity and on account of their character as ambassadors, we do not refuse the privilege of trading beyond the prescribed limits; unless, under the pretext of belonging to an embassy, and having remained for a long time in some province, they do not return to their own country; for, as they engage in trade, the penalty of this law will not unreasonably be imposed upon them, as well as upon those with whom they have contracted while they reside (in Roman territory). (tr. Scott, revised)

In this context we may note the recent discovery of a hoard of jewellery, counterfeit Roman *solidi* (of Arcadius) and silver drachms of Yazdgerd I, at Humayma in Jordan (south of Petra). The excavators have tentatively dated the hoard to the first decade of the fifth century, and have suggested that the Roman *solidi* were forged in Persia; according to them, the hoard 'has provided archaeological confirmation for the literary evidence of political, commercial and ecclesiastical contact between the Byzantine and Sasanian regimes in the early fifth century.' See de Bruijn and Dudley 1995: 683–97 (quotation from 697), Maeir 2000: 172, 180–2.

The organisation of the Persian Church (410)

In February 410 the Council of Seleucia–Ctesiphon took place, the first such assembly of the Persian Church. Instrumental in the organisation of the council was Marutha, as is acknowledged in the proceedings. Yazdgerd was kept informed of the discussions which took place, and agreed to give his support to the head of the Persian Church, the *catholicos* Isaac; he also received considerable powers of intervention in Church affairs. According to the records of the council, Yazdgerd, upon being praised for his favourable attitude to Christianity, declared, 'East and West form a single power, under the dominion of my majesty' – a statement capable of being interpreted in several ways. See Labourt 1904: 92–9, Brock 1985: 126, Sako 1986: 67–70, Synelli 1986: 50–1, Blockley 1992: 54.[14]

A raid on the eastern provinces (411)

Jerome, *ep.*126 describes 'a sudden inroad of the barbarians' which overran Egypt, Palestine, Phoenicia and Syria. Its origin is unclear, and it is possible that the raiders came from Africa rather than the desert to the East. See Graf 1989: 349–50, Shahîd 1989: 22–5, Isaac 1998a: 450.[15]

The role of Marutha in fostering good relations (c.412)

Nonetheless relations between the two powers remained friendly for most of the second decade of the fifth century. See Blockley 1992: 54–5, Schrier 1992: 77, van Rompay 1995: 363–4.

Socr. *HE*VII.8.1–3, 18–20 (353.9–15, 354.20–7): About this time,[16] it happened that Christianity was disseminated in Persia for the following reason. (2) Frequent embassies were constantly taking place between the Romans and the Persians: there were various reasons why they were continuously sending embassies to one another. (3) Necessity led to Marutha, the bishop of Mesopotamia, of whom we have made mention a little earlier (VI.15), being sent at this moment by the Roman emperor to the king of the Persians. (*Various miracles are performed by Marutha, which impress the Persian king Yazdgerd I.*) (18) He (Yazdgerd) loved the Romans and welcomed their friendship towards them (the Persians). He nearly became a Christian himself after Marutha, in conjunction with Yabalaha, the bishop of Persia, had shown him another demonstration <of wonders>;[17] (19) for both men, by taking to fasting and prayers, drove out a demon which was troubling the king's son. (20) Yazdgerd died before he completely embraced Christianity and the kingdom fell to his son Bahram. Under him the treaty between the Romans and Persians was broken, as we shall tell a little later (VII.18, translated below).

The situation on the frontier in the 410s

Even the frontier region in Syria enjoyed peace at this time. The ruler of the Persian-allied Lakhmid tribe, Nu'man I, was on friendly terms with the *dux* of Phoenice Libanensis, Antiochus; according to the *Life* of Symeon the Stylite (the Elder), Nu'man later claimed that he would have become a Christian if he had not been under the control of the Persian king. See Shahîd 1989: 161–4, dating the passage below to between 410 and 420.[18]

***V. Sym. Styl.* ch.101, 596–7:** For Antiochus, the son of Sabinus, came to him, when he was made *dux* at Damascus, and addressed the holy man in front of all (p.597), (declaring) 'Na'man (Nu'man) came up into the desert near Damascus and held a banquet and invited me'. For at this time there was still no enmity between him and the Romans.[19] (tr. M. Greatrex)

Further evidence on life in this same frontier region comes from the Greek *Life of Alexander Akoimetos.* Alexander received his education in Constantinople, but upon deciding to dedicate his life to God moved to the East. After spending some time in Osrhoene and Syria, he assembled some disciples and headed south from Osrhoene into what the *Life* calls 'the Persian desert'

(Euphratesia) (*V. Alex. Akoim.* 32 [682], cf. Gatier 1995: 451).[20] Because he and his followers had brought no supplies with them, they soon began to suffer; many began to complain, but Alexander insisted that God would help them.

V. Alex. Akoim. **33 (683.9–13):** And when they had gone a short distance, God, in accordance with the word of the holy man, sent Roman tribunes and soldiers, carrying good things to them from God. And they asked them to go to their *castella* to bless them; for there are *castella* between the Romans and Persians to ward off the barbarians, (situated) ten and twenty miles from one another.[21]

Alexander then proceeded to journey along the *limes*, blessing the fortifications; mention is also made of a raid by barbarians (no doubt Arabs) when a three-year drought ended and the land was recovering. Clearly this region, although later dismissed by an envoy of Justinian as 'altogether unproductive and barren' (Proc. *Wars* II.1.11), supported farmers, soldiers and nomads in this period (*V. Alex. Akoim.* 33–4 [684–5] with Gatier 1995: 452–4).[22]

Towards the end of Yazdgerd's reign, relations were still sufficiently good for a Roman envoy apparently to play a part in the internal politics of the Sasanian kingdom, if Tabari's account can be trusted. See Bardill and Greatrex 1996: 177 and n.28.[23]

Tabari, I, 857–8/86 (Nöldeke 90–1): Then Bahram informed Mundhir that he was going to return to to his father, (and) he set out to see the latter. But his father Yazdgerd, because of his evil character, paid no attention to any of his children, and merely took Bahram as one of his servants, so that Bahram suffered great hardship in this. At that point an embassy came to Yazdgerd under a brother of the Roman emperor (p.858), called Theodosius, seeking a peace agreement and a truce in fighting for the emperor and the Romans. Hence Bahram asked Theodosius to speak with Yazdgerd and to secure for Bahram (permission) to return to Mundhir. (tr. Bosworth)

The war of 421–2: background

In 417/18 the Persian *catholicos* Yabalaha was sent to Constantinople 'for the peace and reconciliation of the two empires'. Evidently there had been some fraying in the relations between the two powers, perhaps as a result of the success of the Christians in attracting converts among the Persians. Nonetheless, in 419/20, the bishop of Amida, Acacius, was present at the second council of the Persian Church, held at Veh-Ardashir. Even at this late stage there was no sign of imminent confrontation between Rome and Persia, nor of the persecution of Christians in Persia. See Labourt 1904: 100–2, Sako 1986: 71–7 (rightly arguing that Acacius did visit Persia in 420), Schrier 1992: 77–8, van Rompay 1995: 363–4.[24] But over the course of the year 420 the situation deteriorated markedly. High-ranking Persians who had converted to Christianity refused to apostasise and were martyred; a general persecution ensued.[25] Yazdgerd died in autumn 420, and was succeeded by Bahram V once his brothers, and rivals for the throne, had been eliminated.[26]

C.J. **VIII.10.10 (5 May 420):** All persons who desire to do so shall be permitted to surround their own lands, or premises established as belonging to them, with a wall, in the provinces of Mesopotamia, Osrhoene, Euphratensis,[27] Syria Secunda, Phoenice Libanensis, Cilicia Secunda, both the provinces of Armenia,[28] both the provinces of Cappadocia, Pontus Polemoniacus and Helenopontus, where this is most required, and in other provinces.[29] (tr. Scott, revised)

Marc. com. a.420.2–3: In the East the soldiers raised a tumult and killed their general, named Maximinus. In Persia persecution raged violently against the Christians.[30] (tr. Croke)

Augustine, De civ. dei XVIII.52 (652.61–4): What (of recent events) in Persia? Did not persecution rage against the Christians to such an extent – if, however, it has even now stopped – that some refugees fled from there even to Roman towns?

Ps.-Dion. I, 193.10–12: In the year 732 (420/1) there arose a severe, intense and pitiless persecution against the Christians in the country of the Persians.[31] (tr. M. Greatrex)

Cyr. Scyth. Vit. Euthym. 10 (18.15–19.9): Therefore this Terebon the Elder, the grandfather of the Younger, while still very young and beardless, was afflicted with a demon and the whole right side of him from head to foot was paralysed. His father, called Aspebetus, spent much money, but it did not help. This Aspebetus, while a pagan and a subject of the Persians, became an ally of the Romans in the following manner. At the start of the persecution in Persia which then took place (around the end of the reign of the Persian king Yazdgerd), the Magi wished to hunt down the Christians; and they stationed the phylarchs of the Saracens under them at all points on the roads, so that none of the Christians in Persia might escape to the Romans. Aspebetus, then a phylarch, observing the harshness (p.19) and inhumanity of the Magi in the city towards the Christians, felt compassion. He did not prevent some of the Christians from fleeing, but rather the opposite; he cooperated (with them), moved by sympathy, although he was an adherent of paganism, (having inherited this) from his ancestors. When he was therefore accused before King Yazdgerd, he took his half-paralysed son, I mean Terebon, and his whole family and wealth, and sought refuge with the Romans. Anatolius, then *magister militum per Orientem*, received them, made them allies of the Romans, and bestowed on Aspebetus the phylarchate of the Saracens in Arabia allied to the Romans.[32]

Quodvultdeus, Liber promissorum III.34.36 (179.29–37): Indeed in our time we learnt of a persecution undertaken among the Persians while the devout and Christian Emperor Arcadius was reigning.[33] In order not to hand back the Armenians who were fleeing to him, he undertook a war with the Persians. He gained a victory by means of a sign before (the engagement) by which bronze crosses appeared on the clothes of the soldiers as they went into battle.[34] Hence the victor also ordered that a golden coin be produced with the same sign of the cross, which continues in use throughout the whole world, and in Asia especially.[35]

Numismatic evidence concerning the war may also be found in Kent 1994: 256, nos.218–21, *solidi* issued in Constantinople, 420–422, depicting Victory supporting a long jewelled cross, a motif which remained popular for the rest of the century. See Holum 1977: 155, 163–7, connecting the coins with the Persian war and the erection of a large jewelled cross at Golgotha in 420/1; also Holum 1982: 108–9, Grierson and Mays 1992: 142, Kent 1994: 75, Key Fowden 1999: 47.

An interesting insight into Persian fears of potential collaboration between Persian Christians and the Romans comes from one of several martyr acts from this period. See Christensen 1944: 280–1 on Mihrshapur's zeal in persecuting Christians. Peroz was martyred in September, AG 733 (= 422).

Conf. Peroz (*AMS* IV.258–9): (Mihrshapur, the chief priest of the Zoroastrians of Persia) got up in anger and went in to the king, and began his accusation (against Peroz) by flattering the king. 'From this moment on, my Lord,' (he said), 'all the Christians have rebelled against you: they no longer do your will; they despise your orders, they refuse to worship your gods. If the king would hear me, let him give orders (p.259) that the Christians convert from their religion, for they hold the same faith as the Romans, and they are in entire agreement together. Should a war interpose between the two empires, these Christians will turn out as a thorn in your side in any fighting, and through their playing false will bring down your power.' (tr. S. Brock)

The course of the war of 421–2

The fullest account of the events of the war is provided by Socrates; scattered details are to be found in other sources, but confusion soon arose in later historians between the conflict of 421–422 and that of 440. See Synelli 1986: 53–5, Croke 1984: 68–72, Blockley 1992: 56–7 and Greatrex 1993: 2.

Socr. *HE* **VII.18 (363.2–365.24):** When Yazdgerd, the king of the Persians, who in no way persecuted the Christians there,[36] died, his son, Bahram by name, received the kingdom in turn. Persuaded by the Magi, he persecuted the Christians harshly, bringing to bear on them various [Persian] punishments and tortures. (2) The Christians in Persia, oppressed by this coercion, therefore fled to the Romans, entreating them not to allow them to be destroyed. (3) Atticus the bishop (of Constantinople) gladly received the suppliants, and did his utmost to help them in whatever way was possible; and he made the events known to the Emperor Theodosius. (4) It happened that at this time the Romans had another cause of grievance towards the Persians, since the Persians were unwilling to hand back the gold-diggers in their possession, whom they had hired from among the Romans,[37] and they were also seizing (the) wares of (the) Roman merchants. (5) To this grievance therefore was added the flight of the Christians there to the Romans. (6) For immediately the Persian (king) sent ambassadors and demanded (back) the fugitives; but the Romans by no means returned the refugees to them, not only because they wished to save them, but also on account of their eagerness to do anything on behalf of Christianity. (7) For this reason they chose to go to war with the Persians rather than allow Christians to perish. (8) The treaty was therefore broken and a terrible war broke out, which I consider it not inopportune to pass over briefly. (9) The Roman emperor acted first, despatching a special army under the command of the general Ardaburius. He invaded Persia through Armenia and laid waste one of the Persian districts called Azazene.[38] (10) Narses, a general of the Persian king, encountered (p.364) him with a Persian force; he engaged (Ardaburius) in battle and, when beaten, retreated in flight. He realised that it would be advantageous unexpectedly to invade Roman territory, which was unguarded, through Mesopotamia, and thus to repel the Romans. (11) But Narses' plan did not escape the Roman general. And so, having ravaged Azazene at great speed, he himself also marched to Mesopotamia. (12) Consequently Narses, although fielding a large force, was nonetheless not strong enough to invade Roman <territory>. (13) When he reached Nisibis (which is a border city belonging to the Persians) he suggested to Ardaburius that they should make war according to a treaty and fix a place and day for an engagement. (14) To those who came he replied, 'Report (this) to Narses: the Romans shall make war not when you want, <but when they judge it to be in their interests>'. (15) <Narses, having learned this, informed his king of everything, and forthwith, just as he was, the king of Persia made ready to go forth and engage Ardaburius with a large force. But the emperor of the Romans>,[39] learning that the Persian (king) was making ready all his forces, simultaneously despatched reinforcements, placing all his high hopes for the war in God. (16) And because the emperor had faith <in God>, he found him to be beneficent, as became clear henceforth. (17) While the people of Constantinople <were in> suspense and uncertainty as to the fortunes of the war, angels of God appeared to some persons in Bithynia who were travelling to Constantinople on their own business, and bade them announce (to the people) to be of good cheer, to pray, and to have faith in God, since the Romans would prove victorious; for they declared that they had been sent by God as arbitrators of the war. (18) When this was heard, it not only encouraged the city, but also made the soldiers more courageous. (19) When, as I have said, the war was transferred from Armenia to Mesopotamia, the Romans laid siege to the Persians who were shut up the city of Nisibis. (20) They constructed wooden towers and led them slowly up to the walls by some device; and they slew many of those hastening to defend the walls. (21) (p.365) Bahram, the Persian king, learning that his province of Azazene had been laid waste and that those shut up in the city of Nisibis were under siege, made preparations to come to an engagement in person with all his forces; (22) but, struck by the strength of the Romans, he summoned the Saracens to his aid, whose leader Alamundarus (Mundhir) was a noble and warlike man. He led an army of many thousands[40] of Saracens, and bade the king of the Persians take heart. He announced to him that the Romans would not hold out for long against him, and that they would hand over Antioch in Syria (to him). (23) But the result did not fulfil his pronouncement, for God inspired the Saracens with an irrational fear: thinking that the army of the Romans was coming against them, they were thrown into confusion, and having nowhere to flee, they threw themselves, armed, into the Euphrates. Around 100,000 men perished by drowning in the river. (24) This matter (turned out) thus. When the Romans besieging Nisibis heard that the king of the Persians was leading a multitude of elephants against them, they grew very afraid; and having burnt all their siege engines, they withdrew to their own territories. (25) In case, <by going through all the events in turn>, I should seem to digress from the subject, I shall leave to one side the battles which took place after this, and how another Roman general, Areobindus, slew the noblest of the Persians in single combat; (nor shall I mention) how Ardaburius ambushed and killed seven noble Persian generals or by what means another Roman general, Vitianus, vanquished the remainder of the Saracens.[41]

Mal. 14.23 (285.65–286.81/364.3–21): In that year Blasses,[42] king of the Persians, came, making war on the Romans. When the emperor of the Romans learnt of this, he made the patrician Procopius *magister militum per Orientem*,[43] and sent him with an army to do battle. When he was about to engage in battle, the Persian king sent him a message, 'If your whole army has a man able to fight in single combat and to defeat a Persian put forward by me, I shall immediately make a peace-treaty for fifty years and provide the customary gifts'. When these terms had been agreed, the king of the Persians chose a Persian named Ardazanes from the division known as the Immortals, while the Romans selected a certain Goth, Areobindus, (who was) *comes foederatorum*. The two came out on horseback fully armed. Areobindus also carried a lasso according to Gothic custom. The Persian charged at him first with his lance, but Areobindus, bending down to his right, lassoed him, brought him down off his horse and slew him. (p.286) Thereupon the Persian king made a peace treaty. Areobindus returned to Constantinople after his victory with the general Procopius and as a mark of gratitude was appointed consul by the emperor.[44] (tr. Jeffreys and Scott, revised)

Oracle of Baalbek, 112–14: And the Persians will rise up for a mighty war, and they will be tripped up by the Romans and will propose peace for forty years.[45]

Tabari, I, 868/103 (Nöldeke 108) provides a brief account of a war in which Mihr-Narse (Narses), with 40,000 men, entered Constantinople and obliged the Romans to resume the payment of tribute. He then returned home, 'having accomplished everything that Bahram wanted'. See Nöldeke 1879: 108 n.2, Synelli 1986: 55, Bosworth 1999: 103 n.261.[46]

Socr. *HE* VIII.20 (366.3–367.9): Let that much suffice on Palladius.[47] The Roman emperor in Constantinople, knowing clearly that the victory had been provided by God, was so happy that, although his men were having such good fortune, he nonetheless longed for peace. (2) Accordingly he sent Helio,[48] a man whom he treated with great honour, bidding him to come to peace terms with the Persians. (3) When Helio reached Mesopotamia, (he found that) there the Romans had made a trench for their own protection; he sent Maximus, an eloquent man, who was the *assessor* of the general Ardaburius, as an ambassador concerning peace. (4) This man, when he was in the presence of the Persian king, declared that he had been sent concerning peace not by the Roman emperor, but by his generals; for, he said, this war was not known to the emperor, and were it known to him, would be considered of little consequence. (5) When the Persian (king) readily chose to receive the embassy (for his army was oppressed by hunger), there came to him those called by the Persians the Immortals (this is a unit of ten thousand noblemen). They said that he should not accept peace before they had made an attack on the Romans, who were [now] off-guard. (6) The king was persuaded and kept the ambassador shut up under guard; and he sent off the Immortals to lie in ambush for the Romans. When they had drawn near (to the

Romans), they divided themselves into two divisions, intending to surround some section of the Roman army. (7) The Romans, catching sight of one of the detachments of the Persians, prepared themselves for its onslaught; the other division was not observed by them, however, for they attacked (so) suddenly. (8) Just as battle was about to be joined, by the foresight of God a Roman army under the command of the general Procopius emerged from behind a small hill. (9) Noticing that his fellow countrymen were about to be in danger, he attacked the Persians in the rear and they who had just previously surrounded the Romans were themselves surrounded. (10) Once they had destroyed all these men in a short time, the Romans turned against those attacking from their place of ambush; and in like fashion they slew every one of them with their missiles. (11) Thus those known to the Persians as Immortals were all shown to be mortals; <they all fell on one day>, for Christ exacted justice (p.367) on the Persians because they had killed many pious men, who were his servants. (12) The king, apprised of the misfortune, feigned ignorance of what had occurred, and received the embassy, saying to the ambassador, 'I welcome peace, but am not yielding to the Romans; rather, I am doing you a favour, because I have come to the conclusion that you are the most intelligent of all the Romans.' (13) Thus was settled the war which had broken out on account of the Christians in Persia; <it had taken place> in the consulship of the two Augusti, the thirteenth of Honorius and the tenth of Theodosius, in the fourth year of the 300th Olympiad; and the persecution of Christians in Persia also came to an end.[49]

Thdrt. *HE* V.37.6–10 (340.22–341.21): (...) And in the previous war he (God) made these same people (the Persians) look ridiculous when they were besieging the city named after the emperor (Theodosiopolis).[50] (7) (p.341) For when Gororanes (Bahram) had been encircling the aforementioned city with all his forces for more than thirty days, had brought many siege-engines[51] to bear, had employed thousands of devices, and had raised up lofty towers outside (the walls), the godly bishop alone (whose name was Eunomius) stood firm and dissolved the strength of the devices brought to bear.[52] Our generals refused battle with the enemy and did not dare to bring aid to the besieged, (but) this man opposed (the enemy) and preserved the city from being sacked. (8) When one of the kings in the service of the barbarians ventured upon his usual blasphemy, uttering (words like those) of Rabshakeh and Sennacherib,[53] and madly threatening that he would set fire to the temple of God, that holy man did not tolerate his raving; he gave orders that the stonethrower, which was named after the apostle Thomas, be placed on the battlements and bade a huge stone be placed on it. He (then) commanded (the men) to discharge the stone in the name of Him who had been blasphemed. (9) It fell directly upon that impious king, landing right on his foul mouth, destroying his face, smashing his entire head, and scattering his brains on the ground. (10) Having witnessed this, (the king) gathered his army together and left the city he had hoped to capture; he acknowledged his defeat through these events and, in fear, made peace. Thus the great king of all looks after the most faithful emperor. (...)

Evagr. *HE* I.19 (28.8–16) = Eustathius frg.1 (*FHG* IV.138): He (Theodosius II) so defeated the Persians, who had violated (the treaty) at the time when their king was Yazdgerd the father[54] of Bahram or, as Socrates thinks, when Bahram himself was

41

king, that he granted them peace after they had sent an embassy; (the peace) lasted until the twelfth year of the reign of Anastasius. These things have been recounted by others, but are most elegantly abridged by Eustathius of Epiphania the Syrian, who also related the capture of Amida.

Chr. Pasch. 579.19–20 (a.421): In the same year a victory over the Persians was reported, in the month Gorpiaeus, on day 8 before the Ides of September, a Tuesday.[55]

Theophanes, A.M. 5943 (104.1–4): In the bygone times, in which the Persian War was undertaken, Marcian, being a common soldier, set out from Greece with his detachment against the Persians; and when he arrived in Lycia he was struck with an illness.[56] (tr. Mango and Scott, revised)

The conclusion of the war of 421–2

Despite the triumphalist tone of the Roman sources, it is clear that the result of the war was a stalemate. Not much is known of the peace terms agreed in 422. Procopius (below) notes one clause in particular, while Malchus (also below) reports that each side undertook not to accept defecting Arab allies from the other. Holum 1977: 170–1 reconstructs the conditions, although it is unlikely that the Romans agreed to make any regular payments. See also Synelli 1986: 62–4, Letsios 1989: 527, Blockley 1992: 57–8, Rist 1996: 33–4, Isaac 1998a: 443, 451, Winter and Dignas 2001: M19.[57]

Marc. com. a.422.4: The Persians made peace with the Romans. (tr. Croke)

Malchus frg.1.4–7: The Persians and Romans (had) made a treaty after the greatest war had broken out against them (the Persians) during the reign of Theodosius (II), (according to which) neither side would accept the Saracen allies (of the other), if any of them attempted to revolt. (tr. Blockley, revised)

Chr. Arb. 16 (67/91): In consequence of that (war) both parties agreed to give their territories complete liberty in the matter of religion. (tr. Schrier 1992: 83)[58]

Proc. *Wars* I.2.11–15 (9.8–10.8): When Theodosius had grown to manhood and was advanced in years, and Yazdgerd had been taken from the world by disease, Vararanes (Bahram), the Persian king, invaded Roman territory with a mighty army; however he did no damage, but returned to his home without accomplishing anything. (And this came about) in this way. (12) The Emperor Theodosius happened to have sent Anatolius, the *magister militum per Orientem*, as an ambassador to the Persians on his own; as he approached the Persian army, he leapt down from his horse alone and advanced on foot towards Bahram.[59] (13) And when Bahram saw him, he enquired from those who were near who this man could be who was coming forward. And they replied that he was the general of the Romans. (14) Thereupon the king was so dumbfounded by this excessive degree of respect that he himself wheeled his horse about and (p.10) rode away, and the whole Persian host followed him. (15) When he had reached his own territory, he received the envoy with great cordiality, and granted the treaty of peace on the terms which Anatolius desired of him; one condition, however, (he added), that neither party should construct any new fortification in his own territory in the neighbourhood of the boundary between the two (countries). When this (treaty) had been executed, both (sides) conducted their affairs as they saw fit.[60] (tr. Dewing, revised)

The aftermath of the war of 421–2

The good cross-border relations established at the opening of the fifth century were not entirely destroyed by the war – which had, after all, lasted for only two years. The actions of Acacius described by Socrates were in effect a reciprocal gesture for the return of Roman prisoners captured from the Huns by Yazdgerd I (noted at the start of this chapter). But only four years later, at its third council, the Persian Church severed its links with the west: it was no longer possible, in the light of the recent hostilities, to rely on the intervention of western bishops to help resolve the conflicts within the Persian Church. See Labourt 1904: 121–4, Brock 1994: 74–5.

Socr. *HE* VII.21.1–6 (367.10–368.2): At this time a good deed made Acacius, the bishop of Amida, more famous among all men. (2) For the Roman soldiers were by no means willing to return to the Persian king the prisoners they had taken in their ravaging of Azazene (Arzanene); the prisoners were perishing of hunger, being about 7000 in number, and this was a source of great grief to the Persian king. At this point Acacius refused to allow these things to take place; (3) summoning the clerics under his authority, he said to them 'Men, our God needs neither dishes nor cups; for he does not eat nor drink, because he is not in need of anything. Since therefore the church here has acquired many gold and silver treasures through the goodwill of its devotees, it is fitting that we should rescue the prisoners of the soldiers and feed them by means of these.' (4) Once he had gone through all these items and still others like them, he melted down the treasures and paid out the ransom to the soldiers on the prisoners' behalf; he fed them, then gave them provisions and sent them off to their king. (5) This deed of the remarkable Acacius astonished the Persian king all the more because the Romans (thus gave the impression that they) were in the habit of being victorious in both warfare and good works. (6) They say that the Persian king wished that Acacius should come into his presence (p.368), in order that he might enjoy the sight of the man; and, following an order from Theodosius, this took place.[61]

Concern for the *limitanei* of the East (438)

Relations between soldiers and civilians in the East had never been easy, but the peace which prevailed for most of the fifth century did not, apparently, ease tensions.[62] Civilians had tended to get the better of soldiers in civil courts, it appears, and so the *magister militum per Orientem* Anatolius persuaded Theodosius to issue a law by which the soldiers could only be tried before a military judge.

***Nov. Theod.* IV.1:** (*Emperors Theodosius and Valentinian Augusti to Florentius, praetorian prefect.*) The efficiency of the *limitanei* demands the support and assistance of Our Clemency, since they are said to be afflicted by the complaints of certain persons and by being produced before various judges, so that as between private life and military science they are born to neither.[63] Add to this the fact that they are compelled to unlearn the use of arms for the observance of the forum of a civilian office,[64] and they are strangers in an alien life, inexperienced in litigation, ignorant of the court actions which are instituted by shameless eloquence and popular doctrines. These facts were brought to Our attention by the report of the Sublime Anatolius, *magister utriusque militiae per Orientem*. Wherefore We do not allow any further that the loss of so great an advantage shall be disregarded, since it is evident by the arrangement of Our ancestors that whatever territory is included within the power of the Roman name is defended from the incursions of the barbarians by the rampart of the frontier.[65] (1) For this reason We sanction by a law destined to live in all ages that throughout all the region of the East from the farthest solitudes, no soldier of a *dux*, no soldier of the *limitanei*, who with difficulty and hardship wards off the misery of hunger by means of his meagre emoluments, shall be produced at all in Our most sacred imperial court, either by the sacred imperial order of Our Divinity or by Our divine imperial response which has been elicited by the prayers of a person who has approached Us. In short, such soldiers shall not be produced in court by the mandates of Our Eternity nor by the decision of any judge whatsoever. Furthermore, the regulations of the Magnificent man (Anatolius) shall be unimpaired and shall be observed in the future, since he established them by a careful investigation for the welfare of the *limitanei*. All such soldiers shall now be returned to their own service who appear to have been produced in court. (tr. Pharr, revised)

The war of 440

The war of 440 scarcely amounted to a war: a brief incursion by Yazdgerd was quickly deflected by the handover of a sum of money to the Persian king. See Blockley 1992: 61 and Greatrex 1993: 2.[66]

Marc. com. a.441.1: The Persians, Saracens, Tzanni, Isaurians and Huns left their own territories and plundered the lands of the Romans. Against them were sent Anatolius and Aspar, *magistri militum*, and they made peace with them for one year. (tr. Croke, revised)

Thdrt. *HE* V.37.5–6 (340.13–21): Just such a thing (as the repulse of Rua by the forces of nature in 435/40) happened in the Persian war. When they (the Persians) learnt that the Romans were heavily occupied, they marched against the neighbouring towns, violating the peace treaty. No one came to the aid of those under attack, for the emperor, confident in the peace, had sent his generals and soldiers to other wars. By hurling down a very fierce thunderstorm and a great hailstorm (God) hindered the (Persian) advance and impeded the movement of their horses. (6) And in the course of twenty days they were not able to traverse as many stades, and by then the (Roman) generals had arrived and mustered the soldiers.[67]

Mos. Khor. III.67 (347): He (Yazdgerd II), having forgotten the treaty, as soon as he was reigning attacked the forces of the Greeks at Nisibis, commanding the army of Azerbaijan to go into our country (Armenia). (tr. Greenwood)

Elishē 7/61–2: And in his exceeding madness, like a ferocious wild animal, he (Yazdgerd II) attacked the country of the Greeks; he struck as far as the city of Nisibis and he ravaged through assault many districts of the Romans and he set on fire all the churches. He collected plunder and captives and terrified all the forces of the country.[68] Then the blessed emperor Theodosius, because he was peace-loving in Christ, did not wish to go out against him in battle, but sent him a man whose name was Anatolius, who was his commander of the East, with many treasures. And the Persians, those who had fled because of Christianity and were in the city of the emperor, he seized and handed over to him.[69] And whatever he (Yazdgerd) said at the time he (Anatolius) fulfilled in accordance with his wishes and he prevented him from much anger; and he returned from there to his own city Ctesiphon. (tr. Greenwood)

Isaac of Antioch, *Hom.*11.374–80: When the Persians plundered our frontiers, many people from within the city of Nisibis joined (them). But after a little time the army which had come to our border was lost, (together) with those who had joined it, so that their records were destroyed.[70] (tr. M. Greatrex)

Concern for the defence of the frontier (443)

The difficulties experienced by the eastern empire in warding off aggressors on several fronts in the early 440s resulted in a substantial reform of the way frontier defences were administered. From 443 the *magister officiorum* had the responsibility of ensuring that the *limitanei* were able to protect the frontiers, and an annual report was required.[71] As is clear from the following extract, particular attention was paid to distribution of the *annona* (rations) to the Arabs, from which, it appears, unwarranted deductions had been made. Clearly their contribution to the defence of the frontier was judged sufficiently important for them to be specifically mentioned. See Shahîd 1989: 49–50, Isaac 1998a: 446.[72]

Nov. Theod. **XXIV.2 (September 443):** To these (*duces*), together with the commandant (*princeps*) and the provosts of the camps (*praepositi castrorum*), as a recompense for their labours, we assign a twelfth part of the *annona* of the *limitanei* only, to be distributed among them, of course, by the decision of the master.[73] But from the *annona* of the Saracen *foederati* and of other tribes, we grant that such *duces* shall have absolutely no right to abstract and appropriate anything. (…) (tr. Pharr, revised)

The threatening situation in the East (447/8)

Despite the Roman concerns here reported by Priscus, no Persian attack materialised. The Roman government might also have taken heart from some of the acclamations uttered at Edessa in this very period, expressing not only support for Roman rule but also hostility to the Persians (and Nestorians). See Frend 1972: 67 (citing Flemming 1917: 21, 27).

Priscus frg.10.9–15 (cf. Jord. *Rom.* 333): They (the Romans) heeded his (Attila's) every bidding and considered it the command of their master, whatever order he might issue. They were not only wary of starting a war with Attila, but were afraid also of the Parthians who were preparing (for hostilities), the Vandals who were creating havoc on the sea, the Isaurians whose banditry was reviving, the Saracens who were overrunning the eastern parts of their dominions, and the Ethiopian tribes who were in the process of uniting.[74] (tr. Blockley, revised)

Peaceful state of the eastern provinces (450s)

Priscus frg.[19] (Suda A 3803): Ardaburius, the son of Aspar, a man of noble spirit who stoutly beat off the barbarians who frequently overran Thrace. As a reward for his prowess, the Emperor Marcian made him *magister militum per Orientem*. Since he received this office in time of peace, the general turned to self-indulgence and effeminate leisure. He amused himself with mimes and conjurors and stage spectacles, and, spending his days in such shameful pursuits, he took no thought at all for things that would bring him glory. Marcian, having proved himself a good emperor, quickly passed away, and Aspar on his own initiative made Leo his successor.[75] (tr. Blockley, revised)

Roman negotiations with the Arabs (c.452)

The raid of 447/8 was not an isolated incident. The Romans therefore sought to come to terms with the restive Arab tribe or tribes attacking the provinces. See Shahîd 1989: 55–6, dating this passage to 453 and suggesting that the Arabs in question were probably Ghassanids or Kindites rather than Lakhmids.

Priscus frg.26: Ardaburius, the son of Aspar, was fighting the Saracens around Damascus. When the general Maximinus and the historian Priscus arrived there, they found him in peace negotiations with the envoys of the Saracens. (tr. Blockley, revised)

Allegations of treachery on the frontier, c.466

Nothing more is known of the allegations reported here; whether or not they were substantiated, they at any rate indicate Roman suspicions of Persian intentions. See *PLRE* II.136 and Lane Fox 1997: 190 on the date. The Nestorian leader Narsai at Edessa in the late 450s had also excited suspicions, prompting him to move to Persia (Barhadbeshabba *HE* 31, *PO* 9.600).[76]

Vit. Dan. Styl. 55 (53.22–54.1, 54.15–19): At around that time (c.466) someone (called) Zeno, an Isaurian by race, came to the emperor. He brought with him letters written by the then *magister militum per Orientem* Ardaburius, who was encouraging the Persians to (undertake) an attack the Roman state and agreeing to join in assisting (p.54) them. (*The matter is then discussed by Leo and his advisers.*) Having heard these things,[77] the emperor replaced Ardaburius, stripping him of all military office, and ordered him to make for Byzantium as quickly as possible. In his place he appointed Jordanes and sent him off; he also appointed Zeno *comes domesticorum*.

The strengthening of a frontier city (465/6)

Chr. Ede. 70: In the year 777 (465/6) Leo built Callinicum in Osrhoene, which he called Leontopolis after his name; and he also appointed a bishop in it.[78] (tr. M. Greatrex)

Developments in southern Arabia (473/4)

Despite the terms of the agreement which had concluded the war of 421–422, towards the end of his reign the emperor Leo accepted an alliance with an Arab, Amorcesus (Imru' al-Qays) who had defected from the Persians and had installed himself by force in Palaestina Tertia (in the area of the Gulf of Aqaba). To the disapproval of the historian Malchus (frg.1), who alone reports this development, the emperor even invited the ruler to Constantinople, appointed him phylarch of the region and patrician, and bestowed many gifts and further territories on him. Although this region was important economically because of the trade routes leading to the Red Sea, it appears that Leo, in the wake of his disastrous expedition against the Vandals, felt he had little choice but to accept the fait accompli with which he was presented. See Letsios 1989: 525–35, Z. Rubin 1989: 388–9, Shahîd 1989: 59–91, Greatrex 1998a: 28, 227 on these developments. In the late 490s Anastasius restored Roman control to this region.

Arab raids, c.474

Evagrius' rather general notice on Arab raids (referred to as Scenitae, i.e. tent-dwellers) can be supplemented by a homily of Isaac of Antioch, describing an attack on Beth Hur, in the vicinity of Nisibis. See Klugkist 1987: 238–43, Shahîd 1989: 114–15, Greatrex 1998b: 287–91.

Evagrius *HE* III.2 (100.6–9): In these ways therefore did Zeno change his way of life at the opening (of his reign). His subjects both in the East and the West suffered badly, on the one side (on account) of the barbarian Scenitae laying waste everything ... [79]
Isaac of Antioch, *Hom.*11.32–47: Why is our foolish community disquieted, so that it complains against its chastisements? For it pleads with the judge, seeking vengeance from him. Behold captivity and exile, along with the plundering of all our possessions. The Arabs ('Arbaye) harry the land in the portion which they took from it. The whole world is in turmoil because the sons of Hagar, those wild asses, transgressed the boundaries of peace and are slaying the good alongside the wicked. Brothers, let us therefore consider Beth Hur, which was suddenly laid waste by the justice of the ruler of all things, who chastises us in order that he may help us. (tr. M. Greatrex)

Roman financial assistance to Peroz (mid-470s)

The whole of the last third of the fifth century saw the Persians embroiled in a bitter struggle with their new eastern neighbours, the Hephthalite Huns. Peroz conducted several campaigns against them, with little success: in the first he was captured, in the second he was killed. See Szaivert 1987, Luther 1997: 121–4, Greatrex 1998a: 46–8.

Josh. Styl. 10 (243.8–13): By the help of the gold which he received from the Romans, Peroz subdued the Huns, and took many places from their land and added them to his own kingdom; but at last he was taken prisoner by them. When Zeno, the emperor of the Romans, heard (this), he sent gold of his own and freed him, and reconciled him with them.[80] (tr. Wright, rev. M. Greatrex)

Border tensions in Mesopotamia in the 480s

Despite Zeno's assistance, tensions on the Mesopotamian border heightened in the early 480s. The emperor had to contend with an uprising in the eastern provinces in 484 led by Illus and Leontius. The rebels sought the support of the Persians, although whether they obtained it is uncertain; they did, however, receive the backing of all but one of the Armenian satraps. Edessa resisted an attack by the rebels, who were soon defeated by Zeno's generals (Joh. Ant. frg.214.2, Josh. Styl. 15–17, Proc. Aed. III.1.25–6). See Brooks 1893: 227, 231, Stein 1949: 28–31. A renewal of the persecution of Christians by Peroz prompted the outbreak of a revolt in Persarmenia (see Chapter 4), and when in 483 the Persian *catholicos* Babowai sought to bring the plight of Christians in Persia to the attention of Zeno, his message was intercepted at Nisibis and he himself executed. See Blockley 1992: 84–5, Gero 1981: 98–107 (doubting that the bishop of Nisibis, Barsauma, was responsible for betraying the *catholicos*, as later sources allege). On Peroz's persecution, see Labourt 1904: 129–30, Fiey 1977: 92–4, Rist 1996: 37. At the same time, Zeno started to demand the return of Nisibis to Roman control (Josh. Styl. 18, cf.7). See Chapter 1 p.5 and n.22.

The letters of Barsauma throw further light on the situation in Nisibis in the 480s. Two years of drought forced Arabs allied to the Persians to encroach on Roman territory, almost leading to full-scale war between the two powers; only by delicate negotiations was the situation restored, as the letters make clear. The situation was exacerbated, according to Barsauma, by the presence of anti-Chalcedonians (Monophysites) in Nisibis, who appear to have formed a fifth column, eager to surrender the city to the Romans. See Gero 1981: 34–7, Blockley 1992: 85, Isaac 1992: 242–3.[81]

Barsauma, *ep.3* (to Acacius), p.528–9: (...) I have learnt, in fact, from the very things which have happened to me, that as long as Nisibis is not in obedience to and under the direction of the one who occupies the throne of the Holy Church of Seleucia and Ctesiphon, the eastern region will endure damage and grave disasters. Now Nisibis is troubled, shaken and tossed like a stormy sea, and if a letter of excommunication is not promptly despatched by Your Fatherhood and does not pacify the city, I shall not maintain my bishopric of Nisibis; Nisibis itself will not remain subject to the great empire of the Persians. There are, in fact, rebels, and if they are left at

Nisibis, they will destroy themselves and the country they inhabit. They have even suggested to me the idea of rebellion, at the time when we were in opposition to the seat of Your Fatherhood and in opposition to the two (cities),[82] as I indicated above. The *marzban* here supports these (p.529) rebels because he is unaware of their evil intent. I fear that when they apprise him of their plan and inform him of their secret, he will write to the king and tell him of the rebellion of these perverse men and that the king will issue an edict against all Christians on account of the revolt of these men.[83] The matter must be covered up as much as possible and not reach (the ears of) people outside. With your great and divine authority, write a letter of excommunication in an imperious style and smite them, just as the doctor who does an amputation on an ill person to deliver him of his illness. Threaten to denounce them to the king and his officers in your letters if they do not pull back. (...)

Barsauma, *ep.2*, p.526–7: (*To patriarch Mar Acacius, the venerable one and friend of God; your affectionate Barsauma. Peace in (the name of) our Lord.*) We live in a country considered beautiful by those who have not experienced it, where there are many opponents of its tranquillity and where the obstacles to its prosperity cannot be counted, especially at the present time. For now for two successive years we have been afflicted by an absence of rain and a shortage of the necessary commodities.[84] The assemblies of the tribes of the south are present here; the multitude of these people and their animals has destroyed and laid waste the villages of the plains and the mountains. They have dared to plunder and capture people and animals, even in the territory of the Romans. A large army of the Romans then gathered and came to the frontier, with their subjects the Tayyaye; they asked for compensation for what the Tu'aye,[85] the subjects of the Persians, had done in their country.

The glorious and illustrious *marzban* Qardag Nakoragan[86] restrained them from this (demand) by his tact and wisdom. He made a pact for them, (undertaking) that he would assemble the chiefs of the Tu'aye and take back from them the plunder and the captives, as soon as the Tayyaye of the Romans had returned the livestock and captives which they had taken on several occasions in (the country of) Beth Garmai, Adiabene and Niniveh, and they would give back some to the Romans and some to the Persians;[87] and he laid down a law in the treaty that they should establish boundaries (p.527), so that there would be no more of these evils, or others like them.

But God knows when these things which were just mentioned will be completed! With reference to and on account of these things, the king of kings has ordered the king of the Tayyaye and the *marzban* of Beth Aramaye to come here; but the leader of the Romans, with all their soldiers and Tayyaye, remains on the frontier. At the start of August, for the sake of peace and as a sign of great friendship we allowed the *dux* to come to Nisibis, to the *marzban*; and he was received by him with great honour. While they were drinking, eating and enjoying themselves together, four hundred cavalry of the Tu'aye had the temerity to go and fall upon the lesser villages of the Romans. When this was heard about, it caused great distress to both sides – both to the Romans and the Persians. The general and the nobles who had accompanied him grew angry with us, for they believed that this had happened in order to insult the Romans; (he thought that) they had entered Nisibis through our deceitfulness.

It is therefore impossible for us at this time to respond to what Your Excellence wrote until all the present differences between Romans and Persians have been resolved. The *marzban* was completely unable to tolerate the matter, when he heard of the king's edict and your letter. If your wisdom heeds us, you will not summon the other bishops there at this moment when famine reigns everywhere and there is a shortage in every country, lest you should bring rumours and blame on yourself. But this assembly which you are preparing to hold will be kept for the time after you have gone up with the envoys to the country of the Romans and you have returned from there. For thus the solid doctrine established at the previous reunion will give pleasure to your knowledge when you have seen and learnt of the confusion which Satan has sown in the country of the Romans. Even if you are absolutely determined that this (assembly) should take place in the near future, I (shall) uphold by word and my deeds all that they do at the assembly according to the laws of Christ; but it is not possible for me to go there now on account of the difficulties over the frontiers. We have annulled and completely destroyed the Synod of Beth Laphat from our letters; now we are for ever the disciples and subjects of the throne of Your Fatherhood. May you be well in Our Lord and pray for us.[88] (tr. M. Greatrex)

Barsauma, *ep.4*, p.529: (...) After I received the edict in our favour sent by the merciful king of kings, on account of the grave matters taking place here between the Romans and the Persians with regard to the frontiers – matters which demanded our presence and diligence above all – the glorious and illustrious *marzban* Qardag Nakoragan passed on our reply to the Gate of the king of kings and made this declaration: 'The Romans are going to send some of their leaders to make a treaty to maintain peace on the frontiers; the bishop of Nisibis knows about the business of frontiers. His presence is very necessary and he cannot come to the Gate until the treaty is concluded.' (...) (tr. M. Greatrex)

Further confirmation of tensions on the border comes from the *Ecclesiastical History* attributed to Barhadbeshabba 'Arbaya. The two major Christian communities in Persian territory, the Monophysites and Nestorians, vied with one another for royal favour, and did their utmost to impugn the loyalty of the other. The advantage was mainly on the side of the Nestorians, whose doctrines were approved by a council in 486. See Fiey 1977: 118–19, Gero 1981: 52–3, Brock 1985: 126. Three years later, in 489, the School of the Persians at Edessa, a bastion of Nestorian teaching, was expelled from the Roman empire. For as long as the Roman emperors tended towards Monophysitism, it was an uneven struggle, and the Nestorians tended to get the upper hand. See Segal 1970: 94–5, Blockley 1992: 85, Brock 1994: 75–6.[89]

Barhadbeshabba, *HE* 31 (*PO* 9.614): Once, when a messenger (of the king) was passing by, certain people of the city accused him (Narses) of being a hater of the kingdom (of Persia) and of spying for the Romans. When the messenger heard these things, he promised that, once he returned from the land of the Romans, he would crucify him. When the athlete (Narses) learned that punishment had been decreed against him without a trial, he said, 'If you return in peace, it is because the Lord has not spoken to me'. And when he (the messenger) had left (Constantinople), had finished his business and had reached Antioch, he died there in accordance with the saint's word; and he ceased his threat(s) and the (saint's) accusers blushed.[90] (tr. M. Greatrex)

Disruption in the Roman eastern provinces (490–500)

The first years of Anastasius' reign (491–518) were troubled by events in the East. First, certain powerful Isaurians who had been sidelined by the death of Zeno undertook a rebellion which took the emperor's generals until 498 to crush. See Brooks 1893: 231–7, Stein 1949: 82–4, Elton 2000: 300. It was also around this time that the Ghassanids under Jafnid leadership displaced the Salîhids as the Romans' chief partner in the defence of the provinces against Arab raids, although not without inflicting some damage on the provinces first. See Shahîd 1958: 147, Sartre 1982a: 157, Shahîd 1989: 282–5. One such raid penetrated as far as Emesa in c.491. (Cyr. Scyth. *Vit. Abram.* 1 [244]). See Sartre 1982a: 152, Shahîd 1989: 120. In the meantime, successive Persian kings, most notably Kavadh, constantly requested funds from the emperor. See Chapter 4 below.

Arab attacks resumed in earnest around the turn of the century. Our chief source for these razzias is Theophanes, who evidently had access to good contemporary sources, for he provides considerable details on who undertook the raids and what provinces were affected. From his account it appears that the Lakhmids, Jafnids and the banu Tha'laba were all involved in the raids: it soon became clear that the Salihids were no longer capable of countering enemy tribes. But around 502 a new configuration of alliances emerged, in which the Kindites, the Jafnids and the tribe of Mudar were brought into the Roman orbit.[91]

Evagrius, *HE* **III.36 (135.20–6):** The Scenite barbarians launched assaults on the Roman empire, but not to their own advantage; and they plundered the lands of Mesopotamia, of each Phoenice and of the Palestines. They suffered badly, however, at the hands of those in command throughout (the region) and later kept peace with the Romans, having agreed a truce *en bloc.*
Theoph. A.M. 5990 (141.1–17): In this year[92] there was an invasion of the so-called Scenite Arabs into Euphratesia. Eugenius, an earnest man in both word and deed, who commanded the army in those parts, drew up (his forces) against them at a place called Bithrapsa[93] in the first region of Syria and defeated them in battle. The vanquished (Arabs) were tributaries of the Persians of the tribe of the phylarch Nu'man.[94] At that time Romanus was commander of the army in Palestine, an excellent man. By good planning and generalship, he captured in battle Ogarus (Hujr), the son of Harith (the latter being known as the son of Thalabane), together with a great mass of prisoners.[95] Before the battle Romanus had worsted and put to flight another Scenite, Jabala by name, who had overrun Palestine before his arrival.[96] At that time also Romanus set free through fierce battles the island of Iotabe, which lies in the gulf of the Red Sea and was subject to the Roman emperor, paying considerable tribute, but which in the meantime had been seized by the Scenite Arabs, and gave it back to the Roman traders to inhabit under its own laws, to import goods from the Indies and to bring the assessed tax to the emperor.[97] (tr. Mango and Scott, revised)
Theophanes, A.M. 5994 (143.21–5): In this year (501/2) there was again an incursion

51

incursion of the Saracens in Phoenice, Syria and Palestine. After the death of Hujr, his brother Badicharimus (Ma'dikarib) overran these regions like a hurricane and retreated with the booty even more swiftly than he had invaded, so that Romanus, who pursued him, could not catch up with the enemy.[98] (tr. Mango and Scott, revised) **Theophanes, A.M. 5995 (144.3–6):** In this year (502/3) Anastasius made a treaty with Harith (known as the son of Thalabane),[99] the father of Ma'dikarib and Hujr, and thenceforth all Palestine, Arabia and Phoenice enjoyed much peace and calm. (tr. Mango and Scott, revised)

Rivalry between Nestorians and Monophysites in the Persian kingdom

It was around this same time that the rivalry between the Nestorians and Monophysites in Persia came to a head. Deteriorating relations with Rome could only harm the Monophysite community, since the Roman emperor himself was a Monophysite. Unsurprisingly therefore the Nestorians exploited the charge that their opponents were disloyal subjects of the king.[100] See Joh. Eph., *Lives, PO* 17.146–8, on a debate (amid accusations of disloyalty) between Simeon (a Monophysite) and Nestorians at the court of a *marzban* between 499 and 504. On the Roman side of the border, comparable accusations against prominent churchmen were also made (Philoxenus, *Letter to the monks of Senun*, 94–5/79 [dating from 502/5]) and Bardhadbeshabba, *HE* 31 (*PO* 9.614), above. See Labourt 1904: 157–8, Guillaumont 1969–70: 42–3, Frend 1971: 201.

Joh. Eph. *Lives, PO* **17.142:** (The Nestorian bishops said to the king): 'These men are traitors to your majesty, as you can learn, since their faith and their rites (agree) with those of the Romans'. It happened that the Magian (Kavadh) believed them, and he ordered a persecution against the orthodox (Monophysites) in the whole of his kingdom.[101] (tr. M. Greatrex)

4

THE NORTH-EAST FRONTIER IN THE FIFTH CENTURY

The tightening Persian grip on Persarmenia (415)

The division of Armenia in 387 greatly reduced tensions between Rome and Persia in the region, but Sasanian concerns over possible collaboration between Armenians and Romans never receded entirely. When Vramshapur, the king of Persian Armenia, died in 414, he was succeeded briefly by his brother Khosrov III, who had previously been removed from power for his alleged Roman sympathies; and when he in turn died in the following year, the Persian king Yazdgerd I appointed one of his sons, Shapur, to succeed him. See Grousset 1947: 178–9, Chaumont 1987: 428–9 and Garsoïan 1989: 430. Cf. Mos. Khor. III.55.

Łazar 18–19/52–3: And he (Shapur) plotted evil designs in his mind: first, this – that the country of Armenia is large and productive and borders the neighbouring Greek empire, under whose control many of the Arsacid nation are subject. Perhaps (he thought) the people would become sympathetic to each other like brothers – that is, those who were under our rule and those under Greek rule – and then trusting in each other and forming an alliance, they might treat for peace with the Greek king, and willingly becoming subject to him, they might rebel against us. Just as they have often caused us trouble, by the increase of their numbers they would cause us even more worry in war. And secondly, (he thought thus) because they (the Armenians) are strangers to our religion and hate it, whereas they have the same cult and religion as them (the Romans). (tr. Greenwood)

The foundation of Theodosiopolis (420–1)

But upon the death of Yazdgerd in late 420, Shapur did not succeed him. The Armenians took the opportunity afforded them by the brief internal struggles in Persia to eject the Persian garrisons, and for three years Persian Armenia was in a state of anarchy (Mos. Khor. III.56, Łazar 19/53). See Grousset 1947: 180 and Winkler 1994: 328. The Armenians remained in contact with the Romans, in particular with Anatolius, the *magister militum per Orientem* at the time, who was involved in the fortification of the border city of Theodosiopolis c.420. Roman interest in the region clearly remained strong (Mos. Khor. III.57–9, cf. Koriun, *V. Mesrop.* 97).[1] On the war of 421–422 see Chapter 3.

Narratio de rebus Armeniae, 4–9: (4) In his (Arsaces') days Armenia was divided, when Theodosiopolis too was built (5) which was once in ancient times a village called Kalē Archē. (6) For the great apostle Bartholomew, while going off to Parthia, baptised the nephew of the king of the Persians and with him three thousand (people) in the river Euphrates, (7) and built on the spot a church in the name of the most holy; Mother of God (8) and when a town grew up in this place, he called it Kalē Archē. (9) Theodosius the Great, when he beheld it and the water in it, was delighted and built a very famous city, renaming it Theodosiopolis.[2]

Despite the suspicions of his father, Bahram was content to accept an Arsacid king for Armenia, Ardashir, son of Vramshapur. But he proved unpopular with some of the nobility, who accused him of attempting to side with the Romans. He was deposed in 428 and replaced by a Persian *marzban*; the Arsacids were never to return to the throne of Armenia (Mos. Khor. III.64, Łazar 24–5/59–60, *Narratio*, 16 [p.28]). No less importantly, the Armenian *catholicos* Sahak was ousted at the same time, as the Persian king (and the Persian Church) sought to win control of Armenia (Mos. Khor. III.64–7, Łazar 24–5/59–60). See Blockley 1992: 60–1, Garsoïan and Mahé 1997: 40–1, Garsoïan 1999: 59–65.

The defence of Roman Armenia (441)

As is evident from the following piece of legislation, the war of 440 (on which see above, Chapter 3) had some impact on Roman Armenia. Although the *dux Armeniae* had some troops at his disposal, the sale of properties which had belonged to the Armenian crown had evidently led to a reduction in the number of forces available for the defence of the region. Hence measures were required to address the problems which had just been highlighted by the Persian invasion.[3]

Nov. Theod. V.3.1 (June 441): Therefore, since we learn through the well considered report of Your Sublimity that the district of Armenia, which is situated almost upon the very threshold of the border of the Persians, and which was formerly protected by the troops and garrisons of the royal estates,[4] has been exposed at the present time to the invasions of the Persians, because the aforesaid estates, and especially those that are adjacent or neighbouring to the municipalities of Theodosiopolis and of Satala, have been transferred by the petitions of certain persons to their ownership at various times in the past, and the original regular tax has been changed, We decree by this law which shall live for ever that it must be established that all persons who obtained Our munificence in the matter (of these estates) shall be allowed to hold these landholdings as granted, under the condition that they shall duly furnish to the account of the fisc the spearmen,[5] the baggage wagons, the supplementary post horses, the supplies, and also the purchases enjoined upon them according to the former custom by the regulation of your magnificent office, and all the other things, and they shall assume such payment as their responsibility. (...) (tr. Pharr, revised)

Persian repression in Persarmenia (449–51)

The king who had undertaken the war of 440, Yazdgerd II, showed himself to be increasingly hostile to Christians in his kingdom as his reign progressed. In 449, urged on by his minister Mihr-Narses, and encouraged by the Suanian prince Varazvałan, he required that the Armenians embrace Zoroastrianism. See Chaumont 1987: 430, Rist 1996: 34–6. Cf. Ełishe 15–27/69–80.

Łazar, 42–3/78–9: (*From a speech of Varazvałan, a pro-Persian Armenian, to Yazdgerd II.*) And first and foremost, how suitable and productive is the great country of Armenia, and likewise Georgia (Iberia) and Albania. Merely look at the advantages which you receive from those countries. But (to) what is significant and urgent, namely the salvation of so many lost souls, you pay no attention nor do you concern yourself with it. You do not realise this – that you will have to give a reckoning to the gods for such a great number of persons. For if you care about the salvation of so many souls, know that their welfare and prosperity, which would come about, would bring more profit and advantage to you than all the present prosperity of the kingdom which you possess. And I see further profit and very great and significant advantages in this matter for this country of the Aryans (Persia). Indeed you yourself, and all the Aryans, know (p.43) how great and profitable is Armenia; it is a close neighbour of the emperor's realm and has the same religion and cult, for the emperor possesses authority over them. (tr. Greenwood)

The programme of conversion which Yazdgerd introduced for Armenia proved intolerable to the Armenian people. A rebellion broke out late in 449, and the following year was spent in expelling the Persian garrisons. The leader of the uprising, Vardan Mamikonean, sought to involve the Romans in the conflict, but without success; in 450 the Huns still posed a significant threat to the eastern Roman empire, and matters were further complicated by the death of Theodosius II and the accession of Marcian in the same year. See Grousset 1947: 194–9, Rist 1996: 34–6, Luther 1997: 141–2, Garsoïan 1998c: 1138–9.[6]

Łazar 63/105: Immediately (upon hearing of an imminent Persian attack) they (Vasak, prince of Siwnikʻ, and his associates) wrote letters to the emperor and to all the nobles of the Greek court, and also to other princes and governors: to the *bdeashkh* of Ałjnik (Arzanene), to the prince of Angeł-tun (Ingilene), to Tsopk (Sophene) and Hashteankʻ (Asthianene) and Ekełeatsʻ (Acilisene), and to other princes of their respective regions, and to the great *sparapet* of Antioch.[7] (tr. Greenwood)

Armenian forces were involved not only in Armenia itself, but also in Albania, in the eastern Transcaucasus. Vardan Mamikonean seized control of the Derbend pass, and gave control of it to the Albanians; in addition, he established friendly relations with the Huns north of the Caucasus (Łazar 66/108, Ełishe 78/129–30). See Grousset 1947: 199–201.[8] But in June 451 the Persians, assisted by Vasak and other Armenians loyal to them, were able to crush the rebellion at the decisive battle of Avarayr (Ełishe 116–21/169–73, Łazar 69–73/112–17). See Grousset 1947: 202–6.[9] A few rebels continued to resist the Persians even after the defeat, operating from western and northern Armenia; some even managed to induce the Huns to destroy the Persian force garrisoning the Derbend pass and to cause damage to Persian territories beyond it (Ełishe 127–9/180–1). See Grousset 1947: 206–7. The situation in Persarmenia then gradually stabilised under the *marzban* Adhur-Hormizd, who proved more tolerant towards Christians, while Vasak of Siwnik' was executed by Yazdgerd for alleged disloyalty (Ełishe 134/ 185, Łazar 83/129). See Grousset 1947: 209–11, Chaumont 1987: 430.[10]

The defence of the passes through the Caucasus (450s–60s)

Although Yazdgerd II, like his successor Peroz, spent most of his reign campaigning in the north-east of his kingdom, he was not unaware of the growing importance of the main Caucasian passes. It had become evident during the Armenian rebellion of 449–451 that whoever controlled them could bar the Huns from entering the Transcaucasus or could unleash them against an enemy. At the same time, there was always the danger that the Huns, whether in collaboration with the Armenians or Romans or independently, might seek to force the passes and annihilate the Persian garrisons stationed there.[11] It is not surprising therefore to find the Persians, who now held control of most of the Transcaucasus, making repeated attempts to extract men or money from the Romans in order to bolster their defences of the passes. As the Roman grip weakened, tensions arose in the 450s and 460s between the Lazi (in ancient Colchis), who had traditionally come within the Roman orbit, and their allies, as the following fragments from Priscus make clear.[12]

Priscus, frg.33.1: The Romans went to Colchis, made war on the Lazi, and then the Roman army returned home. The Emperor's advisers prepared for a second campaign and deliberated whether in pursuing the war they should travel by the same route or through the part of Armenia bordering on Persian territory, having earlier persuaded the monarch of the Parthians by an embassy (to allow this).[13] For it was considered wholly impracticable to take the sea route along the rugged coast, since Colchis had no harbour. Gobazes himself sent envoys to the Parthians and also to the Roman emperor. Since the monarch of the Parthians was involved in a war with the so-called Kidarite Huns, he dismissed the Lazi who were fleeing to him.[14] (tr. Blockley, revised)
Priscus, frg.33.2: Gobazes sent an embassy to the Romans. The Romans replied to the envoys sent by Gobazes that they would abstain from war if either Gobazes himself resigned his sovereignty or he deprived his son of his royalty, since it was not right that both rule the land in defiance of ancient custom. That one or the other, Gobazes or his son, should rule over Colchis and that war should cease there was the proposal of Euphemius, the *magister officiorum*. Because of his reputation for sagacity and eloquence he was given oversight of the affairs of the Emperor Marcian and was his guide in many good counsels. He took the author Priscus to share in the cares of his office.

When the choice was put to Gobazes, he chose to hand over sovereignty to his son and himself laid down his symbols of office. He sent envoys to the ruler of the Romans to ask that, since Colchis now had one ruler, he should not take up arms in anger on his account. The emperor ordered him to cross to the land of the Romans and give an explanation of what he had decided, and he did not decline to set out. But he asked that the emperor should hand over Dionysius, who had earlier been sent to Colchis over the disagreement with this same Gobazes, as a pledge that no harm should befall him. Therefore, Dionysius was sent to Colchis, and they composed their differences. (tr. Blockley, revised)

Peroz, occupied with constant warfare in the north-east, kept up diplomatic pressure on the Romans to assist in the defence of the Caucasian passes. His repeated demands for money or troops may have elicited occasional contributions, although these are generally reported only in late sources.[15]

Priscus, frg.41.1.3–27: An embassy also arrived from the Persian monarch which complained to the Romans both about those of their people who were fleeing to them (the Romans) and about the Magi who had lived from old in Roman territory.[16] The embassy alleged that the Romans, wishing to turn the Magi from their ancestral customs, laws and rites of worship, harassed them and did not allow the fire, which they called unquenchable, to be kept burning continually according to their law. It also said that the Romans, through a contribution of money, should show interest in the fortress of Ioureiopaach,[17] situated at the Caspian Gates, or they should at least send soldiers to guard it. It was not right that the Persians alone should be burdened by the expense and the garrisoning of the place, since if they gave up (these expenditures), evil would befall not only the Persians but also the Romans at the hands of the neighbouring peoples. They further said that they (the Romans) should help with money in the war against the so-called Kidarite Huns, since they (the Romans) would derive benefit from their victory insofar as (that) people would be prevented from penetrating to the Roman Empire also. The Romans replied that they would send someone to discuss all these issues with the Parthian monarch. They claimed that there were no fugitives amongst them and that the Magi were not harassed on account of their religion, and said that since the Persians had undertaken the guarding of the fortress of Iouroeipaach and the war against the Huns on their own behalf, it was not right that they demand money from them (the Romans). Tatian, who held the rank of patrician, was sent as ambassador to the Vandals on behalf of the Italians, while Constantius, who was prefect for the third time and a patrician as well as a consular, was sent to the Persians.[18] (tr. Blockley, revised)

Roman involvement in Lazica continued in the 460s, at which time the small (but strategically important) kingdom of Suania succeeded in breaking away from Lazic control, an event which was to have repercussions in negotiations between Rome and Persia a century later. There were stirrings too in Persarmenia, where Vahan Mamikonean, nephew of the rebel leader of 450–451, sought help from the Romans. Although Leo agreed to lend his support, none was forthcoming.[19]

Priscus, frg.44: After the fire in the city during the reign of Leo, Gobazes came with Dionysius to Constantinople, with Persian clothing and a bodyguard in the Median manner. The officials at court received him and at first blamed him for his rebellion, but then treated him in a kindly manner and dismissed him. For he won them over both by the flattery of his words and by bearing with him the symbols of the Christians.[20] (tr. Blockley, revised)

Priscus, frg.51: A very serious dispute existed between the Romans and Lazi and the nation of the Suani. The Suani were making war against … ,[21] and the Persians wished to go to war with him because of the forts that had been captured from the Suani.[22] He

(Gobazes) therefore sent an embassy (to the Romans), asking that reinforcements be sent to him by the emperor from amongst the troops who were guarding the borders of that part of Armenia which was tributary to the Romans. Thus, since these were close at hand, he would have ready assistance and would not be endangered while waiting for troops to come from a distance; nor would he be burdened with the expense of supporting them if they came and the war was postponed, should it turn out in this way, as had happened earlier. For when Heraclius was sent with help, and the Persians and Iberians, who were at war with him, were diverted to fighting other active peoples,[23] he dismissed the reinforcements since he was worried about the provision of food. As a result, when the Parthians returned against him, he again called upon the Romans.

When the Romans had replied that they would send help and a man to command it, an embassy arrived from the Persians which announced that the Kidarite Huns had been vanquished by them and that their city of Balaam had been captured. They reported their victory and in barbaric fashion boasted about it, since they wished to advertise the very large force which they had at present. But when they had made this announcement, the emperor straightaway dismissed them, since he was more concerned about the events in Sicily.[24] (tr. Blockley, revised)

The end result of these disputes between the Suani and their traditional overlords, the Lazi, was that the latter were soon afterwards brought into alignment with Persia, while the former retained their independence and their loyalty to the Romans. See Zuckerman 1991: 543, Greatrex 1998a: 126.[25] While Peroz may have been gratified by his success in gaining control of almost the entire Transcaucasus, his joy will have been blunted by the burden this imposed on his armed forces: for since he now ruled the region south of the Derbend and Dariel passes, it fell to him to defend it. And, as is clear from Priscus and Caucasian sources, numerous tribes were active in trying to penetrate the passes in this period.[26]

Priscus, frg.47: The Saraguri, having attacked the Akatiri and other peoples, marched against the Persians. First they came to the Caspian Gates, but when they found that the Persians had established a fort there, they turned to another route, by which they came to Iberia.[27] They laid waste their (the Iberians') country and overran Armenia. As a result the Persians, apprehensive of this inroad on top of their old war with the Kidarites, sent an embassy to the Romans and asked that they give them either money or men for the defence of the fortress at Iouroeipaach. They repeated what had often been said by their embassies, that since they were facing the fighting and refusing to allow access to the attacking barbarian peoples, the Romans' territory remained unravaged. When the Romans replied that each had to fight for his own land and take care of his own defence, they again returned having achieved nothing.[28] (tr. Blockley, revised)

The escalation of Persian demands for subsidies (470s–80s)

Leo's successor Zeno proved more sympathetic, at least initially, to Peroz's requests. Joshua is the first source to refer to a mutual assistance agreement between the two powers; a similar engagement is reported by Malalas, who gives the text of a letter of the Persian king Kavadh referring to the agreement. See Blockley 1992: 75 and n.32, Greatrex 1998a: 15–16.[29]

Josh. Styl. 8 (242.10–23): Further, there was a treaty between the Romans and the Persians, that, if they had need of one another when they had a war with any of the nations, they should help one another, by giving 300 strong men, with their arms and horses, or 300 staters in lieu of each man. This was (to be) according to what the side that had the need wished. Now the Romans, by the help of God, the Lord of all, did not need assistance from the Persians; for there have been believing emperors from that time until the present day, and by the help of heaven their power has been strengthened. But the kings of the Persians have been sending ambassadors and receiving gold for their need; but it was not in the way of tribute that they received it, as many thought. (tr. Wright, rev. M. Greatrex)

Mal. 18.44 (378.32–9/449.19–450.6): see Chapter 6, p.88, below.

Josh. Styl. 9–10 (242.23–243.2): For in our days the Persian king Peroz, because of the wars that he had with the Chionites who are the Huns,[30] very often received gold from the Romans, not however demanding (it) as tribute, (but) by inflaming them with zeal,[31] as if (p.243) he was carrying on his (the emperor's) fights on their behalf, 'that', (he said), 'they may not pass over into your territory.' (tr. Wright, rev. M. Greatrex)

Revolt in Persarmenia (482)

Roman subsidies availed Peroz little. As early as 471 he deposed the Armenian patriarch Giwt, suspecting him on account of the links he had with the Romans (Łazar 113–16/165–9). See Garsoïan 1999: 129. Towards the end of his reign, he not only persecuted the Christians, but also undertook further campaigns against the Hephthalite Huns. While he was away in the north-east, a rebellion broke out in Iberia in 482. The Armenians soon followed suit, and gained the advantage initially. Persian armies were deployed in 483, and succeeded in restoring the situation. The response of the rebel leader, Vahan Mamikonean, was to take refuge in the western regions of Armenia. Here, just as the Romans had operated with circumspection in attacking Lazica in the 450s, the Persians had to proceed with care (Łazar 118–54/172–213). See Sanspeur 1975–6, Luther 1997: 142–3, Greatrex 1998a: 127–8, Garsoïan 1999: 130.

Łazar 136/193: In pursuit of them (Vahan and his forces, then in Taykʿ) came Mihran with his army. He was attempting either to slay them in battle or to seize them by some means, or to persuade them to submit. The camp of the mass of the Aryan (Persian) forces was in the village called Du, on the border of Persian and Roman territory. The Armenian commander Vahan Mamikonean was about two leagues distant in a village called Mknarinch with around one hundred men, or perhaps a few more or less. (tr. Greenwood)

Mihran, the Persian general, therefore sought to negotiate with Vahan, rather than attacking him.[32] Other Persian generals, however, actually entered Roman territory in their pursuit of the rebels. Zarmihr crossed the border to the north of Theodosiopolis in search of Vahan before proceeding against the Iberian king Vakhtang; but the king eluded the Persians by also moving west, into Lazica. Shapur of Ray, another Persian general, actually attacked some labourers in Roman territory south of Theodosiopolis when he was foiled in his efforts to seize Vahan.[33] In a battle fought in this same campaign, Łazar reports that a certain Łerpagos died, 'who was Greek by origin': some assistance from Roman Armenia and the satrapies, perhaps unofficial, may then have been forthcoming. It should be stressed, however, that even at this point, one hundred years after the partition of Armenia, the borders between Roman and Persian territory will hardly have been obvious or precise. And while Shapur was worried in case Vahan should obtain help from the Armenians of the satrapies, it appears that these same regions were becoming involved in the insurrection of Illus and Leontius against Zeno.[34]

The waning of Persian power (484–98)

In late summer 484 the situation changed abruptly. Peroz was decisively defeated once again by the Hephthalites, and on this occasion perished in battle (Josh. Styl. 11, Proc. I.4, Łazar 154–6/213–15).[35] His successor, Balash, proved more conciliatory. Vahan was appointed *marzban* of Armenia, and Christianity tolerated; for their part, the Armenians helped Balash to defeat a challenger to the Persian throne, Zarer (Łazar 170–5/232–7). See Grousset 1947: 226–9, Luther 1997: 129–30, 143, Garsoïan 1998c: 1139–40. Notwithstanding this aid, Balash was faced with an intractable problem – the emptiness of the Persian treasury.

Josh. Styl. 18 (247.25–248.12): After he (Peroz) had been sought out and not found, which I have mentioned above,[36] his brother Balash reigned over the Persians in his stead. He found nothing in the Persian treasury, (p.248) and his land was laid waste by the depopulation (carried out) by the Huns. It is not forgotten by Your wisdom what expenses and outlays kings incur in wars, even when they are victorious, to say nothing about when they are defeated, and from the Romans he had no help of any kind such as his brother had. For he sent ambassadors to Zeno, (asking him) to send gold; but because he was occupied with the war against Illus and Leontius, and because he also remembered the gold that had been sent by them at the start of their rebellion, which still remained there in Persia,[37] he did not wish to send him anything, but he sent word to him, 'The taxes of Nisibis which you receive are enough for you, which for many years past have been due to the Romans'.[38] (tr. Wright, rev. M. Greatrex)

Balash's lack of funds and unpopularity hastened his downfall. In 488 he was deposed and replaced by his nephew, Kavadh. But since he too had no source of funds, he was obliged to make repeated demands of the Romans; unlike Balash, he believed it best to adopt a more aggressive tone in his requests.

Josh. Styl. 19 (248.21–8): (...) For he (Kavadh) sent an ambassador, and a large elephant as his present to the emperor, that he might send him gold. But before the ambassador reached Antioch in Syria, Zeno died, and Anastasius became emperor after him.[39] When the Persian ambassador informed his master Kavadh of (this) change in the Roman kingdom, he sent him (word) to go up with diligence and to demand the customary gold, or to say to the emperor, 'Accept war.' (tr. Wright, rev. M. Greatrex)

Anastasius refused, demanding that Nisibis be returned before he handed over any gold (Josh. Styl. 20). As a result of his failure, Kavadh, like Balash before, found his position weakening. Despite the concessions made to the Armenians by Balash, a rebellion broke out in 491. Joshua ascribes the uprising to discontent with Persian attempts to force Zoroastrianism upon the Armenians once again, although this would have been in contravention of the recent agreement. The Armenians may therefore have been persuaded to rise up instead in the wake of a Church council at Vałarshapat at which they expressed their doctrinal unity with the Church of Constantinople. See Luther 1997: 143–4, Garsoïan 1999: 133, 164–6.

Josh. Styl. 21 (249.15–23): When the Armenians who were under the rule of Kavadh heard that he had not received a peaceful answer from the Romans, they took courage and strengthened themselves, and destroyed the fire-temples that had been built by the Persians in their land, and killed the Magi who were among them. Kavadh sent against them a *marzban* with an army to exact capital punishment from them and make them return to the worship of fire; but they fought with him, and destroyed both him and his army, and sent ambassadors to the emperor, in order to become his subjects. He however was unwilling to receive them, that he might not be assumed to be provoking war with the Persians. (...) (tr. Wright, rev. M. Greatrex)

Like all his predecessors before him in the fifth century, Anastasius refused to undertake anything which might be seized on by the Persians as an excuse to break the peace. In the short term, his refusal to bow to Kavadh's demands paid off: not only the Armenians, but also the Qadishaye (tribesmen living in the vicinity of Nisibis) and Tamuraye (in Persia) revolted against the king (Josh. Styl. 22). See Luther 1997: 145–6, Greatrex 1998a: 76–7 and n.18. The Persian kingdom was also disturbed by the Mazakites, members of a revolutionary sect, to which the king gave some support (Josh. Styl. 20, Proc. I.5.1, Tabari, I, 885–7/132–6). See Winter and Dignas 2001: M11, Crone 1991, Luther 1997: 137–41, Wiesehöfer 1996: 173, 208–10.[40] Kavadh, however, having failed in another attempt to extract money from Anastasius, was ousted from power in favour of his brother Zamasp, and only returned to the throne in 498/9 with the assistance of the Hephthalite Huns (Josh. Styl. 23–4, Proc. I.6.10–11). The stage was then set for the oubreak of hostilities in 502.[41]

5

THE ANASTASIAN WAR AND
ITS AFTERMATH (502–25)

The causes of the war

Several factors underlay the termination of the longest period of peace the two powers ever enjoyed. The Persian king Kavadh, having only just regained his throne in 498/9 with the assistance of the Hephthalite Huns, had more need now of funds than ever: his allies required payment. The situation was exacerbated by recent changes in the flow of the Tigris in Lower Mesopotamia, sparking famine and floods. When Anastasius again refused to provide any help (in 501 or 502), Kavadh had little choice but to try to gain the money by force. See Morony 1995: 76, Luther 1997: 177–8, Greatrex 1998a: 51–2, 76.

Theoph. A.M. 5996 (144.21–3): In this year Kavadh, the Persian king, demanded money from Anastasius. Anastasius said that if Kavadh wanted a loan, he would make a written agreement; but if it were in any other form, he would not pay.[1] (tr. Mango and Scott, revised)

Proc. *Wars* I.7.1–2 (30.7–16): A little later Kavadh was owing the king of the Hephthalites a sum of money; since he was not able to pay it back to him, he asked the Roman Emperor Anastasius to lend him this money.[2] He took counsel with some of his friends and asked whether this should be done. (2) They did not allow him to make the agreement, for they declared that it was disadvantageous to strengthen the friendship of their enemies with the Hephthalites with their own money; rather it was better (for the Romans) to stir them up against each other as much as possible. (tr. Dewing, revised)

The outbreak of war (502)

Once restored to the throne, Kavadh enlisted the peoples who had revolted against him – the Tamuraye, the Qadishaye, the Arabs and the Armenians; some joined his invasion force willingly, others less so (Josh. Styl. 24). The king invaded Roman territory in August 502, quickly capturing the capital of Armenia Interior, Theodosiopolis, perhaps with local support; the city was in any case undefended by troops and weakly fortified (Josh. Styl. 48, Mal. 16.9 [398], cf. Proc. I.7.3). See Luther 1997: 178–9, Greatrex 1998a: 79–80.

Zach. *HE* VII.3 (22.15–22): But Kavadh, who ruled after him (Peroz), and his nobles, had a grudge against the Romans, as they said that they had caused the coming of the Huns, and the pillage and devastation of their country. And Kavadh mustered an army, and went out against Theodosiopolis in Armenia of the Romans, and subdued the city; and he dealt with its inhabitants mercifully, because he had not been insulted by them; but he took (prisoner) Constantine, the ruler of their city. (tr. Hamilton and Brooks, rev. M. Greatrex)

The siege of Amida (502–3)

Anastasius only learnt of Kavadh's preparations after his invasion. He immediately despatched Rufinus to try to dissuade the king from his attack. But Kavadh, having seized Theodosiopolis, quickly moved southwards, overrunning the vulnerable Armenian satrapies. He paused at Martyropolis, where the satrap, Theodore, handed over two years' worth of taxes from the satrapy of Sophanene (Proc. *Aed.* III.2.4–8).[3] Kavadh therefore left Theodore in charge and continued to Amida. Here Rufinus met him, but was unable to deflect him from his course. The siege of Amida, testament to Kavadh's continuing appetite for plunder, proved to be a far more difficult enterprise than he expected; the defenders, although unsupported by troops, repelled his assaults for three months before they were finally beaten (Proc. I.7.5–35, Josh. Styl. 50, 53, *Chr. 1234*, 51 [147–50]). Zachariah of Mytilene provides one of the most detailed accounts of a siege on the eastern frontier.[4] On the siege itself see Luther 1997: 180, 182–6, Greatrex 1998a: 83–94 and the notes in Trombley and Watt 2000: 53–63, 120 with map 5.

Zach. *HE* VII.3–4 (22.22–31.14): In the month of October he (Kavadh) came to Amida of Mesopotamia. (But though he assailed it) with fierce assaults of sharp arrows of bows, and with battering-rams, which pushed the wall to overthrow (it), and roofs of hide, which protected the men who had piled up the mound and raised (it) up and made (it) equal in height with the wall, for three months, day after day (p.23) yet he could not take the city by assault. Meanwhile the people with him had great hardship through work and fighting, and he heard in his ears the abuse of disorderly men on the wall, and ridicule and mockery, and he was reduced to great straits. (He felt) indignation and regret, because the winter came upon him in its severity, and because the Persians, being clad in their loose garments, appeared inefficient; and their bows were greatly relaxed by the moisture of the air;[5] and their battering-rams did not hurt the wall or make any breaches in it, for (the defenders) were tying bundles of rushes from the beds with chains, and receiving upon them the force of the battering-rams, and preventing them from breaching the wall. But they (the defenders) breached the wall from inside, and carried the material of the mound inside from the outside, and they gradually propped up the cavity with beams from underneath. And when chosen Persian soldiers ascended the mound and placed beams upon the wall to effect an entrance (now they had armour, and the king was near with his army outside, and was supporting them with arms[6] and shooting of arrows, and giving encouragement with shouting, and stimulating them and exhorting them by his presence and appearance; they were about five hundred men [in number]), (the defenders) threw strings of skin flayed from an ox, and soaked vetch mixed with myrrh-oil, from the wall upon the beams; and they poured the liquid from the vetch upon the skins to make (them) slippery, and placed fire among the props which were placed beneath (p.24) the mound. When they had fought with each other for about six hours, and (the besiegers) had been prevented from effecting an entrance, the fire blazed up and consumed the wood of the props, and immediately the rest of the material was reduced to ashes by the violence of the fire, and the mound was destroyed and fell. The Persians who were on top of it were burned, and they were also bruised, since they were struck (by stones) from the wall.

And (so) the king withdrew with shame and grief, since he was more and more mocked and insulted by those daring, proud and boastful men. For there was no bishop in that city to be their teacher and to keep them in order, (since) John the bishop, a chaste and noble man of great character, had died a few days before. This man had been summoned from the monastery of Qartmin, and he came (to Amida) when he was elected and became bishop. However, he did not change his asceticism and self-mortification and way of life, but was faithful in service by day and by night. He warned and rebuked the rich men of the city in the days of the famine and the incursion of the Arabs and the pestilence, when he said that they should not keep back the corn in the time of distress, but should sell (it) and give (it) to the poor, in case when they kept (it) back, they might only be hoarding it for the enemy, according to the word of Scripture. And so, in fact, it happened. To him an angel appeared openly, who was standing on the side of the altar-table, and he foretold to him concerning the incursion of the enemy, and that he should be taken away as a righteous man from the presence of the enemy; and he (John) revealed the saying when he published it in the presence of the people of the city, that they might turn and be saved from the wrath.

(p.25) *The fourth chapter of this seventh book explains how the city of Amida was subdued, and what happened to its inhabitants.* When Kavadh and his army had been conquered in the various assaults which they had made upon the city, and many of his soldiers had died, his power gave way and (so) he asked that a small gift of silver should be given to him and he would withdraw from the city. But Leontius, the chief councillor, son of Pappus, and Cyrus the governor, and Paul Bar Zainab the steward,[7] through the men whom they sent to Kavadh, requested from him the value of the garden vegetables which his army had eaten, and for the rest of the corn and wine which they had gathered and brought from the villages. When he was greatly grieved at these things, and was preparing to withdraw since he had been disgraced, the Messiah appeared to him in a vision of the night, as he (himself) afterwards related, and said to him that within three days He would hand over to him the inhabitants of the city, because they had sinned against Him; and this happened in this way.

On the western side of the city by the Tripyrgion was a guard of monks who were appointed from the monastery of John Urtaye, and their archimandrite was a Persian.[8] On the outside, opposite their watch-tower, one *marzban*, Kanarak the Lame, (was) encamped. Day after day, as he vigilantly watched by night and by day, he was diligent and clever in devising craftily how he could subdue the city. For there was a man whom they called in the city Kutrigo, a seditious and thievish man; this (man) was very daring in all kinds of attacks upon the Persians, and he made raids and snatched away from them cattle and possessions, (p.26) so that they too, being accustomed to hear those on the wall crying out, called him Kutrigo. Kanarak watched this man, and perceived that he went out by the streams next to the Tripyrgion and plundered, and went in again. For a time the Persians let him accomplish his will, as they noted and examined his actions, and they ran after him and saw from where he came out and went in.

But it happened that on that night when the city was subdued, there was darkness, and a black cloud sending down soft rain;[9] and a man charitably made entertainment for the monks who guarded the Tripyrgion, and he gave them wine to drink in the late evening. Because of this, sleep overtook them, and they did not watch diligently upon their guard, according to their usual custom. When Kanarak and a few of his army came up as he pursued Kutrigo, and drew near to the wall, the monks did not cry out or cast stones. The man perceived that they were asleep, and he sent for ladders and for his army; and those with him went in by the streams, and ascended the tower of the monks, and slew them. They took the tower and the rampart; and they set up ladders against the wall, and sent (a message) to the king.

But when their neighbours, who were guarding another tower, heard it, they cried out; they sought to come to the monks who were being killed, but could not; but some of them were wounded by arrows from the Persians, and died. When the report was heard by Cyrus the governor, he came up; and torches were close to him and he was easily (struck with arrows (p.27) which (themselves) carried torches).[10] He was struck and wounded by an arrow from the Persians, who stood in the darkness but were unhurt; and he withdrew when he was wounded. But when it was morning, and the king and his army reached the place, they set ladders against the wall, and he ordered the army to go up. Many of those who went up died, since they were wounded by arrows and by stones and driven back by spears. Those who through fear turned from the ladders and went down were killed at the king's behest as cowards and fugitives from the battle. And on account of this the Persians were encouraged and determined either to be victorious by conquering and subduing the city, or, after being wounded in the actual conflict, not to be blamed and killed by their king, who was near and was a spectator of their struggle. But the people of the city tried to loose from beneath the keystone of the arch of the tower in which the Persians were, and they were in the act of loosening the supports. Meanwhile another tower was subdued, and another and another in succession, and the guards of the wall were killed.

But Peter, a man of huge stature, from 'Amkhoro, held the battlement of one side, since he was clad in an iron coat of mail; and he did not allow the Persians, and those who assailed him from outside and inside, to cross over, and repelled and hurled (them) back with a spear, since he was firmly fixed (in place) and stood like a hero until at last, when five or six towers on another side were subdued, he too fled and was not killed. The Persians (thus) first got possession of the whole wall and held it; and for a night (p.28) and a day and the following night (they) killed and drove back the guards. At last they went down and opened the gates, and the army entered after receiving the king's command to destroy men and women, and all classes and ages, for three days and three nights. But a certain Christian prince of the country of Arran[11] pleaded with the king (on behalf of) a church called the Great (Church) of the Forty Martyrs;[12] and he spared it, since it was full of people. After three nights and days the slaughter ceased by the king's command. Men went in to guard the treasure of the church and of the nobles of the city, that the king might have whatever was found in them. He ordered also that the corpses of those who were slain that were in the street, and of those whom they had crucified, should be collected and brought round to the northern (side) of the city, so that the king, who was outside on the south side, might enter in. (So) they were collected, and they were numbered as they went out, eighty thousand, besides those that were heaped up in the taverns and thrown into the streams, and those left in the courtyards. Then the king entered the treasury of the church, and when he saw there an image of the Lord Jesus, who was represented in the likeness of a Galilean, he asked who it was. They said to him, 'It is God'; and he bowed his head before it, and said, 'He it was Who said to me,[13] "Stay, and receive from Me the city and its inhabitants who have sinned against Me."' But he took away many holy vessels of gold and precious items of clothing of Isaac Bar Bar'ai, a consul and a rich man of the city, which had come to the church by inheritance a few years before. But he found there also good wine dried into its dregs, which was brought up (p.29) and placed in the sun for seven years, and at last it became dry; from this the stewards, when on journeys, were accustomed to take some, once it had been pounded, in clean linen pouches. They would pour out a little of it (to make) mingled wine and water, and drank (it) with the sweetness and taste of wine. They told the ignorant it was holy water. The king admired it greatly, and took it. And (so) the technique of (practising) this gluttony was lost to the sons of the church from this time.

The gold and silver of the great men's houses, and the beautiful garments, were gathered together and given to the king's treasurers. They also brought down all the statues of the city, and the clock-towers and the marble; and they collected the bronze and everything that pleased (them), and they placed (them) upon wooden rafts that they made, and sent (them) by the river Tigris, which passes by the east of the city and penetrates into their country. The king sought for the chiefs and nobles of the city; and Leontius, and Cyrus the governor, who had been wounded by an arrow, and the rest of the nobles, were brought to him; but the Persians had killed Paul Bar Zainab the steward so that he did not reveal to the king that they had found much gold in his possession. They clothed Leontius and Cyrus in filthy garments, and put swine-ropes on their necks, and made them carry pigs, and led them along, while proclaiming and exhibiting them, saying, 'Rulers who do not rule their city well nor restrain its people, so that they do not insult the king, deserve such insult as this.' But at last the nobles and all the chief craftsmen were bound (p.30) and gathered together, and set apart as the king's captives; and they were sent to his country with an army which brought them down.[14] But knowledgeable men of the king's army drew near and said to him, 'Our kinsmen and brothers were killed in battle by the inhabitants of the city,' and they asked him that one-tenth of the men should be given to them for the exaction of vengeance. They gathered and counted some of the mass of men and gave to them (this group selected) from the men; and they put them to death, killing them in every way.[15]

The king bathed himself in the bath of Paul Bar Zainab, and after winter he departed from the city. He left in it Glon the general as ruler, and two *marzbans*, about 3000 soldiers to guard the city, and John Bar Habloho, one of the rich men, and Sergius Bar Zabduni, to rule (the people). (tr. Hamilton and Brooks, rev. M. Greatrex)

During the siege Kavadh ordered his Lakhmid allies, under their king Na'man, to ravage the area around Carrhae, while another detachment struck the region around Constantia; these forces encountered Roman resistance, under the *dux* Olympius, but emerged victorious from a battle at Tell Beshme. Na'man's forces, however, penetrated as far as Edessa. The *dux* of Armenia, Eugenius, meanwhile succeeded in recapturing Theodosiopolis (Josh. Styl. 51–2). See Luther 1997: 181–2, Greatrex 1998a: 87–9.

Rufinus, who had been detained by Kavadh during the siege, was then allowed to depart westwards. While the news he brought with him caused alarm in the cities of the East, Anastasius had already reacted to news of the siege (Proc. I.8.1–5, Josh. Styl. 54, Theoph. A.M. 5997, 146–7 [below]).[16]

A composite account of the events of 502

Theoph. A.M. 5996 (145.24–146.15): As a result[17] Kavadh violated the peace treaty that had previously been made with Theodosius the younger, and with a large army of Persians and foreigners invaded first of all Armenia, and captured Theodosiopolis, which was betrayed by Constantine, a senator who had been commander of the Illyrian detachments. Next he went to Mesopotamia and besieged Amida, since no Roman army worthy of note was yet stationed in that region: only Alypius was there with a small force. He was praised by everyone and was a lover of philosophy and took such care as he could both for the defence of the cities and the stores of food. He himself lived at Constantina (Constantia), 507 stades to the west of Nisibis and an equal distance from Amida to the north. But some time having meanwhile elapsed, and several engagements having taken place between the Romans and the Persians, in which the Romans sometimes got the worse and sometimes the better of the foreigners in different places, Amida was finally betrayed to the Persians, after being besieged for over three months by the barbarians. It was betrayed during the night by monks who were guarding one of the towers. The enemy used ladders and thus gained entrance to the city, plundered and destroyed it all and captured considerable riches. King Kavadh came to the city on an elephant on the third day after its betrayal and removed great riches. He left Glon to guard the city while he himself returned to the city of Nisibis and the Persian forces remained between Amida and Constantia.[18] (tr. Mango and Scott, revised)

The Roman reaction

Josh. Styl. 54 (281.6–27): (…) The emperor Anastasius too, when he heard (of the fall of Amida), sent a large army of Roman soldiers to winter in the cities and garrison them. All the booty that he had taken, and the captives that he had carried off, were not, however, enough for Kavadh, nor was he sated with the great quantity of blood that he had shed; but he (again) sent ambassadors to the emperor, saying, 'Send me the gold or accept war.' This was in the month of April. The emperor, however, did not send the gold, but made preparations to avenge himself and to exact satisfaction for those who had perished. In the month of May he sent against him three generals, Areobindus, Patricius and Hypatius, and many officers with them. Areobindus went down and encamped on the border by Dara and Ammodius, facing the city of Nisibis; he had with him 12,000 men. Patricius and Hypatius encamped against Amida, to drive out from there the Persian garrison; they had with them 40,000 (men). There came down too at this time the *hyparchos* Apion, who dwelt at Edessa, to look after the provisioning of the Roman troops that were with them. As the bakers were not able to make (enough) bread, he ordered that wheat should be supplied to all the houses in Edessa and that they should make the soldiers' bread (*bucellatum*) at their own cost. The Edessenes turned out at the first baking 630,000 *modii*.[19] (tr. Wright, rev. M. Greatrex)

The Roman force assembled was the largest the eastern front had seen since Julian's invasion of Persia. While Areobindus initially gained the upper hand in his advance upon Nisibis, his army was eventually forced back from there in July by superior Persian numbers; an appeal to Patricius and Hypatius for support went unheeded, and so he quickly withdrew westwards (Josh. Styl. 55). His two colleagues eventually came to his aid, but arrived too late: Areobindus had already retreated further west, leaving his camp at Apadna to be plundered by the Persians. The two generals therefore returned to Amida (Josh. Styl. 56). See Luther 1997: 187–9, Greatrex 1998a: 96–8.

Zach. HE VII.4–5 (30.14–31.1): And then in the summer the Romans came, and their chiefs of the army were Patricius the great *stratēgos*, an old man, upright and trustworthy, but with slight intelligence, and Hypatius and Celer the *magister*, (and) at last also Areobindus; there was with them also the *comes* Justin, who ruled after Anastasius. They gathered and made war on the city (Amida) with wooden towers and trenches and all kinds of engines. They set fire also to the gate of the city, which was called that of the house of Mar Za'uro, (in order) to come upon the Persians, but they were hindered because they (the Romans) were resting, and they did not go in for the Persians shut (the gate).[20] And the Romans did not subdue it nor take it from them by assault, although the men who were found in it were afflicted by famine, day after (p.31) day, until at last the people in it were eating one another.

Theoph. A.M. 5997 (147.6–24): (...) The army gathered in Edessa, a city of Osrhoene, and at Samosata, a city of Euphratesia.[21] The forces under Hypatius and Patricius were engaged in freeing Amida from the Persian garrison. Areobindus, campaigning with Romanus, the phylarch Asouades and several others against Kavadh himself, who was then staying at Nisibis, prevailed against the Persians in various battles and drove Kavadh out of Nisibis, making him retreat many days' journey inside its territory.[22] In one engagement there fell the greatest of the Persian generals,[23] whose sword and bracelet were brought to Areobindus by the Scythian who had killed him, and then sent to the emperor, a noteworthy and particularly clear token of victory. And so with the Persian army defeated to this extent by the Roman generals, Kavadh got ready and sent against the Romans a very large army, with the result that Areobindus urged the forces under Hypatius and Patricius to hasten to his help from the area round Amida. When they declined out of envy, Areobindus wanted to withdraw and to return to Byzantium; (and he would have done so) had not Apion, the Egyptian, who was second in command of the army and in charge of supplies and general supervision, with difficulty kept him in those parts. (tr. Mango and Scott, revised)

Meanwhile Timostratus, the *dux* of Osrhoene, based in Callinicum, inflicted a defeat on the Lakhmid forces, and Arabs allied to Rome – the Tha'labites – even undertook an attack on the Lakhmid capital at Hira (Josh. Styl. 57). Cf. Robin 1996: 689–90, 697–9, Luther 1997: 189–90, Greatrex 1998a: 99 and n.77, Whittow 1999: 212–13.[24]

Kavadh's counter-offensive (summer 503)

In August, as Kavadh led a renewed invasion from Nisibis, Patricius and Hypatius moved southwards to join forces with Areobindus in the Tur Abdin. They failed to meet up, and while Areobindus decided to withdraw westwards again, the forces of the other two generals were decisively defeated in the area between Apadna and Tell Beshme by Kavadh and retreated towards Samosata (Josh. Styl. 57, Marc. *com.* a.503, Proc. I.8.11–19, Zach. VII.5 [below], Theoph. A.M. 5997 [below]). Kavadh then proceeded due west, coming first to Constantia. There, according to Josh. Styl. 58, the Jewish population sought to betray the city to the invaders, but were thwarted by a message from a Roman officer who was a prisoner of the Persians. Prominent in boosting the morale of the city's defenders was the bishop Bar-Hadad. Kavadh, frustrated in his wish to capture the city, but having received some supplies from its inhabitants (Proc. II.13.8–15), continued west to Edessa; he arrived in its vicinity in early September. The king attempted to extort 10,000 lbs of gold from the city, but Areobindus refused his demands. Although elements of the Persian army, especially the Arabs, overran much of Osrhoene, attempts to storm the city failed (Josh. Styl. 59–60). Following further unsuccessful negotiations, Kavadh was forced to withdraw because of a lack of provisions and the approach of further Roman reinforcements (Josh. Styl. 61–3); passing by Callinicum, he followed the Euphrates back to Persian territory (Josh. Styl. 64). The legendary impregnability of the city had been vindicated again. See Luther 1997: 191–202, Greatrex 1998a: 99–106, Trombley and Watt 2000: 77–82.

Theoph. A.M. 5997 (146.24–147.16):[25] While the generals were at odds with one another, Kavadh came to Nisibis (p.147) and, having learned of the discord among the generals, he himself, in a powerful position with his large force, divided up his own army in many places and overran almost the entire Roman territory, so to speak, pushing as far as the Syrias themselves. Meanwhile he sent many envoys to Areobindus about peace, saying that he would end the war on payment of money. He therefore overran in particular the territory round Edessa, where Areobindus was. However, he did not accomplish anything successfully there but, contrary to expectations, he came off worst in a battle with Areobindus. Knowing, too, that his general Glon, with the garrison at Amida, had been destroyed following a plot against him,[26] he marched back in distress along another route, neglecting the hostages whom he had given to Areobindus during the peace-talks. They also retained, contrary to the agreements, Alypius, that excellent man, and Basil of Edessa;[27] so that after his retreat to his own territory (since winter had already arrived), the Roman generals divided themselves among the various cities of Euphratesia, Osrhoene, Mesopotamia, Syria and Armenia, and encamped for the winter season. (tr. Mango and Scott, revised)

While Kavadh invaded Osrhoene, another Roman commander, Pharesmanes, continued to harry the Persian garrison in Amida. Zachariah's account concentrates on this, but describes some of the other episodes of the campaign as well.

Zach. *HE* VII.5 (31.7–33.21): King Kavadh, as stated above, when he departed with his army from Amida to his own country, left in it Glon, a general, and two *marzbans*, and about 3000 soldiers to guard the city; and also two or three rich men and some (other) independent people. These the Roman generals did not overcome, nor did they subdue the city and take it. But at last Patricius went down to Arzanene of the Persians, and carried off captives, and subdued fortresses in it.[28] And Areobindus and Hypatius (went down) to Nisibis and did not subdue it, although the citizens were pleased with the Romans, and appeared lazy in the fight.[29] However, when the king heard, Kavadh came with an army against the Romans; and they fled from him, and they left their tents and the heavy equipment which was with them. Areobindus (fled) from Arzamon by Apadna, and Hypatius and Patricius and others from Thelkatsro. And they lost many horses and the riders who were on them, who fell from the cliffs of the mountains, and were bruised, and perished, and were injured.[30]

Pharesmanes alone, a warlike man, was successful in battle several times; he was renowned and formidable against the Persians, and his name terrified them. His deeds destroyed and weakened them, and they were found to be cowards and fell in his presence (p.32). This (man) at last came to Amida with 500 horsemen, and he observed the Persians who went out to the villages, and he killed some of them, and he took the animals which were with them, and also their horses.

Now a certain cunning man, whose name was Gadono, of the town of Akhore, whom I know, introduced himself to him, and made a compact with him, that when he acted treacherously, he would bring out to him (Pharesmanes), on some pretext, Glon, the Persian general, with three or four hundred horsemen. Because this man Gadono, who was mentioned (above), was a hunter of wild animals and partridge and fish, he was accustomed to go freely to Glon, carrying in his hands a present of game for him; and he ate bread in his presence, and received from him goods of the city equivalent to the game. At last he told him that there were about 100 Romans and 500 horses nearly seven miles from the city, at a place called Fold of the Shepherds; and as a friend he advised him to go out and take possession of the beasts, having killed the Romans, and to make a name (for himself). He (Glon) sent scouts, and they saw a few Romans and the horses, and returned and informed him. Then he made preparation and took with him 400 horsemen, and this Gadono upon a mule; and he (Gadono) led him (Glon) and set him in the midst of the ambush of the Romans, who were lying in wait. So the Romans massacred the Persians, and they brought away the head of Glon to Constantia.[31]

So then distress and rage (seized) the son of Glon, and the *marzbans* who were there became cautious; they did not allow the inhabitants who happened to be shut up in the city to go out to the market, which was held beside the wall by peasants from the villages. (These peasants) brought wine and wheat (p.33) and other produce, and sold (them) both to the Persians and to the citizens, while horsemen were stationed by them, and escorted them one at a time and conducted them in. By an excellent law of the Persians, no one ventured to take anything from the villagers: they sold what they liked and received payments and goods from the city. They assembled in the market enthusiastically. However, on account of the slaughter of Glon and the horsemen, the market ceased. And the nobles who were left in the city, and about 10,000 people, were seized and shut up in the Stadium, and they were guarded there, and there was no food; some of them died. They ate their shoes and their excrement, and they drank their urine. At last they assailed one another; and when they had been on the point of death for some time, those who were left in the Stadium were let loose like the dead from graves in the midst of the city. Starving women, who were found in groups, laid hold of some of the men by means of solicitation, deceit and trickery, and overcame, killed and ate them; and more than 500 men were eaten by women. The famine which was in this city increased, (so that) the suffering surpassed the blockade of Samaria and the destruction of Jerusalem, which is written in Scripture and Josephus relates. (tr. Hamilton and Brooks, rev. M. Greatrex)

Lakhmid raid on Palestine (late 503)

While Roman forces were heavily engaged in Mesopotamia, the new Lakhmid ruler Mundhir undertook a daring raid further south. Mundhir's father Nu'man died in August or September 503, and this raid probably took place shortly afterwards. See Shahîd 1995: 17–19, Greatrex 1998a: 107.

Cyr. Scyth., *Vit. Ioh.* 13, 211.15–19: Around this time Mundhir the son of Sikika (Shaqiqa),[32] who had acquired the dignity of king over the Saracens subject to the Persians, invaded Arabia and Palestine in great anger against the Romans, laying everything waste, enslaving countless thousands of Romans, and committing many lawless acts, following the capture of Amida.

The Roman response (503–4)

In summer 503 Anastasius despatched further reinforcements to the East, under the command of the *magister officiorum* Celer; he also cancelled the taxes due from Mesopotamia and Osrhoene. When he arrived in Hierapolis in late September, Hypatius and Apion were recalled and the other commanders assigned to winter quarters. During the winter Patricius moved from Melitene to Amida in order to prevent the Persians there from replenishing their supplies; although a Persian force was sent to drive him away, he defeated it and invested the city (Josh Styl. 65–6). At this point Kavadh was obliged to leave the front to deal with a Hunnic incursion, while Celer brought increasing pressure to bear on the remaining Persian forces. From his assembly point at Resaina, Celer moved north in spring 504 to join Patricius in besieging Amida, having meanwhile ordered a successful raid on Persian livestock in the Jebel Sinjar (Josh. Styl. 69). But the defences of Amida, despite the sufferings of the inhabitants, proved too strong for the besiegers, who were unable to sustain the siege in winter (Josh. Styl. 70–3). See Luther 1997: 202–4, Greatrex 1998a: 111–12.

While the siege of Amida continued, Celer harried Beth Arabaye, the Persian territory east of Nisibis (Josh. Styl. 79, Marc. *com.* a.504). Areobindus conducted a simultaneous punitive raid in Arzanene (Josh. Styl. 75). The weakness of the Persian position was highlighted by the defections of the renegade Constantine (Josh. Styl. 74), an Arab chief Adid, and the Armenian Mushlek and his army (Josh. Styl. 75). See Trombley and Watt 2000: 93 n.443. This year, not only was Amida's tribute remitted, but the taxes of both Mesopotamia and Osrhoene were cancelled again; a reduction was also granted to Hierapolis, where Roman troops had mustered (Josh. Styl. 78). See Greatrex 1998a: 112–14.

Now that the war was spilling over into Persian territory, Kavadh had no interest in prolonging it. He sent a *spahbadh* to negotiate the surrender of Amida and returned the Roman hostages taken earlier. Although initially Celer preferred to continue the siege of Amida, believing its capture to be imminent, he decided to agree to a truce when the Roman army proved incapable of sustaining the siege during the winter. A truce was therefore agreed, to be ratified by both rulers (Josh. Styl. 71–3, 75–7, 80–2). See Luther 1997: 206–7, Greatrex 1998a: 114–15.

Theoph. A.M. 5998 (147.31–149.7): In this year the *magister* Celer was sent out by the emperor with a very large force under him and took over almost all authority (p.148) together with the general Areobindus. To them the emperor entrusted the management of the entire war. He recalled Apion and Hypatius with all speed to Byzantium, thinking them to be unnecessary for the army because of their hostility towards the general Areobindus, and he appointed the general Calliopius to be in charge of supplies. Accordingly Celer managed the whole war extremely well together with Areobindus, Patricius, Bonosus, Timostratus, Romanus, and the others in their various regions; for he was a man of good sense and learning of every kind, filled with God's grace, and brave, an Illyrian by race, from where Anastasius also came. Many forts in Persian territory were overrun in the incursions and destroyed by fire or by other means, so that even Nisibis itself nearly fell to the Romans. For hunger was by then seizing the Persians, and besides a tribal uprising of the so-called Kadousioi and other races had occurred. Thus, in short, the Romans prevailed over the Persians, so that Kavadh sent the general Aspetius[33] to discuss peace urgently with the Romans, (instructing him,) even if he gained little or nothing in return, to hand back Amida to the Romans. (For) despite their enormous effort, they had not yet been able to capture it from the Persians, even though hunger was oppressing the garrison, because of the nature of the site and the unbreachable (nature) of the walls. But the generals, seeing that winter was approaching again, and judging that it was preferable to redeem the Roman army for a few talents from the harsh wintry conditions of those places where the discussions with Aspetius took place, handed over three talents[34] and got back Basil of Edessa, who was still being held a hostage by the Persians (the excellent Alypius had died after suffering an illness among them), and returned (p.149) the hostages whom they held. They won back Amida and made the covenants for the peace on the border between the forts of Amudis (Ammodius) and Mardin, and confirmed them in writing. Such was the end of Anastasius' Persian war in the 15th year of his reign. It had lasted for three years and had harmed the territory of the Persians more than previous wars, reaching this conclusion in the 15th year of Anastasius' reign. (tr. Mango and Scott, revised)

Zach. *HE* VII.5 (33.21–34.20): But at last Pharesmanes came to the city, and he made a treaty with the Persians who were in it, for they too were weak. The chiefs of the Romans and the Persians sat by the gate of the city, while the Persians went out carrying as much as they could, and they were not searched. If any of the citizens accompanied them, they were asked whether they wished to remain or would like (p.34) to go with the Persians. So the evacuation of the city (took place). But 1100 lbs of gold was given to Kavadh by Celer the *magister* for the ransom of the city and for peace. And when the documents (were drawn up) they brought the drafts to the king for his signature. The king fell asleep, and it was told him in a vision that he should not make peace; (therefore) when he awoke, he tore up the paper, and departed to his country, taking the gold.[35]

But Pharesmanes remained in the city, since he governed its inhabitants and the country. Now a remission of tribute was (granted) by the emperor for seven years. The emperor dealt mildly with the inhabitants of the city: on those who returned from captivity he bestowed gifts lavishly, and he received (them) peaceably, every man according to his rank. (So) the city was at peace and was inhabited; and more building was done to the wall. There was sent to the city a quiet and pleasant man, Thomas, a monk, councillor (and) merciful bishop, by the advice of Dith. Again the providence of God called and conveyed there Samuel the Just from the monastery of the *katharoi*[36], a miracle-worker and a 'dissolver of doubts'; and he upheld the city by his prayer and also aided its inhabitants. (tr. Hamilton and Brooks, rev. M. Greatrex)

An account of the whole war

John the Lydian provides a very negative assessment of the Roman performance in the war. Since he was commissioned to write a history of Justinian's war of 527–532, he no doubt aimed to diminish the achievements of earlier emperors, just as Procopius and Marcellinus *comes* did. See Greatrex 1998a: 73–6.

Joh. Lyd. *De Mag.* III.53 (214.7–20):[37] In his (Anastasius') time, when the elderly Kavadh led out the whole of Persia against the Romans, war broke out. And though the Romans were capable of victory by force, through the profligacy and weakness of the last Areobindus (for he was a lover of song, of the flute and of the dance) and the inexperience and cowardice of the generals Patricius and Hypatius, they were at first beaten when the Persians suddenly overwhelmed them. Subsequently, when they (the Romans) had pursued the Persians and liberated Amida again, which had been captured, the Persians began talks with Celer, who was the *magister officiorum* for Anastasius, concerning Biraparakh, as we mentioned before, and the expense incurred by the Persians alone on its account. The strife came to an end when certain modest favours were granted to Kavadh by Anastasius; for the magnanimity and organisation of Anastasius piously sustained the loss for the sake of peace.[38] (tr. Carney, revised)

Roman refortification work and the construction of Dara (505)

While Kavadh and Anastasius were consulted about the truce, the Romans took the opportunity of upgrading their dilapidated fortifications. Improvements were made at Edessa, Batnae and Amida, and the governor of Osrhoene, Eulogius, erected a wall to defend the fortress at Batnae (Josh. Styl. 81, 89, 91). The Arab allies of either side attempted to continue hostilities, carrying out raids in (hitherto) enemy territory; but both the Romans and the Persians punished their allies severely for these breaches of the truce (Josh. Styl. 88). Undoubtedly the most important construction project undertaken by the Romans in this period was that at Dara, to the north-west of Nisibis, just inside the Roman frontier; work was begun there in late 505. We are fortunate to possess a wealth of sources concerning why and how it was founded. See Croke and Crow 1983: 148–59, Whitby 1986b: esp. 751–2, Isaac 1992: 254–5, Gregory 1997: C6, Luther 1997: 210–12, Greatrex 1998a: 115–16.

Josh. Styl. 90 (309.12–310.3): The year 817 (505/6). The generals of the Roman army informed the emperor that the troops suffered great harm from their not having any (fortified) city situated on the border. For whenever the Romans went forth from Constantia or Amida to go about on forays in the 'Araba, they were in constant fear, whenever they halted, of the treachery of enemies; and if it happened that they encountered a larger force than their own, and thought of turning back, they had to endure great weariness, in that there was no city near them in which they could find shelter. For this reason the emperor gave orders that a wall should be built for the village of Dara, which is situated on the frontier. They selected workmen from all Syria (for this task), and they went down there and were building it; but the Persians kept going out from Nisibis and stopping them. (p.310) On this account Pharasmenes set out from Edessa, and went down and dwelt at Amida, and went forth to those who were building and gave them aid. (...) (tr. Wright, rev. M. Greatrex)

Zach. *HE* VII.6 (34.24–38.15): The Emperor Anastasius brought heavy criticisms against the Roman *stratēgos* and commanders (p.35) who set out to the royal city after the war with the Persians, because they did not, according to his will, under the Lord, prosper and succeed in the war, and conquer the Persians or drive them out from Amida, save by the gifts and the gold that were sent from him. And they made the excuse that it was difficult for the *stratēlatēs* to fight with a king who, according to the word of God, although he was an Assyrian and an enemy, was sent by the Lord to the country of the Romans for the punishment of sins, and, moreover, on account of the greatness of the army which was with him; and again, that it was not easy for them even in his absence to subdue Nisibis, since they had no engine ready, nor any place of refuge in which to rest. For the fortresses were far away and were too small to receive the army, and neither the water in them nor the vegetables that were left (there) were sufficient.

They (therefore) begged of him that a city should be built at his command on the side of the mountains, as a place of refuge for the army and for their rest, and for the preparation of weapons, and to guard the country of the Arabs from the forays of the Persians and Tayyaye. Some of them spoke on behalf of Dara, and some on behalf of Ammodius.[39] Then he sent (a message) to Thomas the bishop of Amida, and he despatched engineers and he drew up a plan; and this holy Thomas brought (it) up with him to the emperor. It semed good to the emperor and the nobles that Dara should be built as a city. At that time (p.36) Felicissimus was *dux*, a brave and wise man; and he was not covetous (or) a lover of money, but was upright and a friend of the peasants and the poor. Now King Kavadh was fighting with the Tamuraye and other enemies of his country. The emperor gave gold to Thomas the bishop as the price of the Church's village; and he bought it for the treasury. He liberated the settlers who were in it, and granted to (each of) them his land and his house. For the building of the church of the city he gave several gold *centenaria*. He promised with an oath that he would give with a liberal hand everything the bishop might spend, and that he would not deal falsely. And at last he made a royal decree without (resort to) a summary, providing that the city be built immediately according to the word of the bishop; so the craftsmen and slaves and peasants who were required for the collection of material there gained and were blessed. He (Anastasius) sent (to the site) many stonecutters and masons, and he ordered that no man should be cheated of the wages of his labour, because he rightly perceived and cleverly understood that by that agreement a city would quickly be built upon the frontier. When they began by the help of the Lord and made a start, there were there as superintendents and commissaries over the works the presbyters Cyrus 'Adon and Eutychian, and Paphnutius and Sergius and John the deacons, and others from the clergy of Amida. The bishop also was (often to be) found there on visits.[40] Gold was given in abundance without any restraint to the craftsmen and for work of every kind (p.37) in this manner: there was (for each) labourer four *keratia* a day, and if he had an ass with him, eight.[41] And from this many grew rich and wealthy. Since the report was published abroad that (the system) was honest and that the wages were given, from the East to the West workmen and craftsmen gathered together. In addition, the superintendents in charge of the work were well provided for and their purses were filled, for they found the man (Thomas) very generous, gentle and kind: he believed in the just emperor and in his promises which he (had made) to him.

In two or three years the city was built, and, as we may say, suddenly sprang up on the frontier. When Kavadh heard (of this) and sought to bring (it) to a halt, he could not, for the wall had been raised and constructed (high as) a protection for those who took refuge (behind it). A large public bath and a spacious storehouse were built, and a conduit which came along the lower part of the mountain, and wonderful cisterns within the city to receive the water.[42] Persons to hasten (the work) were (sent) from the emperor to the bishop, and they all brought back excellent reports of his integrity and justice to the emperor. (So) he was greatly pleased with the man, and sent gold when he answered his request, fulfilling (it) without delay. At last the hundred pounds which he sent was counted out, and the bishop sent (a report) in writing to the emperor, declaring in the presence of God that (the money) had been spent upon the work, and that no part of it remained in his hand or had reached his church. He (Anastasius) readily sent him a royal decree, which the treasury approved, (acknowledging that) all the gold which had been sent by him (had been spent) on the building work in the city. And Dara was completed, and it was named Anastasiopolis, after the name of the just emperor. He swore (p.38) by his crown that no statement of accounts (should be) required of Thomas or of his church, either by himself or those who were appointed emperors after him. And he (Thomas) appointed there and consecrated as first bishop Eutychian the presbyter, a diligent man, and accustomed to business affairs; and he gave the privilege of (certain) rights to his church (taken) from the jurisdiction of the Church of Amida.[43] To him was attached John, a Roman soldier from Amida. Eutychian tonsured him and made him a presbyter and master of the hostelry; and, when he went up to the royal city, he (John) was with him. When he was presented to the emperor, he (Anastasius) gave (him) an endowment for his church. Abraham bar Kaili of Tel Bande[44] was *notarius* at this time, who was the son of Ephraem of Constantia, and he too was attached to Eutychian the bishop, who made him a presbyter. He was sent as superintendent of the work and the building of the bath, and eventually he became steward of the church.

Marc. *com.* a.518: Dara, a city of this kind, was founded in Mesopotamia. Dara, a certain estate located 60 miles south of Amida and 15 miles west from the town of Nisibis, paid its dues to the church of Amida. So the Emperor Anastasius bought the houses of this modest village at a fixed price for the purpose of founding a city there, and he immediately despatched outstanding craftsmen and ordered (the city) to be built. He put Calliopius, who was later patrician of the city of Antioch, in charge of this work.[45] Indeed, with remarkable insight, he marked out with a hoe a furrow for locating the foundations on a hill ending up on level ground; and he protected (it) on all sides by the construction of very strong walls as far as (this) boundary. So too he enclosed the stream called Cordissus, which takes its name from the estate near which it originates, and which winds its way as it roars along, and at the fifth milestone it divides the same hill and the new city, falling into a concealed entrance at each end.[46] Moreover, he allowed the city which had been endowed with public buildings to retain the name of the village.[47] The city's huge look-out, called the Herculean tower, built on higher ground and connected to the walls, looked up to Nisibis to the east and looked back to Amida to its north.[48] (tr. Croke, revised)

Joh. Diakrin. 558 (157.9–11): The Emperor Anastasius built Dara, and after he built it in a vision he beheld the apostle Bartholomew, saying that he was entrusted with the defence of the city. And for this reason he (Anastasius) sent for his relic and deposited it there.[49]

Joh. Lyd. *De Mag.* III.47 (206.22–8): While many were the things which Anastasius did in the service of the common good, one alone will suffice as an illustration – the city established by him beyond the Euphrates (the natives call it Dara, (but) among us they call it the city of Anastasius after him). If God had not clamped down on the throat of the Persians through that man (Anastasius), the Persians would have taken over the lands of the Romans, since they border on them. (tr. Carney, revised)

Proc. I.10.13–18 also describes Anastasius' construction of Dara. Cf. Proc. *Aed.* II.1.4–3.26 (mostly on subsequent improvements by Justinian, playing down Anastasius' work). See Capizzi 1969: 216–21, Mundell 1974: 219, Whitby 1986b, Greatrex 1998a: 120–1.

Despite these measures and remissions of tax by the emperor (Josh. Styl. 92, cf. Proc. I.7.35 and *Anecd.* 23.7), many inhabitants of the frontier region remained discontented, chiefly because of the behaviour of Gothic soldiers in the Roman army. Billeted on the population of Edessa, and no doubt elsewhere, they had oppressed the population and nearly killed the *dux* Romanus when he tried to limit their exactions (Josh. Styl. 93–4, 96). See Greatrex 1998a: 115–16.

The conclusion of hostilities (506)

Negotiations between the two powers continued, interrupted by the death of the Persian negotiator early in 506. In September that year, the two sides met on the frontier by Dara, each accompanied by their troops. Such was the distrust that remained that the Romans, suspecting treachery, seized the Persian officials; once released, the Persians preferred to stay in Nisibis (Josh. Styl. 97). At last in November 506 terms were agreed. Little is known of what these terms were. Procopius (I.9.24) states that peace was made for seven years; it is likely that some payment was made to the Persians (cf. Josh. Styl. 81 on gifts from Anastasius to Kavadh), but there is no reason to suppose that the annual payments demanded by the Persians were conceded by the emperor. See Luther 1997: 213–16 (who believes in Roman payments) and Greatrex 1998a: 117–18.

The aftermath of the war (506–18)

Celer returned west following the conclusion of negotiations and entered Edessa in triumph (Josh. Styl. 100). Although no further large-scale conflict took place during Anastasius' reign, tensions remained, especially while work continued at Dara. Once Kavadh had concluded his war with the Huns, he accused the Romans of breaching the treaty agreed in 422 (see Chapter 3, p.42), by which no further fortifications were to be erected near the frontier. But Anastasius pursued the project nonetheless, deflecting the king's complaints with money; Kavadh was in any case unable to stop the work. (Proc. I.10.17). The walls were completed by 507/8; later, probably during the reign of Justin, the city became the seat of the *dux* of Mesopotamia and a bishop. See Whitby 1986b: 751, 769, Greatrex 1998a: 121.

The development of Sergiopolis and other sites

Although Justinian is well known for his strengthening of the fortifications of the east, Anastasius too undertook important work in the region. The monastery of Mar Gabriel at

Qartmin, on the southwest flank of the Tur Abdin, was expanded with the assistance of the emperor; work was finished in 512. See Whitby 1986a: 726, Palmer 1990: 113–48.

Between 514 and 518 the city of Resafa, already an important shrine to the growing cult of St Sergius and a meeting point for Arab tribesmen, was granted the status of a metropolis and renamed Sergiopolis. It is possible that the emperor was also responsible for the construction of the great basilica there (Joh. Diakr. 554, p.156.17–19). See Capizzi 1969: 214–15, Whitby 1986a: 724, 726, Whitby 1987: 102–5, Key Fowden 1999: 64–5, 92 and Chapter 3 generally.

For epigraphic evidence of work on frontier defences (notably at Emesa), see Chapter 16 below and Greatrex 1998a: 122.

The northern frontier (506–18)

Already during the war against Kavadh, the Pontic region had suffered at the hands of the mountainous Tzani, perhaps taking advantage of Roman involvement elsewhere (Theod. Lect. *HE* 466). After the war, Anastasius undertook extensive work at Theodosiopolis in Armenia, although Procopius plays down its importance in his *Aed.* (III.5.4–9, cf. *Wars* I.10.19). See Capizzi 1969: 206–7, Whitby 1987: 106–7, van Esbroeck 1997: 367–8. The city of Euchaita in Helenopontus was also fortified by Anastasius, probably before 515. See Mango and Ševčenko 1972: 380–1 and Trombley 1985: 83 n.28.[50] In the wake of a raid by Sabir Huns across the Caucasus mountains in 515, work was started at Melitene, but probably only completed during the reign of Justin I; fortifications in Cappadocia, where the invaders did much damage, were also strengthened (Proc. *Aed.* III.4.19–20, Mal. 16.17 [406]). See Whitby 1987: 101, Greatrex 1998a: 122.

Further north still, in the Transcaucasus, the Persian grip was loosening. Although Kavadh had brought Iberia under control once more around 500, an invasion by the Sabirs distracted him from his war against the Romans in 504. An indication of growing Roman influence in the region is provided by the offer of the Hunnic king Ambazuces to hand over control of the Caspian Gates (i.e. the Dariel pass) to Anastasius, probably soon after the raid of 504 (Proc. I.10.9–12). The emperor refused, however, and Kavadh continued to rebuild his influence in the Transcaucasus, suppressing a minor Armenian uprising in 513/14, erecting fortifications, building a new capital for Albania at Partaw, and installing a *marzban* at Mtskheta in Iberia around 520. See Kramer 1935–7: 613, Greatrex 1998a: 128–30 with bibliography.

Southern Arabia

The conflicts between Ethiopians and Himyarites which occurred in the early sixth century in modern-day Yemen lie beyond the scope of this work. The involvement of the Romans and Persians was extremely limited: the former were called upon by the Ethiopians to assist them against a Jewish Himyarite ruler, Dhu Nuwas, who had persecuted the Christians of his kingdom. Some Roman ships sailed to help in the invasion of Himyar in 525, which swiftly overthrew Dhu Nuwas. But the Ethiopian grip on Himyar did not last long: the ruler appointed by the Ethiopian king was ousted by a certain Abraha in 530 or 531, who went on to reign for approximately forty years. See Vasiliev 1950: 283–302, Smith 1954, B. Rubin 1960: 297–319, Z. Rubin 1989: 383–420, Brakmann 1992: 753–62, Greatrex 1998a: 226–40.

The revival of tensions (518–25)

The accession of Justin I was greeted in the East by a raid of the Lakhmid Arabs on Osrhoene in 519 or 520, perhaps following renewed demands for funds from Kavadh (*Chr. 724*, 111/14, AG 830, Mich. Syr. IX.16 [270–1a/178]). Probably in the course of this raid the Roman commanders Timostratus and John were taken prisoner by the Lakhmid chief Mundhir (Proc. I.17.43–5). The capture of a *dux* and another high-ranking officer is an indication of the return of the Roman frontier to a state of ill-preparedness.[51] Further south, in Palestine and Arabia, Arab raids also caused problems, such that the aged St Sabas in 530 appealed to the Emperor Justinian to build a fortress to protect the monks here, a request Justinian granted (Cyr. Scyth. *V. Sab.* 72–3 [175, 178]). See Magoulias 1990–3: 301–3 (noting some other incidents), Shahîd 1995: 92, Di Segni 1999: 151.

The conference at Ramla (524)

The Emperor Justin despatched the presbyter Abraham to ransom the captured Roman commanders, and at a significant gathering of Arab leaders and Roman and Persian diplomats at Ramla, south-east of Hira, in February 524, their release was negotiated. The 'conference at Ramla' was probably preceded in late 523 by discussions at Hira. Despite Justin's persecution of Monophysites within the Roman empire, Abraham intervened to support them in Persia; their representative at the conference was the energetic Simeon of Beth Arsham. Both gatherings also attracted envoys from southern Arabia. At Ramla, an envoy of the newly installed Jewish ruler of Himyar, Masruq (also known as Dhu Nuwas), who had unleashed bloody persecutions of the Christians at Najran and elsewhere, called upon both the Persian king and Mundhir to persecute the Christians under their control. Although Mundhir was a pagan, he certainly had Christians among his followers, and Dhu Nuwas' request went unheeded. See Vasiliev 1950: 278–83, Shahîd 1964: 115–31, De Blois 1990 (on the dating), Shahîd 1995: 40–2, Evans 1996: 112–14, Greatrex 1998a: 131, 228–30.[52]

The forces of nature and doctrinal disputes had more impact on the eastern provinces in the 520s than any Lakhmid raids. Edessa, for instance, was struck by a devastating flood in 525, while an earthquake destroyed Antioch in May 526. The Monophysite communities meanwhile met with increasing harassment from bishops and imperial troops. See Stein 1949: 241–2, Vasiliev 1950: 221–41, Frend 1972: 247–52, 257–61, Greatrex 1998a: 131–2.

Roman successes in the Transcaucasus

The waning of Persian influence in the Transcaucasus was spectacularly confirmed in 521 or 522. See Whitby and Whitby 1989: 106 n.330, Scott 1992: 162–3, Braund 1994: 276–7, Greatrex 1998a: 132 n.35.

Mal. 17.9 (340.53–341.94/412.16–414.16) (cf. *Chr. Pasch.* 613.3–615.4 and other chronicles noted by Jeffreys and Scott 1986: 233): During his reign Ztathius (Tzath), the king of the Lazi, grew angry and departed from Persian territory. (This was) while the Persians were ruled by Kavadh, a friend of Ztathius, king of the Lazi, who had once been subject to the rule of Kavadh. Thus whenever a king of the Lazi happened to die, his successor, though from the race of the Lazi, was appointed and crowned by the king of the Persians. (p.413) The king of the Lazi had rejected the belief of the Hellenes and so as not to be appointed by Kavadh, the Persian king, and not to perform sacrifices and all the other Persian customs, as soon as his father Damnazes died, he immediately went up to the Emperor Justin in Byzantium, put himself at his disposal and asked to be proclaimed king of the Lazi and to become a Christian. He was received by the emperor, baptized, and, having become a Christian, married a Roman wife named Valeriana, the granddaughter of Oninus the patrician and former *curopalatēs*, and he took her back with him to his own country. He had been appointed and crowned by Justin, the Roman emperor, and had worn a Roman imperial crown and a white cloak of pure silk. Instead of the purple stripe it had the gold imperial border; in its middle there was a <small> true purple portrait bust with a likeness of the Emperor Justin. He also wore a white tunic with a purple border, with gold imperial embroideries, equally including the likeness of the emperor. The red shoes that he wore, which he brought with him from his own country, bore pearls in Persian fashion. Likewise his belt (p.341) was decorated with pearls. He received many other gifts from the Emperor Justin, as did his wife Valeriana, since she had once and for all been forced, or rather urged, to be wedded to him (and to go) to other kingdoms.

When Kavadh, the king of the Persians, learned of this, he sent (p.414) the following message to the Emperor Justin by an ambassador: 'Though friendship and peace between us are being discussed and are now established,[53] your actions are hostile. Witness the fact that you have yourself appointed as king of the Lazi a subordinate of mine, who does not come under the Roman administration but has from time immemorial belonged to the Persian state.'[54] In reply the Roman Emperor Justin made the following statement through an ambassador: 'We have neither annexed nor won over any of those subordinate to your empire. In fact, a man named Ztathius came to us in our empire and begged us as a suppliant to be rescued from some defilement and Hellenic belief, from impious sacrifices and from the errors of wicked demons, and asked to become a Christian, worthy of the power of the eternal God, the Creator of all things. It was impossible to prevent someone who wished to enter a better way and to know the true God, so that when he had become a Christian and worthy of the heavenly mysteries, we sent him back to his own country.' As a result there was enmity between Romans and Persians. (p.414) (tr. Jeffreys and Scott, revised)

Justin's reply, together with the attention lavished on Tzath, clearly shows the important role played by Christianity in dealings with the Transcaucasus. The emperor was being disingenuous, however, in his reply, since it appears from another entry of Malalas that he had also been in negotiations with Huns (presumably north of the Caucasus) and had secured their support. They subsequently shifted allegiance to Kavadh, but Justin was able to turn this to his advantage by claiming that they were planning to betray the Persians. Kavadh therefore killed their king, Zilgibis, and destroyed their army (Mal. 17.10 [414.17–415.19], cf. *Chr. Pasch.* 615.13–616.6). See Vasiliev 1950: 264–5, Fowden 1993: ch.5, Greatrex 1998a: 133–4.

The proposed adoption of Khusro I by Justin I (c.525)

According to Malalas (17.10 [415.19–21], cf. *Chr. Pasch.* 616.6–8), Justin's information concerning Zilgibis inspired Kavadh to enter negotiations with Justin; he therefore despatched an envoy called either Broeus or Labroeus to Constantinople. The priority of the Persian king, now over seventy, was to secure the succession of his son Khusro, whose position was threatened by rival brothers and the still strong Mazdakite sect. His proposed solution was that Justin adopt Khusro as his son, a proposal greeted with enthusiasm by the emperor and his nephew Justinian. The emperor's quaestor Proculus, however, opposed the move, arguing that it would entitle Khusro to inherit the Roman empire (Proc. I.11.1–22, Theoph. A.M. 6013 [167–8]). Whether or not this would formally be the case under Roman law, it is highly unlikely that this was Kavadh's intention; and *de facto* it is difficult to see how Khusro could press his claim in any case.[55] Negotiations proceeded nevertheless, although it was made clear to the Persians that Khusro could only be adopted 'by arms', a procedure already used by the Emperor Zeno for the Ostrogothic king Theoderic. The negotiations are reported in most detail by Procopius and must have taken place in 524 or 525. See Greatrex 1998a: 134–8.

Proc. I.11.23–30 (52.19–54.8): Accordingly the Emperor Justin dismissed the (Persian) envoys, promising that men who were the noblest of the Romans would follow them not long afterwards, who would arrange a settlement regarding the peace and regarding Khusro in the best possible way. (24) He also answered Kavadh by letter to the same effect. Accordingly there were sent (p.53) from the Romans Hypatius, the nephew of Anastasius – who had reigned (until) recently – (who) also held the office of *magister militum per Orientem*, and Rufinus, son of Silvanus, a man of note among the patricians and known to Kavadh through their fathers; (25) from the Persians came a most powerful man, wielding great authority, Seoses by name, whose rank was *adrastadaran salanēs*, and Mebodes (Mahbodh), who held the office of *magister.*[56] (26) These men came together at a certain spot which is on the borderline between the land of the Romans and the Persians; (there) they met and negotiated as to how they should resolve their differences and make a good settlement of the issues surrounding the peace. (27) Khusro also came to the river Tigris, which is about two days' journey from the city of Nisibis, in order that, when the details of the peace should seem to both sides to be as well arranged as possible, he might set off himself in person to Byzantium. (28) Now many words were spoken on both sides regarding the differences between them, and in particular Seoses (referred to) the land of Colchis, which is now called Lazica, saying that it had been subject to the Persians from of old and that the Romans had taken possession of it by violence for no reason. (29) When the Romans heard this, (p.54) they took it ill that even Lazica should be disputed by the Persians. And when they in turn stated that the adoption of Khusro must take place in the manner that befits a barbarian, this seemed intolerable to the Persians. (30) The two (sides) therefore separated and returned home, and Khusro left and went off to his father with nothing accomplished, deeply injured at what had taken place and praying that he might exact vengeance on the Romans for their insult to him. (tr. Dewing, revised)

6

JUSTINIAN'S FIRST PERSIAN WAR
AND THE ETERNAL PEACE (c.525–40)

Despite the breakdown of negotiations about the adoption of Khusro in 524/5, it was not until 530 that full-scale warfare on the main eastern frontier broke out. In the intervening years, the two sides preferred to wage war by proxy, through Arab allies in the south and Huns in the north. Although the Emperor Justin died in August 527, the transfer of power to his co-ruler Justinian was peaceful and straightforward.

The defection of Iberia to the Romans (524/5)

Tensions between the two powers were further heightened by the defection of the Iberian king Gourgenes to the Romans. The successful transfer of allegiance of Tzath in 521/2 had clearly had an impact in the region: Iberia had been securely in Persian hands since the late fourth century. According to Procopius, the only source for this development, the Iberians were discontented with efforts being made by Kavadh to impose Zoroastrian practices on them. Gourgenes received pledges from Justin that the Romans would defend Iberia, and the emperor despatched Probus to recruit Huns from north of the Caucasus to assist the Iberians. Although he proved popular in the region between the Crimea and the Caucasus, he failed to raise any troops (I.12.1–9, Zach. *HE* XII.7 [216]). See Angeli Bertinelli 1989: 123–4.

In 526/7 Justin therefore sent Peter, his former secretary, to Lazica, with some Huns, while Kavadh countered by entrusting a large army to a certain Boes. The Persians easily overran Iberia, forcing Gourgenes and the nobility to flee into Lazica. The Iberians then moved to Constantinople and Peter was soon summoned there himself. In 528 he was sent back to Lazica with other commanders, charged this time with defending Rome's other new allies in the region, the Lazi; evidently it was regarded as impossible to recover Iberia (Proc. I.10.9–14). There was, according to the chroniclers (*Chr. Pasch.* 618, Mal. 18.4 [427], Theoph. A.M. 6020 [174]), heavy fighting, and the Romans lost control of the two forts guarding the approaches to Lazica, Sarapanis and Scanda (Proc. I.12.15–19, although he does not name the forts there). They were later to become important bargaining chips towards the end of the war. See Lordkipanidse and Brakmann 1994: 85, Greatrex 1998a: 142–7.

There were no further developments in the region during the war: the Romans, with Lazic support, retained control of the rest of Lazica, while the Persians had regained Iberia. Negotiations with the Huns north of the Caucasus continued, and, according to the chroniclers, a Roman-allied queen Boa triumphed over a Persian-allied opponent in 528 (Mal. 18.13 [430–1], Joh. Nik. 90.61–5, Theoph. A.M. 6020 [175]). See Greatrex 1998a: 143.

The strengthening of Roman Armenia (528)

Just to the north of Armenia, the Roman commander Sittas spent some years in the early 520s pacifying the mountainous Tzani. Thus the Romans gained control of an important region bordering on both Armenia and Lazica (Proc. I.15.24, *Aed.* III.6).[1] A brief and inconclusive raid on Persarmenia in 526 by the young commanders Belisarius and Sittas may be noted in passing; it may have been intended to relieve pressure on Iberia (Proc. I.10.20–2). See Greatrex 1998a: 147–8.

The new Emperor Justinian, perhaps advised by these two former bodyguards of his, decided on a large-scale reorganisation of Roman Armenia in 528. Hitherto, as has been seen, both Armenia Interior and the former satrapies had had to rely primarily on their own defences: only gradually had the Romans begun to exert their authority in this region. At the highest level, he created a new post – that of *magister militum per Armeniam* – the holder of which supplanted the *magister militum per Orientem* in Armenia and the Transcaucasus. Beneath him were *duces* and Roman forces. See Toumanoff 1963: 133–4, Adontz 1970: 106–11, Garsoïan 1998a: 249, 260–2.

Proc. *Aed.* **III.1.27–9 (86.8–16):** Even so, Roman soldiers did not serve these officials,[2] but rather certain Armenians that had been accustomed to (do so) previously, and consequently they were unable to ward off invading enemies. (28) Having examined these matters, the Emperor Justinian immediately removed the name of 'satraps' from the region and stationed two *duces*, as they are called, in these provinces. (29) He joined to them many *numeri* of Roman soldiers so that they might guard together with them the Roman borders.[3] (...) (tr. Dewing, revised)

***C.J.* I.29.5:** The Emperor Justinian to A. Zeta (Sittas), *vir illustris* and *magister militum* for Armenia, Pontus Polemoniacus and the *gentes*. Having, through God's grace, received the Roman power, and having considered (this matter) with solicitous care and vigilant concern, we have found it appropriate to create by this law a special military commander for parts of Armenia, Pontus Polemoniacus and the *gentes*. We chose your highness, which has been greatly commended to us by its former activity, confident that you would be suitable for such an honour. We have entrusted to your care certain provinces, namely Greater Armenia, which is called Interior, and the *gentes* (namely Anzitene, Ingilene, Asthianene, Sophene, Sophanene, in which lies Martyropolis, Belabitene),[4] as well as First and Second Armenias and Pontus Polemoniacus, together with their *duces*. The *comes Armeniae* is to be abolished altogether. We have placed under your command certain *numeri*, not only those which have now been formed, but also (some) detached from the praesental, eastern and other armies. Furthermore, the number of soldiers in them shall not be diminished; rather, because we have added many (*numeri*) to them without burdening the state or raising taxes, (although) we have now withdrawn some, the result is nevertheless that they remain more numerous than they had been before our blessed time.[5] (tr. Adontz–Garsoïan, revised)

Mal. 18.10 (358.7–359.19/429.16–430.8): In the year of Justinian's reign mentioned above, a man named Sittas was dispatched as *magister militum per Armeniam*, for in previous times Armenia did not have a *magister militum* but satraps, *duces*, governors and *comites*. The emperor gave (p.359) the *magister militum numeri* of soldiers from the two praesental (armies) and (the army) of the East. Sittas enrolled indigenous (p.430) *scriniarii* and made them his own military *scriniarii* in accord with an imperial rescript, having requested the emperor to enroll natives since they knew the regions of Armenia. The emperor granted him this, and the rights of the Armenian *duces* and *comites*, and also their consulars who were formerly *milites castrensiani*; for the former offices had been abolished.[6] He also took four *numeri* from the *magister militum per Orientem* and from that time (Armenia) became a great bulwark and help for the Romans.[7] (tr. Jeffreys and Scott, revised)

There were now therefore *duces* based at Tzanzakon, Horonon, Artaleson, Citharizon, Martyropolis and Melitene, while the headquarters for the *magister militum* lay at Theodosiopolis. Fortifications were also strengthened: Mal. 18.4 (427) notes building work at Martyropolis in 528, and work was probably also carried out at Citharizon, Theodosiopolis and elsewhere (Proc. *Aed.* III). See Adontz 1970: 112–25, Whitby 1984, Whitby 1986a: 727, Howard-Johnston 1989: 218–20, Greatrex 1998a: 154.[8]

Skirmishes along the Mesopotamian border (527)

Here Kavadh, through his Lakhmid vassal Mundhir, was able to continue exerting pressure on the Romans to obtain funds from them: clearly none had been forthcoming since the end of the Anastasian war. But the Roman treasury was in any case being severely drained by the need to fund repairs to several cities of the East (see Chapter 5 above), compounded by a further series of earthquakes which hit the region in 528 and 529. See Stein 1949: 420, Moorhead 1994: 96.

Zach. *HE* VIII.5 (77.9–24): Kavadh, the Persian king, insistently made demands for the payment of the tribute of five gold *centenaria* which was given to him by the king of the Romans on account of the cost of the Persian army guarding the gates facing the Huns; and for this reason he used from time to send his Tayyaye into the territory of the Romans, and they plundered and took off captives.[9] The Romans also crossed into Arzanene, his (Kavadh's) country, and the district of Nisibis, and inflicted damage. Because of this, negotiations (took place), and the two kings sent (envoys), Justin sending Hypatius and the old man Pharesmanes, and Kavadh Asthebid;[10] and much discussion took place on the frontier, which was reported to the two kings by their nobles through couriers; and no peaceful message was sent by them, but (rather) they were enemies of one another.[11] (...) (tr. Hamilton and Brooks, rev. M. Greatrex)

The fact that negotiations took place even after the defection of Iberia is an indication that Kavadh genuinely wished to reach a compromise with the Romans; but their continuing refusal to offer him payments will have rendered such a compromise impossible. Even before the raids of Mundhir described by Zachariah (below, p.86), the Romans launched an attack of their own in mid-summer 527: the *dux* of Mesopotamia, Libelarius, led a force into Beth Arabaye, but failed to take either Nisibis or Thebetha. Roman losses were considerable, and Justinian, having now become sole emperor, replaced Libelarius with Belisarius (Proc. I.12.24). See Greatrex 1998a: 148–9.[12]

Zach. *HE* IX.1 (92.3–17): (...) But since the Persians and the Romans were at enmity with one another in those times, while Timostratus, the *magister militum*, was *dux* on the frontier,[13] the army with its officers assembled around him to fight against Nisibis; and they fought, but could not crush it, and retired from there to the fortress of Thebetha; and the (Roman) army came close up to the wall and breached it; and it was the hot time of the summer. And through some cause they were hindered and did not take the fortress, which was about fifteen parasangs from Dara. And the army was ordered to go to Dara; and, because they greedily coveted as food honey and the flesh of many swine, some of the infantry died of thirst on the march and were lost to the army; others threw themselves into the wells of the desert and were drowned, and the rest were burnt up on the march, but the cavalry reached Dara; and so the army was broken up. (tr. Hamilton and Brooks, rev. M. Greatrex)

This raid may have been intended as a diversionary measure, for the Romans were seeking to strengthen their fortifications elsewhere along the frontier, as is clear from Zachariah's accounts (below). While these efforts were unsuccessful too, other work proceeded unhindered, as to the north (already noted) and at Dara. See Whitby 1986b: 758, Greatrex 1998a: 149–50.

Zach. *HE* IX.2 (92.19–25): During the lifetime of the Emperor Justin,[14] who had learnt that Thannuris was an advantageous place for a city to be built as a place of refuge in the desert, and for an army to be stationed as a protection for the 'Arab against the forays of the Tayyaye, Thomas the *silentiarius* of Apadna was sent to build it. And when he had got ready a certain amount of material, the works which had started to be carried out were halted by the Tayyaye and Qadishaye from Singara and Thebetha. (...) (tr. Hamilton and Brooks, rev. M. Greatrex)

Zach. *HE* IX.5 (96.2–7): In the days of Belisarius the *dux*, in the (year) five,[15] the Romans, having been prevented from building Thannuris on the frontier, wished to make a city at Melabasa.[16] And therefore Gadar the Kadisene was sent with an army by Kavadh; and he hampered the Romans and put them to flight in a battle which he fought with them on the hill of Melabasa. (...) (tr. Hamilton and Brooks, rev. M. Greatrex)

The strengthening of Palmyra (late 527)

One of Justinian's first acts as sole emperor was to take steps to counter Mundhir's raids. See Greatrex 1998a: 151, Gregory 1997: II, 194–5.

Mal. 18.2 (354.13–355.19/425.10–426.5): In the month of October of the sixth indiction the emperor appointed an Armenian named Patricius as *comes Orientis* in Antioch. To him he gave a large sum of money with instructions (p.426) to go and reconstruct the city in Phoenice on the *limes*, known as Palmyra, and its churches and public buildings. He also ordered a *numerus* of soldiers to be stationed there with the *limitanei*, and also the *dux* of Emesa, to protect (p.355) the Roman territories and Jerusalem. (tr. Jeffreys and Scott, revised)

Cross-border warfare in the south (528–529)

In late 527 or early 528 Harith, the phylarch of Palaestina I, quarrelled with the local *dux* and fled eastwards into the desert. There he was defeated and killed by Mundhir. Justinian reacted swiftly, writing personally to the *duces* of Phoenice, Arabia and Mesopotamia and to various phylarchs, instructing them to avenge Harith's death. Their force failed to encounter Mundhir, but sacked several Persian forts, and returned with much booty in April 528 (Mal. 18.16 [434–5]). See Shahîd 1995: 70–6, Greatrex 1998a: 152.[17] Mundhir's riposte followed in spring 529. Clearly the *dux* recently moved to Palmyra was unequal to the task of deterring Mundhir. See Shahîd 1995: 43–4, 79–80, Greatrex 1998a: 152–3.[18]

Zach. *HE* VIII.5 (77.24–78.4): (...) And Mundhir, the Tayyaye king, went up into the territory of Emesa and Apamea and the district of Antioch twice;[19] and he carried off many people and took them down (p.78) with him. And four hundred virgins, who were suddenly captured from the congregation (of the church) of Thomas the Apostle at Emesa (?), he sacrificed in one day in honour of 'Uzzai.[20] Dada the ascetic, an old man, who was captured from the congregation, saw it with his eyes, and told me. (tr. Hamilton and Brooks, rev. M. Greatrex)

Theoph. A.M. 6021 (178.7–15):[21] On March 21st of the 7th indiction, Mundhir son of Zekikē, prince of the Saracens, invaded and looted Syria I as far as the boundaries of Antioch, up to a place called Litargon, and the estates of Skaphathae. He killed many people and burned the territory outside Chalcedon and the Sermian estate and the Kynegian country.[22] And, hearing (this), the Roman commanders went out against him. When they realised this, the Saracens, with the Persians, took their booty and prisoners and fled through the inner *limes*.[23] (tr. Mango and Scott, revised)

In response, Justinian deployed contingents of Lycaonian infantry in the East (Mal. 18.34 [445], Theoph. A.M. 6021, 178.15–18). See Greatrex 1998a: 152–3.

The attempt to fortify Thannuris (528)

The most important Roman initiative on the southern front in 528 was Belisarius' expedition to Thannuris. Here he tried, albeit unsuccessfully, to protect Roman workers undertaking the construction of a fort right on the frontier. (Zach. *HE* IX.2, p.85 above) The region to the south of Dara was poorly defended, and had always been subject to Arab or Persian raids (cf. Ammianus XIV.3). Now measures were being taken to plug this gap in defences. Although this effort failed, it is clear from Proc. (*Aed.* II.6.14–16) that at a later stage Justinian did succeed in establishing a fort there. See Kennedy and Riley 1990: 118–21 (on the site), Shahîd 1995: 76–9 and Greatrex 1998a: 150 n.33, 156–9.

Zach. *HE* IX.2 (92.25–93.27): Now because, as we have made known above, the Romans had equipped themselves (p.93) and fought against Nisibis and Thebetha, afterwards the Persians also similarly came and made an entrenchment[24] in the desert of Thannuris. And when the *dux* Timostratus, the *magister militum*[25] had died, Belisarius had succeeded him; and he did not hanker after bribes, and was kind to the peasants, and did not allow the army to injure them. For he was accompanied by Solomon, a eunuch from the fortress of Edribath;[26] he was a shrewd man, and accustomed to the affairs of the world. He had been notary to the *dux* Felicissimus, and had been attached to the other governors and had gained cunning through experience of difficulties.

Accordingly, a Roman army was gathered in order to enter the desert of Thannuris against the Persians; with (it were) Belisarius, Coutzes, the brother of Bouzes, Basil, Vincent and other commanders, and Atafar, the chief of the Tayyaye.[27] When the Persians heard, they craftily dug several ditches among their trenches, and concealed them[28] all round outside by triangular stakes of wood, and left several openings. When the Roman army arrived, they did not foresee the Persians' deceitful strategem, but the generals entered the Persian entrenchment at full speed; and when they fell into the pits, they were seized, and Coutzes was slain. Of the Roman army those who were mounted turned back and, fleeing, returned to Dara with Belisarius; but the infantry, who did not escape, were killed or taken captive. Atafar, the Tayyaye king, during his flight was struck from nearby and died;[29] he was a warlike and skilful man, and he was very practised in Roman arms, and in various places had excelled and was celebrated. (tr. Hamilton and Brooks, rev. M. Greatrex)

Mal. 18.26 (441–2) describes an invasion by 30,000 Persians, who were opposed by Coutzes, Sebastian, Proclianus, *dux* of Phoenicia, the *comes* Basil, Belisarius and the phylarch Tapharas. Proc. I.13.1–8 refers to the fort as Minduos, apparently situating it near Nisibis, and mentions, apart from Belisarius, the two *duces* of Phoenice, Coutzes and Bouzes. See Greatrex 1998a: 156–9 for an attempt to reconcile these three sources.

While continuing work at fortresses already constructed, such as Dara and Martyropolis (above), Justinian shored up defences in the East still further by transferring soldiers from the Balkans and entrusting the defence of Beroea, Sura, Edessa, Amida and Constantia to specific nobles despatched from Constantinople for the purpose (in late 528) (Mal. 18.26 [442]). See Greatrex 1998a: 159.

Attempts at a compromise (529)

So far no significant campaigning had taken place anywhere along the eastern frontier. Armies had clashed close to the border, Roman fort-building had been thwarted on several occasions, and Arab raids had been carried out, but nothing more. The considerable Roman building programme in the late 520s should be seen as a defensive effort, designed to allow the Romans to refuse Persian demands for money with impunity – not as a measure with which to threaten Persian territories.[30] After the hard winter of 528–529, during which Antioch and Laodicea were struck by earthquakes, followed by Mundhir's daring raid in March 529, Justinian was eager to negotiate. Already by the time his envoy Hermogenes had reached the Persian court, a large uprising of the Samaritans had broken out, which was suppressed only with difficulty (Mal. 18.35 [445–7], Theoph. A.M. 6021, 178–9).[31] The response of Kavadh to Hermogenes is recorded by Malalas. See Scott 1992: 160, Greatrex 1998a: 160.

Mal. 18.44 (378.32–47/449.19–450.15): Koades (Kavadh), king of kings, of the rising sun, to Flavius Justinian Caesar, of the setting moon.[32] We have found it written in our ancient records that we are brothers of one another and (p.450) that if one of us should stand in need of men or money, the other should provide them. From that time to the present we have remained constant in this. Whenever nations have risen against us, against some we have been compelled to fight, while others we have per-suaded by gifts of money to submit (to us), so it is clear that everything in our treasury has been spent. We informed the Emperors Anastasius and Justin of this, but we achieved nothing. Hence we have been compelled to mobilize for war, and having become neighbours of Roman territory, (we have been compelled) to destroy the peo-ples in between on the pretext of their disobedience, even though they had done noth-ing wrong. But, as pious Christians, spare lives and bodies and give us part of your gold. If you do not do this, prepare yourselves for war. For this you have a whole year's notice, so that we should not be thought to have stolen our victory or to have won the war by trickery. (tr. Jeffreys and Scott, revised)

Justinian received this reply in late 529. In response he did not send money, but despatched Hermogenes again, this time with Rufinus. In March 530 they were in Antioch, from where they proceeded to Dara. They appear to have expected negotiations to continue, but Kavadh had now mustered an army and was prepared to back up his demands with force. The Romans too had an army ready at Dara, commanded by Belisarius, recently promoted to the post of *magister militum per Orientem* (Mal. 18.50 [452], Theoph. A.M. 6022, 180, Proc. I.13.9–11). See Scott 1992: 161, Greatrex 1998a: 162–3.

The promotion of Harith the Jafnid (529)

The opening of Justinian's reign saw significant changes of command on the eastern frontier: men of Justin's generation, such as Pharesmanes, Hypatius and Timostratus disappear from the scene. Sittas and Belisarius were entrusted with high commands, as was the Jafnid ruler Harith. According to Procopius, who in general is critical of the chief, Harith received 'the dignity of king' from the emperor. He thus became a supreme phylarch, wielding authority not just in Arabia, his own phylarchate, but over the phylarchs of other provinces too. Justinian thereby hoped to make him a match for the Lakhmid Mundhir, who exercised undisputed control over the tribes allied to Persia, and whose power was extended by Khusro in 531 to cover the whole Arabian coast of the Persian Gulf (Proc. I.17.46–8, Tabari 958/253). See Sartre 1982a: 170–2, Potts 1990: II 249, 334–5, Shahîd 1995: 95–124, Greatrex 1998a: 160.

The battle of Dara (June 530)

Kavadh's decision to cross the border in force in June took the Romans by surprise: Hermogenes, who was with Belisarius at Dara, had expected negotiations to continue, and Rufinus was waiting at Hierapolis to take part in a diplomatic mission (Proc. I.13.10–11). But when Kavadh's army advanced as far as Ammodios, 7.7 km from Dara and in Roman territory, Belisarius prepared his army for battle outside Dara; the fact that he chose to fight in the field, rather than defending the city from within, probably indicates that work on the city's defences was continuing. To compensate for the uncertain quality of his forces, Belisarius dug protective trenches in front of his infantry (Proc. I.13.12–18). See Whitby 1986b: 758–9, Greatrex 1998a: 168–72.

Belisarius positioned his forces with care, assigning a key role to the Hunnic forces. 600 Huns were stationed on each side of the centre, just in front of the trenches and the infantry. From there they could help either the infantry in the centre or the cavalry on the flanks. The Persians divided their forces into three parts, the central section of which was under their commander-in-chief Mihran. When both sides were ready for battle, some skirmishing and single combat took place; in the latter, a Roman former bath attendant emerged victorious in two duels, despite having been forbidden to fight again after his first victory (Proc. I.13.19–39). On the next day, reinforcements arrived for the Persians from Nisibis, bringing their force up to 50,000; the Romans faced them with 25,000 men. Nevertheless, no fighting took place. Belisarius and Hermogenes sought to reopen negotiations, but the Persian general Mihran rebuffed the attempt (Proc. I.14.1–12). The two sides therefore prepared for battle on the following day. Mihran kept some of his forces in reserve, so as to relieve those who were hard pressed in the fighting, thus exploiting his superiority in numbers. On the Roman side, Belisarius accepted a suggestion from Pharas, a Herul, that he should position his men behind a hill on the edge of the battlefield, from where he might fall on the Persians unexpectedly (Proc. I.14.13–33). See Greatrex 1998a: 173–85 (with diagrams). Procopius' eyewitness account of the battle itself provides an important description of the tactics and habits of the two sides.

Proc. *Wars* I.14.34–55 (70.23–74.4): But up to midday neither side began battle. As soon, however, as the noon hour had passed, the barbarians began operations, having postponed the engagement to this time of day for the reason that they (p.71) are accustomed to partake of food only towards late afternoon, while the Romans have their meal before noon; and for this reason they thought that the Romans would never hold out so well, if they assailed them while hungry.[33] (35) At first, then, both sides employed arrows against each other, and the missiles by their great number made, as it were, a vast cloud; and many men were falling on both sides, but the missiles of the barbarians fell much more thickly. (36) For fresh men were always fighting in turn, giving the enemy the least possible opportunity to observe what was being done; but even so the Romans did not have the worst of it. For a steady wind blew from their side against the barbarians, and did not allow their arrows to be very effective. (37) (Then), when all the missiles of both sides had been exhausted, they began to use their spears against each other, and the battle had come still more to close quarters. On the Roman side, the left wing was suffering especially. (38) For the Kadiseni, who with Pityaxes were fighting at this point, came to (his) assistance suddenly in great numbers, routed their enemy, and, pressing hard upon the fugitives, were killing many of them. (39) Seeing this, the men under Sunicas and Aigan advanced against them at great speed. But first the 300 Heruls under Pharas from the high ground got in the rear of the enemy and made a wonderful display of valorous deeds against all of them, and especially the Kadiseni. (40) And the Persians, seeing the forces of Sunicas too already coming up against them from the flank, (p.72) turned to flight. (41) And the rout became complete, for the Romans here joined forces with each other, and there was a great slaughter of the barbarians. (42) On the Persian right wing not fewer than 3000 perished in this action, while the rest escaped with difficulty to the phalanx and were saved. (43) And the Romans did not continue their pursuit, but both sides took their stand facing each other in line. Such then was the course of these events. (44) But Mihran secretly sent to the left wing many men and the so-called Immortals. And when Belisarius and Hermogenes saw them, they ordered the 600 men under Sunicas and Aigan to go to the angle on the right, where the troops of Simmas and Ascan were stationed, and behind them they placed many of Belisarius' men. (45) So the Persians who held the left wing under the leadership of Baresmanas, together with the Immortals, charged on the run against the Romans opposite them, who failed to withstand the attack and turned to flight. (46) Thereupon the Romans in the angle, and as many as were behind them, advanced with great ardour against the pursuers. (47) But inasmuch as they came upon the barbarians from the side, they cut their army into two parts, and the greater portion of them they had on their right, while they kept some also who were left behind on their left. Among these happened to be the standard-bearer of Baresmanas, whom Sunicas charged and struck with a spear. (p.73) (48) And already the Persians who were leading the pursuit perceived in what straits they were, and, wheeling about, they stopped the pursuit and advanced against them (the Romans), and thus became exposed to the enemy on both sides. (49) For those (Romans) in flight before them understood what was happening and turned back again. The Persians, on their part, with the detachment of the Immortals, seeing the standard inclined and lowered to the earth, rushed all together against the Romans at that point with Baresmanas. There the Romans held their ground. (50) And first Sunicas killed Baresmanas and threw him from his horse to the ground. As a result of this the barbarians were seized with great fear and thought no longer of bravery, but fled in utter confusion. (51) And the Romans, having made a circle as it were around them, killed about 5000. Thus both armies were all set in motion, the Persians in retreat, and the Romans in pursuit. (52) In these straits all the infantry who were in the Persian army threw down their shields and were caught in disorder and killed by (their) enemy. However, the pursuit of the Romans took place only for a short distance. (53) For Belisarius and Hermogenes refused absolutely to let them go further, fearing lest the Persians through some necessity should turn about and rout them while pursuing recklessly, and it seemed to them sufficient to preserve the victory unmarred. (54) For on that day the Persians had been defeated in battle by the Romans after a long time (without any such success).[34] Thus the two armies separated from one another. (55) And the Persians (p.74) were no longer willing to fight a pitched battle with the Romans straightaway. However, some sudden attacks were made on both sides, in which the Romans were not at a disadvantage. Such, then, was the fortune of the armies in Mesopotamia. (tr. Dewing, revised)

Zach. *HE* IX.3 (94.1–95.2): (*The third chapter of the ninth (book), concerning the battle by Dara.*) The Persians were proud and puffed up and boastful indeed; the *mihran* and the *marzbans* assembled an army and came against Dara and encamped at Ammodius, being justifiably confident in thinking they could subdue the city because the Roman army had been diminished by their sword. Their cavalry and infantry approached and came up on the south side of the city, (in order) to encompass it all around for the purpose of blockading it; but a Roman army encountered them by the help of our Lord, who chastises but does not utterly deliver over to death. For a certain Sunicas, a general who was a Hun (and) had been baptized when he took refuge with the Romans, and Simmas, a Roman tribune, and their armour-bearers with twenty men drove the whole Persian army away from the city several times, passing boldly and vigorously from one side to the other, and slaying (men) right and left. They were practised with the spear and the sword; their cry was vehement and powerful, and they seemed terrible to the Persians, so that they fell before them; and two of their leaders were killed, along with a not inconsiderable force of cavalry, while the Heruls who were with Bouzes to the east of the city slew and hurled back the *faige*, who are the Persian infantry.

The Persians, when they realised how many had been killed, craftily sent (a message) to Nisibis, asking them to bring as many (pack animals) as they could, and to come at once to Dara and take as much spoil as they were able. And when many came, they loaded up the bodies of the slain, and they returned in shame. (p.95) However the rest of the Persian force poured over the Roman 'Arab and burned it with fire.[35] (tr. Hamilton and Brooks, rev. M. Greatrex)

The battle of Satala (summer 530)

Kavadh did not attack Roman territory only in Mesopotamia. To the north, the Persians had gained ground recently, having retaken Iberia and advanced into Lazica. An advance into Roman Armenia therefore seemed appropriate. Mihr-Mihroe (Mermeroes) was placed in command of a mixed force of Persians and allies, including Persarmenians, Sabirs and Sunitae. Ranged against them were the *duces* and troops of the *magister militum praesentalis* Sittas and his successor as *magister militum per Armeniam* Dorotheus. Even before the Persians invaded, they were able to inflict some losses on the enemy, having heard of the preparations underway. Mihr-Mihroe, when his 30,000 troops were assembled, made no attempt on Theodosiopolis, preferring to penetrate as far as possible into Roman territory. The Romans took a stand at the important base of Satala, where they succeeded in defeating their more numerous opponents by a ruse (Proc. I.15.1–17). The Roman successes of 530 then began to have an impact on the region: first, two Persarmenian chiefs, the brothers Narses and Aratius, defected to the Roman side. They received a generous welcome from the Romans at the hands of the eunuch Narses, and this in turn persuaded their youngest brother, Isaac, to follow suit, handing over control of the fortress of Bolum at the same time. The Romans also gained the fort of Pharangium, which was a particular blow to the Persians, since it lay in a gold-producing region (Proc. I.15.18–19, 26–33).

The resumption of negotiations (autumn 530)

In August 530, probably after the defeat at Satala, Rufinus and the *comes* Hermogenes arrived at Kavadh's court. The king complained bitterly of the continuing Roman refusal to pay for the defence of the Caspian Gates, as well as of the construction of Dara. He was now obliged, he claimed, to maintain two armies – one to defend the Caspian Gates, and one to defend against the Romans in Dara. He therefore demanded that the Romans either dismantle Dara or contribute towards the costs of defending the Caspian Gates; he hinted to the envoys that the latter was the option he preferred (Proc. I.16.1–10). When the ambassadors returned to Constantinople in winter 530, Justinian believed the peace was within his grasp: he may have been assured that a one-off payment to the Persians would satisfy Kavadh, without the obligation to contribute money every year. He wrote a letter to the king, welcoming the development; but when Rufinus reached the frontier in early 531, it soon became clear that Kavadh was no longer interested in peace. The defections and losses in Armenia may have changed his mind, as may exaggerated rumours of the Samaritan uprising: some Samaritans had contacted the king, urging him to march on Jerusalem, but were intercepted on their way back to Roman territory (Mal. 18.54 [455–6], Theoph. A.M. 6021 [179]). See Scott 1992: 161, Greatrex 1998a: 190–2.[36]

The campaign of Callinicum (spring 531)

According to Procopius, the inspiration for Kavadh's next line of attack was the Lakhmid chief Mundhir. A Persian army of 15,000, under Azarethes, consisting exclusively of cavalry, together with 5000 men under Mundhir's command, crossed into Roman territory by Circesium. They advanced up the Euphrates, meeting no resistance. Only when they passed Callinicum was Belisarius informed; he instantly moved west with 3000 men and 5000 Ghassanid allies under Harith. The remainder of his forces he left behind to defend Dara. The Persians had by this time reached the region where the Euphrates runs north–south and proceeded to ravage the provinces of Euphratesia and Syria I, but the arrival of Belisarius at Chalcis barred any further advance. The *dux* Sunicas harried the Persians near Gabbulon successfully, although Belisarius had given orders not to engage the enemy. Meanwhile Hermogenes arrived at Hierapolis with reinforcements, and from there proceeded south to Barbalissus. Here the Roman army assembled, and Hermogenes tried to reconcile the *magister militum per Orientem* with his subordinate commanders. This proved to be a difficult task, since Belisarius was inclined to let the Persians now withdraw unmolested. Local commanders felt differently, no doubt spurred on in part by the fact that prisoners seized by Mundhir in 529 had only just been ransomed for a large price; others had been killed in captivity (Mal. 18.59 [460–1]). Furthermore, when the citizens of Antioch had heard of the recent Persian advance, they had fled to the coast in panic. Hermogenes therefore led the army forward against the invaders, who were now withdrawing eastwards. The Roman army shadowed the Persians as far as a site opposite Callinicum, on the south side of the Euphrates. Here Belisarius was prevailed upon to engage the Persians, just before they retreated into the uninhabited regions beyond Callinicum (Mal. 18.60 [460–3]; Proc. I.17.1–3, 29–39, 18.1–13). See Greatrex 1998a: 193–9.

The Roman army, having set off from Sura early on Saturday 19 April 531, came upon the Persians as they were about to leave their camp opposite Callinicum. Although the Roman troops had already marched some distance that day and were fasting during Holy Week, they insisted on engaging the enemy immediately in spite of the objections of both Belisarius and Hermogenes (Proc. I.17.14–29). The ensuing battle was a substantial victory for the Persians. Both Procopius and Malalas offer a detailed account of events, but their emphasis is somewhat different: the former exonerates Belisarius as far as possible, insisting that he prevented a rout by drawing up his infantry in dense formation to ward off the Persian cavalry, and that the Persians suffered considerable losses (I.17.30–56).[37] Malalas, on the other hand, accuses Belisarius of fleeing the battle early, leaving Sunicas and Simmas to wage a successful infantry struggle against the Persians (Mal. 18.60 [463–5]). Both accounts agree on the poor performance of the Lycaonian or Phrygian infantry and note suspicions of treachery on the part of the allied Arabs. Procopius insists that although Roman firepower was less rapid than the Persians', it was more effective, but the evidence of Zachariah (below) implies otherwise, at least in this instance.[38] On the battle itself see B. Rubin 1960: 287–9, Shahîd 1995: 134–42, Greatrex 1998a: 200–7.

Zach. *HE* IX.4 (95.4–26): The Persians, since they had become wise from experience on account of the great (damage) which they had suffered from the attacks of the Romans whenever they approached the city and went out against them, went up into the desert land of the Romans and encamped on the Euphrates; and according to their usual practice they made a trench. Belisarius at the head of a Roman army and tribunes came up against them to battle; and they (the Romans) arrived in the last week of the fast. The Persians were found to be like a little flock, and so they appeared in their (the Romans') eyes; and the *astebid*, their commander, was afraid of them, and those who were with him; and he sent (a message) to the Romans, (asking them) to honour the fast, 'for the sake of the Nazarenes and Jews who are in the army that is with me, and for the sake of yourselves who are Christians.'[39] And when Belisarius the *magister militum* had considered this, he was willing (to agree); but the commanders complained greatly, and would not consent to delay and honour the day. When they prepared for battle on the eve of the first day of the week, (the day) of unleavened bread, it was a cold day with the wind against the Romans, and they appeared feeble, and turned and fled before the Persian attack. Many fell into the Euphrates and were drowned, and others were killed; Belisarius escaped, while the nephew of Bouzes was seized (for he himself was ill at Amida, and did not go to the battle, but sent his army to Abgersaton with Domitziolus), and went down to Persia. But he eventually returned; and how this happened I shall relate in the chapter below. (tr. Hamilton and Brooks, rev. M. Greatrex)

The Roman failure was followed by a commission of enquiry, the result of which was the dismissal of Belisarius from his post in May or June. See Greatrex 1998a: 194–5, questioning the impartiality of the commission.

The aftermath of Callinicum (April–June 531)

Hermogenes visited Kavadh immediately after the battle to reopen negotiations, but without success (Proc. I.20.1). The Persians were meanwhile pressing home their advantage elsewhere, seizing the fortress of Abgersaton in Osrhoene (Mal. 18.61 [465–6], Zach. *HE* IX.4, above). Justinian therefore took steps to bolster the Roman position. Sittas was charged with the defence of the entire East in the wake of Belisarius' dismissal; and the former praetorian prefect Demosthenes was sent to the frontier with funds to provide the cities with adequate granaries (Proc. I.20.3, Mal. 18.63 [467]). At the same time the emperor continued to try to engage Kavadh diplomatically. The role of Mundhir as intermediary is interesting, as is Justinian's attempt to enter into relations with the Lakhmid chief. See Scott 1992: 163–4, Shahîd 1995:

142–3 (suggesting that Sergius should be identified with a Sergius, bishop of Sergiopolis), Greatrex 1998a: 208.

Mal. 18.61 (390.86–8/466.18–467.14): In the month of June, while the Roman *magistri militum* were making preparations against the Persians, Alamundarus (Mundhir), the prince of the Saracens, wrote to the Romans for a deacon called Sergius to be sent to him so that he could convey peace terms through him to the Roman emperor. Sergius was sent to the Roman emperor with the letter (p.467) sent by Mundhir. The emperor, having read the letter, did not stop his campaign against the Persians. He sent Rufinus as an ambassador to Persia with a letter for him (the king, recommending) that he accept friendship: 'for it is honourable and glorious to make the two states to live in peace. If he does not do this, I shall seize the Persian land for myself.' At the same time Sergius the deacon was sent to king Mundhir with imperial gifts. In that year gifts were sent from the emperor of the Romans to the Persian king. Likewise the Augusta sent gifts to the Persian empress, who was his sister.[40] When Rufinus and Strategius reached the city of Edessa, they sent a message to Kavadh, the king of the Persians. He put off receiving them, since he had secretly sent a force against the Romans.[41] (tr. Jeffreys and Scott, revised)

Campaigns in Armenia (summer 531)

The Persians were also active further north, as Zachariah relates.

Zach. *HE* IX.5 (96.7–27): (…) And he (Gadar) was in the confidence of Kavadh, and had been stationed with an army to guard the frontier eastwards from Melabasa in the country of Arzanene as far as Martyropolis. This man boasted and talked nonsense against the Romans, and blasphemed like Rabshakeh, who was sent by Sennacherib. He brought about 700 armed cavalry and infantry, who accompanied them to amass plunder; and they crossed the Tigris into the district of Attachas (in the territory) of Amida. Bessas was *dux* in Martyropolis, and it was summer in this year nine (531). With Gadar was Yazdgerd, the nephew of the *bdeashkh*, who, as a neighbour, knew the region of Attachas. When Bessas heard (of this), he went out against him with about 500 horsemen from Martyropolis, which was about four stades distant.[42] He encountered him at Beth Helte and massacred his army by the Tigris, killed Gadar, took Yazdgerd prisoner, and brought him to Martyropolis. This man after the peace, which was (made) in (the year) ten, was given in exchange for Domitziolus, who returned from Persia. But Bessas the *dux*, after massacring Gadar and the Persian cavalry, who were guarding the frontier of Arzanene, entered the country and did much damage there; and he carried off captives and brought (them) to Martyropolis.

Cf. Mal. 18.65 (468–9) for an account of the same events, taken from a report compiled by Hermogenes. He claims that 6000 Persians invaded, of whom 2000 were killed. Malalas also (18.66 [469]) refers to successes of Dorotheus in Persarmenia, where he defeated Persians and Persarmenians and captured fortresses. These events spurred Kavadh to make a further attempt to redress the position: his victory at Callinicum had been narrow, little booty had been gained, and no major fortresses captured. He therefore now despatched an army under Aspabedus, Mihr-Mihroe and Khanaranges to take Martyropolis, a city vexingly close to the frontier and recently strengthened by Justinian, and to avenge Bessas' raid on Arzanene. See Greatrex 1998a: 209–10.

Zach. *HE* IX.6 (97.2–98.18): The villages in the country of Arzanene belong to the Persian kingdom, and no small sum is collected as poll-tax from their inhabitants for the king's treasury and for the office of the *bdeashkh* who is stationed there (he is the king's prefect). To this country, as related above, Bessas the *dux* did much injury; he captured the nephew of the *bdeashkh*, and also kept him prisoner in Martyropolis. King Kavadh was much distressed when he learned from the *bdeashkh* about the devastation of the country. This same Hormizd left no stone unturned in order to subdue Martyropolis by force and cunning,[43] for it acts as a (place of) ambush and refuge for a Roman army (from which) to damage Arzanene. And an army was, so to speak, equipped by the Persian army: Mihr Girowi was sent to hire a large number of Huns and bring them to their assistance. They got ready and were gathered together by Martyropolis at the beginning of the (year) ten;[44] and they made a trench against it, and a 'mule' and many mines; and they pressed hard upon it in an attack and oppressed it. In it was a Roman force of no small size and Bouzes, and they drove large numbers of Persians back in battle. But Nonnus, the bishop of the city, had died.

Now Belisarius, because he was blamed by the king on account of the massacre of the Roman army by the Persians at Thannuris and by the Euphrates, had been dismissed and had gone up to the king; and after him (the commander) at Dara was Constantine.[45] A large Roman army was assembled, and Sittas was *stratēgos*, and Bar Gabala, the Tayyaye king was with them.[46] And they reached Amida in November[47] of the year ten; and John, the hermit of Anastasia, (p.98) a man of honourable character, who had been called (to the bishopric) accompanied them. When they had gone to Martyropolis and the winter came on – the country is northerly and cold – the Persians were held back by rain and mud, and endured hardship, while they were also afraid of the multitude of the Roman army; (in addition), Kavadh their king had died while they were there, and (so) they made a truce with the Romans to withdraw from the city.

Soon after they had withdrawn and Martyropolis had been relieved, and the Roman army had returned, the Huns, who had been hired by the Persians, arrived. This great people suddenly entered the territory of the Romans, and massacred and slew many of the tillers of the soil, and burned villages and their churches. They crossed the Euphrates and advanced as far as Antioch, and no one stood before them or harmed them, except only this Bessas, the *dux* of Martyropolis, who fell upon some of them while they were leaving, and killed them, and captured about 500 horses and much spoil; and the man became rich. At the fortress of Citharizon the *dux* there repulsed some of them – about 400 men – and captured their baggage animals. (tr. Hamilton and Brooks, rev. M. Greatrex)

Proc. I.21.6–8 also mentions the siege; he plays up the weakness of the fortifications, probably excessively. Cf. *Aed.* III.2 with Whitby 1984: 182. Mal. 18.66 [469–70] provides more details, describing how the defenders foiled all the tactics pursued by the besiegers. As Zachariah describes, the arrival of Sittas and another Roman army at Attachas, 20 km from Martyropolis, forced the Persians to withdraw in November or December 531 (Proc. I.21.9–11). Procopius (I.21.11–16) adds that the Romans encouraged the Persian decision to withdraw by suborning a Persian spy, who reported that the approaching Sabir Huns were allied to the Romans rather than them. A further factor prompting the Persian withdrawal was news of the death of Kavadh; Malalas (18.68 [471.4–10]) actually attributes his death (in September) to news of Persian losses. See Greatrex 1998a: 210–11.

In autumn 531 Rufinus and Strategius were still at Edessa, having been refused access to Kavadh while the attack on Martyropolis proceeded. Justinian, learning of the attack on Martyropolis, forbade them to proceed to the king with their gifts until he so ordered (Mal. 18.66 [470.16–18]). When Khusro, having succeeded to the throne, therefore invited the envoys to proceed, they refused, citing the emperor's command. Khusro was obliged to write to Justinian through Hermogenes, asking to see the envoys and to arrange terms. The emperor refused, answering Khusro: 'We do not give permission for our ambassadors (p.472) to come to you, nor do we recognize you as king of the Persians.' (Mal. 18.68 [471.22–472.2], tr. Jeffreys and Scott). Justinian thereby hoped to destabilise Khusro's position, clearly aware of the instability within Persia. However, Khusro was able to purge his brother and his Mazdakite supporters swiftly, and Justinian therefore agreed to a three-month truce and the exchange of hostages, presumably at the very end of 531 or in early 532 (Mal. 18.69 [472.7–14]). See Crone 1991: 31–3, Scott 1992: 164, Greatrex 1998a: 211–12.

Before peace was agreed in the following year, several eastern provinces had to endure one further invasion – that of the Sabir Huns described by Zachariah (above). They had been summoned by the Persians earlier in the year, but only arrived in December, after the Persians had withdrawn from Martyropolis. According to Malalas (18.70 [472–3]) they penetrated as far as Euphratesia, the region around Cyrrhus, and Cilicia. Little effort was made to repel them, perhaps because their arrival was unexpected so late in the year. But as they withdrew counter-operations got underway, and Dorotheus, the *magister militum per Armeniam*, retook much of the booty they had plundered (Mal. 18.70 [472–3], Proc. I.21.28 [playing down the raid], Zach. *HE* IX.6 [above], *Chr. Ede.* 103 [AG 843]).

The Eternal Peace (532)

In spring 532 negotiations began in earnest to end the war. The new Persian king, Khusro, needed to devote his attention to securing his own position, while Justinian may already have been looking westwards and have been intending to redeploy his forces now engaged in the East. The Roman envoys Rufinus, Hermogenes, Alexander and Thomas met Khusro in Persian territory and soon came to an agreement. The Persians would receive 110 *centenaria* (11,000 lbs of gold), and the Romans would withdraw the base of the *dux* of Mesopotamia from Dara to Constantia. Khusro insisted on retaining control of Sarapanis and Scanda, the forts in Lazica, and would also receive back the Armenian forts of Pharangium and Bolum. Khusro underlined that the payment was to be made to cover the expense of defending the Caucasian passes. Before the agreement was finalised, Rufinus returned to Constantinople to acquire permission to concede the forts to Khusro (Proc. I.22.1–8). Justinian at first agreed to the terms, but soon afterwards ordered his ambassadors not to give up the Lazic forts to Khusro. The negotiations were therefore broken off, and Rufinus recovered the money already paid only with difficulty (Proc. I.22.9–14). In summer that year, however, Hermogenes and Rufinus succeeded in concluding a treaty by which the Romans recovered the Lazic forts and the Iberians who had fled their country were allowed to remain in Roman territory or to return to their native land (Proc. I.22.15–19, Zach. IX.7 [99–100]).[48]

Mal. 18.76 (401.19–33/477.13–478.7): In that year Hermogenes and Rufinus returned from Persia, bringing with them a peace treaty between the two states of Rome and Persia for the duration of the life of both.[49] The region of Pharangium was restored to the Persians with all their prisoners, while the forts that had been captured by the Persians were restored to the Romans, with those captured in them. The two rulers agreed and stated explicitly in the treaty that they were brothers according to the ancient custom, and that if one of them required money or men in a military alliance, they should provide it without dispute.[50] After these proceedings (p.478) both armies, the Roman and the Persian, withdrew. The war had lasted 31 years from the time that Kavadh, the king of the Persians, had advanced in hostility into Roman territory, as was mentioned above during the reign of Anastasius, and the capture of Amida, mentioned above, and the restoring of that city of Amida to the Romans, and the local wars with raiding Saracens.[51] (tr. Jeffreys and Scott, revised)

Chr. Ede. 104: In the year 843 (532) in the month of September the patrician Mar Rufinus made peace between the Romans and Persians; and this peace lasted until the year 851 (539/40). (tr. M. Greatrex)

A column from Hierapolis, with a fragmentary inscription on every side, commemorates the conclusion of the peace.

Roussel 1939: I (366) The lord Justinian alone, by divine counsel, made peace, and he put a stop to the lamentations of war (which had been) upon (the) cities for three decades[52]. With Rufinus the general ... .

Roussel 1939: II (367) By the good will of the Lord Christ and for the preservation of our city of the holy apostles Peter and Paul, peace was made. Being consul ... .

Roussel 1939: III (367) + The cross extinguished the terrible roarings[53] of war and the measureless hardships of life, as if (they were) a rough wave or a fire.

Roussel 1939: IV (367) Peace was made between the Romans and Persians with (the help of) holy God; the money was handed over and ... .

The peaceful state of relations in the 530s

By the mid-530s, Justinian could take pride in his achievements on the eastern front alongside his more recent successes in the West. He appears, however, not to have taken the current peaceful state of relations with the Persians for granted.

*Nov.J.*1.proem: While we have been busied with the concerns of the whole state and have preferred to concentrate not on trivial matters, but (on) how the Persians may remain at peace, (how) the Vandals, along with the Moors, may obey us, (how) the Carthaginians, having regained their former liberty, may enjoy (it), (and how) the Tzani, for the first time (brought) under the Roman state (something which God had not granted to the Romans until now, only during our reign) may be enrolled among its subjects, individual concerns from our subjects have constantly been reported and have flooded in; to each of these we give an appropriate response.[54]

The following passage describes a meeting between the anti-Chalcedonian bishop of Constantia (Tella), John, who had been captured in the Jebel Sinjar by a joint Roman and Persian force, and the *marzban* at Nisibis.[55] John's replies to the *marzban*'s questions clearly show how good relations were between the two states, at least up to 537, and how permeable the frontier was at this time. It is not surprising therefore that envoys from the Gothic king Vitiges were able to make their way from Italy to Persia in order to establish relations with Khusro.[56]

Elias, *V. Joh. Tel.* 71.21–73.11: When the *marzban* heard this (that John was a bishop) he at once gave an order (summoning him) and sat down on the ground in his presence. And he spoke with him through an interpreter, who said to him in Greek: 'How did you dare, a man such as you, to cross over into our territory without our (permission)? Do you not know that this is another state?' The blessed man replied, speaking to him through (p.72) the interpreter in Greek, 'It is not the first time that I have crossed over into this land. This is the third time that I have crossed over, in order that I might pray among these saints who have lived for many years on the mountain (Jebel Sinjar) from which you took me away as an evil-doer. For who am I that your greatness knows of me and (knows that) I had crossed over then? For I am a poor man, just as you see me. Today, while there is complete peace between these two kingdoms, I did not know one state from another. For the two kings are brothers in love; and, if I am here, I think I am among Romans, and, if I am among Romans, I am here on account of (that) peace.' The *marzban* said, 'How is that you say your are a poor man, when much gold was retrieved from you by those who came to you?' The confessor replied, 'Lo! Suddenly those whom you sent seized me; let them tell what they found with me when they seized me and searched me. And again I ask that, if it is easy while I am imprisoned here, your greatness send trustworthy men to go round our whole land. Let them question both my enemies who have accused me, and my friends, and let them show that anything has been taken by me from any man. And if any of those (charges) with which I have been accused are found (to be true), let me be crucified in the middle of this city. What I had from my parents I have given away, and have received (items) from others.' The *marzban* said, 'Why have you rebelled against Caesar and those who hold authority (p.73) in his land? Do you not know that the man who rebels against his masters behaves wrongly? And, if you wish, I shall reconcile you with the Romans and you will behave according to their will, and live in peace and quiet.' The holy man said, 'I have not rebelled against our victorious and peaceful emperor, who is beloved by men. I, according to my duties, as we are bound, am his servant, since I am of the world. And I pray on his behalf that he may judge his empire in accordance with God's will.' And when (the *marzban*) had heard him praising the emperor (so) fully, he shouted out and said, according to their custom of praise, 'May the fortune of the king of kings, who is the equal of God, be with you.'[57] (tr. M. Greatrex)

The *Martyrdom of Grigor* confirms this picture. Cf. Joh. Eph. *Lives*, *PO* 18.543–4 (*Life of Susan*), also in Brock and Harvey 1987: 134–5 with Lee 1993a: 56–7 on the openness of the frontier at this time.

Mart. Grig. 360.5–10: God made peace between these two kingdoms. In the year forty (of Kavadh's reign)[58] King Khusro came to the throne, and in the third year of his reign[59] he ordered an ambassador to go to the Roman emperor, in order to confirm the peace between the two kingdoms. (For this mission) Zabergan, one of the nobles of the kingdom, was chosen.[60] (tr. M. Greatrex)

Deterioration of Roman defences

Although Bury confidently ascribed Justinian's refortification and upgrading of cities in Mesopotamia, Osrhoene and Syria to the period of the Eternal Peace, there is no evidence to support this. On the contrary, given that in the fifth century a ban on fortifications near the frontier had been part of a peace agreement (see Chapter 3 above), and that Justinian had been obliged to move the headquarters of the *dux* of Mesopotamia from Dara to Constantia, it is highly unlikely that Khusro would have tolerated such a building programme.[61] Furthermore, Justinian seems to have wished to cut his expenditure on the defences of the East to the maximum possible extent.

Proc. Anecd. 24.12–14 (148.11–149.14): And I shall add one further item to those I have mentioned, since the subject of the soldiers leads on to it. Those who had ruled the Romans in earlier times stationed a very great multitude of soldiers at all points of the state's frontier in order to guard the boundaries of the Roman domain, [and] particularly in the eastern portion, thus checking the inroads of the Persians and Saracens; these troops they used to call *limitanei*. (13) These the Emperor <Justinian> at first treated so casually and meanly that their paymasters were four or five years behind in their payments to them, and whenever peace was made between the Romans and the Persians, (p.149) these wretches were compelled, on the supposition that they too would profit by the blessings of peace, to make a present to the Treasury of the pay which was owing to them for a specific period. And later on, for no good reason, he took away from them the very name of an army. (14) Thereafter the boundaries of the Roman empire remained without guardposts, and the soldiers suddenly found themselves obliged to look to the hands of those accustomed to works of piety.[62] (tr. Dewing, revised)

Reorganisation of Armenia (536)

Following his military reforms in Armenia, Justinian now undertook a systematic reorganisation of the Roman Armenian territories, seeking to integrate the former satrapies and Armenia Interior into the empire. He established four provinces of Armenia. The frontier provinces were Armenia I, which incorporated both Theodosiopolis and Satala, and Armenia IV, which took over the old satrapies and had its chief city at Martyropolis (*Nov.J.*31, tr. in Adontz 1970: 133–6). See Toumanoff 1963: 174–5, Adontz 1970: ch.7, Hewsen 1992: 18 (with a map), Garsoïan 1999: 195–6. Roughly simultaneously with these developments in Armenia, the Roman grip on the Transcaucasus tightened. Roman troops were deployed in Lazica and a city established at Petra. In addition, the new commander there, John Tzibus, restricted trade, to the vexation of the Lazi (Proc. II.15.1–26). See Lordkipanidse and Brakmann 1994: 85–6, Braund 1991: 222–3, Braund 1994: 290–5.

*Nov.J.*28.pr.: (…) Pontus Polemoniacus comprises five other (cities) – Neocaesarea, Comana, Trapezus, Cerasus and Polemonium, for Pityus and Sebastopolis are to be counted among forts rather than cities. As far as these extend the two Ponti (i.e. Pontus Polemoniacus and Helenopontus). After these, our Lazica is established, in which is also the city of the Petraeans, which has taken its civic identity and title from us, using the name of our piety and being called Justiniana. (There lie also) Archaeopolis and Rhodopolis, very large and ancient forts. Amid these are also the forts of Scandis and Sarapanis, which we took from the Persians, and Mourisius[63] and Lysiris and whatever works we have undertaken among the Lazi. Thereafter the land of the Tzani takes over, now in our day, for the first time, held by the Romans, which is receiving recent civic foundations, and which will receive foundations yet to be made. But after that land the peoples are the Suani and Scymni and Apsilae and Abasgi and others now, by the grace of God, friendly and ours.[64] (tr. Braund, revised)

Justinian clearly had his sights on the whole western Transcaucasus. From Procopius (VIII.3.13–21) we know that it was at just this time that the Abasgi were converted to Christianity through the efforts of the Abasgian Euphratas. See Colvin 2003.

Euphratesia threatened by an Arab incursion (536)

The fragility of the eastern frontier is well illustrated by this rare glimpse of border negotiations.[65]

Marc. Com. *Addit.* a.536.11: Indeed in that very year, on account of the excessive drought, pasture land in Persia was refused and about 15,000 Saracens with the phylarchs Chabus (Ka'b) and Hezidus (Yezid) were driven across the borders of Euphratesia by Mundhir. There the *dux* Batzas encouraged them partly by flattery and partly by peaceful restraint and repressed their desire for war. (tr. Croke, revised)

Roman–Persian cross-border cooperation (late 536)

According to Elias, the biographer of John of Tella, the patriarch of Antioch, Ephraem, was so eager to seize the anti-Chalcedonian bishop of Constantia that he enlisted the help of the Persians (albeit by a deception).

Elias, *V. Joh. Tel.* **65.24–66.21:** (p.66) And, in order that he (Ephraem) might altogether block (that) fount of benefits, he schemed and found men to perform his will; and he sent them to the *marzban* of Nisibis of the Persians. He persuaded him through them, since he had agreed (to pay) a not inconsiderable bribe to him, to send urgently some of his soldiers, and the Romans with them, (in order that) this blessed man, famous for (his) victories of the spirit, might be seized from the mountain called Sinjar (Singara). For the saint had retreated here on account of the many things of use (to him) in that hard time. Those who had been sent to that pagan *marzban* by Ephraem repeated to him many lies against that man, and supposed that he had acquired a lot of gold. That pagan, whose name was Mihrdades, inflamed by desire, sent off many cavalrymen against him with a certain commander from among his own (men), who was also himself a pagan. And the Persians and Qadishaye and some of the Romans reached the mountain, since they had also brought scouts with them, comprised of Romans and Persians who knew the place. And, furthermore, there was (a man) who had been sent by Ephraem to complete the task, who was from the fortress of Barbalissus (Beth Balash) and who had been made what it called a brigand-hunter in the territory of Antioch, whose name was Cometas.[66] (tr. M. Greatrex)

A coup at Dara (537)

The most detailed source for the uprising is Procopius (*Wars* I.26.5–12), according to whom the initiator of the coup, John, was an infantry soldier, and enjoyed only limited support for his venture. See Greatrex 1998a: 220.

Marc. Com. *Addit.* **a.537.4:** In the East too, John Cottistis was killed at Dara while usurping power, before he could undertake any hostile action. (tr. Croke, revised)
Zach. *HE* **X.1** (176.8–15): Now there went up ... in <the year fif>teen, and also ... the king ... much ... he told him about <a ... man> named But ... <organis>ed a rebellion in Dara in the summer of the year, who was ... And he freed the king from distress of mind, <but> in what way I cannot truthfully state, and therefore keep silence. (tr. Hamilton-Brooks, rev. M. Greatrex)

7

JUSTINIAN'S SECOND PERSIAN WAR

The southern front (540–5)

The background to the war

The second Persian war of Justinian broke out in early summer 540, when a large Persian army commanded by Khusro invaded Roman Mesopotamia and Syria. According to Procopius, Khusro was encouraged to undertake the campaign both by an emissary from the Gothic king Vitiges and by Armenians discontented with Roman rule (Proc. II.2–3).[1] Justinian's continuing campaigns in North Africa and Italy and the consequent reduction in manpower on the Roman eastern front must have encouraged Khusro's ambitions; he may too have been aware of the poor morale among the *limitanei*, whose pay had been cut since the Eternal Peace.[2] Another likely contributory factor was Khusro's continuing need for funds, since his kingdom was still having to make tributary payments to the Hephthalite Huns.[3] Khusro initially (in 539) attempted to exploit a dispute between the Lakhmid and Ghassanid Arabs (over ownership of grazing land known as the 'Strata', i.e. the region through which passed the *Strata Diocletiana*) to justify an attack on Roman territory, but the Romans successfully defused the issue by prevaricating. Next the Persian king alleged that Justinian had sought to bribe the Lakhmid ruler Mundhir through his envoy Summus, and that he had encouraged some Huns to invade Persian territory (Proc. II.1). See Bauzou 1993: 36 (on the name of the *Strata*), Shahîd 1995: 210–16 (critical of Proc.'s portrayal of the affair), Key Fowden 1999: 66.

The Persian tradition is also aware of the quarrel between the two Arab leaders, but (unsurprisingly) portrays the Jafnid ruler Harith as the aggressor. See Shahîd 1995: 216–18 (noting an acccount similar to Tabari's in Firdausi, tr. Mohl 1868: 195–201).

Tabari, I, 958/252–3 (Nöldeke 238–9): Between Khusro Anushirvan and Justinian, emperor of the Romans, there was, as has been mentioned, a total cessation of hostilities. But enmity arose between a certain Arab whom Justinian had appointed king over the Arabs of Syria and who was called Khalid ibn Jabala,[4] a man of Lakhm whom Khusro had appointed king over the territory between Oman, Bahrain and Yamama as far as Ta'if and the rest of the Hijaz together with its Arab inhabitants and who was called Mundhir ibn al-Nu'man. Therefore Khalid ibn Jabala invaded Mundhir's domain, killed a great number of his men and took much of his wealth as booty. Mundhir complained of that to Khusro and asked him to write to the king of the Romans that he might obtain justice for him from Khalid. So Khusro did write to

Justinian, mentioning the treaty of peace between them and informing him what Mundhir, his prefect over the Arabs, had met with at the hands of Khalid ibn Jabala, whom he (Justinian) had appointed king over the Arabs in his lands, and asking him to order Khalid to return to Mundhir the booty he had taken from his domain and to pay him bloodmoney for the Arabs belonging to it, whom he (Harith) had killed. (In short Khusro asked that) he (Justinian) obtain justice for Mundhir from Khalid and that he not treat lightly what he had written to him about, in case the peace treaty between them thereby be nullified. Repeatedly he wrote letters to Justinian to obtain justice for Mundhir, but he (Justinian) did not heed them. (tr. Hoyland)

The Persian invasion, early summer 540

In late 539 Justinian, aware of Persian plans, despatched a message to Khusro through Anastasius of Dara to dissuade him from his expedition (Proc. *Wars* II.4.14–26).[5] But in May 540[6] Khusro entered Roman territory nonetheless. He invaded Euphratesia at the confluence of the Khabur and Euphrates, proceeding along the southern bank of the Euphrates, thus avoiding the fortress at Circesium (II.5.1–6). He made a half-hearted attempt to induce the fortress of Zenobia to surrender (II.5.7), but when he met with no success, he quickly moved on to Sura. The garrison of Sura, under the commander Arsaces, resisted the first Persian attack with some sucess, but Arsaces himself was slain in the fighting. Dispirited by this development, the inhabitants sent their bishop to negotiate with Khusro. He appeared to accept the entreaties of the bishop, but instead seized the opportunity of taking the city by surprise and sacking it (II.5.8–27). The Roman prisoners were then ransomed by the bishop of nearby Sergiopolis, Candidus, who pledged to pay the Persian king two *centenaria* (II.5.28–33).

The general in charge of the Roman defences in Belisarius' absence was Bouzes. He proposed to defend his base at Hierapolis by positioning some of his forces in the neighbouring hills; but having led off the best troops to do this, he lost contact entirely with those remaining in the city (Proc. II.6.1–8). Justinian, apprised of the invasion, despatched his cousin Germanus to bolster the defences of Antioch, but provided him with only 300 men. Discovering that the city was vulnerable to assault, Germanus and the city's inhabitants decided to negotiate with Khusro through the agency of Megas, bishop of Beroea (II.6.9–16).[7] Despite Megas' intervention, Khusro proceeded to threaten Hierapolis, whose defenders quickly agreed to buy off the king for 2000 lbs of silver. Following further entreaties from Megas, Khusro agreed to call off his invasion if the Romans paid him ten *centenaria* (II.6.17–25). While Megas returned to Antioch to report back to Germanus, the Persians advanced against Beroea and sacked the city; most of the population gained refuge in the acropolis, however. At Antioch, the bishop discovered that his offer could not be followed up because John, the son of Rufinus, and Julian, Justinian's *a secretis*, had arrived in the meantime and forbidden (on the emperor's orders) that any money be handed over to the enemy. The patriarch Ephraem, having been accused of favouring the city's surrender, withdrew to Cilicia, where he was joined soon afterwards by Germanus (II.7.1–18).[8] Other sources offer scraps of additional information.

Mal. 18.87 (405.65–9/479.23–480.5): In the month of June of the third indiction Antioch the Great (p.480) was captured by Khusro, the Persian king. Germanus was sent with his son Justin to carry on the war, after being appointed *magister militum*.

Having achieved nothing, he stayed in Antioch buying silver for two or three *nomismata* a *litra* from the Antiochenes.[9] (…) (tr. Jeffreys and Scott, revised)
Evagrius, *HE*IV.25 (172.11–14): He (Ephraem) is said to have preserved the church and everything around it by adorning (it) with the holy offerings, so that they might be a ransom for it.[10]

Megas returned to Beroea and attempted to negotiate the release of those besieged in the city's acropolis. Khusro allowed them to depart (II.7.19–35). The defection of some soldiers to the Persians, noted here by Procopius, is remarkable, and indicates the low level of morale in the East at the time, perhaps resulting from the cut-backs in pay implemented in the wake of the Eternal Peace. See p.99 above.

Proc. *Wars* II.7.36–7 (183.19–184.4): Then the Beroeans, after coming into such great danger, left the acropolis free from harm, and departing went each in the direction he wanted. (37) Among the soldiers a few followed them, but most (p.184) came as willing deserters to Khusro, putting forth as their grievance that the government owed them their pay for a long time; and with him they later went into the land of Persia. (tr. Dewing, revised)

The sack of Antioch (June 540)[11]

As Khusro approached Antioch, many of the population fled. Some were encouraged to remain, however, by the arrival of 6000 Roman troops under the *duces* of Phoenice Libanensis, Theoctistus and Molatzes. Once Khusro had arrived, he proposed to depart from the city for the payment of ten *centenaria*. His offer was vigorously rebuffed by the Antiochenes, and Khusro ordered that the city be attacked. Thanks to a fatal weakness in the city's defences, the Persians succeeded in gaining control of the walls; the newly arrived Roman forces therefore immediately abandoned the city to the king. Despite the valour of the citizens of Antioch, and in particular of the circus partisans, the city was taken by storm (Proc. II.8.1–35). Once enough plunder had been removed from the city, it was razed to the ground with the exception of one church (II.9.14–18). See Downey 1961: 542–4, Stein 1949: 489–90, Evans 1996a: 156–7.

V. Sym. Styl. Iun. 57 (50–2): At that time what God intended to do in the city of the Antiochenes was revealed to the holy man – that he intended it to be burnt from gate to gate by the Assyrians, through whom the impending devastation (would occur). And the servant of God prayed on its behalf, and God said to him, 'Lo, the shouting of the residents in it (Antioch) has gone up into my presence and the time for its requital is at hand, on account of the lawlessness which they practise: they set forth a table, libations, and a sacrifice to demons. Their excuse is the fortune of the city, (but) they provoke me to jealousy against them. For that reason I shall hand them over to a sense-less[12] people.' And lo, he beheld the Spirit, sent bearing a dagger into the city. This vision the servant of God related to the brothers and certain Antiochenes devoted to a pious life who had come to him. After a short interval of time, God aroused Khusro, the Persian king, and the saying of the just man was close (to fulfilment), for a substantial multitude of Persians encamped outside the gates of the city of Antioch. And the holy man cried out to (p.51) the Lord, (asking) whether he had changed his mind about the things he had shown him earlier, and whether he would hand the city over to the Assyrians (i.e. the Persians); and there was no explanation from the Lord, because his heart was filled with anger. Again, therefore, for a second (time), he (Symeon) earnestly prayed about this (event) and the Lord said to him, 'I shall hand over the city; nor shall I conceal from you what I intend to do. I shall fill it with the enemy and hand over most of those who inhabit it to the slaughter; many of them will also be led off as prisoners of war. Now therefore I dispense to you the prize of peace – the symbol of my cross – as a protection for you, and in a short time you will see what this vision (is).' And again, in a trance, the Spirit, bearing the life-giving cross, came to the holy man. And he saw two angels wearing linen robes and (bearing) drawn bows in their hands and masses of arrows; and the servant of God asked what these things were, and they said, 'The cross is salvation and security against any enemy. The arrows are for the heart of those wielding daggers in battle as they come against you, so that they may be turned back in fright and so they may not prevail against you, through the power of the Lord who sent us to guard you.' After this divine vision had appeared to him, he again beheld the city being besieged and captured by means of ladders (placed) on the wall, and (he saw) the barbarians arriving inside. And (he saw) that wailing and shouting rang out, and a massive flight from the town took place, while many threw themselves from the wall; then (he saw) that the two gates of the city – the one facing the sea and (the one facing) south – being opened; for on account of the clamouring of the holy men, God forbore to destroy everyone down to the last man. He also saw two of the monks with him deserting their posts and retreating; the head of one was cut off, while the other was taken prisoner. (p.52) The divine vision, then, took this form, and the event itself followed not long afterwards. For it happened that the city was besieged and taken by the Assyrians and set alight from one gate to the other, through not all of it was burnt. And some threw themselves from the wall, while others, once the two gates were opened, fled to the south and south-west.[13] And two monks, growing afraid, retreated, and one of them was decapitated, while the other was taken prisoner. Not one person of those remaining with him (Symeon) on the mountain fell, because the prayer of the holy man was a strong tower for them in the face of the enemy.[14]

Joh. Lyd. *De Mag.* III.54 (216.14–22): But as the city (Antioch) was recovering, as if from a nether gloom, through much effort, an abundance of resources and collaboration between crafts, Justin (I) met his end, and the evil genius Khusro (came through) Arabia with a countless host and fell upon Syria.[15] The recently demolished city itself, which appeared to him an easy prey since it was not fortified, he took in war and burned, wreaking countless slaughter. The statues, however, with which the city was adorned, he seized as booty, along with slabs of marble, precious stone and pictures; it was the whole of Syria that he carried off to Persia. There was not a farmer or a tax-payer left to the treasury.[16] (tr. Carney, revised)

Negotiations for a Persian withdrawal

After the capture of the city, Khusro was approached by Roman ambassadors who urged him not to continue his attacks on the empire; the king, in response, claimed that it was Justinian who had violated the treaty (Proc. II.10.1–18).

Proc. *Wars* II.10.19–24 (196.16–198.4): Finally Khusro made the demand that the Romans give him a large sum of money, but he warned them not to hope to secure peace for all time by giving money at that moment only. (20) For friendship, (he said), which is made by men on terms of money (p.197) is generally spent as the money (is used up). (21) It was necessary, therefore, that the Romans should pay some fixed annual sum to the Persians.[17] 'For thus,' he said, 'the Persians will maintain a constant peace with them, guarding the Caspian Gates themselves and no longer feeling resentment at them on account of the city of Dara, in return for which the Persians themselves will be in their pay forever.' (22) 'So,' the ambassadors said, 'the Persians desire to hold the Romans liable to the payment of tribute to them.' (23) 'No,' Khusro said, 'but the Romans will have the Persians as their own soldiers for the future, providing them with a fixed payment for their service; for you provide an annual payment of gold to some of the Huns and to the Saracens, not as tributary subjects to them, but in order that they may guard your land unplundered for all time.'[18] (24) After Khusro and the ambassadors had held such discussions with one another, they later came to an agreement by which Khusro should forthwith take from the Romans fifty *centenaria* and receive a tribute of five more *centenaria* annually for all time. (In return) he should do them no further harm, but taking with him hostages from the ambassadors (as pledges) for the keeping of the agreement, he should make his departure (p.198) with his whole army to his native land. There ambassadors sent from the Emperor Justinian would put the peace terms on a firm (footing) for the future. (tr. Dewing, revised)

The progress of Khusro's invasion

From Antioch Khusro continued westwards to Seleucia, the port of Antioch, where he bathed in the Mediterranean. Having explored further the suburbs of Antioch, he then proceeded to Apamea. Despite pledges given to the Roman ambassadors, he extracted great wealth from the city, but forbore from taking the fragment of Christ's cross (Proc. II.11.1–38, Evag. *HE*IV.26). Khusro continued his predatory tour past Chalcis, which deflected him by a payment of two *centenaria*. Crossing the Euphrates at Obbane, north of Barbalissus, and passing through Batnae *en route*, he headed towards Edessa. Here he extracted a further two *centenaria* and agreed not to damage the surrounding countryside (II.12.1–34). At this point Justinian confirmed in writing the terms negotiated by his ambassadors earlier. Khusro therefore prepared to ransom his captives, and the citizens of Edessa collected money for this purpose; but Bouzes, who was in the city, prevented the exchange. The Persian army now moved south-east to Carrhae, and from there to Constantia. Here too Khusro received a sum of money. Before returning to Persian soil the king undertook an assault on Dara, despite the agreement made with Justinian. A Persian mining operation was nearly successful, but was thwarted by a Roman counter-mine;[19] Khusro therefore left the city, having received 1000 lbs of silver from the defenders, and passed back into his own kingdom. His attempt on Dara had brought to nothing the agreement reached earlier, and the two powers consequently remained at war (II.13.1–29).

The inhabitants of Antioch, whom the citizens of Edessa had been unable to ransom, were given their own city, Veh-Antioch-Khusro (the better Antioch of Khusro) near Ctesiphon by the king (II.14.1–4).[20] And just as Justinian had adorned the Chalke in Constantinople with mosaics depicting Belisarius' triumphs, Khusro commissioned a mural of the fall of Antioch for the throne room of his palace in Ctesiphon.[21]

General notices on the campaign of 540

Chr. Ede. 105: In this year (AG 851 = 540), in the month of May, Khusro, the Persian king, broke the peace, invaded the lands of the Romans and took by force Sura, Beroea and Antioch. He also gained control of Apamea; and, as he returned, he reached as far as Edessa. But the grace of God protected it, and he inflicted no damage on it; but once he had received two *centenaria* of gold,[22] which the leading citizens held out to him, he returned to his (own) land. (tr. M. Greatrex)

Jord. *Rom.* 376 (49.25–50.4): When the Parthian (i.e. Khusro) discovered this (Justinian's victories in the West), he blazed with the flames of envy and moved (his army), mobilised for war, into Syria; laying waste Callinicum, Sura and Neocaesarea,[23] he came to Antioch. When Germanus, the patrician, together with his son Justin, the same man who was consul, (reached Antioch) after returning from the province of Africa, he left the city and withdrew to the region of Cilicia since he was unable to block the arrival of the Parthians. The Persians, having gained control of Antioch, (which was) devoid of an army, looked on as the populace, mingled with soldiers, fled along the course of the Orontes to Seleucia Maritima. They did not pursue (them), but zealously seized plunder throughout the city. They passed by the neighbouring cities and towns, attacking some and exacting a sum of money from others; and (so) the Parthian gathered for himself the wealth of the whole of Coele Syria within the space of one year.

Marc. Com. *Addit.* a.540.1–2: The Parthians invaded Syria and overthrew many cities. Germanus took up arms against them, and brought with him his son Justin the consul, while he was actually in office. (2) Antioch the Great was ravaged and demolished by the Persians (tr. Croke, revised)

Ps. Dion. II, 69.7–15: The year 850 (538/9): there was a siege by the Persians of Antioch and it was subdued, ravaged and burnt. Thus at that time, in the fourteenth year of Ephraem's (period as bishop), powerful Persian troops, coming with their king Khusro, attacked and subdued the city of Antioch. They burned it with fire and pulled it down. They stripped it and removed even the marble slabs which overlaid the walls, and took them away to their country, since they also were building in their country a city like this one and named it Antioch (as well).[24] (tr. M. Greatrex)

Tabari, I, 898/157–8 (Nöldeke 165–6): When his (Khusro's) rule was on a firm footing and all countries were subject to him, he moved, after a few years of his rule, against Antioch, inside which were the commanders of Caesar's army. He captured it, then he ordered that a plan be drawn up for him of this city of Antioch, taking account of its dimensions, of the number of its dwellings and roads, and of everything that was in it, and (he ordered) that a city be constructed for him according to this plan, next to Mada'in. Thus was the city know as Rumiya[25] built, on the model of Antioch, and he transported the people of Antioch to take up residence in it. When they entered the gate of their city, each resident proceeded to a house which so resembled his own in Antioch that it was as though he had never left it. Then he (Khusro) headed for the city of Heraclea and captured it, next Alexandria and its environs.[26] He left a portion of his army behind in the land of the Romans after Caesar had submitted to him and conveyed to him the ransom.[27] (tr. Hoyland)

The Roman invasion of Assyria (541)

Two campaigns took place in the following year. While Belisarius undertook an invasion of Persian territory in retaliation for Khusro's attack, the Persian king opened up a new theatre of war in the Transcaucasus (on which see Chapter 8). Belisarius arrived in the East to take charge of the Roman campaign and quickly sought to bring his forces up to strength: according to Procopius (II.16.3), many soldiers had no weapons or armour. Learning that Khusro was elsewhere, he prepared to invade Persian territory at once. The two *duces* of Phoenice Libanensis, Theoctistus and Rhecithancus, were unwilling to join the expedition because of anticipated raiding by Mundhir, but were obliged to do so by Belisarius, who was aware that the (pagan) Lakhmid Arabs were in the habit of abstaining from raids in spring for religious reasons.[28] He agreed, however, to release their forces when this period was ended (II.16.1–19). The Roman army approached Nisibis from Dara and encamped a few miles away; two commanders, Peter and John Troglita, the *dux* of Mesopotamia, insisted on taking their troops much closer to Nisibis, despite Belisarius' warnings. They were therefore easy victims to a sally by the Persian garrison, led by the general Nabedes; but the attackers were quickly driven back by the forces under Belisarius which came to the rescue (II.18.1–26). A tendentious account of the incident is preserved in Corippus' poem in praise of John, the *Iohannis*.

Corippus, *Ioh.* I.56–67: For the glory of the man (John Troglita), and the signs of distinguished service, and the wars won please (the emperor), as well as the more weighty (conflicts) against a proud kingdom.[29] (The emperor considers) how he expelled the Persians, striking down and wounding the confident Parthians, and standing up to the dense (volleys of) arrows on the occasion when the broad fields of Nisibis ran with the blood of the Persians. Nabedes, second (in importance) only to the Parthian king, relying on (his own) courage in the fierce battle, lost his allied units, even as he himself was winning; and, in his flight, fearing for his post, he was barely able to shut the gates (in time), so that the Roman cavalry was unable to burst into the midst of the citadel of Nisibis.[30] And the victorious John shook his spear at the lofty gates of the Persians.

Passing by the well defended Nisibis, Belisarius made instead for Sisauranon, a smaller Persian fort to the east. Here he divided his forces, sending off Harith with 1200 Roman troops under John the Glutton and Trajan to plunder Assyria (Beth Aramaye) and then report back to him. With the remainder of his men, Belisarius soon brought the defenders to surrender; the Persian garrison he sent to Justinian, while the Christian inhabitants were permitted to depart and the city-walls razed (Proc.II.19.1–25).[31] Harith's forces meanwhile pillaged Assyria, but the Jafnid leader sent off the Roman detachment which had accompanied them; John and Trajan therefore returned to Roman territory along the southern bank of the Euphrates, ending up, having crossed the river, at Resaina. Belisarius, lacking information on Harith's progress, and under pressure from his commanders to withdraw, moved back westwards (II.19.26–46). The limited success of the Roman invasion of Assyria in 541 was controversial. In the *Wars*, Procopius accuses Harith of deliberately concealing his whereabouts from Belisarius in order to keep his spoils;[32] he also stresses the poor condition of the Roman forces, as well as the fact that other commanders insisted that the Romans withdraw. But in the *Anecdota* (2.18–22) he claims that Belisarius' decision was driven entirely by his desire to meet his wife Antonina, who, he had heard, was on her way to the East. In this context he makes the following assertion.[33]

Proc. *Anecd.* 2.25 (17.4–10): And yet if he had been willing in the first place to cross the Tigris river with his whole army, I believe that he would have plundered all the lands of Assyria and have reached the city of Ctesiphon without encountering any opposition whatever, and, after rescuing the prisoners from Antioch, and all the other Romans who chanced to be there, he would finally have returned to his native land. (…) (tr. Dewing, revised)

General notices of the campaign of 541

Agap. *PO* 8.431: In this year[34] a certain Arab called al-Harith ibn Jabala attacked the Persians. Since Khusro was afflicted with these ulcers, he (Harith) despatched troops against him and the Persians were defeated. He destroyed many of their cities and took captive a great number of them. Then one of Khusro's *marzbans* marched against them and defeated them and recovered all the captives from them. (tr. Hoyland)

Marc. Com. *Addit.* a.541.1: Since the Parthians continued to be hostile, Belisarius undertook the eastern campaign after Germanus had returned to the royal city. (tr. Croke, revised)

Jord. *Rom.* 377 (50.4–9): And he (Khusro) did not therefore desist (then), but continuously attacked the Roman state. Against him was appointed the consul, the victor over Vandals and Goths, as usual.[35] Although he did not subdue him (Khusro) as he had other peoples, he nonetheless forced him to regroup his forces within his own territory; and the fortunate commander would have obtained a victory from this people too, had not the disaster in Italy, which had broken out after his departure, required him to be swiftly replaced by Martin. (…)

Jac. Ede. *Chr.* p.320: (…) And the Romans <also> laid waste the lands of C<orduene> and Arzanene and 'Arabaye.[36] (tr. M. Greatrex)

The campaign of 542

The eastern provinces, already reeling from the rapacious invasion of Khusro of 540, received a double blow in 542. For not only did a Persian army return to Euphratesia and Osrhoene, but the whole eastern Roman empire was visited by plague. Although the extent of depopulation brought about by the plague remains a matter of dispute, its arrival was sufficient to persuade Khusro to withdraw from Roman territory not long after his invasion had begun.[37]

Khusro invaded Euphratesia in early summer. As the army advanced towards Roman territory, a Persian convert to Christianity, Pirangushnasp (who had taken the name Grigor), was martyred near Pirisabora.[38] Candidus, the unfortunate bishop of Sergiopolis, unsuccessfully pleaded for forgiveness from Khusro, having failed to hand over the money he had promised by way of ransom for the prisoners taken at Sura. The inhabitants of Sergiopolis therefore handed over many treasures,[39] but no Persians were allowed in the city. A Persian attempt to capture the city with 6000 men failed; although there were only 200 soldiers stationed there, all the citizens took part in the defence of the city walls (Proc. II.20.1–16, Evagr. *HE* IV.28 [a more pious version]). See Key Fowden 1999: 133–4.

Proc. *Wars* II.20.17–19 (240.13–241.3): But when Khusro arrived at the land of the Commagenae, which they call Euphratesia, he had no desire to turn to plundering or to the capture of any stronghold, since he had previously taken everything to hand as far as Syria, some things by capture and others by exacting money, as has been set forth in the preceding narrative. (18) And his purpose was to lead the army straight for Palestine, in order that he might plunder the treasures (there) and especially all those in Jerusalem. For he had it from hearsay that this was an especially rich land with wealthy inhabitants. (19) And all the Romans, both leaders and soldiers, were in no way inclined to confront the enemy or (p.241) to stand in the way of their passage, but taking to their strongholds as each one could, they thought it sufficient that they should guard these and be safe themselves.[40] (tr. Dewing, revised)

Justinian again despatched Belisarius to retrieve the situation. He established Europus on the Euphrates as his base, and there he summoned Bouzes and the other Roman commanders who had sought refuge in Hierapolis (Proc. II.20.20–28). Belisarius' presence just to the west of the Euphrates effectively prevented Khusro from advancing further, and the king, over-estimating the forces available to the Romans, decided to retreat. He crossed the Euphrates and returned to Persian territory, receiving John of Edessa as a hostage.[41] Although Khusro had agreed in return not to damage Roman territory as he withdrew, he could not resist the opportunity afforded by the weakness of Callinicum. Belisarius was nonetheless acclaimed throughout the East for his success in repelling the Persians (II.21.1–29).[42]

Proc. *Wars* II.21.30–32 (248.12–25): But in the meantime Khusro, disregarding what had been agreed, took the city of Callinicum which was defended by absolutely nobody. For the Romans, seeing that the wall of this city was altogether unsound and easy of capture, were constantly demolishing some portion of it in turn and restoring it with a new construction.[43] (31) Now just at that time they had demolished one section of it and had not yet built in the space left; when, therefore, they learned that the enemy were close at hand, they carried out the most precious of their treasures, and the wealthy inhabitants withdrew to other strongholds, while the rest without soldiers remained there. (32) And it happened that a very great number of farmers had gathered there. These Khusro enslaved and razed everything to the ground.[44] (tr. Dewing, revised)

Jac. Ede. *Chr.* **p.320:** Khusro went up and laid waste Callinic<um> and all the southern land(s) of Mesopotamia. (tr. M. Greatrex)

Roman efforts to refortify the East (540–65)

The defences of Callinicum were not alone in receiving attention at this time. Inscriptions from above the gate of the citadel at Cyrrhus testify to building work being carried out there in the 540s, which has been connected with Belisarius' presence at nearby Europus in 542.[45] From 540 onwards serious efforts were made to upgrade Roman fortifications, and particularly those in Syria which had been neglected during Justinian's earlier phase of construction (527–532). See Lauffray 1983: 35, Whitby 1986a: 729–30, Whitby 1988: 211–12 and Chapter 16 below.

IGLS **145:** Up with the victory of the general Belisarius.[46]

IGLS **146:** Many years to Justinian the emperor and to the Augusta Theodora many years.

IGLS **147:** Many years to Eustathius the *domesticus*, by the grace of God.[47]

The conclusion of Khusro's invasion of 542

While Khusro himself presumably continued his retreat along the Euphrates to Persian territory, he may have detached some of his forces, under the command of Mihr-Mihroe (Mermeroes), to strike at fortified cities further to the north-east.[48]

Zach. *HE* **X, index (173.23–174.2):** The eighth (chapter),[49] concerning Khusro, who went up (p.174) and took Callinicum and the other camps on the frontier of the Euphrates and the Khabur.

Agap. *PO* **8.431:** In year 17 of Justinian('s reign), Khusro, son of Kavadh, attacked Kafr-tut and Resaina. But Belisarius[50] marched against them with the Byzantine army and drove him back before he (Khusro) could take them (the two cities).[51] (tr. Hoyland)

Corippus, *Ioh.* **I.68–98:** Before the eyes of the emperor all the brave deeds of the faithful man pass by. He considers and ponders (his) labours. (He recalls) how a thick (mass of the) enemy had blockaded Theodosiopolis in an oppressive siege, and how, in the shadows of night, he (John) had swiftly brought aid to the ramparts of the endangered city, entering the friendly gates (having passed) through the midst of the enemy. (The emperor was) terrified as the huge Mihr-Mihroe moved off from those walls, and as, with weapons bristling, he more fiercely headed for Dara, where the leader (John) kept his standards, (a place whose) towering ramparts are surrounded by a brilliant wall, and put the Roman formations to test in battle. But after the watchful leader had snatched the first city from the enemy, he then followed those fleeing and occupied the roads and took control of all the fields, so that the cruel enemy might not lay (them) waste or harm anyone. He reached the ramparts of the lofty wall (of Dara) first, and he did not allow (the issue) to be delayed for long. For at once he boldly ventured to engage the enemy in the middle of the plains and, in a favourable battle, he struck down innumerable formations, eminent leaders and allied nations. He put to flight the vanquished and confounded leader of the Parthians, Mihr-Mihroe. In the plains every Persian, in fear of the pursuing Romans, cast his sword from his hand (and threw off) his gleaming decorations into the midst of the fields. A Median sword and an empty scabbard gleam on every expanse of sand; and spears, shields, hairs[52] and bodies, as well as the horse of the armour-bearer of the proud commander, (all) tangled up with his weapons. He too (Mihr-Mihroe) would have lain there, laid low in the plains, had not the magnanimous leader (John) wished to take him alive. Mihr-Mihroe, however, saw the towering ramparts (of Dara), as he entered (the city) with a few companions.

Harith's involvement in ecclesiastical matters (542/3)

John of Ephesus, in his *Life of James and Theodore* (*PO* 19.153–4), recounts how the Jafnid phylarch Harith appealed to Justinian's wife Theodora to appoint some bishops for the Monophysites of Syria: few now remained in the wake of the persecutions in the 520s and 530s. Theodora therefore arranged for the consecration of Jacob (known as Jacob Baradaeus) and Theodore as bishops for the region, the former of whom proved to be an energetic convert of pagans and organiser of the Monophysite community. Jafnid support of the Monophysite Church was consistent throughout Harith's reign and that of his successors. When, under Maurice, an attempt was made to convert the Jafnids, it proved wholly unsuccessful. See Shahîd 1995: part 2 (on ecclesiastical history), esp. 755–75 on this episode, cf. Evans 1996a: 185–6 (dating Harith's intervention to 541), Stein 1949: 625, Frend 1971: 285, Bundy 1978: 78–9.[53]

The Roman counter-offensive of late summer 542

This took place in Armenia, but involved troops from Mesopotamia. See below, Chapter 8 with n.8 (for the dating of this campaign, usually placed in 543).

The defection of a Persian prince (c.543)

Kavadh, the grandson of King Kavadh and son of Zames, who had rebelled unsuccessfully against Khusro, sought refuge at the Roman court soon after the death of his protector, the *kanarang* Adhurgundadh (Adergoudounbades). See Mosig-Walburg 2000: 69–70.[54]

Proc. *Wars* I.23.23–4 (121.26–122.6): Not long after this (the death of Adhurgundadh) (p.122) either Kavadh himself, the son of Zames, or someone else who was assuming the name of Kavadh came to Byzantium; yet he resembled very closely king Kavadh in appearance. (24) And the Emperor Justinian, though in doubt (concerning him), received him with great friendliness and honoured him as the grandson of Kavadh.[55] (...) (tr. Dewing, revised)

The campaign of 543

Khusro, presumably again in spring, directed his next invasion at Edessa. Despite initial losses, he energetically laid siege to the city, erecting a huge mound to tower over the walls; elephants were also employed in the operations. Attempts by the defenders, and in particular a doctor, Stephanus, who had served Kavadh, to induce the king to raise the siege proved vain (Proc. II.26.1–46, VIII.14.35–7). The defenders destroyed the Persian mound by undermining it and then setting fire to it (II.27.1–17),[56] and so another Persian attack was brought to nothing. Further assaults had no more success, and negotiations were begun; a Roman envoy, Rhecinarius, had arrived during the siege. The Edessenes paid five *centenaria* to Khusro, and the Persians departed after nearly two months (II.27.18–46, *Chr.1234* 56, 192–3 [below]). See Bury 1923: II, 107–10.

Jac. Ede. *Chr.* **p.321:** Khusro continued to wage w<ar> against Edessa and laid waste Batnae.[57] (tr. M. Greatrex)

A truce is declared, 545

In the wake of the Persian retreat, two Roman envoys, the newly appointed *magister militum* Constantianus, and Sergius, then proceeded to Ctesiphon to arrange a truce with Khusro (Proc. II.28.1–6).

Proc. *Wars* **II.28.7–11 (283.7–23):** But Khusro said that it was not easy for them to come to terms with each other, unless they should first declare an armistice. Thus they might go back and forth to each other more securely and resolve their differences and henceforth arrange matters for a peace in safety. (8) And it was necessary, (he said), that in return for this continuous armistice the Roman emperor should give him money and should also send a certain physician, Tribunus by name, with the condition that he spend some specified time with him.[58] (9) For it happened that this physician at a former time had rid him of a severe disease, and as a result of this he was especially beloved and greatly missed by him. (10) When the Emperor Justinian heard this, he immediately sent both Tribunus and the money, coming to twenty *centenaria*. (11) In this way the truce was made between the Romans and the Persians for five years, in the nineteenth year of the reign of the Emperor Justinian (545–546). (tr. Dewing, revised)

Marc. Com. *Addit.* **a.546.4:** In the East a treaty was entered into with the Parthians through Constantianus, the *magister militum*, and the army returned to Constantinople.[59] (tr. Croke, revised)

Jord. *Rom.* **377 (50.9–11):** (...) He (Martin), though unequal in strength (to Belisarius), was not inferior in planning (even if he was collaborating with Constantianus), and although he was not strong enough to resist the Parthians, he brought about peace, so that he would not have to maintain hostilities for a long time.

In fact, hostilities resumed in Lazica in 548, and it seems most likely that, as at other times, the northern sector of the frontier (or in fact just Lazica in this case) was excluded from the truce.[60]

Composite entry concerning the war in Mesopotamia, 540–545

Chr. 1234 56, 192.29–193.10: At this time Khusro, the Persian king, went up against (p.193) Edessa. And he besieged it for 55 days;[61] and when he proved unable to subdue it, he laid waste the whole region, and Sarug (Batnae), as far as the Euphrates. From there he set out and laid siege to Antioch, and subdued it, dismantled it and laid it open; and he took all the treasure of the churches, even the marble tablets which were covering the walls, and brought them back to Persia. And on his way back he came and crossed the Euphrates, and reached Callinicum; and he laid waste Balash (Barbalissus)[62] and all the banks of the Euphrates and the region of Callinicum. And he took away the bones of Mar Bacchus and the gold covering the reliquary of Mar Sergius of Rusafa (Sergiopolis) and all the treasure of the church.[63] (tr. M. Greatrex)

8

JUSTINIAN'S SECOND PERSIAN WAR

The northern front (540–62)

The invasion of Lazica (541)

One factor behind Khusro's breaking of the Eternal Peace was the prevailing dissatisfaction with Roman rule in Transcaucasia. The Armenians had previously complained to him of their treatment at the hands of Justinian, while the Lazi now also came forward to urge Persian intervention, having been forced to endure the quartering of Roman troops on their territory and the rapacity of imperial officials (Proc. II.15.1–30).[1] Accordingly Khusro made preparations to invade Lazica, masking his intent by claiming that he was instead intending to campaign against Huns who had attacked Iberia (II.15.31–5).[2] Having entered Lazica, Khusro was met by the Lazic king Gubazes, who formally handed over control of the kingdom to him. The Persians next moved to seize control of the chief Roman base in the region, the newly founded city of Petra. Despite an initial setback here, Khusro took the city, but did not destroy it. The Roman defenders, having negotiated a truce with the king, joined his army (II.17.1–28). The Roman garrisons at Pityus and Sebastopolis also withdrew after destroying their bases. (VIII.4.4–5).[3] See Braund 1994: 292. When news reached the Persians of Belisarius' capture of Sisauranon and Harith's attack on Assyria, Khusro installed a garrison at Petra and withdrew to his own lands (II.19.47–9). See Bury 1923: II, 101–2, Stein 1949: 493–4, Braund 1994: 294–6. Elsewhere Procopius sheds further light on the interrelationship between the campaigns of 541.

Proc. *Anecd.* 2.29–31 (18.7–19.2): It happened also that Khusro had sent an army of Huns against the Armenians subject to the Romans, in order that by reason of their preoccupation with this (force) the Romans there might not notice what was going on in Lazica. (30) Other messengers brought word that these barbarians (the Huns) had come to battle with Valerian and the Romans, who had come forth (to meet them), and had been heavily defeated by them, and as a consequence most of them had perished. (31) When the Persians heard these things and, partly because of the miseries which they had suffered in Lazica, and partly because they feared that they might during the withdrawal chance upon some hostile forces among the cliffs and the regions overgrown with thickets and all be destroyed in the confusion, they became exceedingly anxious for the safety of their wives and children and native land. Then whatever (section) of the Medic army that was fit began to heap abuses upon Khusro, charging him with having violated his oaths and the common laws of all men by invading Roman territory, (territory) to which he had no claim. (And they said that) he was wronging a state which was ancient and worthy, above (all states), of the highest honour, (p.19) one which he could not possibly overcome in war; and they were on the point of revolution.[4] (tr. Dewing, revised)

Jac. Ede. *Chr.* p.321: Khusro again went and took Petra, a city in Lazica, and placed an army there. (...) And thenceforward it happened that the Romans fought against it for a time; and <after> seven years they overcame the Persians and took it f<rom them>.[5] (tr. M. Greatrex)

Return of the Armenians to allegiance to Rome (542)

Khusro's second invasion of Euphratesia accomplished little, and was soon repelled by Belisarius. Already those who had urged the Persians to begin the war were changing sides.[6]

Proc. *Wars* II.21.34 (249.1–3): And the Armenians who had gone over to Khusro received pledges from the Romans and came with Vasak to Byzantium. (...)[7] (tr. Dewing, revised)

The Roman invasion of Persarmenia (late summer 542)

During his invasion of Mesopotamia in 542, Khusro had entered into negotiations with Justinian and had withdrawn after concluding a truce (see Chapter 9). Later the same year, Khusro awaited the arrival of Roman emissaries in Atropatene,[8] but they were delayed *en route*. The Persian general in Armenia, Nabedes, therefore sent the Armenian patriarch at Dvin to the *magister militum per Armeniam* Valerian, to hasten the progress of the envoys. But the patriarch's brother, who had accompanied him, informed Valerian that Khusro's rule was under threat; and when news of this reached Justinian, he immediately ordered all the commanders in the East to unite and invade Persian territory (Proc. II.24.1–11). Khusro and his army had meanwhile withdrawn to Assyria, worried by the arrival of the plague.[9] Numerous Roman commanders along the frontier readied their forces and set off into Persian territory in haphazard fashion; 30,000 men are said by Procopius to have taken part in the invasion. Only once the Romans were in Persian territory did the various leaders converge and make for the chief city of Persarmenia, Dvin (II.24.12–21).[10] Nabedes, whose force numbered only 4000, therefore took refuge at a mountain fortress at Anglon and prepared an ambush for the Romans there. The Roman army, attacking the Persian position in haste and poor order, was forced back with heavy losses. The Persian victory was complete (II.25.1–35). See Stein 1949: 499–500.[11]

The war resumes in Lazica, 547–9

The Lazi did not prosper under Persian domination. Their zealous Christianity was at odds with their masters' Zoroastrianism, while they also found themselves cut off from trading in the Black Sea. Khusro, aware of the rising discontent in Lazica, decided to take measures to ensure that his grip on the region was secure (Proc. II.28.15, 25–9). See Braund 1994: 296–7.

Proc. Wars II.28.18–24 (285.2–286.2): For it seemed to him that it would be a lucky stroke and a really important achievement to win for himself the land of Colchis and to have it in secure possession, reasoning that this would be advantageous to the Persian empire in many ways. (19) In the first place they would have Iberia in security thereafter, since the Iberians would not have anyone with whom, if they revolted, they might be safe;[12] (20) for since the most notable men of these barbarians together with the king, Gourgenes, had looked towards revolt, as I have stated in the preceding pages, the Persians from that time did not permit them to appoint a king for themselves, nor were the Iberians autonomous subjects of the Persians, but they (the two peoples) bore much suspicion and distrust towards one another.[13] (21) And it was evident that the Iberians were most thoroughly dissatisfied and that they would attempt a revolution a little later, if they could only seize upon some favourable opportunity. (22) Furthermore, the Persian empire would be forever free from plunder by the Huns who lived next to Lazica, and he would send them against the Roman domains more easily and readily, whenever he should so desire. (For he considered that), as regards the barbarians dwelling in the Caucasus, Lazica was nothing else than a bulwark against them. (23) But most of all he hoped that the subjugation of Lazica would afford this advantage to the Persians, that starting from there they might overrun with no trouble both by land and by sea the countries along the Euxine Sea, as it is called,[14] and thus win over the Cappadocians and the Galatians and Bithynians who adjoin them, and capture Byzantium by a sudden assault with no one opposing them.[15] (24) For these reasons, (p.286) then, Khusro was anxious to gain possession of Lazica, but in the Lazi he had not the least confidence. (tr. Dewing, revised)

Khusro's solution, according to Procopius, was to assassinate Gubazes, the Lazic king, and to deport all the Lazi. He is also said to have made preparations to build a navy on the Black Sea. Neither venture was successful, and the Lazi switched their allegiance to the Roman camp once again (Proc. II.29.1–9).[16] Accordingly, in 548 Justinian despatched an army of 8000 men to Lazica under the *magister militum per Armeniam* Dagisthaeus; in conjunction with Gubazes, these forces laid siege to Petra, but were unable to take it (II.29.10–12). See Stein 1949: 505 n.2. In response, Khusro sent Mihr-Mihroe to relieve the garrison (II.29.13). While Dagisthaeus prosecuted the siege of Petra, sending only 100 soldiers to defend the borders of Lazica to the south, Gubazes sought to block the Persian advance further north. By offering the Alans and the Sabir Huns three *centenaria*, he secured an agreement from them that they would attack the Persians in strength in Iberia; Justinian, however, delayed in sending the money (II.29.27–32). Meanwhile, Dagisthaeus proved unable to capture the city, despite the desperate straits in which the garrison found itself (II.29.33–43). Mihr-Mihroe's relief force, having with difficulty pushed back the Roman force guarding the pass leading into Lazica, at last reached Petra, which had continued to withstand Dagisthaeus' efforts to storm it; the *magister militum* quickly withdrew before the Persians arrived (II.30.1–14).[17] Mihr-Mihroe restored the battered defences of Petra and installed a garrison of 3000; but he and his forces were then ambushed nearby by Dagisthaeus and some Lazi (II.30.15–22). Unable to sustain his army, over 30,000 strong, with adequate supplies, he withdrew with most of his forces to Persian territory, leaving 5000 men to ensure supplies to Petra (II.30.30–3). Gubazes remained on guard by the river Phasis, protecting Lazica; and Justinian now at last paid the money promised to the Sabirs, as well as providing Gubazes with a handsome reward for his defection. In addition, he sent another army to the region, commanded by Rhecithancus (II.30.23–9). The 5000 Persians left near Petra soon fell victim (probably in spring 549) to the combined forces of Gubazes and Dagisthaeus, numbering 14,000; they were heavily defeated and their supplies captured. The victors then penetrated into Iberia, leaving a substantial garrison of Lazi to guard the pass leading into Lazica before returning westwards (II.30.34–48). See Stein 1949: 505, Braund 1994: 298–9 on this campaign (which was over by 1 April 549, Proc. II.30.48).[18]

The campaign of summer 549[19]

Khusro's response to the mixed Persian fortunes of the previous campaign was to send a large army under the command of Khorianes, supplemented by Alan forces, to invade Lazica. They penetrated as far as Mocheresis and there encamped in the region of the river Hippis (Proc. VIII.1.3–6).[20] Dagisthaeus and Gubazes marched against the invaders, and prepared to attack them; the Lazic and Roman cavalry were now operating separately. Initial cavalry skirmishes proved indecisive (VIII.8.1–20). The arrival of the Roman and Lazic infantry turned the battle to their advantage; the Roman cavalry dismounted, and the Persian cavalry was unable to break the Roman formation. Once the Persian general Khorianes was killed in the engagement, the Persians broke and fled. The Roman victory was complete (VIII.8.21–38). But in the meantime another Persian army had succeeded in delivering supplies to the garrison at Petra (VIII.8.39).

The campaign of 550

The Lazi, unhappy with Dagisthaeus' failure to retake Petra, accused him to Justinian of siding with the Persians. He was recalled and replaced by the veteran commander Bessas; further reinforcements were sent at the same time (Proc. VIII.9.1–5). Bessas' first task was to put down a rebellion by the Abasgi, who had gone over to the Persians, unhappy with their treatment at the hands of the Romans. A Persian army under Nabedes had even succeeded in reaching Abasgia and there obtaining hostages (VIII.9.6–14). John Guzes and the Herul commander Uligagus were therefore charged by Bessas with the mission of subduing the rebels. They sailed along the Black Sea coast and took possession of the Abasgian fortress at Tracheia, which they razed to the ground (VIII.9.15–30).[21] The Persians also succeeded in gaining control of an important fort among the Apsili, the neighbours of the Abasgi, thanks to the treachery of a Lazic noble named Terdetes. The Persian garrison was soon ejected by the Apsili, who were unwilling then to return to their allegiance to the Lazi. John Guzes, however, was able to effect a *rapprochement* between the Apsili and the Lazi (VIII.10.1–7).[22]

The Persian campaign of 551

Since the five-year truce had now expired, the two powers were once again formally at war. While negotiations proceeded in Constantinople (see Chapter 9 below), Bessas attempted to wrest Petra from Persian hands. He vigorously prosecuted the siege, assisted by some Sabir allies; his forces amounted to 6000 men, matched against 2600 inside the city. After a bitter struggle, the city fell, although a few Persians sought refuge in the acropolis (Proc.

VIII.11.1–64). When they refused to surrender, the acropolis was burnt. The Romans captured large quantities of supplies and equipment, a testament to Khusro's desire to maintain control of the city (VIII.12.1–20). Bessas then razed the city's walls to the ground, an action commended by the emperor (VIII.12.28–9).

Mihr-Mihroe, meanwhile, who had been marching south of the Phasis to relieve Petra, turned instead to cross the river close to the border with Iberia, seizing the forts of Sarapanis and Scanda. With an army of Persian cavalry and 4000 Sabir Huns, he made for Archaeopolis, to the north of the Phasis. The Romans had 3000 men stationed in the city, while a further 9000 were encamped at the mouth of the river under Venilus, Uligagus and Varazes. Mihr-Mihroe passed by the fortress, aiming to deal first with the larger force, but was thwarted when it withdrew across the river. He therefore returned to lay siege to Archaeopolis (Proc. VIII.13.1–30).[23] Despite the useful support of Dilimnite troops and elephants, Mihr-Mihroe's attack was driven back with heavy losses; many of his forces died from lack of supplies rather than in the actual fighting (VIII.14.1–44).[24] He therefore proceeded to the more fertile region of Mocherisis, to the west, and set about rebuilding the fortress which had earlier existed at Cotaeum; at the same time he invested the nearby Lazic fortress, Uthimereos, which was guarded by a joint garrison of Romans and Lazi. Thus he was able not only to blockade the Roman stronghold, but also to assure himself of adequate supplies and to bar the Romans access to Suania, a strategic kingdom to the north of Lazica (VIII.14.45–54). See Braund 1994: 305 (noting, however, that other routes to Suania existed).

Despite the peace negotiations taking place in Constantinople, both powers continued to manoeuvre to secure the advantage in Transcaucasia. The Persians initially gained the upper hand, seizing Uthimereos through the defection of a Lazic noble; they were now masters of eastern Lazica, Suania and Scymnia (Proc. VIII.16.1–15).[25] Further details on the Persian annexation of Suania are provided by Menander, who is here reporting the words of a Roman envoy, Peter the Patrician. Since he was seeking to prove that Suania had always been a dependency of Lazica, and hence should be returned to the Romans along with Lazica, his words must be treated with caution.[26]

Menander frg.6.1.249–67: Actually, when Tzath was chief of the Suani, a certain Deitatus was commander of the Roman troops there, and there were other Romans also living among the Suani. When some ill-feeling <arose> between the king of the Lazi and Martin, at that time the general of the Romans there, on account of this the Colchian did not send to the Suani the usual supply of grain (for (it was) the custom that grain be sent by the king of the Colchians). The Suani, therefore, angry that they had been deprived of the customary items, made known to the Persians that if they came there, they would hand over Suania to them. Meanwhile, they told Deitatus and the other Roman commanders that 'a large mass of Persians is reported to be advancing against the Suani, against which we do not have a battleworthy force. Your best course of action is to retreat before the Median army with the Roman units here.' By means of so great a deception and by gifts the Suani convinced the army commanders and rid themselves of the Roman garrison, and the Persians quickly arrived and took over Suania. (tr. Blockley, revised)

Menander also reports the counter-claims of Khusro.

Menander frg.6.1.495–507: I (Khusro) subdued Lazica, but did not make an attack on the Suani. I only heard (of them) when Mihr-Mihroe reported to us that it (Suania) was a country not worthy of consideration, nor even worth fighting over, nor a (suitable) object for a royal expedition, but (that) it was (inhabited by) one of the peoples around the Caucasus, and that they have a petty king, and that the land is a thoroughfare for the Scythians. Mihr-Mihroe died, and the *nakhveragan* succeeded to the command. He too then wrote about them in no different fashion, (reporting) that they lived on the ridges of the Caucasus, that they were actually thieves and plunderers and perpetrators of cruel and impious deeds. I decided, therefore, to send an army against them, when they in fear became Persians instead of Suani. As a result the land obviously belonged to me from that time, and I do not refuse to keep it. (tr. Blockley, revised)

In winter 551–552 Mihr-Mihroe consolidated his grip on eastern Lazica, even threatening to move against the Roman forces assembling at the mouth of the Phasis. They dispersed upon hearing of his plan; the Romans perhaps withdrew to the south, while the Lazi took refuge in the mountains. A diplomatic overture by Mihr-Mihroe to Gubazes met with no success (Proc. VIII.16.16–33). See Braund 1994: 305–6.

The Persian campaign of 552

According to Procopius, Khusro used the money paid to him by Justinian by the terms of the truce of 551 to hire a large force of Sabirs, which was to take part in a further campaign by Mihr-Mihroe aimed at further entrenching the Persian position in Lazica. But the Persians had arrived at the limits of their expansion: while the main Roman force, now under Martin, remained in place at the mouth of the river Phasis, the garrisons at an unnamed fortress, Tzibile and Archaeopolis were able to withstand all Mihr-Mihroe's attacks (Proc. VIII.17.11–19).

The Persian campaign of 554

There is no record of any significant military activity in 553, although an Armenian source, the martyrdom of Yazdbozid, notes the arrival in Persarmenia of three high-ranking Persian nobles, sent by Khusro to investigate complaints concerning the behaviour of Persian officials in the region; evidently the Persians were determined to maintain their grip on Persarmenia, and were prepared to conciliate the Armenians if necessary.[27] Further Roman troops arrived in the Transcaucasus, some of whom will have been transferred from the now quieter western theatre of war. They were under the joint command of Bouzes, Martin and Bessas and accompanied by Justin, the son of Germanus. See Stein 1949: 511 and Braund 1994: 306 with Agath. II.18.8. In 554 Mihr-Mihroe decided to try to penetrate further into Lazica, although aware of the strength of the Roman defences; their most advanced position lay at Telephis, where Martin guarded a narrow pass (Agath. II.19.1–4). When Mihr-Mihroe captured it by a ruse, the Roman forces stationed behind it withdrew westwards along the Phasis as far as Nesos, a fortified island at the confluence of the Doconus and the Phasis (Agath. II.19.5–21.11). Mihr-Mihroe did not follow up his victory, aware of the difficulties in supplying his forces so far west, and, having reinforced a Persian fort at Onoguris, near Archaeopolis, returned to Mocheresis; he died in Iberia from an illness the following summer (Agath. II.22.1–6).[28]

Events of 555–6

Both sides then underwent a change of command. Mihr-Mihroe was succeeded by a general whose name is given by Agathias as Nakhoragan, which probably in fact represents the Persian title *nakhveragan*. See Stein 1949: 514 n.2 and Christensen 1944: 21 and n.3. Following a complaint from Gubazes about the incompetence of the Roman commanders, Bessas was recalled and sent into exile; Martin and Rusticus, the two other individuals criticised by Gubazes, remained in post, and formed a plot to rid themselves of the king (Agath. III.2.1–11).[29] After Gubazes had been killed, in September or October 555,[30] the Lazi refused to cooperate with the Romans any further (Agath. III.3.1–4.8). Martin nonetheless undertook an assault against the Persian fortress at Onoguris, while detaching a small force to ward off a Persian army said to be coming from Mocheresis and Cotaeum to relieve the garrison. It proved unequal to the task, and the besiegers were forced back in a disorderly retreat; the Roman camp outside Archaeopolis was then plundered by the pursuing Persians (Agath. III.5.6–8.1). Although the loyalty of the Lazi was wavering, they preferred to inform Justinian of what had happened and to demand justice, rather than to defect to the Persians once again. Justinian accordingly despatched the senator Athanasius to resolve the situation (Agath. III.8.4–14.3).[31] See Stein 1949: 513–14 and Braund 1994: 308–9.

The campaigning of 556

The *nakhveragan* was in Mocheresis in spring 556. Gubazes' younger brother and successor, Tzath, arrived in Lazica from Constantinople at the same time, having been invested with the regalia of office by Justinian. He was accompanied by the *magister militum* Soterichus (Agath. III.15.1–5).

Agath. III.15.6 (103.31–4): The general Soterichus set out immediately on the journey on which he had been despatched. He was bearing gold from the emperor for distribution among the neighbouring barbarians according to the treaty of alliance, since this had been the custom for a very long time and occurred annually.[32]

In this instance, however, Soterichus encountered hostility among the Misimians, a people subject to the Lazi, according to Agathias; and having killed him, they felt they had little option but to embrace the Persian cause (Agath. III.15.7–17.2). Meanwhile, the *nakhveragan* advanced down the Phasis, towards Nesos, with (according to Agathias) 60,000 men including Dilimnite allies.[33] The Romans, on the other hand, enjoyed the support of a contingent of 2000 Sabirs, serving as heavy infantry (Agath. III.17.3–5). An attempted ambush of the Sabirs by the Dilimnites proved disastrous, and the Persian commander sought, without success, to come to terms with Martin (Agath. III.17.6–19.7). The *nakhveragan* then turned against Phasis, which, he had learnt, was vulnerable to attack.[34] He crossed the river, bypassing the forces at Nesos, and marched on Phasis; most of the Roman forces, however, reached the town before him and made preparations for a siege. There, a morale-boosting trick by Martin routed the besiegers, who hastily fled eastwards (Agath. III.19.8–28.5). The *nakhveragan* himself withdrew as far as Iberia, leaving a subordinate in command of the forces remaining in Mocherisis (Agath. III.28.5–10). See Stein 1949: 514, Braund 1994: 310.

While the formal trial, condemnation and execution of Rusticus and his brother John were taking place, the Misimians implored the aid of the *nakhveragan* (Agath. IV.1.1–12.7).[35]

The Romans counter-strike, summer 556

The *nakhveragan*'s retreat gave the Romans the opportunity to recover lost ground. While Bouzes and Justin remained on guard at Nesos, a Roman force of 4000, including 2000 Tzani, set off to recover Misimia. Under two low-ranking leaders, it advanced no further than Apsilia, while the Persians moved on Misimia. A stand-off ensued, punctuated only by a minor Roman success against some Sabirs allied to the Persians (Agath. IV.13.1–14.5). A Roman cavalry force, operating from Nesos, regained control of Rhodopolis without a struggle (Agath. IV.15.1–3). As winter drew on, the Persians withdrew from Misimia, and Martin arrived at the border fortress of Tzibile to take charge of the Roman force in Apsilia. Although he fell ill, his subordinates proceeded against the Misimians. They successfully overran Misimia and laid siege to Tzakher, the stronghold where the Misimians had assembled. When John Dacnas, sent by Martin, arrived to take charge of the siege, the Romans succeeded in inflicting such damage on it and the surrounding the region that the Misimians sued for peace. John agreed to their petition and recovered the money which had been in Soterichus' possession, which amounted to 28,800 *solidi* (Agath. IV.15.4–20.10).[36] See Stein 1949: 515 and Braund 1994: 310. While Martin was then replaced as *magister militum per Armeniam* by Germanus' son Justin, the *nakhveragan* was cruelly executed for his failures. (Agath. IV.21.1–23.3).

Truce agreed (autumn 557)

See Chapter 9, below.

A Tzanic revolt subdued (558)

The Tzani, having returned to their previous habits of predatory raids on the surrounding provinces, were with difficulty brought to heel by Theodore, a Tzan who had remained loyal to the empire. They were henceforth obliged to pay an annual tax, a burden from which they had hitherto been exempt (Agath. V.1.1–2.3). See Stein 1949: 516 and n.2.

The dispute over Suania, 562

The peace negotiations which brought the war to a close are dealt with elsewhere (below, Chapter 9). A particular point which exercised the negotiators was control of the kingdom of Suania, which had at one stage been subject to the Lazi. In the end, when the treaty was agreed, the question of Suania left open.[37]

9

JUSTINIAN'S SECOND PERSIAN WAR

Diplomatic relations (545–62)

The continuing war between the Ghassanids and the Lakhmids (545–50/1)

Despite the truce of 545, the Arab allies of both sides remained at war. Nothing more is known of the progress of their struggle in this period than what is recorded by Procopius.[1] See Shahîd 1995: 237–9.

Proc. *Wars* II.28.12–14 (284.1–13): And a little later Harith and Mundhir, the rulers of the Saracens, continued the war against each other by themselves, unaided either by the Romans or the Persians. (13) And Mundhir captured one of the sons of Harith in a sudden raid while he was pasturing horses, and straightaway sacrificed him to Aphrodite;[2] and from this it was known that Harith was not squandering Roman chances (in favour of) the Persians. (14) Later they both came together in battle with their whole armies, and the forces of Harith were overwhelmingly victorious, and turning their enemy to flight, they killed many (of them). And Harith came within a little of capturing alive two of the sons of Mundhir; however, he did not actually capture (them). Such then was the course of events among the Saracens. (tr. Dewing, revised)

The Persian attempt to seize Dara (547)

Despite the armistice in force since 545, Khusro remained eager to seize control of Dara, and sought to do so by a ruse. He sent Yazdgushnasp (Isdigousnas) as an ambassador to Constantinople; *en route* he would stay at Dara and, with the assistance of his large retinue, take possession of the city in conjunction with forces based at Nisibis. The plan was thwarted by George, a former adviser of Belisarius, who insisted that Yazdgushnasp would be allowed in the city with only twenty followers. He then continued to Constantinople, where he was cordially received by Justinian, and received lavish gifts from the emperor (Proc. II.31–44).[3]

Justinian seeks an end to hostilities (551)

After the five-year truce had ended, Justinian sent Peter the Patrician to the Persian court to obtain a full-scale settlement. Khusro, who had just had to suppress a revolt by his eldest son

Anoshazadh (Anasozadus),[4] refused to enter negotiations immediately, but sent Yazdgushnasp to Constantinople soon afterwards. As in 547, he brought with him a large retinue, including several relatives, and, to the annoyance of Constantinopolitans, was treated with great honour. But Yazdgushnasp proceeded to accuse the Romans of violating the truce, on account of Harith's recent attack on Mundhir (Proc. VIII.11.1–10). See Shahîd 1995: 239–40. The negotiations continued, however, and a limited armistice was agreed in late 551; in Lazica alone would hostilities continue.[5]

Proc. Wars VIII.15.1–7 (566.5–567.5): In Byzantium, meanwhile, Khusro's envoy Yazdgushnasp, in conferring with the Emperor Justinian regarding the peace, wasted a vast amount of time. (2) And after disputing many (points) thoroughly, they finally reached an agreement by which there would be a truce in the realm of each sovereign for five years, while envoys passed back and forth from each country to the other, fearlessly carrying on negotiations for peace during the period in order to settle their differences regarding both Lazica and the Saracens. (3) It was further agreed that the Persians receive from the Romans for this five-year truce twenty *centenaria* of gold, and for (the) eighteen months which had elapsed between (the expiration of) the former truce and this one – while they were sending embassies to one another – six *centenaria* more. (4) For the Persians declared that (only) on this understanding had they agreed that negotiations for the truce proceed. (5) Yazdgushnasp further demanded that he should receive these twenty *centenaria* on the spot, but the emperor wished to give four each year, for the reason that he might have surety that Khusro would not violate the agreement. (p.567) (6) Later, however, the Romans gave the Persians outright the entire amount of gold agreed upon, in order not to appear to be paying them tribute each year. (7) For it is disgraceful names, and not deeds, which men are wont as a general thing to be ashamed of. (tr. Dewing, revised)

A detailed account of a mission of Yazdgushnasp, perhaps this one, is provided by Peter the Patrician, in an account embedded in a work compiled by Constantine VII Porphyrogenitus. It is clear that an elaborate diplomatic protocol had emerged by this point; and, as others have noted, the measures taken to protect Dara may have been inspired by the recent attempt of the Persians to seize control of it under the guise of an embassy.[6]

De Cer. **89–90 (398–410):** (*What should be closely observed upon the arrival of a great ambassador of the Persians.*) When a great ambassador is announced, the *magister* should send to the frontier one *illustris* magistrate, or a *silentiarius*, or a tribune, or indeed one of the nobles or *magistriani*, or whomever he sees fit to send for the honour of the personage coming, so that he may receive and guide him safely from one place to another. He who is sent comes (p.399) to Nisibis, and greets him, and, if he has a letter from the emperor, he hands (it) over; if not, then (he hands over one) from the *magister*, summoning him. Equally, the *magister* may not write either, but the invitation is issued only by *mandata*, (bidding him) come with good spirits and a retinue; and he (the Roman envoy) goes out with him (the ambassador). The commanders of Dara should meet him with (their) soldiers at the frontier, and receive the ambassador and his men. And if there is anything that must be discussed at the frontier, it is discussed, while the ruler of Nisibis has come with him (the Persian ambassador) as far as the frontier with a force of Persians. If nothing is discussed, in this case too it is absolutely necessary for him to come with a force, and while the Romans receive him and those with him, the rest of the Persians must stay in Persian territory and he alone with his followers is to come to Dara and be entertained. It is the duty of the commanders of Dara to display much alertness and foresight, so that a force of Persians does not come along too, by a pretext of the ambassador, and closely follow after (him) and gain control of the city by cunning. The magistrates must pay great attention to this contingent (p.400) and be discreetly vigilant and guard against this plan. The *ducici*, according to custom, pay the cost of the journey here (Constantinople) for 103 days. This many (days) have been determined from the start as sufficient for an ambassador going up (to Constantinople), and as many for one going down. Sometimes he is slow on the road, and the emperor issues a command, and an extra payment is made to him. The record of expenses for him is conserved in the *scrinium* (office) of the barbarians.[7]

Five post-horses and thirty mules are assigned to him, according to the agreements (reached) when Constantine was praetorian prefect. The emperor, should he wish to entertain him (the ambassador), orders a lot more to be given to him. And should he wish to honour him as well, he should send for and receive him through men of good repute in Galatia and Cappadocia and provide food (for him); similarly he should send (a message) to Nicaea to look after him and entertain (him). The *magister* too, when (the ambassador) reaches Antioch,[8] should send a *magistrianus*, charged with greeting and welcoming him, and to learn how he is being guided from place to place. If the emperor wishes, he does this once, and then for a second time, writing (to him) and greeting (him), and asking how he is being looked after. Both beasts and *dromons* should be made ready for him at Helenopolis, so that, if he wishes (p.401) he may depart on foot for Nicomedia, or, if he wishes, he may cross over in the *dromons*. It is vital that horses and beasts be made ready in Dakibyza so that they may receive him and convey him to Chalcedon. In Chalcedon the *magister* should prepare lodgings both for him and his men; he should also send the *optio* of the barbarians and entrust to him[9] ready cash for expenses incurred in the day or days in Chalcedon. And he sends gifts to him. It is the duty of the *magister* to send (a message) to him to greet him and to ask him how his journey was, whether he is weary or not, and simply to entertain him in suitable fashion.

His (the ambassador's) lodging in Constantinople must be prepared in advance in accordance with the man's rank and the escort he brings with him; and there must be made ready in it beds, bedclothes, ovens, fireplaces, tables, and buckets to carry water and help with other hygienic services.[10] But the *comes rei privatae*, that is the *sacellarius* of the emperor – for now this duty has been transferred to him – provides the mattresses in accordance with a token of the *magister*. The *praefectus urbi* (city prefect) provides the beds and small cans and tables (p.402) and ovens and pots, again in accordance with a tablet of the *magister*. The men of the arsenals provide the braziers. Workmen are also allotted to him by the prefect from warehouses. And the bath of that house where he is to stay must be made ready, or one near him, so that he himself and those with him may bathe when they want; and for them alone is the bath available.

Whenever he comes ashore, the *magister* should send imperial horses (to him); the *spatharius* (bodyguard) of the emperor provides them. They receive him off the *dromons* and they carry him off to his house. And immediately the *magister* sends (a message) to him and greets him and again asks him how he was looked after. He also sends small gifts – the things he wishes – through the *optio*; generally the ambassador too sends (a message) to the *magister* and greets him in return. And the *magister* should receive kindly him who comes and should give a fitting reply to the greeting. The *magister* through his own man informs him (the ambassador), 'Refresh yourself, and when you see fit, I (shall) greet you.' And that man on the next day or the one after makes an announcement in advance and comes and greets the *magister*, and the *magister* receives him in person and (p.403) asks him before anything (else) about the health of his king, and then about the children of his king, and about the magistrates and about his own health and that of his household. (He also asks) how his journey was, whether anything was amiss *en route*, if anything was passed over and says 'We have been charged by our pious master to do everything for your entertainment. If therefore anything was remiss, that is our failure. We invite you not to be aggrieved or silent, but to tell us, so that correction may be made.' And all those with the ambassador too do obeisance to the *magister*, throwing themselves to the floor.

And when the emperor decides to receive him, the *magister* sends for him and informs him 'The master has bid you come to (him).' The master (emperor), when he (the ambassador) is in Chalcedon, and when he has come here, should send a decurion[11] to greet him and to enquire concerning the health of the king, and how he himself was looked after. When he (the emperor) receives him, the *magister* sends a *subadiuva*[12] in the evening and informs him that 'The emperor has bid you come forward, and (so) come forward.' And the emperor similarly sends a decurion and greets him and informs him that (p.404) 'On the morrow we (shall) receive you, and (so) come forward.' *Mandata*[13] are given in the evening for a *silentium*,[14] and it receives the ambassador of the Persians. The *admissionalis*[15] should go and ask the *magister* about the *labaresioi* (standard-bearers), and *mandata* are given, so that they too come and meet (him), and they must stand in their positions with the chariot. All the magistrates who have worn silk garments go forward, and the ambassador enters through the Regia (Royal Door), and the *magister* receives him in his *schola*[16] and asks him whether he has the gifts of the king; he must see everything before they go in and receive a record of them. The *magister* goes to the emperor and reports to him concerning the gifts, and hands over to him the record. The ambassador waits in the *schola* of the *magister*. Then after that the magistrates are received and advance to the *consistorium*; the *admissionalis* and the *chartularii* of the barbarians and the interpreters must conduct the ambassador and must seat him in the *anteconsistorium*;[17] the *chartularii* and interpreters must give a decree (*citatorium*) of the *magister* to the *admissionales*, and the other (proceedings) take place as in a *silentium*.

The *magister* should (p.405) prepare armed *candidati*[18] and handsome boys to follow them. And the emperor comes out of the *cubiculum*, preceded by the patrician, and takes his seat in the great *consistorium*; the magistrates come in, naturally with dark brown (cloaks) according to custom.[19] At this point the *admissionalis* should lead the ambassador and bid him stand at the wall opposite the curtains of the great summer *consistorium*. The three doors of the *consistorium* are opened, if he (the ambassador) has horses among the gifts; and three all-silk curtains are hung. After the magistrates are received, the *magister* pronounces (as an example), 'Let Yezdekes, the ambassador of Khusro, the king of the Persians, and those coming with him, be called.' And he brings forward the guards.[20] The (*chartularii*) of the barbarians[21] should give this pronouncement to the *admissionales*, as has been said; and the *admissionales* make two tablets, one inscribed with large letters, and (this) they give to the *silentiarius*, and he in turn to the *ostiarius*.[22] And it is read to the emperor by the *chartularius* in the *cubiculum*.[23] The other tablet they give to the *magister* for his acknowledgement. The *tertiocerius*[24] receives a copy of the decree, stands behind the *magister*, and informs him (of it). Therefore, according to the pronouncement of (p.406) the *magister*, the decurion enters the small *consistorium* and takes (with him) the armed *candidati*; and he moves them on, placing them on the right and left in front of the magistrates, with the consulars. At that point he goes out, and if he observes that the ambassador is ready, the decurion shouts, 'Leva'.[25] When the curtain is raised, the ambassador outside throws himself to the floor, where (there is) purple marble, does obeisance, and arises. And then he enters the gate, (and) again he throws himself (down) and does obeisance on the floor and arises. Again in the middle of the *consistorium* he does obeisance likewise, and then he comes and adores the feet (of the emperor) and stands in the middle; he hands over the letter and declares the greeting of his king. The emperor should then ask, 'How fares our brother in God? We rejoice in his good health.' And he says to the ambassador any other words he wishes that occur to him. After this, the ambassador says 'Your brother has sent you gifts and I invite you to receive them.' The emperor permits this. The ambassador goes out, and, with his men, carries the gifts; and he enters (again), himself carrying either a mantle or an ornament or whatever, if it is valuable, and each of the other men carries one sample. They (the men) should (p.407) be prepared by the interpreters in the *anteconsistorium*, and all go in carrying (something). All of them stand at the wall opposite the chair outside the curtain; when the curtain is raised, they throw themselves to the floor, and again go through the door, and throw themselves down again, and do this for a third time. Then the *silentiarii* accept all the gifts, and they have the task of conveying them to the *vestosacra*[26] according to the record of the *magister*, and of handing them over; and the evaluation of the gifts takes place. The *vestosacrani* must immediately take the evaluation of the gifts to the *magister*, so that he may know what has been brought, and, at the time of the exchange of gifts, he may remind the emperor what he should send in return through his own ambassadors. When therefore the gifts have been offered, the emperor says to the ambassador, 'Refresh yourself for a few days, and if we have some-thing to discuss, we (shall) discuss it; and with good manners we (shall) dismiss you to our brother.' The ambassador thanks (him), and does obeisance, and again does obei-sance at the same places, and withdraws. When the curtain has been released, the decurion stands up, (and) the *magister* pronounces (the command) 'Transfer',[27] and the decurion takes the armed *candidati*, and moves (them) to the small *consistorium*. And (p.408) then the emperor rises and the rest (of the proceedings) take place as usual. The ambassador must remain below at the *schola* of the *magister*, and the *magister* must go down and bid him farewell and dismiss him.

(90): (*What should be observed with regard to the ambassador during the other days.*) The emperor, once he has read the letter, permits, when he wishes, the *magister* to inform the ambassador that he may come to the palace on the following day. And he (the *magister*), if he wishes, informs him[28] through a *silentiarius* that he may come. A *silentium* is held, the band of troops is held still, and the *labaresioi* stand, and when he comes forward, the *magister* receives him in his *schola*; and he leaves him seated and goes up and reports to the emperor. He receives him (the ambassador) within, either in the portico or in the Augusteus itself.[29] If the ambassador has gifts of his own, he asks the day before through the *magister* that they may be received; and if the emperor allows, he (the ambassador) shows them to the *magister* in the *schola*, and a record is made for him. And the *magister* should go first to the emperor and show the record of the gifts to him. The ambassador, if he wishes his gifts to be received, goes in and asks the emperor to receive them; and if the emperor allows, his (the ambassador's) men go in, carrying his gifts, following the same plan as for the royal gifts; and a conversation is held. The emperor should again continuously recall the Persian king in pleasant fashion, as well as (asking about) his health; and if there is peace, they talk of such things, and the emperor dismisses him, and he awaits the *magister* outside. (Then) the *magister* comes out and takes his leave of him, and also himself dismisses him.

On the other days, he (the emperor) summons him, and they discuss matters. And if he sees fit, he allows the *magister* or even other magistrates with him to hold discussions with the ambassador outside. If there is complete peace between the states, the emperor should send (messengers) to him to visit him continuously and to find out how he is; (p.410) and he should send to him portions (of food) and gifts both on our feast days and on his notable ones; and in every way he should look after him.[30]

We may take this opportunity to note also the recommendations in the treatise *Peri Stratēgias*, which is assigned by many (though not all) scholars to the sixth century (*Peri Stratēgias* 43.1–13 [= *Peri Presbeias*]). See Lee and Shepard 1991: 32 (who assign the work to the tenth, rather than the sixth, century). It stresses that while foreign embassies in Constantinople should be well treated, they should also be kept under close watch, especially if they come from powerful states. Procopius complains, however, that Yazdgushnasp, in addition to the generous gifts he received from the emperor (see above), was also allowed to wander around the city freely (VIII.15.19–21). See Tinnefeld 1993: 207–8.

The armistice, and in particular the payments to the Persians, were (according to Procopius) highly unpopular in the imperial capital, partly because it allowed the Persians to consolidate their grip on Lazica (VIII.15.13–15), and partly because it conceded regular payments to the Persians, something which Roman emperors had always sought to avoid. This latter issue in particular would continue to arise for some time to come.[31]

Proc. *Wars* VIII.15.16–18 (568.9–569.4): They (the people of Constantinople in 551) (were also moved by the fact) that the very thing which the Persians had been striving for from ancient times, but which had seemed impossible to achieve either by war or by any other means – I mean, having the Romans subject to the payment of tribute to them – this had been most firmly achieved at the present juncture in the name of an armistice. (17) For Khusro imposed upon the Romans an annual tribute of four *centenaria*, which he had clearly been aiming for from the start, and now forty-six *centenaria* have been handed over for (a period of) eleven years and six months on the pretext of the armistice, giving to the tribute the name of treaty, although in the meantime he had, as stated, been carrying on a campaign of violence and war in Lazica.[32] (18) From this (plight) the Romans had not the least hope of rescuing themselves in the future, (p.569) but they perceived that they had in no hidden sense become tributary to the Persians. Thus were these things done. (tr. Dewing, revised)

The Romans acquire the silk-worm (c.552)

Right from the start of his reign Justinian wished to free the Romans from the need to purchase silk from the Persians, realising that it was an important source of revenue for the Sasanians; for it was almost impossible for any silk to reach Roman territory without passing through their hands. In the 540s, when it appears that the Persians increased the charge for raw silk, or perhaps earlier, he had commissioned some monks, who had been to 'Serinda' (probably Sogdiana), to bring back the eggs of the silk-worm to Roman territory; and this they accomplished in 552. Thus Justinian at last brought to an end the Persian monopoly in the provision of the Roman empire with silk; but the dependence of the empire on imported silk continued for some decades afterwards[33] (Proc. VIII.17.1–8, Theoph. Byz., *FHG* IV.270, tr. Wilson 1994: no.64). See Stein 1949: 769–73 (773 n.2 for the Sogdian provenance of the silk-worms), Pigulewskaja 1969: 158–9, Evans 1996a: 234–5.

The victory of Harith over Mundhir (June 554)

While in Mesopotamia and Armenia the armistice was untroubled, Mundhir evidently continued his raids deep into Roman territory, south of the Euphrates. The precise location of Harith's victory is uncertain. See Shahîd 1995: 240–4, Nöldeke 1879: 170 n.1.

Mich. Syr. IX.33 (323–4a/269): In year 27 of Justinian, Mundhir (the son) of Shaqiqa went up into the territory of the Romans and devastated many regions. Harith (the son) of Jabala encountered him, fought against him, defeated and killed him at the source (p.324) of the 'Udaye in the region[34] of Chalcis. The son of Harith, called Jabala, died, killed in battle. His father buried him in a *martyrion* of this fort.[35] (tr. M. Greatrex)

According to the *V. Sym. Styl. Iun.*, a Roman embassy went to Khusro in the early 550s to resolve the ongoing conflict between Mundhir and Harith; the author claims, however, that the attempt was foiled by the personal intervention of Mundhir, who pledged that he would imminently launch another raid.[36]

V. Sym. Styl. Iun. 186–7 (164–6): After a short interval of time he (Mundhir) set up camp and went up to the frontier (lands) of the Romans, exulting in (his) great army and rulership. (p.165) And all the inhabitants of the East were greatly troubled. Then Symeon, the servant of God, went into a trance and beheld a vision (which) he related to us, saying, (ch. 187) 'I saw myself today being snatched up by the Spirit and arriving on some small hill, near the frontier (lands) of the Saracens, Persians and Romans; and I was standing in the middle of an encampment[37] of soldiers and Saracens,[38] where the phylarch Harith had his camp. And, lo, I saw on the opposite side (that) a mass of many cavalrymen had come with the tyrant Mundhir (as numerous) as the stars in the sky and the grains of sand on the shore; and fear descended on all those with Harith and the sinews of their arms grew slack. And, lo, I saw the mêlée begin and the formations clash with one another, and in (the battle) Mundhir had it in his power to slay all of them; (but) the spirit of strength stood in my presence, bearing a ball of fire, and, at my behest, he threw it at his (Mundhir's) head and struck him down. Be of good cheer therefore, children, for today the Lord has done a great service[39] to the entire East.' When he had related this, we made a note among ourselves of the day and the hour. Within one week a victory bulletin arrived in the city of Antioch, announcing how, on that day and at that time at which the holy man had related these things to us, the impious Mundhir had been struck down. And some (men) from the Roman camp afterwards came to the holy man, who said that in that battle which had taken place opposite the hill, about (p.166) which the holy man had spoken publicly, they had been in dire straits and had called upon the servant of God; and they knew well that that great service had been performed by the Lord through him. And, in addition to this, they related all that had happened in the same battle. Some of them even remained with the holy man until their death. We, along with all those who had heard (Symeon's vision), remembered (the words) prophetically spoken by him and praised God for revealing to his holy servant events far off and close at hand. Henceforth the entire East enjoyed peace and remained in great calm.

General armistice agreed (557)

As a result of the stalemate in the Transcaucasus (see Chapter 8), Khusro despatched his senior ambassador Yazdgushnasp (here referred to as Zikh) to negotiate an armistice.[40]

Agath. IV.30.7–10 (163.1–21): Khusro calculated that it was not possible for him to deploy (his forces) against the Romans in the Colchian land (Lazica). (For) while they had control of the sea and could easily send for all the things they needed from that quarter, he was obliged to send even the smallest (quantities) of food to his troops by a long and deserted road by means of porters and beasts of burden. Therefore, considering these things, he resolved to put aside the war, so that the peace which had been limited for a long time to certain regions might not continue (to be) incomplete and ineffective, but might be strengthened everywhere equally. (8) So he sent on an embassy to Byzantium Zikh, (who was one) of the most distinguished men among them (the Persians). (9) When this Zikh arrived and came into the presence of the Emperor Justinian, he spoke much about the current situation and heard much (about it). At length they came to an agreement by which the Romans and Persians would keep possession of everything they had already happened to capture in the country of the Lazi according to the custom of war, whether they were towns or fortresses. They would keep peace with each other and make ready for battle against one another as little as possible until the authorities on each side should come to another, more important and authoritative, agreement. Zikh, having therefore carried out the aim of his embassy, went home to his own land. (10) When these matters were announced to the generals, the forces for a long time remained completely at peace; and what had previously occurred spontaneously was then reinforced by treaty.[41]

Embassies continued to pass to and fro between Constantinople and Ctesiphon, resulting, after a few years, in a comprehensive peace treaty.[42]

The strains of life on the frontier (559/60)

Although the Mesopotamian front had been free of campaigning since the 540s, the inhabitants of Amida in particular were afflicted by 'an abominable and hideous affliction' in 559/60. Pseudo-Dionysius of Tel-Mahre, our chief source for the episode,[43] describes a sort of mass-panic which struck the city: a rumour arose that the Persian king was about to attack Amida, and so the citizens fled in panic. The panic therefore spread in turn to the surrounding area. Various other types of unusual behaviour are noted by Pseudo-Dionysius, who reports too that Constantia and Edessa were similarly affected (Ps.-Dion. II.115–18/104–7, *Spurious Life of Jacob Baradaeus*, *PO* 19.259–62). See Harvey 1980: 3–4.

The conclusion of the war, 561–2

From late 561, high-level negotiations took place on the frontier between the two states, at Dara.[44] The Roman representative was the long-serving *magister officiorum* Peter the Patrician; that of the Persians was Yazdgushnasp, also a veteran of many previous diplomatic missions. The peace agreed in the end comprised three treaties, the first of which concerned the most pressing issue – the return of Lazica to the Romans and Roman payments to the Persians. See Verosta 1965: 153–4, Verosta 1966: 600–1, Antonopoulos 1990: 110–11, Winter and Dignas 2001: 164–77.

Menander frg.6.1.134–54: The Persians maintained that the treaty should be continuous and that they should receive a fixed amount of gold every year from the Romans in return for their not taking up arms. Moreover, they wished to lay down their arms (only) after receiving in a lump sum forty, or at least thirty years' instalments of the money to be paid. The Romans for their part wanted the treaty to be a short one and, in addition, to pay nothing for peace.[45] There was a long dispute over this in which many words were expended, but finally they decided to make peace for fifty years; Lazica should be ceded to the Romans; the terms of the treaty should be firm and strong, and prevail on both sides, not only in the East and Armenia, but also in Lazica itself; the Persians would, however, receive 30,000 gold *nomismata* per year from the Romans for the peace.[46] It was also established that the Romans should provide in advance the amount for ten years at one go in this way: that for seven years would (be paid) immediately, and after the elapse of the seven years, the contribution for the three remaining years would be paid without delay. Thereafter the Persians in this way would receive annually the payment due. (tr. Blockley, revised)

The detailed treaty

Once the matter of Lazica and Roman payments had been dealt with, it remained to hammer out detailed terms designed to ensure that the peace would not be broken by either side or its allies.[47] Two items, passed over in the treaty, provoked much debate; one was the question of the ownership of Suania (whether it formed part of Lazica, and should thus be returned to the Romans), which was left unsolved. The other concerned Roman payments to Khusro's Lakhmid ally 'Amr, which the Persians, on behalf of the Lakhmids, asserted should be made on a regular basis. Peter the Patrician denied that the payments had ever been regularised and it seems that Yazdgushnasp did not succeed in extracting any subsidies for the Lakhmids.[48]

Menander frg.6.1.314–97: (1) Through the pass at the place called Tzon[49] and through the Caspian Gates the Persians shall not allow the Huns or Alans or other barbarians access to the Roman empire, nor shall the Romans either in this area or on any other Persian borderlands send an army against the Persians.

(2) The Saracen allies of both states shall themselves also abide by what has been agreed and those of the Persians shall not take up arms against the Romans, nor those of the Romans (against) the Persians.[50]

(3) With regard to Roman and Persian merchants of all kinds of goods, they and tradesmen of this kind shall conduct their business according to established practice through the specified customs posts.[51]

(4) Ambassadors and all others using the public post (to deliver) messages, when they reach either Roman or Persian territory, shall be honoured each according to his rank and (according to) what is appropriate, and shall receive the necessary attention. They shall depart without delay, but shall be able to exchange the trade goods which they have brought without hindrance or any impost.[52]

(5) It is agreed that Saracen and barbarian merchants of whatever kind of either state shall not travel by strange roads but shall go by Nisibis and Dara, and shall not cross into foreign (territory) without official permission. But if they dare anything contrary to the agreement – that is to say, if they engage in smuggling, so-called – they shall be hunted down by the officers of the frontier and handed over for punishment together with the merchandise which they are carrying, whether Assyrian or Roman.[53]

(6) Should any persons during the period of hostilities have defected either from the Romans to the Persians or from the Persians to the Romans, and if, having defected, they wish to return home, there shall be no obstacle to them and they shall meet with no hindrance. But those who in time of peace defected, or rather fled, from

one side to the other shall not be received, but every means shall be used to place them, even against their will, in the hands of those from whom they have fled.[54]

(7) Those who complain that they have suffered some hurt at the hands of subjects of the other state shall settle the dispute equitably: either those who have suffered harm themselves or their representatives shall meet on the frontier before the officials of both states, and in this manner the aggressor shall make amends for the damage.[55]

(8) Henceforth the Persians shall not complain to the Romans about the foundation of Dara. But in future neither state shall fortify, i.e. protect with a wall, any place along the frontier, so that no pretext for trouble shall arise from this and the treaty thus be broken.

(9) The forces of one state shall not attack or make war upon a people or any other territory subject to the other, but without inflicting damage or suffering any harm whatever they shall remain where they are so that they too might enjoy the peace.[56]

(10) A large force, beyond what is adequate for the defence of the town, shall not occupy Dara, and the *magister militum per Orientem* shall not have his seat there, in order that this not lead to incursions against or injury to the Persians. It was agreed that if some such offence should happen, the commander at Dara should deal with the offence.

(11) If one city damages another or in any way destroys its property not in accordance with rules of war and with a regular military force but by guile and theft (for there are such godless men who do these things so that there might be a pretext for war), it was agreed that the judges stationed on the frontiers of both states[57] should make a thorough investigation of such acts and remedy them. If these prove unable to check the damage that neighbouring cities are inflicting on each other, it was agreed that the case should be referred to the *magister militum per Orientem*[58] on the understanding that if the matter of dispute were not settled within six months and the injured party had not recovered what he had lost, the offender should be liable to the victim of the injustice for a double indemnity. It was agreed that if the matter was not terminated in this way, the injured party should send a deputation to the sovereign of the offender. If within one year satisfaction is not forthcoming from the sovereign and (the injured party) does not receive the double indemnity due to him, let the treaty be broken in respect of this clause.[59]

(12) Here you might find prayers to God and imprecations to the effect that may God be gracious and ever an ally to him who abides by the peace, but if anyone with deceit wishes to alter any of the agreements, may God be his adversary and enemy.

(13) The treaty is for fifty years, and the terms of the peace shall be in force for fifty years, the year being reckoned according to the old fashion as ending with the 365th day.

It was also the practice, as I have said, that letters be sent by both rulers stating that they, too, ratified everything upon which the envoys had agreed. When the terms had finally been settled, the so-called 'sacred letters' were exchanged. (tr. Blockley, revised)

The status of Christians in Persia after 561

The reign of Khusro had seen a certain tendency towards persecution of Christians, at first between 542 and 545 and then later in the 550s; during the most recent outbreak St Shirin had suffered martyrdom in 559.[60] The treatment of Christians in Persia had long been a cause for concern to the Romans, and their omission from the detailed part of the treaty may be interpreted either as a concession to the Persians or, perhaps, an awareness of how easily any such clause might prove to be a pretext for war. As it turned out, even the separate annex[61] did not succeed in settling the issue, and among the factors which prompted the resumption of war in 572 was the treatment of Armenian Christians.[62]

Menander frg.6.1.398–407: When these matters had been agreed and ratified, they turned to a separate consideration of the status of Christians in Persia. (It was agreed) that they could build churches and worship without fear and sing their hymns of praise unhindered, as has been our custom. Furthermore, they would not be compelled to take part in Magian worship nor against their will to pray to the gods revered by the Medes. For their part, the Christians would not by any means venture to convert the Magians to our beliefs.[63] It was also agreed that the Christians would be permitted to bury (their) dead in graves, as has been our custom. (tr. Blockley, revised)

Explicit confirmation of this agreement is provided by Tabari, I, 1000–1/314–15 (Nöldeke 288). See Bosworth 1999: 314 n.737.

Khusro's encouragement of Arab Christians (c.565)

The *Life* of Mar Ahudemmeh, combined with the discovery of a church at Qasr Serij in Beth 'Arabaye, sheds an interesting light on Persian willingness not only to tolerate Christianity, but even to encourage it for political ends. Ahudemmeh was appointed (Monophysite) bishop of Beth 'Arabaye by Jacob Baradaeus in 559 and enjoyed great success in converting the Arabs to Monophysitism.[64] See Key Fowden 1999: 121–8.

V. Ahudemmeh, PO 3.29.4–12: He (Ahudemmeh) built a great and beautiful house of dressed stone in the middle of Beth 'Arabaye, in a place called 'Ain Qenoye; and he placed in it an altar and some holy relics, and called the house by the name of Mar Sergis, the famous martyr, because these Arab (Tayyaye) peoples were greatly devoted to the name of Mar Sergis, and sought refuge in him more than in all other men. The saint (Ahudemmeh) attempted by means of this house which he had built in the name of Mar Sergis, to cut them off from the shrine of Mar Sergis of Beth Resafa (Sergiopolis), on the other side of the Euphrates, since it was far distant from them. He made it, as far as he was able, resemble the other, so that its appearance might hold them back from going to the other. (tr. M. Greatrex)

It has been suggested, from the evidence of the *Life*, that the church was founded c.565. Its style is close to that of churches in northern Syria, and there is no reason to doubt that it was intended to be an alternative focus to Sergiopolis for devotees of St Sergius. Such a centre would, as has been noted, reinforce Persian influence among Monophysites in this border region, as well as reducing the need for cross-border movement – something both powers were keen to keep to a minimum, as is clear from the treaty of 562.[65]

10

THE FAILURE OF THE PEACE OF 562 (562–73)

From the Peace to the death of Justinian (562–5)

For the rest of Justinian's reign the eastern frontier of the Roman empire was untroubled. There was just one minor infringement of the terms of the treaty: the Lakhmid king 'Amr attacked Harith's territory in 562 or 563, about which Harith complained during a visit to Constantinople in November 563. Justinian apparently resolved the problem by offering a subsidy to 'Amr.[1] No further progress was made on the possession of Suania.[2] See Stein 1919: 6.

The opening of Justin II's reign

Justin II, one of Justinian's nephews, ascended the throne the day his uncle died, 14 November 565. He at once embarked on a foreign policy quite at odds with the more diplomatic approach of his predecessor. See Stein 1919: 4–5, Whitby 1988: 250–1.

Soon after becoming emperor, Justin determined to resolve the Suanian question for good. He despatched John, the son of Domnentiolus, to announce his accession to Khusro and to re-open negotiations about Suania; he also empowered him to buy back the country, if this was possible. On his way to the king, John restored the water supply of Dara. In July 567 the two met,[3] and the king complained of Justin's failure to supply the Arabs with subsidies; John successfully rejected the charge, arguing that there was no reason why Justin should continue Justinian's generous policy. John later brought up the matter of Suania and negotiated the sale of the country to the Romans; the Persians, however, attached conditions to the transaction, which Peter was persuaded to accept (Menander frg.9.1). See Turtledove 1983: 293–5. Another account of John's mission is to be found in Michael the Syrian.[4]

Mich. Syr. X.1 (331a/282): In this period[5] the Persian king was Khusro. And in the beginning they enjoyed a true peace. For this reason, in the second year of Justin, according to the kings' practice of sending one another gifts when they started to reign, the patrician John of Callinicum was sent to bring gifts of honour to the Persian king, and to make peace and unify the churches.[6] (tr. M. Greatrex)
Theoph. Byz. 1 (*FHG* IV.270): In this book[7] he (Theophanes) recounts in full how the truce was ruptured when Justin, through the agency of Comentiolus, demanded from Khusro the return of Suania. (Khusro) himself had suggested this but had not

restored it. He also records how the whole of Mesopotamia was shaken (by an earth-quake),[8] a prelude to the evils which followed. (tr. Donovan, revised)

Justin was incensed by John's action, which had given the Suani the opportunity of rejecting Roman rule, thus strengthening the Persian claim to the territory (Menander frg.9.2). The emperor therefore informed Khusro and his envoy Yazdgushnasp, then *en route* to Constantinople, that he would not accept the terms agreed by Peter. Following the deaths of Yazdgushnasp and John, Khusro despatched Mahbodh (Mebodes) to Justin in late 567, accompanied by a contingent of Arabs sent by 'Amr. Neither obtained what they had hoped from Justin: Suania, apparently, was not raised, and Mahbodh accepted Justin's insistence on ceasing payments to the Arabs. 'Amr in turn retaliated, ordering his brother Qabus to attack the territory of Mundhir the Jafnid (Menander frg.9.3). See Shahîd 1995: 308–14, Stein 1919: 7, Turtledove 1983: 295–6.

The conflict between Lakhmids and Ghassanids and Mundhir's withdrawal from frontier defence (569–75)

The Lakhmids saw an opportunity to regain the initiative against their rivals after the death of Harith in 569 or 570. The new Lakhmid ruler, Qabus, invaded the territory of Mundhir, son of Harith, but sustained a heavy defeat (probably in 570). Mundhir followed up his victory by taking the war into Lakhmid territory, where he gathered much plunder. A further attack by Qabus in the following year was also decisively defeated; Mundhir informed Justin of these developments, but was unable to secure any assistance from the emperor (Joh. Eph. *HE* VI.3).[9] See Shahîd 1995: 340–7. Justin's reaction was rather to attempt to have Mundhir assassinated; the attempt was never made, however, because Mundhir accidentally received the letter sent to Marcian, ordering him to kill the Jafnid chief. He therefore withdrew from defending the southern Roman provinces for two or three years (572–575) (Joh. Eph. *HE* VI.4; *Chr. 1234*, 67 [205/161–2]).[10] The Romans had come to rely heavily on their allies here, so that Mundhir's action greatly weakened the defences of Syria and Euphratesia. See Liebeschuetz 1977: 494–9, Whitby 1988: 210–11.

Unsuccessful attempts to reconcile Monophysites and Chalcedonians (566–8)

It would be inappropriate to enter into the details of the efforts made by Justin II and his wife Sophia to bring about a *rapprochement* between the opponents of Chalcedon (themselves divided) and its supporters. We may note, however, that the consequences of the continuing division between the two parties was by this point leading to the emergence of a separate Monophysite hierarchy; and this increasingly distinct church enjoyed the support of much of the population of the East, on both the Roman and Persian sides of the border. These disputes would be exploited to good effect by Khusro II in the early seventh century.[11]

Roman negotiations with the Turks

In late 568 or early 569 an embassy from the Turks arrived in Constantinople. Its leader was a

Sogdian, a nation now subject to the Turks, called Maniakh, who had earlier attempted to enter into friendly relations with the Persians in order to sell them raw silk. This had been rejected by Khusro, and so the Turkish leader Sizabul had permitted Maniakh to establish contact with the Romans. The Sogdian asserted that the Turks had crushed the Hephthalites and now wished to form an alliance with the Romans; he also strongly hinted that they would be prepared to co-operate against the Persians (Menander frg.10.1).[12] In August 569 Justin sent off the *magister militum per Orientem* Zemarchus on an embassy to the Turks in response (Menander frg.10.2). He was well received and accompanied Sizabul on an expedition against the Persians, after which he was sent back to Roman territory (Menander frg.10.3). The Roman envoys success-fully regained Roman territory, avoiding a Persian ambush in Suania (Menander frg.10.4–5).[13]

Zemarchus returned to Constantinople towards the end of 571. See Blockley 1985: 269 n.170 with *PLRE* III, Zemarchus 3. His report to the emperor was to have far-reaching consequences.

Menander frg.13.5: There were many other reasons for the war between the Romans and the Persians, but the Turks were the nation which most encouraged Justin to open hostili-ties against the Persians. For they attacked the land of the Medes and laid it waste,[14] and sent an embassy to Justin to urge him to fight with them against the Persians. They asked him to destroy, in concert with them, those hostile to both of them, and (so) to embrace the cause of the Turks. For in this way, with the Romans attacking from one direction and the Turks from another, the (state) of the Persians would be destroyed in the middle. Aroused by these hopes, Justin thought that the power of the Persians would easily be overthrown and annihilated. He therefore made every preparation to keep his friendship with the Turks as firm as possible. (tr. Blockley, revised)

More immediate reasons also impelled the emperor to attack the Persians. First, there was the Persian intervention in southern Arabia, where in 570 Khusro had given assistance to a Himyarite prince in expelling the Ethiopians, who were the allies of the Romans. Cf. Tabari, I, 945–58/235–52 (Nöldeke 219–37) with Turtledove 1983: 298, Bosworth 1983: 606–7, Rubin 1995: 284–6, Shahîd 1995: 364–72.[15]

Theoph. Byz. 3 (*FHG* IV.270–1): Justin sent Zemarchus as an ambassador to the Turks. (p.271) He entertained them[16] magnificently and was treated with the greatest kindness; he (then) returned to Byzantium. For this reason Khusro launched a cam-paign against the Ethiopians, allies of the Romans, formerly known as Macrobioi but now called Homerites. Through the agency of Miranus,[17] a Persian general, he took captive Sanatourkes,[18] the king of the Himyarites, pillaged their city and made the people subject to him. (tr. Donovan, revised)

The outbreak of the Armenian revolt (571–2)

Thus the arrival of the Turkish/Sogdian embassy of 568/9 had set in motion a chain of events which eventually led to the outbreak of war. The evident hardening of the Roman stance towards Persia appears to have had an impact on the Persarmenians, who had been suffering at the hands of Persian *marzbans* for some time, and particularly so under the *marzban* Chihor-

Vshnasp.[19] A secret pact between the Romans and the Persarmenians was concluded in late 570, and the Armenians openly revolted in late summer 571, supported by the Iberians; in February 572 the rebels killed Chihor-Vshnasp. See Stein 1919: 23–4, Turtledove 1983: 299; on the Iberians, see Toumanoff 1963: 379–80.

Stephen of Taron, 84.23–86.7 (59.24–60.24): Then in accordance with the sequence of princes, after Mžež Gnuni Persian *marzbans* came to Armenia. First Denshapuh, who contented himself in adultery and lit the Ormizdean fire in Rshtunikʿ; he forced the Christians to worship the flame, on account of which many died. And after him one Varazdat, a Persian from the same family, in whose time a grievous plague with sufferings (occurred). And then a terrible sign, sparkling and blood-like, began to appear in the sky, which frequently flashed across the northern district from the west to the east during the whole night in the shape of a column, and went on for eight months.

And then Khusro, king of Persia, raised to the office of *hazarapet* of Armenia one Suren, his kinsman, whose name was Chihor-Vshnasp, who, when he came, occupied our lands by greatly oppressing the Armenian nobles. For he committed adultery with the wives of the nobles, not accepting the husband as lord of his wife. With him the *bdeashkh* Vardan, son of Vasak, who was from the family of the Mamikoneans, became enraged; having waited for a suitable occasion, he killed Suren the *marzban* with the sword (and) threw him to the ground in the forty-first year of the kingship of Khusro, which was the seventh year of the kingship of Justinian, in the month of Areg, the 22nd of the month, which is of February, on a Tuesday.[20] And the Armenian princes all rebelled from the Persians; they received assistance from the Greek(s) and opposed them in a violent struggle. Then Vardan, having taken his relations and other nobles, took flight to the country of the Greeks, to the royal city Constantinople. And he came before the king Justinian who built Saint Sophia. And he took the sacrament with him. And he (Justin) named in his name the main door of Saint Sophia, which up until today is called the Armenian Gate.[21] (tr. Greenwood)

Narratio de rebus Armeniae 77–8: After a long time, a certain Vardan, a ruler, killed the Persian tyrant Surenas, left the Armenians, and (**78**) ran off to Constantinople in the fortieth year of Khusro and the thirtieth year of Justinian, who also built Hagia Sophia.[22]

Evagr. *HE* V.7 (203.3–26): While this man (Gregory) was holding the episcopacy in his first year,[23] the inhabitants of what was once called Great Armenia, but afterwards Persarmenia – which was recently subject to the Romans, but when Philip, the successor of Gordian, had betrayed it to Shapur, what is called Lesser Armenia[24] was possessed by the Romans, but all the remainder by the Persians[25] – (whose people) revered (the practices) of the Christians and were being cruelly treated by the Persians, especially with regard to their faith, sent an embassy to Justin in secret. They begged to become subject to the Romans, in order that they might freely perform the honours (due) to God without anyone hindering (them). When the emperor had admitted (their overtures), and certain points had been agreed by the emperor in writing and guaranteed by solemn oaths, the Armenians massacred their governors; and with their whole army, bringing (with them) their neighbours, both of kindred and foreign race, they united themselves to the Roman empire, Vardan having a precedence among them by birth, dignity and experience in wars. In reply to the complaints of Khusro on account of these transactions, Justin alleged that the terms of the peace had expired, and that it was impossible to reject the advances of the Christians who defected to (other) Christians. Such was his reply. Notwithstanding, he made no preparation for war, but was caught up in his habitual luxury, regarding everything as secondary to his personal enjoyments. (tr. Anon., revised)

An interesting sidelight on the events in Armenia is provided by Gregory of Tours. Although his information is regarded with suspicion by some, his mention of the destruction of the church of Saint Julian, passed over by other sources, is corroborated by *Chr. 724*.[26]

Greg. Tur. *Hist.* IV.40 (172.10–173.12): (…) After this, Antioch of Egypt and Apamea of Syria, very great cities, were captured by the Persians, and the people carried off as captives. At this time the church of the martyr Julian of Antioch was burnt down by a serious fire. To the Emperor Justin (p.173) came Persarmenians with a great mass of woven silk,[27] seeking his friendship, and assuring him that they were hostile to the Persian king. For his envoys had come to them, saying, 'The emperor in his concern inquires whether you are preserving the peace entered into with him.' When they replied that all that had been promised was being adhered to, the envoys said, 'In this (matter) it will be plain that you preserve his friendship – if you will worship fire, as he does.' When the people replied that they would never do this, the bishop, who was present, said, 'What divinity is there, which might be worshipped, in fire? God created it for the use of men. It is kindled by touchwood, extinguished by water, burns when attended to and grows warm if neglected.' As the bishop continued with these (words) and (others) like them, the envoys were inflamed with anger, and attacked him with insults and beat him with clubs. Seeing their priest stained with his own blood, the people rushed upon the envoys, came to blows with and killed them, and, as we said, sought the friendship of this emperor.

John of Ephesus offers a detailed account of the circumstances leading up to the defection of the Persarmenians, which he claims is based on the narrative of the Armenian *catholicos* and his followers. John asserts that Khusro's decision to force a fire-temple on the Armenians was based on advice from the Zoroastrian clergy, who had heard of the coercion being exerted by Justin to ensure all his subjects were orthodox (Chalcedonians).[28]

Joh. Eph. *HE* II.20 (81.28–82.6, 83.15–84.3): After all this (had happened) – as the *catholicos* and his companions proceeded to relate – he (Khusro) sent a *marzban* to our region, accompanied by (p.82) (a force of) 2000 cavalry, who came first of all to us, to our city, delivering the directive that he should erect a fire-temple there for worshipping the king.[29] When he, as the *catholicos* related and said, showed me and the people of the city the directive, I burned with zeal and rose up against him, I and all the people of the city, and we said … (*The Christians fail to dissuade the* marzban *from proceeding with his task, although they point out to him that Shapur (III) had allowed* *them their religious freedom and even show him a copy of the document.*)[30] But when he saw their readiness and determination against him, and perceived moreover that they outnumbered him, he retired with threats and protests against them and in great anger went to inform the king of all that had taken place. And he, on learning it, was roused in anger and burned with indignation. Vowing death against all the people of the region, he sent against them, accompanying his *marzban*, 15,000 men to do battle and ordered that they be exterminated if they would oppose his command and that he should erect there a shrine of a fire-temple. But the people of the region, when they had heard of these (matters), all assembled together, about 20,000 (in number) and were prepared for battle (and) to fight to the death for the sake of their Christianity. When these had arrived and had all drawn up in line against them (the Persians)to do battle, they cried out 'In the name of our Lord Jesus Christ' and moved onward to attack them. And Christ shattered them before the people of the region, and they destroyed them all as one man (p.84); they slew the *marzban* and took off his head, and brought it to the patrician Justinian, who was stationed at that time at the border at Theodosiopolis. (...) (tr. van Ginkel)

Mich. Syr. X.1 (331–2a/282–3): (...) Afterwards (p.332a) the Persians began to oppress the Armenian people again, in order that they should worship fire, like the Magi; for the Armenians were subject to the power of the Persians in this period. For this reason, the Armenians revolted against the Persians and sought help from the Romans. And when the Romans helped the Armenians, they defeated the Persians. Khusro demanded that Justin return the Armenians to him, stating, 'It is not right that you give (succour) to a people which has revolted against its king. And if you do not return the people to me, make the land tributary to me'. Justin replied, 'I will not deliver into your hands a Christian people which has forsaken the worship of demons and has sought refuge with me'. Khusro responded and wrote to Justin for a second time, saying, 'If you do not give me the people and do not return the country to us, give the gold which your kings gave by way of tribute for Armenia; and may peace endure between us'. Justin replied again in harsh terms, saying, 'I demand from you even the tribute which you have formerly received. For it is for him who requests peace to give tribute; and since you ask me for the country of the North, so we also demand Nisibis; for it belonged to the Romans, and it was given to the Persians conditionally, as is written in the archives.'[31] (tr. M. Greatrex)

Joh. Bicl., a.567?.3 (211.18–21): When the Armenian and Iberian people, who had received the faith from the preaching of the apostles of Christ, were forced by the Persian king Khusro into the worship of idols, they refused such an impious order and handed themselves, together with their provinces, over to the Romans. This affair broke the treaties of peace between the Romans and the Persians.[32]

Theoph. Byz. 3 (*FHG* IV.271): He (Theophanes)[33] recounts in full also how the Armenians, because of the hostile treatment which they had received at the hands of Surena, particularly in matters concerning their religion, united and slew Surena through (the actions) of Vardan, whose brother Manuel he (Surena) had killed, and of a certain other man, Vardes. They then revolted from the Persians and went over to the Romans. They left the town of Dvin in which they were living and entered Roman territory. This action in particular was the cause of the Persians' breaking of the treaty with the Romans. Immediately the Iberians rebelled, and under their leader Gorgenes[34] went over to the Romans. At this time Tiflis was the capital city of the Iberians. (tr. Donovan, revised)

Notwithstanding the events in Persarmenia, Khusro attempted to maintain the peace and in early 572 sent a Christian ambassador, Sebokht, to Constantinople to receive the payment due for that year and to confirm that the Romans were still prepared to abide by the treaty. Justin made clear, however, that he had given his backing to the Persarmenians, as fellow Christians, and that he was prepared to invade Persia if necessary (Menander frg.16.1).[35] As is noted by John of Epiphania (below), Justin had no intention of submitting to the indignity of making yearly payments to the Persians.[36] A summary of the factors which induced Justin to go to war is offered by several sources.

Joh. Eph. *HE* VI.23 (321.26–322.2): The first cause why the peace was broken was that the Persarmenians surrendered themselves (and their country) to the Romans. The second cause of bitter enmity was the fact that the emperor of the Romans had sent ambassadors to the barbarous tribes who live more inland[37] from the lands of the Persians, whom they call (p.322) Turks (Turkioi), together with many other causes (...) (tr. van Ginkel)

Joh. Epiph. 2 (*FHG* IV.273–4), cf. Th. Sim. III.9.3–10:[38] When the Emperor Justinian had ruled the Roman empire for 39 years in all, he died. At the end of (that) time, he lived in peace with everyone including the Medes also. Upon his death, Justin the younger, who was his nephew, succeeded to the Roman empire, and the treaty which had previously been made between the Romans and the Persians was broken. (Justinian had made (the treaty) with Khusro, the son of Kavadh, and it was for a duration of 55 years.)[39] They fought a great war against each other, which began in the seventh year of Justin's reign and lasted for twenty (p.274) years. It ended in the ninth year of the reign of the Roman Emperor Maurice. (Each nation) attributed to the other the causes for the strife between them. The Romans were angry because the Persians intended to bring about the revolt of the Himyarites – an Indian tribe allied and subject to them – to rebel. When they (the Himyarites) refused to take their (the Persians') side, they made an attack on them at a time when the treaty was still valid.[40] Besides this, when the Turks had sent an embassy to the Romans, the Emperor Justin had even admitted it into his presence. He had also sent out Zemarchus, a man of senatorial rank, with them, (and so) the Persians wanted to bribe the Alans, through whose territory they (the Romans) intended to travel, in their eagerness to murder Zemarchus and the Romans and Turks with him. In similar fashion the Medes made counter-accusations, blaming the Romans for the outbreak of war, since when the Armenians, their tributaries, were looking to rebel, having killed the governor, Surena by name, and went over to join the Roman empire, they had received them with hospitable treaty terms and accorded them a close alliance.

The strife between them was greatly exacerbated, if anyone should wish to know the least obvious, but nonetheless the true cause (of the war), because the Emperor

Justin no longer deigned to make an annual payment to the Medes of the 500 lbs of gold, on which condition the treaty had previously been agreed, or to make the Roman state tributary to the Persians in perpetuity.[41] (tr. Donovan, revised) **Menander frg.13.5:** See above, p.137.

The opening of war, 572–3

In the wake of Sebokht's embassy, Justin made the fateful decision to launch a full-scale war on Persia. As is clear from John's account, the newly appointed *magister militum per Orientem* therefore had little opportunity to go on the offensive in this year. See Whitby 1988: 254 and *PLRE* III, Marcianus 7.

Joh. Epiph. 3 (*FHG* IV.274), cf. Th. Sim. III.10.1–3: Therefore when the period had come to an end for which Khusro, the Persian king, had received the money in accordance with the terms agreed (for it was decided to advance the total amount for ten years at one and the same time),[42] and since in addition no one had attempted to come to an agreement, Justin, the Roman Emperor, speedily despatched the general Marcian to the east. He was among the patricians of the senate and related to Justin. He was not without experience of the dangers of war and besides was brave in appearance and in reality. Marcian crossed the Euphrates and reached Osrhoene. When the height of summer had already passed, and the barbarians had not so far foreseen any hostility, he dispatched 3000 infantry to the area called Arzanene. He put in command of them Theodore and Sergius, whose family was from Rhabdion,[43] and Juventinus, who was in command of the units in Chalcis. They made a sudden attack and laid waste the Persian territory, and having captured sufficient booty, they retreated as quickly as possible. (…) (tr. Donovan, revised)

The failure to take Nisibis, 573

Only in spring 573 was Marcian in a position to undertake a campaign in Mesopotamia; and by then the Persians had made ready their defences.

Evagr. *HE* V.8–9 (203.27–205.28): The emperor sent out his relative Marcian, appointing him commander of the forces in the East, but did not give him a battleworthy army or other equipment for war. He occupied Mesopotamia amid obvious danger and the (possible) ruin of everything, stringing along with him very few troops, and these without weapons, and with some diggers and cattle-drivers pressed into service from among the provincials.[44] There were (some) small engagements with the Persians near (p.204) Nisibis, although the Persians were not ready for war. Having gained the upper hand, he laid siege to the city, though the Persians did not think it necessary to close the gates, and mocked the Roman army quite disgracefully.[45] And many strange things were observed, indicating the troubles to come, and among them we saw a newly born ox at the start of the war, from whose neck hung two heads. (V.9) Khusro, when sufficient preparations for war had been made, accompanied Adarmahan for a certain distance, and after transporting him across the Euphrates within their own country, sent him into Roman territory through (the place) called Circesium. Circesium is a most important town to the Romans, lying at the outer limits of the state. Not only do the walls, rising up to a limitless height, make it strong, but also the rivers Euphrates and Khabur which surround it and make the city a sort of island.[46] He (Khusro) himself, with his own force, crossed the river Tigris and made his expedition towards Nisibis. These events were unknown to the Romans to a great extent,[47] and so Justin, convinced by a rumour which said that Khusro had either died or was at his very last gasp, was vexed at the supposed slowness of the siege of Nisibis; and he sent men to urge Marcian on, and to bring him the keys of the gates as soon as possible. To Gregory, the bishop of Theopolis (Antioch), it was first announced that the matter was making absolutely no progress, and that he (Marcian) was bringing disgrace (on the Romans), seeking the impossible against such a great and notable city with such a contemptible army. For the bishop of Nisibis[48] was a great friend (p.205) of Gregory, having been honoured by him with great gifts, and was especially discontented with the senseless violence of the Persians towards the Christians, which they constantly suffered at their hands.[49] He desired that his own city be subject to the Romans, and provided information to Gregory of all that took place in enemy territory, supplying everything at the appropriate time. These things he (Gregory) immediately reported to Justin, informing (him) of the swift advance of Khusro.[50]

But he (Justin), wallowing in his usual pleasures, paid no heed to what had been written, and did not wish to believe (it), thinking what he wanted. For meanness and confidence towards outcomes are the norm for dissolute men, and disbelief if they turn out contrary to their wishes. He therefore wrote to him (Gregory) at last, passing over these matters as if they were entirely false, or if they were true, as if the Persians would not arrive in time (to lift) the siege, or if they did, as if they would be badly beaten. He therefore sent a certain wretched and arrogant man, Acacius, to Marcian, ordering him to remove him from office, even if Marcian should have put one foot in the city before (he came). This he accomplished punctiliously, serving the commands of the emperor to no advantage. For having reached the camp, he dismissed Marcian from office in enemy territory, having made no announcement to the army. The captains and unit commanders, when, having passed the night, they learnt that the commander had been dismissed, no longer came before the multitude, but withdrew in scattered flight, breaking the absurd siege. (...)

Chr. 1234, 65 (202.7–203.20): And with the envoy[51], the emperor Justinian sent his aunt's son Marcian[52] with an army to lay siege to Nisibis. But when they set out and reached the city of Dara, he (Marcian) sent a part of the army to invade the borders of the Persians; they took captives and pillaged and returned to Dara. And when the Persians who were at Nisibis saw (this), they were greatly afraid. But the *marzban* of Nisibis, since he was a shrewd man, schemed to go out to Marcian, the leader of the army, (went) up to the border and, talking with him, asked for a period of four months while he apprised the king (of the situation).[53] But Marcian, because he was a gentle and simple man, granted (this) to him, and returned to Edessa. But the Persians

143

brought provisions to Nisibis, and cut down the parks and gardens which were around the city, as far as a missile can be thrown. They expelled the Christians who were in the city and apprised King Khusro (of the situation). But the emperor Justinian, when he heard that Marcian had returned to Edessa, wrote to him that he should swiftly and without delay go down to lay siege to Nisibis. And Marcian set out when the emperor's letter reached him, and reached Dara on the Saturday of Holy Week; he celebrated the Sunday of the Resurrection (i.e. Easter) in the city of Dara,[54] and on the Tuesday went down to lay siege to Nisibis. And he surrounded it on all sides and put up a strong fight against it; and the city was close to being crushed. But the emperor Justinian was extremely angry that Marcian had turned back and arrived at Edessa, (thus) allowing Nisibis a time of respite. After he wrote to him, so that he would go and lay siege to Nisibis, and when Marcian had arrived and put up a strong fight against it, (p.203) in those days all thought that Nisibis had been taken; but Khusro was by the river Tigris, and ready to come against the Romans, and when the city was close to being taken Acacius Archelaus, a savage man, came, who had been sent by the emperor Justinian to remove Marcian from (his) command, without consideration for rank, and to take his place. And when Marcian heard the emperor's order, he asked Archelaus to allow him two days until the city was taken. But he was angered and did not agree. And at night, when no one was paying attention, Marcian and those of the officers who were with him left and came to the city of Dara. And at daybreak the Roman army saw the tent of Marcian[55] overturned, and his standard which was taken from its place, they thought that they had fled before the Persian army coming up against them; and a commotion and disturbance fell on the camp; they turned to flight and abandoned (their) tents, laying down their weapons and engines and provisions, and fled to Dara. But when the Persian army, which was at Nisibis, had opened the gates, it went out and pillaged the tents and everything that had been left behind. And this evil end happened to the Roman forces in the year 880 (568/9).[56] (tr. M. Greatrex)

Joh. Epiph. 3 (*FHG* IV.274), cf. Th. Sim. III.10.4–5: (…) When the winter season had passed, Marcian assembled his forces again and set out from Dara. The Persians, under the generalship of Baramanes,[57] who had been appointed to command the units there, came out to meet (Marcian) in front of the city of Nisibis. A hotly contested battle ensued in the vicinity of a Persian place called Sargathon,[58] in which the Romans vigorously put the barbarians to flight and slaughtered many of them in the battle. They then made an attempt on the fort at Thebetha and spent ten whole days there. Since they could not capture it by any means, they returned again to the fortress of Dara. While the spring was still at its height, they invaded the enemy's territory for a second time, and, by the order of the Emperor Justin, they decided to besiege Nisibis. (tr. Donovan, revised)

Joh. Eph. *HE* VI.2 (278.8–280.5): Of the events which are now happening in the eastern territories, we will present some short accounts. First we will start the exposition of our stories with the illustrious patrician Marcian, a relative of the Emperor Justin, one of the army commanders who at that time were sent to the East. Burning with zeal for the nation of Christians, he gathered his army and descended and laid siege to the city of Nisibis, which until now was held by the Persians. He attacked vigorously in order to take it. He built against her ramparts all around, and because he also had engineers with him, he raised against her siege engines, namely lofty towers and strong bulwarks. The city was in distress. And its inhabitants together with the Persian garrison despaired of their lives, seeing that at that moment it was on the verge of being captured by the Romans. When those inside despaired, (and) when those outside prepared themselves to take the city and destroy it, (and) when all the Romans thought to be ready to enter it, behold, a violent-tempered man arrived, named Acacius Archelaus, sent by Emperor Justin against Marcian for no just reason to deprive him of his command[59] and cut his girdle and send him away from the regions of the East. As soon as he had arrived and shown his order, when Marcian with his army was about to take Nisibis by storm and they expected to enter it (p.279) the next day and take possession of the city, the entire army was perplexed and their arms became weak. The illustrious Marcian, who had been assiduously making his preparations and was on the verge of capturing Nisibis, when he heard the order, said to Acacius, 'Behold, you see what great labour we have taken upon us for the purpose of capturing this city. Right now, be patient, and grant us a delay of two days only, and then do what you have been ordered. It is lawful that what the emperor orders will be done.' But he became angry with him and insulted him and was furious and in front of all his troops he grabbed him and pulled him about, and threw him down and cut his girdle, insulting him and even, as was said, struck him on the cheek. The whole army was indignant and the entire corps lowered their arms. While sneering because they had seen an unfair act, they took his banner, lowered it and turned it upside down. Immediately the entire army fled and turned around and retreated from the city, lamenting and grieving about what had happened to their commander, a good man and a believer[60], and also because at the very moment that they were expecting to enter and take the city, they had turned their backs, while they were not pursued by their enemies, and they had become (an object of) laughter and scorn to their haters.

But when the Persian army, which was in the city, saw this, the breaking up and sudden retreat of the Romans, and the overturning of the banner of Marcian, they were astonished and became encouraged and armed themselves and pursued after them and fell upon a body of infantry which had remained behind, and defeated and slew many of them.

Thus they returned to their city laughing and mocking at what had happened to the Romans of their own doing. Forthwith, too, they wrote and informed their king of all these (things), saying, 'Come immediately, and let us cross over (p.280) into Roman territory, because our noble gods, the sun and the fire, have thrown them down, namely thus, in that they have fallen upon one another because of an order from their emperor and they have dismissed Marcian with scorn, and have all fled away from the city.' (tr. van Ginkel)

The Persian counter-strike (mid-573)

Khusro's response to the Roman invasion was two-fold. He led an army up the Euphrates, which divided near Circesium. While he continued northwards, up the Khabur, ready to drive off the Romans from Nisibis and strike at Dara, a detachment under Adarmahan continued up the Euphrates into Euphratesia and Syria.[61] See Stein 1919: 44, Downey 1961: 561–2, Whitby 1988: 257.

Evagr. *HE* V.9 (205.29–206.16): (…) Adarmahan, therefore, with a considerable force of Persians and Scenite barbarians, having passed by Circesium, inflicted every possible injury (p.206) with fire and sword on Roman territory, setting no limits to his intentions or actions. He also captured fortresses and many villages. No one stood in his way, in the first place because there was no one in command, and secondly, because, since the Roman troops were shut up in Dara by Khusro, his foragings and incursions were made in perfect security. He also directed an advance upon Theoupolis (Antioch) through his subordinate, but did not go there himself. These (troops) were repulsed most unexpectedly; for scarcely anyone, or indeed very few persons, remained in the city; and the bishop had fled, taking with him the sacred treasures, because both the greater part of the walls had fallen to ruins,[62] and the populace had revolted, wishing to take control by means of a revolution, as often occurs, especially at times like this. They themselves (the populace) also fled, leaving the city deserted; and no one at all took thought for (any) preparation or counter-attack (against the Persians). (tr. Anon., revised)

Joh. Eph. *HE* VI.6 (292.12–293.13): When the Persian king was still besieging the city of Dara and saw that there was nobody trying to stop him, he immediately sent a *marzban* named Adarmahan against the city of Apamea with a large army. *En route* he seized many fortresses and destroyed and burnt important and strong villages until he arrived at Apamea. After the Persian (i.e. Khusro) had conquered Antioch (in 540) he had besieged Apamea and had caused great hardship, and Apamea had also surrendered to him after it had received his word (of honour). When the king had entered it (Apamea) and had been a spectator at the horse-races, he had not destroyed nor burned anything in it. For this reason they (the citizens of Apamea) were full of confidence that he (Adarmahan) who had come (now) would also do them no harm. Because of this trust the leaders of the city and the bishop went out to him and paid homage. He said cunningly to them, 'Because the city is ours, open the gates for me, that I may enter and see it.' They, trusting him, and not expecting that he would do anything evil, opened the gates for him and he entered (p.293) the city. Immediately he seized the gates and started seizing and binding men and women and plundering the city. They brought the entire booty and all the people outside and placed them outside the city. After they had plundered the entire city of Apamea, which was full of riches, (accumulated) over a long period, and far more prosperous than most cities,[63] and had led its entire population and its entire booty outside and also the bishop with them, they then set it on fire and burned it down completely. Thus they led away all the captives and all the booty from it and from elsewhere and went down to the king, while he was still encamped against Dara. And the captives, who were led down from it and from elsewhere, were counted before the king (and they numbered) 292,000.[64] They were divided (up) and crossed over to Persia.[65] (…) (tr. van Ginkel)

Joh. Epiph. 4 (*FHG* IV.275), cf. Th. Sim. III.10.6–11.1: While they (the Romans) were encamped near the city, King Khusro set out from Babylon with the Median army. Having crossed the Tigris, he made his way through the desert so that his[66] movement should not be detected by the Romans. When he drew near to Ambar, a Persian fort (which was situated a five-day journey's distance from Circesium)[67] he speedily dispatched the general, Adarmahan by name, who crossed the Euphrates at this very spot (Ambar), to lay waste <Roman> territory. Khusro had provided him with 6000 Persians and nomad barbarians.[68] Khusro himself <followed the river> Khabur and hastened <to make an unexpected attack> on the Romans besieging Nisibis. Adarmahan, then, crossed the Euphrates in the vicinity of Circesium, and went out plundering the Roman possessions. For as a result of the previous peace and the ease which they had enjoyed in abundance during the reign of Justinian, the practice of war had been neglected by them, and their courage thoroughly corrupted. Since no one dared to join battle with the barbarians, Adarmahan got very close to the city of Antioch and after ravaging the districts and fields lying close to the city, he pushed on into Coele Syria. He made camp not far from the large city of Apamea. When the inhabitants sent out an embassy and <offered a ransom for the city, he deceived the men (sent)> by announcing that he would preserve the town unharmed. Once, however, he was inside the town, the Medes plundered its possessions, enslaved its inhabitants, and consigned it to the flames. Then as quickly as possible they returned to their own territory.[69] After these events the Emperor Justin sent out Acacius (whom the Romans were accustomed to call (the son) of Archelaus) and relieved Marcian of his command while he was still besieging Nisibis, suspecting him of being slack in his duty, since nothing had been done to bring about the capture of the city. (tr. Donovan, revised)

Mich. Syr. X.9 (349a/312): At once Khusro despatched the *marzban* Adarmahan, and he plundered and laid waste Barbalissus, Qasrin, Beth Dama, Gabbulon, the (region) surrounding Chalcis, Gazara, the mountain, and the territory of Antioch.[70] (tr. M. Greatrex)

See also Greg. Tur. p.139 above, and *Chr. 724* p.150 below.

The siege and fall of Dara (summer–autumn 573)[71]

***Chr. 1234*, 66 (203.20–205.7):** Concerning the siege of the city of Dara by the Persians. But when King Khusro, who had been encamped on the river Tigris with his army, heard what had happened to the Roman army and about their flight from the city of Nisibis, he set out and came to Nisibis and found all the weaponry of the Romans; he took everything and came to smite the city of Dara. Khusro had with him 23,000 cavalry, 40,000 infantry and 120,000 farmers to help in the work.[72] And when he had reached Dara and laid siege to (it), he sent stonecutters to cut through the eastern mountain, and he cut off the aqueducts from it; and with great labour he diverted the river, which flowed in a deep valley and entered it (p.204). Afterwards he forced the workmen to build a wall of bricks outside the surrounding wall (of the city). But when the mountain rock turned out to be hard, they kindled a fire above it, and afterwards poured vinegar on it, and thus they cracked it. He fought against the city, night and day, for a period of six months, and he built two mounds against it. And after six months, when he had been unable to crush the city, he decided to go. He sent (a message) to the Romans, asking for five *centenaria* of gold from them – as a fine which he had imposed on the city – so that he might leave them.[73] But there was no reply to him from the citizens. For it is said that that the envoy who had been sent for the gold did not report the matter to them (the citizens of Dara) because he thought that the city could not hold out. Therefore Khusro was angry and began to fight fiercely. They (the Persians) tied pieces of wood from the mounds to the wall, and crossed over the wall, and overran it. But the Romans who were in the city fled, so that they might enter the citadel;[74] but the leaders did not open the gates, and so the Persians who had entered the city and the Romans fell upon one another, and began to slaughter and be slaughtered for seven days. Other men were not able to enter until the city was foul on account of the dead. Then a battle raged against the city; and against a high tower, which was called Hercules', they (the Persians) set up three mounds and *ballistae* which hurled huge stones. And the citizens were much enfeebled, and could not get near the tower; and the besieged relented. So now Dara was taken on account of our sins.[75] When the king saw the dead in the middle of the city, he forbade a slaughter of the leaders of the city; (rather,) he carefully bound their hands. And he gathered up the gold and silver of the city and amassed a weight of 200 *centenaria*. When Khusro saw (this), he said to the leaders, (p.205) 'God will seek from you all the blood which has been shed; when you possessed all this gold, why did you not give one hundredth of it to me, and I would have left you ?' And they swore that the envoy, who had been sent, had said nothing to them about any gold.[76] And the number of captives, beyond those who died by the sword, was 98,000.[77] From the building of Dara until this capture (there were) 72 years. (tr. M. Greatrex)

John of Ephesus (*HE* VI.5) offers a lengthier version than that of *Chr. 1234*, adding a few details.[78] According to John, Khusro's initial camp was on the northern side of the city; he commends the competence of the Roman commander John, the son of Timostratus, in contrast to Evagrius (*HE* V.10), who states that John either did little to save the city or actually betrayed it.[79] He further states that the Romans slackened in their defence on account of their increasing confidence and the cold season. According to John, at the end of the siege, after the mêlée in the city, the Romans were tricked by the Persians into dropping their guard and allowing the besiegers to enter the city unhindered. In this way they gained possession of Dara.

Joh. Epiph. 5 (*FHG* IV.275), cf. Th. Sim. III.10.2: After the Romans had retreated and reached a fortress situated on a mountain (it was called Mardin by those living there) King Khusro suddenly applied himself <to> the siege <of Dara and assailed the township for six months>. He di<verted> the water-(supply) of the city <and

surrounded (it) with ramparts>; he also erected great <mo>unds alongside the wall and employed ramming devices as siege engines.[80] When no help came for the inhabitants from outside, he took the city after the Medes had ascended the walls by force. He plundered the entire city and enslaved the population including John, the son of Timostratus, who surpassed all the others in power and rank and had assumed the control and administration of the city. He (Khusro) left behind a sufficiently strong force and retired to his home territory. Meanwhile the Romans were still tarrying at the fortress of Mardin with Magnus, the keeper of the imperial purse,[81] who had been entrusted with overall command. (...) (tr. Donovan, revised)

The war in Armenia, 572–3

In the wake of the assassination of Chihor-Vshnasp, the Armenians had seized control of Dvin, but it was soon retaken by the Persians. Later in 572 it changed hands again, as Vardan, in conjunction with Roman forces under Justinian, successfully expelled the Persians. In the process, however, the Romans burned down the church of St Gregory outside Dvin, which the Persians had been using to store supplies (Sebeos 68/7).[82] See Whitby 1988: 254–6 and Stein 1919: 38. The extent of Roman gains in the Transcaucasus should not be underestimated: the defection of the Persarmenians and Iberians gave them a huge advantage in the region, and immediately rendered the dispute over Suania irrelevant. Henceforth, as will be seen in the following chapter, Roman armies were able to penetrate deep into Azerbaijan and even to pass the winter there.[83]

Sebeos, 67.27–68.8/6–7: And it happened in the 41st year of the kingship of Khusro, son of Kavadh, (that) Vardan rebelled and withdrew from submission to the Persian kingdom, together with all the Armenians in unison. They killed the *marzban* Suren by surprise in the city of Dvin, and took much plunder and went into submission to the Greeks. At a time before this, one named Vahan, prince of the country of Siwnikʿ, rebelled and withdrew from the Armenians. He requested from Khusro the Persian king that they should transfer the chancery of the country of Siwnikʿ from Dvin to the Pʿaytakaran city,[84] and that he should assign the city to the census (p.68) of Atropatene so that the name of Armenians would not be applied to them. And the order was fulfilled. Then the Greek king made a vow with the Armenians and confirmed the same pact which had existed between the two kings, the blessed Tiridates and Constantine. He gave them an imperial army in support. And when they received the army, they attacked the city of Dvin and, having besieged it, destroyed it from top to bottom, and expelled the Persian force which was located in it. (tr. Greenwood)[85]
Joh. Bicl. a.571?.1 (212.20–1): The Emperor Justin made Armenia and Iberia Roman provinces after the Persians had been driven back,[86] and the Persian king prepared for war through his commanders.

In the following year, Justinian, perhaps as a consequence of complaints over the destruction of the church of St Gregory, was replaced by John, while the ineffectual Vardan Vshnasp (who had replaced Chihor Vshnasp as *marzban*) was succeeded by Gołon Mihran, the father of Bahram

Chobin. As is clear from Theophanes of Byzantium (below), John had among his forces Lazi, Abasgi and Alans. Whether he also had any Roman troops is uncertain, since it is possible that they had been sent south to help in the Mesopotamian campaign. See Stein 1919: 38–9 and 49 n.2 on the tribes listed in Theoph. Byz. In August 573 Khusro despatched Gołon Mihran against the rebels, but only gradually did he restore some Persian control to the region (Sebeos, 68/7, 70/10–11).[87]

Composite account of events, 572–3

Chr. 724, 145.12–19: And again in the year 884 (572/3) Khusro and his troops went up and laid siege to Dara. He sent Adarmahan[88] his *marzban* and went up as far as Antioch. He set on fire ?Amos and the house of Mar Julian. And he went to Seleucia and subdued it.[89] He went to Apamea and it surrendered to him of its (own) free will. He set fire to it, captured its inhabitants and went away. And when he went down to his lord (Khusro), he subdued Dara and captured its inhabitants and emptied it; and he made some of the people of the Persians dwell in it. (tr. M. Greatrex)

Theoph. Byz. 4 (*FHG* IV.271): (He reports) that Marcian the nephew of the emperor Justin was appointed *magister militum per Orientem* and in the eighth year of the reign of Justin was sent out to fight against Khusro. John, the *magister militum per Armeniam* and Miranes, the general of the Persians, also known as Baramaanes, mustered their forces.[90] The Colchians, the Abasgi and Saroes,[91] the king of the Alans, allied themselves with the Armenians, while the Sabirs, the Daganes and the Dilimnite people[92] (joined) Miranes. Marcian fought against Miranes near the city of Nisibis and put him to flight, killing 1200 men in the battle and taking captive 70 men; seven Romans were killed. Already he was laying siege to the walls of Nisibis. When Khusro learned of this, he assembled 40,000 cavalry and over 100,000 infantry, and hastened to bring help and to combat the Romans. Meanwhile Marcian was slandered to the emperor as one who was desirous of usurping (the throne).[93] The emperor was persuaded (of the charge) and dismissed him from his command. He appointed in his place Theodore, surnamed Tzirus, the son of Justinian.[94] As a result of this, disorder ensued and the Romans lifted their siege. Khusro besieged the city of Dara and captured (it). (tr. Donovan, revised)

It is also worth noting that Firdausi (tr. Mohl 1868: 509–21) offers a brief overview of this war, unlike Tabari, who omits it altogether. Firdausi reports that war broke out when the new Roman emperor (i.e. Justin II) no longer wished to be a vassal of Persia. Khusro therefore attacked the Romans, capturing Beroea (Halab) and Sakila (? Seleucia), despite some problems in furnishing his troops with pay. The war was brought to an end when Roman envoys brought the required payments to Khusro in return for a cessation of hostilities.[95]

11

THE WAR UNDER TIBERIUS (574–82)

Continuation of negotiations (574–5)

The fall of Dara affected the Emperor Justin severely; he became insane, although he retained occasional moments of lucidity. Henceforth effective control of affairs was in the hands of Tiberius, assisted by Justin's wife Sophia. Early in 574 they received an embassy from Khusro, seeking to renew negotiations; Sophia replied by despatching Zachariah as an ambassador (Menander frg.18.1). At the same time Tiberius undertook an extensive recruitment drive, mainly in the Balkans, to bolster the Roman forces in the East, while Justinian was appointed *magister militum per Orientem* and given overall command of the whole eastern front (Th. Sim. III.12.3–4, Evagr. *HE* V.14 [209.27–210.2]).[1]

Joh. Epiph. 5 (*FHG* IV.275–6), cf. Th. Sim. III.11.3–4: (…) Not many days later[2] the Emperor Justin, when an illness of the body suddenly afflicted (him), grew fearful of everything, and made a truce for the present year with the Persians. Since the ailment (continued to) trouble him, he proclaimed Tiberius, the commander of the imperial guard – the Romans call this man *comes excubitorum* – as his son, and chose him to share control of the empire. He declared him Caesar and handed over to him responsibility for ruling. (p.276) Of all the things done by Justin during the course of his rule this decision was the best and the one most promising of future security; it was the cause of very many benefits in the affairs of the Romans. As he deliberated on the present situation, Tiberius decided to take matters vigorously in hand, so that nothing else intolerable would occur … .[3] (…) (tr. Donovan, revised)

Menander frg.18.2: The Empress Sophia, the wife of Justin, sent <Zachariah>, who ranked among the court physicians, as envoy to the Persian king Khusro. When he arrived there offering 45,000 *nomismata*,[4] he made a one-year agreement in the East, so that there might be a truce.[5] He said that during this period a major embassy[6] would be sent by the empress, which would discuss everything in greater depth, and which would in addition put an end to the war, if it should also happen that the Roman emperor in the meantime returned to health. Thus Zachariah made a one-year truce in the Roman dominions in the East, but not for those in Armenia, paid over the 45,000 gold *nomismata* for this (concession) alone, and departed. When these matters had been settled, the general Eusebius was recalled to Byzantium.[7] (tr. Blockley, revised)

In late 574[8] a further embassy was sent from Constantinople, in which served the *quaestor sacri palatii* Trajan and Zachariah. Their mission was to secure a general truce for three years to allow further time for negotiations to continue; their top priority was to gain respite for the Mesopotamian frontier. The Persians, however, wished for a more enduring period of peace, and the Romans agreed to a five-year pact, for which the Romans would pay 30,000 *nomismata* annually, subject to ratification by the emperor (Menander frg.18.3).

Menander frg.18.4: When affairs of state had already encompassed Tiberius,[9] Trajan and Zachariah the envoys wrote to him that the Persians were unwilling to make a three-year agreement, but wanted it to be for five years. And he did not assent (to this), since he did not wish to make a longer truce, and he told them preferably to make the agreement for two years, and, if this were impossible, not to accept (one) for more than three years. When, therefore, the letter to this effect had been sent to the envoys and they had read what the letter revealed, Mahbodh, who had come to the border near Dara for this purpose, when he learned that the Romans were not satisfied with the terms approved by Trajan and Zachariah, sent Tamkhusro against the Roman domains.[10] He immediately overran and burned the territory close to Dara until Mahbodh was persuaded to accept the 30,000 gold *nomismata* each year for the three-year peace on the understanding that during this period the high officials of both states would meet to discuss how arms might be put aside completely. The Caesar accomplished these things aiming, with some forethought, for his own advantage, since he knew that within three years his forces would be sufficient for him and would be clearly battleworthy (to face) the Persians. The Persians, too, were aware of the Caesar's forethought, realising that the respite had been (agreed to) by him for no other reason than that he was looking to the future so that forces for what was necessary might be prepared in advance by him. Nevertheless, they were contemptuous of the Romans, thinking that they would not be able to retrieve their defeat, even if they were given more time.

When a truce had been made in the East,[11] all the tumult (of war) was transferred to Armenia, which was partitioned between the two sides, and at the beginning of spring the war began. (tr. Blockley, revised)

Joh. Epiph. 5 (*FHG* IV.276), **cf. Th. Sim. III.12.6–9:** (…) He (Tiberius) sent Theodore,[12] who had been in charge of affairs in Armenia and had held many other distinguished offices and was adequately endowed with reason and especially well able to recognise at a glance what was necessary, on an embassy to the barbarians. According to the usual practice therefore he explained what had taken place concerning him (Tiberius) and urged Khusro to enter into negotiations. A little later he (Tiberius) in the same way speedily despatched to the East Justinian, the son of Germanus, who had been enrolled among the patricians in the senate, entrusting the whole conduct of the war to him. He was inured to the dangers of war, having reached that (point) in life where he was tripped up neither through the rashness of youth nor by the weakness of old age. Justinian therefore arrived as quickly as possible in the East and took charge of the discipline and order of the soldiers, while Tiberius Caesar speedily sent out a not inconsiderable force and continually worked hard at making preparations for war. He distributed an unlimited amount of money and assembled the strongest and most warlike soldiers from among the nations, giving very careful consideration to everything to do with the war which was upon him.[13] While these matters were progressing in this way, and it was a short time into the period of the truce, the Persians, after assembling opposite Dara, arrived in the vicinity of Constantina, 490 stades to the west of Dara.[14] (tr. Donovan, revised)

At some point in 575 the Ghassanid ruler Mundhir met Justinian at Sergiopolis, and there a reconciliation was effected between the two parties. In the wake of their meeting, Mundhir launched a raid deep into Lakhmid territory, seizing and plundering their capital at Hira (Joh. Eph. *HE* VI.4).[15] See Stein 1919: 61–2, Whitby 1988: 264, Shahîd 1995: 373–83 (placing the raid in spring 575, before the three-year truce was agreed).

Continued fighting in the Transcaucasus (574–5)

While negotiations continued in Mesopotamia, the war was vigorously pursued to the north. In 575 Roman commanders took hostages from the Sabirs, the Alans and other tribes, who were brought to Constantinople and welcomed by Tiberius. The Sabirs, however, rejoined the Persians soon afterwards (Menander frg.18.5). See Stein 1919: 62–3, Turtledove 1977: 231–2, Whitby 1988: 264. Help from the Turks, in whom Justin had placed such hopes, never materialised; rather, following the unsuccessful mission of Valentinus in 576–577 to Turxanthus, they attacked and seized the Roman city of Bosporus in the Crimea (Menander frg.19.1–2). See Blockley 1985b: 274–8, Sinor 1990: 304. Persian efforts to regain control of Armenia were only partially successful. See Chapter 10, p.150 with Toumanoff 1963: 380.

The campaign of Melitene (576)

In 575 or early 576 Theodore son of Bacchus[16] was sent on a minor embassy to Khusro, partly to thank the king for his good treatment of Zachariah and Trajan's mission, and partly to indicate the emperor's willingness to resume high-level negotiations on the border (Menander frg.18.6.1–12). Khusro, however, decided to accept the ambassador and simultaneously to attack the Romans in Armenia, where the truce did not apply. Arriving from the south earlier in the year than usual, he took the Romans completely by surprise: the generals Curs and Theodore were still operating around Albania, ensuring the loyalty of the tribes there, while the *magister militum per Orientem*, Justinian, had yet to move his forces north from Mesopotamia to the front (Menander frg.18.6.13–47).[17] Khusro passed through Persarmenia unopposed, bringing Theodore with him; in late spring he arrived outside Theodosiopolis, determined to take it in order to restore his grip on Persarmenia and Iberia. He was opposed by a Roman force to the south of the city, and preferred therefore to open negotiations rather than risk an assault on the city. Theodore was released to go to Tiberius and enjoined to return within thirty days, if an invasion was to be avoided (Menander frg.18.6.48–116; Joh. Eph. *HE* VI.8).[18]

Khusro's despatch of Theodore was only a ruse. Passing by Theodosiopolis, he continued westwards.

Joh. Eph. _HE_ VI.8 (298.1–300.9): (...) When they[19] had blocked him in and were preparing to do battle with him, he (Khusro) became afraid and turned away from them to go against another city. They also hastened there against him and opposed him and repulsed him also from there.[20] After they had tested his army, they took more courage (in their struggle) against him and they despised him. After these (events), when he saw that it (the campaign) did not go according to his wish, he marched to the northern mountains and focused his eyes on Cappadocia in order to enter and conquer Caesarea.[21] When the armies of the Romans saw (it), they marched against him and in front of him also to Cappadocia. They positioned themselves against him and blocked him in the mountains of Cappadocia and stopped him and did not let him pass. For many days they encamped opposite one another, while he did not dare to fight an open battle with them. When he saw that they were more numerous and powerful than him and that he was not able to pass them and march on Caesarea, he was alarmed and very troubled. Therefore he began to plan whether he could pass (them) and make his escape to his own country. His Magi reproached him and quarrelled with him. Then he turned around and headed towards Cappadocia against Sebastea, while all were afraid of the Roman armies. Out of shame for being mocked that he had not been able to achieve anything of what he had planned, he attacked and burned Sebastea with fire, for he could not find booty and prisoners because the entire territory had fled from before him.[22] When he marched on from there, he made clear that he was retreating and therefore marched eastward in order to make his escape, if possible, to his own country. Therefore the Roman armies treated him with contempt when they came into contact with his army, and despised him and took courage against him. When he saw that they had surrounded him and taken up positions against him on all sides, he was forced to flee hastily to the mountain, leaving behind his entire camp and his pavilion, (p.299) which is his tent, and his entire equipment and his baggage-train of gold and silver and pearls, and all his majestic state garments, departing empty-handed. The Romans hastened and entered the camp and took possession of it, slaying whomever they encountered there. And they seized his entire equipment and that of his nobles and also the place of worship of his fire, in which he used to worship, and the horses, which carried and transported it. There some became rich, as some of the Romans found and took royal goods, banded together and took what they had found and fled. And they were never found or seen again. Those who fled and escaped from the camp of the Persians went to their king, crying and saying, 'My lord, the Romans have fallen upon us and have slain many of your servants and have plundered our entire camp and have looted it.' When he had heard these (matters), he replied to them, 'Let them.' For he had ordered that his entire army should surround him and should erect a wall of shields for him. He positioned them in lines while riding between them and beseeched them showing his white hair to them saying, 'My brothers and sons, take pity on my grey hair, attack and fight for the empire of the Persians, lest it be mocked and ridiculed. Behold, I as a

horseman, as one of you, will fight with you.' For his nobles were constantly quarrel-
ling with him, saying, 'Whether we live or die, in us the Persian has gained a bad reputation, because none of the kings of the Persians has ever done what you have done,
that is, you have brought us to die in these mountains.' From these people themselves
the Romans learned what was said amongst them. The Persians had made a plan and
marched (down) on the other side in order to flee (p.300) to a city[23] and moved away
against Melitene. Had there not been hatred and dissension between the commanders
of the Romans, had they but agreed with each other, they would have destroyed him
and his entire army there. After having pledged their word to one another, they split
up and surrounded him. They[24] faced the Patrician Justinian, son of Germanus, and
Justinian became scared and fled from before him, and his fellow (commanders) did
not follow him closely and help him. When he (Khusro) and his army saw (this), they
became encouraged and took heart and attacked Melitene and set fire to it. (tr. van
Ginkel)

Eustratius, *V. Eutychii,* 1719–32: We all know about the incursion into our state by
the godless Persians, when Khusro, the new Nebuchadnezzar, came to Sebastea and
Melitene. There was therefore at that time much suffering and violence: nearly all the
neighbouring peoples – both those around Nicopolis and Neocaesarea, and Comana
as well as Zela, and (those) of other cities nearby – sought refuge in Amasea, as in the
strongest city, encouraged not so much by the city as by the prayers of the holy man
(Eutychius). For both all the local inhabitants and the foreign peoples – most of them
were Iberians – as well as the citizens of other cities placed their hopes, after God, in
him; and paying heed to his mouth and to what was said by him, they were saved.[25]

Evagr. *HE* V.14 (210.20–211.16): (…) But while he (Khusro) was lingering and
whiling away the time,[26] and evading battle, Curs, the Scythian, who was in command
of the right wing, advanced upon him; and since the Persians were unable to stand his
charge, and were most obviously abandoning their formation, he made an extensive
slaughter of his opponents. He also attacked the rear, where both Khusro and the
whole army had placed their baggage, and captured all the royal stores and indeed the
entire baggage. Khusro beheld (this) and endured (it), deeming it more bearable than
a charge of Curs against himself.[27] He (Curs), having together with his troops made
himself master of a great amount of money (p.211) and spoils, and carrying off the
beasts of burden with their loads as well, among which was the sacred fire of Khusro
which was established as a god, made a circuit of the Persian camp, singing songs of
triumph. Around nightfall he arrived at his own army, which had already broken up
from its position. Neither Khusro nor they (the Romans) had begun battle; there had
only been some skirmishing, or just even one man from each camp had joined battle,
such as usually happens. During the night Khusro, having lit many fires, made preparations for a night assault; and since the Romans had formed two camps, he attacked
those in the northern section at the dead of night. On their giving way under this
sudden and unexpected (onset), he advanced upon the neighbouring town of
Melitene, which was undefended and deserted by its inhabitants, and having fired the
whole place, prepared to cross the Euphrates. (…) (tr. Anon., revised)

Sebeos, 68.18–69.8/7–8: This is that Vardan, against whom the Persian king, called

Khusro Anushirwan, came in person with a multitude of armed men and many elephants. Having advanced through the province of Artaz, he crossed Bagrevand and passed beside the city of Karin.[28] And he advanced and came to Melitene and camped opposite it. On the morning of the following day, with great speed they drew up, contingent facing contingent and line facing line, and they engaged one another in battle. The battle intensified over the face of the earth and the battle was fought fiercely. And the Lord delivered defeat to the Persian king and all his forces. They were crushed before the enemies by the edge of the sword and fled from their faces in extreme anxiety. Not knowing the roads of their flight, they went and threw themselves into the great river which is called Euphrates. The swollen river carried away the multitude of fugitives like a swarm of locusts, and not many were able to save themselves on that day. But the king escaped by a hair with a few others, taking refuge in the elephants and cavalry. He fled through Ałznik' (Arzanene) and arrived back at his own residence. And they seized the whole camp with the royal treasures. (p.69) And they took the queen and the women and they took possession of the whole pavilion, the golden carriage of great weight which had been adorned with precious stones and pearls, which having been (so) named was called by them the carriage of glory. The Fire was seized which the king used to take about with him continually for his assistance, which was considered greater than all fires, (and) which was called by them At'ash. It was drowned in the river with the *mobadhan mobadh*[29] and a further multitude of the most senior people. At all times God is blessed.[30] (tr. Greenwood)

Th. Sim. III.14.1–9 also recounts the battle at Melitene and Khusro's retreat, but adds nothing to the sources already cited. See Schreiner 1985: 285 n.426, Whitby and Whitby 1986: 95 n.65.

Following this defeat west of Melitene, Khusro was forced to retreat eastwards in haste, sacking the city *en route*. Much of his army was destroyed as it attempted to ford the Euphrates; such an impression did the expedition leave on Khusro that he passed a law forbidding future Persian kings from undertaking similar campaigns in person.[31]

Joh. Eph. *HE* VI.9 (300.12–302.10): After the Persian had attacked the city of Melitene, he immediately gave orders to set fire to it completely. But when he left in order to cross the Euphrates, heading towards his own country, the commanders of the Roman armies sent him the following message: 'This, what you have done, namely attacking and burning a city, is not in accordance with the stature of a king, namely to create ruins and run away. Even for us ourselves, servants of the emperor, it would be very disgraceful if we were to do what you have done. How much more (is it disgraceful) for you, because you not only think of yourself as a king, but even as the king of kings. For it is not proper for a king to do such deeds, to come with a band of robbers, to plunder, flee, set fire and burn. But it befits a king authoritatively, confidently and regally to take up position openly in battle, and whenever he wins, let him subsequently triumph as a king, and let him not enter as a thief, cause damage, steal and run away. But prepare yourself and we will do battle against one another in the open in order that both victory and defeat will clearly be known to the others.' After he had heard these (things), he ordered a battle on the next day on the plain[32] to the east of the city at some distance from it. (p.301) Before dawn, both parties were lined up against each other a short distance apart. They were lined up, arrayed and facing each other from the dawn until the sixth hour. No man moved from his position and the king was standing behind his army and they looked at each other (wondering) who would start. Certain people have told us these (things) under oath and have narrated to us all these (events). They were the interpreters[33] of the Persians and Romans. (They said): 'Finally we, the three of us, kicked our horses and left the ranks of the Romans for the area in between both parties and we came at full speed up to the edge of the Persian ranks and turned around at full speed without making contact, three times, and we were fast because of the pace of our horses. Both parties were looking intently and staring at us. For we went out in order to provoke them to do battle. Even then none of them moved from his position and went out against us, while they were lined up and arrayed as a wall. They did not even utter a word to each other.' Finally he (Khusro) sent word: 'At the moment there cannot be a battle today, because too much time has passed.' Therefore the armies[34] turned away from each other. At night, before dawn reddened, the king and his army were found near the river Euphrates, making plans and labouring about how he would cross the river, six miles from Melitene, for the Romans pursued him in order to vex and destroy him. This they did achieve. The Persians were pressed together and when the Persian army saw the Roman army in pursuit, they threw themselves on their horses into the river and more than half of his army submerged and drowned. He and the rest, on horses and by swimming, saved themselves with difficulty and got across (the river) and hastily drove on into Roman Armenia. While they marched on quickly, he ordered all villages which they came across (p.302) to be burnt down with fire. In this manner he bent his course to the high mountains of Qurha,[35] where there never had been any road, and he was forced to position his army in front of him in order that they would make a road for him. Therefore they cut timber from the woods and at some places levelled mountains and cut through them and made a road. Thus, confused and worn out, he barely escaped out of the hands of the Romans and entered his own territory. For this reason he made a ruling and made a law that a king should not go out to war, if he does not go out against (another) king. (tr. van Ginkel)

Evagr. *HE* V.14 (211.17–25): When the Roman army had assembled and followed him (Khusro), however, he feared for his own safety, mounted an elephant, and crossed the river. A great multitude of his army found a grave in the waters of the river; realising these men had drowned, he went off and left. Having paid this extreme penalty for his great insolence towards the Roman power, Khusro, with the survivors, regained the eastern (lands), where he had a truce that provided that no one should attack him.[36] (...) (tr. Anon., revised)

Joh. Bicl. a.575?.1 (214.7–16): The Persian king Khusro, with an overwhelming multitude, moved his armies forward to lay waste the Roman borderlands. Against him Justinian, appointed by Tiberius as leader of the Roman army and *magister militum per Orientem*, prepared for war; he had with him extremely brave peoples, who are called Herina[37] in the barbarian language. In the plains which lie between Dara and Nisibis he

157

(Justinian) met him (Khusro) in a fierce engagement and overcame the aforementioned king in battle.[38] When he (Khusro) turned in flight with his army, he (Justinian) overran his camp. The victorious Justinian laid waste the borders of the province of Persia and sent (back) the weapons (taken) from them to Constantinople for the triumph. Among other things (sent) were 24 elephants,[39] which provided a great spectacle for the Romans in the royal city. To the huge benefit of the public purse a multitude of the Persians – the booty from the spoils of the Romans – was put on sale.

Th. Sim. III.14.10–11 (140.5–19): And so the Babylonians (i.e. the Persians), having been defeated, fled as fast as they could, while the Romans, keeping on the offensive, gave the Parthians an experience of evils. Furthermore, in addition to this they also plundered the Persian camp, pillaged the king's tent, and gloriously carried off all their equipment. They captured the elephants and despatched them to the Caesar together with the Persian spoils. (11) When the king of the Persians had been defeated and made his retreat homewards in shame, on coming to Melitene he set fire to the beauty of the city, since he found that it was undefended[40] and enjoying complete quiet. After crossing the Euphrates and making his withdrawal through Arzanene, he inscribed the disgrace of the failure in a law: for he decreed that in future it did not befit the Persian king to travel on expeditions of war.[41] (tr. Whitby and Whitby, revised)

The Roman counter-attack (576–7)

In the wake of Khusro's withdrawal, the Romans went on the offensive; their counter-attack lasted until mid-577. See Whitby 1988: 267.

Evagr. *HE* V.14 (211.25–30): (...) Nevertheless Justinian made an irruption into Persian territory with his entire force, and passed the whole winter season there without anyone troubling (him) at all. He withdrew about the summer solstice without having sustained any loss whatever, and passed the summer near the border, amidst much comfort and renown. (tr. Anon., revised)

Th. Sim. III.15.1–2 (140.20–9): And so when the king of the Persians had thus paraded his misfortune in the law, he was at a loss as to what he should do. But the Roman (army) seized on the Persian disasters and marched towards the interior of Babylonia, ravaged and removed everything in their path, and what they encountered became a victim of destruction. (2) Then they became marines on the Hyrcanian (Caspian) Sea and, after great achievements and the infliction of misfortunes on the Parthians, they did not return to their own (territory); for the winter season intervened on their actions, and disaster waxed fat in Persia. With the arrival of spring the Romans retired, carrying off bravery too as travelling-companion.[42] (tr. Whitby and Whitby, revised)

Joh. Bicl. a.576?.2 (214.25–7): Romanus, the *magister militum*, son of the patrician Anagast, captured the king of the tribe of the Suani alive; he brought him, together with his treasury, his wife and his children, to Constantinople, and subsumed his province within the dominion of the Romans.[43]

The resumption of negotiations (577)

Roman fortunes were at their height in late 576, following Khusro's inglorious retreat.[44] The Persian king therefore sent off Nadoes to reopen negotiations; in response Tiberius despatched Theodore, son of Peter the Patrician, John, Peter and Zachariah to Constantia. The Persian envoy for these talks was the *sarnakhorgan* Mahbodh. Little progress was made at first, as discussion centered around the attribution of blame for the outbreak of war (Menander frg.20.1; Joh. Eph. *HE* VI.12). Probably in 577 Mahbodh proposed that the Romans could obtain peace by resuming their annual payment of 30,000 *solidi*, ceding Persarmenia and Iberia, and handing over those who had rebelled there (Menander frg.20.2.1–15).[45]

Menander frg.20.2.15–69: When Mahbodh made these (proposals), the Roman envoys, as they had been enjoined by the Caesar, immediately said that this could not be called a peace if the Persians hoped to keep the Romans (liable) for a certain sum, as if for the payment of tribute.[46] The Caesar would not accept to pay any of this money nor would he buy peace like something openly for sale. For if this was the case, (the peace) would be neither enduring nor stable. The Roman envoys said that he (Mahbodh) should first therefore renounce this (demand) and thus explore on what terms the (cause) of peace might progress.

And again, for this reason, much verbal sophistry was expended by both sides. Initially the Persians did not give way, but argued that they (the Romans) should either pay the 30,000 *nomismata* (mentioned) above or make one large payment, if needs be. Finally, however, Mahbodh decided to show them a letter which had recently been sent to him by his king, in which he insisted that, on account of (his) friendship for the Caesar, he would offer to renew the peace on equal terms without any money (involved). When news of this spread through the capital, all became excited, and both the authorities and the rest of the populace thought that swords would at once become idle and peace firmly established, since the Caesar too was very ready to hand over Persarmenia and Iberia to the Persians. For he saw very clearly that if they were deprived of this considerable tract of territory, they would never give up, even if Persian fortunes should completely decline and grow weak. (He declared), however, that he would surrender neither the princes of the Persarmenians nor their relatives, nor indeed anyone at all who had willingly deserted to the Romans, and, moreover, that he would make peace only on condition that there should be no impediment to those of the Persarmenians and Iberians who wished to leave their country and migrate to the Roman empire. For the Caesar laid great store by the oaths of the Emperor Justin to the Persarmenians and those of the Iberians who had come over (to him). The emperor had sworn that as far as he was able he would use every means to make their native land subject (to him), but if he proved unable to sustain the war to the end, he would never hand over those who had raised the revolt, their blood relatives and, in short, all those who wished to have a share in the Roman empire.

The Persian king decided to be content with these terms: that the Romans evacuate Persian Armenia and Iberia and that he allow that the inhabitants here should go wherever they wished – not unreasonably, I think – for he knew that, with the exception of a very few of those in office who had initiated the revolt, none of the Persarmenians and Iberians, out of love for their native land, which resides and is lodged in men by nature, would migrate to foreign parts. Furthermore, he also hoped that when the war was ended, he would soon settle the situation in Persarmenia and Iberia. For these lands were highly productive and brought him a very large income. For these reasons therefore the Persian king was willing to end the war on these terms. (tr. Blockley, revised)

Tiberius also sought to regain Dara, offering to buy it back from the Persians (Menander frg.20.2.68–78). A deal was at the point of being struck when a surprise victory of the Persians in Armenia (in summer or autumn 577) brought all the negotiations to nothing. See Whitby 1988: 219 and *PLRE* III, Tamchosroes.

Sebeos, 71.1–4/11: Then came Tamkhusro, and he had two campaigns, one to Basean, at Bolorapahak, where the Murts‘ and Araxes join, and one to Bagrevand, at Kt‘in.[47] And in both he achieved a very great victory. He stayed for two years and he went.[48] (tr. Greenwood)

Th. Sim. III.15.8–9 (141.21–142.4): At that time then, a fierce battle was joined between Romans and Parthians for Armenia, with Tamkhusro commanding the Babylonian force and Justinian leading the Roman throng; the Romans fell short of (their) (p.142) former glory. (9) It was for this reason that the Medes gave up on the peace treaty and their love of war was rekindled again, since they were incapable of moderation because of their recent successes.[49] (tr. Whitby and Whitby, revised)

These Roman defeats, combined with their ill-treatment of the Armenians reported by John of Ephesus (*HE* VI.10, II.24) and alluded to by Menander (frg.23.4), persuaded many to return to their former allegiance (Joh. Eph. *HE* VI.11).[50] See Stein 1919: 70, Turtledove 1977: 265–6.

A raid into Osrhoene, ravaging the area around Constantia, Resaina and Tell Beshme, was undertaken by Adarmahan in 577; the attackers drew off, however, when the people of Constantia warned of the imminent arrival of more forces under Justinian (Joh. Eph. *HE* VI.13).[51]

The resumption of the war in Mesopotamia (578)

Late in 577 Tiberius appointed Maurice *magister militum per Orientem* to succeed Justinian, bestowing on him in addition overall command in the East in an attempt to eliminate the internal dissensions which were plaguing the eastern army.[52] On his way to the frontier, he recruited fresh forces in Cappadocia, and proceeded to Citharizon, where he met up with his fellow commanders (Joh. Eph. *HE* VI.14, 27).[53] Forewarned of the arrival of more Roman troops, Khusro decided to launch a pre-emptive strike in Mesopotamia (probably in June 578); his chief negotiator, Mahbodh, was put in charge of the operation, a calculated insult to the Romans. Mahbodh's army, consisting of 12,000 Persians and 8,000 Sabir and Arab allies, laid waste the region around Resaina and Constantia; it then retreated to Persian territory by way of Thannuris, a Roman fortress now in Persian hands. Simultaneously the Persian commander in Armenia, Tamkhusro, having tricked Maurice into expecting an attack on Theodosiopolis, instead skirted Citharizon and headed south. In a quick raid, lasting under three weeks, he despoiled the country around Martyropolis and Amida (Menander frg.23.1.16–43, 23.6, Joh. Eph. *HE* VI.14, 27, Th. Sim. III.15.11–12).[54] See Honigmann 1935: 22 and Szádeczky-Kardoss 1976: 109–10.

Neither raid brought the Persians any significant advantage (Menander frg.23.5), and Maurice was quick to respond. See Stein 1919: 74. Despite having a fever, he set off eastwards into Arzanene, deporting much of the (Christian) population. He laid siege to the fortress of Chlomaron, but was unable to capture it either by force or by persuasion; he did, however, take Aphumon, and installed a Roman garrison there (Joh. Eph. *HE* VI.15, 34; Menander frg.23.7). A passage from Agathias clearly shows that Maurice penetrated well into Arzanene, reaching almost as far as Corduene.[55]

Agath. IV.29.7–8 (161.7–15): (…) For he (Khusro) happened at that time[56] to be moving towards the Carduchian mountains, to the village of Thamnon, to take up residence (there) for the summer season because of the mildness of the region. (8) Maurice the son of Paul, appointed *magister militum per Orientem* by the Roman emperor Tiberius (II) Constantine, suddenly invaded the land of Arzanene, which is adjacent and close to the territory surrounding the village,[57] and indeed did not cease ravaging and plundering the whole (country) without mercy. After crossing the waters of the river Zirma, he moved up further still, despoiling and burning (whatever) lay close by.[58]

Th. Sim. III.16.1–2 (143.13–21): Accordingly, after Arzanene had thus suffered harm from the Roman spear, the general (Maurice) changed course and invaded the lands of Arabia situated not far from Nisibis in the most direct fashion.[59] (2) Next, after laying waste as far as the river Tigris, he dispatched Curs and Romanus across to the other bank to ravage the entire enemy (territory); but, after he himself had laid waste the fort of Singara, since the winter season was peeping in,[60] he collected his forces and arrived among the Romans. (tr. Whitby and Whitby, revised)

Tiberius followed up Maurice's remarkably successful first campaign with an invitation to the Persians to come to terms. In late 578, around the time of the Emperor Justin's death, he again sent Zachariah, on this occasion accompanied by another Theodore,[61] to Khusro, simultaneously releasing many Persian captives taken during the war[62] (Menander frg.23.8.1–12).

Menander frg.23.8.13–24: 'I too want peace and welcome (it) because it is God-given, just as within me there is a natural friendship with you. Therefore I am prepared to give up all Persarmenia and Iberia, save indeed those of the Persarmenians and Iberians who wish to be subject to us. I both give up the fortress of Aphumon and shall concede Arzanene[63] to you, recovering from you only Dara in exchange for so many things.' These things the Emperor Tiberius indicated to Khusro, and he sent off Zachariah and Theodore with the powers of major envoys[64] to arrange a peace as best they could. (tr. Blockley, revised)

In the meantime, the inhabitants of the Roman frontier provinces prepared for the worst.

Chr. 1234, 73 (209.4–8): (…) At this time,[65] there was anxiety in the cities beyond the Euphrates; and they were steadfast, by night and day, on Sundays and feast-days, in building the walls of the cities; and all were in distress and fear.[66] (tr. M. Greatrex)

Continued negotiations (579)

Khusro had also been sufficiently impressed by Maurice's campaign to despatch an envoy of his own, Ferogdath, in an effort to re-open negotiations on the frontier. He arrived in Constantinople while Zachariah and Theodore were still on their way to Persia, and was offered the same terms as Tiberius had outlined to his own emissaries (Menander frg.23.8.25–57). According to Menander, peace would have been agreed at this point, had not Khusro died before the Roman ambassadors reached Persia (in February or March 579). They proceeded with their mission nevertheless, armed with a further letter from Tiberius, stating that he was willing to make peace with the new king, Hormizd IV, on the same terms as with his father. At the same time Maurice returned to the East from Constantinople, to await developments there (Menander frg.23.9.1–23). But Hormizd proved to be uncompromising and refused to accept Tiberius' terms; he insisted upon the payment of the yearly sums agreed by Justinian, thus undoing all the progress made in negotiations over the previous years. The Roman ambassadors were treated with contempt, and their mission returned to Roman territory after a long and unpleasant stay in Persia (Menander frg.23.9.24–125).[67] The length of time taken up by the fruitless embassy meant that no campaigning was undertaken on the Mesopotamian front in this year.[68] Fighting continued in Armenia meanwhile, where Tamkhusro was succeeded by Varaz Vzur. But the Romans continued to have the upper hand; a notable victory of the commanders Curs and John Mystacon is reported, although so too is a Roman defeat (Sebeos 71/11, Joh. Eph. *HE* VI.28).[69]

Hormizd and the Christians of Persia

Roman sources display a hostile attitude to Hormizd, during whose reign there was a continual state of war with Rome. His son and successor, Khusro II, did nothing to improve his father's image while he was a refugee on Roman soil. The Persian tradition is more varied, and Tabari in particular preserves some material quite favourable to the king.[70] See Nöldeke 1879: 264 n.5, Christensen 1944: 442–3, Bosworth 1999: 295 n.696.

Tabari, I, 991/298 (Nöldeke 268):[71] 'Just as our royal throne cannot stand on its two front legs without the two back ones, our kingdom cannot stand or endure firmly if we cause the Christians and adherents of other faiths, who differ in belief from ourselves, to become hostile to us. So renounce this desire to persecute the Christians and become assiduous in good works, so that the Christians and the adherents of other faiths may see this, praise you for it, and feel themselves drawn to your religion.' (tr. Bosworth)

The Roman offensive of 580

Early in 580, following a visit to Constantinople, Mundhir scored another victory against the Lakhmids, who had sought to exploit his absence from the front (Joh. Eph. *HE* IV.42). See Shahîd 1995: 398–406, Stein 1919: 92, *PLRE* III, Alamundarus.

Only one source, Theophylact, reports the events of 580.[72]

Th. Sim. III.17.3–4 (145.21–146.3): When Hormizd's boastfulness was made plain to the Emperor Tiberius and summer had again arrived, Maurice collected his forces and moved into Persia, after sending Romanus, Theoderic, and furthermore Martin to the far side of the Tigris to lay waste the interior of Media. (4) And so they invaded with the mass of the army, and pillaged the fertile and most fruitful (areas) of the Persians; after spending the whole of the summer season in the slaughter of Persians, they ravaged Media, and wrought destruction with great firmness. (tr. Whitby and Whitby, revised)

The Sasanian diplomatic offensive in the Transcaucasus (c.580)

Soon after the accession of Hormizd, the Persians regained the initiative in the Transcaucasus. As the excerpt below attests, Hormizd's despatch of his son Khusro to Albania successfully loosened the Roman grip on the region. In the light of this manoeuvre, Hormizd's intransigence with Roman peace efforts becomes more understandable. See Toumanoff 1963: 380–2.

HVG 217/228–9: Then Hormizd, the king of the Persians, gave Ran (Albania) and Movak'an to his son, who was called Kasre Ambarvez (Khusro II). He came and took up residence at Partaw, and he began to hold talks with the *erist'avebi* of K'art'li (Iberia). He promised them great benefit and put in writing for them the patrimony of their eristavates from child to child, and thus did he win them over by blandishment. The *erist'avebi* apostasised and began to give individual tribute to Kasre Ambarvez. The children of Bakur remained in the mountainous part of Kakhet'i; and as for the descendants of Mirdat, son of Vakhtang, who ruled in Klarjet'i (Cholarzene) and Javakhet'i, they remained amongst the rocks of Klarjet'i. The Persians took all the rest of K'art'li, Somkhiti (Armenia) and Asp'uragan (Vaspurakan) and began to wage war on the Greeks. (tr. G. Hewitt)

The campaigns of 581

Theophylact also provides the most credible account of the campaign of the following year.[73]

Th. Sim. III.17.5–11 (146.3–28): With the arrival of winter (580), the Roman leader came to Caesarea in Cappadocia, but as the summer (581) came round again, he arrived in the east with the whole army at Circesium, a city of the Romans. (6) Next, he subsequently hastened through the desert of Arabia to reach the land of Babylonia and then to steal a victory by the shrewdness of the enterprise. (7) In this he was accompanied by the leader of the nomadic barbarians (his name was Alamoundarus [Mundhir]) who, they say, revealed the Roman position to the Persian king; for the Saracen tribe is known to be most unreliable and fickle, their mind is not steadfast, and their judgement is not grounded in prudence. (8) Therefore, as a result of this, the king of the Persians transplanted the war to the city of Callinicum, after appointing Adarmahan as a not untalented custodian of the expedition. (9) Then, after Mundhir had like a drone destroyed the beehives (full) of honey, or in other words had ruined Maurice's enterprise, the manoeuvres of the expedition against the Medes became unprofitable for the Romans: for they returned to quench the disasters at home. (10) And indeed the general consigned to burning flames the grain ships which had accompanied him down the river Euphrates; he himself, with the pick of the army, came with all speed to the city of Callinicum. (11) When the Parthian contingents came to grips, the Roman spear won supremacy; then flight came upon the Persians, and their insolence received a check. (tr. Whitby and Whitby, revised)

Joh. Eph. *HE* VI.16–17 (312.15–314.4): Then Maurice and Mundhir, the son of Harith, king of the Arabs, together gathered their armies as one and crossed over into the territories of the Persians by the route through the desert. They penetrated many day-marches into the territories of the Persians, as far as Beth Aramaye. When they had reached the great bridge of Beth Aramaye, full of confidence to cross over it and to capture the important cities of the Persian Empire, it was found that the bridge had been broken down. When the Persians had heard (of their plan), they had broken it down. After they (Maurice and Mundhir) and their troops had seen much hardship, especially the Romans, they came to an argument with one another and turned back without being able to achieve anything to their advantage. Worn out, they could but barely escape and leave for the territory of the Romans. They wrote heavy accusations against one another. Maurice was of the opinion about Mundhir that he had given notice in advance and had informed the Persians (of their plan) and that they had (therefore) broken down the bridge lest they should cross. This was a lie. (p.313) The emperor was deeply concerned, sending messengers to both commanders, and with difficulty he reconciled them with one another. Eventually Maurice went up to the emperor and it is not known whether he accused Mundhir (or not).[74] (17) When the Persians saw that Maurice and Mundhir were descending upon their land and saw that the (Roman) territory was without an army, the *marzban* of the Persians, named Adarmahan, crossed over into the territory of the Romans with many troops and arrived in the territory of Constantia and Resaina. He destroyed and burnt the rest of what they had left the first time. They crossed over into the territory of Edessa, a wealthy region, and burnt and destroyed and ruined the entire region of Osrhoene. Full of confidence and without fear he moved through the region for many days as if he was staying in his own country, while he did not leave one house standing everywhere he passed by, sneering at the entire army of the Romans because it was incapable of guarding it (i.e. the region). Eventually, when Maurice and Mundhir came up from the territory of the Persians, worn out, and he (the *marzban*) heard that they intended to march against him, he sent them the (following) message: 'Since I have heard that you are coming against me to do battle, do not exhaust yourselves by coming, because you are tired from the exertions of the journey, but rest and I will come to you.' Eventually, after the destruction and plunder and the capturing of people which he had accomplished, and after he had led away the captives and had done whatever he wanted, and after he had heard that they intended to march against him, he took with him his loot and all the captives which he had made, and moved to his own territory (p.314), while nobody of the 200,000 Romans who were eating the emperor's meal had attacked him. When he had made up his mind to go, they marched out to go up against him. When they did not catch up with him, they said that he had fled. (tr. van Ginkel)

According to John, Mundhir himself then proceeded to exact revenge on both his Lakhmid and Persian opponents; following a victory in the field, he captured and plundered the Lakhmid camp (Joh. Eph. *HE* VI.18).[75]

***Chr. 1234*, 74 (209.21–210.15):** And Mundhir took forces of the Romans and Saracens and entered Persian territory. They laid siege to a certain fort which was called 'Anat (Anatha). They fought greatly against it; they armed themselves and got on small boats in the waters of the Euphrates, and made war from the boats. But the Persians fought them from the wall with the stones of ballistae, and many were drowned and perished. And they withdrew from there, while taking captives and pillaging the territory. But the leader of the Persians, whose name was Adarmahan, who had gone to Apamea and destroyed it, (p.210) had been left at Nisibis by Khusro. And while the Romans were laying siege to Anatha, he came to Edessa and laid it waste and set fire to it, took captives, slew many, overturned many churches, and came against Callinicum.[76] But the forces who were with Mundhir assembled there; and when they fell upon each other, many of the Persians were slaughtered.[77] And at dawn on the following day, when they were ready to join battle, Adarmahan, knowing that he could not fight with Mundhir, cleverly sent (to him), saying, '(Since) tomorrow is Sunday, let us not go into battle, but on the next day, Monday, let us prepare for battle.' And the Romans agreed. When it was dark the Persians ate and drank, and lit a fire in front of the gates of the tents, as was customary, so that they should be thought to be there; but in the evening they set off and fled. And in the morning none of them was found. But they crossed over to Constantia; they laid waste the monastery of Qartmin and the region of the Tur Abdin and came to Nisibis.[78] (tr. M. Greatrex)

Chr. 819 (10.13–14): And in the year 891 (579/80) the Persians went up again and set fire to the monastery of Qartmin, and Constantia, Carrhae and Edessa.[79] (tr. M. Greatrex)

Evagrius (*HE* V.20 [215.27–216.5]) claims that Maurice defeated Adarmahan, and that Theoderic, who was probably serving as *comes foederatorum*, and his men behaved in a cowardly fashion at the battle.[80]

At the same time as Maurice invaded Lower Mesopotamia, Roman forces were involved in a campaign in Persarmenia, which also met with failure[81] (Menander frg.23.11).

The Persian offensive of 582

As a result of the recriminations which followed the failure of the previous year's campaign,

Mundhir was arrested at Huwwarin (Evaria), south-east of Emesa, and taken to Constantinople. Henceforth the Ghassanids turned their fire against the Romans under the leadership of Mundhir's son Nu'man; Arabia, Syria and Palestine suffered at his hands, and he even laid siege to Bostra. A Roman attempt to appoint another ruler for their allies proved fruitless, and although Nu'man soon voluntarily came to Constantinople, the Ghassanid federation was never again united under the leadership of one chief (Joh. Eph. *HE* III.40–3, 54–6 [chapter-headings only], VI.41–2, Evagr. *HE* VI.2).[82] See Shahîd 1995: 455–78, Stein 1919: 93–5, Sartre 1982a: 190–2, Allen 1981: 246–7.

Tiberius sought to revive negotiations after the campaigning of 581, and Zachariah was despatched to the frontier once again. His interlocutor was Andigan.[83] While the talks were underway, Maurice occupied his troops with the fortification of Shemkhart in eastern Sophanene.[84] Andigan and Zachariah met on the frontier – in tents made ready for the occasion – and went over the same ground as before. Andigan tried to intimidate the Romans through his knowledge of Roman difficulties elsewhere in their empire, but was rebuffed by Zachariah. After Andigan then attempted to put pressure on Zachariah by drawing attention to the army of Tamkhusro mobilised nearby, just outside Nisibis, negotiations were abandoned in favour of conflict. Tamkhusro, accompanied by Adarmahan, advanced westwards towards Constantia, where Maurice, from his base at Monocarton, had been preparing for just such an attack (Menander frg.26.1).[85] Outside Constantia the Romans met Tamkhusro's forces in June 582; in the ensuing battle the Persian commander was killed and his forces defeated. The Persians withdrew, but remained in Roman territory for a further three months (Joh. Eph. *HE* VI.26, Menander frg.26.5, Th. Sim. III.18.1–2).[86] See Whitby 1988: 274, Turtledove 1977: 330.

12

THE REIGN OF MAURICE (582–602)

After ten years of largely inconclusive conflict, neither side ventured on any large-scale campaigns in the following few years. While the Romans tightened their grip on Arzanene, the Persians maintained pressure south of the Tur Abdin, but without any significant gains. Almost the only source available for much of the campaigning is Theophylact Simocatta, who was himself reliant on earlier accounts.[1] See Olajos 1988 and Whitby 1988: 222–42.

The Roman offensive in Arzanene (late 582)

Maurice's successor as *magister militum per Orientem*, John Mystacon, led an army into Arzanene, and was met at the border, at the junction of the rivers Nymphius and Tigris, by the Persian general Kardarigan. The battle which ensued initially favoured the Romans, but dissension among the commanders led to a Roman defeat (Th. Sim. I.9.4–11).[2] See Whitby 1988: 277.

Further campaigning in Arzanene (583)

Arzanene continued to be the focus of military activity in the following year. While the Persians attempted to recapture Aphumon, a Persian fort taken by Maurice in 578, the Roman general Aulus laid siege to Akbas, a recently constructed Persian fortress just east of the river Nymphius and thus right on the Roman border. The Persians besieging Aphumon were able to join the defenders of Akbas in repelling the Romans initially, but by the end of the year the fortress had fallen into Roman hands. Rather than occupy it, the Romans chose to destroy it (Th. Sim. I.12.1–7, Joh. Eph. *HE* VI.36).[3] See Whitby 1988: 277–8, *PLRE* III, Aulus.

The Roman offensive into Beth Arabaye (584)

Much of this year was taken up in unsuccessful negotiations, known only from chapter headings of lost parts of John of Ephesus' *Ecclesiastical History* (VI.37–9) and from a short entry in Michael the Syrian (X.21 [379b/361]).[4] While the talks proceeded, the new *magister militum per Orientem*, Maurice's brother-in-law Philippicus, strengthened the fortifications of Monocarton (Th. Sim. I.14.6). In the autumn came a new Roman strategy: having assembled his forces at Monocarton, Philippicus proceeded to the Tigris. After a lengthy march, he arrived at a place called Carcharoman, from where he proceeded to lay waste the region around Nisibis. Kardarigan, who was about to undertake an offensive into the Tur Abdin, was forced to return eastwards to deal with the incursion. Philippicus withdrew his forces before meeting Kardarigan; some, it appears, went north, while others returned to Roman territory south-west-wards to Resaina (Th. Sim. I.13.1–12, Evagrius, *HE* VI.3 [224.2–6]).[5]

Joh. Eph. *HE* **VI.43** (277.3–5): Concerning famous princes among the Persian *marzbans*, who were taken prisoner and went up in chains to the royal city (i.e. Constantinople).[6] (tr. M. Greatrex)

In this year too the power of the Jafnids was divided following the arrest and deportation of Nu'man.

Joh. Eph. *HE* **VI.41–2** (276.32–277.3): Concerning (p.277) the elevations and abasement of the chiefdom of the Tayyaye of the Romans. (42) Concerning those of the leaders of the Tayyaye who went off (and) surrendered to the Persians. (tr. M. Greatrex)
Mich. Syr. **X.19** (375a/350–1): The kingdom of the Tayyaye was divided between fifteen princes, and many of them inclined towards the Persians; and the empire of the Christian Tayyaye came to an end and ceased to exist because of the treachery of the Romans.[7] (tr. M. Greatrex)

The campaigns of 585

Philippicus resumed campaigning in Arzanene in this year, but then fell ill and entrusted his forces to Stephen and Apsich. The Persians, meanwhile, went on the offensive. Kardarigan moved westwards from Nisibis and laid siege to Monocarton. After failing to capture the fort, he moved northwards across the Tur Abdin and Sophanene towards Martyropolis, where Philippicus was; but having sacked a monastery to the west of the city, he swiftly returned to Persian territory (Th. Sim. I.14.1–10).[8] See Whitby 1988: 279–80.

The campaign of Solachon (586)[9]

When Philippicus returned to the front from Constantinople in spring 586, he was met by the Persian envoy Mahbodh at Amida. The Persians again demanded money in return for peace; and the bishop of Nisibis, Simon, was also sent to convey the same proposals. But Maurice rejected the Persian demands, and the *magister militum* therefore moved southwards, first to Mambrathon, then to Bibas (Th. Sim. I.15.1–15).[10] The Persian commander, Kardarigan, advanced westwards to meet the Romans, but Philippicus had so positioned the Roman forces that the Persians would have to traverse a waterless plain before engaging them (Th. Sim. II.1.1–7).[11]

The Persians, taking with them adequate water supplies, moved towards Constantia and Monocarton. Philippicus, apprised from captured Persians of Kardarigan's movements, arranged his forces for battle in the plain of Solachon, a few miles east of the Arzamon.

Theophylact provides a very full account of this battle, perhaps derived from the campaign journal of Philippicus and/or a source associated with Heraclius, the father of the Emperor Heraclius (Th. Sim. II.2.1–7).[12]

Evagr. *HE* VI.3 (224.6–11): Battle was also joined with the Persians, and, after a hard battle had taken place and many of the most noteworthy Persians had fallen, he (Philippicus) took many prisoners and let go unharmed a detachment which had retreated to one of the opportune hillocks (there), (and) which he could have destroyed; they promised that they would persuade their king to send (an embassy) for peace as quickly as possible. (tr. Anon., revised)

Joh. Eph. *HE* VI.44 (277.5–7): Concerning another war in the third year, and the victory which was given by God to the Romans.[13] (tr. M. Greatrex)

Th. Sim. II.3.1–4.14 offers a detailed account of the battle, drawing attention to Philippicus' use of the 'image of God Incarnate' to inspire his troops.[14] Although the Roman right wing under Vitalius was initially victorious, the desire of the Roman troops to loot the enemy camp might have led to disaster for the Romans in the centre and on the left. Philippicus was able to draw Vitalius' troops back into the fray, however, and the Romans eventually emerged triumphant. Kardarigan escaped to a hill, where he remained for several days. See Whitby 1988: 281. The defeated Persians were refused admission to Dara as they fled. Philippicus, once he had ascertained that no Persian reinforcements were in the vicinity, rewarded soldiers who had distinguished themselves in the battle. Kardarigan and his men escaped from the hill, but not without further losses (Th. Sim. II.5.1–6.13).

Philippicus followed up his victory by an incursion into Arzanene. Although some of the inhabitants of the region offered to collaborate with the Romans, a Roman attempt to capture Chlomaron was thwarted by the arrival of Kardarigan and the union of his forces with those stationed in the city (Th. Sim. II.7.1–8.12). Philippicus was therefore obliged to withdraw his forces to Aphumon, and from there he proceeded to Amida. He then attended to the strengthening of fortifications in the Tur Abdin (Th. Sim. II.9.1–17).[15] When Philippicus fell ill again, it was left to Heraclius to conduct a further invasion of Persian territory. He proceeded across the Tigris, penetrating as far as Thamanon in Corduene before turning southwards, crossing the Tigris once more, and despoiling Beth Arabaye. From there he returned to Amida by way of Resaina (Th. Sim. II.10.1–5).[16]

The campaigns of 587

Philippicus, still unwell, entrusted most of his army to Heraclius, while giving a third of his forces to Theodore, a native of the Tur Abdin, and Andrew[17] (Th. Sim. II.10.6–7). Heraclius undertook a further expedition into Persian territory and succeeded in capturing a well-defended unnamed Persian fortress. Theodore and Andrew for their part, having received intelligence from a local, recaptured the fort of Beiuades (Sina), north-east of Dara, from the Persians and restored that of Matzaron (to the north of Dara). Philippicus then moved to Constantia for the winter (Th. Sim. II.18.1–26).[18]

Mutiny on the eastern front (588–9)

Philippicus, as he returned to Constantinople for the winter (587–588), learnt that he had been replaced as *magister militum per Orientem* by Priscus. He therefore made public Maurice's decree reducing the pay of soldiers by a quarter. Priscus meanwhile advanced to Monocarton, where he had ordered the troops to gather, by way of Antioch and Edessa. In April 588 he arrived at Monocarton, but his demeanour angered the soldiers, and such was his unpopularity that he was forced to withdraw to Constantia (Th. Sim. III.1.3–15, Evagr. *HE* VI.3–4).[19] The soldiers elected Germanus, the *dux* of Phoenice Libanensis,[20] as their leader; efforts at mediation by Priscus through the bishops of Constantia and Edessa met with failure. Maurice therefore restored Philippicus to his command (Th. Sim. III.2.1–11, Evagr. *HE* VI.5–6). The mutiny persisted nonetheless, and 5000 soldiers set out against Edessa. The arrival of Philippicus at Monocarton did nothing to calm the situation; and the Persians exploited it by marching on Constantia.[21] The mutineers, however, repelled the incursion, and proceeded to launch an attack into Persian territory. Tensions within the Roman camp were at last eased by the arrival of Maurice's envoy Aristobulus (Th. Sim. III.3.1–11). The Roman army then moved north to Martyropolis, from where a force was sent out to attack Arzanene; it may have been this force which was defeated by the new Persian *marzban* in Armenia, Aphrahat (Armenian Hrahat), to the west of Lake Van at Tsalkajur (Sebeos 71/12). See Higgins 1939: 32–3. At any rate it was also opposed by the Persian general Maruzas and withdrew towards Martyropolis; near the city a battle was fought, in which the Romans were overwhelmingly victorious. Much booty was captured and sent on to Maurice in Constantinople (Th. Sim. III.4.1–5, Evagr. *HE* VI.9).[22] In October (588) Antioch was struck by a severe earthquake, which, according to Evagrius, killed as many as 60,000 people, and thus inflicted a further financial and demographic blow to the largest city of the East (Evagr. *HE* VI.8). See Allen 1981: 251, Downey 1961: 568–9. In spring 589 the emperor paid the soldiers promptly, while Germanus and other leaders of the rebellion were summoned to Constantinople; there they were tried, convicted, but pardoned (Th. Sim. III.4.6, Evagr. *HE* VI.10).

If Theophylact is to be believed, a remarkable Roman feat took place around the time of the mutiny: Romans captured at Dara in 573, together with imprisoned Qadishaye, succeeded in effecting an escape from the 'Prison of Oblivion' in Khuzistan and fighting their way back to Roman territory (Th. Sim. III.5.1–7, Theoph. A.M. 6080, 261.29–262.2).[23]

The renewal of war (589)

Perhaps prompted by the need to deploy more troops in the Balkans to face the growing Avar threat, Maurice set in motion a co-ordinated Roman offensive to bring about an end to the eastern conflict. Four strands will be noted below: a Roman-sponsored raid by the Iberians and their allies into Albania, the appointment of Romanus to a command in Lazica, an offensive into Persarmenia by the *magister militum per Armeniam* John Mystacon, and an incursion into Beth Arabaye by the Roman forces in Mesopotamia. This last was disrupted by the Persian capture of Martyropolis, but took place later in the year.[24] See Higgins 1939: 40 for this plan.

In April a reconciliation between Philippicus and the troops in the East was brought about at Litarba by Gregory, the bishop of Antioch. The rebels and Philippicus then met at Antioch, and an amnesty was granted (Th. Sim. III.5.10, Evagr. *HE* VI.10–13).[25] Despite their setback near

Martyropolis of the preceding year, the Persians now gained control of the city through the defection of a Roman officer, Sittas. Although Philippicus at once laid siege to the city, he was unable to take it or to prevent a Persian army under Mahbodh and Aphrahat from joining the defenders. Maurice therefore replaced Philippicus with Comentiolus (Th. Sim. III.5.11–16, Evagr. *HE* VI.14, *Chr. 1234*, 78 [214/113–14]).[26] In autumn 589 the new *magister militum per Orientem*, having captured the Persian fort of Akbas and thus tightened the Roman blockade of Martyropolis, undertook an invasion of Beth Arabaye and confronted the Persians at Sisauranon; the outcome was a decisive Roman victory, attributed largely to Heraclius by some and to Comentiolus by others (Th. Sim. III.6.1–5, Evagr. *HE* VI.15).[27]

Events in the Transcaucasus (589)

Since the late 570s the chief theatre of war between the two powers had shifted southwards to the former Armenian satrapies (Justinian's Armenia IV), Mesopotamia and Beth Arabaye. The Persians had in the meantime regained control of Persarmenia, and Hormizd sought to tighten his grip on the region by appointing his son Khusro as the ruler of Albania and Iberia. See p.163 above and Toumanoff 1963: 380–1.[28] Trouble even broke out in Roman Armenia at this time: a plot was formed to murder the commander John (Mystacon), which was foiled by the arrival of the imperial agent Domentziolus. The leader of the rebels, Smbat, was taken to Constantinople but pardoned for his sedition (Th. Sim. III.8.4–8). See Whitby 1988: 291, *PLRE* III, Symbatius 1 (dating the uprising to 589), Higgins 1939: 38–9.

In April 588 the Persian general Bahram Chobin gained a decisive victory over the Turks threatening Persia's north-eastern frontier. From there he proceeded westwards to the Transcaucasus, where he arrived in the following year to repel the Iberians and their allies, who were just beginning to embark on a raid of Albania (Th. Sim. III.6.9–14, Sebeos 73–4/14–15). See Higgins 1939: 38, Thomson and Howard-Johnston 1999: 168.

HVG 217–18/229: After a few years, great troubles arose among the Iranians, for the king of the Turks entered into Iran. The Greeks came and harassed the Persians in Mesopotamia and, penetrating into Persia, began to devastate (it). Then Kasre Ambarvez (Khusro II) left Ran (Albania) and K'art'li (Iberia) and went to the aid of his father. While the Iranians were thus occupied, all the *erist'avebi* of Iberia, of the Upper and Lower (country), conferred and dispatched an envoy to the emperor of the Greeks, asking him to place a king over them from the Iberian royal family, but leaving them as *erist'avebi*, one and all, undisturbed in their principalities. (p.218) The Caesar fulfilled their wish and gave to them as king the son of the brother of Mirdat, Vakhtang's son by (his) Greek spouse, who was named Guaram and who ruled over Klarjet'i (Cholarzene) and Javakhet'i.[29] The Caesar conferred upon this Guaram the dignity of *curopalates* and sent him to (the city of) Mts'khet'a.[30] (Toumanoff, rev. Rapp)

Having received financial support from the emperor, Guaram enlisted some allies and invaded Atropatene in spring 589 (*HVG* 219–20/230). But when news came that Bahram Chobin had defeated the Turks decisively, many of the invaders withdrew, including the Iberians themselves. As anticipated, Bahram then turned his attention to Roman (and allied) territory, undertaking a plundering expedition into Suania. A Roman force under Romanus, operating in

Albania, was forced to withdraw to Lazica after a minor defeat; but in a subsequent engagement by the river Araxes in Albania Romanus gained a notable victory over the Persians. Bahram was then dismissed and insulted by Hormizd, and therefore determined to rebel (Th. Sim. III.6.15–8.3, 8.10–11).[31] See Whitby 1988: 291, Thomson and Howard-Johnston 1999: 168–9, *PLRE* III, 1091.

The rebellion of Bahram Chobin and its impact on the frontier (589–90)

Among the first supporters of Bahram's revolt were the soldiers of Nisibis, recently defeated by Comentiolus, who feared punishment from Hormizd. Supporters of Hormizd were killed and preparations made to march southwards to the heartlands of the Persian kingdom (Th. Sim. IV.1.1–9). Comentiolus naturally profited from the divisions in the Persian camp, and at the end of the campaigning season of 589 captured Akbas (Th. Sim. IV.2.1). John Mystacon for his part, who had been besieging Dvin, proceeded further into Persian territory, overrunning Atropatene (Sebeos 74/16). See Higgins 1939: 39, Thomson and Howard-Johnston 1999: 169. In February 590 Hormizd was deposed before Bahram could oust him, and his son Khusro crowned in his stead. Bahram refused to come to terms with Khusro and, having defeated him in battle on 28 February, seized the throne for himself. Khusro fled to Roman territory and sought Maurice's help in regaining his position (Th. Sim. IV.2.2–12.8, Evagr. *HE* VI.17, *Chr. 1234*, 80 [215–16/115–16]).[32] See Whitby 1988: 292–6 and Higgins 1939: 27–30 (for precise dates).

Naturally Khusro attempted to prove his goodwill to the Romans, sending a message to the garrison of Martyropolis to surrender to the Romans, initially to no effect (Th. Sim. IV.12.9–13.1).[33] In a second petition to the emperor, sent probably in summer 590, Khusro proposed an alliance so that he could be restored to the throne (Th. Sim. IV.13.2–26).[34] On the territories conceded by Khusro to Maurice see Garsoïan 1999: 264–7.

Th. Sim. IV.13.24 (177.23–7): In exchange we give back Martyropolis, we shall forthwith freely offer up Dara, and we shall lay war in the tomb without payment, having established peace by bidding farewell to Armenia, on whose account war ill-fatedly gained free rein among men. (tr. Whitby and Whitby, revised)

Sebeos 76.8–18/18–19: Then king Khusro sent to king Maurice prominent men with gifts and wrote as follows: 'Give me the throne and royal place of my fathers and ancestors and send me an army in support through which I shall be able to defeat my enemy and restore my kingdom, and I shall be your son. I shall give you the regions of Syria – all Aruastan[35] as far as the city of Mcbin (Nisibis) – and out of the land of Armenia the area of Tanuter authority[36] as far as Ayrarat and the city of Dvin, and up to the shore of the lake of Bznunik' and to Arestawan;[37] and a great part of the land of Iberia, as far as the city of Tpklis (Tiflis). Let us observe a pact of peace between us until the death of us both; and let this oath be secure between us and between our sons who will reign after us.'[38] (tr. Greenwood)

Narratio de rebus Armeniae **93–6:** The general Mushel the Mamikonean, called the Taronite, went away to Persia and, once victorious, confirmed Khusro in his rule.[39]

(94) He reigned for 38 years. This man gave all of Armenia, as far as Dvin, to the Emperor Maurice,[40] in return for which he was established as king beneath him. (95) And he received many great gifts and honours from him – he himself and his armies. (96) In the same year the Persian king Khusro sent Mushel to Maurice.

Thus Maurice was presented with the chance not only to obtain peace without any payments but also to make territorial gains unparalleled since 298. See Goubert 1951: 169–70. Despite some opposition,[41] he decided to back Khusro and sent Domitian, bishop of Melitene and a relative of his, to the king at Hierapolis (Th. Sim. IV.14.1–6, Evagr. *HE* VI.18).[42] Bahram meanwhile, having crowned himself king in March, outbid the offer of his rival and proposed to hand over Nisibis and Beth Arabaye to the Romans – to no avail, however (Th. Sim. IV.14.8).[43] News of the emperor's backing for Khusro only emerged late in the year,[44] but as it did, defections to his camp multiplied: his supporters gained control of Atropatene, while the forces of Nisibis also rallied to his side. In late 590 (or early 591) Martyropolis was duly surrendered to the Romans, and Sittas arrested and executed (Th. Sim. IV.15.1–17, Evagr. *HE* VI.19).[45] See Whitby 1988: 298–300, Higgins 1939: 46–7 (suggesting that the handover may not have occurred until early 591). The restoration of the city to Roman control was apparently commemorated by an inscription set up on Khusro's instructions, only fragments of which survived until the nineteenth century. See Mango 1985: 91–104.

Section 1: mention of the Euphrates.
Section 2: … which they had from ancient ?times … to our army it was handed over … to us and …
Section 3: (?In this) manner [we] wrote to our slaves … your state came back to life and waged war against … happened you know. But it is not necessary that what was seized … lest in any way a greater injury follow … those who accomplished such things.
Section 4: mention of the Romans and of Nekra and of today.[46]
Section 5: mention of 'the god, king of kings', which is interpreted as a reference to Khusro himself.[47]
Sections 6–7: … your state … cities by the providence of the gods and fortune … through the army and the might of … which the Romans had at Nekra and now … because we appeared considerate to … I confirmed as we said and because …
Section 8: I wrote to the Romans and … [so that] he might better know (that) we ordered … to be affixed on the gate and just as on the tablet … it was inscribed and affixed in the same manner and to the … of the cities of which by the providence and help … we received for (?) one and each … to be inscribed on a tablet.

The tide continued to turn in Khusro's favour in 591. The Persian king implored the aid of St Sergius, and was careful throughout his stay in Roman territory to appear favourable to Christianity;[48] and soon after his prayer to St Sergius (7 January 591), Zatsparham, one of Bahram's commanders, was killed by forces loyal to Khusro while *en route* to Nisibis. Maurice replaced Comentiolus with Narses at Khusro's request, as well as furnishing him with a loan and troops (Th. Sim. V.1–2, *Chr. 1234*, 81 [216/116]).[49] In February Khusro was acclaimed king at Mardin, close to the Persian border, an event of sufficient magnitude to cause many Syriac sources to date his reign from this point (rather than the previous year). See Higgins 1939: 47–9. The Roman army crossed the frontier in spring 591 and was admitted into Dara, which

Khusro then handed back to Roman control. In response to this gesture, Maurice called Khusro his son – a fateful gesture, as it turned out (Th. Sim. V.3).[50] While the king and the Roman forces of Mesopotamia advanced to the Tigris, probably in June, Mahbodh was sent southwards to seize control of Ctesiphon (Th. Sim. V.6). The main field of conflict was Chnaitha, a region west of Atropatene. Here Bahram unsuccessfully sought to prevent the Roman–Persian army of Khusro and Narses from linking up with the Roman army under John Mystacon advancing from Armenia. The final battle at Ganzak, by the river Blarathos, in late summer was a decisive victory for Khusro and his allies. The bulk of the Roman forces then returned to Roman territory (Th. Sim. V.7–11; Sebeos 79/23).[51] See Higgins 1939: 53–4, with Whitby 1988: 302–3. Bahram himself, having escaped his defeat, continued to oppose Khusro, but to little effect (Th. Sim. V.15.1).[52]

The conclusion of the war (591)

Th. Sim. V.15.2 (216.10–13): The treaty between Romans and Persians proceeded on equal terms, and thus indeed that great Persian war was gloriously brought to an end for the Romans.[53] (tr. Whitby and Whitby, revised)

Sebeos 84.20–32/28–9: Then king Khusro gave gifts to them all according to each one's status and dismissed them from him. He himself set out from Atropatene and reached Asorestan, his own royal residence. He was confirmed on the throne of the kingdom, and he carried out his promise of gifts for the emperor. He transferred to them all Aruastan as far as Nisibis; and the land of Armenia which was under his authority, the Tanuter tun as far as the river Hurazdan, the province of Koteik' as far as the town of Garni, and up to the shore of the lake of Bznik' and up to Arestawan, and the province of Gogovit as far as Hats'iwn and Maku. The region of the Vaspurakan gund was subject to the Persian king. Out of the Armenian nobles, many were in the Greek sector, and a few in the Persian. But the king summoned Mushel to the palace, and he saw his country no more.[54] (tr. Greenwood)

On the territories ceded by the Persians to the Romans, see also p.172 above. Iberia was probably divided between the two powers, each acquiring a zone of influence in a theoretically independent kingdom (*HVG* 221/230–1). See Toumanoff 1963: 384–6, Martin-Hisard 1998b: 1178. Maurice reorganised the whole of Roman Armenia following these gains. Because these new arrangements were only fully operational for at most a decade, their impact on frontier defence and organisation is unclear.[55]

The optimism which attended the peace is well brought out in a *Life* of St Golinduch, a Persian convert to Christianity who came to Roman territory in the 580s, which was compiled in 602 by Eustratius.[56]

Eustratius, *V. Golinduch* 23 (170.1–26): Nor were these things alone in this condition.[57] And through the help of God, the aforementioned most holy man (i.e. Domitian) well directed the movement of affairs; and 'he broke down the wall that separated them' (Eph. 2:14) and 'he abolished the law of the commandments in decrees' (Eph. 2:15). Christ our God, again in person through those worthy of himself, that is, through the priest and the king,[58] pacified the states. Both (nations), belonging by nature to God and granted by him to those worthy (of him) came to an agreement, both according to the kinship of the union in the flesh and according to the purpose of the gifts of the Holy Spirit (cf. 1 Cor. 12:1–4), that is, of the high priesthood and the kingship.[59]

Hence Christ is both our high priest and king and is named according to Melchizedek (cf. Heb. 5:5–10 and elsewhere), and the angel which told the good news to the mother of God and ever-virgin Mary said: 'Behold, you will conceive in your womb and bear a son, and you shall call his name Jesus. He will be great and will be called the Son of the Most High; and the Lord God will give to him the throne of his father David, and he will reign over the house of Jacob for ever; and of his kingdom there will be no end.' (Luke 1:31–3) When therefore through the assistance of the true and natural high-priest and king Christ our God and through both his servants, both we and the Babylonians gained a peaceful end (to the war), the cities – both that of the Holy Martyrs (i.e. Martyropolis) and Dara – were given back to our Christ-loving state. (The peace was accomplished) through their embassy and the recently slain martyr Golinduch,[60] also known as Mary; (and) the aforementioned most holy man (Maurice) invited the victorious woman to present herself in the ruling city of the Christians … .[61]

The years of peace (591–602)

The situation of both powers in the last decade of the sixth century favoured peace. Maurice was occupied in combatting the serious Avar threat in the Balkans, while Khusro was faced with a rebellion by Bestam, whose brother Bindoes he had executed.[62] Just as in the opening years of the fifth century, the two powers were in constant contact. See Sako 1986: 106.

Between late 591 and early 592 Khusro despatched gifts to the shrine of St Sergius at Sergiopolis. The text which accompanied the gifts is preserved by both Theophylact and Evagrius.[63]

Evagr. *HE* VI.21 (235.10–236.16), cf. Th. Sim. V.14.4–6 (212.21–213.20): Khusro, having become master of his own kingdom, sent to Gregory a cross, adorned with much gold and with precious stones, in honour of the victorious martyr Sergius; this (cross) Theodora, the wife of Justinian, had dedicated, and Khusro had carried off with the other treasures, as has already been mentioned by me. He also sent another golden cross, and Khusro engraved these things on the cross in the letters of the Greeks: 'This cross I, Khusro, king of kings, son of Khusro (have sent).[64] Because[65] of the diabolic action and evil-doing of the most ill-fated Bahram Gushnasp and the cavalrymen with him, we fled to Roman territory;[66] and because the ill-fated Zatspharam came with an army to Nisibis to incite the cavalry of the district of Nisibis, we too sent cavalrymen[67] with a commander to Charcha. And through the fortune of the all-holy and famous saint Sergius, since we had heard that he was the granter of petitions,[68] in the first year of our reign,[69] on 7th January, we petitioned that, if (p.236) our cavalrymen should slay or capture Zatspharam, we would send a jewelled cross to his home. And on 9th February they brought the head of Zatspharham to us. Therefore, having gained our request, because each element was unambiguous, we sent to his all-holy name this cross,[70] which had come into our possession, together with the cross sent by Justinian, emperor of the Romans, to his house, and which, in the time of the estrangement of the two states, had been brought here by Khusro, king of kings, son of Kavadh, our father, and was found among our treasures. (These crosses we have sent) to the house of the all-holy saint Sergius.' Gregory, having received these crosses, with the approval of the Emperor Maurice, dedicated them with much ceremony in the sanctuary of the martyr.

Persecution of Monophysites in the Roman East (590s)

Gregory then seized the opportunity to strengthen the Chalcedonian position in the frontier region, where opposition to the council had always been strong. Khusro's patronage of St Sergius may have been loosening the natural bonds between Christians (especially Monophysites) and Romans.[71]

Evagr. *HE* VI.22 (238.22–8): Gregory too, after Khusro had given the crosses, visited the wastelands of the (areas) called *limites* (i.e. frontiers), where the doctrines of Severus extensively prevailed, with the approval of the government. He expounded the doctrines of the church and brought into union with the Church of God many garrisons, villages, monasteries, and entire tribes.[72] (tr. Anon., revised)

Soon afterwards, in 598/9, stronger measures were taken by Domitian at Edessa and throughout Mesopotamia to enforce adherence to the Council of Chalcedon; Monophysite sources allege that the persecutions inflicted were brutal (*Chr. 724*, 145/17, AG 910, *Chr. 819*, 10/76, AG 910, *Chr. 1234*, 82 [217–18/117–18], Mich. Syr. X.23 [386–7b/118 n.270]).[73] Such policies can hardly have endeared the imperial government to the inhabitants of the region, the majority of whom were opposed to Chalcedon. As will be seen, when the Persians took over Osrhoene and Mesopotamia, they were able to restore Monophysite bishops to their sees and thus gain useful support.[74]

Khusro's continuing patronage of the shrine of St Sergius (593/4)

Even once secure on his throne, Khusro continued to honour the shrine of St Sergius. Between spring 593 and the following spring he sent a further collection of gifts, including a gold paten, to Sergiopolis, to thank the saint for the conception of his Christian wife, Shirin (Th. Sim. V.14.1–12, Evagr. *HE* VI.21 [236.20–238.12]).[75] Both Sebeos (85/29–30) and Tabari (1000/314) emphasise Khusro's toleration of Christianity, leading to legends according to which he was even converted.[76] The king also built three churches, which were consecrated by Anastasius, the patriarch of Antioch (*Chr. 1234*, 81 [217/117], Mich. Syr. X.23 [387a/117 n.267], *Chr. Seert* 58, *PO* 13.466–7, cf. Agap., *PO* 8.447). See Labourt 1904: 209, Flusin 1992: II, 101–2.

At some point after the conclusion of peace, probably in 592, tension rose again between the two powers. The cause was a raid by Arabs allied with the Romans on Persian territory.[77]

Th. Sim. VIII.1.3–8 (283.19–284.19): For this reason the Emperor Maurice despatched to Persia as ambassador George, who held charge of the tax collection of the eastern cities; Romans call this man praetorian prefect. (4) And so Khusro, complaining at what had happened, made trouble for the ambassador and brought about for him a long delay in the barbarian country; (p.284) George therefore was harshly treated for many days in Persia without gaining any access to the king. (5) Then, since affairs for Khusro were still in confusion,[78] the notion occurred to the barbarian, (quite) reasonably, that he should not begin a war against the Romans for the moment; then the Babylonian king admitted George into the palace. (6) And so George, gaining the moment as his ally,[79] persuaded the barbarian not to dissolve the peace treaty. And so, in this way, Khusro 'willingly yet with unwilling heart', according to the poem,[80] welcomed quiet. (7) And so the ambassador reported in full to the emperor all that had occurred, but his exposition of the conversation did not gain a good conclusion. For in addressing the emperor George said: 'The king of the Persians stated these things in the hearing of the satraps: "On account of the ambassador's excellence, I grant deliverance from war."' (8) On hearing this, the emperor grew angry with the ambassador, and the success of his mission became perilous for George. For, in truth, speech that is not regulated by moderate (words) knows how to provide great misfortunes for its practitioners. (tr. Whitby and Whitby, revised)

Joh. Epiph. 1 (*FHG* IV.273): Book 1 of the Histories of John of Epiphania, *scholasticus* and former prefect, concerning the attack by Khusro (II) on Maurice, the Roman Emperor.

The losses, which the Romans and the Persians bore and inflicted when they were fighting each other during the reign of Justinian, the Roman Emperor, have been related by Agathias of Myrina, a man who was outstanding amongst the lawyers in Byzantium. Writing later than Procopius of Caesarea, he related what had been achieved against the barbarians. Since this is the most momentous event of which we have heard, I shall relate how the Persian king, after he had been expelled from his own kingdom, became a refugee from his native country and approached the Roman state and how he requested the Emperor Maurice to grant him an alliance and to restore him to his kingdom. (I shall do this) not relying on any superiority of style or indeed as a result of (my) earlier <training>, but in order that so momentous an event should not remain unknown to posterity, since even the greatest deeds, if they are not in some way or other preserved in writing and handed down by memory, are extinguished in the darkness of silence. For written accounts give life to events that have passed.

I did not consider it strange therefore to give, as far as I was able, an account of what took place to those who did not know about these matters, since I had a part in some of the events which took place and I had been in talks with Khusro the younger himself as well as with other very distinguished Medes; previously, as an *assessor* to Gregory, the archbishop of Antioch, I happened frequently to have taken part with him in conversations with them (the Persians) and later, after the end of the war, I also happened to go to Persia, accompanying George, who was making a concord for what had happened.[81] It is necessary for the understanding of (generations) to come to have an accurate knowledge also of the main events that had happened previously, not least of those relating to the rising against Hormizd, the father of Khusro. Therefore I think that first I should recall briefly previous events, and then come to the remaining narrative, so that those who (already) know should call to mind the disturbances, and that those who have not heard (about them) at all should be able to obtain a clear knowledge of the origins from which the subsequent events arose. (tr. Donovan, revised)

Embassies continued to journey between Constantinople and Ctesiphon, the majority of them undertaken by churchmen. Thus in c.596/7 Probus, bishop of Chalcedon, visited the Persian court and was well received by Khusro; the Persian king responded in kind, despatching Milas, bishop of Senna, to Maurice (Th. Sim. V.15.8–11, *Chr. Seert* 67, *PO* 13.494, 78, *PO* 13.514).[82] Concrete political ends were served by some of these missions, for the Persian *catholicos*, who was in regular correspondence with Maurice, asked the emperor to release captives he had taken in Arzanene, Bezabde, Beth Arabaye and Singara in order to elicit a reciprocal gesture from Khusro and to strengthen the good relations between the two rulers (*Chr. Seert.* 67, *PO* 13.493).[83] See Sako 1986: 113.

The increasingly prominent role of Christians in Persia may have intensified the disputes which had always plagued them. After the *catholicos* Sabrisho gave his support to Henana of Nisibis against the city's bishop, Gregory of Kashgar, the latter left the city. Around the year 599, the city rose in revolt and slew the Persian governor; how far this was connected to disputes within the Nestorian Church is uncertain. Khusro soon quelled the uprising, despatching a *nakhveragan* with an army to retake the city. Promises of clemency made by bishops sent with the army proved to be empty, and a massacre ensued (*Chr. Khuz.* 18–19, *Chr. Seert* 75, *PO* 13.514).[84]

Armenia and Iberia between the two powers (591–602)[85]

The Armenian nobles, under Musheł Mamikonian, supported Khusro in his campaign against Bahram. Although the king soon fell out with Musheł, who therefore left Armenia to serve the Romans in the Balkans (Sebeos 81–4/25–9, 90–1/36),[86] Khusro made great efforts to ingratiate himself with the Armenians who remained in Persian territory. He was assisted in this by Maurice's wish to move large numbers of Armenians to the Balkans, a policy fiercely resisted by most Armenians (Sebeos 86–7/31–2). See Goubert 1951: 204–6, Thomson and Howard-Johnston 1999: 176–7. But Khusro's attempt to exploit this anti-Roman feeling was thwarted by the Armenians themselves, who robbed an official sent to win them over, and a joint Roman–Persian force soon crushed this rebellion (Sebeos 87–8/32–4). See Grousset 1947: 256–7, Thomson and Howard-Johnston 1999: 176, dating the episode to 594–595. A further rebellion in Roman Armenia was also put down by the Roman commander Heraclius after the rebels had sought refuge in the mountains of Corduene (Sebeos 89–90/34–5).[87] While Smbat Bagratuni proved to be a loyal servant of Persian interests (on the north-east frontier of the Sasanian kingdom),[88] Atat Khorkhoruni, who was summoned to Constantinople in 601 to serve in the Balkans, proved less obedient. He returned to Armenia while on his way to the capital, and withdrew as far as Nakhchawan, in Persian territory. A Roman army was sent against him, and even advanced to Nakhchawan, thus crossing the frontier; it retreated, however, upon the approach of a Persian army (Sebeos 104–5/55–6). See Goubert 1951: 204–6, Thomson and Howard-Johnston 1999: 189.[89] Maurice's last effort to effect a large-scale transplantation of the Armenians to the Balkans was foiled both by Atat's flight and by his own sudden death in the following year (Sebeos 105/56).[90]

As we have seen, Maurice had restored Roman influence in Iberia through the appointment of Guaram as *curopalates* in 588. But his descendants did not prove loyal, and in the early seventh century Stephen I aligned himself with Khusro II in his attacks on the Roman empire (*HVG* 223/232). Iberian Christianity remained unaffected, however. Coins were issued in the late sixth century, modelled on the silver drachms of Hormizd IV, but making use of Christian images. See Toumanoff 1963: 389–90, 428–34, Lang 1983: 523. It was also in this period that the Iberian Church broke from the Armenian, but remained in communion with the Church of Constantinople. See Martin-Hisard 1998b: 1222–33, Garsoïan 1999: 307–53.

The Roman view of the Persians and their army (late sixth century)

The *Stratēgikon* attributed to the Emperor Maurice offers a glimpse of Roman intelligence and the methods devised to counter Persian tactics. Although the account is clearly hostile, the description given reflects an awareness of Persian customs and methods. See Dagron 1987: 209–13, Lee 1993a: 103–4.[91] Many of the observations made here correspond to what is known of the Persian campaigns outlined in this work.[92]

(Maurice), *Stratēgikon* XI.1 (354–60): The Persian nation is wicked, dissembling, and servile, but at the same time patriotic and obedient. The Persians obey their rulers out of fear, and the result is that they are steadfast in enduring hard work and warfare on behalf of the fatherland. For the most part they prefer to achieve their results by planning and generalship; they stress an orderly approach rather than a brave and impulsive one. Since they have been brought up in a hot climate, they easily bear the hardships of heat, thirst and lack of food. They are formidable when laying siege, but even more formidable when besieged. They are extremely skilful in concealing their injuries and coping bravely with adverse circumstances, even turning them to their own advantage. They are so intractable in negotiations that they will not initiate any proposal, even one they regard as vitally important for themselves, but will wait until the proposal is made by their opponents.

They wear body armour and mail, and are armed with bows and swords. They are more practised in rapid, although not powerful, archery than all other warlike nations. Going to war, they encamp within fortifications. When the time of battle draws near, they surround themselves with a ditch and a sharpened palisade. They do not leave the baggage train within, but make a ditch for the purpose of refuge in case of a reverse in battle. They do not allow their horses to graze, but gather the forage by hand.

They draw up for battle in three equal bodies, centre, right, left, with the centre having up to four or five hundred additional picked troops. The depth of the formation is not uniform, but they try to draw up the cavalrymen (p.356) in each company in the first and second line or phalanx and keep the front of the formation even and dense. The spare horses and the baggage train are stationed a short distance behind the main line. In fighting against lancers they hasten to form their battle line in the roughest terrain, and to use their bows, so that the charge of the lancers against them will be dissipated and broken up by the rough ground. Before the day of battle a favourite ploy of theirs is to camp in rugged country and to postpone the fighting, especially when they know their opponents are well prepared and ready for combat. When it does come to battle, moreover, especially during the summer, they make their attack at the hottest hour of the day. They hope that the heat of the sun and the delay in beginning the action will dampen the courage and spirit of their adversaries. They join the battle with calmness and determination, marching step by step in even and dense formation.

They are really bothered by cold weather, rain, and the south wind, all of which ruin the effectiveness of their bows. They are also disturbed by a very carefully drawn-up formation of infantry, by an even field with no obstacles to the charge of lancers, by hand-to-hand combat and fighting because volleys of arrows are ineffective at close quarters, and because they themselves do not make use of lances and shields. Charging against them is effective because they are prompted to rapid flight and do not know how to wheel about suddenly against their attackers, as do the Scythian nations. They are vulnerable to attacks and encroachments from an outflanking position against the flanks and rear of their formation because they do not station sufficient guards in their battle line to withstand a major flank attack. (p.358) Often, too, unexpected attacks at night against their camp are effective because they pitch their tents indiscriminately and without order inside their fortifications.

To do battle against them our forces should be drawn up as prescribed in the book on formations. Select open, smooth and level terrain, if you can do so, without any swamps, ditches or brush which could break up the formation. When the army is pre-pared and lined up for battle, do not delay the attack if you have really decided to fight a pitched battle on that day. Once you get within bowshot make the attack or charge in even, dense, regular order, and do it quickly, for any delay in closing with the enemy means that their steady rate of fire will enable them to discharge more missiles against our soldiers and horses.

If it is necessary to fight on very rough ground, it is better not to have the whole battle line on horseback in such places, but to draw some up in infantry formation while others remain mounted. When lancers attack archers, as we have said, unless they maintain an even, unbroken front, they sustain serious damage from the arrows and fail to come to close quarters. Because of this they require more even ground for such fighting. If the army is not really ready for combat, it must not engage in a pitched battle. Instead, employ it safely in skirmishes and raids against the enemy, which can be done smoothly on favourable terrain. Neither the enemy nor our own troops should be allowed to discover the reason for putting off a pitched battle, since it would embolden the one and make cowards out of the other. Wheeling or turning around in withdrawals should not be directed against the enemy's front, but to turn up their flanks and take their rear. For as a result of their efforts not to break up their formation while in pursuit, (p.360) the Persians easily expose their rear to forces wheeling around against them. By the same token, if a force withdrawing before them wants to turn about and attack the front lines of the pursuing Persians, it will suffer injury on running into their well-ordered ranks. For the Persians do not attack in a disorderly fashion as the Scythians do in pursuing, but cautiously and in good order. For this reason, as has been said, forces wheeling about should not attack their front, but should be sure to go by the flanks against their rear. (tr. Dennis, rev. Burgess)

13

THE PERSIAN TAKEOVER OF THE NEAR EAST (602–22)

Unrest in the Roman army in the Balkans led to Maurice's downfall in 602. Phocas seized the imperial throne in November that year, executing Maurice and all his family (with the possible exception of his eldest son, Theodosius). As protocol had established, Phocas informed the Persians soon afterwards of the change of ruler.[1]

Th. Sim. VIII.15.2–7 (313.16–314.16): In the fifth month,[2] having set out his own proclamation in writing, the tyrant dispatched Lilius[3] to Khusro, selecting him as the messenger of his tyrannical election: for it was customary for Romans and Persians to do this whenever they ascended to the royal might. (3) Lilius came to Dara, carrying regal gifts. Germanus, who was adorned with the rank of the consuls and had received charge of the army arrayed there, received him with exceptional splendour. (4) For shortly before the time of the tyranny, when the Persian king Khusro had been roused to hatred of[4] the commander Narses, the Emperor Maurice had relieved the leader Narses[5] of custody of Dara (p.314) and had appointed Germanus instead; Maurice wished thereby to calm the Babylonian ill-temper. (5) Now while Germanus and Lilius were out riding, forming a pair, during the third day a military man struck the mounted Germanus with a sword. (6) And so Germanus dismounted from his horse and arrived home carried in a litter; but since the consequences of the sword-thrust did not gain influence in a vital place, Germanus was cured of the blow in a few days. Then, after he had been made better by medicines, he gave an exceptionally notable feast for Lilius, and sent him on to Khusro. (7) And so Khusro exploited the tyranny as a pretext for war, and mobilised that world-destroying trumpet: for this (tyranny) became the undoing of the prosperity of the Romans and Persians. For Khusro decided to pretend to uphold the hallowed memory of the Emperor Maurice. And so in this way the Persian war was allotted its birth, and Lilius remained among the Persians in great hardship. (tr. Whitby and Whitby, revised)

Sources from 603

With the end of Theophylact's *History* the evidence available to us on the eastern front diminishes appreciably. The chronology of the following twenty years at least is difficult to determine with any precision; nearly all dates must be regarded as approximate. A few contemporary sources may be mentioned here, the most important of which are in Syriac. The *Chronicle of 724* (also known as that of Thomas the Presbyter and referred to by Palmer [1993] as 'a chronicle composed about AD 640') contains some useful notices. See Hoyland 1997: 118–20. The *Chronicle of Guidi*, also known as the *Khuzistan Chronicle*, composed slightly later in the seventh century, furnishes a different perspective – that of a Nestorian Christian, living and writing in what was, at the time of these events, Sasanian territory. Cf. Hoyland 1997: 182–5, arguing for a date of composition not later than the 660s. The *Chronicon Paschale*, composed in Greek in Constantinople around 630, contains some useful entries, particularly for events later in the reign of Heraclius. See Whitby and Whitby 1989: xi, 190–1. But the source most commonly used to construct an account of this period is the early ninth-century Byzantine chronicler, Theophanes, supplemented by material in still later Syriac sources, such as the *Chronicle of 1234* and Michael the Syrian. Recent studies have shown, however, that all these three sources, as well as the Christian Arabic chronicler Agapius of Manbij (Hierapolis), were drawing much of their information on this period from a common source, identified convincingly as Theophilus of Edessa, who composed a chronicle around the year 750.[6] The tenth-century Nestorian work, the *Chronicle of Seert*, may well also have drawn on this common source.[7]

For the history of this period,[8] two obvious conclusions impose themselves. On the one hand, insofar as by a comparison of these later sources we can arrive at some sort of reconstruction of Theophilus' chronicle, we can gain access to an earlier (and clearly quite well informed) source. On the other hand, these various sources cannot now be seen as independent witnesses: if Michael the Syrian and Theophanes agree on a certain event, this merely shows that they were almost certainly here both deriving their information from a common source, Theophilus of Edessa. No greater weight should be given to a date or event below simply because it is reported by several of these sources.[9]

We should also point out that we have offered few translations of the relevant Syriac sources, since they are for the most part readily accessible in Palmer 1993. In Chapter 15 we have offered, however, a translation of the whole first part of the *Khuzistan Chronicle*, of which none (in English) is yet available.

Khusro's invasion and the rebellion of Narses

The usurpation of Phocas gave Khusro an ideal opportunity to turn the tables on his former allies and helpers.[10] Having recently suppressed the rebellion of Bestam and quelled the uprising in Nisibis, he was further assisted by the relative quiet of the north-eastern front since Bahram Chobin's successes. The defence of the Roman east was complicated by several factors: first, opposition to Phocas. Narses, unhappy at his removal from Dara, at some point rebelled openly against Phocas and seized control of Edessa. Second, Khusro sent someone purporting to be Maurice's son Theodosius with his invading armies, thus appealing to those of the population who looked back with favour on Phocas' predecessor. See Thomson and Howard-Johnston 1999: xxii.[11]

Narses' revolt broke out in late 603. See Stratos 1968: 59, *PLRE* III, Narses 10. It seems highly unlikely (despite the report of Pseudo-Dionysius below) that he actively collaborated with Khusro: when the Persians advanced westwards, he withdrew to Hierapolis (rather than unite with the Persian forces). See Olster 1993a: 93.

Chr. 819 (10.23–4), cf. *Chr. 846* (230.16–17): And in the following year (AG 913 = 601/2) Narses entered Edessa, occupied it and there stoned the bishop Severus.[12]

Ps. Dion. 148.9–12: In the year 914 (602/3) Narses, commanding the army of the Persians, crushed Edessa, entered it and captured Severus, the bishop of the city; and he stoned him, and he (Severus) died. (tr. M. Greatrex)

Theoph. A.M. 6095 (291.27–292.1): Narses the Roman general rose up against the tyrant and seized Edessa. And so Phocas wrote to the general Germanus to lay siege to Edessa; Narses wrote to Khusro, the Persian king, to collect his forces (p.292) and make war on the Romans. (tr. Mango and Scott, revised)

Khusro probably invaded Roman territory towards the end of 603. Whether Germanus was sent to besiege Narses in Edessa is uncertain, since *Chr. 1234* (85, 220/121) and Michael the Syrian (X.25, 390b/379) state that it was a certain John (Iwannis) who attacked and took the city. See Olster 1993a: 93–4.

The siege and capture of Dara (604)

After a siege of at least nine months, Dara fell to Khusro in summer 604; Khusro must therefore have begun his attack in November 603 at the latest[13] (*Chr. 724*, 145/16, AG 915, Mich. Syr. X.25 [390a/122 n.279], AG 915, *Chr. Khuz.*, 21).

The fullest account of the events of 604 is provided by Theophanes. The provenance of his material is uncertain: it is not to be found in any of the Syriac sources.

Theoph. A.M. 6096 (292.6–25): (…) And Khusro, the Persian king, collected a great force and sent it against the Romans. When Germanus heard of this, he was afraid, but began the war under compulsion. When Germanus was wounded in battle, his bodyguards brought him safely to Constantina; and the Romans were defeated.[14] And on the eleventh day Germanus died. Phocas conveyed the forces from Europe to Asia after increasing the tribute to the Khagan, thinking the Avar nation to be at rest. Dividing the armies, he sent <one part> against the Persians and the other part to the siege of Edessa, against Narses, under the command of the eunuch Leontius, who was one of his magnates.[15] Khusro collected his forces and came against Dara. Narses departed from Edessa and took refuge at Hierapolis. Khusro met the Romans at Arxamoun[16] and, putting together a fort from (his) elephants, began the war[17] and won a great victory. He captured many of the Romans and beheaded them. When these things had been done, Khusro returned to his own land entrusting his forces to Zongoes.[18] When Phocas learnt of this, he was angered at Leontius and brought him ignominiously to Byzantium in iron fetters; and he appointed Domentziolus, his own nephew, as general, and made him *curopalates*.[19] (tr. Mango and Scott, revised)

Further information on Phocas' attempts to deal with the eastern frontier are provided by a contemporary source, the *Life of Theodore of Sykeon* composed by the saint's disciple George; it is a work of immense value as an account of life in Asia Minor in the period immediately preceding the Persian invasions in the 610s. Theodore's monastery lay close to the main road between Constantinople and Antioch, not far from Ancyra, and he therefore received visits from many important figures travelling to and from the East.[20]

V. Theod. Syk. ch.120.1–11 (96): And not many days later the Emperor Maurice was slain, and Phocas took over the kingdom. When his nephew Domitziolus became a patrician and *curopalates* he was sent by the emperor to the East to take over the army and to marshal his forces against the Persian people, which was attacking and pillaging our territories. The aforementioned illustrious man, when he had come as far as Heliopolis,[21] learnt of the raid of the Lazi as far as Cappadocia and of the plot of the patrician Sergius, the father-in-law of the emperor, and was in much grief and fear, not daring to complete the remainder of the journey.[22]

Following the capture of Dara, Khusro took no further part in the campaigning. His place was taken by Rasmiozan, a Persian general more commonly known by his title of Shahrvaraz.[23]

Between 604 and 610 all the remaining Roman cities east of the Euphrates were taken. It is impossible to arrive at any firm chronology of this conquest, and the following dates should therefore be regarded only as approximate.[24] The Persians, it is clear, were operating in both Osrhoene and Mesopotamia, assaulting the Roman fortresses of the Tur Abdin (which had never before fallen to them), such as Cephas, and Amida further north, and Resaina, Edessa and Callinicum in the south. Given the large Roman expenditure on fortifications over the sixth century, especially under Justinian, it should not occasion surprise that the conquest took so long even in the absence of a Roman army in the field.[25] The crumbling of the Roman defences brought about a large emigration westwards, across the Euphrates (*Chr. 724*, 146/17, AG 922),[26] as it became ever clearer that Khusro's war was going to be very different from that waged by his grandfather. Roman resistance will have been further weakened by the capture and execution of Narses in 604 or 605. See *PLRE* III, Narses 13 and Stratos 1968: 60.

In either 606/7 (*Chr. 1234*, 86 [221/122], AG 919,[27] Mich. Syr. X.25 [391a/122 n.279], AG 918, cf. Jac. Ede. *Chr.* 324/38)[28] or 608/9 (*Chr. 724*, 146/17, AG 920, cf. Agap. *PO* 8.449) Mardin and Amida fell, followed by Resaina in summer 607 or 609. Cephas was captured six months before Mardin, and upon learning of this, the Roman garrison at Mardin withdrew, leaving the fortress's defence to local monks (Mich. Syr. X.25, 390–1a/122 n.279). Thus both the inability of the Romans to relieve the embattled cities and the tenacity of their inhabitants are in evidence; but as the campaigns continued, their zeal waned. Khusro, no doubt in an effort to win the support of the inhabitants of his newly conquered territories, restored the anti-Chalcedonian bishops to their sees, removing those who supported the council. Some bishops who had been expelled by Domitian in 598/9 and had sought refuge in Egypt now crossed into Persian territory to resume their positions. Allegiance to their creed now took precedence over loyalty to the empire, and the victories of the Persians were seen as a judgement on the beliefs of the Chalcedonians (*Chr. 1234*, 89 [224/125–6], Geo. Pis. *Contra Severum*, *PG* 92.1625, 47–55, Mich. Syr. X.25 [389–91c/126 n.283], Barhebraeus, *Chronicon ecclesiasticum*, 263–7).[29] There were no Roman counter-attacks, perhaps because of the rebellion of Heraclius, which began in 608; but even before then, Roman forces may have preferred to remain west of the Euphrates. This war was thus already quite different from those of the sixth century: not only were there no Roman counter-strikes, but the Persians clearly aimed at annexing the cities and territories they overran. As the *Chronicle of 1234* mentions (86, 221/122), tribute was exacted; anti-Chalcedonian bishops were installed; and, unlike previously, the Persians systematically captured every fortress east of the Euphrates before proceeding further.[30]

In 609/10 (*Chr. 724*, 146/17, AG 921, cf. *Chr. Pasch.* 698/149, a.609), Edessa, Carrhae, Callinicum and Circesium were taken: the Persians were now clearly concentrating on mopping up the remaining cities of Osrhoene. Some at least seem to have surrendered to the Persians rather than face a protracted assault. The capture of Edessa – a city thought to be impregnable, protected by Jesus' promise to King Abgar – must have had a particularly crushing effect on Roman morale.[31] Then, on 7 August 610 (*Chr. 724*, 146/17, AG 921), Shahrvaraz captured Zenobia, the first city west of the Euphrates to fall. See Stratos 1968: 63, Flusin 1992: II, 74.[32]

We may note in passing that a reference in the Syriac common source (taken up by Theophanes, A.M. 6100 [296], Mich. Syr. X.25 [391–2a/125 n.282], *Chr. 1234*, 88 [224/ 125], to which should be added Niceph. Call. XVIII.43 [416b]) to a Persian invasion of Asia Minor in 610, penetrating as far as Chalcedon, is inaccurate.[33]

Armenia, 601–10

The Persian annexation of Roman Armenia was as slow and systematic as that of Mesopotamia. Here the Persians had to regain territory ceded in 591, and it was not until the end of Phocas' reign that they were in a position to penetrate beyond Roman Armenia. By far the most important source available for events in Armenia is Sebeos, whose chronology is unfortunately often obscure. A certain amount of approximation is therefore inevitable in the dates here offered. See Thomson and Howard-Johnston 1999: lxi–lxxvii, esp. lxxii.[34]

In the winter of 603, while the siege of Dara was being pursued, a Persian commander named Džuan Veh was appointed to the command of Persian forces in Armenia. Setting forth from his base at Dvin in the spring of 604, he fought an unsuccesful battle against the Romans at Ełevard (near Erevan) (Sebeos 107–8/59).[35] In the following year, Khusro appointed Datoyean to replace Džuan Veh, and under his leadership the Persians defeated the Romans at the village of Getik to the west of the plain of Shirak. The Armenians, who had loyally supported the Roman forces, were massacred after the battle in their fort at Erginay. The victorious Persians then withdrew to Atropatene. (Sebeos 108–9/59–60).[36] Datoyean was in turn succeeded by Senitam Khusro (in 605/6), who outflanked the forces of Theodosius Khorkhoruni, the Roman commander, at Angł (Anglon).[37] The Romans tried to negotiate terms for a withdrawal, but were surprised by a Persian attack and forced to flee. Theodosius was captured, and the Persians continued to advance westwards. Following a further Persian victory in Basean, to the west of Theodosiopolis, various forts fell into Persian hands. (Sebeos 109–10/60–2).[38] The next Persian commander in Armenia was Ashtat Yeztayar, who was accompanied by Maurice's son (or pretender) Theodosius. In 606/7 Ashtat defeated the Romans in Basean and pursued them as far as Satala. He then returned eastwards, invested Theodosiopolis, and persuaded the city to surrender by presenting Theodosius to the defenders. Other Roman fortresses fell soon after-wards, including those of Citharizon, Satala and Nicopolis. (Sebeos 110–11/63).[39]

Narratio de rebus Armeniae, 109–13 (p.41): After his (Maurice's) death, the Persian king Khusro took over the land of Armenia; (110) at that time[40] the heretic Abraham was established as patriarch.[41] (111) And in the same year he obliged the bishops and priests and *hegoumenoi* to anathematise the Council in Chalcedon and to depart from the country. They pronounced the anathema and the controversy ended. (112) After three years there was warfare in Phasiane (Basean) and the Persians slaughtered the Romans, and the city Kitris (Citharizon) was besieged, as was Theodosiopolis, in the fifth year of Phocas and the twentieth year of Khusro.[42] (113) And they took many other cities, in one of which was the *catholicos* John, who was in Armenia, but subject to the Romans.[43]

The Persians had now penetrated deep into Roman Armenia. Probably in the following year, 607/8, Shahin, the new Persian commander, defeated the Romans near Theodosiopolis and expelled them from Armenia (Sebeos 111/64).[44] That each year battles continued to be fought seems to imply that the Romans were more willing (or better able) to defend Armenia than Mesopotamia.[45] Two years later, in 609/10, perhaps after continuing Roman resistance, the inhabitants of Theodosiopolis, including the *catholicos* John, were deported to Hamadan (Sebeos 112/64). See Garsoïan 1999: 356–64.[46] While the Armenian Church was able to regain its unity and even prosper under Persian rule, the way now lay open for the invaders to push deeper into Asia Minor. See Garsoïan 1999: 368–84.[47]

The continuing Persian advance (610–12)

It was not until the autumn of 611 that the Persian advance was pursued further. Their progress beyond the Euphrates was greatly assisted by the unrest which had broken out in Syria and Palestine in the wake of Heraclius' revolt in Africa and the invasion of Egypt by his ally Nicetas in 608. The outbreak of rebellion sparked off conflicts between circus factions, leading to the intervention of imperial troops, and in 609 or 610 to the murder of the patriarch of Antioch, Anastasius II. According to many sources, the Jews were heavily involved in the fighting, although whether as faction members or as opponents of Christians is unclear.[48] Phocas responded by appointing Bonosus as *comes Orientis* in 608 or 609 to repress the violence, and he exacted savage retribution on the Green faction in Antioch. But in 609 he was forced to move into Egypt to oppose Nicetas' forces advancing from the west. Although initially victorious, he was defeated by Nicetas outside Alexandria in late 609.[49] Heraclius overthrew Phocas and was crowned emperor in October 610, but this did not mark the end of his struggle for power. Comentiolus, one of Phocas' brothers, and the commander of a Roman army in the East, refused to accept the new ruler and undertook a rebellion at his winter quarters in Ancyra late in 610. Heraclius, whose régime was still insecure, quickly opened negotiations, first through a monk named Herodian, and then through the former *magister militum* Philippicus. Probably early in the new year the revolt came to a swift end with the assassination of its leader by Justin, the commander of the Armenian forces under Comentiolus.[50]

While the details of Heraclius' revolt and seizure of power are not strictly relevant to our theme, it is clear that they had a considerable impact on the ability of the Romans to resist further Persian attacks. Several points may be noted. First, and most obviously, Roman forces which might otherwise have been available for the defence of Syria and Palestine were taken by Bonosus to Egypt, thus leaving the field open to the Persians. Other troops which might have defended Armenia withdrew to Ancyra in 610. This would help to explain the willingness of cities such as Antioch to capitulate to the invaders. Second, the bloodshed between 608 and 610 was considerable. Not only were there fewer soldiers left in the Levant after Bonosus' departure, but those civilians remaining were weakened after the strife and reprisals, and no doubt reluctant to engage in further conflict.[51] Divisions must have remained within the populace, and thus some at least will have welcomed the opportunity afforded by an enemy attack to take revenge. The Persian armies were therefore faced with a weakened and divided enemy, and against this background their rapid and sweeping conquests become more comprehensible.[52]

The accession of a new emperor failed to persuade Khusro to end hostilities. According to some sources, Heraclius asked for peace upon gaining power, but Khusro refused, killing the Roman ambassadors (Sebeos 113, *Chr. 1234*, 91 [226/127], Mich. Syr. XI.1 [403a/128 n.287], Agap., *PO* 8.450, *Chr. Seert* 82, *PO* 13.527).[53] The Persian advance westwards continued in earnest in 611; the preceding year had perhaps been spent clearing the southwest bank of the Euphrates (the Roman province of Euphratesia), where Roman strongholds such as Zenobia and Sergiopolis may still have been holding out.[54] In Armenia, meanwhile, the deportation of the population of Theodosiopolis was being carried out.

The Persian onslaught in 611 was two-pronged. In the north, Shahin proceeded to Caesarea in Cappadocia, which he captured without difficulty: the Christians, according to Sebeos, evacuated the city, while the Jews welcomed the invaders. Here, however, the Romans made an attempt at a counter-strike. Probably in autumn 611 Priscus, whose attempt to take command in the East in 589 had proved so disastrous, was sent to surround the Persians in Caesarea. The blockade proved effective, but in summer 612 the Persians managed to escape back to Armenia (Sebeos 113/66, Nic. 2.9–22, Theoph. A.M. 6103 (610/11), 299, *Chr. 1234*, 91 [226/127]).[55] Heraclius, who had visited Priscus during the siege, therefore decided to take over command of the eastern front in person, something no emperor had done since Valens in the 370s.

V. *Theod. Syk.* ch.153–154.9 (123–4): When now the disorder of the army had been brought to an end and had reached a peaceful outcome, not much afterwards the Persian people made an incursion as far as Caesarea, the metropolis of Cappadocia. We of the monastery and all in our territory were in great fear, suspecting that they would venture even as far as us. And when the servant of God was called upon to move us from the monastery because of this great fear, he prayed to God and said to us, 'Do not fear, children, the onrush of the (Persian) people. For God has been called upon by me and will not allow them to come against our territory; nor shall I see with my eyes a foreign invasion here.' After this, Priscus, the most glorious patrician and *comes* of the excubitors, went off with an army against the Persians; (and) again a rumour arose that they had surrounded (p.124) this people in Caesarea and that they were dying of hunger and would either swiftly surrender or be destroyed. To these things the servant of Christ said, 'None of these (things) will come about, but they will completely escape and depart. And if we do not turn back to God and repent so that he may be reconciled with us as with the Ninevites, they will come again with a great force and lay waste all the land as far as the sea. However, confident in my God, I say to you that in my lifetime God will not abandon my old age nor will a barbarian incursion take place in my time.'[56] And this was the case by the grace of God. (154) There came to him letters from the most pious Emperor Heraclius and the patriarch Sergius (to urge) him to come to the capital city so that they might receive his blessing. He therefore went out from the monastery and reached the capital. It happened that before his arrival the emperor departed and went off to Caesarea to join forces with the protopatrician Priscus and our army which was with him, against the Persians, with the result that the holy man was thenceforth obliged by the patriarch Sergius to await the return of the emperor.[57]

In the south, the Persian advance under Shahrvaraz was swift. Its progress is difficult to follow with precision, however. Perhaps in May 611 Apamea and Antioch fell, followed by Emesa, which surrendered after receiving a guarantee of safety. Again, there was some Roman resistance: in a battle at Emesa, following the city's capture, a Roman army was defeated (*Chr. 724*, 146/17, AG 922, cf. *Chr. 1234*, 91 [226/127], Theoph. A.M. 6102 [609/10], 299, Agapius, *PO* 8.450).[58] At both Caesarea and Emesa it is interesting to note that it was only after the fall of a city that Roman forces intervened – perhaps because it was not until mid-611 that Heraclius was able to organise a response. Clearly the Persians were driving southwards towards Palestine, a region famous for its wealth.[59]

The Roman counter-strike (613)

Although Caesarea had fallen to the Persians in 611, the important fortress of Melitene still remained in Roman hands. It was against this city therefore that Shahin directed his army, by way of Theodosiopolis, in 613; and, having captured it, he proceeded to join forces with Shahrvaraz (Sebeos 113/66).[60] At this point Heraclius embarked on a bold counter-attack, having elevated his infant son Heraclius Constantine to the rank of Augustus. Philippicus, succeeding to Priscus' command as he had 24 years earlier, led the Roman army at Caesarea eastwards into Roman, then Persian, Armenia, penetrating as far as the province of Ayrarat. Khusro was therefore obliged to recall his armies, which hastened to deal with the Roman incursion. Philippicus then withdrew to Roman territory via Theodosiopolis, while the Persians, wearied by the forced marches undertaken to overtake the Romans, turned instead to Mesopotamia (Sebeos 114/67–8).[61] Philippicus' campaign was probably merely a diversion, allowing Heraclius, his brother Theodore, and Nicetas to combine forces in Syria. There, in a closely fought battle, they were finally defeated by the invaders (Sebeos 114/67–8, Agap. *PO* 8.450).[62] See Pernice 1905: 68–9, Baynes 1914: 36–7 (placing the episode in 611), Thomson and Howard-Johnston 1999: 205–6.

V. Theod. Syk. 166 (153–4): During the days of Lent, when the Emperor Heraclius, beloved of Christ, was going down from the royal city to Antioch of the East, to marshal his forces against the Persians, he came up to the monastery to get his (Theodore's) blessing. The blessed man arose and met him at the entrance of the church of the holy martyr George; and they embraced one another, and went into the church of the glorious martyr and into the church of the Archangel, and the blessed man gave him a blessing, commending him to God. And he gave gifts of blessing to him (p.154) – fine flour, apples and choice wine – and urged him to taste (them). But the emperor, because of (his) great haste, declined to taste them and to receive the gifts bestowed on him, saying 'Keep these things for me, father, and pray for us. And on my way back I shall come and then take these things, and shall stay here as long as you bid; and I shall enjoy at great leisure both your gifts and your all-holy prayers.' But the blessed man said to him, 'Now listen to my exhortation, child, for on your return you will not find me. I have a great road (to travel) and I intend to be away.' But the emperor said to him, 'God will so arrange (things), holy father, that I will find your holiness here and will feast with you[63] at leisure.' He then received his (Theodore's) blessing and went off to the city of Antioch, in which he began (his) war against the Persians, (together with) Nicetas the patrician and *comes* who was there also. The blessed man grieved that he had left behind his gifts, saying, 'If he had taken them, it would have been a token of his victory, and he would have returned with joy. His leaving these things behind is a sign of our defeat, and if he had not come up and received the blessing of the saints, then great sorrow would have overtaken him and all of us.' Having sat down for a short time in the chapel of the Mother of God, bowing (his head) and becoming thoughtful, he soon raised (his head) and said to me, 'Know, George, (my) child, that by the command of God this emperor will be long-lived, for he will reign for at least thirty years.' And indeed it occurred in accordance with his word.

The Romans withdrew northwards after their defeat, closely followed by the Persians. In another engagement fought near the Cilician Gates, the Romans, although initially victorious, were defeated. The Persians then took over the province of Cilicia (Sebeos 115/68). See Stratos 1968: 106–7, Kaegi 1973: 329, Flusin 1992: II, 79.

Once the Romans had been pushed back from Syria, the way southwards, towards Palestine and Egypt, lay open to the invaders. Later in 613 the city of Damascus was captured by Shahrvaraz. Like Emesa, it surrendered to the Persians, agreeing to pay tribute; according to Theophanes, however, many prisoners were taken (*Chr. 724*, 146/17, AG 924, *Chr. 1234*, 91 [226/128], Mich. Syr. XI.1 [401a/128 n.287], Theoph. A.M. 6105, 300). See Stratos 1968: 107–8, Flusin 1992: II, 79 and n.54.

The fall of Jerusalem (614)

The following year, Shahrvaraz's drive southwards continued. From Damascus he proceeded southwards to the vicinity of Bostra and Adraa.

Tabari, I, 1007/327 (Nöldeke 300):[64] Qaysar (Caesar) sent a man called Qatma with an army of Romans[65] and Khusro sent one with Shahrvaraz, and they fought a battle by Adhri'at (Adraa) and Busra (Bostra), and it is the nearest part of the al-Sham to you (Arabs).[66] The Persians joined with the Romans, and the Persians overcame them. The unbelievers of Quraysh disliked it; then God revealed 'Aliph lam mim' ... [67] (tr. Hoyland)

Qur'an, 30.2–5: Aliph Lam Mim. (3) The Romans have been defeated (4) in the nearest part of the land, but after their defeat they will be victorious (5) after many years – government belongs to Allah before and afterwards – and on that day the faithful will greatly rejoice. (...).

Passing through Phoenice and Galilee, Shahrvaraz first directed his march to Caesarea, on the Mediterranean coast; from there he proceeded to Jerusalem via Diospolis (Lydda) (Sebeos 115/68, Ant. Strateg. 3 [503], *V. Georg. Khozeb*. VIII.33 [133]).[68] Although the new patriarch of

Jersualem, Zachariah, was inclined to come to terms with the invaders, the circus partisans insisted on resistance. Roman troops were summoned from nearby Jericho, but fled upon seeing the number of Persians surrounding the city (Ant. Strateg. 5–7 [504–5]).[69] The Persian siege, which began in mid- or late April, lasted twenty days. When the city walls fell, a massacre ensued (Sebeos 115–16/69, Ant. Strateg. 8 [506–7]).[70] A mass grave of Christians recently uncovered near the Pool of Mamilla has been associated with the capture of the city. See Reich 1996: 26–33, 60.

The contemporary evidence of Sophronius shows that resistance at Jerusalem was stiff nevertheless. Cf. *Hist. Her.* 429/228 with Mahé 1984: 223. See Clermont-Ganneau 1898: 36–7 and Baynes 1914: 198.

Sophronius, *Anacr.* 14.69–102 (105–7): On top of the ridges of the walls stood the population, (like Mount) Olympus, (so that) all the children and wives felt (only) trivial concerns. (p.106) O Christ, grant (us) to see Persia burning soon instead of the holy places! Possessed of a steadfast mind, they kept the approaching Mede from the strong walls by showers of missiles and rocks. Then indeed, with raging spirits, the Persian, barbarian that he was, after thousands of clashes, employed siege engines. Having set fires everywhere beneath the wall, (as well as) an army of siege engines,[71] he destroyed the strong wall and came to be inside the city. Equipped with bloody sword, he cut down the people – the city of sacred and holy old men, children, and women. (p.107) O Christ, may you curb by the hands of Christians the ill-fated children of impious Persia! Accomplishing everything with cruelty, he despoiled the holy city and with blazing fire burnt the holy places of Christ. After shouting an insult to God, who had once died there, he despoiled the sacred spoil and with the spoil marched (off). O Christ, may you curb by the hands of Christians the ill-fated children of the dreadful parent, Persia!

Most sources report that the Jews collaborated with the Persians, both before and after the siege, and took the opportunity to settle scores with their Christian oppressors. Many inhabitants, including the patriarch, were deported to Persia (Ant. Strateg. 9–18 [507–11]). Outside Jerusalem, the Jews may have undertaken some campaigns in Palestine themselves, laying siege to Ptolemais and Tyre according to Eutychius (ed. Breydy, 121–2/101–2).[72] Churches in the vicinity show signs of destruction which have been associated with this episode. See Schick 1995: 27–9, Russell 2001: 47. The Persians for their part withdrew to Damascus by way of Jericho after the capture of the city (Ant. Strateg. 15 [510], *V. Georg. Khozeb.* VI.29 [127], VII.31 [130]). See Schick 1995: 21.[73]

Both Palestine and Syria also suffered at the hands of Arab raiders at this time. The collapse of the frontiers will have meant that normal arrangements between the Romans and neighbouring tribesmen will have broken down. With no subsidies on offer, both tribes hitherto allied to Rome and their opponents may have sought to profit from the unsettled conditions. See Sartre 1982a: 193, Kaegi 1992: 52–6, Shahîd 1995: 640–1.[74]

General accounts of the fall of Jerusalem, with widely varying casualty figures (from 36,500 to 90,000) are to be found in numerous sources; the various versions of Antiochus Strategius' account also offer differing figures. Mention is generally made of the seizure and removal of the

True Cross from Jerusalem; Nicetas succeeded in salvaging the sacred sponge and the spear which had pierced Christ's side (Ant. Strateg. 23 [515–16], Theoph. A.M. 6106 [613/14], 300–1, Chr. 724, 146/17, AG 925, Chr. 1234, 93 [226–7/128], Mich. Syr. XI.1 [403–4a/400], Chr. Pasch. 704–5, Tabari, I, 1002/318 [Nöldeke 291]).[75]

The Life of George of Khozeba offers a glimpse of the panic in the region at the time of the siege of Jerusalem. The Persians probably withdrew northwards past Jericho and Bostra. See Vailhé 1901: 646, Baynes 1914: 199, Di Segni 1991: 144.[76]

V. Georg. Khozeb. **VII.30 (127.19–129.13):** When the Persian invasion had then reached (p.128) as far as Damascus, there was no inconsiderable confusion in this country. At one (moment) therefore our holy father – this George – while sitting on a rock and warming himself by the ray of the sun (for he was withered through excessive abstinence), (and) completely burning with the longing of spiritual love for the fulfilment of the divine will, called upon merciful God, imploring him with tears to spare his people. And a voice came to him: 'Go to Jericho and you (will) see the works of men.' And he arose and finding some from the monastery going down to Jericho, went down with them. When they arrived at the gardens near the city, suddenly he heard in the air a great sound of crowds (of people) throwing one another into confusion, striking and crying out, as if in combat. Raising his eyes to the air, he beheld it filled with some Indians attacking one another as though under arms, and striking (one another) as in war.[77] And the earth shook and trembled beneath him. The brothers said to him: 'Come here, father, (and) let us go to the city. Why have you been standing there for so long, gazing at the sky?' But he said to them with tears and lamentation, 'Let us flee, brothers, and return (home). Do you not see and sense the earth shaking?' And when he had said this, lo, suddenly some armed men on horseback came forth from the city, and other young men on foot, and youths wearing greaves, and spears were in their hands, running hither and thither.[78] (p.129) And the brothers realised that this was the shaking of the earth of which the old man had spoken. They returned to the monastery in great fear, for he reported to them the vision in the air. When the old man came back to his cell, he grieved and lamented the coarseness of the people rather than their foolishness or impiety. Then, going outside, seated on a rock (facing) towards the ray of the sun (for this was his task on account of the slightness of his body), he called upon and besought God, saying: 'Lord God of mercies and Lord of pity, who wants all to be saved and to come to the recognition of the truth, raise your rod and strike your people, because they wander in ignorance.' At once he beheld a rod of fire in the air stretching from the holy city (Jerusalem) to Bostra.[79] And the holy man knew that the people would be heavily punished; and he grieved and lamented over all these things.

The Persians soon afterwards gave permission for the rebuilding of the city, and the patriarch of Alexandria, John the Almsgiver, even sent materials to assist in this (Leontius, V. Ioh. Eleem. 20).[80] Extensive reconstruction took place after 617, when the Persians barred further Jews from migrating to the city. Zachariah's replacement in office, Modestus, raised funds from Christians throughout the region, while according to the *Khuzistan Chronicle* Khusro's minister

Yazdin contributed generously to the rebuilding (Sebeos 116–18/70–2, *Chr. Khuz.* 27). See Flusin 1992: II, 174–7, Schick 1995: 41–4 and Thomson and Howard-Johnston 1999: 208–9.[81]

Many refugees from Palestine sought refuge in Egypt at this time, where they received a kind reception from the patriarch.[82]

Anon., *V. Ioh. Eleem.* 9: After Rasmiozan (Shahrvaraz), the governor – or rather the chief general – of Khusro, the Persian king, had sacked the holy places of Jerusalem, this grievous report came to the ears of the thrice-blessed patriarch. When he heard of this outrageous and audacious deed, and learnt that all the holy places had been committed to flames, he sat down and composed a lament as though (he were) one of the inhabitants of (those) places. He lamented the desolation of these (places) not for one day, nor two nor twenty or twice this amount, but for a whole year, grieving and groaning bitterly as he struggled to surpass in his laments Jeremiah, who had once lamented the capture of this city. This lament he did not compose (to put it simply) just as it occurred (to him), so that it might be consigned to oblivion, but rather he is said to have committed it to writing. In addition to this he sent a certain man, Ctesippus by name, who at that time ran the monasteries of Ennaton,[83] a man most beloved of God, to see the destruction of the holy places in Jerusalem. And through him he sent a great quantity of gold, a mass of grain, wine, oil and beans, and he provided clothes for lay-people and monks, and a large amount of food for the sake of the sick, as well as very many beasts of burden for the transport of these things.[84]

He did not concern himself only with those captured in the cities, but also cared with great attention for those in monasteries, and above all those in convents, who had suffered in this way. Of these (monastic buildings) a great number had been destroyed by the Persians, and about a thousand of the nuns had been taken captive; he (John) sent a great amount of gold on their behalf and, having taken a record of them, he restored them all to monasteries. The governors of the Persians, when they learnt of the exceeding charity and sympathy of the man who was in truth well named 'the almsgiver' – for even the foe respected the virtue of the man – they greatly desired to see him; they provided money for Dion, who happened to be governor at the time, so that he might go off and see him.

Furthermore, he despatched Theodore, the bishop of Amathus, to rescue those who had been taken prisoner by the Madieni,[85] as well as Anastasius, the superior (of the monastery) of the mountain of Antony the Great, and Gregory, the bishop of Rhinocolura.[86] Through them he effected the rescue of very many men and women captives by ransoming them in return for the payment of a great quantity of gold.[87]

The Persians at Chalcedon (614–15)

The capture of Jerusalem imbued the Persians with still greater confidence. In the summer or autumn of 614 Shahin set off from Ctesiphon, bound for the heart of the Roman empire; among his troops was a certain cavalryman, Magundat, who during the campaign deserted the army and made his way to Hierapolis. By the end of 614 or early 615 Shahin had reached

Chalcedon on the Bosporus, and proceeded to invest the city; elements of his army may well have been despatched to devastate other parts of Asia Minor, since archaeological evidence establishes that Ephesus was destroyed in 614 (*Acta Anast.*, ch.8, *Chr. Pasch.* 706, Theoph. A.M. 6107 [614/15], 301, Nic. 6, Sebeos 123/79, Tabari, I, 1002/319 [Nöldeke 292]).[88] The Roman response was two-fold. First, the tactics already employed in 613 were repeated: Philippicus undertook another incursion in the East, and thereby forced Shahin to abandon his siege and follow him (*V. Anast.* ch.8).[89] Second, taking advantage of the proximity of the Persians, Heraclius sought to open negotiations to end the war. The emperor visited Shahin outside Chalcedon, and the Persian general received him courteously (Nic. 6, Sebeos 122-3/ 78-9, Thom. Arts. 89-91/156-8). Three Roman ambassadors were therefore sent by the Senate to Khusro, and Shahin withdrew from the city (*Chr. Pasch.* 706, Nic. 7, cf. Sebeos 122-3/78-9). The text of the letter borne by the ambassadors is preserved in the *Chronicon Paschale.* See Stratos 1968: 115-17, Thomson and Howard-Johnston 1999: 211-12.[90]

Chr. Pasch. 707.1-709.24: God, who created all things and maintains (them) with his own power, has bestowed a gift worthy of his own goodness on the race of men – providential care for the kingdom, by means of which we have been considered worthy to live without disturbances, or, falling upon certain difficulties, we find a solution. Giving thought to this divine thing – we mean the royal care – and before anything else, we beseech your very great Clemency to consider us worthy of forgiveness, since we have dared to undertake the present appeal to your might contrary to the previous system which operated. For we know the custom which prevailed in previous times, which ordained that when some strife arose between the two states, the rulers of each of them would resolve the points at issue through reports (presented) to one another. But Phocas, once he became a traitor to the Roman state, broke this arrangement. For, having gradually corrupted the Roman army in Thrace, he suddenly attacked our royal city and slew Maurice, who piously reigned over us, and his wife, as well as his children and relatives and many of those in charge. And he was not content with the great evils he had committed, but also did not pay fitting honour to your very great Clemency, with the result that then you, aroused by our errors, brought the affairs of the Roman state to such dire straits.[91] (p.708) Our current piously reigning emperor and his ever-memorable father, realising the things done by that corruptor, resolved to free the Roman state from the excessive violence of that man. And this they did, discovering (then) how it (the state) had been humbled by your might. And after the death of the tyrant, when our emperor wished to take his own relatives (with him) and return to his own father in Africa, urging us to select the man we wished as emperor, he was only just persuaded by our entreaties to accept the kingdom. Because of the confusion which prevailed in the two kingdoms, as well as the civil strife,[92] he did not have the opportunity, as should have been done, to pay the honour owed to the very great might of your Serenity through an embassy.[93] We therefore resolved to disregard the custom which we mentioned above, and, being mere men, to employ entreaty towards so great a supreme king, despatching some of our number who should be considered worthy of your footsteps. But because of what has been happening in the meantime, we have not dared to do this until now. When, however, Shahin the most glorious Babmanzadag,[94] the commander of the Persian army, was in the region of Chalcedon and met our most pious emperor and us, and was asked by all to hold talks about peace, he said that he himself did not have such authority, but that he required (authority) about this matter from (p.709) your Clemency. And now he has sent an answer to us through the Spadadavar,[95] promising under oath that your very great might will receive those sent by us as is fitting, and will release them unharmed to return to us, and that he was ordered by your Beneficence to do this. Encouraged again by this sequence of events, and above all by God and by your greatness, we sent your slaves Olympius, the most glorious ex-consul, a patrician and praetorian prefect, and the most glorious Leontius, a patrician and city prefect, and Anastasius, the most God-beloved priest and *syncellus*, who, we beseech you, may be received as befits your very great might;[96] and (we entreat that you) restore to us quickly and safely peace, which is pleasing to God and which befits your peace-loving might. We beg your Clemency to hold our most pious Emperor Heraclius as (your) genuine child,[97] for he eagerly wishes to do the service of your Serenity in all things. In doing this, you gain a double glory for yourself, both for your valour in wars and for the gift of peace. And henceforth we shall enjoy peace through your eternally remembered gifts, taking the opportunity to offer prayers to God on behalf of your long good health, and holding your good deed in remembrance through the ages of the Roman state.

Neither Roman initiative bore fruit. The ambassadors were executed by Khusro, while Shahin returned to Chalcedon, having presumably dealt with Philippicus' incursion, and captured the city (either in late 615 or 616) (Theoph. A.M. 6108–9, 301, Mich. Syr. XI.1, 404a/128 n.289 [year 7 of Heraclius], Nic. 7.20–2).[98]

Consolidation of the Persian position (615–18)

Little is known of specific campaigns in this period; we are reliant for the most part on the evidence of numismatics and archaeology in reconstructing the history of these years. Sardis was destroyed in 616,[99] and in the same year the Roman mint at Cyzicus ceased operation. But a Roman army continued to hold out in Seleucia in Cilicia Tracheia, as is clear from the presence of a mint there between 616 and 617. In the following year (and perhaps later) coins were minted instead at Isaura Vetus in Isauria, away from the coast;[100] the cause of this retreat may have been the construction of a Persian fleet, since it seems that Constantia (Salamis) came under attack around 617. Thanks to the intervention of the patriarch of Alexandria, John the Almsgiver, who was in Cyprus at the time, the situation was resolved peacefully.[101]

Anon., V. Ioh. Eleem. 13: Hearing of the utter destruction of the Roman state at the hands of the Persians, he (the patriarch John) wished to journey to the emperor and to be an ambassador concerning a peace. And indeed he put together a valedictory speech and addressed everyone, (but) it was not accepted by the people that he should leave the city. When therefore the Persian armies had utterly devastated Syria, Phoenice and Arabia and still other cities, the evil men threatened to take Alexandria itself. At that point indeed he became aware through God of a deadly plot being hatched against him, and he sailed away to his fatherland, Cyprus. A certain general,

Aspagourius by name, after being sent against Constantia in Cyprus and not being received by those in the city,[102] had armed himself for war against them, and they in turn had armed themselves against him. They intended to proceed at once to close quarters for a great slaughter of one another, had not the disciple of peace, the all-admirable John, anticipated (events), reconciled (them) and turned both sides to peace, bringing them together.

If it was the Persians who were attacking Constantia, they do not appear to have gained control of the whole island.[103] Instead, they concentrated their efforts on the invasion of Egypt, the richest province of the eastern empire. Shahrvaraz probably began his assault in 618, passing by Pelusium on the well-trodden invasion route into the country.[104]

Heraclius' measures (615–19)

The situation in Constantinople itself was fraught; according to Nicephorus (8), Heraclius even considered abandoning the capital and moving to Carthage instead.[105] With the devastation of Asia Minor by the Persians and the assaults on the Roman Balkan provinces, and even Greece, by the Avars and Slavs, the economic resources of the empire were shrinking alarmingly. The city of Thessalonica survived a siege by the Avars in c.618, but only with difficulty.[106] See Haldon 1990: 43–4, Foss 1994: 49, Whittow 1996: 76–7. Desperate measures were called for, even as the Persian attack on Egypt removed the one remaining significant source of grain and wealth. Heraclius therefore introduced a new silver coin, the hexagram, in 615. This allowed official salaries to be halved when paid in the new coin, which was also inscribed on the reverse with the appropriate entreaty *Deus adiuta Romanis* ('God help the Romans') (*Chr. Pasch.* 706, a.615). See Grierson 1968: 17–18, 101, 270–4 with pl.10, Yannopoulos 1978: 2–8, Hendy 1985: 494.[107] At the same time, the weight of the copper *follis* was reduced from approximately 11 grams to 8 (and still further later in the war).[108] In 618 a charge of 3 *folles* per loaf of bread was introduced at Constantinople; hitherto it had been free. Later in the same year the distributions were suspended altogether (*Chron. Pasch.* 711 [a.618]). See Whitby and Whitby 1989: 164 n.449, Stratos 1968: 100–1.[109]

The Persian conquest of Egypt (618–19)

Probably because Egypt was now cut off from the remainder of the Roman empire, the Roman sources offer no account of the fall of Alexandria.[110] The most complete account is to be found in the *Khuzistan Chronicle* (see Chapter 15 below), according to which the city was betrayed by a certain Peter; that in Severus' *History of the Patriarchs of Alexandria* (*PO* 1.484–5) is of little worth.[111] Leontius' *Life of John the Almsgiver* (52, Dawes and Baynes 44b) further informs us that Nicetas and the patriarch were able to flee the city before its fall, probably in June 619 (*Chr. 724*, 146/17, AG 930).[112] The Persians gradually extended their control of Egypt southwards; by mid-621 the whole province was in their hands. See Altheim-Stiehl 1991, 1992a (noting that the Persians were already in Oxyrhynchus in January 620), 1998 (a convenient summary). The serious economic consequences of the province's fall have already been noted. As elsewhere, following the destruction which accompanied the invasion, a period of peace and even reconstruction followed.[113] We may note also that copper *dodecanummia* minted in Alexandria under the Persians feature a bust of Khusro between a sun and a crescent (common Sasanian motifs on coinage) on the obverse, and a cross on the reverse: here too the king was clearly prepared to conciliate local opinion. See Grierson 1968: 233–4, 336–8 with pl.18 and Flusin 1992: II, 127.

The Persian conquest of Asia Minor (619–22)

The noose around Constantinople now tightened further; nor was there any obvious source of hope for those remaining in the capital. The Balkans continued to suffer devastation at the hands of Avars and Slavs.[114] In Asia Minor the last functioning mint – that at Nicomedia – ceased operating in 619. See Hendy 1985: 416. Perhaps in 620, but more probably in 622, the important central Anatolian city of Ancyra fell into Persian hands. A Persian fleet was also active, and the island of Rhodes fell to the invaders in 622/3 (*Chr. 724* 147/18, AG 934, Theoph. A.M. 6111 [618/19], 302, *Chr. 1234*, 96, 230/133, Mich. Syr. XI.3, 408a/133 n.300, Agap. *PO* 8.458).[115] Evidence for Sasanian activity along the Aegean coast is also provided by a hoard of coins discovered on the island of Samos, probably buried in 623. See Oeconomides and Drossoyianni 1989: 163–75.

It should be noted, however, that the Persians did not have a secure hold of all of Asia Minor: Roman troops were clearly able to assemble and operate in many provinces there later in the 620s without hindrance. Archaeology similarly confirms that some cities at least, such as Aphrodisias, were spared destruction.[116] In general the Persians seem to have preferred to lay waste Asia Minor, while keeping Palestine, Syria, Mesopotamia and Egypt more or less intact under their own administration. See Morony 1987: 91–2, Flusin 1992: II, 95, Kaegi 1992: 45.[117]

14

THE ROMAN RECOVERY UNDER
HERACLIUS (622–30)

Sources

The source material for the final phase of the last Roman–Persian war is more extensive than for the first phases. Theophanes offers a continuous account of several campaigns, and the *Chronicon Paschale* provides similarly detailed information. The poems of George of Pisidia commemorate certain episodes during the war, but tend to focus more on the emperor's personal involvement in masterminding the Roman recovery. It has been plausibly suggested that behind all three sources, as well as (Pseudo-)Sebeos' notices, lie campaign reports by Heraclius and his staff, sent to the capital from the front in order to boost morale and to reassure anxious citizens. See Howard-Johnston 1994: esp. 72–8 and Thomson and Howard-Johnston 1999: lxviii, M. Whitby 1994 and 1998. Speck 1988 offers a more sceptical perspective.[1] For the other sources used, see the notes on pp.182–3.

The campaign of 622[2]

In the spring of 622 Heraclius was at last ready for a counter-offensive against the Persians. A costly peace had been agreed with the Avars in 620, and Heraclius had therefore transferred the Roman forces in the Balkans across to Asia Minor in the following year (Theoph. A.M. 6112, 302.27–30).[3] In 622 the emperor, with the backing of the patriarch Sergius, took over the candelabra and vessels of the church and melted them down to make gold and silver coins (Theoph. A.M. 6113, 302.34–303.3, Nic. 11.21–3). See Haldon 1984: 171–2 and Whitby and Whitby 1989: 158–9 n.441 (accepting the date of 622 for this measure).[4]

Parast. synt. chron. **42.7–10:** And after the same Phocas was burnt, the ox[5] was melted down by Heraclius for the treasury of the guards (*skoulkatameion*) and in order to cross over to Pontus for the sake of raising troops; for there was a guardpost (*skoulkaton*) in Pontus.[6]

On 5 April Heraclius left Constantinople, entrusting the city to the patriarch Sergius and the general Bonus as regents for his young son Heraclius Constantine. On the following day he reached Pylae, on the gulf of Nicomedia, by sea. He then assembled his forces somewhere in Asia Minor, probably in Bithynia (Geo. Pis. *Exp. Pers.* I.154–II.11, Theoph. A.M. 6113, 302.32–4, 303.6–12). See Oikonomides 1976: 2, Howard-Johnston 1999: 3 and n.11,

Thomson and Howard-Johnston 1999: 213.[7] The size of this combined army is unknown, but it clearly must have been the largest force fielded by the Romans in the recent past: Theophanes rather vaguely states that Heraclius 'collected his forces and added a new army to them' (303.11–12), while George of Pisidia specifically mentions the diverse nature of the forces assembled by the emperor (*Exp. Pers.* II.165).[8] But before he could lead them into battle, it was necessary to revitalise their broken morale and to increase their effectiveness. Military exercises, described by George of Pisidia (followed by Theophanes), were held; the image of Christ, not made by human hands,[9] was displayed to the troops; and Heraclius roused his troops for battle by emphasising the religious nature of the struggle against a barbarian who had plundered the holy sites of Christianity (Geo. Pis. *Exp. Pers.* II.12–202, Theoph. A.M. 6113, 303.12–304.13).[10]

Probably in July Heraclius proceeded to Armenia, where he inflicted a defeat on an army led by a Persian-allied Arab chief (Geo. Pis. *Exp. Pers.* II.203–34, Theoph. A.M. 6113, 304.13–18).[11] The emperor was prevented from pushing further east by the arrival of the Persian general Shahrvaraz, who had wintered in Pontus and quickly seized control of the passes leading east from Armenia (Geo. Pis. *Exp. Pers.* II.256–60).[12] Heraclius then outmanoeuvred his opponent, prompting him to try to deflect the emperor by invading Roman territory, moving south through the Cilician Gates (Geo. Pis. *Exp. Pers.* II.261–344, Theoph. A.M. 6113, 304.20–5).[13] Shahrvaraz soon reversed his plan, fearing an invasion of Persia through Armenia, and took to shadowing Heraclius' army. An attempt at a night attack by the Persians was abandoned, but soon afterwards, probably in early August, the two sides finally met in an open battle from which the Romans emerged victorious (Geo. Pis. *Exp. Pers.* II.345–III.304, Theoph. A.M. 6113, 304.25–306.7).[14]

Almost immediately after this victory Heraclius was forced to leave his army to winter in Armenia, while he returned westwards to deal with the renewed Avar threat (Theoph. A.M. 6113, 306.7–8).[15] It is doubtful whether Heraclius had done much to reverse the Persian tide in the East by his victory, but the effect on morale of the first Roman success of the war must have been considerable. See Oikonomides 1976: 7–9, Howard-Johnston 1999: 4.

Distractions in the west (623)

Continuing pressure from the Avars obliged the emperor to arrange a meeting in June with their ruler, the khagan, at Heraclea in Thrace. Heraclius got only as far as Selymbria before learning that the Avars planned to ambush him. He was forced to flee, while the invaders penetrated as far as the walls of Constantinople. Nevertheless peace terms were agreed, by which the Romans agreed to pay 200,000 *solidi* a year to the Avars and to hand over high-ranking hostages (*Chr. Pasch.* 712.12–13.14, Nic. 10, 13.1–9, Theoph. A.M. 6110, 301.26–302.4).[16]

The Persians meanwhile continued to whittle away at Roman possessions in Asia Minor. Shahrvaraz captured Ancyra, while a Persian fleet seized Rhodes and deported the island's inhabitants (Theoph. A.M. 6111, 302.22–3, *Chr. 724*, 147/18, AG 934, *Chr. 1234*, 96, 230/133, Mich. Syr. XI.3 [408a/133 n.300], Agap., *PO* 8.458).[17] However at the same time, perhaps as a result of Heraclius' successes in the previous year, Khusro started to take a harder line in his newly conquered territories, as well as in his whole kingdom generally. In particular, he seized the wealth of the churches of Mesopotamia and Syria, and increased taxes to provide funds for his continuing campaigns (Theoph. A.M. 6112, 302.25–7, A.M. 6116, 314.23–6, *Chr. 1234*, 96, 230/133, Mich. Syr. XI.3 [408a/408], Agap. *PO* 8.451, 458).[18]

Heraclius' first counter-offensive in the north-east (624)

On 25 March 624 the emperor left the capital with his new wife Martina and his two children by his previous marriage. They celebrated Easter on 15 April in Nicomedia, from where he and Martina set off for Caesarea in Cappadocia (*Chr. Pasch.* 713.19–714.8, Theoph. A.M. 6114, 306.19–21, Sebeos 124/81).[19] From Caesarea Heraclius proceeded north, first to Theodosiopolis, then eastwards to Dvin in Persarmenia, which he sacked, and then southeast to Nakhchawan (Geo. Pis. *Her.* II.160–72, Sebeos 124/81, Thom. Art. 92–3/159).[20] At the same time, Shahrvaraz continued to campaign in Roman territory, from where he was recalled because of the emperor's incursion (Theoph. A.M. 6113, 306.21–3, 306.27–307.1).[21]

Theoph. A.M. 6114, 307.19–308.25: So the emperor, taking up his army straightaway made for inner Persia, burning the towns and villages. And there happened at this stage an awesome miracle. For at the time of the summer solstice the air became damp, refreshing the Roman army with the result that fair hopes revived them. When Heraclius heard that Khusro was in the town of Ganzak[22] with 40,000 fighting men, he rushed against him. He sent forward some of his subject Saracens as an advance party and they encountered the watch of Khusro, some of whom they killed, whilst others they captured and brought to the emperor together with their commander. When he had learnt of this, Khusro, abandoning the town and his army, took to flight. Heraclius gave pursuit, and some he overtook and killed, whilst the rest escaped and scattered. And when the emperor reached the town of Ganzak (308) <he refreshed his army in its suburbs. The Persians who had taken refuge with him said that Khusro had destroyed with fire all the crops in those parts on his way to the town of Thebarmais>[23] in the east, wherein were the temple of Fire and the treasure of Croesus, king of the Lydians, and the deceit of the coals.[24] Having seized these items, he (Khusro) had marched to Dastagerd.[25] Setting out from Ganzak, the emperor reached Thebarmais; and he entered (it) and burnt down the temple of Fire and burnt down the entire city; and he followed hard behind Khusro into the defiles of the land of the Medes.[26] And in this difficult terrain Khusro went from place to place. Heraclius, as he was pursuing him, plundered many towns and lands. When winter had set in, he deliberated as to where he should winter together with his army. Some said that they should do so in Albania, others that they should push ahead against Khusro himself. The emperor ordered that the army should purify itself for three days, and then, opening the holy Gospel, found a passage that directed him to winter in Albania.[27] So immediately he turned back and hastened to Albania. As he had with him numerous Persian captives, he was the object of several attacks by the Persian armies on the intervening journey, but with God's help he gained a victory against all of them. In spite of the severe winter cold that overtook him on the way, he arrived in Albania with 50,000 captives whom, in his compassionate heart, he pitied and liberated. He granted them proper care and repose so that all of them prayed with tears (in their eyes) that he should become the saviour even of Persia and slay Khusro, the destroyer of the world.[28] (tr. Mango and Scott, revised)

Movsēs Daskhurants'i II.10 (130.3–132.5): Now since, in accordance with his desire, he (Khusro) had successfully imposed his will over all peoples and kingdoms, and had become so powerful and behaved so arrogantly and believed that he had derived his formidable and wonderful kingdom through his own deeds of valour, he did not comprehend that the Most High is lord of an earthly kingdom and He gives it to whom He wishes.

So he began gradually to grow weak and to lose strength before the king of the Greeks and he was not able to raise his head in accordance with his former power. For the emperor suddenly notified all his commanders and officers of God's favour in front of him. Straightaway he ordered (them) to assemble in one place with all the strength which was under their control. Everyone responded to the assembly that had been arranged. No man had time for his friend, but without delaying they hastily beat their ploughshares into swords and their scythes into spears. The weak and the mild were encouraged saying, 'We are strong and warriors.' Having arisen with his whole army, he himself became commander and leader in front of his forces. Leaving the court of his palace in the hands of his son, he fastened a crown on him and established him upon the throne of his kingdom in his place.

He did not strike against the Persian forces, which had surrounded and blockaded his countries and cities, and were holding them in submission, and he did not pass near (p.131) to them and he did not provoke them to battle. Rather, having left them there in his land, he came and went across the sea and having fashioned a route through the land of the Egerians, he went through Armenia and passed across the river Araxes. And he planned to take the great king Khusro unprepared.[29]

And when it was reported to Khusro, he marvelled in his mind and said, 'Is this not he who was driven into an abyss from fear of me? What now is this?' And he took flight from his face, from the fortresses on the borders of Media; he went from there to the country of Asorestan. And immediately he sent swift-arriving couriers and wrote to his great commander Shahrvaraz very great oaths and threats. 'My great dishonour and wrath will be expiated if in this way you are able to hasten to arrive and not to spare a single man or beast out of those who have dared (to come) into my presence.' And the commander undertook the command, having read and heard the terrible news. Straightaway he reviewed all the Persian forces. Having left in the control of garrisons the cities of the Romans and the Palestinians which had become subject to (his) control, carefully he charged them to hold (them) until his return from the matters which had arisen. And he himself set in motion the forces with chosen armed men, and with swift horses he made haste to accomplish the command of the king.

Now the great emperor Heraclius, when he saw that the Persian king had fled from his face, refrained from pressing after him. And he raided (p.132) through the regions of Atropatene as far as the place called Gayshavan, a fortified place chosen by the Persian kings in the months of heat for its healthy coolness, which is on the borders of the country of Media. He plundered, ruined and enslaved the whole land and turned from there; he intended to winter in the districts of the countries of Albania, Iberia and Armenia. (tr. Greenwood)

Stalemate in the Transcaucasus (625)

Over the winter Heraclius sought to win support from the Transcaucasian kingdoms; he also entered into negotiations with the Turks to the north of the Caucasus. See Howard-Johnston 1999: 17.

Movsēs Daskhurants'i II.10 (132.5–21):[30] Consequently he (Heraclius) composed a letter to the princes and leaders of (the) countries, (stating) that they themselves should go out willingly to meet him, and that they should receive him and serve him together with his forces in the days of winter. But if not, they would be reckoned before him like heathens, their strongholds would be taken and the regions of those countries would be enslaved by his forces. And when all the heads and princes of this country of Albania heard this, they abandoned the great city of Partaw to the same person (Heraclius) at the command of Khusro, (and) departed and secured themselves in various places.[31] Many of the Christians and heathens, skilled inhabitants of the city, who by reason of their incapacity and infirmity were not able to escape and flee from their presence, remained there in the city.

A certain priest, named Zachariah, a holy man, who was a monk of the church of Partaw, a mild and quiet man, placed himself over them and through oaths and various means, he caused many Christian persons to be saved; through his prayers, he acted as their surety. (He did this) also for the sake of Jews and heathens. Consequently afterwards his action was praised and having been attested by everyone, he was appointed to the office of chief bishop of the see of Albania. (tr. Greenwood)

Heraclius spent most of the campaigning season of 625 in the Transcaucasus, eluding three Persian armies sent to overtake him, and seeking to defeat them individually. In addition to Theophanes and Movsēs (below), Sebeos (125–6/81–4) provides important details concerning the campaigns. See Manandjan 1950: 138–44, Stratos 1968: 159–63, Howard-Johnston 1999: 17–18, Thomson and Howard-Johnston 1999: 215–16 and Zuckerman 2002.

Movsēs Daskhurants'i II.10 (132.21–133.11): Now when the force of Romans arrived, a countless, immense multitude camped in the province of Uti, beside the torrent which was inside the boundaries of the village of (p.133) Kałankatuk.[32] They trampled and ruined the fine properties of vineyards and village possessions through which they passed. And travelling from there, they camped beside the torrent Trtu near to the village of Diwtakan.[33]

Then the Persian force, which they called 'New Force', came and caught up with them. And its commander was Shahraplakan.[34] And from the faithful nobles of the king there was an inspector and governor among them, one man whom they used to call Granikan Sałar; he came and descended upon him (Heraclius). The other commander of the Persians came from Rome and turned Heraclius backwards and drove him out through the country of Siwnik'.[35] For although very great losses had occurred to the Persian forces, nevertheless they displaced, drove away and threw him (Heraclius) into his own country and reoccupied the cities which they had taken from him by force. (tr. Greenwood)

Theoph. A.M. 6115 (308.27–312.8): In this year Khusro, king of the Persians, appointed as his commander Shahraplakan, an energetic man puffed up with great vanity; and having entrusted him with an army (consisting of) the so-called Khosroēgetai and (p.309) Perozitai, sent (him) against Heraclius in Albania. Having advanced to the peaks of Albania, they did not dare face the emperor in battle, but seized the passes that led to Persia, thinking to trap him. At the beginning of spring (625) Heraclius set out from Albania and made (his) way towards Persia through level plains that provided an abundance of food, even if, by this lengthy route, he was covering a great distance. Shahraplakan, on the other hand, pushed ahead by the narrow and shorter way so as to anticipate him in the territory of Persia.[36]

Heraclius exhorted his army, saying: 'Let us be aware, O brethren, that the Persian army, as it wanders through difficult country, is weakening its horses and debilitating them. As for us, let us hasten with all speed against Khusro so that, falling upon him unexpectedly, we may throw him into confusion.' The troops, however, did not consent to do this, especially the Lazic, Abasgian and Iberian allies. For this reason they fell into misfortune. For Shahrvaraz, too, had arrived with his army, whom Khusro had armed in full strength and sent against Heraclius by way of Armenia. (As for) Shahraplakan, he was following Heraclius from behind and did not engage him, expecting, as he did, to join Shahrvaraz and in this way give battle. When the Romans had been apprised of the approach of Shahrvaraz, they turned to cowardice and fell at the emperor's feet, repenting with tears of their misguided disobedience; for they knew how great an evil it is for a servant not to yield to his master's wishes. And they said: '(Stretch out) your hand, O lord, before we miserable ones perish. We obey you in whatever you command.' Then the emperor hastened to engage Shahraplakan before the latter had been joined by the army of Shahrvaraz and, having made many sorties against him both by night and by day, reduced him to a state of timidity. Leaving both of them to his rear, he pushed on with all speed against Khusro. Now two of the Romans deserted to the Persians and persuaded them that the Romans were fleeing out of cowardice. Another rumour had also reached them, namely that Shahin, the Persian commander, was coming with another army to (their) aid.

(p.310) When Shahraplakan and Shahrvaraz learnt this, they strove to engage Heraclius in battle before Shahin arrived and transferred to himself the glory of victory. Trusting also the deserters, they moved against Heraclius and, when they drew near to him, encamped, wishing to engage him in the morning. But Heraclius set out in the evening and marched all night; and when he had gone a long distance from them, he found a grassy plain and encamped in it. The barbarians, thinking that he was fleeing out of cowardice, pushed on in a disorderly manner so as to overtake him. But he met them and gave battle. Having occupied a certain wooded hill and gathered his army there, he routed the barbarians with God's help and slew a multitude of them after pursuing them through the ravines. <Shahraplakan fell, too, struck with a sword

in his back.>[37] As these struggles were going on, Shahin also arrived with his army, and the emperor routed him and slew many of his men, whilst the rest he scattered as they were fleeing; and he captured their camp equipment. Shahrvaraz then joined forces with Shahin and gathered together the barbarians who had survived. And, once again, they made plans to move against Heraclius. (As for) the emperor, he pushed on to the land of the Huns[38] and their difficult terrain, through rough and inaccessible places, (while) the barbarians followed him from behind. Now the Lazi, together with the Abasgi, took fright; they severed themselves from their alliance with the Romans and returned to their own country. Shahin was pleased at this and, together with Shahrvaraz, eagerly marched on against Heraclius. The emperor, having gathered his army, encouraged his men and spurred them on with advice, saying: 'Brothers, do not let the multitude <of the enemy> disturb you. For when God wills it, one man will rout a thousand. So let us sacrifice ourselves to God for the salvation of our brothers. May we win (p.311) the crown of martyrdom so that the time to come will praise us and God will grant (us) our reward.' Having encouraged the army with these and many other words, he arranged the battle order with joyful countenance. The two sides stood a little distance from each other from morning until evening, but did not engage with each other. When evening had fallen, the emperor kept to his march; and again the barbarians pressed on behind him. Wishing to overtake him, they changed route, but fell into marshy ground, went astray and came into great danger. So the emperor passed through the regions of Persarmenia. That country being under Persian control, many men joined Shahrvaraz and increased his army. And when it was winter, the multitude was dispersed in their own lands so as to take rest <in their houses>.[39] Heraclius, learning of this, planned to steal a battle by night. And when the winter, then, had set in, and Shahrvaraz was not suspecting anything, he selected the strongest horses and the bravest soldiers of the army and divided them into two; the first part he ordered to move ahead against Shahrvaraz, whilst he himself followed behind with the rest. So they hastened through the night and reached the village Salbanon at the ninth hour of the night.[40] The Persians who were there became aware of the attack: they rose up and rushed against them (the Romans). The Romans slew all of them, except one, who informed Shahrvaraz. Shahrvaraz, rising up and mounting his horse, naked and unshod as he was, obtained his salvation by flight. Heraclius overtook and destroyed by fire his wives and the flower of the Persians, i.e. the commanders, satraps and picked soldiers, after they climbed onto the roofs of their houses and were preparing to fight; some he slew, some he burnt, whilst others were bound in fetters, so that nearly no one escaped except for Shahrvaraz. (p.312) They took the arms of Shahrvaraz, (namely) his golden shield, his dagger, spear, gold belt set with precious stones, and boots. When Heraclius had taken these things, he moved against the men scattered in the villages. These men, on learning of the flight of Shahrvaraz, (also) fled without restraint. He pursued them, killed or captured many of them, whilst the remainder returned to Persia in disgrace.[41] (As for) the emperor, he joyfully collected his army and wintered in those parts. (tr. Mango and Scott, revised)

Sebeos 125–6/81–3 offers more geographical precision than Theophanes. Shahrvaraz moved from Nisibis, through Media, to P'aytakaran in Albania. He and Shahin, with 30,000 troops, nearly surrounded Heraclius near Gardman, east of Lake Sevan. Heraclius eluded both of them, first moving south to Nakhchawan and then northwest into Bagrevand. With an élite force of 20,000 men, the emperor inflicted a crushing defeat first on Shahrvaraz's vanguard (of whom only one survived) and then on the main body of the Persian forces at Archesh (in the battle described by Theophanes, immediately above). Shahrvaraz escaped, while Heraclius continued west for the rest of the winter.[42] See Thomson and Howard-Johnston 1999: 215–17 (noting probable use of the same source by Theoph. and Sebeos) and Howard-Johnston 1999: 18.

The turning of the tide (626)

While Heraclius continued to outmanoeuvre Khusro's armies, the Avars were advancing towards the imperial capital. Shahrvaraz too reached Chalcedon and entered into communication with the Avars. But the city, already strongly fortified at the emperor's orders, stoutly resisted the attacks of the Avars and Slavs in late July and early August. See Barišić 1954, Stratos 1968: ch.14, Howard-Johnston 1995b.

The Persians, lacking a fleet, were unable to do any more than observe.[43] It is possible, however, that they deliberately failed to intervene: according to Theophanes (A.M. 6118, 323.22–324.16), Mich. Syr. XI.3 (408–9a/408–9), Chr. 1234, 98, 232–3/136–7, and Agapius (PO 8.461–2),[44] Khusro wrote to the second-in-command at Chalcedon, Kardarigan, ordering him to kill Shahrvaraz and lead the army back to Persia. The letter was intercepted by the Romans, and Heraclius Constantine invited Shahrvaraz to Constantinople to show it to him. The general therefore entered into an alliance with the Romans, altered the letter to state that Khusro wanted 400 commanders killed, and by making it public secured the backing of his army against the king. Whether because of such an arrangement, which may well have been fabricated when Shahrvaraz entered into friendly relations with Heraclius in 629, or because he was threatened by the Roman army which had defeated Shahin (see Theoph. below), Shahrvaraz's forces then withdrew from Constantinople. See Mango 1985: 106–9 (accepting the alliance) and Speck 1988: 144–52, 293–8 and Howard-Johnston 1999: 19–22 and n.68 (rejecting it).[45]

Theoph. A.M. 6116 (312.19–314.23): In this year, on the 1st of March, the emperor Heraclius collected his army and took counsel as to which road he should follow: for two roads lay before him, both narrow and difficult, one leading to Taranton, the other to the land of Syria.[46] And whereas the one to Taranton was superior, it lacked every kind of food supply, whereas the one to Syria that went over the Taurus provided a plentiful abundance of food. Everyone gave preference to the latter, even though it was more precipitous and covered with much snow. Having traversed it with great toil, in seven days they reached the river Tigris, which they crossed and arrived at Martyropolis and Amida.[47] Both the army and the captives rested (there). From there the emperor was able to send letters to Byzantium (p.313) and to set out everything from his point of view, and to cause great joy in the City. Shahrvaraz, having collected his scattered army, went after him. The emperor picked a band of soldiers and sent them forth to guard the passes leading to him; and sallying forth to the eastward passages,[48] he came face to face with Shahrvaraz. Having crossed the

Nymphius river, he reached the Euphrates, where there was a pontoon bridge made of rope and boats. Shahrvaraz, having untied the ropes from one bank, shifted the whole bridge to the other.[49] When the emperor came and was unable to cross by the bridge, he went by (it) and found a ford which he safely traversed – an unexpected feat in the month of March – and so reached Samosata. Once again he went over the Taurus and arrived at Germaniceia; and, going by Adana, he came to the river Sarus.[50] Now Shahrvaraz stretched the bridge back to its former place and, crossing the Euphrates without hindrance, followed him from behind. The emperor crossed the bridge of the Sarus and, finding an opportunity to rest his army and horses, encamped there and gave them rest. Shahrvaraz (then) reached the opposite bank. Finding the bridge and its forward bastions occupied by the Romans, he encamped. Now many of the Romans made disorderly sorties across the bridge and attacked the Persians, among whom they caused much slaughter. The emperor forbade them to sally forth indiscriminately in case a way might open for the enemy to enter the bridge and cross it at the same time they did, but the army did not obey the emperor. Shahrvaraz set up ambuscades and, feigning flight, drew many of the Romans to cross over in pursuit of him against the emperor's wish. He then turned round and routed them, (p.314) and killed as many as he overtook outside the bridge – (and so) they paid the price for their disobedience. When the emperor saw that the barbarians had broken ranks in pursuit and that many of the Romans who were standing upon the bastions were being slain, he moved against them. A giant of a man confronted the emperor in the middle of the bridge and attacked him, but the emperor struck him and threw him into the river. When this man had fallen, the barbarians turned to flight and, because of the narrowness of the bridge, hurled themselves into the river like frogs, whilst others were being killed by the sword. The bulk of the barbarians, after being scattered to the edges of the river, shot arrows and stood firm, preventing the Romans from crossing. The emperor did cross to the other side and bravely opposed the barbarians with a few men of his guard, fighting in a superhuman manner so that even Shahrvaraz was astonished and said <to> one Cosmas (a runaway Roman and an apostate) who was standing close to him: 'Do you see, Cosmas, how boldly the Caesar stands in battle, how he fights alone against such a multitude and shrugs off blows like an anvil?' For he was recognized by his particular boots, and received many blows, although none <of a serious nature in this battle. After they had fought in this battle all day,> when evening came, they drew apart. Shahrvaraz became frightened and retreated through the night. As for the emperor, he collected his army and hastened to the city of Sebastea. After crossing the river Halys, he spent the whole winter in that land.[51] (tr. Mango and Scott, revised)

Since Heraclius will have reached Sebastea in April or May 626, Theophanes' final statement above must be rejected. His next entry in fact continues to recount events from the same year.

Theoph. A.M. 6117 (315.2–26): In this year Khusro, king of the Persians, made a new army by conscripting strangers, citizens and slaves, raising the levy from every nation. He placed this levy under the general Shahin and, taking another 50,000 men chosen from the phalanx of Shahrvaraz, attached them to him. He called them the Golden Spearmen and sent them against the emperor. (As for) Shahrvaraz, he despatched him with his remaining army against Constantinople, so that after establishing an alliance between the western Huns (whom they call Avars) and the Bulgars, Slavs and Gepids, they would advance on the City and lay siege to it. When the emperor learnt of this, he divided his army into three contingents: the first he sent to protect the City (Constantinople); the second he entrusted to his own brother Theodore, whom he ordered to fight Shahin; the third part he took himself and marched to Lazica.[52] During his stay there he invited the eastern Turks, whom they call Khazars, into an alliance.[53] Now Shahin with his newly recruited army overtook the emperor's brother and prepared for battle. With God's help (through the entreaties of the all-praised Mother of God), when battle was joined a storm of hail fell unexpectedly on the barbarians and struck down many of them, whereas the Roman array enjoyed calm weather. (So) the Romans routed the Persians and slew a great multitude (of them).[54] When Khusro learnt of this, he was angered at Shahin. And Shahin, because of his great despondency fell ill and died. By order of Khusro his body was preserved in salt and conveyed to him; and he subjected the corpse to many outrages. (tr. Mango and Scott, revised)

The following extract from an account of the life and miracles of St Theodore the Recruit has been connected with the victory of Heraclius' brother. See Howard-Johnston 1995b: 134. Zuckerman 1988: 206–10 associates it rather with Heraclius' campaign of 622.

V. S. Theodori, ch.11 (53): Miracle three. For while the Persians remained before the city (Euchaita),[55] they were suddenly hit by a Roman expeditionary force. Boiling with anger, they slaughtered many of the captives with the sword and set fire to the city and the shrine of the holy man. But they were not quite able to escape (him), (and) the warrior martyr overtook them. They had not yet marched far (from the city) when another column of Roman soldiers attacked them on the mountain called Omphalimus. They (the Romans) destroyed many, (while) a mass of stones sent from the sky, like hailstones, killed the others by divine judgement when they reached the river called Lycus.[56] Thus none of those who had done such things returned to his lands. (…) (tr. Zuckerman, revised)

In the eastern Transcaucasus, Heraclius' contacts with the Turks began to bear fruit in the same year: an invasion of Albania took place in mid-626, and the yabghu khagan demanded from Khusro that he withdraw from Roman territory. See Baynes 1914: 665–6, Howard-Johnston 1999: 21.

Movsēs Daskhurants'i II.12 (140.17–143.20): Then, after that, in the thirty-sixth year of Khusro (625/6), Caesar Augustus decided to contemplate ways how perhaps he might be able to be cured from the terrible sorrow and dishonour. And during the whole (p.141) period of his kingship he united to himself the whole Roman army which he summoned to his assistance, in order to breach the great mount Caucasus, which shuts in and dominates the regions of the north-east and in order to open the gates of Ch'or[57] to draw out various peoples of barbarians and through these to drive out the king of the Persians, the proud Khusro. Then he prepared and briefed one of his nobles (whose) name (was) Andrē,[58] a highly talented and intelligent man, and sent him with many promises of innumerable and countless treasures; 'On condition that they shall assist me out of great envy (of Khusro), I shall undertake to satisfy the thirst of the savage, gold-loving people of long hair.'

Now when the heir to the king of the north, who was second to his kingship and named Jebu Khak'an (yabghu khagan),[59] heard this, and saw the promises of very valuable presents in return for plundering in a raid all the countries which were under the control of the Persian king, then with great eagerness he gave a reply saying, 'I shall take revenge against the enemy. I shall leave and arrive in person as an assistant to him (Heraclius) with my valiant forces, and I shall please his mind with military engagements, with my sword and bow, just as his person desires.' Then he sent with the same noble, in order to satisfy the purpose of that agreement, select mounted men, powerful in strength and skilled archers, in number about one thousand. They rushed suddenly against the gates of Ch'or and did not pay attention to the militia and garrison of the king of Persia, who were arranged at the great gate. Rather, swooping like (p.142) eagles beside the great river Kur, sparing no one who came against them, they took a route through the country of Iberia and Eger; they cut across the great sea as far as the royal palace.[60] And being in the presence of the great emperor Heraclius, they affirmed to each other oaths in accordance with the custom of each one. Having received from him an order concerning their issuing forth, they returned from there on the same route to their country, nothing being suspected by anyone.

Now at the entering of the thirty-seventh year of the same Khusro (626/7),[61] the king of the north sent the promised fighting force, appointing his brother's son as commander, whose princely title they give (as) Shat'. When he came, he galloped through all the borders of this country of Albania and through a part of Atropatene. He put to the edge of the sword many individuals, Christian and heathen alike. Who will be able to discover and set down in writing the number of those who were made prisoner by them?

When they had encamped beside the river Araxes, he despatched messages to the great king Khusro, revealing their uniting with the emperor and their coming to his assistance. And the transcripts of the messages to one another are as follows. 'If you will not turn your face from the king of the Romans and yield to him all the countries and cities which you have seized through your violence, and (if) you will (not) despatch all the prisoners taken from his land, which you have at present under your control, together with the wooden cross which all (p.143) Christian peoples worship and glorify, and (if) you will (not) summon outside his borders all your forces, the king of the north speaks in this way, the lord of all the earth, your king and (king) of all kings, "I shall set my face against you, you governor of Asorestan, and in place of one evil which you employed against him, I shall pay you back double. I shall move against all your borders with my sword in the same way that you moved with your sword against his borders. I shall not release you, and I shall not hesitate to act against you according to that statement which I have relayed to you.'"

Then when the great Khusro heard all this, he was provoked like a terrible flood, or like a lion against hunters, or like a bear bereft of young; so was he. Although he saw them united and risen against him, despite this, in accordance with his cunning, he did not display his fear or his hiding from his face, but with arrogance and great rebuke, he replied, 'Depart, say to your king and our brother khagan that your house has been venerated and honoured long since by my ancestors and by me as if our beloved brother. For this reason we have been grafted onto one another in alliance through sons and daughters.[62] So it was not right or worthy for you to cast off your limbs and be led astray by the words of my servant, the valiant one[63] of the Romans.' The messenger returned to his country. (tr. Greenwood)

The final Roman counter-strike (627–8)

Heraclius probably returned to Constantinople for the winter of 626–627, allowing his troops some rest before returning to the offensive. Then in spring 627 he set off for the Transcaucasus once more, arriving first in Lazica. In the meantime, his diplomatic overtures to the Turks continued to bring results, and a large-scale invasion of Albania was undertaken by the Turkish yabghu khagan. The two sides then converged at Tiflis in Iberia. See Howard-Johnston 1999: 22–4.

Theoph. A.M. 6117 (315.26–316.16) (cf. *Chr. 1234*, 98, 233/137, Mich. Syr. XI.3 [409a/409], Agap. *PO* 8.463–4):[64] Now the Khazars, after breaking through the (p.316) Caspian Gates, invaded Persia, i.e. the land of Adraigan,[65] under their commander Ziebel[66] who was second in rank after the khagan. And in whatever lands they traversed, they made the Persians captive and consigned the towns and villages to the flames. The emperor, too, set out from Lazica and met them. When Ziebel saw him, he rushed forward, embraced his neck and did obeisance to him, while the Persians were looking on from the town of Tiflis. And the entire army of the Turks fell prone to the ground and, stretched out on their faces, reverenced the emperor with an honour that is unfamiliar among (foreign) nations. Likewise, their commanders climbed on rocks and fell (flat) in the same manner. Ziebel also brought his adolescent son to the emperor, and he was delighted by the emperor's conversation and struck by his appearance and wisdom. After picking 40,000 noble men, Ziebel gave them in alliance to the emperor, while he himself returned to his own land. Taking these men along, the emperor advanced on Khusro. (tr. Mango and Scott, revised)

Nic. 12.16–43 also describes the meeting of Heraclius and the yabghu khagan in some detail. According to his account the emperor betrothed his daughter Eudocia to the khagan in return for his assistance; and with the troops he received from the Turks he invaded Persia. See Mango 1990: 180–1 and Zuckerman 1995: 120–3 (on the significance of this dynastic marriage, which came to nothing when the khagan was assassinated in late 629).[67]

HVG 224–6/233–5 offers a few details from the Iberian perspective. It describes how the Iberian ruler Stephen remained loyal to the Persians and fortified himself in Tiflis. He opposed the Romans courageously but he was killed and the city captured. In his place Heraclius installed Adarnase as king of Iberia, a kingdom reduced in size in the west after Heraclius' victories in 627–628. See Toumanoff 1963: 389–91.[68]

Movsēs Daskhurants'i II.11 (135.5–140.14): Now in the thirty-eighth year (of Khusro), which was a year of crisis and misfortune (and) of the murder of Khusro, the same man came himself, whom we mentioned above, who was Jebu Khak'an, bringing with him his son as well. And no one was able to quantify the number of his force. When the terrible, sorrowful news reached this land of Albania, it was decided to defend this country of ours in the fortress of the great capital city Partaw. That came about from the order of one man, whose name was Gayshak', who had been sent by Khusro as head and prince of this country. He surrounded the majority of the neighbouring provinces and wanted to consolidate himself by means of an alliance with the magnates of this country and the inhabitants of the city (in order) to oppose them (the raiders). But he watched to see what events would occur to the garrison of the great city of Ch'or, and to the garrison of the wonderful walls (for) which the kings of Persia had exhausted their country through vast expenditure, collecting architects and devising various materials for the construction of the astonishing project (by) which they barred and enclosed (the pass) between mount Caucasus and the great sea of the east.[69]

Now at the approach of the universal wrath which was facing us all, however, the waves of the sea extended and struck it (the city of Ch'or) and demolished it from (its) foundations. Because (their) terror increased on seeing the ugly, insolent, (p.136) broad-faced (men), without eyelashes, in feminine dress with locks of hair, as they charged, trepidation possessed them (the defenders), especially on seeing in front of them the well-drawn, expertly aimed (bows) which were showering (arrows) upon them like very heavy hail.

When these ravenous shameless wolves charged against them, they (the defenders) were massacred indiscriminately in the streets and passages of the city. Their eye did not spare the handsome, the beautiful, the young men or women, nor the insignificant or useless. They did not pass over the crippled or the old, nor did they show pity nor did their heartstrings writhe with compassion for the children, those who embraced murdered mothers and suckled blood from their breasts rather than milk. But like having lit a fire in straw, they went in through one gate and went out through the other. They left work for the beasts of the field and birds of the air in it. Then gradually the waves were stirred against us.

Now when our head and prince heard about all this, who was guarding and holding the city of Partaw, he wanted to speak to the multitude who had fortified themselves, who had gathered in the great fortress, because (their) terror had increased, as to what it would be right to do. He opened his mouth but from great fear at that time, he was unable to repeat his plan, because his courage had disappeared and shaking seized him from foot to head, and his knees were knocking together. And when the multitude perceived that the man had completely lost courage, they raised a clamour and said, 'Why have you shut us in completely at this time, to give us with our wives and children into the clutches of bloodthirsty animals? Also how shall we be able to (p.137) leave and flee before them, such a large common crowd of this city, because behold the exterminating enemy has come and is three miles from us?' Then each man said to his neighbour, 'Why are we (so) passive (as) to make this city a tomb for ourselves? Let us abandon our goods and wealth, let us leave and depart; perhaps we shall be able to save ourselves.' And having raced in common to the four gates of the city, they hastened to escape to the mountainous region of the province of Arts'akh.[70]

When the enemy became aware of what had happened, they strained after the fugitives and caught up with one group at the foot of the mountain which is opposite the village of the large region of Kałankatuk',[71] which is in the same province of Uti, from which I also am. And at the darkening of the day, they were not able to spend time injuring many, but a few fell into their clutches, some of whom they massacred; having placed others forcibly behind the baggage, the carts and the beasts of burden, they returned from there to their camp. And by the protection of God, they did not continue to press after the multitude of fugitives. During that night, everyone crossed, just as in an earlier time, the Hebrews (crossed) through the Red Sea, and they slipped away into the inaccessible province of Arts'akh. In the same way, that prince, by name Gayshak', saved himself along with his whole house and he slipped away to the regions of the Persians, but he was not able to establish himself in the same office of prince.

After all this, the mountain streams rose, and a rapid river gushed against the country of Iberia, and they surrounded and blockaded the fine, commercial, renowned great city of Tiflis. And it was brought to the attention of the great emperor (p.138) Heraclius. He assembled all the forces of his power, (and) straightaway he came to his assisting ally. On drawing near, they received gifts and royal presents; they rejoiced on seeing one another. Then from that time there was visible the miseries of the unfortunate persons, those who were shut in the fortress. Calamity upon calamity apprehended them. But because the time (of the city's capture) had not yet arrived, which stood in the future, it happened in this way, that when Khusro learned about the meeting of both great kings at that city, before the siege (began) he sent rapidly a force to their assistance for the defence of the city, the eager and valiant warrior, his commander Shahraplakan, and elite cavalry of his bodyguards and courtguards with him, about one thousand men (in number). When the inhabitants of the city saw the reinforcements despatched, consisting of strong experienced warriors, they grew much stronger in themselves and began to deride the two kings. For although they could see the countless multitude of the forces of the north and west, drawn up around the city in the likeness of mountains – the land trembled and shuddered from the multitude – and with the same (army) engines and four-wheeled (machines) and various other devices prepared by the hands of Roman engineers, by which they threw stones accurately in order to demolish the circuit wall by means of very large stones; and (although they could see) the very large bloated skins full of stones (and) full of sand, by which they (their besiegers) had compelled the great river Kur, which surrounds one side of the city, to rush and burst against the circuit wall, they were not at all faint-hearted at any part of the proceedings;

(p.139) rather they encouraged one another and they rebuilt and reconstructed the demolished parts of the wall.

Now when the forces of the two kings were dispirited and used up and exhausted, and a considerable number of infantry had fallen in battle, the kings consulted one another and said, 'Why is this loss to our forces (taking place)? Is it not the case that when we have bound the strong man, we shall pillage his house as we may wish?' Then the zealous great emperor Heraclius organised and arranged whatever it should be right to do. He said to that man who had come to his assistance, 'Turn, go peacefully with your forces this year to your place. For we see your cool disposition, and behold you will not be able to endure at the coming of summer time the burning heat of the country of Asorestan, where the royal residence of the Persians is, beside the great river which is the Tigris. And at the coming of another year, at the diminishing of the months of heat, may you hasten to advance to here so that we may realise our plans. I shall not cease to contend with the king of the Persians and having ventured forth, I shall harass this country and his subjects, and I shall contrive in such a way through cunning that he will be killed by his own people.'

And it happened that when the inhabitants of the city learned of their disheartenment and weakening, they became even more arrogant in themselves and they began to mock the (eventual) cause of their own destruction. They brought one large pumpkin and they painted upon it a picture of the king of the Honk' (Huns), one cubit long and one cubit wide. They stretched one vine branch in the place of his eye lashes, which no one was able (p.140) to make out. And in the place of his beard, an impudent baldness and in the place of his nose, nostrils one span wide, and with a number of moustache hairs so that anyone could recognize him. Having carried that (out), they placed it upon the circuit wall opposite them and they shouted to the forces and said, 'Here's the emperor your king, where he is standing. Turn, worship this one. It is Jebu Khak'an.' And having taken a spear in hand, they pierced the pumpkin in front of them – the one which had been made similar to his figure. In the same way, they ridiculed the other king, made a mockery and jeered and called him impure and a sodomite. When the kings saw and heard this, they nourished resentment and became swollen (with rage); they hoarded and collected rancour in their own persons (in their determination) that not a single soul out of all of them should be saved – (of) those who were under their rule[72] – until revenge should have been exacted for those insults with which they had been ridiculed by them. Having turned their faces, they left with insults. (tr. Greenwood)

Movsēs describes the actual fall of the city at II.14 (151–3/94–5). He apparently dates it to the following year, but it seems more probable that it took place later in 628. See Howard-Johnston 1999: 24 and n.77.

While the yabghu khagan prosecuted the siege of Tiflis, Heraclius moved southwards with an army comprising Roman forces and a substantial Turkish escort; he also secured the support of many Armenians.[73] In the late summer and early autumn, Roman control was restored to the region, while the Persians sought to muster more armies to meet the new threat. See Howard-Johnston 1999: 24, Speck 1988: 135–8.

Theoph. A.M. 6118 (317.11–26): In this year Heraclius, by invading Persia together with the Turks starting in the month of September – an unexpected move, since it was winter – threw Khusro into a state of distraction when he learned this. But the Turks, seeing the winter and the constant attacks of the Persians, could not bear to toil together with the emperor and started, little by little, to slip away, and (eventually) all of them had left and returned home.[74] Now the emperor addressed his own army, saying: 'Know, brothers, that no one wishes to ally with us, except God and His Mother who bore Him without seed, and (and) so that He may show His might, <since salvation does not lie in the abundance of armies and weapons, but to those who trust in His mercy> He sends down His aid.'

(As for) Khusro, he collected all his armies and appointed Rahzadh commander over them, a most warlike and brave man, whom he sent against Heraclius. The emperor (meanwhile) was burning the towns and villages of Persia and destroying by the sword the Persians he captured. On the 9th of October of the 15th indiction he reached the land of Chamaetha,[75] where he rested his army for one week. (As for) Rahzadh, coming to Ganzak, in the emperor's rear, he followed him, while the Romans, in front, were destroying the crops. Trailing behind, like a hungry dog, he was sustained with difficulty on the emperor's crumbs. (tr. Mango and Scott, revised)

Sebeos 126/83 describes Heraclius' route in more detail. Initially he moved westwards, into Gogovit, the region south of Dvin, but then turned southeast, passing to the west of Lake Urmia towards Ganzak. See Manandjan 1950: 148–53, Stratos 1968: 205–6, 208–9 and Thomson and Howard-Johnston 1999: 218–19. From Chnaitha Heraclius moved west across the Zagros through the Keli Shin pass, heading down towards the river Tigris; one detachment at least may have employed a more northerly route, passing through Marga (*Hist. Rabban bar 'Idta*, 1280–1319, p.67–8/253–5). See Howard-Johnston 1999: 25, Fiey 1966: 7–9.

Theoph. A.M. 6118 (317.32–323.22, 324.16–325.10): On the 1st of December the emperor reached (p.318) the Great Zab river, which he crossed, and encamped near the town of Niniveh. Following him, Rahzadh, too, reached the ford and, going three miles downstream, found another ford and crossed. The emperor sent out the commander Baanes[76] with a few picked soldiers; the latter encountered a company of Persians and, after killing their captain, brought (back) his head and his sword, which was all of gold. He killed many more and made 26 captive, among whom was the sword-bearer of Rahzadh. This man announced to the emperor that Rahzadh was intending to attack him, (since) thus Khusro, who had sent him 3000 armed men, had commanded; but these men had not yet arrived. Learning these things, the emperor first sent away his camp equipment and himself followed,[77] seeking a place in which to give battle before the 3000 had joined (the enemy). And when he had found a plain suitable for fighting, he addressed his army and drew it up in battle order. Upon arriving there, Rahzadh also drew up his army in three wedge formations and advanced on the emperor. Battle was given on Saturday, the 12th of December. The emperor sprang

forward in front of everyone and met a commander of the Persians in battle, and, by
God's might and the help of the Mother of God, threw him down; and those who had
sprung forward with him were routed.[78] Then the emperor met another (Persian) in
combat and cast him down also. Yet a third assailed him and struck him on the lip
with a spear, wounding him; but the emperor slew him too.[79] And when the trumpets
had sounded, the two sides attacked each other and, as a violent battle was being
waged, the emperor's tawny horse, called Dorkon, was struck in the thigh by the
infantry, receiving a spear (blow) to its thigh. It also received several blows of the
sword on the face, but, wearing as it did a coat of armour made of fibres, it was not
hurt, nor were the blows effective. (p.319) Rahzadh fell in battle, as did the three divi-
sional commanders of the Persians, nearly all of their officers and the greater part of
their army. As for the Romans, fifty were killed and a considerable number wounded,
but they did not die, save for another ten. The battle was waged from morning until
the 11th hour. The Romans captured 28 standards of the Persians, not counting those
that had been broken, and, having despoiled the dead, took their corselets, helmets
and all their arms. And the two sides remained at a distance of two bowshots from one
another, for there was no rout.[80] The Roman forces watered their horses at night and
fed (them). But the Persian horsemen stood until the seventh hour of the night over
the bodies of their dead; and at the eighth hour of the night they moved (off) and
returned to their camp; and taking it up, they went away and encamped in fear at the
foot of a rugged mountain. The Romans took many all-gold swords and belts interwo-
ven with gold and set with pearls, and the shield of Rahzadh, which was all of gold and
had 120 laminae, and his all-gold breastplate; and they brought in his caftan together
with his head, and his bracelets and his all-gold saddle. And Barsamouses, the prince
of the Iberians who are subject to Persia, was taken alive.[81] <No one can recall such a
battle having taken place between Persians> and Romans in that the battle did not
cease for the whole day. The Romans won, but this occurred only by God's help.[82]

After encouraging his army, the emperor pushed on against Khusro with a view to
frightening him and so that, having sent (him) forth, he might summon Shahrvaraz
from Byzantium.[83] On the 21st of December (p.320) the emperor learned that the
army of Rahzadh – as much of it as had escaped from the battle – had been joined by
the 3000 men despatched by Khusro and had reached Niniveh as it followed behind
him. After crossing the Great Zab, the emperor <despatched the turmarch George[84]
with 1000 men to ride forward and seize the bridges of the Lesser Zab> before Khusro
had become aware (of it). After riding 48 miles in the night,[85] George seized the four
bridges of the Lesser Zab and, finding Persians in the forts, took them alive. On the
23rd of December the emperor reached the bridges, crossed them and encamped in
the mansions of Yazdin; he rested both his army and his horses and celebrated the feast
of Christ's Nativity in that place.[86]

When Khusro became aware that the Romans had seized the bridges of the Lesser
Zab, he sent a message to the army (that had been) under Rahzadh that they should
try very hard to overtake the emperor so as to return to him. Making haste, they
crossed the Lesser Zab in another place and anticipated the emperor, and (now)
marched in front (of him). (As for) the emperor, he came upon <a palace called

Dezeridan, which he destroyed and handed over to the flames, (while) the Persians crossed the bridge of the river Tornas and encamped there.[87] The emperor came upon> another palace of Khusro called Rousa[88] and this, too, he destroyed. He suspected that the enemy were going to fight him at the bridge of the river Tornas; but when they saw him, they abandoned the bridge and fled. (So) the emperor crossed without hindrance and reached another palace called Beklal;[89] here he built a hippo-drome and destroyed it.[90] Several of the Armenians who accompanied the Persians came to the emperor <at night> and said: 'Khusro with his elephants and his own army (p.321) is encamped five miles from the palace called Dastagerd, in a place called Barasroth,[91] and he has given instructions that his forces should assemble there and fight you. There is a river there that is difficult to cross, and a narrow bridge, and many cramped spaces between buildings, and fetid streams.' The emperor, after taking counsel with his officers and his army, remained in the palace of Beklal. He found therein in one enclosure 300 corn-fed ostriches, and in another about 500 corn-fed gazelles, and in another 100 corn-fed wild asses, and all of these he gave to his army. And they celebrated the 1st of January there. They also found sheep, pigs and oxen without number, and the whole army rested, enjoying (these things) and praising God. They caught the herdsmen of these cattle and accurately learned from them that Khusro had learned on the 23rd of December that the emperor had crossed the bridge of the Tornas, and forthwith set out from the palace of Dastagerd <going away to Ctesiphon with great speed,[92] loading all the money he had in the palace on the elephants, camels and mules that were in his service, and he wrote to the army of Rahzadh that they should enter that same palace and the houses of the noblemen and take away anything they found therein. Therefore the emperor sent one half of his army to Dastagerd>, while he himself went by a different road to another palace called Bebdarch,[93] and having destroyed this too and consigned it to flames, they thanked God for having wrought such wonders by the entreaties of the Mother of God. For who had expected that Khusro would flee before the Roman emperor from his palace at Dastagerd and go off to Ctesiphon, when, for 24 years, he would not suffer to behold Ctesiphon, but had (p.322) his royal resi-dence at Dastagerd? In his palace of Dastagerd the Roman forces found 300 Roman standards which the Persians had captured at different times. They also found the goods that had been left behind, namely a great quantity of aloes and big pieces of aloes wood, each weighing 70 or 80 lbs, much silk and pepper, linen garments beyond counting, sugar, ginger and many other goods.[94] Others found silver bullion, silken cloaks, woollen rugs and woven carpets – a great quantity of them and very beautiful, but on account of their weight they burnt them all. They also burnt the tents of Khusro and the porticoes he set up whenever he encamped in a plain, and many of his statues. They also found in these palaces an infinite number of ostriches, gazelles, wild asses, peacocks and pheasant, and in the hunting park huge live lions and tigers. Many of the captives from Edessa,[95] Alexandria and other cities sought refuge with the emperor, (as did) a large multitude from other cities. The emperor celebrated at Dastagerd the feast of the Epiphany,[96] cheering and refreshing the army and horses while destroying the palaces of Khusro. These priceless, wonderful and astonishing structures he demolished to the ground so that Khusro might learn how great a pain the Romans had suffered when their cities were laid waste and burnt (by him).[97]

Many of the palace stewards were also seized and, on being interrogated as to when Khusro had departed from Dastagerd, they said: 'Nine days before your arrival he heard of your presence and secretly made a hole in the city wall near the palace.[98] In this way he went out unhindered (p.323) through the gardens, he and his wife and children, so there should not be a tumult in the city.' And neither his army was aware of it nor his noblemen until he had gone five miles from there, at which point he announced that they should follow him in the direction of Ctesiphon. And this man who was incapable of travelling five miles in one day, travelled 25 in his flight. His wives and children, who previously had not laid eyes on one another, now fled in disorder, jostling one another. When night had fallen, Khusro entered the house of an insignificant farmer to rest, but could scarcely be admitted through the door. When, later, Heraclius saw that (door), he was amazed. In three days Khusro reached Ctesiphon. Twenty-four years earlier, when he besieged Dara in the days of Phocas, the Roman emperor, he had been given an oracle by the magicians and astrologers, namely that he would perish at whatever time he went to Ctesiphon; and although he would not suffer to go one mile in that direction from Dastagerd, he now returned to Ctesiphon as he fled. Even there he did not dare stop, but crossed the pontoon bridge over the river Tigris to the town on the other side, which is called Seleucia by us and Gouedeser[99] by the Persians. He deposited all his money there and remained there with his wife Shirin and three other women who were his daughters. His remaining wives and his many children he sent to a stronghold forty miles further east.

(A (misplaced) section on the siege of Constantinople in 626 and a deal between Heraclius and Shahrvaraz is omitted here.)

Now Heraclius wrote to Khusro: 'I am pursuing you as I hasten towards peace. For I do not willingly raze Persia, but after being forced by you. Let us, therefore, throw down our arms even now and embrace peace. Let us extinguish the fire before it consumes everything.' When Khusro did not accept these proposals, the hatred of the Persian people grew against him.[100] He conscripted all the retainers of his noblemen and all his servants and those of his wives and, having armed them, sent them to join the army of Rahzadh and take a stand at the river Narbas, 12 miles from Ctesiphon.[101] He commanded them that when the emperor had crossed the river, they should cut the bridge and the pontoon bridge. (As for) the emperor, he moved from Dastagerd on the 7th of January and, after marching three (p.325) days, encamped 12 miles from the river Narbas, where the Persian camp lay and where they had 200 elephants. The emperor despatched George, turmarch of the Armeniacs, to go as far as the river and ascertain whether the Narbas had a ford. And when he had found that they had cut the bridges and that the Narbas had no ford, he returned to the emperor. Setting forth, the emperor came to Siazouros and, for the whole of the month of February, he went about burning the villages and the towns.[102] In the month of March he came to a village called Barzan,[103] where he spent seven days; and he despatched the commander Mezezius[104] on a foray. (tr. Mango and Scott, revised)

Sebeos 126–7/83–5 (cf. Thom. Arts. 93–5/160–2) reports in similar fashion the battle of Niniveh and Khusro's flight across the Tigris and downfall; see Thomson and Howard-Johnston 1999: 219–20. Nic. 14 recounts Heraclius' duel with Rahzadh slightly differently from Theophanes, cf. Mango 1990: 182 and Speck 1988: 317–21. On other sources dealing with Khusro's fall (in much less detail) see Flusin 1992: II, 265–6 and n.6 (and add Tabari 1004–5/322–3). Heraclius' withdrawal northwards was probably prompted by several factors, among them his concern that Shahrvaraz might arrive on the scene (cf. Sebeos 127/84), his inability to reach Ctesiphon, the opportunity to damage Persian lands in the Diyala valley, and perhaps an awareness that events at the Persian court might overtake Khusro. See Baynes 1914: 674, Stratos 1968: 218–20, Howard-Johnston 1999: 5–6.[105]

Movsēs Daskhurants'i II.12–13 (143.21–148.24): Then the emperor took his forces and marched into the regions of the Persians. Being obdurate and determined, he hastened to reach the court of the Persian king. Now when (p.144) the Persian king saw that it (the campaign against Heraclius) had not been carried out in that way, but that (the emperor had) been daring, had marched, and was coming against him, he took flight before him and slipped away to his own capital, to the great Ctesiphon. He transported his wives and concubines and children to the far side of the river Tigris. He assembled his permanent force, which was small in size (and) close to him, prepared it and sent it against the emperor. He attracted an individual through distinctions and wealth, who was acknowledged at his court because of his valour – he transferred another name to him and called him Rochveh (Rahzadh) – (and) he promoted him by way of inducement and he struck against the waves. He appointed him as commander of the force about to be sent against it (the Roman army). Out of fear of his order, he reluctantly agreed, but he himself anticipated the vanquishing of the hastily assembled and weak force of Khusro before the emperor. He wrote once and twice and four times to his king Khusro out of concern and said, 'If not of my own death, I shall at least warn you in advance about the destruction of your forces. For if you do not supply to me straightaway a force to assist me, although I am not afraid of dying, then you will learn of (my death).'

Then the king ordered this reply to be composed: 'Do not be frightened in the face of them, but fight and overcome.' But on the last occasion, being extremely disdainful, he wrote to him saying, 'If you will not be able to overcome, why should you not be able to die?' When he saw that harsh order, having raised his hands with his forces to the sun and moon, he shouted with a loud voice and said, 'My gods, judge between me and my merciless king.' (p.145)

And having plunged into battle, he and his forces fell before the Greek forces and became like dust which a storm carries away.[106]

Now when the Persian nobles witnessed that great rout which happened to the Persian forces, they began to complain to one another, 'For how long will the streams of blood flow in various places on account of battle, (the blood) of Aryan persons of this country? For how long will we be in fear and trepidation of this blood-letting king? For how long will our possessions and property be amassed to the royal treasury, our silver and gold to his treasuries? For how long will the passes of roads remain constrained and blocked, damaging the profits of trade of various regions? For how long will our souls remain quaking and emptied from our persons by his terrible command? Did he not in fact consume and swallow like the sea our most excellent companions, the leaders of countries? Did not in fact many of our brothers perish on various occasions, in companies, in divisions, in various torments by his command, some even being drowned? Did he not snatch a man from his wife, and a father from his son, and scatter (them) to distant peoples in the capacity of a servant or female domestic, and have (them) assembled against ferocious enemies?'

They muttered this and much similar about him, but no one dared to speak anything openly until the time for the end of his life was reached. Then someone from his trusted friends, a noble, arose, who was protector of the first-born of Khusro who was called Kavadh.[107] Having formed a plan with him, he had (them) destroy the reputation of his father Khusro and the multitude of his brothers. And he took the office of the king of Persia. Through the striving and directing (p.146) of his protector he seduced and disturbed the very decorous ranks of the members of the court of Khusro. And he diverted the hearts of everyone unawares in favour of his foster-child Kavadh, in order to make him king in place of his father.

II.13. But listen to me for a moment and I shall describe briefly the cunning of the man, how or by what way he was able to arrest in a cage of death the terrible hunter, the lion of the east, at whose roar alone distant peoples shook and trembled and those close to his presence shrank, like melted wax. And that man[108] in that way in a moment stole the hearts of everyone and rose up against him as if (he was) an orphan. In performing all this, he did not summon another king or prince to his assistance, nor did he organize distant peoples and tribes to bring reinforcements to his foster-child against him. He merely sent secretly to the emperor Heraclius for him to stay put there where he was with his forces for a few days.[109]

He ordered official letters to be written on behalf of Kavadh to the magnates and the leading members of the various contingents of the great court of the Persian kingdom. 'The authority over this kingdom has been removed from my father and given to me; be prepared with a few cavalry.' He established them at the head of the bridge of the river Tigris near to the city of Veh-Ardashir opposite the gate of (p.147) Ctesiphon where his father Khusro was, being guarded by his personal forces. A herald proclaimed loudly from the right and the left of Kavadh, saying 'Whichever man who loves life and wants to see his days in mildness, let him hasten to come before this new régime of Kavadh, for this man is king of kings.' And they opened the gates of the fortress of Oblivion[110] and he summoned outside audaciously all the prisoners of the king – those who had been held in the shadows of death for a long time, in a huge countless multitude. And he said to them, 'Come out, you unfortunate people, touched by Khusro, for the gates of life have been opened for you by this newly-dedicated king, by his son Kavadh.' And each one having broken his chains, they rushed outside together. The noise of their praise being shouted went up to heaven; they praised Kavadh saying, 'O king, may you live for ever.' Having driven (off) the most select horses of the stables of Khusro, they mounted (them) with their chains in their hands, and galloped this way and that, abusing Khusro.[111]

Then many of the various contingents of house-guards and bodyguards and others similar to them[112] of the court of Khusro seized the symbols of their banners and rushed to Kavadh his son. And (as for) those who remained in the court, the messengers of Kavadh urged them to behave prudently and to arrest Khusro, because otherwise they would perish. Now when Khusro heard the clamour of that shouting, he said to those who were standing nearby, 'What are the sounds of those cries?' And they were silent because they were ashamed to explain (them) to him. And the mixed sound of trumpets pressed more and more. Again he said to those who were nearby, 'What are the disorderly (p.148) sounds of cries?' And they said, 'Because your son Kavadh intends to become king in place of you, and everyone is running to him. Behold, he has drawn up opposite this city beside the bank of the river and has released all the prisoners of the great prison, those arrested by your command. And with joy everyone is saluting him, calling (him) king.'

When he heard all this disastrous news, especially the release of the prisoners, he was exhausted, he sighed, he lamented and was uncertain of himself. He was (not able to) think when sitting nor contemplate when standing, because he saw the immense force that had arrived against him. He went out on foot through the gate of his garden; he went and hid among the trees of the garden and he stood concealing himself; his soul was emptied by sudden fear. His eyes watched the merciless sword raised above him. Then the whole contingent came against him and arrived around the palace. Searchers went in after (him) and found him at that place where he had been hesitating. Having conducted him outside the palace, they threw him into a hall which they call K'ataki Hndukn, the house of the Indians, in the palace of the one called Maraspand.[113] When he entered, he enquired about the place and the lord of the house; having beaten his breast, he said groaning, 'Woe is me, how unfortunate I am! How I have been deceived by sorcerers, those who divined that I would be arrested in India! And now behold it has been allotted to me in accordance with the description of their vision, albeit metaphorically.'

Having kept him for that day, on the following day they removed his head with a sword. The evil one was exterminated. And in the same way King Kavadh, having mutilated his brothers' feet and hands, intended to spare their lives in a crippled state, but then after the complaint of many, these too were removed with the sword.[114] (tr. Greenwood)

As described above (and below), in late February Heraclius withdrew northwards to Atropatene, leaving events in Persia to take their course. The devastation wrought by the Roman army in the heart of the kingdom and the manifest failure of their king accelerated the demise of Khusro.[115] He was replaced in a coup during the night of 23–24 February and executed five days later; he was succeeded by his son Kavadh II Shiroe, who immediately entered into negotiations with Heraclius. It was not until the arrival of Kavadh's embassy on 24 March, as emerges from the *Chronicon Paschale*, that Heraclius learned at Ganzak of the fall of Khusro. The account of the *Chronicon Paschale* below is the text of a despatch sent by Heraclius, which was read out in St Sophia in Constantinople on Sunday 15 May 628; it is therefore a contemporary source of the highest value. On the events described see Christensen 1944:

493–6, Stratos 1968: 226–8, Howard-Johnston 1999: 5–6, 26, Thomson and Howard-Johnston 1999: 221.

***Chr. Pasch.* 727.15–734.17:** May you, the whole world, shout to God (in victory), may you serve the Lord in merriment, enter His presence in exultation and know that the Lord himself is God. He made us and not we ourselves. We are His people and the sheep of His pasture. Enter His halls with hymns and give thanks to Him. Praise His name, since Christ (is) Lord and His pity (endures) for ever, and His truth (endures) through the generations. Let the heavens rejoice (p.728) and the earth exult and the sea make merry and all things in them.[116] And let all of us Christians, praising and glorifying (Him), give thanks to God alone, rejoicing greatly in His holy name. For the arrogant Khusro, who fought with God, has fallen. He has fallen and has been overthrown, down to the underworld; and his memory has been obliterated from the earth. He who was puffed up and spoke unjustly in his arrogance and contempt against our Lord Jesus Christ the true God and his undefiled mother, our blessed Lady, the Mother of God and ever-virgin Mary, he, the impious one, has perished with a crash. His labours rebounded on his own head, and onto his head descended his injustice. For on the 24th of February past of the first indiction (628), there was an uprising against him by Shiroe, his first-born son, as we indicated to you by another despatch; and all the Persian nobles and armies, and the whole force assembled from various places by the accursed Khusro, joined the side of Shiroe with Gusdanaspes too, the former commander of the Persian army. That God-hated Khusro prepared to turn to flight, but was prevented and taken prisoner in the new fortress which had been built by him for the guarding of the monies collected by him.

(p.729) And on the 25th of the same February Shiroe was crowned and proclaimed king of the Persians, and on the 28th of the same month, after he had placed the iron-bound God-hated Khusro in great pain for four days, he killed this same arrogant, proud blasphemer, who fought against God, by a most cruel death so that he might know that Jesus, born of Mary, crucified by the Jews, as he himself had written in blasphemy, is almighty God;[117] and he treated him (Khusro) according to how we had written to him (Kavadh Shiroe). And thus did that man who fought against God perish in this life. He departed by the road of Judas Iscariot who had heard from our almighty God that 'it would have been better for that man if he had not been born';[118] he departed to the unquenchable fire prepared for Satan and those worthy of him.

Through our other despatch to you from our camp near Ganzak which contained the account (of events) from the 17th of October up to the 15th of March, we indicated how God and Our Lady the Mother of God acted with us and our Christ-loving expeditionary forces (in a way) beyond human comprehension; and how the God-hated and accursed Khusro fled from Dastagerd to Ctesiphon, and how his palaces were destroyed along with many districts of the (p.730) Persian state; and in what manner Shiroe was able to make his move against him.

After we had composed that despatch and sent it on the 15th of the present month of March, we were concerned to know the subsequent events surrounding Khusro and Shiroe, and we sent (letters) to various places, as far as Siarsuron[119], and as far as the

Lesser Zab, Kalkhas, (the mansions) of Yazdin, by both roads (leading from) our most successful expeditionary forces, as well as through the Saracens who are in the control of our Christ-loving state.[120] (This we did) in order, as has been said, to know precisely what had taken place there. On the 24th of the same month of March scouts brought to us at our camp near Ganzak one Persian and one Armenian, who handed over to us a memorandum (addressed) to us from a certain *a secretis* of the Persians with the name Khosdaes and the rank (of) Rasnan.[121] It contained (the news) that Shiroe, having been proclaimed king of the Persians, had sent him to us, along with other nobles too, and this memorandum of Shiroe to us, and that, having reached Arman,[122] he (Khosdaes) had resolved to despatch to us the two aforementioned men so as to have some men sent (to him) who would keep him and those with him safe. It was realised by us that he had observed many corpses of Persians along the road, slain by our most successful (p.731) army – about 3000 men from the Narbas (onwards);[123] frightened by this, he feared to reach us without an escort. And on the 25th of the same month of March we sent to them the most glorious *magister militum* Elias called Barsoka and the most magnificent Theodotus the *drungarius*[124] with younger soldiers and twenty pack-horses with saddles, who would meet and bring them safely to us. With them we had resolved to send also Gusdanaspes Rhazei, the commander of a thousand men who had come to us when trouble broke out between Shiroe and Khusro. On the 30th of March we received a reply at our camp near Ganzak from Elias and Theodotus and Gusdanaspes that they had found much snow in the Zagros mountains and that they had brought Persians and horses out from their forts and had thus dug through the snow; (they added) that it had come to their attention that the envoys sent by King Shiroe were nearby, but that they had were unable to cross the Zagros mountains. From this we – and all the men of our Christ-loving expeditionary forces – realised all the more that the favour and goodness of God had guided us and guides us and preserves (us yet). For if it had fallen out that we had tarried (p.732) in the Zagros mountains, and if the storm had taken place in this way, our most successful expeditionary forces would have come to great harm, since adequate provisions are not to be found in these places. For from the time when we moved from Siarsuron, that is from the 24th of February, until the 30th of March, it did not cease snowing. But coming to the districts of Ganzak through God('s help) we found many provisions for men and horses; and we stayed in the city of Ganzak, which is suitable and has about 3000 houses, and in the surrounding villages, so that we were able to reside for many days in one place. We ordered our Christ-loving expeditionary forces to place their horses in the houses of the city during the winter and to keep one each in our camp; for our fortified camp is near the city. The superintendent of the city of Ganzak and all its landowners, when they learned that we had crossed the Zagros (mountains), withdrew and departed to mountain regions to more secure forts.

When we received the two men sent by the Persian king Shiroe, we despatched one of them – that is the Persian – with other men too, to the superintendent of Ganzak, who was forty miles away and in a secure fort; and (p.733) we addressed a memorandum to him, to the effect that he should prepare sixty horses for the envoys, so that they might depart immediately and without hindrance to the Persian king Shiroe.

The superintendent, receiving those sent by us and this memorandum of ours, praised us and the Persian king Shiroe for many hours – he himself and all to be found there. For they had been informed by the Persian who had been sent as an envoy that Khusro, who fought against God, had perished and that Shiroe had become king of the Persians. And the superintendent replied to us that he was making ready the horses of the envoys in response to our commands to him, and that when he received our second order containing (the news) that the envoys had arrived, he himself in person would come, bringing the requisite horses; (and he said that) he would undertake every task and service. While we stayed in our camp near Ganzak until the 3rd of April, Phaiak the *a secretis* and Rasnan[125] arrived around the second hour, on a Sunday. And that same hour we received him and he gave us the memorandum of Kavadh Shiroe, the most clement Persian king, which contained his proclamation and (announced) that he wished to have peace with us and with every man. We resolved therefore to attach after our present despatch a copy of the memorandum of Kavadh Shiroe the most clement (p.734), as well as to attach beneath our reply to him. We stayed in this same camp of ours near Ganzak until the 7th of April, that is for 27 days, and on the 8th of the same month we despatched the same Phaiak the *a secretis* and Rasnan, having attended to him and all those with him as far as possible, for he had with him distinguished personages; and we despatched with him the most magnificent *tabularius* Eustathius.[126] And thus we have faith in our Lord Jesus Christ the good and almighty God and in our Lady the Mother of God, because they have arranged all our affairs by their goodness.

And with (the help of) God we moved our camp on the 8th of the same month, intending to make our way to Armenia. But may you fare well, unceasingly and zealously praying on our behalf, so that God may grant us, as we desire, to see you (again).

(p.735) Copy of the memorandum from Kavadh Shiroe, most clement king of the Persians, to our most pious emperor Heraclius, protected by God. 'From Kavadh Sadasadasakh to Heraclius, the most clement Roman emperor, our brother, we offer the greatest thanks.[127] To the most clement emperor of the Romans and our brother. We, through the support of God, have with good fortune been vested with the great diadem and have attained the throne of our fathers and forebears. Since we have been so beneficently deemed worthy by God to attain such a throne and dominion, we have decided that if there is anything for the good and service of mankind which can be done by us, we have, as is fitting, beneficently ordered that it be done. When God honoured us with this great throne and dominion, we had the policy of releasing each and every person held in prison. And for the future, if there is anything for the good and service of mankind and this state which could be ordered by us, we have ordered (it), (p.736) and it has been done. And we have a policy of such a kind that we shall live in peace and love with you, the emperor of the Romans and our brother, and the Roman state, and the other peoples and other petty kings around our state. Because of the delight of your brotherhood, the emperor of the Romans, at our accession to this same throne[128] ... directly ... your brotherhood and we sent orders to your brotherhood that Phaiak the *a secretis* and Rasnan, our (advisor), be present. But your brotherhood knows the disposition, love and friendship which we hold towards your brotherhood, not only towards it but also towards your state. Because of your love, may you order that the men from this state who have been captured (p.273) by the army of your brotherhood be released. In addition, may you order these men by every means to come to our ancestral state. And concerning the firm and eternal peace to be (established) ... '

(p.737) 'In the name of our Lord Jesus Christ and God. Emperor Caesar Flavius Heraclius, faithful to Christ, emperor of the Romans.[129] We offer the greatest thanks and report that we received the memorandum sent to us by your filiality[130] through Phaiak Khosdaes the *a secretis* and Rasnan. And we recognise that with the support of God you have been vested with the royal diadem for the good fortune (of all), and are seated on the throne of your father and forebears. We have rejoiced all the more and devote ourselves to God so that he may deem you worthy to occupy the throne of your fathers and forebears for many years in good health, in eternal good fortune and in great peace. And that which you disclosed to us through your memorandum, (namely) that when you sat on so great a throne and took power, you had the policy of releasing those held in prison for various causes; and furthermore that you had ordered that those things be done which were for the good and benefit of men (p.274) and had such an intention ...

Nic. 15 briefly reports the imprisonment and death of Khusro, as well as the exchange of letters between Heraclius and Kavadh Shiroe. According to Nicephorus, Heraclius called Kavadh his child (15.15) and asked for the return of the Holy Cross; he also enquired about the fate of the ambassadors sent in 615. Kavadh replied that he would return the cross when he found it and that the ambassadors had all died, all but one executed by Khusro. See Mango 1990: 182–3 and Speck 1988: 322–4.

Theoph. A.M. 6118 (325.10–327.16):[131] Gusdanaspes,[132] who was captain of a thousand men in the army of Shahrvaraz,[133] went over to him (Heraclius) together with five others, three of whom were captains and two officers of other rank; and he brought them to the emperor. This man Gusdanaspes announced some vital news to the emperor, saying that 'When Khusro fled from Dastagerd and went to Ctesiphon and Seleucia, he fell ill with dysentery and wanted to crown his son Mardanshah who was born to Shirin. And he crossed the river again and brought with him Mardanshah along with Shirin and her other son Shahryar. As for his first-born son Shiroe[134] and his brothers and wives, he left them on the other side of the river. When Shiroe became aware that Khusro was intending to crown Mardanshah, he was troubled and sent his foster-brother to Gusdanaspes with this message, 'Come across the river that I may meet you.' But Gusdanaspes was afraid to cross on account of Khusro and declared to him, 'Write to me through your foster-brother, if you wish.' So Shiroe wrote him the following: 'You know how the Persian state has been destroyed by this evil man Khusro, and now he intends to crown Mardanshah and has scorned me, the first-born. If you tell the army (p.326) that they should accept me, I shall increase their pay and make peace with the Roman emperor <and with the Turks>, and we shall live in plenty. (So) strive with your men that I should become king. I will then promote and acclaim all of you, and yourself in particular.' I informed him through his foster-brother that I would speak to the army and labour to the best of my ability. And I spoke to 22 captains and won them over to my views, as well as other officers and many soldiers. I announced this to Shiroe, who instructed me that on the 23rd of March[135] I should take some young regulars and meet him at the pontoon bridge of the Tigris river, take him to the army and move against Khusro. (He stated also) that Shiroe had with him the two sons of Shahrvaraz, the son of Yazdin, and many other sons of noblemen, and the son of Aram – all picked men. If they are able to kill Khusro, well and good; but if they fail, all of them, with Shiroe, will go over to the emperor. He sent me to you, O lord, because he feels ashamed before the Roman Empire; for, once upon a time, it saved Khusro and, on his account, the land of the Romans has suffered many ills. Because of his arrogance, he says, the emperor will not trust me.'

Now the emperor sent this man back to Shiroe and indicated that he should open the prisons and let out the Romans confined therein, and give them arms, and so move off against Khusro. Shiroe obeyed the emperor and, after releasing the prisoners, attacked his parricide father Khusro. The latter tried to escape, but failed and was captured. They bound him securely with iron fetters, with his hands tied behind his back, and placed iron weights on his feet and his neck, and so led him into the House of Darkness, which he himself had fortified and rebuilt for the deposit (p.327) of monies therein; and they starved him by giving him a paltry amount of bread and water. For Shiroe said, 'Let him eat the gold he collected in vain, on account of which he starved many men and made the world desolate.' He sent to him the satraps that they might insult him and spit upon him, and he brought Mardanshah, whom he had wished to crown, and slew him in his presence, and they killed all his remaining children in front of him, and he sent all his enemies that they might insult him, strike him and spit upon him. After doing this for five days, Shiroe commanded that he should be killed with bow and arrows, and thus slowly and in suffering he gave up his wicked soul. Then Shiroe wrote to the emperor to give him the good tidings of the slaying of the foul Khusro; and after making with him a permanent peace, he handed back to him all the imprisoned Christians and the captives held in every part of Persia together with the patriarch Zachariah and the precious and life-giving Cross that had been taken from Jerusalem by Shahrvaraz, when the latter captured Jerusalem.[136] (tr. Mango and Scott, revised)

As the *Chronicon Paschale* (p.734) relates, while Heraclius returned westwards, an envoy was sent to Ctesiphon to arrange terms for concluding the war. Although Kavadh Shiroe released Roman prisoners (Theoph. 327.12–13 above), he lacked the power to give orders to Shahrvaraz to evacuate his conquests in the west.[137] (Sebeos 128/86). Heraclius was therefore obliged to despatch forces to reconquer the occupied territories. The *praefectus sacri cubiculi* Narses was entrusted with a large force, which, according to Ant. Strateg. 24 (516), drove the Persian into flight.[138] More information is provided by *Chr. 1234* (below), cf. Theoph. A.M. 6119, 327.19–24, Mich. Syr. XI.3 (409a–10/409–10), Agap. *PO* 8.465–6.[139] See Flusin 1992: II, 285–7, placing these events in 628, before the death of Kavadh Shiroe.

Chr. 1234, 100–2 (234.26–236.12): (...) He (Shiroe) made with him (Heraclius) a treaty and agreement, so that Heraclius would receive all the lands which belonged at that time to the Romans, and the Persians would stay inside their former boundaries, and those of them who were in the lands of the west would go over to the country of the Persians. (p.235) Shiroe became king of the Persians in the year 19 of Heraclius and 7 of Mohammed. After this, Heraclius marched from the east to arrive in Syria, and he sent before him Theodoric (i.e. Theodore) his brother, to cast out Persians who were living in the cities, according to the agreement which existed between him and Shahrvaraz from before[140] and confirmed between him and Shiroe.

(101) Theodoric, the brother of the king, went over into the cities of Mesopotamia and told the Persians who were in them to leave and go to their land. In addition, they had already been informed in letters from Shahrvaraz and Shiroe of the treaty between the Romans and the Persians. Then the emperor advanced in the footsteps of his brother and, when he had arrived, he set up governors and Roman garrisons in the cities. When Theodoric reached Edessa, he notified the Persians there of those things which were (happening) and of the coming of the emperor; but the Persians scorned him and did not listen to his words, and replied to him, 'We do not know Shiroe and we will not surrender the city to the Romans'. There were Jews who dwelt in Edessa standing with the Persians on the wall, and because of their hatred for Christians, and to ingratiate themselves with the Persians, they insulted the Romans and mocked Theodoric and made him listen to bitter taunts. After this, Theodoric incited a violent attack against the city and beset it with a hurling of rocks from a siege engine, and when the Persians (who were) in the city were crushed together, they accepted an amnesty to return to their land. A certain Jew, whose name was Joseph, when he feared the destruction of his people, threw himself down from the wall and went off to Heraclius, and found him at Constantia. He came before him and sought to persuade him to forgive his people (p.236) the offence of insulting Theodoric, his brother, and to send (instructions) to him so that he would not take vengeance on them. Theodoric had entered Edessa and had taken control of it, and made the Persians go to their land. He sent (men) to gather all the Jews who had insulted him, and then he began to kill them and to plunder their houses. Suddenly Joseph the Jew arrived, bearing a letter from the emperor, which ordered his brother not to harm them.

(102) Afterwards Theodoric left Edessa and crossed the Euphrates and arrived at Mabbug (Hierapolis), where he expelled the Persians who were in Syria and Phoenice. In those days, Emperor Heraclius reached Edessa and began to dwell in the palace at the head of the source (of the river). (...) (tr. M. Greatrex)

At Edessa Heraclius hoped to heal the divisions between supporters and opponents of the Council of Chalcedon by taking communion from the bishop of Edessa, Isaiah, but he was brusquely rebuffed. Henceforth the emperor was to prove more forceful in his dealings with the Monophysites (*Chr. 1234*, 102, 236/140, Mich. Syr. XI.3 [408–9c/411–12], Agap. *PO* 8.466–7).[141] The situation was further complicated by Kavadh's death in October 628, upon which he was succeeded by his young son Ardashir (*Chr. Khuz.* 29, Sebeos 129/87–8).[142]

The peace treaty of 629

Despite the inglorious death of Khusro almost a year earlier, Roman control of the Near East had not been fully restored by January 629 by any means. Mesopotamia, Osrhoene, and presumably Syria and Phoenice had been regained by Theodore, but Shahrvaraz remained in Egypt.[143] Nothing is known of Persian troops stationed north of Syria. Heraclius was forced therefore to deal with Shahrvaraz, clearly now a more powerful figure than the new king in Ctesiphon (Sebeos 129/88, Thom. Arts. 96/162). On 17 July 629 the emperor met Shahrvaraz at Arabissus to arrange terms. Since already in June Shahrvaraz had started to evacuate Egypt, the two leaders had evidently been in contact for some time before their meeting (*Chr. 724*, 146/17–18). A western Turk invasion around the same time failed to dissolve the good relations now established. See Flusin 1992: II, 290–1, Zuckerman 1995: 118 and n.30, Howard-Johnston 1999: 27–8.[144]

Chr. 724, 147.18–24, cf. 139.13–18 (AG 940 = 629): In that year, in July, Heraclius, emperor of the Romans, and Shahrvaraz the *patricius* of the Persians, met each other at a pass in the north, which is named Arabissus Tripotamus. They built a church there and called it Eirene (Peace) by name, and they spoke about peace there with each other, and it was determined that the Euphrates was the boundary between them. Thus they made peace with each other. (tr. M. Greatrex)

Nic. 17.1–19: Shahrvaraz, when he had heard that Khusro and Shiroe, Kaboes and Hormizd had died, returned from the land of the Romans and wrote an apology to Heraclius, (claiming) that what he had done to the Romans he had not performed willingly but according to the order of the one who sent him, and he sought permission to come to him (Heraclius) and to present (himself) as a slave. After being reassured by a sworn assurance from the emperor, he came to him and promised to give him money from Persia with which he might repair whatever he had destroyed in the land of the Romans. Meanwhile the son of Hormizd fell victim to a plot and was slain, and Shahrvaraz sought from the emperor the Persian crown.[145] He granted him (this), and they agreed between themselves that all the Roman territory under the Persians should be restored to the Romans. When peace had been concluded, Shahrvaraz immediately returned to the Romans both Egypt and all the eastern lands after withdrawing the Persians (that were) there; and he sent the life-giving Cross to the emperor. Heraclius conferred the dignity of patrician upon Nicetas, the son of Shahrvaraz, and gave the latter's daughter Nike in marriage to his own son Theodosius, born of Martina.[146] (...) (tr. Mango, revised)

Sebeos 129–30/88, cf. Thom. Arts. 96/162 reports that Shahrvaraz agreed to evacuate the eastern provinces after Heraclius offered him the Persian crown and military support if he should need it.[147] When they met (i.e. at Arabissus, presumably) Shahrvaraz pledged to return the Cross as soon as he found it and to fix the frontier where Heraclius wished it. See Thomson and Howard-Johnston 1999: 224.

The significance of the terms reported in *Chr. 724*, if correct, should not be underestimated: the Roman frontier would have been shifted further west than it had been since the first century

AD. The whole of the Roman provinces of Mesopotamia and Osrhoene, including the city of Edessa, so recently retaken by Theodore, would be handed over to the Persians, and Antioch would lie within striking range of Persian armies. We think it more likely that its reference to the Euphrates is an error. Cf. Flusin 1992: II, 290 and n.145; *contra*, Howard-Johnston 1999: 28.[148] There are indeed scraps of evidence to indicate a continuing Roman presence on the Tigris, as far south as Tagrit. See Fiey 1987: 98–9, Kaegi 1992: 153–7.

It remained for Shahrvaraz to wrest the Persian throne from the young Ardashir. From the *Khuzistan Chronicle* (p.29) the *Chronicle of Seert* (below), Sebeos 129/88, *Hist. Her.* 432/231, and *Chr. 1234*, 103, 238/142, it appears that Heraclius provided military assistance to his ally.[149] The chronology of Shahrvaraz's march to Ctesiphon is uncertain; the only well established date is that he seized the throne on 27 April 630. Given that he had to assemble his army and march from the Roman East to the Persian capital, he is unlikely to have reached it until the end of 629. See Flusin 1992: II, 306–9, Zuckerman 1995: 119 n.30, Thierry 1997: 172–6 (on the general David), Thomson and Howard-Johnston 1999: 223–4.

Chr. Seert 93, *PO* 13.556: Then troubles (at the Persian court after the assassination of Kavadh Shiroe) began to brew. And so they wrote to Shahrvaraz, who resided in the country of the Romans in the service of the Emperor Heraclius. And they asked him to return to them because he was the only survivor from the progeny of Sasan. But he declined out of fear for himself, and because he did not relish violating his compact with Heraclius that he would stay with him. When the latter knew of this, and of his staunch loyalty to him, he gave him a large force[150] and sent with him a commander, known as David. And Shahrvaraz headed towards al-Mada'in with the intention of fighting with Ardashir, son of Shiroe. When he came near al-Mada'in, they closed the gates before him and prevented him from entering it. But he continued to employ deceitful devices until he had the gates opened, and so he entered (the city), killed Ardashir and seized the kingdom from him. Because of this, the army's commander-in-chief was angered and a group of soldiers went over to him and refused to recognise Shahrvaraz. So Shahrvaraz fought with him victoriously, and captured him, and thus the kingdom incontestably became his. And Shahrvaraz honoured those of the Romans who were with him and returned the wood of the Cross which Khusro had taken from Jerusalem, and placed it in the box, which he despatched with David, who had been sent with him from the country of the Romans.[151] Forty days later he killed Shamta, son of Yazdin, and crucified him.[152] Then one of the relatives of Khusro assailed him unawares, and secretly assassinated him. (tr. Shahîd)

Tabari, I, 1062/401, offers more details on how Shahrvaraz, with 6000 men, captured Ctesiphon by securing the loyalty of the son of Adhur Gushnasp, Ardashir's leading general, and another commander. See Flusin 1992: II, 306–7.

The return of the Cross and the fall of Shahrvaraz (630)

The date of the return of the Cross to Jerusalem has been the cause of much controversy. As has been noted, at some point in late 629 or early 630, Shahrvaraz captured Ctesiphon, and the young Ardashir was overthrown. But not until 27 April did Shahvaraz make himself king. It is possible therefore that he ruled as a regent for Ardashir before killing him, or that he ruled the kingdom for some months before formally becoming king. The date of Shahrvaraz's seizure of power bears on the return of the True Cross, for it is generally now agreed that it was carried into Jerusalem by the emperor himself on 21 March 630 and then deposited in the church of the Holy Sepulchre. Since the *Khuzistan Chronicle* (p.29), Nicephorus (above) and the *Chronicle of Seert* (above) all credit Shahrvaraz with the restoration of the Cross, it must be supposed that he was in a *de facto* position of power before his formal accession – whether as a regent for Ardashir or simply as uncrowned king. See Flusin 1992: II, 293–309 (arguing for a regency), Zuckerman 1995: 119 n.30 (noting that no ancient source refers to a regency) and Thomson and Howard-Johnston 1999: 224 (accepting the regency).

The return of the Holy Cross to Jerusalem, escorted by Heraclius from Hierapolis, made a huge impression on contemporaries. It was even asserted that the Cross had been preserved intact throughout its time in Persia. Accounts are found in Sebeos 131/90, Geo. Pis. *In Restitutionem S. Crucis*, Ant. Strat. 24 (516), Sophronius, *Anacreontica* 18, *Translat. Anast.* 1, Theoph. A.M. 6120 (328.13–15), Nic. 18, *Chr. 1234*, 103, 238/142. See Frolow 1953: 94–105, Thierry 1981: 205 and 206 fig.1, Speck 1988: 336–77 (dating the restoration to September 628), Flusin 1992: II, 309–19.[153]

On 9 June 630 Shahrvaraz was assassinated and his place taken by Boran, a daughter of Khusro II. To bolster support for her régime, the new ruler sent several prominent churchmen as envoys to the Romans, including the *catholicos* Isho-Yab. They met the emperor at Beroea and conceded all the territories which the Persians had gained – not only Mesopotamia and Osrhoene, if these had indeed been ceded by the Romans (see p.227 above), but even those which Maurice had annexed in 591 (*Chr. Khuz.* 30, *Chr. Seert* 93, PO 13.557–60, *Translat. Anast.* 3, Sebeos 131/90).[154] The future had seldom looked better for Roman rule in the East. See Sako 1986: 121–4, Flusin 1992: II, 320–1, Howard-Johnston 1999: 29 and n.92, Thomson and Howard-Johnston 1999: 227.

15

THE *KHUZISTAN CHRONICLE*[1]

(First part)

Some events from *(Ec)clēsastikē* (i.e. from ecclesiastical accounts) and *Cosmostikē* (i.e. accounts relevant to secular matters) from the death of Hormizd, the son of Khusro, to the end of the Persian kingdom.[2]

Hormizd reigned for twelve years, and imposed the yoke (of servitude) on the nobles and on all the world. One of the chiefs of his troops, Bahram by name, (of) Rhagae, who had been sent by him to the regions of the Turks, rebelled against him; and having assembled many troops, he prepared for war with the king. But when the nobles who were at the royal court,[3] who hated Hormizd, heard of the rebellion of Bahram, they conspired with each other, took Hormizd from his throne, and put out his eyes; and in his place they appointed his son Khusro. When the news reached Bahram, he was very angry, not because he liked Hormizd, but because he (himself) had not performed the deed. (Therefore), having prepared his troops and got ready for war with Khusro, he proceeded to march against Khusro. Since Khusro saw that Bahram's side was stronger than his own, he fled from him and hurried along the south road,[4] that is, through Peroz-Shapur (Pirisabora), 'Anat (Anatha), Hit and Circesium, and went to take refuge with the Roman emperor Maurice. While he was making his journey in flight, the *catholicos* Mar Isho-Yab did not set out with him;[5] and (so) Maurice greatly blamed Khusro, in that he was not joined by the patriarch of his kingdom, (p.16) and all the more in that Mar Isho-Yab of Arzanene was a wise and clever man.[6] Khusro developed a great hatred of the *catholicos*, (firstly) because he had not set out with him, and secondly because he had not met him on the road when he heard that he had set out, after Maurice had given him troops. But the *catholicos* did not meet the king because he feared the wickedness of Bahram, in case he should ruin the Church and stir up a persecution against the Christians.[7] Maurice handed over many troops to Khusro, and they set off to the east; when Bahram heard (this), he set off from Mahoza[8] with his troops and fled to Azerbaijan (Atropatene).[9] Khusro, with Persian and Roman troops, encountered him (in battle); the Romans gained a victory and Bahram's contingent was defeated. But Khusro with great joy turned back (to Persia). For it was said that the image of an old man appeared to Khusro, as he seized the bridle of a horse and was going forth to war; and when he told his wife Shirin (of this) after his return from the war, she said to him, 'This is Sabrisho, bishop of Lashum'; and (Khusro) considered the matter and was silent.[10]

At that time the brothers Bindoes and Bestam, who were imprisoned by Hormizd, left prison, and were of great help to Khusro, because they were from the family of his mother.[11] Then (Khusro) sent Bestam with a large army to the regions of the Turks, but he (Bestam) left Bindoes at his (Khusro's) court. When Bindoes rebuked Khusro about matters of state, he (Khusro) planned to kill him; Bindoes fled, going forth in the direction of his brother Bestam. But when he was passing through the region of Azerbaijan, the *marzban* there heard (about him), made dinner for him, and seized him; and he sent him to Khusro. Having learnt (of these things), his brother gathered forces from the Turks and Dailamites and proceeded as far as Mahoza; but a certain Turk plotted against him, killed him, and sent his head (p.17) to Khusro.[12] As for Bindoes, the king ordered that they (his men) cut off all the limbs of his right side; and he sent him to Beth Lapat[13] and crucified him there. They also placed the head of Bestam on the neck of Shapur, the son of Bahram, who had opposed him (Khusro); and they mounted (Shapur) (on) a camel and led him around the royal court.

But Isho-Yab, the leader of the Christians, because Khusro had a great hatred indeed of him[14] in that he had not set out with him for the territory of the Romans, and furthermore on account of the slander of Timotheus the chief doctor of Nisibis,[15] strenuously protected himself from the king. After a little time, when the patriarch went down to Hira of the Tayyaye to see Nu'man, king of the Tayyaye, who had become a Christian,[16] and when he reached the place of Hira, he was struck down by disease and died in the area whose name is Beth Qushi. But when Hind, the sister of Nu'man,[17] heard (of this), she left Hira with the priests and the faithful, and with a great procession they brought the body of the holy man into (the city); and Hind placed it in the new monastery which she had built.[18] The Church was for a time without a leader, and then the synod was gathered by the command of the king to elect the head. The king sent (a message) to them that they should bring forth Sabrisho (the bishop) of Lashum and appoint (him) as (their) chief; they hurriedly brought him forth and appointed him as their head.[19] And he was greatly honoured all his days, both by the king and by both his (the king's) Christian wives, that is by Shirin the Aramaean[20] and Maria the Roman.[21]

There was at Nisibis the metropolitan Gregory the Kashgarite. It is not possible for the tongue to narrate the disputes and many quarrels which Satan caused between these two good men (Gregory and Sabrisho).[22] But (when) at <first> Gregory was at Nisibis for a short time, they excommunicated Gabriel the son of Rufinus because he was well-versed in the course of the stars and the signs of the Zodiac;[23] and they seized (p.18) and brought over Gregory, the bishop of Kashgar. (Now) at Nisibis, which is (also known as) Antioch of Mygdonia, which is named thus[24] because of the gardens and parks which are there, since it is <on the borders> of the Persians and the Romans, stupid, troublesome and quarrelsome men gathered from every region, especially on account of the famous school which was there. But there was (a certain) Henana of Adiabene, an interpreter (of Scripture);[25] (and) because (regarding) various matters he had blamed in his teachings the ecumenical interpreter,[26] the zealous Gregory did not tolerate this.[27] He wished also to correct clergy who corrupted their practices along with the rest of the faithful, but they did not obey him. But they arrested a certain deacon, who was called Bar Taʻlē (son of foxes), while sacrificing a white cock in a grove which is outside the city; (Gregory) summoned and punished him. He also disgraced and scattered everywhere certain monks who (had committed) disgraceful acts (and) lived around Mount Sinjar; they were Messalians.[28] From that time there were many accusations against him from the Nisibenes and from those outside (the city); (therefore) the king sent for him to come (to him), and ordered that he stay in the Shahdost monastery. (Gregory) shook the dust from his feet at the gates of Nisibis, and then departed.[29] Mar Sabrisho wished to depose Gregory (from his office), but the bishops did not give in to him; then the king ordered him to return to his land.[30] He set out (there) and built a monastery for himself in the region of Kashgar, in the place which is called Bazza of the Euphrates;[31] there he founded a monastery, and he brought many to the fear of God. For they say that after the abdication of Gregory it was not accorded to Mar Sabrisho to perform miracles as previously.

Then Nisibis seceded from Khusro; when the king heard (this), he sent the *nakhveragan*, a royal leader, against them with (p.19) a great army and elephants, and with him Mar Sabrisho. The inhabitants of the city shut the gates before him; then, through the wheedling of the *catholicos*, and because the *nakhveragan* gave an oath to them that he would not repay them with evil, they opened the gates to him. But when he entered, he went back on his agreement, and he took the notables who were with them and tortured them; he plundered their houses, destroyed all they possessed, and finally slew them by every manner of death. And (thus) the curse of Gregory against them was fulfilled, and Mar Sabrisho himself understood this.[32]

There was at that time (a certain) Gabriel Derustbadh[33] from Singara, a chief doctor, beloved by the king for the reason that he had drawn blood from the arm of Shirin, and she had had a son and had called him Mardanshah, when previously she had not had sons;[34] Gabriel, although previously he had been a heretic,[35] wished to be enrolled in the side of the orthodox;[36] but because he had put away the lawful wife whom he had taken, who was a confessor of noble lineage, and had taken in marriage two pagan wives, with whom he lived in pagan fashion, the *catholicos* urged him to put away the pagans and to take (back) the lawful (wife), but he refused; then he returned to the side of the heretics, and brought many evils upon the followers of our side.[37]

When Khusro was fleeing from Bahram and had reached Roman territory, he is said to have asked Nuʻman, the king of the Tayyaye, to travel with him, but he (Nuʻman) refused; he also requested a very noble horse from him, which he did not give him.[38] And Khusro also asked for the daughter of Nuʻman, who was most beautiful, and Nuʻman did not agree; but he (Nuʻman) replied, 'I would not give my daughter as a bride to a man who enters marriage in the manner of beasts.' Khusro put all these things together and kept them in his heart. When (p.20) Khusro had a pause from wars, he wished to exact vengeance on his enemies, and among them Nuʻman. One day he invited Nuʻman to dinner, but in place of food he broke scraps made of hay before him; and Nuʻman was very embittered, and sent (word) to his fellow tribesmen, the Maʻadd.[39] They devastated many places and took captives from Khusro; and they penetrated as far as the ʻArab.[40] When Khusro heard (of these things), he was disturbed, and enticed him (Nuʻman) to come to him by all sorts of means, but he refused. But one of Nuʻman's interpreters, (who was) from the island of Derin,[41] Maʻne by name, conspired with Khusro and said to Nuʻman, 'The king really loves you', and swore by the gospel, 'The king will not hurt you'. Mawiyah too, the wife of Nuʻman, said to him, 'It is more fitting for you to die with kingly status than to live expelled and driven away from kingly status.' But when he reached the royal court, (Khusro) did not kill him, but ordered him to remain at the gate; afterwards, however, it is said that he slew this illustrious confessor by deadly poison.[42]

Then a certain man, Phocas by name, rose against Maurice, the emperor of the Romans, and slew him together with his sons and wife; but one of his sons escaped, Theodosius by name, and came to Khusro. He was received with great honour by the king. He ordered the *catholicos* to admit him to the church, (where) the royal crown was placed on the altar, and then placed on his head, according to the ritual of the Romans.[43] Then Khusro handed over an army to him (Theodosius), and he went against the Romans. Phocas too sent many troops, who pitched camp in Beth Washe, beyond the city of Dara;[44] and they fought a battle with Theodosius and crushed his troops. He reported to Khusro, 'I do not have the strength to stand against the Romans'. And Khusro set off in winter with many troops from Mahoza and assailed Roman territory (p.21); and the *catholicos* was with him.[45] The forces of Phocas went out against them, and after the detachments fell upon each other, many on both sides were killed. They threw down a noose for Khusro,[46] but one of his (Khusro's) bodyguards, Mushkan by name, cut it; on the next day, the battle (line) was drawn up, and the Romans gave way before the Persians.[47] (Then) the king fought against Dara and constructed mounds; (soldiers) made tunnels beneath the wall and set fire (there). And through the many things they did they broke through the wall; and in this (city) they poured out blood like water. But the bishop of Dara struck with an iron bar the vein which is known as the 'catholicos' of the body,[48] and while he lay on his bed, the blood flowed out and he died. For he was fearful of the king, who had sworn, 'I will kill him by forty means of death'. From that time Khusro had power over the Roman territory. Dara was crushed in the fourteenth year of Khusro.[49]

But when the king was fighting against Dara, a certain Radh[50] came down to the churches of Seyarzur[51] and overturned them; and when the faithful, together with their bishop Nathaniel, saw (this), they did not tolerate it; and they rose up against Radh and expelled him. He came to Khusro at Nisibis, and spurred him on, saying to him, 'You are fighting on behalf of Christians, while I am persecuted by Christians.' And without consideration, the king summoned Nathaniel, the bishop of Seyarzur, and gave an order to imprison him for six years; and afterwards he crucified him. For although Khusro in appearance showed favour to the Christians for the sake of Maurice, he was, however, the enemy of our people.[52]

But Mar Sabrisho was seized by a serious illness at Nisibis; and the king sent (a message) to him and asked him to release Gabriel from his (sentence of) excommunication, but he refused. He made a will and sealed (it), and he ordered that they carry him to his monastery. The Nisibenes, however, wanted to deposit (p.22) the body of the holy man in their church, but the king refused them, since he had heard the order of the catholicos; and his (Sabrisho's) disciples placed his body on a camel, and carried it to his monastery.[53]

Then Gregory, (who was) from Porath,[54] was made *catholicos* at the instigation of Shirin, who was a (fellow) native, although all the clergy, along with the king, sought out Gregory of Kashgar, who had been expelled from Nisibis. But he undertook unacceptable practices in his pontificate, lived on for a few years, and (then) died.[55] On account of the scheming and hatred of Gabriel towards the Church, the Church remained for a while without a leader and was not allowed a voice on account of the accusations of Gregory; and they appointed in the Church Mar Aba the archdeacon, (who was) from Ctesiphon, to lead it, an upright and wise man. The Church remained for a long time without a head.[56] But Gabriel, (who was) from Singara, much threatened the orthodox, and expelled our people from the monastery of Mar Pethyon and the monastery of Shirin and from other (monasteries), and these he colonised with followers of the party of the heretics.[57]

At that time Ionadab the Adiabenean was distinguished in the Church through the freedom of speech which he had before God and (through) his love for the king[58] and he obtained a letter from the king by which he had power over all the mountain where (the monks) lived in the monastery of (St) Matthew, the deceivers of Mosul.[59] But when his desire had been fulfilled by the king – to expel and persecute them in every way – the cunning plots of Gabriel did not allow (him to finish the operation). Bar Hadbeshabba of Holwan[60] published his writing(s); and for practices of virtue Shubalemaran of Karka de Beth Selokh was famous, and Aphrahat of (the region of) the Zab (rivers) and Gabriel of Nehargul, a great man and performer of miracles.[61]

(p.23) Then Gabriel roused the king against us, so that we should (have to) come to debate with the followers of his party. And since there was no *catholicos* in the Church, there voluntarily came down in person to the debate Ionadab the metropolitan of Adiabene, Shubalemaran of Karka de Beth Selokh, George of Mount Izala, and also the bishop of Nehargul and Sergius of Kashgar, (who was) from Tell Pahare.[62] They held the debate in the royal court; Gabriel and the followers of his side came off worse, while our orthodox men triumphed. The king reproved Gabriel, (urging him) to desist from this impertinence, but he refused. But Gabriel uttered bitter insults against the orthodox and denounced Gregory of Izala in the presence of the king, because he had abandoned the law of the Magi and become a Christian and reviled (the gods) Hormizd and Saturn. The king sent (a message) and put him in prison for one year; then he crucified him in Veh-Ardashir (Seleucia), in the middle of the hay market. The faithful then seized his body and deposited it in the monastery of St Sergius in Mabrakhtha.[63]

Notable at the royal court at this time was Yazdin, from Karka of the Garamaei;[64] this man was a defender of the Church like Constantine and Theodosius, and built churches and monasteries everywhere, as an equivalent of a heavenly Jerusalem. He was as beloved by Khusro as Joseph in the eyes of Pharaoh and more besides, and in consequence of this he was famous in both kingdoms – that is of the Persians and of the Romans. It is said that this Yazdin each day from one morning to the next used to send one thousand staters to the king.[65]

By practices of virtue there flourished at this time Mar Babai of (Mount) Izala. He became the priest for the monastery after Rabban Mar Abraham of Kashgar.[66] Many industrious brethren came forth from the monastery, such as Mar Jacob, who founded the monastery of Beth 'Abe,[67] Mar (p.24) Elias, who built a monastery on the bank of the Tigris at Hesna 'Ebraya,[68] and Mar Babai bar-Nesib[n]aye.[69] That blessed man (Babai the Great) abandoned all he owned, and went up to the monastery of Mar Abraham and became an anchorite; finally he departed from there, and set out to build a monastery in the vicinity of the monastery (of Mar Abraham) itself. Large numbers of brethren settled there; and although he was (one) of the notables in the (secular) world, he chose to occupy himself in the holy labours of penitence, his practices surpassing the written word.[70] When Yazdin learnt of this, he came to see him. When he saw him (practising) every (form) of asceticism and dead (in) body, Yazdin stood at his feet; (but) the holy man sent him away. After a while Yazdin brought to him a golden cross which had many settings in it like rubies, and many emeralds, and in its middle was placed a fragment of the actual wood of the cross on which our saviour was crucified, together with other items to adorn his monastery.[71] But Satan, the lover of controversy, caused much bickering and great disputes between those two fortified towers of the fear of God;[72] and it did not settle down or end until the end of their lives. The followers of Mar Babai the Great did not allow anyone to enter their monastery until they should pronounce an anathema against the excellent Mar Babai the Nisibene, whom they named Babai the Small (lesser). We have said these things briefly, for their practices arose and blazed forth more than the sun, and bear witness that they have many doctrines concerning their party and the purity which they possess.[73] Mar Babai the Great published many doctrines, debates and interpretations. The holy Mar Babai the Nisibene published books on the practices of anchorites, which greatly fascinate their listeners, as well as sermons on penance, which were made in metrical (style).[74]

(p.25) Then Khusro gathered his troops and entered Roman territory. He appointed two commanders, (whom) he sent to the west. They crushed Mardin, Amida, Martyropolis (Mayfarqet) and Edessa, made bridges over the Euphrates, (and) crossed opposite Mabbug (Hierapolis). One of the commanders, whose name was Shahrvaraz, hurried to Jerusalem and struggled to make (the inhabitants) open the gates to him, but they refused. And he prepared an assault against (the city) and, having built mounds against it and broken through the wall, he entered it. He seized the bishop and the nobles of the city and punished them on account of the wood of the cross and the items in the treasury. Because the divine power had broken the Romans in the presence of the Persians, and because they had shed the pure blood of the Emperor Maurice and his sons, God left no place hidden, but rather they[75] revealed (each one) to them (the Persians). They revealed to them the wood of the cross, which had been placed and hidden in a herb garden.[76] They made many chests and sent (the wood) to Khusro with many vessels and items of great worth. When it (the furniture) reached Yazdin, he held a great festival, and with the permission of the king, he took a piece of (the wood for himself), and sent (the wood) to the king. The king placed it as a token of honour with the sacred vessels in the new treasury which he had built at Ctesiphon.[77]

Then the Persian troops besieged Alexandria, which is enclosed by walls and surrounded by the water of the Nile[78] and has weighty doors. Alexander built it on the advice of his teacher Aristotle. For a while they (the Persians) fought against it but were unable to capture it; then a certain man, Peter by name,[79] went over to them. He had (earlier) come down to Alexandria from Qatar, so that he might be instructed in philosophy; and he said to the Persian commander, 'I will hand over the city to you'. This Peter had one day found (p.26) at the bottom of some book in the public archives of the city (a passage) written thus: 'When affliction arises for Alexandria, (the city) will be seized from the west gate which looks towards the sea.' The Persians prepared themselves, and seized (some) small fishing vessels, and embarked in them. With the fishermen, they entered the city in the early morning while it was (still) dark, protected by the fishing (vessels).[80] They killed the guardians of the gates, opened (the gates) to their allies, and announced the victory of Khusro on the wall. All the men were seized by fear; and the wind took hold of many ships onto which had been loaded the treasures of the Church and the nobles (of the city), so that they might be taken to sea for safety, and brought them to the camp of the Persians. They sent the (treasures) to Khusro, along with the keys of the city.[81] But when an envoy bearing keys reached Yazdin, he had golden keys made in the night in place of the (keys) and sent them to the king, to entice the king further to favour him. But after Jerusalem had been crushed, the detestable Jews threw fire into all the churches in it (the city). In this way the conflagration destroyed the church of the Resurrection, which had been built by Constantine and Helena and adorned with marble and priceless mosaics. In addition, the sons of the crucified one (the Jews) went up to the Persian commander, and said to him, 'Behold! All the gold and silver and treasures of Jerusalem were placed beneath the tomb of Jesus'. For they were contriving to destroy the place of (his) tomb. And when he (the commander) had given them the opportunity, they dug down three cubits around (the tomb), and found a box inscribed with these words: 'This is the box of Joseph, the counsellor who gave burial to the body of Jesus.' But when the commander heard of the Jews' plot he threw them out sternly.[82] When Yazdin heard, he made it known to the king; and he issued an order concerning the Jews, by which their wealth was confiscated and they were crucified. But as regards the body (p.27) of Joseph, he (Joseph) had ordered before his death that his body be deposited at the side of the grave of our Lord. Then Yazdin sought from the king (permission) to rebuild the churches of Jerusalem and, having sent not inconsiderable moneys, he renovated (them) with all their beauties; and everywhere he built churches as well as monasteries.[83]

When the Persian commander also heard that many riches were to be found in the church of St George of Lydda,[84] he sent a large number of his soldiers, but they were unable to enter, however, being held back by divine power. But at last he (himself) went (forth) with great anger, and when he reached the door of the church, he urged on his horse to enter by force; but the hooves of the horse stuck to the ground and he could neither move on forwards nor go backwards. (Thus) God showed that although he had allowed him to enter Jerusalem, (he had not done so because) his power was weak, but in order to punish the Romans, who said that Khusro could not hold power over Jerusalem. He (the Persian commander) vowed, 'If I escape, I shall make an object of silver in the likeness of the church of St George'. And so it turned out, and, behold, this miraculous object has hung in the church until now.

Afterwards, while Khusro was living in Dasqartha de Malka,[85] the Caesar Heraclius gathered many troops and came down against him; Khusro was disturbed by his presence and was in great fear. Heraclius went down to the northern regions; and he ravaged, devastated and took captives (in) all the northern regions. When he drew near to Dasqartha, Khusro fled from him and went to Mahoze. But it was said that when he (Khusro) had determined to take flight from Dasqartha, he heard the sound of a wooden bell; and he was disturbed and struck (p.28) his loins, and his stomach was relieved. Shirin said to him: 'Do not fear, O God', to whom he (replied): 'Now am I a God, when I am persecuted by a priest?' This he said because he had heard that Heraclius had taken the office of priest;[86] but he swore, 'If I obtain victory, I will leave no church and no wooden bell in my entire kingdom'. Yet the apprehension and anxiety which had seized him from the sound of the bell (did so) because he supposed that the Romans had wooden bells with them, and, behold, had come already to Dasqartha. He (Heraclius) removed all the royal treasure (and) led off captives; and, having devastated many places, he withdrew.[87]

Then many of the (Persian) troops revolted against Khusro; but Shamta, the son of Yazdin and Nehormizd, rose up and made Shiroe the son of Khusro king and gathered many troops around him.[88] But when Khusro heard (of these things), terrors seized him and fatal pains struck him. Having abandoned his kingdom in the night, he escaped; and he had two servant boys with him, who joined him from his household. They fled and hid in the royal garden, and when he saw the troops following him, the boys cried to each other.[89] He (Khusro) reached out his hand into a hedge, so that he might proceed further alongside it and escape, but he could not go on because of his fear. And they seized him and led (him) off and imprisoned him in the house of a certain man whose name was Mihraspend;[90] they gave bread to him to sustain (his) life. Then Shamta and Nehormizd sought (permission) from king Shiroe the son of Khusro to kill Khusro; and when he allowed them, they came and entered (the place) where he was guarded. Shamta lifted the sword to strike him, and Khusro, weeping before him said to him, 'How did I wrong you, that you would kill me?' And Shamta did not strike him, but Nehormizd struck him on his shoulder with an axe, and repeated (the blow) on the other (shoulder). His son Shiroe mourned for him, (p.29) and they brought him into the tomb of the kings. This Shamta accomplished, because when his father Yazdin had died, Khusro had plundered his house and inflicted many tortures on Yazdin's wife;[91] but Nehormizd (acted) because he (Khusro) had slain his father.[92] But Khusro, the son of Hormizd, reigned for 38 years.

There was peace and tranquillity in the days of Shiroe, his son, for all the Christians. But the nobles of the king, together with Shamta, formed a plot and killed all the children of Khusro; and Merdanshah, the son of Shirin, (was) among them.[93] Afterwards Shamta was accused in his (Shiroe's) presence of wishing to take over the kingdom; and he (the king) sent (men) to imprison him. Shamta then escaped, but they followed (him) and came upon him in the city of Hirtha of the Tayyaye (Hira). The king cut off his right hand and put him in prison.[94]

Isho-Yab, from Gedhala, was made head of the Church.[95] Although in early youth he had married a woman, he had not been barred because of this and was made bishop of the city of Balad. Finally he was elevated to the rank of *catholicos*, being endowed with every virtue.

Shiroe, when summer came, set off for Media, according to the custom of the king; a pain in the stomach seized him, and he died on the journey.[96] He had reigned eight months.[97]

Then they made reign in his stead Ardashir, his son – his son by the Roman Anzoy[98] – although he was still a small boy.[99] But one of the leaders of the Persian army, who was aligned with the Caesar Heraclius, Feruhan by name (Shahrvaraz),[100] when he heard of the boy Ardashir's rule, equipped Roman and Persian troops, entered Mahoza, overcame the army of the Persians, and went up and killed Ardashir. He brought Shamta, the son of Yazdin, out of prison and crucified him in front of the gate of the church of Beth Narqus,[101] because he had insulted the daughter of this (p.30) general (i.e. Shahrvaraz).[102] He dismissed the Romans who had accompanied him, and they returned to Heraclius.[103] Together with them he sent to Heraclius the wood of the Lord's cross, which they had brought back from Jerusalem and had been deposited in the Persian treasury, along with a countless number of presents.[104] Ardashir had reigned one year and six months; this Feruhan (Shahrvaraz), the general who killed Ardashir, reigned forty days.[105] As he was leaving Mahoza one day, a certain body-guard struck him from behind with a spear, and he died and was reviled by all the people.[106]

The Persians made Boran, the wife of Shiroe,[107] rule over them. When she came to rule, she wisely sent Mar Isho-Yab the *catholicos* to Heraclius in order to make peace with him. Cyriacus of Nisibis accompanied him (Isho-Yab), as well as Gabriel of Karka of Beth Garmai and Marutha of the city of Qastra.[108] They were received in a very friendly fashion by the Emperor Heraclius, who did for them everything they wanted.[109] Boran the wife of Shiroe, who ruled over the Persians, died by strangulation in the end.[110] (tr. M. Greatrex)

16

THE EVIDENCE OF EPIGRAPHY

The eastern frontier (363–630)

The epigraphic record of the eastern frontier is markedly uneven. Large numbers of inscriptions from Syria and Phoenice Libanensis allow us to build up a fairly detailed picture of local defences and reactions to enemy invasions in this region. But elsewhere, including Mesopotamia, Osrhoene, Armenia and the Transcaucasus, very few inscriptions have been found. Inevitably, therefore, this chapter will concentrate on the southern part of the frontier, a region where Arab raiders were often more of a threat than Persian armies.[1] It should be emphasised that we offer here only a selection of inscriptions, concentrating on those which are most often referred to in the secondary literature, but have not always been translated. It is not our aim to provide an exhaustive assessment of Roman defensive work along the frontier, which would involve a systematic examination of literary and epigraphic evidence. See Mouterde and Poidebard 1945: 237–40, Liebeschuetz 1977, Whitby 1986a, Gregory 1997.

Fourth–fifth centuries

It is difficult to discern any particular pattern to building work in the East in the late fourth and fifth centuries, partly because most of our evidence is clustered in the sixth century. Under Valens, however, there is record of building work at Amida, no doubt partly required by the swelling of the city's population with refugees from Nisibis.

CIL III.213, Amida (367/75): see Chapter 1.

In Syria, on the other hand, it has been suggested that some forts were abandoned by troops and were taken over by hermits. At any rate the desert area around Chalcis became the haunt of anchorites and Arab tribesmen.[2] Other places, however, such as Zebed, at the eastern approach to the Jebel Shbeyt, were strengthened in the second half of the fourth century. See Mouterde and Poidebard 1945: 167. Further south, we have clear evidence for continuing investment in frontier defences: the following inscription testifies to the building of a *mansio*, a hostel, to protect travellers in the desert. See Isaac 1992: 176–7, Gregory 1997: 94–5.

IGLS 2704 = *AAES* 355, Khan al-Abyad, south-west of Qaryateyn:[3] A plain that is dry indeed, and hateful enough to wayfarers, on account of (its) long wastes and (its) chances of death close at hand, for those whose lot is hunger, than which there is no graver ill, you have made, my lord, a camp, adorned with greatest splendour, O

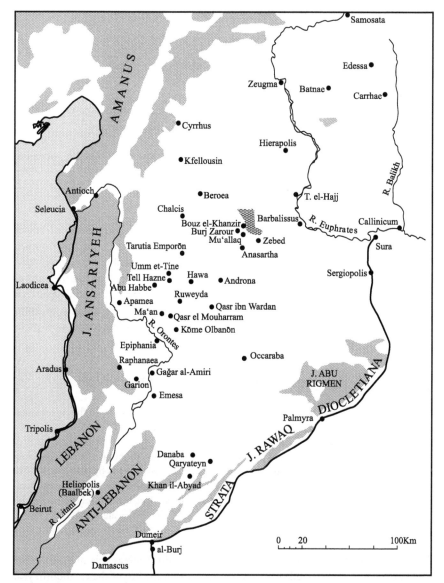

Map 6 Provenance of inscriptions discussed in Chapter 16

Silvinus, guardian of the most strong *limes* and of the cities by the trust of (our) masters, revered in all the world; and you have contrived that it abound in water celestial, so that it may be taken under the yoke of Ceres and of Bacchus. Therefore, O guest, with joy pursue your way, and for benefit received sing with praise the doings of this great-hearted magistrate, who shines in peace and in war. I pray the gods above that he, enjoying higher rank, may continue to found for (our) masters such camps,

239

arduous though they be, and that he may rejoice in children who add honour to their father's deeds.[4] (tr. Prentice, revised)

The fifth century, in general a peaceful one for the eastern frontier, provides occasional glimpses of defensive building work.

IGLS 2090, Burj el-Qai: + In the year 768, in the month Xandikos (April 457), through the effort of Maximus and Bassumus (this lintel) was erected.[5]

The following inscription from the fifth century testifies to the problems besetting communities of Phoenice and Syria (and even Palestine), among which were both Arab raiders and the Roman troops entrusted with guarding the region. See (e.g.) Mayerson 1989, Isaac 1992: 235–49, Whittaker 1994: 135–41.[6]

IGLS 2501bis, region of Emesa:[7] ... of asylum ... But we wish that this same (?) place be inviolate and unaffected by violence in every way possible, and in no way troubled by anyone in any way, and we decree that for the future (its inhabitants) should resist any damage, ill-treatment or annoyance either by the armed forces or (on the part) of those of the Saracen race or of anyone else attempting to wrong them, and again that they should have certain rights of ownership under whatever form it might be, completely immune from tax save for the capitation tax ... Donation of the most pious (emperor ?) ... granted ... '

The reign of Anastasius (491–518)

Under Anastasius a more coherent policy of defence emerged, most notably in the construction of the powerful stronghold at Dara on the frontier (see Chapter 5).

Granaries and depots were important to troops and inhabitants in the event of enemy invasion. It is clear that they were constructed not only by imperial officials but also by churchmen.[8] The role of the church in public building projects is noteworthy: churchmen were used on several occasions to supervise building work even of a military nature (as at Dara, but also at Scythopolis after the Samaritan revolt of 529–530. See Di Segni 1995: 321–2, Trombley and Watt 2000: xlviii-l, Feissel 2000: 88.

IGLS 2081, Arethusa: (Under the most) holy bishop Andreas this most beautiful (public) granary (was erected) from its foundations on the 9th of the ... month, year 810, indiction 6 (498).[9]

In general, funding for defensive works came either from city or provincial funds. The former were limited, and so recourse to the latter, which were administered by the province's governor, was frequent. Often the emperor would be thanked for channelling this money into a city's infrastructure. See Di Segni 1995: *passim*, esp. 330–1, Jones 1964: 759. Outside the cities, military officials might engage in the construction of forts or barracks, as might also the church. But here wealthy local individuals might also come to the assistance of their region, as in this case from Taroutia Emporōn (modern Kerratin, south of Chalcis).[10] See Di Segni 1995: 326–8, Gregory 1997: I, 93, Di Segni 1999: 150–2. On the context of the inscriptions below see Foss 1997: 234.

IGLS 1630 = *PUAES* III B 992, Taroutia Emporōn, a lintel from a tower: Thus wisely guarding his country, John, abounding in good counsels, supplying the gold unsparingly, provides a tower, a place of safety for (his) friends, through the effort of Paul (the) deacon, in (the) year 821 (AD 509/10), in (the) name of God (the) Saviour. (tr. Prentice)

IGLS 1631 = *PUAES* III B 993, Taroutia Emporōn, a lintel found close to the preceding inscription: He who in the emperor's business has proved a faithful servant in toils, John, has made this guardhouse secure, a defence of safety in this region, being son of Azizos by name, brother of Paul ... (tr. Prentice)

IGLS 1725, Umm et-Tine, south of Taroutia Emporōn, a lintel: May the Lord guard your entrance and your exit. (This building) was (built) under (the direction) of the most glorious [C]apito[l]inus. Indiction 10, in the month Gorpieus, year 828 (September 516).[11]

The reigns of Justin I, Justinian and Justin II (518–78)

A wealth of evidence for building work during the reigns of Justin I and Justinian survives. On the one hand, there is the detailed account provided by Procopius' *Buildings (De Aedificiis)* II–III, recording the extensive building activity of Justinian on the eastern frontier. At the same time, the epigraphic record from Syria for this period exceeds that of any other in antiquity: northern Syria was more densely inhabited at this time than ever before.[12] The inscriptions frequently attribute the initiative for the defensive work to individuals who do not appear to be imperial officials; much work in particular seems to have been undertaken by churchmen. The two sources – inscriptions and Procopius – must both be taken into account in assessing imperial involvement in frontier defence; although there are few references to imperial involvement in the epigraphic record, it is clear from Procopius that much work was undertaken by Justinian in the East.[13]

In general, it is only inscriptions which allow Justinian's fortification work to be dated: Procopius' *Buildings* merely ascribes a wide range of projects to the emperor without assigning any date to the work involved.[14] Three phases may be distinguished within the period 518–578.

(1) 518–32

In this phase there was a considerable amount of defensive work undertaken in Syria and along the frontier with Persia, see Chapter 5. Fortifications were also restored further south, as at Scythopolis: see Di Segni 1995: 318–19, translating the relevant inscriptions. An uneasy period of peace with Persia prevailed up to the late 520s, but raids by Lakhmid Arabs presented a significant threat to Syria. See Whitby 1986a: 727 (who regards 518–27 as a period of peace), Lauffray 1983: 38–9 and 141 (suggesting that work was also carried out at Zenobia in this period).

IGLS 481 = *PUAES* III B 1105, Kfellousin, a four-storey tower: + In the year 570 (?), the third of Xanthikos, indiction 15 (April ?522) through Sabatius, deacon, contributing of his own toil.[15]

IGLS 2155, basalt lintel from Garion (Gour), between Emesa and Raphanea: station-post (*metaton*) of St Longinus and St Theodore and St George, year 836 (AD 524/5).[16]

IGLS 1768, Hawa, north of Ruweyda, among important ruins, lintel of a tower: The tower was erected (?) with God's (help) for the safety and health of the brothers and servants (?), year 840, 6th (?) indiction (528/9).[17]

Seyrig 1950: 239, Palmyra: Under the supervision of Flavius Platanius Serenianus the most eminent *dux* of the East ... [18]

Roussel 1939, Hierapolis: inscription commemorating the Eternal Peace. See p.97 above.

(2) 532–40

During the period of the Eternal Peace, there was little building work in the East. Justinian concentrated his efforts in the West, and by the time of Khusro's invasion in 540, Roman defences were in a poor state. See Chapters 6–7.

IGLS 1789, Ruweyda, lintel of a tower: + Chi-mu-gamma. Lord, help your servant Thomas (the) deacon. + Year 851, indiction 3, Jesus Christ. (AD 539/40).[19]

(3) 540–78

Following Khusro's devastating invasions in the early 540s, more effort was invested in fortifying the eastern provinces, particularly towards the end of Justinian's reign (the early 560s).[20] See Whitby 1986a: 728–9, Lauffray 1983: 35–7, Sauvaget 1939: 122, Tate 1996: 334. However, the construction of city defences and forts could not compensate for a general reduction in troop numbers in the region. The Roman presence on or near the *Strata Diocletiana* had been decreasing well before this period, and Justinian intensified this trend by relying on the Jafnid kings to defend much of the southern section of the frontier. In noting the inscriptions below therefore, we must keep in mind that 'there is practically no inscriptional evidence for the presence of the Roman army'.[21]

SEG 41.1510 = **Mango and Mango 1991: 466, perhaps from Tell Beshme, possibly from a work of fortification:** Under our lord of the world, Flavius Justinian, eternal Augustus and the most glorious *dux* Thomas, through the effort the most glorious *comes domesticorum* Cyrus, (this work) was completed in the month of Audynaeus, indiction 5.[22]

IGLS 1889 = *PUAES* III B 871, Kōme Olbanōn (Halban), north-east of Epiphania, lintel of a tower facing north: + In the year 854, the month of Dystrus, indiction 6 (March 543). + (This is) the work of John and Symeon, stonemasons from Kōme Olbanōn.[23]

Humann and Puchstein 1890: 405 no.5, Constantia: Thomas, the most holy bishop, putting his hope in God, began the labour (of building) this granary in the month of Artemisium, indiction 6, of (the) year 854 (May 543).[24]

IGLS 145–7, **Cyrrhus:** see p.111.

IGLS 1598, **Idjaz, about 3 km south of Taroutia Emporōn, lintel on a wall that terminates in a tower:** I shall not fear the myriads of people besetting me on every side, because the Lord is my protector. Lord my God I hope in you. Save me from those who persecute me and deliver me. You, Lord, will protect and keep me. Protect me, Lord, like the maiden of (your) eye. In the shadow of your wings shelter me. Some (enemies) are in chariots and others on horses, but for our part we glory in the name of our Lord God. Play the man and let your heart be strong, all of you who hope in the Lord. (Chi-Rho). I am a house of peace, keeping the children of prosperous people safe with walls of stone. + In the tenth indiction of the year 858 (546/7).[25] (tr. Trombley)

IGLS 1809, **Ma'an, east of Apamea, lintel of the west gate of the fortress in three fragments:** Justinian, our most pious and gloriously triumphant emperor, who saves all the cities by his unsparing munificence, restored this fort also in the year 859 (AD 547/8). Many years to the most distinguished count John, who takes delight in building. Many years to Theodore the renowned *a secretis*.[26]

IGLS 348 = *AAES* 305, **Chalcis, on the east side of the north tower:** With the aid of God the whole eastern face was built from its foundations out of the pious generosity of our most serene … master Flavius Justinian, Eternal Augustus and Emperor and under the supervision of Longinus, the most glorious and most renowned former governor, ex-consul and most glorious *magister militum* and of the most glorious former consul Anastasius and of the most magnificent and illustrious engineer Isidore in the 14th indiction, year 862 (= 550/1).[27]

IGLS 1811, **Qasr el-Mouharram (Qasr el-Berouj), north-east of Emesa, tower B, lintel of the gate:** Christ Jesus, become for us a protecting God, a house of refuge and a mighty tower in the face of the enemy. Raise up this house, plant in it the glory of your name for eternity (through) the prayer of Mary the Mother of God and all your saints. Amen. This lintel was placed in the year 862, in the month of Artemisius, indiction 14 (May 551).[28]

IGLS 1682, **Androna, lintel across the main gate:** + This is the gate of the Lord. Just men shall enter within it. + + It is customary for others to serve the many by (the) contribution of funds. May you, Thomas, best and most wonderful (of men), illuminate the daily life of your fatherland. You appear as a saviour through the acts in which you are prudent, while God our Saviour takes care to share in your plans. + + We laid the foundations of the fortress with (the help of) God, through the munificence of Thomas and the effort of Jacob his nephew in May, on the twentieth day, in the sixth indiction of the (year) 869 (AD 558). + + The lintel was set in place in November, on the first day, with the help of God in the eighth year of the indiction of the year 871 (November 560). + +[29] (tr. Trombley, revised)

The peace concluded in 562 did not mark an end to defensive work in the East; the Romans had perhaps learnt their lesson after the Eternal Peace of 532.[30]

IGLS 1841–4, **Qasr ibn Wardan:** extensive ruins have been discovered here, in a style more similar to buildings in Constantinople than surrounding Syrian constructions. *IGLS 1842* offers a date of November 564; recent work indicates continuing construction under Justin II, apparently under the supervision of a *stratēlatēs* George. The site contains a church, a palace and barracks for troops. See M. Mango, *ODB* III.1764 (with references), C. Mango 1976: 151 and now de Maffei 1995: 109–12.[31]

IGLS 1726, **Tell Hazne, about 18 km north-west of Ruweyda, lintel of a gate of the tower:** + I, Thomas, *periodeutes* by the grace of God, having prayed and besought God for a means of atonement for my sins, erected this tower for the glory of his name, praising (him) for its foundation (…). Indiction 13 of the year 874 (563). + (The) Lord of the armies (is) with us; our protector is the God of Jacob. Holy God, holy (and) mighty, holy (and) immortal, (who) was crucified for us, have mercy on us, who was crucified for us, have mercy on us. (*In a cross in the middle: Light. Life. Alpha. Omega.*)[32]

IGLS 1743, **Abu Habbe, north-east of Apamea, a fortress of which only the north wall remains:** … (The God of the armies is with us); our protector is the God of Jacob. + In the name of the father and of the son and of the Holy Spirit this good work (was accomplished) under Macedonius through John, his *notarius*, in the month of Daisius, indiction 14, year 877 (June 566).[33]

The role of the Ghassanids on the frontier

The Ghassanid allies of the Romans assisted in defending the frontier not only with their forces, but also by undertaking building work themselves. See Shahîd 1995: 489–518, cf. 258–61, Foss 1997: 250–2, Sartre 1982a: 183–8, Key Fowden 1999: 149–73 (on the so-called *praetorium* of Mundhir the Jafnid at Sergiopolis).

Waddington 1870: 2562c, al-Burj (just south of Dumayr), on a stone on top of the entrance to the fort: Flavius Alamundarus (Mundhir), (the) renowned patrician and phylarch, giving thanks to the Lord God and saint Julian for the sake of his salvation and that of his most glorious children, built (the tower).[34]

The late sixth and early seventh centuries

Defences continued to be worked on in the period after Justin II (from 578 to the 610s), although the number of inscriptions decreases. Whether it should be inferred from this that less work was being carried out is uncertain.[35]

IGLS 288 = *AAES* 318, **Anasartha, lintel:** By the gifts of (his) majesty (the) city, despising the inroad of the barbarians, set up at its gates its benefactors, (the) Saviour Christ, (her) gloriously victorious sovereigns, (the) renowned (commander), the prefects of the praetorium, also (?) its most holy bishop, (and the?) most glorious engineer, in the month Gorpieos (September), in the 906th (?) year, indiction 13. + Jesus Christ, Emannuel. + God over all.[36] (tr. Prentice)

Imperial involvement continued nevertheless, as the following inscription, and others from the same site, clearly attest.[37]

IGLS 2125: Gağar al-Amiri, south-west of Arethusa, part of a huge lintel: (in accordance with) the decision of Constantine (Tiberius Augustus?), (as) the (aforementioned) Tiberius, (the emperor) of pious reputation (and memory, and as too) our Emperor (Maurice) beloved of Christ, having inherited the piety of his aforementioned father (decreed), and once Gregory the venerable (patriarch was involved), the surrounding wall (*peribolos*) (was erected) from its foundations by the generous (?) (gift of the most beloved of God) Sergius, son of Leontius, presbyter and *paramonarius* ... year 894 (582/3).[38]

IGLS 281 = AAES 319, Anasartha, city gate: + (Phocas) and Leontia,[39] our most pious sovereigns, O Lord protect! + A pious branch that sprang from noble stock, Gregory, the renowned, and adorned with the fruits of his virtue, presented to God this wall also, in sparing his own country (the expense). Indiction 8, in the 916th year (604/5).[40]

Building work went on in the early seventh century, and the inscriptions thus provide evidence for Roman resistance to the Persian invasions.

IGLS 271, Mu'allaq, north-east of Anasartha, a monastery church: + Chi-Mu-Gamma. (Chi-Mu-Gamma). ++ This is the gate of the Lord. The just shall enter within it. Upon this rock I shall build my church, and the gates of hell shall not prevail against it. + This house of St Barapsabba was built through the efforts of the most distinguished ... in the tenth indiction in the year 918 (606/7), ... being the stonecutter.[41] (tr. Trombley)

Worthy of note too is *IGLS* 2068 from Bserin, south of Epiphania, recording construction of a barracks dedicated to St George in November 928 (616).

NOTES

PREFACE

1 Cf. Robin 1996: 698 n.118 and Key Fowden 1999: 142.
2 Cf. Garsoïan 1998b: 1110, 1998c: 1158.

CHAPTER 1

1 Cf. also Paschoud 1979: II, 218 n.91 (noting that several of the regions surrendered to the Persians were not east of the Tigris). The precise status of Armenia in the treaty of 363 is unclear, and may well have been deliberately left ambiguous: see the perceptive comments of Seager 1996: 283–4 and idem 1997: 267. For a general account of events see (e.g.) Curran 1998: 78–9; on the chronology of the withdrawal see Dodgeon and Lieu 1991: 237, with Matthews 1989: 185–6, Dillemann 1962: 308–12 on the geography.
2 Turcan 1966 considers the differing attitudes of the sources. Whitby 1988: 205 n.14 believes that attitudes softened as time passed, but the passages of Agathias and Joshua the Stylite below imply otherwise. See also Chrysos 1993, Teixidor 1995: 499–504.
3 Reading *memorabant* with Fontaine 1977: I, 195, cf. II, 254–5 n.636.
4 The Tigris.
5 Surena was the name of one of the seven most noble families of Persia, but, like other family names, was frequently misunderstood by Roman sources as a title. See Christensen 1944: 105 and n.3. On the Persian initiative see Chrysos 1993: 168–9 (noting that Ammianus is supported by other sources).
6 A detailed analysis of this section of Ammianus is provided by Seager 1997: 266, who notes some internal inconsistencies (over the strength or weakness of the Roman position).
7 The four days are 8–11 July. As Fontaine 1977: II, 256–7 n.645 and Matthews 1989: 186 note, Ammianus is guilty of serious exaggeration here: Corduene lay some 280 km away and had been evacuated by the Romans four years earlier, cf. also Dillemann 1962: 304.
8 I.e. the emperor more commonly known as Galerius.
9 Location uncertain, but Fontaine 1977: II, n.648, following Dillemann 1962: 213–14 identifies it with Rhabdion. Ball 1989 proposes an identification with Seh Qubba on the Tigris in Iraq. As noted above (n.1), not all these regions are on the eastern side of the Tigris; cf. also Chrysos 1993: 174–82, 187–8, noting that, contrary to what Ammianus alleges, Shapur did not obtain all that he wanted. See Dillemann 1962: 219–20 on the fifteen fortresses.

10   Procopius was a relative of Julian, who in 365 unsuccessfully attempted to wrest power from Valens. Cf. *PLRE* I.742–3.

11   Reading *nimium* with Fontaine 1977: II, 259 n.650 for *nimia*.

12   A district of Atropatene: see Fontaine 1977: II, 29 n.58 and Dillemann 1962: 300–1.

13   So Seyfarth. Fontaine 1977: I, 198, has the more likely Nevitta, on whom see *PLRE* I.626–7.

14   Dillemann 1962: 304–5 and fig.18 for the Roman route back. On the duration of the peace see Chrysos 1993: 186–8, arguing that it was a crucial point gained by Jovian (and that Nisibis and the other cities were therefore liable to be returned to Roman territory after this time). We find this point unconvincing: the peace may have been intended to last thirty years, but there is no reason (despite later Roman claims) to suppose that any territory was ever due to be handed back.

15   Millar 1993: 102, 129, on these earlier attacks on Hatra. By the 230s, however, a Roman garrison had been installed there.

16   Dillemann 1962: 310–11 on the Roman route here and Fontaine 1977: II, 264 n.663 on the types of food mentioned by Ammianus.

17   30 km east of Singara, cf. Dillemann 1962: 311 and Fontaine 1977: II, 264–5 n.664.

18   The text of this may be found also in the Suda, I.401; a similar extract in *Exc. de Virt.* 63 = Joh. Ant. frg.181.

19   Libanius has just referred to earthquakes in Syria.

20   Very similar complaints may be found in *Or.*24.9 (tr. in Dodgeon and Lieu 1991: 261).

21   This reference to Roman defeats is directly at odds with Ammianus' account, XXV.7.5.

22   The agreement to hand back Nisibis after 120 years is a clear fabrication, cf. Blockley 1992: 84 and 215 n.37. But the story persisted, finding its way into the Roman archives, it appears: so Justin II claimed to Khusro I in the 570s, cf. Mich. Syr. X.1 (below, p.140). See Chrysos 1976: 31–2, Luther 1997: 99 and below (d).

23   Or 'generalship': the Greek is ambiguous.

24   The names seem to have been somewhat garbled by Zos. Zalene is presumably a misunderstanding of Arzanene, and Moxoene is omitted. Cf. Blockley 1984: 35 for a list. The Greek term *ethnē* has here been translated as 'provinces', although it literally means 'peoples'. These Armenian principalities or satrapies were known as *ethnē* (Latin *gentes*), and were not technically provinces: cf. Paschoud 1979: II, 218 n.91 and Chrysos 1993: 174–6. They had not been under direct Roman control.

25   The tone of this excerpt, and the list of previous Roman surrenders contrasted with this one (III.32), is more pessimistic than hostile. Cf. Paschoud 1975: 188–97 for a comparison of Zos.'s treatment of the peace with other sources (esp. Ammianus, Eutropius and Festus).

26   A reference to the three eastern provinces annexed by Trajan in his Parthian campaign, but given up voluntarily by Hadrian upon his accession in 117. Millar 1993: 100–2 notes how numerous fourth-century sources make this same comparison.

27   We take this as a reference to contemporary debate about the peace treaty and the events leading up to it.

28   An allusion to Herodotus VIII.6, where the expression is used of Persian expectations of their victory over the Greek navy shortly before the battles of Artemisia and Salamis in 480 BC.

29   An ironic criticism of Julian rather than Jovian.

30   Essentially the same account in *Chr. Pasch.* 553–5; a more garbled version in Joh. Nik. 80.34–6.

31   As Turcan 1966: 884, 886 notes, Theodoret is plainly in error in making such positive claims for the state of the Roman army on its way back, as is clear from the eyewitness account of Ammianus.

32 Cf. Drijvers 1994: 201–14. On the generally more positive attitude of the Syriac sources towards Jovian, see Teixidor 1995: 503–4.

33 I.e. the Romans had caused the more damage. Cf. Chrysos 1993: 171–2 on this tradition, which Chrysos is inclined to accept.

34 Cf. Chrysos 1976: 31 and Nöldeke 1874: 280 on these details; also Josh. Styl. 7 (above) and n.22 on this invention of a time-limit.

35 Cf. Ehling 1996 on Jovian's emissions (for which see Kent 1981: 393 nos.109–12, 424 no.229); also Chrysos 1993: 170.

36 Tabari is here drawing on the *Julian Romance*, cf. Nöldeke 1874: 291–2 and Chrysos 1976: 31.

37 Cf. Teixidor 1995: 504–5 on this population transfer. He emphasises rightly that neither the departure of many Romans from Nisibis nor the arrival of immigrants from the east had a significant impact on the character of the city.

38 See Matthews 1989: 1–4 for an excellent modern evocation of the scene. Ammianus and Ephrem were certainly eyewitnesses; Zosimus himself, equally certainly, was not, but he is clearly relying on a first-rate source which shows notable parallels with Ammianus. Cf. Paschoud 1979: II, 226 n.97, 228–32 n.99. See below on the work at Amida. Edessa was another place of refuge for those forced to move, as is noted by Chr. 724 (in vol.1); see Chrysos 1976: 27–8 and 27 n.1 on the destinations of the refugees.

39 Fontaine 1977: II, 269 n.678, following Dillemann 1962: 312, identifies the place with Thebetha.

40 If the reading *ad Hibitam* is accepted, it is probably another reference to Thebetha, cf. Fontaine 1977: II, 271–2 n.686 and Dillemann 1962: 312.

41 The implication seems to be that the Persians tolerated the Christian community in Nisibis. Presumably either some people remained in the city or others from the countryside nearby were moved there, along with the Persians tranferred to the city (on whom see Tabari, p.9 above). This would account for the continuing pro-Roman sympathies of the city, cf. Blockley 1992: 28.

42 The body of Julian on its way to Cilicia. The city referred to is Nisibis.

43 *Chr. Pasch.* 553–4 offers the same account.

44 Cf. Ps.-Dion. and Mal. (above) on the resettlement of the citizens of Nisibis at Amida; Gabriel 1940: 178–82 notes an extension to Amida's city walls around this time (see below), cf. Oates 1968: 106, Gregory 1997: II, 65. Other Nisibenes, such as Ephrem, emigrated to Edessa. See Chrysos 1976: 27 n.1.

45 Vanderspoel 1995: 168 for the date.

46 AD 370. In fact Valens arrived in the spring, and was back in Constantinople in winter 370/1; cf. Barnes 1998: 251. An earlier trip to Antioch (in 365) had had to be abandoned on account of Procopius' revolt, cf. Gutmann 1991: 166 and Greatrex 2000a: 35–6.

47 Dillemann 1962: 105 connects this cession (otherwise unattested) with the return of Rhabdion (identified with Ammianus' Castra Maurorum, 304–5) to the Romans. No other source knows of a peace treaty under Valens nor of the handing over of territory in Mygdonia (i.e. the area around Nisibis).

48 Bird 1986 argues that the *Breviaria* composed by both Festus and Eutropius and presented to Valens in 369/70 were intended to incite the emperor to exact vengeance on the Persians. Note (e.g.) Festus, *Breviarium* 30.2 (the closing lines of the work, hoping for an imminent victory over the Babylonians, i.e. the Persians).

49 As Paschoud 1979: II, 355–6 n.128 argues, Zos. must be referring to Valens' journey in spring 370. Zos. rightly refers to the emperor's visit to Hierapolis that year – the traditional mustering point for eastern campaigns – but fails to record his trip back to Constantinople in winter 370–1. See Barnes 1998: 251–2 on Valens' movements at this time. The case mentioned at the end of 13.2 took place in winter 371/2.

50 Vanderspoel 1995: 177 for the date (March 373; March 374 is also possible) of Themistius' speech.

51 Themistius Or.11.149b appears to refer to Valens being in Mesopotamia in late March 373. *CTh* XIV.13 places him at Hierapolis in August that year (cf. Seeck 1919: 245 and *PLRE* I.212), although the date of the law is not entirely secure.

52 The version translated here is that printed by Gabriel 1940: 136. On archaeological evidence for the expansion of Amida at this time, see n.44 above.

53 For a useful recent assessment of the role of the Arabs in this period see Isaac 1998a: 444–52. Graf 1989: 350 cautions against views of 'increasing pressure' on the frontier here. A brief and judicious summary of the debate surrounding the term Saracen is provided by Bowersock in *LA* 680–1; cf. Matthews 1989: 349.

54 Mayerson 1980 is rightly sceptical about how much reliance can be placed on the surviving accounts of Mavia's uprising, since their primary interest is doctrinal matters. Although the passage from Socr. below refers to Valens' departure from Antioch (378), this seems too late for the outbreak of the revolt, cf. Woods 1996: 268, putting the ending of the revolt in 377, shortly before Valens' departure from Antioch (dated to 378 by Barnes 1998: 253 and n.16). Note also that a contingent of Arabs was present near Constantinople shortly after the battle of Adrianople, Ammianus XXXI.6.5–6 (and perhaps before, cf. Shahîd 1984: 175–83). The account of Thdrt. *HE* IV.23.1 has been omitted, since it is of little worth, as too is that of Theodore Lector and those who followed him: cf. Shahîd 1984: 197–8 and Bowersock 1980: 481–2. The Tanukhids seem to have been replaced by the Salihids as the chief allies (*foederati*) of the Romans around 383. Shahîd 1984: 203–16 rather overplays the meagre information provided by Pacatus, *Pan. Lat.* II (XII) 22.3 concerning a successful campaign against the Arabs at this time.

55 Lucius was the Arian successor of Athanasius as patriarch of Alexandria, who oppressed his orthodox opponents. Rufinus, writing in the first decade of the fifth century, is the first source to write on Mavia; as Mayerson 1980: 124–6 notes, he was more interested in the monk Moses and events in Alexandria than Mavia.

56 Socrates goes on to describe how the (orthodox) monk Moses was appointed as bishop for Mavia and her tribesmen.

57 Soz. may be exaggerating in the extent of Mavia's raids, but cf. Shahîd 1984: 146. On the term *klima* here used for 'region', cf. *ODB* II.1133 (misunderstood by Shahîd, loc. cit.).

58 Woods 1998: 329 identifies the *magister equitum et peditum per Orientem* as Julius and his subordinate with Maurus, *dux Phoenices*.

59 cf. Bowersock 1980: 490–3. See also Millar 1998: 85 on the importance of Sozomen's evidence here, noting that it is the first-ever reference to poetry in Arabic. Frye 1977: 11 oddly interprets the word 'odes' as a non-Greek term meaning 'regions'.

60 As Sartre notes, Sozomen's reference to 'the present reign' is ambiguous, since it could refer to Valens (in whose reign the episode of Mavia took place) or Theodosius II (in whose reign he was writing). Isaac places the episode 'in the last quarter of the fourth century'. Shahîd 1984: 141 identifies Zocomus as the 'first of the Salihids', the confederation allied to Rome during the fifth century (doubted by Sartre 1982a: 143).

61 Weissbach, *RE* II.1 (1920), 618–19 and II.5 (1934), 1922–3 and Matthews 1989: 51–2 on Resaina. Since it had a bishop earlier in the fourth century, it was clearly not an insignificant place even before Theodosius' work, cf. Dillemann 1962: 107. Mal.'s claim that Theodosius I extended the walls of Antioch is a confusion with Theodosius II, however: see Downey 1961: 437 and 1941. Van Esbroeck 1997: 364–5 attributes the foundation of both this Theodosiopolis and that in Armenia (see Chapter 4) to Theodosius I, dating them to 383/4. For Litarba and Gindarus see Talbert 2000: 67 D4.

62 Valens perished in 378 at Adrianople, while Shapur II died in 379, to be succeeded by his brother Ardashir II (379–83). Not all the embassies sent during this period are noted

here. That undertaken by Sporacius is to be found in Chapter 2; that by Stilicho (Claudian, *De cons. Stil.* I.51–4) cannot be placed with certainty, cf. Blockley 1987: 230 and n.35.

63 The passage comes between a report concerning the death of King Athanaric (Jan. 381) and one concerning the elevation of Arcadius to the rank of Augustus (Jan. 383).

64 This oration is dated to 1 January 383, cf. Vanderspoel 1995: 205.

65 i.e. previous emperors.

66 Cf. Seeck 1920: 453 on this passage.

67 Parallel notices in *Chr. Pasch.* 563, Hyd. a.384, *Cons. CP* a.384, Socr. *HE* V.12.2. See also Marc. com. a.385, a possible allusion to the division of Armenia, and certainly evidence of further negotiations with Persia; cf. Croke 1995: 59.

68 Nixon in Nixon and Rodgers 1994: 475 n.73 rightly connects this passage with the embassy of 384. Pacatus later (32.2) seems to allude to the division of Armenia; see Chapter 2 below.

69 The brief notice comes just before Theodosius' campaign against Maximus in 388. Libanius, *Orr.*19.62, 20.47 confirms that the Persians were seeking peace at this time. The division of Armenia (Chapter 2) cemented the peace. Following the accession of Bahram IV in 388, a further Persian delegation confirmed the peace with Theodosius in Rome in 389, cf. Claudian, *VI cos. Hon.* 69–72 with Greatrex 2000a: 43.

70 Lee 1993a: 133 considers the invasion to be directly linked to the absence of Roman troops, but since the Huns attacked the Persians as well, who did succeed in rebuffing them, there is no need to attribute knowledge of Roman troop dispositions to them. Note also that, as the notice preserved in Ps.-Dion. (below, p.18–19) makes clear, sufficient troops were left to defeat at least part of the invasion force of 395.

71 Maenchen-Helfen 1973: 52 for this chronology. On the impression left by the invasions, note also the poems composed by Abhsamia, the nephew of the great Syriac hymnographer Ephrem some ten years after the event: the references to this are assembled in Witakowski 1984–6: 495 (cf. e.g. *Chr. Ede.* 47 [a.715 = 403/4]). On the derivative nature of some sources, cf. Levy 1971: 131 and Maenchen-Helfen 1973: 10–15. Not included here is Priscus frg. 11. 596–619. Despite the doubts of Blockley 1983: 386 n.66, the passage probably does refer to this invasion, but adds few details. Cf. Maenchen-Helfen 1973: 53–4 and note the references to the defeat of the Huns by the Persians, paralleled by *Chr. 724* below.

72 The Dariel pass probably, instead of the Derbend to the east. So Maenchen-Helfen 1973: 57.

73 The river Phasis is the modern Rioni, which flows into the Black Sea in ancient Lazica (modern Georgia). The other references to the places where the prisoners have been taken are to the lands north of the Caucasus. Argaeus is a mountain in Cappadocia.

74 The letter (to Heliodorus) was written in 396, cf. Scourfield 1993: 230–1.

75 *Ep.*77.8 (tr. in Thompson 1996: 31–2), lengthier and more sensationalist, adds little of substance, save to confirm that the Roman army was absent from the region and that there was a rumour that the invaders considered making for Jerusalem on account of its wealth. As Levy 1948: 62–8 notes, Jerome's description may well be influenced by Claudian.

76 Here, according to Markwart 1930: 97 n.2, in the sense of Mesopotamia.

77 The Armenian Antitaurus, cf. Markwart 1930: 99.

78 Markwart 1930: 99 thinks a reference to Arsamosata more geographically probable.

79 Dillemann 1962: 238 and now Greatrex and Greatrex 1999: 73–5 on its location, cf. Ammianus on its use as a refuge, XIX.6.1.

80 Chabot in his translation (p.140) unnecessarily emends the river's name to Zab. He thus seems to place Ziatha much further down the Tigris (in Persian territory).

81 The location of Ziatha the great is a matter of dispute: cf. now Greatrex and Greatrex 1999: 73–5, where this translation first appeared.

82 Of the Persian king Peroz, in the 470s or early 480s. He was demanding money from the Romans to defend himself from the (Hephthalite) Huns. See Chapter 3 below.

83 Cf. Kettenhoffen 1998: 161 for this translation.

84 Maenchen-Helfen 1973: 56–7 plays down Eutropius' victory, arguing that there were no Huns left south of the Caucasus by 397. Cf. also Braund 1994: 266–7 and *PLRE* II.441–2.

CHAPTER 2

1 For the opposite view see Rubin 1986a: 38–9, placing Sporacius' negotiations in 442 (arguing that the Theodosius referred to is Theodosius II, not I).

2 Luther 1997: 104 n.28 argues that this Yazdgerd should be identified with neither king of this name, but is rather a Persian envoy.

3 Probably an allusion to the invasion of 395 (on which see Chapter 1 above).

4 There is much debate on the meaning of this name, complicated by the question as to whether the fortress is located in the Dariel pass (as John almost certainly means here) or the Derbend pass. Priscus (e.g. frg.41.1.10) refers to the place as Ioureiopaach. See Marquart 1901: 99–106, Dillemann 1962: 92 and Synelli 1986: 102–4.

5 As Blockley 1985a: 65–6 argues, it is not clear that the Persian claims for Roman contributions were justified. Luther 1997: 106 n.30 suggests that the attacks on Syria and Cappadocia allude to the Hunnic invasion of 395.

6 Blockley 1985: 64 n.10 rightly rejects Wuensch's emendation of the manuscript text here, according to which the Romans became tributaries of the Persians. Bandy's translation is likewise flawed.

7 On the differing interpretations of Jovian's peace, see Blockley 1984: 36–8, Gutmann 1991: 164. Seager 1996: 276, 283–4 concludes that the Persians were not explicity entitled to intervene in Armenia, while Chrysos 1993: 187–8 argues that although the peace barred the Persians from intervening in Armenia, it was dissolved by the emperor's death. Note Ammianus XXVI.4.6 (where he is critical of Persian attacks on Armenia in 365, cf. Seager 1996: 276–7); also Chrysos 1976: 35–6.

8 Cf. *Epic Histories* IV.52–4 for a slightly different account; also Mos. Khor. III.34. On the death of Arsaces (referred to as Arsak III by some modern scholars, as Arsak II by others), see Marié 1984: 271 n.303, Hewsen 1978–9: 114, and Garsoïan 1989: 352–3.

9 The Persians might have regarded it as part of Armenia, however. Zuckerman 1991: 533–5 argues, on the basis of identifications of places listed in the *Notitia Dignitatum* (for which see Dodgeon and Lieu 1991: 347–8), that Valens also established Roman strongholds on the eastern shores of the Black Sea, at Pityus and Sebastopolis, to reinforce the Roman position in the region. See also Gregory 1997: II, 11–18.

10 The expulsion will have taken place in 368/9, since Sauromaces' restoration took place in 370. Cf. Braund 1994: 260 and *PLRE* I.809. Heather and Matthews 1991: 23 argue that Them. *Or.*8.116c (175) refers to the arrival of an Iberian prince named Bacurius in Roman territory and suggest that Shapur may have been encroaching on Iberia as early as 367/8.

11 Cf. Mos. Khor. III.35 for his version; only a part of that contained in the *Epic Histories* is offered here. See Baynes 1955: 200 and Grousset 1947: 143–5 on the Persian takeover in 369–70. The capture of Artogerassa (the Armenian Artagers in the district of Arsharunik', north of the river Araxes, cf. Garsoïan 1989: 447) and Arsaces' wife is reported by Ammianus at XXVII.12.12 (below, p.23). Gutmann 1991: 171 dates these events to 368/9.

12 Arrabannus is probably a corruption of the Armenian name Ardavan (Artabanus).

13 On the transfer of allegiance of Cylaces and Arrabannus (in 368 or early 369), see Gutmann 1991: 171–2.

14 Both of these are names of noble houses of Iran, cf. Garsoïan 1989: 382–3, 433.

15 Garsoïan 1967: *passim*, esp. 304–9, argues that Valens' support for Pap was linked with their shared adherence to Arianism; cf. Gutmann 1991: 172–3. Shapur's support came from elements of the Armenian nobility unhappy with the Roman-backed monarchy, cf. Gutmann 1991: 168–70.

16 Cf. *Epic Histories* IV.58 for the invasion undertaken by the king himself. Terentius' restoration of Pap took place in 369, and the winter referred to here is that of 369–70; cf. Gutmann 1991: 172–3.

17 Artogerassa fell in 370: so Baynes 1955: 201. Gutmann 1991: 173 seems (implicitly) to place it in 369, however.

18 As Seager 1996: 278 notes, Valens' war with the Goths was now over and he was therefore in a better position to deploy forces in the East. Arintheus, it may be noted, was in fact *magister peditum praesentalis*, cf. Woods forthcoming, ch.3b: Ammianus' terminology is imprecise here.

19 This is Musheł Mamikonean, later the chief general of King Varazdat.

20 Cf. Mos. Khor. III.36–7 and *Vit. Ners.* 11, who ascribe the plea for Roman intervention to the patriarch Nerses; Garsoïan 1989: 307 n.4 compares this passage with the account of Ammianus. Gutmann 1991: 173 sees in Pap's coronation a deliberate Roman response to the escalating situation. The count Adē may be a confused reference to Arintheus, or, as Garsoïan suggests (1989: 344), to another commander, Trajan. Baynes 1955: 201–2 connects Adē with Addaeus, the *magister utriusque militiae per Orientem* in the 390s, cf. *PLRE* I, Addaeus. Woods, forthcoming ch.3b, argues persuasively that Adē is Ammianus' Vadomarius, however; he also notes that Terentius was *comes et dux Armeniae*, cf. *PLRE* I, Terentius 2.

21 Working back from Ammianus XXIX.1.4 (winter 371–2), cf. Blockley 1987: 225–6 for this dating. Baynes 1955: 202 preferred to place these events in 372. *Epic Histories* V.2 notes a remarkable victory by Pap's general Musheł Mamikonean in this year, apparently without Roman assistance, but his account must be treated with caution: see Garsoïan 1989: 34–5 on such episodes which highlight the Mamikonean family.

22 The executions may rather have been an attempt by Pap to reduce Roman military influence in Armenia, cf. Gutmann 1991: 174–5. According to Azarpay 1981–2: 188–9, the rock relief of Shapur II at Bishapur, depicting captive Armenians, refers to Persian successes in this period and the allegiance of Pap to the king.

23 The Armenian Kur and Georgian Mtkvari, which flows into the Caspian Sea: cf. Garsoïan 1989: 476.

24 On the settlement, see Toumanoff 1963: 460–1 and Braund 1994: 260–1.

25 On these events see Gutmann 1991: 175–6 and Seager 1996: 278–9.

26 Trajan was *comes domesticorum* at this time, Vadomarius the *vicarius* of the *magister peditum praesentalis* Arintheus, cf. Woods, forthcoming ch.3b.

27 The Armenian Bagavan, cf. Seyfarth 1971: 336 n.3 (with Garsoïan 1989: 452). One of the two battles described in the *Epic Histories* (IV.4) is set at the foot of mount Niphates (Npat), where the town of Bagavan is situated. On the two battles described in the *Epic Histories* (V.4–5) see n.29 below. As Seager 1996: 280 points out, the Roman forces, although adopting a defensive posture, were apparently operating deep in eastern Armenia.

28 Ctesiphon on the Tigris was the traditional winter residence of the Sasanian king.

29 Cf. *Epic Histories* V.4–5 (two battles) with Mos. Khor. III.37 and *Vit. Ners.* 11 (p.33) and the comments of Garsoïan 1989: 308. See also Gutmann 1991: 176–7.

30 On the date of Pap's death, see Blockley 1987: 226 and Garsoïan 1989: 397; see also Gutmann 1991: 178–82. As Garsoïan 1967: 316–20 argues, Pap's fall from favour with

the Romans was probably due to the machinations of orthodox commanders, such as Terentius and Trajan, rather than any malice on Valens' part (but cf. Gutmann 1991: 182 n.117).

31 Garsoïan 1967: 315 suggests that these *gentiles* were the satraps of the Armenian territories under Roman control.

32 As Garsoïan 1967: 314 points out, these letters may have been genuinely amicable.

33 *Epic Histories* then relates the seizure and slaying of Pap at a banquet held by the Romans still in Armenia. Mos. Khor. III.39 has Pap order the Romans out, who then return and capture the king.

34 Reading *deleri* rather than *deseri*, with Blockley 1987: 226 n.18, Seyfarth and Chrysos 1976: 37–8. See also now Seager 1996: 281–2 for a discussion of this passage. On Shapur's rather unclear proposal, see Blockley and Seager, loc. cit. and Gutmann 1991: 183.

35 This embassy probably took place in late 375, cf. Gutmann 1991: 182. Zuckerman 1991: 535 n.35 interprets Shapur's alternatives as an attempt by the king to point out to Valens that he could not maintain his claim to be keeping Armenia independent while at the same time sending forces to Iberia (which could almost only be reached by traversing Armenia).

36 The resolutions referred to are probably those of 363, cf. Gutmann 1991: 183 and n.128, Seager 1996: 282, *contra* Blockley 1987: 227.

37 This message was received in early 376.

38 We adopt the translation proposed by Blockley 1987: 227 n.24.

39 As Gutmann 1991: 184 notes, Armenia would have in effect been under Roman supervision after the accession of Varazdat (on which see below).

40 The Latin is ambiguous as to whether it was the Armenians (as Blockley 1987: 227 n.25 argues and Seager 1996: 283 assumes) or the Persians (as Greatrex 2000a: 39 argues, cf. Chrysos 1976: 39 and Gutmann 1991: 187 n.144) who made the offer. Zuckerman 1991: 535–6 n.35 suggests that the regions were 'most probably a corridor which connected the empire to Iberia'. The two regions may well have been Belabitene and Asthianene, satrapies which came under Roman control at some point in the fourth century but are not mentioned in the treaty of 363. Cf. Toumanoff 1963: 171–2, Adontz 1970: 37, Garsoïan 1998a: 241 n.9.

41 The two embassies took place over late 376–early 377, cf. Gutmann 1991: 187.

42 Valens started to prepare for war in 377, cf. Gutmann 1991: 188.

43 Cf. Gutmann 1991: 188–9 on these events. The attack on Thrace referred to is the revolt of the Goths admitted to Thrace, on which see Heather 1991: ch.4.

44 On Varazdat, cf. Garsoïan 1989: 423–4 and Baynes 1955: 205. He reigned from c.375 to c.377. Chrysos 1976: 38–9 is sceptical of the worth of the *Epic Histories* here.

45 Garsoïan 1989: 326 places this activity c.377, cf. Grousset 1947: 153 on the fortification measures here described.

46 *Epic Histories* V.42 for the seven years of peace (378–85). Although Manuel apparently clashed with Surena, complete political independence from Persia was extremely unlikely, cf. Gutmann 1991: 190–1. Blockley 1992: 43 argues that the bestowing of two crowns by Shapur 'signalled a willingness to abandon the Sasanid aim of suppressing the Arsacid kingship and which also hinted at the possibility of division.'

47 Ammianus XXXI.7.1 for Victor's mission, cf. Blockley 1987: 229 and Gutmann 1991: 189. As Blockley notes, the references in Eunapius (frg.42.78–9) and Zosimus (IV.21) to the conclusion of a peace with Persia are suspect.

48 Cf. Gutmann 1991: 226–7, placing this development before 379/80. As he notes, the existence of two opposing Armenian kings could have led to war between the two powers, but neither was in a position to resume hostilities.

49 Pacatus, *Pan. Lat.* II (XII) 32.2 may well allude to the partition – so Nixon in Nixon and

Rodgers 1994: 496 n.115. Garitte 1952: 73 notes the divergences between the *Narratio* and Procopius and the main Armenian historical tradition. Mos. Khor. III.42–5 has a somewhat confused account of the partition and its aftermath, on which see Garsoïan 1989: 430; cf. also Łaz. 12–13/45–6 and Chaumont 1987: 428. Perhaps before the partition Shapur III had granted religious toleration to the Christians in Armenia, cf. Chaumont 1974: 71–6, Maraval 1995: 941 (citing *Chr. Seert* 43, *PO* 5.261). Some scholars date the foundation of the fortress of Theodosiopolis (Erzurum) to this period, cf. Chapter 4 n.1.

50   The allusion is to territorial losses of Armenia to the south and east, where lands were ceded to the Albanians and Persians. See Toumanoff 1963: 132.

51   The text is uncertain here and could alternatively refer to the 'Siwnik' provinces', on the location of which see Garsoïan 1989: 490–1.

52   The boundary ran from Karin (modern Erzurum, the later Theodosiopolis) down to just east of Amida in the south, cf. Chaumont 1987: 428 with Hewsen 1992: map 2 and Greatrex 1998a: map 3. The kingdom once ruled by the Arsacids was also shorn of other territories, cf. Garsoïan 1989: 334 and Toumanoff 1963: 131–2.

53   This account follows a description of the foundation of Theodosiopolis by Theodosius II, which leads the author into mistakenly associating the partition with the wrong Theodosius; cf. Greatrex 1993: 6 (*contra*, van Esbroeck 1983). The reference to King Shapur (III), however, confirms a date in the 380s. On Arsaces (Arshak IV), son of Pap, Garsoïan 1989: 353; he died c.390. Cf. also Garitte 1952: 70–3 on this passage.

54   On the 'History of the Armenians' used by Procopius see Garsoïan 1989: 10, 20, Greatrex 1994b: 74, Yuzbashian 1999: 195–6.

55   Proc. *Aed.* III.1.24 on the independence of the satraps (curtailed in 485, however), cf. Adontz 1970: 84–9, 91–3. Garsoïan 1998a traces the whittling away of Armenian autonomy in both regions through the fifth century. There were no Roman forces under the *comes Armeniae*, cf. Adontz 1970: 89–91, Greatrex 1998a: 22, 79–80, Zuckerman 1998: 110–11, but Garsoïan 1998a: 254–5, 261 argues that the *comes* only emerged in the late fifth century and that there were some local forces under his command.

56   Khosrov, however, was also replaced c.389, cf. Garsoïan 1989: 430.

57   Lordkipanidse and Brakmann 1994: 35–6 note continuing contacts between Iberia and the Romans in the fifth century, e.g. in the arrival of the Iberian king Pharesmanes in Constantinople during the reign of Arcadius. Despite Persian control, Christianity remained strong in Iberia.

CHAPTER 3

1   In late sources there are references to persecution of Christians early in Yazdgerd's reign: Marcus 1932: 61 (the Armenian life of Marutha) and ibid.: 53 (the late historian 'Amr). Cf. Sako 1986: 63–5.

2   In fact Shapur III's reign had ended in 388, when he had been succeeded by Bahram IV. Bahram was assassinated by his own soldiers in 399 – the event here referred to – to be followed on the throne by Yazdgerd I. Cf. Schippmann 1990: 40, and Nöldeke 1879: 418. Claudian is probably using 'Shapur' as a stock Persian name, as Cameron 1968: 410 suggests. 'Medes' and 'Parthians' are also merely poetic references to the Persians.

3   Literally 'of the stomach'.

4   For the date see Bardill and Greatrex 1996: 174.

5   Referring to Arcadius' decision to ask Yazdgerd to look after his son.

6   Procopius wrongly dates Arcadius' arrangement to his deathbed, cf. Bardill and Greatrex 1996: 172–3.

7   See (e.g.) Blockley 1998: 118–25 on the difficult situation in Italy at this time.

8 Cedrenus' account continues with a slightly condensed version of what is reported by Theophanes (below).

9 Theoph. is the first source to mention Antiochus, Yazdgerd's emissary, by name; see Bardill and Greatrex 1996: 177–80 for an attempt to explain how he disappears from the historical record for so long. He later enjoyed a long career at Theodosius' court, ibid. 180–97.

10 The word here used is *epitropos*; elsewhere in Theoph. 'guardian' translates the Latin *curator*. On the legal significance of the terms see Bardill and Greatrex 1996: 174 and n.15.

11 The passage follows an account of Stilicho's death, which occurred on 22 August 408. Synelli 1986: 63 needlessly tries to place this treaty in 422; Blockley 1992: 54 rightly accepts its occurrence in 408.

12 The measure probably had more to do with trade restrictions than spying. The statutes of the school of Nisibis (from AD 496) also bar students from crossing into Roman territory to trade, cf. Vööbus 1962: 75–7 with idem 1965: 114–15 and Lieu 1996: 134–5 (on the vigilance of the [Nestorian] Christians in Nisibis). See also Teixidor 1995: 505–8 on the school and the legislation of 408.

13 The date of the treaty is uncertain: cf. Lee 1993a: 64 and n.75 and Synelli 1986: 92–4 (arguing that it was in 400, and that the Roman initiator was Anthemius).

14 The *Synodicon Orientale*, as it is usually known, contains the records of nearly all the councils held by the Persian Church. Although the compilation dates from the eighth century, it is a source of great value, cf. Fiey 1977: 77, Gero 1981: 2–3 and Sako 1986: 49. The acts of the first council are in Chabot 1902: 17–36/253–75; quotation from 19/256. The term *catholicos* used in the *Synodicon Orientale* is likely to be anachronistic, cf. Brock 1994: 74.

15 Jerome provides a fuller account of an Arab raid in his *Vita Malchi*, ch.4, cf. Millar 1993: 484–5.

16 Around 412, cf. Hansen 1995: 352.

17 On this episode see Labourt 1904: 90.

18 *V. Sym. Styl.* 597 for Nu'man's claim (which need not be believed). See also *PLRE* II, Naamanes I and Antiochus 9 on the individuals involved. The historical worth of the Syriac life of Symeon, drawn up in 474, is stressed by Peeters 1943: 48, cf. Festugière 1959: 357.

19 The Lakhmids later played a significant role in the war of 421–2 (see below, p.39).

20 On Alexander's life up to this point, Gatier 1995: 435–50. It is very difficult to date Alexander's movements with any precision, but Gatier places his period in the East between 397/8 and 427/8 (p.439). Since he spent twenty years in Osrhoene (ibid. 449), his move into Euphratesia must have taken place around the time of the war of 421–2; Zuckerman 1998: 117 puts it c.425. Gatier (p.440) also suggests that the *Life* of Alexander was originally written in Syriac.

21 Gatier 1995: 452 notes how this description of a regular series of fortifications along the frontier from Palmyra to Sura is supported by archaeology. See also Peeters 1934: 373 and Zuckerman 1998: 118.

22 A good map of the frontier here may be found in Kennedy and Riley 1990: 40. On the implications of the references to the *limes* in the *Life* for the debate as to its nature see Zuckerman 1998: 118. Alexander also visited Palmyra, whose inhabitants refused to admit him; but he and his companions were saved by the arrival of *camelarii* with supplies (perhaps coming from Emesa to provision Palmyra), V. *Alex. Akoim.* 35 (685–6) with Gatier 1995: 454–5.

23 That the embassy took place late in Yazdgerd's reign may be inferred from the fact that Tabari immediately goes on to relate the death of Yazdgerd and the struggle for the succession which followed. Sako 1986: 62 incorrectly places it in Arcadius' reign.

24 The acts of the council are in Chabot 1902: 37–42/276–84; quotation from 37/277. On the problem of converts, see van Rompay 1995: 368–71 (with e.g. *Conf. Peroz, AMS* IV.255). It was probably internal Persian circumstances therefore, as van Rompay suggests, rather than a Christian militancy at Theodosius' court (as Holum 1977: 153–72, argues) which led to the outbreak of war.

25 Cf. van Rompay 1995: 364–75, successfully rebutting earlier views (e.g. in Labourt 1904: 104–8) that over-zealous Christians brought the persecution on themselves. The persecution had a considerable impact on Roman Christian writers, as can be seen from some of the extracts below, as well as the contemporary account of Theodoret of Cyrrhus, *Graec. curat.* IX.32–3. See also Rist 1996: 32–3.

26 Christensen 1944: 273–6 on the succession, though he places the death of Yazdgerd in 421. For the correct date see Nöldeke 1879: 419. It should be noted that it was with assistance from the Zoroastrian clergy that Bahram gained the throne, which helps to explain the severity of the persecutions at the start of his reign (cf. *Conf. Peroz, AMS* IV.253–4, tr. Braun 1915: 163 with Williams 1996: 44–5, noting other instances of this phenomenon).

27 The province of Euphratensis (= Euphratesia) was established in the reign of Constantius II, cf. Sturm in *RE* 12 (1925), 194 and Mango in *ODB* II.748. It lay to the west and south of the river Euphrates, between Osrhoene and Syria.

28 I.e. Armenia I and II; Armenia Interior, further to the east (around Theodosiopolis) is omitted, since it had not yet been fully integrated into the empire as a province. Cf. Zuckerman 1998: 112 and n.10.

29 This law is clearly defensive in nature; since Theodosius had to commit additional troops to the war quickly, it may have been a measure designed to compensate for inadequate defences. Holum 1977: 162 argues that the law was needed to allow all available forces to be thrown into the attack, but see Schrier 1992: 77 and Isaac 1998a: 443–4.

30 Nothing further is known of this Maximinus, cf. Croke 1995: 73. Instability among the Roman forces in the East would help to account for the fortification measure noted above. Some problems in maintaining discipline among officers in Euphratesia at least are attested by *C.Th.* VII.11.2 and XV.11.2, both issued in July 417; the first of these laws in particular shows that officers had been making illegal exactions from the provincials there for three years (which they were now obliged to pay back).

31 On Pseudo-Dionysius' account of the war, see Schrier 1992: 84–5 (adding little to Socrates).

32 For an extensive commentary on this episode, see Shahîd 1989: 40–9; cf. Sartre 1982a: 149–50, Letsios 1989: 527 and Isaac 1998a: 450–1.

33 An error for Theodosius II: cf. (e.g.) Holum 1977: 155.

34 There are textual problems with this sentence, on which see Braun 1964: 558 n.6.

35 Quodvultdeus was writing c.450. As Holum 1977: 156 notes, he appears to have misunderstood the sign on the coins. Holum 1977: 163–7 links the cross rather with the erection of a large cross in Jerusalem and the Christian militancy of Theodosius' court.

36 Socrates is alone, and generally disbelieved, in this assertion: cf. Labourt 1904: 109 n.1 and van Rompay 1995: 365.

37 The gold being dug may have been in Armenia, in a region disputed between the two sides; cf. Greatrex 1998a: 190 and n.53 for a similar dispute in 530.

38 The Syriac text here has *Arzōn*, i.e. Arzanene, as does Theophanes: cf. Hansen 1995: 363. Ardaburius (probably the *magister militum per Orientem*, cf. *PLRE* II, Fl. Ardabur 3) made his invasion in 421, cf. Greatrex 1993: 2.

39 Restored from the Armenian translation of Socrates, cf. Hansen 1995: 364.

40 Literally, 'tens of thousands'.

41 Areobindus was *comes foederatorum*, cf. *PLRE* II, Fl. Ariobindus 2; Vitianus' position is uncertain.

42 The year is apparently 450, following an entry concerning an earthquake in Constantinople also reported in *Chron. Pasch.* 590; but, as is noted by Whitby and Whitby 1989: 80 n.262, both sources are mistaken in assigning an earthquake to that year. The reference is rather to the war of 421–422. The name Blasses is one of the Greek renderings of the Persian Balash (the Persian king between 484 and 488), here given in error for Bahram, cf. *PLRE* II, Valas. For a parallel text of this entry from the *Exc. de Virt.* see Thurn 2000: 285–6.

43 In fact, Procopius was promoted to the post of *magister militum per Orientem* after the war, in 422, cf. *PLRE* II, Procopius 2. His rank at the time of the war must have been inferior.

44 As Holum 1977: 171 notes, Malalas' anecdotal account may owe something to the epic tradition concerning the war, alluded to by Socr. *HE* VII.21.7–8. Wiesehöfer 1996: 198–9, however, links it to Sasanian notions of 'chivalrous single combat'.

45 Alexander 1967: 88 is uncertain whether this refers to the war of 421–2 or that of 440. Since, however, the latter conflict was on such a minor scale (see below), the former is by far the more probable. With the reference to the forty years' peace may be compared Mal.'s reference to the proposal of 'Blasses' for a peace of fifty years.

46 Quotation from Bosworth's translation, 103.

47 A messenger who had brought news to Theodosius concerning the war in a remarkably short space of time.

48 Helio was *magister officiorum* (*PLRE* II, Helion 1), an office often associated with diplomacy in late antiquity, cf. Lee 1993a: 41–7.

49 In fact, as Hansen 1995: 367, notes, the correct date by Olympiads would be 300.2 not 300.4. Sidonius Apollinaris, *Carm.* 2.75–93 gives Procopius a large role in the negotiations; no doubt he exaggerates, since the poem is a panegyric to Procopius' son Anthemius. He also alludes to Procopius' promotion after the war. Cf. *PLRE* II, Procopius 2.

50 This could be Theodosiopolis in Osrhoene (Resaina), in which case the siege might have followed the retreat of the Romans from Nisibis; so Schrier 1992: 79–81. But it could be Armenian Theodosiopolis (modern Erzurum), attacked perhaps in 421, while Narses was in Mesopotamia; so Greatrex 1993: 6–8.

51 The term used is *helepolis*, on which see Ammianus XXIII.4.10–14 with Matthews, *Ammianus*, 293–4.

52 Cf. Isaac 1998a: 444 on Eunomius' role – typical of the growing role of bishops in the defence of the cities of the eastern frontier.

53 Cf. 2 Kings 18.17–19.37.

54 The manuscripts say 'the father', which would refer to Yazdgerd I, but in Greatrex 1993: 4 and 10 n.11 Greatrex argued for the proposed emendation to 'the son', so that the reference would be to Bahram V's son, Yazdgerd II (following Müller in *FHG* IV.139). We are now inclined to suppose Eustathius/Evagrius to be referring to the 421–422 war, in a rather confused fashion; it should be noted that by the time of Mich. Syr., Socrates' account of the war had been sufficiently distorted by the tradition to cause him to give reports of it in three quite separate years. See also Schrier 1992: 85–6.

55 The date is 6 September 421.

56 Marcian's unit was presumably among the reinforcements mentioned by Socr. *HE* VII.18.15 (above, p.39).

57 It is generally supposed that both sides undertook to cease persecuting adherents of the other's religion (note Priscus frg.41.1 [from 464/5] reporting the complaints of a Persian embassy to Leo concerning both the flight of refugees and the treatment of Zoroastrians within the Roman empire, on which see Chapter 4 below), but this is far from certain. As Holum notes (1977: 171 n.76) persecutions continued in both empires; and, according

to the *Conf. Peroz* (*AMS* IV.254, tr. Braun 1915: 163), Bahram exposed the bodies of dead Christians for five years after his accession.

58 Cf. Schrier 1992: 82 n.26 for a defence of the reliability of this work.

59 For another case of the respect shown by dismounting cf. Theoph. Sim. III.1.7–8 (when the Roman commander Priscus fails to do so when entering camp for the first time, and thereby angers his own troops).

60 This brief passage could refer to either the 421–422 war or that of 440: Anatolius played a part in both. Since Procopius explicitly places it in the reign of Bahram rather than Yazdgerd, we have inserted it here; the episode must have taken place towards the end of the war. Cf. Croke 1984a: 70 n.45 on Anatolius (arguing that he was *magister militum per Orientem* at this time, *contra* PLRE II.84–6 and Synelli 1986: 59–61); also Greatrex 1993: 8–9, tentatively assigning the passage to 421–422. The treaty term barring further fortifications may have been introduced on account of recent Roman work at Theodosiopolis in Armenia, undertaken by Anatolius, cf. Greatrex 1993: 5, 8. The ban is also referred to by Joh. Eph. *HE* VI.36, where mention is made of a specified distance from the frontier within which fortification work was prohibited.

61 Acacius visited the Persian court in 422: see Sako 1986: 78–80, Blockley 1992: 58. In April 428 the new patriarch of Constantinople, Nestorius, declared to Theodosius, 'Help me destroy the heretics, and I will help you destroy the Persians' (Socr. *HE* VII.29.5, cf. Barhadbeshabba, *HE* 25, *PO* 9.555, tr. Holum 1982: 150), which might imply continuing hostility between Rome and Persia. How much significance should be attached to the patriarch's words is uncertain, however: Socrates at least was critical of his pronouncement, *HE* VII.29.6–7, and his tenure of office was short.

62 Cf. complaints about the conduct of officers in Euphratesia in 417, noted above n.30. See Matthews 1989: 281–2, citing Ammianus XX.11.5, the critical remarks of the *comes sacrarum largitionum* Ursulus concerning the expenses incurred by the army.

63 I.e. they fall between the two, cf. Pharr 1952: 490 n.3. On the position of *limitanei* in general, see Isaac 1988: 139–46 (= 1998b: 366–78).

64 When they attend a trial in a civil tribunal, cf. Pharr 1952: 490 n.4.

65 Zuckerman 1998: 119 rightly notes how this passage implies the notion of a linear defensive frontier (against the views of Isaac).

66 On the date of the war, cf. Croke 1984a: 65 and Lee 1987: 88. Luther 1997: 106 and Zuckerman 1998: 110 and n.1 prefer 441, however; cf. Zuckerman 1994: 164-8 on the various attacks suffered by the Romans in this period. See also Luther 1997: 102–3 and n.21, arguing that the war was concluded with a peace treaty (more plausibly associated with the end of the previous war). That the passage of Isaac of Antioch cited below refers to this war is argued by Greatrex 1998b: 287–91.

67 Croke 1984a: 67–8 believes that this episode refers to the war of 421–2, but cf. Greatrex 1993: 2–5 for a detailed refutation.

68 The attack is dated to the second year of Yazdgerd II's reign, i.e. 439–40.

69 Note the Persian accusation in the 460s, according to Priscus frg.41 (below, Chapter 4), that the Romans were harbouring refugees from Persia. Evidently the bar on defecting Saracen allies (noted above) did nothing to stem the flight of others into Roman territory. Cf. Luther 1997: 103 n.21.

70 I.e. they vanished without a trace.

71 *Nov. Theod.* 24, section 5 for the annual report. See Clauss 1980: 54–5 and Jones 1964: 369 on this measure; also Isaac 1988: 145–6 (= 1998b: 376–8) on this Novel and the *limitanei*.

72 Cf. the contempt for the Arabs expressed by a Byzantine eunuch, who refused to give them their customary pay in 630/1 (Theoph. A.M. 6123, 335–6).

73 Presumably the *magister militum*.

74 Blockley 1981: 119, cf. 168–9 n.48, places the fragment in 448, while Shahîd 1989:

39–40 dates it to 447. See also Zuckerman 1994: 179–80. As Shahîd, *loc. cit.*, notes, the identity of the Arabs is uncertain.

75　Archaeology lends substance to these allegations against Ardaburius: a mosaic at Yakto (Daphne) depicts a large building, labelled the *privaton Ardabouriou*, apparently representing his own private bath complex. See Downey 1961: 472.

76　The date of Narses' departure is uncertain: Vööbus 1962: 19 and Asmussen 1983: 944 put it in 457, while Brock 1994: 75–6 dates it to 471. See also Gero 1981: 60–1.

77　Ardaburius' father advised the emperor to do as he saw fit.

78　The extent of Leo's work is unknown, cf. Whitby 1987: 93.

79　Cf. Theoph. A.M. 5966 (120.9–10).

80　A late Nestorian source, Mari (tr. Gismondi, 35–6), claims that the Romans gave financial assistance to Peroz for his campaigns against the Hephthalites (in the 460s or 470s). Josh. Styl. 9 (below, Chapter 4) stresses that Zeno's payments were voluntary. See Greatrex 1998a: 15–16 and Blockley 1992: 83 and 215 n.30 on this cooperation.

81　On the chronology of Barsauma's letters, see Gero 1981: 120–2, dating *ep*.3 to 485 and *epp*.2 and 4 to late 485/early 486. Luther 1997: 131–3 prefers 486. On Roman sympathisers in Nisibis, see Segal 1955: 575, 583 and Joh. Eph., *Lives*, PO 17.147–53, and ch.1 n.41. Barsauma had an interest in equating Monophysites with traitors in order to boost the cause of the Nestorian Church: see Guillaumont 1969–70: 42–3 and n.11. Barsauma's correspondent, the *catholicos* Acacius, went on an embassy to Constantinople in 486/7, perhaps partly to restore relations: see Sako 1986: 87–9.

82　This is the suggestion of Chabot to fill the evident lacuna in the text.

83　Chabot 1902: 536 n.2 is no doubt right to see this as a reference to Monophysites in Nisibis, cf. Fiey 1977: 120.

84　Peroz's reign was marked by a severe drought: see Greatrex 1998a: 46, Harper and Meyers 1981: 18 and n.18.

85　Shahîd 1989: 117 (cf. idem 1984: 421 n.17) suggests that the Tuʿaye will have been members of the Tayy tribe (to be distinguished from the Tayyaye, the generic Syriac term for Arabs).

86　Christensen 1944: 21 n.3 on the name Nakoragan, a frequent western rendering of the Persian title *nakhvadhar*.

87　The lands east of the Tigris north of Ctesiphon. Cf. Fiey 1968a: 11–16 with pl.1 (a map).

88　On the doctrinal issues here see Gero 1981: 51–2.

89　We use the term Nestorian because it is conventional. Brock 1985: 126 and 1996: 28–9 rightly points out that it is misleading.

90　The date of this episode is unclear. The termini are (at the outside) 470s and 502. The date of Narses' arrival in Nisibis is uncertain, cf. n.76 above.

91　The discussions of Shahîd 1989: 121–31, idem 1995: 1–12 and Sartre 1982a: 156–60 have been superseded by those of Robin 1996: 696–9, who argues that the Arethas mentioned by Theoph. was a member of the banu Thaʿlaba (a ruler of the Mudar tribe, he suggests) and should not be identified with the Kindite ruler (with whom Anastasius did, however, come to an agreement, as Nonnosus, *FHG* IV.179, reports), cf. Whittow 1999: 212. See also Key Fowden 1999: 64 and now Shahîd 2000: 135.

92　Theoph. places this in 497/8, a date accepted by Shahîd 1989: 121.

93　Unconvincingly identified by Shahîd 1989: 123–4 with Sergiopolis (Rusafa), a city in Euphratesia (not Syria); accepted, however, by Key Fowden 1999: 61. See Honigmann 1923: 24 no.114.

94　I.e. the Lakhmid king Nuʿman II (498–503).

95　Ogaros is the Arabic Hujr, a ruler in north-west Arabia; cf. Shahîd 1989: 127–8, Sartre 1982a: 156 and Olinder 1927: 51. The meaning of Thalabane is disputed, cf. Mango and Scott 1997: 217 n.4 and Shahîd 1995: 6–8. Robin 1996: 696–7 argues persuasively that it refers to the banu Tha'laba and that this Arethas (Harith) was ruler of the Mudar tribe of north-western Arabia. On Romanus, *PLRE* II.948.

96   The father of Arethas (Harith) the Jafnid, cf. Shahîd 1989: 125–6 and Robin 1996: 698. Sartre 1982a: 159 notes evidence for the construction of shelters for the population at Oboda (in Palestine), which have been dated to this period.

97   On this recovery of territory which had been Roman up to 473, see Shahîd 1989: 125–7 and Greatrex 1998a: 227.

98   Badicharimus is the Arabic name Ma'dikarib. Shahîd 1989: 128 notes that Ogarus (Hujr) had probably not died by this point; cf. also Olinder 1927: 74–6.

99   Shahîd 1995: 6–7 argues that Theoph.'s text should be emended here to 'with Arethas (known as the son of Thalabane) and Arethas, the father of Badicharimus and Ogarus'. See, however, Robin 1996: 696 and n.113, against this, and above n.91 on the identity of the Arethas here mentioned. Cf. also Sartre 1982a: 161–2, Blockley 1992: 87 and Shahîd 1995: 3–12, although Robin's treatment is to be preferred.

100   Cf. Labourt 1904: 157–8 on the vulnerability of the Monophysite community, which had enjoyed a revival of fortunes following the death of Barsauma (in the mid-490s). Cf. Barhadbeshabba, *HE* 31 (*PO* 9.613) for another instance of accusations, dated to late 502 (while Kavadh was besieging Amida, with p.63 below.

101   According to John, Simeon (of Beth Arsham) succeeded in bringing the persecutions to a halt by appealing to the Emperor Anastasius, who wrote to the Persian king to ask him to desist from his policy. John notes that this occurred while the two powers were at peace, but offers no further chronological indicators. It seems likely therefore that this episode took place in the 490s, or at any rate before war broke out in 502 (if the account is to be credited). See Brooks' note in *PO* 17.143. Charanis 1974: 58–9 places Anastasius' intervention in 499, apparently confusing Simeon's visit to Constantinople with Philoxenus' (which probably did not take place in 499 anyway: see Tisserant 1933: 1513). See also Greatrex 1998a: 77 and n.16.

CHAPTER 4

1   See Winkler 1994: 329–30 on the visit of Mesrop, the inventor of the Armenian alphabet, to Constantinople in 423/5; cf. also Grousset 1947: 181–2. Mos. Khor. III.59 offers a detailed account of the work carried out at Theodosiopolis. *PLRE* II, Anatolius 10 does not register his eastern command at this time, but see Greatrex 1993: 5. Garsoïan 1998a: 245 n.31 and van Esbroeck 1997: 364–5 place the foundation of Theodosiopolis in c.387, however.

2   Cf. Garitte 1952: 66–7, noting that no other source makes mention of Bartholomew or Kalē Archē; from the account of Procopius, perhaps derived from a similar source, it is clear that the Theodosius concerned is Theodosius II (*Aed.* III.1.8–13 and 5.1–2). Both Procopius and the *Narratio* similarly confuse the division of Armenia and the construction of Theodosiopolis, cf. p.255 n.53. On Bartholomew's association with Theodosiopolis (and other fortresses) see van Esbroeck 1997: 363–4.

3   This Novel has recently been translated and commented on by Zuckerman 1998: 108–12. See Dodgeon and Lieu 1991: 347–8 for a translation of *ND* 38.10–30, the Roman forces in Armenia. Adontz 1970: 79–82 notes that the forces of the *dux* lay in Armenia Minor, well to the west of Theodosiopolis and Armenia Interior, but cf. Garsoïan 1998a: 255–6 on the presence of some troops in Armenia Interior.

4   Presumably those that had once belonged to the Arsacid house, cf. Zuckerman 1998: 110–11. The transformation of Armenia into a Roman province was a gradual process and had not been finished by this date, cf. Garsoïan 1998a and Zuckerman 1998: 112.

5   Latin *contati*, which Zuckerman 1998: 110–12 and n.7 identifies with the Armenian *nizakawork'* (lancers).

6 On the threats to the eastern empire generally at this time, see (e.g.) Zuckerman 1994: 180–90. Thdrt. *ep*.77–8, to bishops in Persarmenia, alludes to Yazdgerd's persecutions, cf. Garsoïan 1999: 125 n.261. See also Nigosian 1978: 431–3.

7 Vasak, according to the Armenian tradition, was a traitor who initially feigned an alliance with Vardan. Cf. Ełishe 71–3/122–4, who gives the text of a letter sent by various Armenian princes to Theodosius, and claims that the Romans made an agreement with the Persians not to intervene. Łazar 73–4/117–18, on the other hand, reports that Theodosius agreed to send assistance, but died before any measures could be taken. As Thomson 1991: 105 n.5 notes, all the districts mentioned by Łazar lie in Roman territory (but they are in Armenia Interior and the satrapies rather than Armenia Minor); cf. Garsoïan 1998a: 249–50 on the ties between Roman and Persian Armenia. The great *sparapet* of Antioch refers to the *magister militum per Orientem*.

8 On the Huns (Armenian Honkʿ) see Garsoïan 1989: 380, 389–90.

9 Thomson 1991: 112 n.5 places the battle on 26 May, Chaumont 1987: 430 and Garsoïan 1998c: 1138 on 2 June.

10 The Armenian princes of Arzanene, Corduene and Zabdicene seem to disappear from the historical record in the mid-fifth century, perhaps as the Persians now tightened their grip on the country after the rebellion; cf. Hewsen 1992: 158.

11 Christensen 1944: 287–8 on Yazdgerd's campaigns. Ełishe 197–9/242–3 offers an excellent example of how control of the two passes (Dariel and Derbend) might be exploited: the Albanian king Vachʿe, when he revolted against the Persians c.459, allowed the Huns to pass through the Derbend pass on their way to attack the Persians, while Peroz countered this by inviting other Huns – Khaylandurkʿ – through the Dariel pass; cf. Bíró 1997: 53–6 for a full analysis. See also Braund 1994: 274.

12 Cf. Greatrex 1998a: 124–5 (where n.14 should refer to frgs.33.1–2 and not 36.1–2) and Zuckerman 1991: 536–8. Thdrt, *Graec. affect.* IX.14, notes however that the Lazi, Sanni (Tzani) and Abasgi were loyal to Rome at the time of the work's composition (427/31 according to Canivet 1958: 27–9). See Priscus, frg.41.1 (given below) for a Persian attempt to obtain help from the Romans – not long after the Albanian incident, noted above n.11; cf. Luther 1997: 113–14.

13 Cf. Zuckerman 1991: 535–6 and n.35 for Roman difficulties in reaching Iberia and Lazica without intruding on Persian territory. Bíró 1997: 57 connects this second Roman campaign with *HVG* 146/161, which describes a Greek invasion eastwards from Abkhazia.

14 Blockley 1981: 120 dates these two fragments to c.456, but Bíró 1997: 57–9 argues for a date in the early 460s. Gobazes was the king of the Lazi.

15 E.g. Mari (tr. Gismondi), p.35, where the captured Peroz is ransomed by Marcian in the 470s (although Marcian died in 457). A late Armenian source, Łewond, reports the discovery of an inscription at the Derbend pass which recorded the involvement of Marcian in the construction of fortifications there; this account is generally discounted, cf. Braund 1994: 271 n.14 (though cf. Josh. Styl. 10 below). See too Harmatta 1996: 82–3 on evidence for Sasanian defensive works in the north-west Caucasus (in the Kuban valley north of Karachayevsk) in the second half of the fifth century.

16 On Zoroastrian communities in the Roman empire, especially in Cappadocia, see Mitchell 1993b: 29–30, 73.

17 I.e. John the Lydian's Biraparakh, cf. p.20 above.

18 Dated by Blockley 1981: 121 to 464–5. See also Luther 1997: 113.

19 On the importance attached to Suania, see Zuckerman 1991: 542–3. On Persarmenia, see Łaz. 112–13/165, with Sanspeur 1975–6: 148. Vahan's request will have been made in 465/6.

20 Dated by Blockley 1981: 121 to 465/6, cf. *V. Dan. Styl.* 51, reporting that the stylite helped reconcile Gobazes and Leo; see also *PLRE* II, Gobazes.

21 The text here is corrupt, cf. Blockley 1983: 398 n.177 and Zuckerman 1991: 543 n.55.

22 Blockley prefers to insert the word *hypo* and thus considers that it was the Suani who had been taking forts; but the objections of Zuckerman 1991: 543 and n.56 and Braund 1992: 64–5 are convincing.

23 Bíró 1997: 60 associates this diversion with Priscus frg. 47 (below), the invasion of the Saraguri. She argues also that the Persian and Iberian attacks described here are those described in *HVG* 157/172 (which assign the primary role to the Iberian king Vakhtang).

24 Dated by Blockley 1981: 122 to 467.

25 Or so the Romans claimed (Men. Prot. frg.6.1.553–4). Colvin 2003 is sceptical of these claims.

26 Greatrex 1998a: 126 n.17, cf. *HVG* 145–6 with Toumanoff 1963: 362 and Braund 1994: 274.

27 The term Caspian Gates is problematic, cf. Greatrex 1998a: 126 n.19. Probably the invaders were deterred by the Sasanian fortifications at the Derbend pass, constructed by Yazdgerd II, on which see Frye 1977: 12 and Kettenhoffen 1996a: 15. See also Bosworth 1999: 113 n.290 on further fortification work here under Peroz.

28 Dated by Blockley 1981: 121 to 467, by Bíró 1997: 60 to 466.

29 Mari (tr. Gismondi), p.36, refers to a peace concluded between Leo and Peroz, dated by Labourt 1904: 129 to 464. Luther 1997: 102–3 argues that the agreement dates from 441, but places too much weight on vague references in Ełishe.

30 Peroz had to deal first with the Kidarite Huns, whom he overcame, and later with the Hephthalites. The former must be referred to here. See Greatrex 1998a: 46–7.

31 Strikingly confirmed by a passage later in the letter, the opening of which is quoted below, Malalas, 18.44, 'But, as pious Christians, spare lives and bodies and give us some of your gold' (tr. Jeffreys-Scott).

32 So Grousset 1947: 222 (also on the location of Du, to the north-east of Theodosiopolis).

33 Łazar, 145–6/204–5 for Zarmihr's attack and Vakhtang's flight, with Grousset 1947: 223–4. Łazar, 148/207–8 on Shapur's inroad, with Grousset 1947: 224–5. *Contra* Grousset, *loc. cit.*, these campaigns took place in 484: see Sanspeur 1975–6: 161.

34 Łazar 153/212 for Łerpagos, with Grousset 1947: 226, who renders the name as Hipparchus. For the fluidity of the border see Greatrex 1998a: 22–3 and Proc. *Aed.* III.3.9–13. Łazar 153–4/213 on Shapur's concerns; Proc. *Aed.* III.1.24–6 for the satraps' adherence to Illus and Leontius, for which they were punished by Zeno, cf. Blockley 1992: 85.

35 Many other sources report the battle. See Greatrex 1994b: 60–4, Luther 1997: 116–24 and Sanspeur 1975–6: 142.

36 Peroz died in battle, falling into a trench dug by the Hephthalites; his body could not be found afterwards. See Josh. Styl. 11.

37 The rebels Illus and Leontius had, according to Josh. Styl. 15, sent 'a large sum of money' to Peroz in order to receive Persian backing for their rebellion (in 484).

38 On this Roman fabrication – that the Persians were due to hand back Nisibis 120 years after its cession to Shapur II in 363 – see p.5 and n.22 above.

39 Anastasius was crowned emperor on 11 April 491: *PLRE* II.79.

40 The bibliography on Mazdak and his followers is large. The works noted in the text provide recent summaries. See also Bosworth 1999: 132 n.342 and Yarshater 1983.

41 Blockley 1992: 89 dates Kavadh's request to 491/2, but Josh. is clearly referring to a time when Anastasius was waging war against the Isaurians, somewhat later in the 490s. Kavadh was expelled in 496, and so his request probably fell c.495. On the expulsion of Kavadh and the reign of Zamasp, see Christensen 1944: 347–9 and Greatrex 1998a: 50–1.

CHAPTER 5

1 Cf. Joh. Diakrin. 552. Theoph. places the episode just before Kavadh's invasion, while Joh. Diakrin.'s entry comes somewhat earlier (before Kavadh's expulsion). Hence (cf. next note) some doubt the existence of any demand just before war broke out.

2 The discrepancy between these two sources over whether a loan was requested or offered cannot be resolved. Josh. Styl. 23 has Anastasius offer a loan to Kavadh before he was expelled, which leads Blockley 1992: 89 and 218 to suggest that Theoph./Joh. Diakrin. and Proc. have erred in placing a further demand from Kavadh in 502. But there is no need to suppose that the king did not make one final bid before going to war.

3 Cf. Greatrex 1998a: 81 and n.31. Marcus 1932: 69–70, a translation of an Armenian life of Marutha, relates how the citizens of the city secured Kavadh's goodwill by presenting him with a gold cup they had received from Yazdgerd I. See Key Fowden 1999: 57–8.

4 For a list and assessment of the available sources, see Greatrex 1998a: 84 and n.16. *Chr. 1234*, it should be noted, is largely derived from Zach. Proc. too shows similarities to Zach., cf. Greatrex 1998a: 66, 73–4.

5 Persian dislike of winter weather was well known to the Romans, cf. Greatrex 1998a: 83.

6 Text uncertain; a variant reading has 'pomp'.

7 See Segal 1955: 110–14 on these officials and their role in city life.

8 Brooks suggests that Beth Urtaye may be equated with Byzantine Anzitene, the region north of Amida and west of Arzanene. Cf. *PO* 17.135 n.2 and Witakowski 1996: 5 n.38. Rumours of treachery arose from this Persian connection: see (e.g.) Josh. Styl. 53, Marc. *com.* 502.2, with Greatrex 1998a: 91 and n.5.

9 Cf. Proc. I.7.23. The night of Friday 9 January 503, cf. Greatrex 1998a: 91.

10 The bracketed section is restored to Zach.'s text from Mich. Syr. by Brooks.

11 Caucasian Albania.

12 On this church, constructed not long before this siege, see Greatrex 1998a: 83.

13 The fall of the city soon acquired this moralising element, cf. Luther 1997: 185–6 and Greatrex 1998a: 84.

14 On the deportation of these people to a new city founded by Kavadh (Veh-az-Amid-Kavadh) see Luther 1997: 183–4 and Greatrex 1998a: 93.

15 On the capture of Amida and its aftermath see Greatrex 1998a: 92–3.

16 Cf. Greatrex 1998a: 93-4 on the timing of Anastasius' reaction. Jacob of Serug, *ep.*20 (129–35), wrote a letter (as noted by Josh. Styl., *loc. cit.*) to encourage the citizens of Edessa not to flee their city and to have faith in the pledge of invulnerability offered to their city by Christ (on which see Greatrex 1998a: 106). A translation of Jacob's letter may be found in Davis 1999.

17 Of Anastasius' failure to give Kavadh money. The passage follows directly from that translated at the start of this chapter.

18 See Greatrex 1998a: 94 and n.64 on Theoph. here: it is doubtful whether the whole Persian army remained in Roman territory for the winter. Theoph's Alypius is generally identified with Josh. Styl's Olympius, cf. n.26 below.

19 On the implications of this figure for Roman troop numbers, see Greatrex 1998a: 96 n.69, Trombley and Watt 2000: 65–6.

20 The precise meaning here is unclear: it is hard to see how the Persians could have shut a gate that had been burnt down.

21 We have omitted the first part of the year's entry here which provides the most detailed list of Roman commanders who fought in the war; cf. Greatrex 1998a: 73, 94.

22 An apparent exaggeration, compared with the other sources. Cf. Mango and Scott 1997: 227 n.4 on the Greek here.

23 The Greek actually says, 'He slew...', and so the reader would suppose that Areobindus was meant.

24 With these Tha'labites the Romans had concluded a peace in 502, cf. p.52 above. Their

leader was Harith (Arethas), a chief of the Mudar tribe of north-west Arabia; *contra* Shahîd 1995: 12–13, they were not Jafnids.

25   This follows immediately from the earlier passage from A.M. 5997 translated above, p.69.

26   See the excerpt from Zach. below.

27   Josh. Styl. 61 confirms the handing-over of Basil. On Alypius see *PLRE* II, Olympius 14.

28   Not attested in other sources, but inherently plausible. See Greatrex 1998a: 97 and n.72.

29   Hypatius clearly did not serve with Areobindus in this campaign, cf. Greatrex 1998a: 97 and n.72.

30   This is the battle near Tell Beshme, referred to above, p.69. See Greatrex 1998a: 100–1.

31   Proc. I.9.5–19 offers a similar and detailed account of this episode. Cf. Greatrex 1998a: 98–9.

32   Presumably the mother of Mundhir, cf. Shahîd 1995: 5. Proc. I.17.1 refers to him in the same way.

33   I.e. the *spahbadh*.

34   The sources vary on the sum handed over. See Greatrex 1998a: 115 n.120. Zach. Myt. (below) gives 1100 lbs of gold, Proc. I.9.4 has 1000.

35   Unlikely. There was no further fighting before the truce was concluded, and Kavadh was no longer near Amida.

36   I.e. 'the pure ones'.

37   The passage follows directly from that in Chapter 2 p.20–1.

38   Despite Luther 1997: 214 these payments need not have been fixed. See further p.77 below.

39   Dara lay 10.4 km from the Persian frontier and 26 km from Nisibis. Amudis (variously spelt: Zach. has Amuda, Proc. refers to it as Ammodius) lay due south of Dara, on the main route from Nisibis to Constantia and Edessa. See Dillemann 1962: 159, 228 and the map on 156.

40   The large role assigned to the church in the building work is not unusual. See di Segni 1995: 322, noting Cyr. Scyth. *V. Sab.* 72–3, where the bishop Barachus of Bacatha is entrusted with the funds to build a fort. As Croke 1984b: 84 points out, however, Calliopius, mentioned below in Marc. *com.*'s account, may have overseen the day-to-day running of operations on site.

41   The *keration* was worth 1/24 of a *solidus*. This would be the normal month's wage for unskilled work, and hence represents a very large payment. See Morrisson 1989: 258.

42   Cf. Whitby 1986b: 749–50 on these buildings.

43   Subsequently the bishop was raised to metropolitan status, cf. Whitby 1986b: 751.

44   The place name is unclear. This Abraham bar Kaili later became bishop of Amida himself and a fierce persecutor of the Monophysites, cf. Zach. *HE* X.2 and Ps.-Dion. II, 32–3.

45   Cf. Croke 1984: 86–8 on this Calliopius, whom he identifies (rightly) with the Calliopius in Josh. Styl.

46   Cf. the description of the city in Whitby 1986b: 739. The hill in question must be the eastern one. See also Croke 1984b: 84 and Proc. *Aed.* II.2.1–7, *Wars* VIII.7.7 on the Cordissus/Cordes and the measures taken to protect its entrance and exit in the city.

47   In fact, the city was renamed Anastasiopolis, cf. Croke 1984b: 84–5. We have translated Marc.'s *moenia publica* as public buildings, not 'communal walls' (as Croke does): cf. Ward-Perkins 1984: 46 n.39 for this translation. We owe this reference to Sam Barnish.

48   On this tower see Croke 1984b: 85–6. It is mentioned again by Joh. Eph. during Khusro's siege of Dara in 573.

49   Cf. Whitby 1986b: 769. The Great Church at Dara was probably only completed after Anastasius' death. Van Esbroeck 1997: 369 argues that Proc. attributes the building of the church of Bartholomew (and the other large church at Dara) to Justinian because he

rededicated them; he also, 363, notes how Bartholomew is associated with the foundation of Theodosiopolis (Armenia) and Martyropolis.

50 Mango prefers to place the fortification before the raid, but Trombley argues that the mention in the *Acta S. Theodori* of the defence of the city against Scythians and Huns implies a successful defence and that therefore the walls were already in place by 515.

51 One need not infer, however, a withdrawal of the Ghassanids from Roman service, as does Shahîd 1995: 32–6 and elsewhere. See the criticisms of Whittow 1999: 213. Luther 1997: 218 puts the capture of the two commanders in 523.

52 The primary literature on these events is extensive: see Shahîd 1964: 115 n.1 and Shahîd 1971. Note also Ps. Dion. II, 56–69/52–64, for the text of the 'shorter' letter of Simeon, which attests Abraham's support for the Persian Monophysites. Cedrenus I.638 appears to refer to a peace treaty agreed in 521 which might be a garbled reference to Abraham's negotiations, cf. Greatrex 1998a: 131. Some prefer a date of 519 for the conference, e.g. Shahîd 1971: 235–42 (cf. idem 1995: 40), Z. Rubin 1989: 393 and Greatrex 1998a: 229, but the consensus now certainly favours 524, cf. De Blois 1990 and Whittow 1999: 213.

53 It is uncertain what is being referred to here. Cedrenus I.638 refers to peace terms being agreed in 521/2, but they are not mentioned in any other source.

54 A gross distortion, since Lazica had been under Roman control up until late in the fifth century, cf. Braund 1994: 269–73, Greaterex 1998a: 133 and n.37.

55 On the legal aspect of the adoption see Pieler 1972: 422–33. According to Theoph., Justin referred the matter to the Senate, which followed the advice of Proculus. Of course Khusro II seized on just such a pretext for invading the Roman empire after the death of his self-proclaimed father Maurice, cf. Chapter 13 below.

56 On these offices (*arteshtaran salar* and, probably, *spahbadh*) and individuals see Greatrex 1998a: 136 n.46.

CHAPTER 6

1 Cf. Greatrex 1998a: 130 and n.28.

2 The reference is to Roman officials appointed by Zeno to replace the satraps in all the satrapies save Belabitene; all the other satraps were removed for having supported the rebels Illus and Leontius (*Aed.* III.1.24–7).

3 Proc. goes on to identify the bases of the two *duces* as Martyropolis and Citharizon.

4 See Garsoïan 1998a: 243–4 on the precise number of satrapies (five or six), which varies between sources. As she points out, there was considerable imprecision.

5 In other words, the praesental and eastern armies had been augmented by Justinian (or Justin) previously. Therefore the removal of some units from them will not reduce their numbers (compared to what they had been before Justinian's reign).

6 This is incorrect: 'only the office of Count of Armenia [*comes Armeniae*] and the autonomy of the satrapies were abolished' (Adontz 1970: 110). The civilian governors of Armenias I and II and the *duces* already in existence remained in place.

7 Bulgar prisoners were also transferred to Armenia in 529, cf. Theoph. A.M. 6032 (219) and Mal. 18.46 (451) with Greatrex 1998a: 154 n.42.

8 Howard-Johnston prefers to date construction work earlier, in peace time. But in fact there was no significant fighting before 530, and it seems more plausible to suppose that in the late 520s, as outright war seemed increasingly likely, such work was conducted. Unfortunately Proc.'s *Aed.* provides no chronological indicators to help.

9 Confirmed by Mal. 17.20 (423), cf. Greatrex 1998a: 148. The raids will have taken place in 525–6.

10 I.e. the *spahbadh* probably.

11 The negotiations probably took place between April and June 527, cf. Greatrex 1998a: 138, 148.

12 Cf. the unsuccessful Roman attack in 572, also launched in late summer.

13 Timostratus' precise post at this point, just before his death, is unclear. See Shahîd 1995: 174–5 and Greatrex 1998a: 149 n.30.

14 Emending Zach.'s text from 'Justinian' to 'Justin', as Brooks suggested, cf. Greatrex 1998a: 150 and n.33.

15 I.e. indiction year 5. The new indiction year began on 1 September, and so this attack, placed after the attempt to build a fort at Thannuris, must have taken place in August 527. Note that Belisarius is not recorded as having participated in the attempt. See Greatrex 1998a: 150.

16 On the north side of the Tur Abdin, next to the Tigris, and therefore threatening Arzanene (the region under Gadar), cf. Greatrex 1998a: 150 and n.35 on the text of Zach. here.

17 The identity of this Harith is uncertain. He is conventionally identified with Harith the Kindite, who at some point seized Mundhir's kingdom and ruled it for about four years. See Potts 1990: II, 248–9 (dating this interregnum to 525–8), but cf. Robin 1996: 697–8.

18 Shahîd dates the raid to 527, but we prefer 529. See Greatrex 1998a: 153 n.39 (against, e.g., Shahîd 1971: 242).

19 A possible reference to his earlier raid in 525/6, noted above n.9. Shahîd 1995: 44 argues for an emendation of the Syriac text here, suggesting we read 'for the second time' instead of 'twice' (in Syriac literally 'a time and twice').

20 See Shahîd 1995: 722–6, 732–3 on this episode. He suggests that Zach. may here be referring to a convent at Emisa rather than the city of Emesa (the reading is uncertain).

21 This is a fuller account than that of Mal. 18.32 (445.1–7).

22 On the places mentioned here see B. Rubin 1960: 492 n.820, Greatrex 1998a: 152 n.39. Litargon is Litarba, Chalcedon is Chalcis; the other places are also near Antioch. Joh. Nik. 90.79–80 claims that Chalcis too was burnt by Mundhir.

23 Mal. has 'outer' *limes*, which is probably correct. See Mayerson 1988: 182–3.

24 The text is uncertain here, but some sort of trench is probably indicated.

25 The titulature of Timostratus is uncertain. See Greatrex 1998a: 149 n.30.

26 Near Dara and Solachon, cf. *PLRE* III, 1168.

27 Shahîd 1995: 63–7 identifies this Atafar with Jabala, the father of Harith the Jafnid. Whittow 1999: 214–15 is sceptical.

28 The meaning of the verb is uncertain: cf. Hamilton and Brooks, 223 n.7.

29 Shahîd 1995: 174–5 proposes a drastic emendation to the Syriac text here to read 'shaken from his horse'.

30 Cf. Greatrex 1998a: 149, cf. 160, 164, *contra* Howard-Johnston 1989: 220.

31 Phylarchs of the Roman provinces concerned played an important role in crushing the uprising. See Sartre 1982a: 168–70, Shahîd 1995: 82–92; also Rabello 1987: 403–22 for a detailed consideration of Mal.'s account. The last known dated military building inscription in Arabia (*PUAES* III A 18), from Qasr al-Hallabat, refers to work by the *dux* of Arabia Anastasius in 529, which may be connected to the uprising. See Sartre 1982a: 80, Gregory 1997: I, 226.

32 Or 'of the sun of the East' and 'the moon of the West', cf. Frendo 1992: 66 n.34.

33 Cf. Greatrex 1998a: 180 for this frequently used tactic.

34 I.e. it had been a long time since the last Roman victory over the Persians. Although the Romans had enjoyed some successes in the Anastasian war (see Chapter 5 above), it is true that there had been no major victory in the field since the war of 421–2. See also Greatrex 1998a: 184–5, noting how the victory was commemorated in Constantinople.

35 Despite the Roman victory, the Persian army remained poised on the frontier, cf. Greatrex 1998a: 185.

36 Rabello 1987: 421–2 is sceptical as to whether the Samaritans had contacted the king: the accusation may have been fabricated to justify harsh measures against them.

37 Jord. *Rom.* 363 also seeks to exculpate Belisarius.

38 See Greatrex 1998a: 38–9 on this question.

39 An interesting reference to Christians and Jews in the army of the notoriously pagan Mundhir. Cf. Shahîd 1995:722–6 on Christians among his forces.

40 Cf. Proc. *Anecd.* 2.32–6 where a letter from Theodora to a Persian noble, Zabergan, is referred to by Khusro; also *Anecd.* 30.24 on the empress' involvement in foreign policy generally, with Greatrex 1998a: 208 n.41. Scott 1992: 164 suggests that Mal. may here mean that Theodora was calling the Persian queen her sister.

41 A reference to the campaign against Martyropolis at the end of 531, on which see below.

42 The Syriac text is unclear here as to whether the distance is 4 or 40 stades. Beth Helte is not otherwise known. See Greatrex 1994b: 211 n.108.

43 The precise meaning is unclear here, cf. Hamilton and Brooks 1899: 228 n.4. Hormizd, the *bdeashkh* of Arzanene, was the uncle of Yazdgerd (Zach. *HE* IX.5, above).

44 I.e. September 531, cf. Greatrex 1998a: 210.

45 The identity of this Constantine is uncertain, cf. Greatrex 1998a: 195 n.6.

46 Bar Gabala (Jabala), the son of Jabala, is Harith (the Jafnid).

47 Or October, the Syriac being ambiguous here: cf. Hamilton and Brooks 1899: 228 n.11.

48 Cf. Greatrex 1998a: 213–18. Zach. emphasises Rufinus' friendship with Kavadh and his consequent influence over Khusro.

49 Omitting the needless phrase 'of the two states' with Festugière 1979: 236–7, Thurn 2000: 394. Cf. Jeffreys and Scott 1986: 282 and Greatrex 1998a: 217.

50 Cf. Greatrex 1998a: 15 on this 'ancient custom', which Malalas and Josh. Styl. refer to elsewhere. See p.59 above.

51 On Mal.'s sources here, most probably the records of the *comes Orientis*, and perhaps also contact with the ambassadors, see Scott 1992: 166. On the events in the war of 502–6 here alluded to, see Chapter 5 above.

52 Literally 'into a third decade'.

53 Or, metaphorically, 'outrages'.

54 Agathias V.2.4 notes Justinian's pride here in having subjugated the Tzani.

55 John of Tella was seized on 1 February, 537, cf. *PLRE* III, Cometas 2.

56 Proc. *Wars* II.1.1–11. Cf. Lee 1993a: 64 and Lieu 1996: 134–5 on the permeability of the frontier, with Lieu 1986: 491–3 for earlier examples of cross-border travel. In wartime, however, security could be tightened considerably, cf. ibid. 493–4; and note that one of the two Gothic envoys was intercepted in 541 near Constantia by John Troglita, Proc. *Wars* II.14.11–12.

57 John was then taken to Antioch, where he was martyred in February 538, cf. Frend 1971: 284. See also Greaterex 1998a: 218.

58 Hoffmann 1880: 80 suggests 'of the peace' (for the Christians) rather than 'of Kavadh's reign', but the latter is clearly more appropriate. The year is 531.

59 This should be 533/4, if the date is correct. The author of the *martyrium*, however, appears to synchronise the Seleucid year 850 (538/9), referred to at the opening of the work, with the tenth year of Khusro's reign (540/1), since he uses both datings for the renewal of persecutions. Hence this embassy should be dated to the mid-530s (Proc. *Anecd.* 2.33 places it 'not much before' 541).

60 This mission is alluded to by Proc. *Anecd.* 2.33, cf. *PLRE* III, Zaberganes 1 (omitting this source entirely, however).

61 Bury 1923:II, 90, but see now Whitby 1986a: 727–8 and Greatrex 1998a: 196 n.11.

62 The chronology of these measures is unclear. Casey 1996 argues, on numismatic and

archaeological evidence, that Proc.'s assertion is borne out only in southern Palestine in the period after 545, when Justinian preferred to use Arab allies to the *limitanei* here. See, however, Greatrex 1998a: 219 n.18, arguing that Proc. may be referring to the 530s here: note (e.g.) the defection of much of the garrison of Beroea in 540, below p.104.

63 Identified by Braund in Talbert 2000: 1261 with Mocheresis. Lysiris remains unidentified.

64 These last two adjectives point up the difficulty of categorising the status of these peoples – whether part of the empire or aligned with it. See Greatrex 2000b: 281 n.27 and Colvin 2003.

65 Cf. Greatrex 1998a: 219 and Shahîd 1995: 194–6. Shahîd suggests that the two phylarchs were Kindites.

66 *PLRE* III, Cometas 2.

CHAPTER 7

1 Both these developments are dated by Stein 1949: 362–4 to 539.

2 On Justinian's campaigns in the West up to 540, see (e.g.) Stein 1949: 311–68, Evans 1996a: 126–54. On the *limitanei* see p.99 above.

3 Cf. Greatrex 1998a: 48–9 and n.26. It is uncertain whether Khusro's extensive reforms of the Sasanian state (including important measures to improve the army) were sufficiently advanced by 540 to have had any bearing on the timing of the invasion, cf. Stein 1949: 485. Recent research (see Rubin 1995: 283) suggests that even after the reforms, the Persian army was by no means so reinvigorated as has traditionally been supposed.

4 I.e. Harith, cf. Nöldeke 1879: 238 n.3.

5 As Lee 1986: 457 notes, Justinian was clearly aware that an attack was imminent by late 539.

6 Stein 1949: 486 (with n.2) gives the month as March, basing himself on the *Chr. Ede.* As can be seen from the translation below, the chronicle actually puts the breaking of the peace in May (Iyar), not March, despite Guidi's translation. This fits better with the capture of Antioch in June (see Mal. below).

7 See Downey 1953: 340–2 with Downey 1961: 535–6. Although Downey 1939: 370 is sceptical of Proc.'s assertions concerning the weakness spotted in the city's defences, Whitby 1989: 541–2 has shown that Antioch's defences may well have been in the poor condition described by Proc. in 540. On the prominent role of bishops in negotiations see Liebeschuetz 1997: 113–23.

8 Justinian's envoys no doubt also summoned the forces from Phoenice Libanensis which soon arrived to defend the city (see below), cf. Downey 1953: 345 (failing to note that the forces summoned were cavalry, Proc. *Wars* II.8.18–19). On Ephraem's role, see below and Downey 1938: 369–70.

9 See Downey 1953: 346 on this, suggesting that Germanus was profiteering during the crisis. Downey 1961: 539–41 is more hesitant about Germanus' behaviour, suggesting that he may have been buying silver 'for official purposes'. As he notes, the Persians appear to have preferred silver to gold; by far the majority of Sasanian coins were silver, cf. e.g. Göbl 1983: 328–9.

10 See Downey 1938: 368–70 (and Downey 1961: 544, though cf. Stein 1949: 488 n.3) on this, noting how the accounts of Proc. and Evagrius agree over the preservation of the church, although the former gives no credit to the patriarch. Evagrius was doubtless here relying on local information, cf. Tricca 1915: 286.

11 The date is known from Mal. 18.87 [479.23–480.1], cf. Downey 1953: 340.

12 See van den Ven 1970: 61 n.2 for the meaning of *asynetos* (senseless), a word with biblical echoes.

13 Greek *notos*, which can also mean south. See van den Ven 1970: 63 n.5.

14 The chapters following this narrate several episodes concerning the period after the capture of Antioch, and clearly show the extent to which the region was overrun by the Persians, cf. van den Ven 1970: 65 ch.59 n.1 and Trombley 1997: 157–8.

15 John's chronology is seriously amiss here (cf. Stein 1949: 734), since he clearly implies that Antioch was captured by Khusro in the first Persian war of Justinian, i.e. between 527 and 532. Thus, three chapters later, he appears to refer to the invasion of 540, but merely notes that Khusro invaded Syria while the Roman forces were occupied in the West (III.57). The recovery referred to by John is from the effects of the earthquakes of 526 and 528.

16 Manpower was a valuable resource for the Sasanians to seize, cf. below n.20. See Lieu 1986: 478–9 on deportations in the third century, Kettenhoffen 1996b: esp. 301.

17 Firdausi, tr. Mohl 1868: 221, also refers to Persian demands for a regularised tribute.

18 On this tendency for enemies of the Romans to demand the regularisation of payment see Blockley 1992:149–50 with 248–9 n.80.

19 The Persian mine was betrayed to the defenders by one of the besiegers; according to some, however, it was a supernatural being (Proc. *Wars* II.13.22). It is possible that the betrayer was a Roman soldier who had defected to Khusro earlier in his campaign (e.g. at Beroea).

20 For its location, just south of Ctesiphon, see Fiey 1967: 26–8 with the map at p.37; also Simpson 2000: 60–1. Cf. Christensen 1944: 386–7 and Firdausi, tr. Mohl 1868: 215–17. Joh. Eph. *HE* VI.19 gives a figure of 30,000 living in this Antioch (but after their numbers had been swollen by further deportations in the 570s). See n.16 above on Sasanian deportations; in this instance the Persians had been prepared to ransom the captives they had taken, however.

21 Shahîd 1995: 235–6 on Khusro's mosaic (commemorated in a ninth-century *ekphrasis*), Proc. *Aed.* I.10.16 on Belisarius' victories. Neither set of depictions survives.

22 Similar (derivative) entries are to be found in *Chr.846*, 229.14–21 and elsewhere. Guidi's Latin translation wrongly refers to two lbs of gold, cf. Stein 1949: 492 n.1.

23 No other source reports an attack on Callinicum in 540, and Stein 1949: 487 n.1 is probably right to reject the information as erroneous. But the city, lying on the northern bank of the Euphrates, could have been attacked by Khusro (note Proc. II.21.22–3 on the Persian capacity for bridge-building). The Neocaesarea referred to lies south-east of Barbalissus.

24 Cf. *Chr.724*, AG 871 (in error for 851, cf. Stein 1949: 490 n.1), 145.6–11.

25 I.e. 'the Roman', cf. Fiey 1967: 26. See n.20 above on the city itself.

26 As Nöldeke 1879: 166 nn.1–2 notes, Tabari here confuses Khusro's attack with that of Khusro II in the early seventh century. Cf. Bosworth 1999: 159 n.399, noting that the reference to Heraclea (in Pontus) is also incorrect.

27 Tabari describes the invasion for a second time at I, 959/253–5 (Nöldeke 239), where he mentions the capture of Dara, Edessa, Hierapolis, Chalcis, Beroea, Antioch, Apamea, Emesa and 'many neighbouring places'. He puts Khusro's army at 90,000 men, an evident exaggeration, cf. Downey 1953: 344 and Howard-Johnston 1995a: 166–7.

28 On this hiatus to raiding, see Nonnosus, *FHG* IV.179–80 with Lee 1993a: 105 and Hitti 1970: 93–4.

29 Cf. Goodyear 1968: 70 for this translation of *regni graviora superbi*, referring to the following lines.

30 The text is very uncertain here. We have translated the suggested reading of Diggle and Goodyear, *mediae ne in Nitzibis arcem/Romanus rupisset eques*.

31 The captured Persian soldiers were sent on to Italy by Justinian (see *PLRE* III, Bleschames), according to the same principle by which Gothic soldiers (from Italy) accompanied Belisarius on this campaign, Proc. II.14.11.

32 Shahîd 1995: 220–30 is highly sceptical of Proc.'s account of Harith's actions.

33 Cf. *Anecd.* 3.31 with Stein 1949: 495–6. Shahîd 1995: 228–9 is sensibly sceptical of this assertion by Proc., cf. ibid.: 437 n.144.

34 I.e. 541 (although Agapius wrongly also places the arrival of the plague in this year). Shahîd 1995: 230, however, takes Agapius as referring to events in 542 (otherwise unattested).

35 The reference is to Belisarius, consul in 535. On the titles *Vandalicus* and *Gothicus* here applied to him, see *Getica* 315.

36 The bracketed items are supplied from Mich. Syr. IX.24 (287a/205), cf. IX.29 (309b/ 244). Although this entry follows immediately from the one quoted below (p.111), it must refer to the 541 campaign of Belisarius; it implies that another Roman offensive took place north of where Belisarius was operating, in Arzanene. This may have been undertaken by Valerian, the *magister militum per Armeniam*, after his victory over the Huns (*Anecd.* 2.30, see Chapter 8 below).

37 Stein 1949: 497 and Kislinger and Stathakopoulos 1999: 84 for the connection between Khusro's withdrawal and the arrival of the plague. The bibliography on the plague is extensive. See (e.g.) Allen 1979: 5–20, Durliat 1989: 107–19, Evans 1996a: 160–5 and the bibliography at http://www.unipissing.ca/department/history/orb/justplag.htm.

38 From the martyrdom of Grigor (ed. Bedjan 1895: 383, tr. Hoffmann 1880: 83–5) we know that Grigor was martyred on Good Friday (18 April) 542, cf. Peeters 1951a: 136 and Martin-Hisard 1998a: 495. Grigor's martyrdom was witnessed by Yazdbozid, who suffered the same fate later in Khusro's reign; cf. Peeters 1925: 192. Martin-Hisard 1998a: 495–9 notes that Grigor's Christianity had long been known to the Persians by 542 and argues that Khusro actually made little active effort to persecute the Christians at this time; cf. Guillaumont 1969–70: 48.

39 Among which was a gem-studded gold cross, later returned to the city by Khusro II, cf. Th. Sim. V.13.2 and Chapter 12 below.

40 This passage is considered in Greatrex 1998a: 32.

41 John never returned to Roman soil alive, cf. Proc. *Anecd.* 12.7–10 and *PLRE* III, Ioannes 30.

42 Belisarius took no part in any further campaigns in the East, having been recalled to Constantinople late in 542 under suspicion of making treasonable remarks about the emperor; and although he apparently wished to return to the East (Proc. *Anecd.* 4.38), he was sent to Italy instead in 544. See *PLRE* III, 211.

43 Cf. *Anecd.* 3.31 for a similar account of Callinicum's capture, *Aed.* II.7.17 on its rebuilding, with Whitby 1987: 93–4.

44 On the deportation of farmers (cf. craftsmen in 614), see Morony 1984: 267.

45 The editors of IGLS I, p.91 suggested 542, cf. Whitby 1987: 95, who notes the existence of a further unpublished metrical inscription (mentioned in Frézouls 1969: 90 n.2), which records the thanks of the citizens to Justinian for rebuilding their city.

46 The Greek *auxi* (translated by *LSJ* as 'prosper') is tricky to translate here, since it is usually applied to individuals; cf. Roueché 1984: 195 on the word and its frequency in acclamatory formulae.

47 This is Eustathius 3 in *PLRE* III, who is likely to be identical to Eustathius 4, a *magister militum* who is acclaimed in an inscription, probably also concerned with fortification work, at Hierapolis dated to 527/48, cf. Mouterde and Poidebard 1945: 209 no.39 and Feissel 2000: 98.

48 Stein 1949: 501–2 and 502 n.1 prefers to put John Troglita's successes (recounted below) in 544/5, shortly before the signing of the truce with Khusro. This is possible, since there are no chronological clues in Corippus' account. In favour of the dating adopted here is the fact that Khusro does not feature in Corippus' poem; and, given that Khusro did take part in the siege of Edessa in 544, one would expect that he would also have taken the lead in any attacks made on Resaina and Dara in the same campaign (since

they would both be close to his route back to Persian territory). In 542, on the other hand, his most direct route back was along the Euphrates, and so he could have split his forces, thereby reducing supply problems (note Proc. *Wars* I.18.13–14).

49 Which does not survive save for this summary.

50 The form given is Basiliyus, which could also be a rendering of the Greek *basileus*, king/emperor.

51 Kafr-tut lies almost due north-east of Resaina, on the way to Dara (see Honigmann 1935: Karte 1). Although Agapius refers to Belisarius and Khusro being involved in this campaign, this is because they were the leading commanders on either side: neither Mihr-Mihroe nor John were sufficiently significant to be recorded here. Hence, largely on geographical (and chronological) grounds, it seems plausible to identify Agapius' notice with Corippus' account.

52 Presumably a reference to horse hairs used in the plumes of helmets, cf. Bishop and Coulston 1993: 61 on the use of horse hair in Roman helmets of an earlier period. The few surviving Sasanian helmets do not seem to have borne plumes, cf. Grancsay 1963: 253–62 (though note 261 fig.15, the rock-carving of a king at Taq-i-Bustan, whose helmet appears to display some sort of plumage).

53 On the failed attempt to convert the Jafnids under Maurice, Shahîd 1995: ch.14 and Sartre 1982a: 189–91.

54 Adhurgundadh's fall came after Khusro's Lazic campaign in 541, cf. *PLRE* III, Adergoudounbades.

55 Cf. the welcome accorded to Hormizd, the brother of Shapur II, who had been imprisoned in Persia but fled to the Roman empire c.324. See Dodgeon and Lieu 1991: 147–9 and Lieu 1986: 494. Cf. also Khusro II's use of someone claiming to be Maurice's son Theodosius, below Chapter 13.

56 According to Evagr. *HE* IV.27, the image of Edessa, not made by human hands, came to the rescue of the defenders when the wood beneath the mound failed to light: the image was brought down, sprinkled with water, and the timber immediately caught fire. But as Cameron 1983: 84–5 notes, Proc.'s omission of the episode implies that it was only after his account was written that the image was 'found', probably in the 550s. See also L.M. Whitby 1998: 198–9.

57 The *Spurious Life of Jacob Baradaeus*, *PO* 19.262–4, also mentions Khusro's attack on Batnae and Edessa. It claims that Jacob, now the Monophysite bishop of Edessa, was in the city at the time of the siege and saved it by his prayers; a certain Cometas, a spy who advised Khusro in his attacks on Syria, is mentioned too. However, the work is generally not accorded much credence and Jacob is not believed to have ever visited his see. See Bundy 1978: 71–2.

58 *PLRE* III, Tribunus 2. At *Wars* VIII.10.14–16, Proc. adds that the time allotted to Tribunus at the Persian court was one year. When the time had elapsed, Khusro repaid the doctor by freeing more than 3000 prisoners at his request.

59 As Croke 1995: 137 notes, Marcellinus' continuator is a year out here: the truce was arranged in spring 545, cf. Stein 1949: 502 n.2.

60 We follow Stein 1949: 502 n.2 in supposing that Agath. II.18.3 refers not just to the truce of 551 but also to that of 545. No recriminations or complaints followed the resumption of hostilities in Lazica, which implies that neither side had expected the area to remain peaceful.

61 Agapius, *PO* 8.432, puts the siege at two months, cf. Stein 1949: 501 n.1. *Chr. 1234* must be referring here to the siege of 544, despite the placing of the event even before the capture of Antioch; for in 540 Khusro did not lay siege to Edessa.

62 Honigmann 1923: 20 for this identification.

63 A similar account is offered by Mich. Syr. IX.24 (287a/205) and IX.26 (296a/220), no doubt derived from the same source. See also n.39 above.

CHAPTER 8

1 See Stein 1949: 492–3, Braund 1994: 292–4. Among the points made by the Lazi to Khusro (according to Proc. *Wars* II.15.27) was that their country could act as a springboard for a Persian naval attack on Constantinople; as Lee 1993a: 23–4 notes, this is more interesting as a reflection of the fears of some Romans than as a reference to a serious threat, cf. Braund 1994: 297–8. Wheeler 1999: 436 argues that the Sasanians did have larger ambitions in Lazica, however.

2 See Lee 1993a: 116–17 on Khusro's ruse.

3 Sebastopolis was regarrisoned and rebuilt at some point before 554 (the composition of *Aed.*), *Aed.* III.7.9.

4 Cf. *Wars* VIII.7.1–5.

5 There is, as Brooks notes, a confusion in the manuscript here, since the 'it' in the second sentence apparently refers to Edessa, which the Persians never captured in the sixth century.

6 Bryer and Winfield 1985: 182 note inscriptional evidence (*CIG* 8636) for the completion of repairs to civic buildings in Trapezus in 542, cf. Proc. *Aed.* III.7.1–2 (reporting the construction of an aqueduct and the restoration of churches). There is no evidence for military building work there, however.

7 It may well have been in the same year that a certain Artabanes (*PLRE* III, Artabanes 1) defected to the Romans, at the same time handing over a fortress previously held by the Persians (Proc. *Wars* VIII.8.22–5). His transfer of allegiance took place while Valerian was *magister militum per Armeniam*, i.e. 541/7.

8 According to the life of Mar Aba (tr. Braun, 197), Khusro was in the region to campaign against barbarians (anachronistically referred to as Khazars), cf. Peeters 1951a: 138 and Tabari, I, 895/151, 898/159 (Nöldeke 157–8, 166). These events have traditionally been dated to 543, but Kislinger and Stathakopoulos 1999: 95 prove that Proc. must be referring to later in 542 (cf. II.26.1).

9 A detailed account of the tribulations of the *catholicos* of the Persian Christians, Mar Aba, at Khusro's court at this time survives (tr. Braun 1915: 197–205), cf. Peeters 1951a: 138–45, who also suggests (148) that Khusro's army brought back the plague from Roman territory in 542. See also Labourt 1904: 181–4, Martin–Hisard 1998a: 494–9.

10 Justus, along with some fellow commanders, started off from Pheison (near Martyropolis), and so were too far to the south to take part in this campaign. It should be noted how Justinian diverted forces from throughout the East into this campaign (Martin, who invaded from Citharizon, was *magister militum per Orientem*, cf. *PLRE* III, Martinus 2). This helps to account for the large size of the Roman force noted by Proc. *Wars* II.24.16.

11 Anglon is the Armenian Angł, near Vagabanta, south-west of Dvin, cf. Hübschmann 1904: 399 and Adontz 1970: 241 and n.21. Proc. emphasises the prosperity of Dvin as a trading centre, II.25.3, cf. Lee 1993a: 64–5, Manandian 1965: 82–3 and Synelli 1986: 96.

12 There are some vague references to Persian intervention in Iberia in *HVG* 206–7/225, cf. Toumanoff 1952: 37, idem 1963: 378.

13 On the imposition of Persian rule in Iberia see Greatrex 1998a: 144–5.

14 I.e. the Black Sea.

15 Cf. *Wars* VIII.7.12 for this last point, and see n.1 above on its implausibility.

16 Braund 1994: 297–8 is rightly sceptical of Khusro's plans for the construction of a navy on the Black Sea. Procopius' reference to the deportation of the Lazi may also be an invention, although the Sasanians frequently did move populations (cf. e.g. Blockley 1992: 145–6).

17 Mihr-Mihroe's route to Petra may have been through Persarmenia, but Proc.'s

geography of this area is difficult to interpret, since he confuses the rivers Boas and Phasis (II.29.14–19, 30.1). cf. Greatrex 1998a: 186 n.43.

18 Rhecithancus' forces may never have actually reached the region: see *PLRE* III, Rhecithangus.

19 Braund 1994: 299 places this campaign in 550, without discussion, although Stein 1949: 506 rightly dated it to 549. Braund may have been misled by Proc.'s reference at VIII.1.3 to 'the succeeding year', which he seems to understand as reference to the next calendar year. In fact, from the context, it must refer to the next year of the truce, i.e. 549–50.

20 The Hippis is generally identified with the modern Tshkenistsqali (Horse river), cf. Braund 1994: 300 n.1 and Stein 1949: 506. On the location of Mocheresis, see Braund 1994: 291 and n.98 (inland from Phasis); the name is applied by Proc. to both a city and a region. See Talbert 2000: 88 A2.

21 Cf. Braund 1994: 300–1 on this campaign, noting the uncertainty of the location of Tracheia (to be found at Talbert 2000: 87 F2).

22 Cf. Braund 1994: 301, identifying the fort (Tzibile) with 'a large fortified crag above the River Kodori, some 20 km behind Sebastopolis', where coins of Justinian have been discovered. See Talbert 2000: 87 G1.

23 Cf Braund 1994: 302–3, who notes (from Proc.) how the Persians had improved communications between Iberia and eastern Lazica, where they had occupied the fort of Scanda. Ibid. 304 for a plan of the fort at Archaeopolis.

24 On the Dilimnites (Proc.'s Dolomites), a tribe from the mountainous region around modern Tehran, west of Tabaristan, see Felix 1996 and Nöldeke 1879: 479 n.1.

25 On the location of Suania and Scymnia and their status (within the Lazic empire), see Braund 1994: 279.

26 The date of the Persian takeover is provided by the second passage from Menander here quoted – ten years before 561, i.e. 551. Cf. Blockley 1985b: 255 n.43, *PLRE* III, Deitatus and Martinus 2; Zuckerman 1991: 541 dates it to 552. Braund 1994: 313, however, puts the withdrawal of the Roman garrison in 554/5 (without explanation); he may have had in mind Khusro's apparent dating of the event to the period when the *nakhveragan* had succeeded Mihr-Mihroe, Menander frg.6.1.501. These two dates are difficult to reconcile, although 551 seems more plausible, since it is clear from Proc. (VIII.14.53, 16.14) that the Persians cut off the Romans from Suania in this year, which would then explain why no grain was forthcoming from the Lazi. See also Braund 1994: 311–13, noting that the Suani were far from being mere tributaries of the Lazi (as the sending of grain from the latter to the former suggests). As Zuckerman 1991: 544 n.61 points out, Blockley (1985b: 259 n.75) is wrong to assert that the Persians established a *marzban* in Suania.

27 Yazdbozid, who was martyred at this time (in 553, cf. Peeters 1925: 198), was a Persian, not an Armenian. The Persians seem to have been wary of provoking rebellion among the Armenians, cf. ibid. 194 (noting the apparent absence of a fire-temple in Dvin). See also Garsoïan 1999: 228–31.

28 Cf. Stein 1949: 511–13 and Braund 1994: 307. See also Agath. II.27.9 and *PLRE* III, Mermeroes on the date of his death (summer 555); his illness may explain his lack of activity earlier in 555. See Stein 1949: 812 on the chronological difficulties of Agathias' account here.

29 Rusticus had charge of disbursing reward money to Roman soldiers, according to Agathias; he may have held the post of *sacellarius*, cf. *PLRE* III, Rusticus 4, but note the uncertainty expressed by Stein 1949: 512 n.2 (apparently ignored by *PLRE*).

30 See Stein 1949: 513 with 811–13 on the chronology here.

31 Stein 1949: 511 is sceptical of Agathias' figure of 50,000 men (III.8.2) operating in the Transcaucasus at this point, and it should also be noted that it is deployed in a markedly rhetorical context (emphasising the thoroughness of the Roman defeat). Cf. also

Treadgold 1995: 59–64 on Agathias' troop figures in general. Archaeopolis itself remained in Roman hands, cf. Agath. III.18.10.

32 Cf. Braund 1994: 309–10 on this incident. This type of regular payments falls under Blockley's third category: Blockley 1992: 149. Colvin 2003 argues, however, that Misimian allegiance to both Romans and Lazi was largely nominal (despite Agath. III.15.8).

33 See n.31 for uncertainty surrounding Agathias' figures. The territory in this region, as the Persians had already discovered, did not favour the use of large forces, cf. (e.g.) Whitby 1988: 201–2 (concerning Armenia).

34 Wrongly, it appears, since the region was well defended by the surrounding marshes, cf. Proc. VIII.17.12, Braund 1994: 306 and Cameron 1970: 46–7, 53.

35 As Stein 1949: 812 notes, this is the same defection as that noted above (at Agath. III.15–17).

36 The figure for the sum is at IV.20.9; it is the equivalent of 400 lbs of gold, i.e. 4 *centenaria*. For the (uncertain) location of Tzakher see Braund in Talbert 2000: 1228 and note the sixth-century wall marked on map 87 G1–2.

37 It continued to come up in negotiations between the two powers, e.g. in 567/8 (Menander frg.9.1). As Zuckerman 1991: 541 notes, the difficulty lay in determining whether Suania counted as part of Lazica (which was returned to the Romans by the peace of 561).

CHAPTER 9

1 There is no reason to suppose, however, that the victory of Harith mentioned by Proc. is that achieved in 554: *Wars* I–VII were published in 550/1, cf. Cameron 1985: 8–9.

2 The Arabic al-'Uzza, cf. Shahîd 1995: 238 and n.9.

3 Proc. alleges that as much as ten *centenaria*'s worth of gifts were given to Yazdgushnasp. Cf. Stein 1949: 503–4 (dating the embassy to 547), with *PLRE* III, Isdegousnas Zich and Georgius 4.

4 Cf. Stein 1949: 510, Peeters 1951b: 157. Anoshazadh, who was in Susiana at the time, had been inspired to rebel by a rumour that Khusro had died; he received some support from Christians in Beth Lapat (Gundeshapur), but was defeated by Phabrizus. See also *PLRE* III, Anasozadus, Nöldeke 1879: 467–74 and Pigulevskaja 1963: 221–8.

5 Proc. VIII.15.12 for the date, the 25th year of Justinian's reign, i.e. 551–552 (not, as Dewing gives, 552–553), cf. Stein 1949: 510. Agath. II.18.3 makes clear that the truce did not extent to Lazica. Yazdgushnasp was in Constantinople from late 550 to autumn 551, cf. Stein 1949: 510 and n.2 and *PLRE* III, Isdigousnas Zich.

6 Cf. Stein 1949: 510 n.2 on the (probable) association of this passage with the embassy of 550–551 (but noting that Peeters doubted that the Iesdekos of Peter's text could be equated with Yazdgushnasp); Antonopoulos 1990: 203–4 prefers to associate the passage with the mission of 556 or 557, arguing that the one of 551 was merely the continuation of a mission begun by Peter the Patrician in Ctesiphon in the previous year. Tinnefeld 1993: 195 and Stock 1978: 167 associate the passage with the mission of 547, however. On the attribution of this section of the work to Peter the Patrician, see Bury 1907: 212–13, Antonopoulos, *loc. cit.* and Clauss 1980: 182. Güterbock 1906: 19–24 provides a detailed analysis of these two chapters, cf. Clauss 1980: 64–5 (on the role of the *magister officiorum* in particular).

7 Cf. Clauss 1980: 137 on this role of the *scrinium barbarorum*. The *ducici* were officials attached to a *dux*.

8 Güterbock 1906: 19 n.2 suggests that Antioch in Pisidia is meant here, since Syrian Antioch would not be on the ambassador's route; it is more probable, however, that a visit to Syrian Antioch, the most important city of the diocese of Oriens is indicated.

Justinian had rebuilt (Syrian) Antioch on an impressive scale after the Persian sack of 540, cf. Proc. *Aed.* II.10.19–25 with Foss 1997: 191–3.

9 Presumably the *optio* (a military official), but perhaps the ambassador. A *dromon* was a Roman military ship.

10 Literally 'dirty services'. Cf. Tinnefeld 1993: 199 on the identification of the items mentioned here (to which our translation is indebted).

11 Here the term refers to a high-ranking member of the corps of *silentiarii* (palace attendants, cf. *ODB* III.1896), cf. Jones 1964: 571–2, Clauss 1980: 102. As the *ODB* notes, the emperor Anastasius was a decurion just before his elevation to the throne.

12 On the *subadiuva* see Güterbock 1906: 20, Clauss 1980: 136–7. Jones 1964: 579, 597 translates the term as 'deputy assistant'.

13 'Orders' in Latin.

14 The gathering of the most important bodies of state, the senate and the *consistorium*, the latter consisting of the chief advisers of the emperor, including officials such as the praetorian prefect, the *magister officiorum* and others. See *ODB* I.496 and III.1896.

15 An official in one of the *officia* (bureaux) under the *magister officiorum*, cf. Clauss 1980: 16.

16 The progress of the ambassadors is best followed in Bardill 1999: 220 fig.2 (and see 218–19). See too Mango 1959: 23 fig.1, 29 fig.4, 79. The precise location of the *schola* is uncertain. The ambassadors, assuming they approached the Chalke from the Mesē, would have been able to admire a statue on top of the Augustaeum, depicting Justinian on horseback, raising his right hand to the East, 'and spreading out his fingers, he commands the barbarians in that quarter (i.e. the Persians) to remain at home and advance no further' (*Aed.* I.2.12, tr. Dewing), cf. Mango 1959: 174–9 and Feissel 2000: 90.

17 On these officials see Clauss 1980: 136–7 (all from the *scrinium barbarorum*, the bureau which dealt with foreign affairs). On the route of the ambassadors (and the location of the *consistorium*), Bardill 1999: 220, cf. Güterbock 1906: 21.

18 Imperial bodyguards, cf. *ODB* II.1100.

19 Cf. Joh. Lyd. *De Mag.* I.17 on these robes (of the patricians).

20 Reiske takes this sentence as part of the *magister*'s pronouncement, translating, 'and may he (the decurion) summon the guards.'

21 Reiske suggests that something has dropped out of the text here. On these *chartularii* see Clauss 1980: 65, 137.

22 'Doorkeeper', cf. *ODB* III.1540.

23 The *cubiculum* is the bedroom. A whole array of officials were concerned with the 'sacred bedchamber' of the emperor, cf. Jones 1964: 566–71.

24 The third rank in the imperial *notarii* (secretaries), cf. Clauss 1980: 22, Jones 1964: 575.

25 Latin for 'Raise!'.

26 The place of the *vestosacrani* (referred to below), who were connected with, if not identical to, the *vestitores* (courtiers associated with the emperor's dress), on whom see *ODB* III.2164.

27 The Latin for 'change (position)'.

28 It is ambiguous as to who is informing whom. Reiske believed it was the emperor (informing the ambassador); we think it more probable to be the *magister*, since the emperor has already communicated his wish to the *magister*.

29 The portico (peristyle) and Augusteus have been uncovered by archaeologists: see Bardill 1999: 227, who notes other evidence for the use of the Augusteus for entertaining dignitaries.

30 Güterbock 1906: 24–5 offers a brief description of the reception of Roman envoys in Persia as a comparison with that here given.

31 Cf. Menander frg.20.2.17–20 for Roman unwillingness to become apparent tributaries of the Persians, with Blockley 1992: 150–1.

32 The period of 'the meantime' (Greek, *metaxu*) refers to the interval between the two truces, from early 550 to late 551, which Proc. has reported. It follows from the fact that

the Romans had already handed over the full amount (Proc. VIII.15.6 above) that this passage cannot be taken to imply that Proc. was writing after the elapse of eleven and a half years (i.e. in 557), as Evans 1996b: 306–8 argues.

33 The date of the arrival of the silk-worm in Roman territory is unclear: Proc.'s chronological indicator at VIII.17.1 seems to place the commissioning of the monks in 552 (accepted by Stein 1949: 772); but given the time involved for them to return to Sogdiana and bring back the silk-worms, a date in the 540s seems more plausible, and is not incompatible with the vague 'around this time'. Evans 1996a: 235 suggests 'about 553' for the arrival of the silk-worms. A useful recent survey of the silk trade in the sixth century is provided by Tate 1999.

34 The Syriac word *bnwra* here makes little sense, and so it is best to read *bathra* (apparently with Chabot, who translates here 'région'). We are grateful to John Watt for advice on this point.

35 Two parallel versions of this entry are to be found in *Chr.1234*, 56 (192.24–7) and 62 (200.15–20). As Shahîd 1995: 249 argues, John of Ephesus was probably Michael's source here.

36 The embassy is nowhere else reported but cannot simply be ruled out for that reason, cf. Shahîd 1995: 245 and van den Ven 1970: 190 n.1.

37 The Greek term is *parembolē*, on which see Shahîd 1989: 212–13.

38 Shahîd 1995: 246 doubts whether Roman soldiers took part in the engagement, and therefore proposes to translate 'in the middle of the camp of the Saracen soldiers.' Since, however, the battle took place well within Roman territory and close to the city of Chalcis, the presence of at least some Roman soldiers does not seem unlikely.

39 The Greek word is *sōtēria*, salvation.

40 Zikh may be a family name, cf. Christensen 1944: 105 n.3 and *PLRE* III, Isdigousnas Zich.

41 Cf. Stein 1949: 516 and Braund 1994: 311. Menander frg.2.1–12 summarises the passage. Another (unnamed) ambassador was present in Constantinople in May 556, where he joined the emperor in watching games and witnessed demonstrations against Justinian (Mal. 18.121 [488.6–9]); Stein 1949: 517 n.2, probably rightly, argued against identifying this ambassador with Yazdgushnasp and the mission of 557 (*contra* Antonopoulos 1990: 100 n.28).

42 The *martyrium* of St Shirin offers a brief glimpse of this, cf. Devos 1946: 124 ‡17 (tr. in Devos 1994: 26) with Stein 1949: 517 n.2 (placing the mission in 558).

43 No doubt deriving his account here, as often, from John of Ephesus (cf. Witakowski 1991: 266). Amida had been afflicted also by a plague (in which 30,000 are said to have died) and continuing persecutions of Monophysites, cf. Harvey 1980: 3–4. The translation quoted is that of Witakowski 1996: 104.

44 The date of the treaty, whether 561 or 562, is disputed. Antonopoulos 1990: 102–6, having considered the arguments in detail, prefers the later dating (*contra*, e.g., Blockley 1985: 259 n.70 and Stein 1949: 518 n.2). This seems preferable, since the negotiations on the border, as he notes, required ratification from the monarchs at more than one point, and thus must have taken a considerable amount of time. They may thus have started late in 561 and only have reached a definite conclusion in late summer 562, after which the peace still required final confirmation. Peter will then have proceeded to Persia in time for Epiphany early in 563 and have returned to Constantinople in summer that year (cf. Theoph. A.M. 6055 [239]). On the procedures involved in the negotiations see Stock 1978: 168–71.

45 As Blockley notes (1985b: 254 n.36), the Persians almost invariably demanded money from the Romans, who were equally consistently reluctant to pay it. The fact that the Romans wanted only a short-term peace, whereas the Persians wanted a longer one, perhaps indicates the relative strength of the former at this point; clearly the Romans no longer had any expectation of agreeing to an 'Eternal' peace. Stein 1949: 518 (cf. Schippmann 1990: 58 and Widengren 1952) notes the victory of the Turks and Persians

over the Hephthalites which occurred c.560, which extended Persian territory in the East and suggests that Khusro may have desired peace to consolidate his conquests.

46 Güterbock 1906: 63–5 suggested that the 30,000 *solidi* were the equivalent not of 416.67 lbs of gold (as one would expect, there being at this time 72 *solidi* to 1 lb of gold), but of 500 lbs (using the older system of 60 *solidi* to the lb); for Joh. Epiph. 2, *FHG* IV.274, gives the figure of 500 lbs of gold. Cf. however Stein 1919: 30 n.6.

47 Blockley 1985b: 255–6 n.49 sees the omission of the items covered earlier (such as the Roman payments) as a concession to Roman pride; it seems preferable to suppose, however, that since these matters had already been agreed on, there was no cause to return to them in this document. General accounts of the peace terms are to be found in Bury 1923: II, 120–3, Stein 1949: 519–21, Synelli 1986: 96–8.

48 On Suania, see below, Chapter 10. On the Arabs, see Menander frg.6.1.288–303, 515–44, with Shahîd 1995: 273–7, rightly pointing out that the Romans were in a strong position in refusing the Lakhmids following the defeat and death of Mundhir in 554. A detailed consideration of both topics may be found in Antonopoulos 1990: 129–36.

49 Procopius' Tzur, i.e. the Derbend pass, cf. Blockley 1985b: 255 n.48 and Marquart 1901: 105–7.

50 *Contra* Stein 1949: 519, this clause should be interpreted as laying down that Arab allies of each side must refrain from hostilities between each other, cf. Shahîd 1995: 267–8 with idem 1956: 197–202 and Blockley 1985b: 256 n.50.

51 Cf. *C.J.* IV.63.4 (above, Chapter 3). Güterbock 1906: 78 argues that these posts were Callinicum, Nisibis and Dvin (the last having replaced Artaxata), cf. Synelli 1986: 96–7. On the wealth of Dvin, linked to trade, see Chaumont 1987: 433.

52 The Greek here could also mean, as Blockley translates, 'They shall be sent back without delay'. Cf. Güterbock 1906: 78–9 on this clause.

53 See Shahîd 1995: 268–72 on this clause, with Blockley 1985b: 256–7 n.54, Shahîd 1956: 192–7, Verosta 1966: 605–7. It is worth emphasising that part of the salary of the *dux* of Mesopotamia came from the revenue raised by the *commerciarius*, the customs official of the province, cf. *IGLS* 9046 with the comments in Sartre 1982b: 115. See also Antonopoulos 1990: 117.

54 See Güterbock 1906: 80–3 and Blockley 1985: 257 n.55. Antonopoulos 1990: 121 compares this clause with the agreement of 422 not to accept defecting allies from the other side.

55 See Güterbock 1906: 83–6.

56 Blockley 1985b: 257 n.58, cf. Güterbock 1906: 66–7, interprets this as referring to peoples such as the Lazi and Armenians, since the Arabs are covered by their own separate clause.

57 Blockley 1985b: 258 n.61 takes these to be provincial governors (*iudices*) or 'specially appointed judicial commissioners'.

58 Blockley 1985b: 258 n.62 suggests that only a Roman official is named here because this is a copy of the agreement destined for the Romans; the Persian version would name a Persian official.

59 See Güterbock 1906: 86–90, Antonopoulos 1990: 119–21.

60 Cf. Lee 1993b: 580–2. But persecutions were no more than intermittent, cf. Labourt 1904: 196 n.1 and Martin–Hisard 1998a: 494–9, and (as shown below) Khusro was prepared to support Christians in some circumstances. Goubert 1951: 172–3 points out that Armenian sources even asserted that Khusro converted to Christianity late in life.

61 Verosta 1965: 154 describes it as a 'Zusatzprotokoll', cf. idem 1966: 608–10.

62 Cf. Eusebius, *Vita Constantini* IV.8–13, tr. in Dodgeon and Lieu 1991: 150–1 (Constantine's letter to Shapur). Part of the background to the war of 421–422 had been the persecution of Christians in Persia, on which see above, Chapter 3, with Antonopoulos 1990: 123–4; cf. also Guillaumont 1969–70: 49–50.

63 How Justinian could guarantee that Persian Christians would not engage in proselytising is unclear.

64 See *V. Ahudemmeh* for a full account of his life, with Oates 1968: 106–17, Shahîd 1984: 420–1 and Frend 1972: 321. Ahudemmeh has been identified with the homonymous Nestorian bishop of Niniveh in 554, but see Fiey 1968b: 156 against this view.

65 So Oates 1968: 116–17. Ahudemmeh himself fell from favour after baptising a prince of the Sasanian dynasty, and was martyred in August 575 (*V. Ahudemmeh, PO* 3.46).

CHAPTER 10

1 See Shahîd 1995: 282–8, 309, cf. Stein 1949: 521 (with Menander frg.9.1.79–82). Theoph. A.M. 6056 (240) for Harith's visit.

2 The subject was raised by Peter immediately after the conclusion of negotiations, but no progress was made: see Menander frg.6.1.435–603 with Turtledove 1983: 292.

3 Scholarly consensus places the mission in 567 rather than 566, identifying it with the embassy reported by Mich. Syr. (below) and Theoph. Byz. (below): see Stein 1919: 31 n.8, cf. Shahîd 1995: 308 and *PLRE* III, Ioannes 81. Turtledove 1983: 293 opts for 566, however, and argues that the mission reported by Mich. Syr. was different from that referred to by Menander (cf. the following note). It should be noted that Justin's delay in announcing his accession to Khusro (noted, e.g., by Shahîd 1995: 308 n.2 and Turtledove 1983: 297) is not without parallel: Justinian's accession was only reported to Kavadh in July 529, almost two years after he became sole emperor (cf. Greatrex 1998a: 160).

4 Turtledove 1983: 296–7 argues that Michael the Syrian is here referring to a different mission from that of John, son of Domnentiolus, and that the gifts referred to were actually the payments agreed for the three years 569–71. Mich. Syr. places the mission in Justin II's second year, but places his accession in 566, and so the mission is dated to 567/8. The consensus, however, identifies the two Johns, cf. e.g. *PLRE* III, Ioannes 81 and Stein 1919: 31 n.8 (arguing that John is called 'of Callinicum' by Michael because it was here that he held his discussions with the Monophysites, on which see below, p.136).

5 Mich. Syr. dates this mission to the second year of Justin II's reign. Although, as Turtledove 1983: 297 points out, Mich. Syr. dates Justin's accession to AG 878 (566/7), it is still quite possible that the mission did indeed take place in Justin's second year (rather than in 567/8).

6 On this (unsuccessful) ecclesiastical mission see Allen 1981: 23–4 and below n.11. It may be Justin's gifts on this occasion which are mentioned in one of the *Sirat Anushirwan* (no.9 in Grignaschi 1966: 24). Rubin 1995: 282 suggests that the gifts mentioned in the *Sirat* were the second instalment of the payments due to the Persians by the terms of the treaty of 562, cf. Turtledove 1983: 297.

7 The first book of his *Histories*.

8 The Greek word could be taken metaphorically instead of literally, i.e. referring to disturbances in Mesopotamia (so R. Henry in his translation of Photius). But given that there was an earthquake in the East in November 570 (*Chr. 724*, 143, tr. in Palmer 1993: 15), the Greek should be translated literally.

9 Mundhir's victory of May 570 is also reported by *Chr. 724*, 143, AG 881 (tr. Palmer 1993: 15), which Shahîd erroneously refers to as the *Chronicon Maroniticum*. Shahîd, who places Harith's death in 569, dates the two campaigns to 569 and 570. Stein 1919: 42 identified the first attack with the victory reported by *Chr. 724*, and so put the two campaigns in 570 and 571. Stein's dating is preferable, since Marcian became *magister militum per Orientem* in 572.

10 Cf. Shahîd 1995: 348–56, arguing that Gregory, the patriarch of Antioch, was involved in the plot. Whitby 1988: 257–8 is rightly sceptical of John's account, seeing in it an

attempt by John to deflect blame from Mundhir; cf. also van Ginkel 1995: 121 and Stein 1919: 42–3. The Jafnid withdrawal began in 572, cf. Shahîd 1995: 356 and Stein, *loc. cit.* with 51 n.6.

11 See Frend 1972: 317–21 on the negotiations, with fig.2, 258–9. Whitby 1988: 213–15 is rightly cautious concerning the impact of imperial policy on local loyalties, cf. Palmer 1990: 152. See also p.185–6 below.

12 Cf. Turtledove 1983: 297–8 and Sinor 1990: 302. Parallel evidence of Persian contact with the Turks in 568 is found in the Sasanian tradition (the *Sirat Anushirwan*, on which see Rubin 1995: 278–80): cf. Grignaschi 1966: 23–4 with Rubin 1995: 280–2 and Grignaschi 1980: 244–5. See also Schreiner 1985: 278 n.367.

13 A detailed commentary on the envoys' route is provided by Blockley 1985b; cf. Joh. Eph. *HE* VI.22. Grignaschi 1966: 24–5 provides the text of an Arabic source recording these contacts between Turks and Romans. The oriental sources record negotiations between Khusro and the Turks north of the Caucasus in 569/70, during which a raid was launched by the Turks and their allies against Armenia and Atropatene; it was, however, repulsed by the fortifications of the Persians. See Widengren 1952: 73–4, 91–2, Nöldeke 1879: 158 and n.2, Sinor 1990: 303–4 and n.12 above; the more peaceful exchanges recorded in the *Sirat* may be an alternative account of the same events.

14 Cf. Grignaschi 1980: 244–5, suggesting that this (successful) invasion entered Media by passing east of the Caspian Sea, rather than through the well guarded Derbend Pass; he therefore appears to distinguish this invasion from a later (unsuccessful) one of Sizabul in 572/3 (p.235).

15 The Himyarites had initially approached the Romans for help against the Ethiopians, according to Tabari (I, 952/244) but had been refused (since the Ethiopians were traditional Roman allies).

16 Wilson 1994: 54 n.6 notes that there may be something wrong with the text here, since it is surprising to find a Roman ambassador entertaining Turks (on Turkish territory).

17 Identified by *PLRE* III with Bahram Gushnasp, the subsequent opponent of Marcian in Mesopotamia, but by Shahîd 1995: 366 with Abu Murra, the Himyarite leader who asked the Persians to intervene.

18 I.e. Masruq, son of Abraha, the last king of Himyar, cf. Shahîd 1995: 370–1 and Nöldeke 1879: 220 n.2.

19 It is clear from Stephen of Taron (below), cf. Grousset 1947: 242, that the Armenian Christians had been suffering for a while (since the late 540s) before they approached the Romans; Chihor-Vshnasp himself had taken charge of Armenia c.564. This implies that the initiative of the Armenians was prompted by wider developments rather than local events in the late 560s, although the secessionist efforts of Vahan of Siwnik' (to be dated between 552 and 558, cf. Garitte 1952: 211–13) probably also played a part (on which see Sebeos, 67–8/6, translated below with Stein 1919: 36 n.22 and Hewsen 1992: 190). The presence of Justinian, the *magister militum per Armeniam*, at Theodosiopolis at this time may have helped lay the foundations for the uprising, cf. Stein 1919: 22 and *PLRE* III, Iustinianus 3.

20 An error for 2 February, according to Stein 1919: 37 n.23. The reference to both an Armenian and a Julian month is confusing, and it is uncertain how much store can be set by such a precise date. For a detailed discussion see Akinean 1913: 79–80 n.19.

21 The references to Justinian are in error for Justin II.

22 See Garitte 1952: 184–5, 189 and Garsoïan 1999: 250–1 on this account; the chronology is clearly awry. As he notes, only one source, Ananias of Shirak, attributes the murder of Chihor-Vshnasp not to Vardan but to Zawrak Kamsarakan.

23 Sometime between September 569 and August 571. The dealings between the Persarmenians and the Romans took place between September and November 570, cf. Stein 1919: 22–3. Turtledove 1977: 176–7 prefers to place the pact in late 571, which

would be compatible with Joh. Eph., who frequently antedates events by one year. Whitby 1988: 251, however, argues that Joh. Eph. has conflated the secret Armenian appeal with the flight of the Armenian leaders. The earlier dating should be preferred, since it allows more time for the negotiations and for preparations for the rebellion.

24 Literally, 'Small Armenia', i.e. Armenia Minor or Lesser Armenia. The reference should in fact be to Armenia Interior, to the east of Armenia Minor. Cf. Stein 1919: 82 n.7 for a similar error in Menander.

25 As Allen 1981: 219 notes, cf. Kettenhoffen 1982: 35 n.72, this must be a reference to the division of Armenia in the 380s (although Philip reigned from 244 to 249). The passage is translated in Dodgeon and Lieu 1991: 45 as referring to the third century (so too Potter 1990: 221–2, Chaumont 1976: 168).

26 Cameron 1975: 421–6 is generally positive concerning Gregory's information on eastern affairs, but cf. Whitby 1988: 8 n.9. Stein 1919: 52 n.9 on the mention of the church. The church of St Julian lay just outside Antioch, cf. Stein 1919: 44 and Downey 1961: 544–5 and 657; it was one of the few monuments which had survived the sack of 540 (cf. Proc. II.10.8). In the translation below we read *narrantes* and *infensos* at 173.2 and *legatos* at 173.11.

27 Stein 1919: 24 suggests that Gregory may here have confused the Armenians with the Sogdians, cf. Turtledove 1977: 180, but see also Manandian 1965: 81.

28 Whitby 1988: 252 suggests that there was no deliberate policy of persecution in Armenia (cf. Stein 1919: 21), and that the temples may have been destined for Persian colonists (cf. Tabari, I, 895/151, Kramers 1935–7). Even if this interpretation is correct, the Persian actions would clearly have been perceived by the Armenians as an aggressive act; it is significant that in the 540s there was (apparently) no fire-temple in Dvin, while in 553 Khusro had even been prepared to despatch envoys of rank to Persarmenia to address grievances. See Peeters 1925: 194 and cf. Lee 1993b: 583. On the persecution of opponents of Chalcedon under Justin II, following the failure of an attempt at conciliation, see Averil Cameron 1976: 62–4 (placing the start of persecutions in 572) and Allen 1981: 22–7. Joh. Eph. *HE* II.18–19 links Justin's persecutions of opponents of Chalcedon with Khusro's decision to turn against the Christians, but his account must be treated with caution (note the very different emphasis of *HE* VI.20-1).

29 Lit. '(as it were) for the adoration of the king', probably referring to acknowledging his authority.

30 Cf. Stein 1919: 37 n.23 and Allen 1981: 219. Cf. Chaumont 1974: 167–8 and Greatrex 2000a: 42 on this concession of religious toleration (at the time Armenia was divided between Rome and Persia; see Chapter 2 above).

31 *Cf. Chr. 1234*, 65 (201–2/158–9). As Turtledove 1977:184 notes, Michael's account complements Menander frg. 16.1 (discussed below). The treaty concerning Nisibis referred to is, of course, an invention (despite Turtledove 1983:300 n.84): see above ch.1 n.22 and Whitby 1988: 206.

32 John may imply that the oppression of the Armenian Christians violated the peace treaty, cf. Menander frg.6.1.398–407 (translated above, Chapter 9). Although John's chronology is often unreliable (cf. Whitby 1988: 87 n.54 and 264 n.22), Campos 1960: 107 argues that contacts between the Persarmenians and Romans may have begun as early as 567.

33 Photius is here reporting what Theophanes said concerning the war.

34 Identified by *PLRE* III, Guaram I, with the Guaram of *HVG* (218/229), cf. Toumanoff 1952: 39, idem 1963: 380.

35 Cf. Turtledove 1983: 299–300, Stein 1919: 24–5; see also Sako 1986: 96–7 on Sebokht. It was presumably to Sebokht that Justin made the declarations reported (above) by Evagrius, Mich. Syr. and Gregory. Firdausi (Mohl 1868: 509–11) also refers to an arrogant letter sent by the new emperor to Khusro. Turtledove 1977: 186–7 argues that

the dismissal of Sebokht marked the opening of war, which Stein preferred to place later in the year. Whether or not there was a formal renunciation of the peace by the Romans before the invasion of Arzanene later in 572 may be doubted.

36 Cf. Whitby 1988: 250–1; note Joh. Eph. *HE* VI.23, where the Persians insist to the Turks that the Romans are their tributaries, whereas Corippus, *In laud. Just.* pref.30–4 makes the claim that the Persians were subject to the Romans. Joh. Eph., *loc. cit.*, mentions how at this time Khusro demolished a statue which Trajan had erected in Persia, since Zemarchus had argued that it demonstrated the Persians' subjection to the Romans. On this interesting episode, see Olajos 1981: 379–83.

37 With this phrase cf. Mal. 18.15 (433) and Ps.-Dion. II, 54/50 (referring to southern Arabia).

38 Th. Sim. follows Joh. Epiph. very closely here, cf. Olajos 1988: 17–32 and Whitby 1988: 222–7.

39 A scribal error for 50 years, cf. Hertzch 1884: 34 and Stein 1949: 519 n.1.

40 Shahîd 1995: 364–72 offers a recent account of the struggle for southern Arabia. Ibid. 367–8 specifically on this passage, dating the start of the Roman alliance with Himyar to the 540s; Shahîd also notes that no other source refers to a Persian attempt to win the Himyarites over to their side.

41 Theoph. Sim. III.9.11, who paraphrases John's analysis, adds that the payments were justified, since they were made to cover joint defence costs (referring, no doubt, to the Caspian Gates); cf. Whitby and Whitby 1986: 86 n.41 and Olajos 1988: 26. Schreiner 1985: 279 n.371 notes that by the terms of the peace of 562, the Romans were supposed to pay 30,000 *solidi* a year, whereas 500 lbs of gold is the equivalent of 36,000 *solidi*; see ch.9 n.46 above.

42 In fact, as has been seen, there were two instalments.

43 The text refers to Rhabdion, but Szádeczky-Kardoss 1976: 113–14 argues that the Greek should read Tourabdion. Whatever the correct Greek form, the reference is to Rhabdion, a Roman fort north-east of Nisibis, also known as the Castle of Tur Abdin (cf. Palmer 1990: 6–7).

44 Cf. Whitby 1988: 254 on Marcian's unreadiness to go on the offensive (wrongly doubted by Turtledove 1977: 198–9). Whitby 1995: 88 n.112 suggests that Evagrius is here referring to 'conscripts drawn from provincial tax registers'.

45 As Turtledove 1977: 199 notes, Evagrius' assessment of Marcian's efforts seems unduly harsh (cf. the other accounts below).

46 Cf. Proc. *Aed.* II.6.1–11 on the defences of Circesium.

47 Or 'for a long time': so Lee 1993b: 571, who offers a translation of 204.18–205.17.

48 *Chr. Seert 36, PO 7.193*, names him as Paul, cf. Lee 1993b: 576–7.

49 See Lee 1993b: 580–4 on Persian oppression of Christians at this time. As has been noted, however (Chapter 9 n.60, above), Khusro was far from being a consistent persecutor of Christians.

50 This episode is analysed in detail by Lee 1993b, who argues that Evagrius' information is reliable.

51 Demanding the return of Nisibis, as reported also by Mich. Syr. (above, p.140).

52 Justinian is a mistake for Justin.

53 On this episode see Lee 1993b: 583–4.

54 9 April 573, cf. Stein 1919: 43.

55 The Syriac text has 'the tent and Marcian' (line 12), but the reading of a *waw* instead of a *daleth* is most unlikely.

56 The date is inaccurate: the correct year is 573.

57 *PLRE* III, Bahram 1, identifies him with Bahram Gushnasp, from the Mihran family, cf. Stein 1919: 39 and 49 n.2. It is possible, however, that the name here is just a Greek rendering of the office *marzban*, cf. Proc.'s Baresmanas with Greatrex 1998a: 176 n.22.

58 It may be this victory which is alluded to by *Anth. Pal.* XVI.72 and *Anth. Gr.* IX.810. The latter refers to an Assyrian triumph, cf. Turtledove 1977: 485 n.15. The former has been dated to 566, however, by Cameron 1966: 101–3, but cf. Olajos 1981: 381–2.

59 Joh. Eph. ascribes Marcian's dismissal to his failure to kill Mundhir earlier in the year (see Joh. Eph. *HE* VI.4 and n.10 above, p.279), cf. Turtledove 1977: 195. This is unlikely, however, since his dismissal occurred only in spring 573, half a year after the bungled attempt to execute Mundhir. More probably his dismissal was due to his (perceived) failure to press the siege of Nisibis sufficiently vigorously.

60 Often 'a believer' = orthodox = Monophysite, although not in this case.

61 The brief passage of Mich. Syr. (below, p.147) shows that Adarmahan's route followed a course similar to that of Azarethes' in 531 and Khusro's in 540. Trombley 1997: 176–82 argues that the capture of the inhabitants of Apamea led to a significant depopulation in northern Syria, cf. Balty and Napoleone-Lemaire 1969: 89 on the damage caused to a church in Apamea apparently by the sack of the city. Tate 1992: 342 and n.8 argues, however, that this (and other) disasters tended to cause only temporary difficulties.

62 Downey 1961: 561–2 notes that the defences of Antioch will have suffered in the earthquakes of 551 and 557.

63 On the wealth of Apamea see Allen 1981: 222, noting evidence from other sources such as the *Itinerarium* of Antoninus of Placentia ‡46, p.190, who refers to Apamea (c.570) as a *civitas splendidissima*, 'a most splendid city'. See Foss 1997: 213–26 for an attempt to combine the literary and archaeological evidence for the sack.

64 Around AD 6 a census registered Apamea as having 117,000 people, *ILS* 2683 (tr. in Sherk 1988: 22). As Millar 1993: 250 notes, this 'must imply a total population of the territory [of Apamea] of several hundred thousand.' Although Foss 1997: 206 dismisses John's figure, Trombley 1997: 176–7 is prepared to take it seriously.

65 Cf. *Chr. 1234*, 68 (205–6/162), with no additional details. Evagr. *HE* V.10 (206) notes that Magnus, the commander in the East at the time, tried unsuccessfully to oppose Adarmahan, cf. *PLRE* III, Magnus 2.

66 Literally, 'the king's'.

67 As Whitby 1988: 257 n.11 notes, the two places are about 200 miles (320 km) apart, and so the reference to a five-day journey implies a particularly quick march on this occasion. Ambar (more usually referred to as Anbar) is Pirisabora, cf. Whitby and Whitby 1986: 87 n.45.

68 Khusro advanced up the east bank of the Euphrates as far as Circesium, where Adarmahan crossed the river (thus avoiding the fort of Circesium, and following the traditional Persian invasion route), and Khusro followed the Khabur north. Cf. Whitby and Whitby 1986: 87 n.45 on the Persian line of advance.

69 Theoph. Sim. III.10.9, apparently supplementing Joh. Epiph. from another source, adds that the sack took place on the third day after the agreement, cf. Olajos 1988: 21.

70 Shahîd 1995: 357–8 plausibly suggests that these details came from a lost section of Joh. Eph. *HE*. Barbalissus is Beth Balash in the Syriac, cf. Honigmann 1923: 20 n.95. Qasrin is probably Neocaesarea, cf. Honigmann 1923: 48 no.229 and 64 no.322, south-east of Barbalissus. Beth Dama lies near Hierapolis, cf. Honigmann 1935: 15 n.5 with Th. Sim. IV.12.8. Gazara might be the Greek Gephyra, a crossing of the Orontes to the east of Antioch, cf. Honigmann 1923: 40 no.189.

71 A detailed narrative is provided by Turtledove 1977: 205–11.

72 Cf. Turtledove 1977: 207 and 489 n.121 on Khusro's use of local labourers for the construction of the counter-walls round the city.

73 Stein 1919: 53 n.10 (cf. 80 n.5) calculates this as the equivalent of 50,000 *solidi* (rather than 36,000, working at the usual rate of 1 lb of gold = 72 *solidi*).

74 According to Joh. Eph. *HE* VI.5, the soldiers were trying to flee out of the city in their panic (rather than into a citadel). This fits much better with the account which follows.

On the relationship between the two sources, see van Ginkel 1995: 80 and n.69. Although *Chr. 1234* clearly had access to a good source here, perhaps the same as that used by Joh. Eph (both place the fall of Dara 72 years after its foundation).

75 Agap., *PO* 8.436 gives 11 November as the date for the fall of Dara; Mich. Syr. X.9 (349a–b/312) gives 15 November. Cf. Stein 1919: 53 n.10. Nicholson 1985: 667–71 suggests that the dead defenders were exposed (according to Zoroastrian practice) in the quarries just outside Dara, where they were buried in 591.

76 Joh. Eph. *HE* VI.5 (followed by Mich. Syr.) gives the envoy's name as Cometas. Khusro blinded him for having failed to pass on his offer.

77 Mich. Syr. X.9 (349a–b/312) offers the figure of 90,000 captives and 150,000 dead (Romans) in addition to many Persians. This section is filled with inflated figures, however.

78 Given the similarity of the two sources on certain points, it is likely that they were drawing on a common contemporary source: cf. van Ginkel 1995: 80.

79 Cf. Turtledove 1977: 208. It is not surprising that the fall of so important a fortress as Dara should have led to accusations of treachery, whatever their accuracy; Evagrius notes that both stories about John were circulating. Evagrius otherwise adds little to our knowledge of the siege.

80 We have followed the restoration of Hertzsch 1884: 36, based on Th. Sim. III.11.2. Although Hertzsch has *kharaka* (rampart), de Boor's text reads *kharakas* (plural) here, which we have therefore followed.

81 I.e. *comes sacrarum largitionum*, cf. *PLRE* III, Magnus 2.

82 Sebeos 68/7 also refers to an Armenian victory at Khałamakh over Mihran Mihrewandak after the recapture of Dvin, cf. Thomson and Howard-Johnston 1999: 163, placing it in late 574. The destruction of the church, combined with Roman pressure on the Armenians to enter communion with their church, strained relations between the two sides. See Garsoïan 1999: 250–62.

83 Menander frg.18.6.46–8 notes how Khusro was able to pass through Persarmenia in 576 unopposed, implying that opposition to him was a possibility, and therefore that the region was seen now as being Roman. Henceforth the Romans were able to use both Persarmenia and Iberia as bargaining-chips in their dealings with Khusro (cf. e.g. Menander frg.20.2.58–9). Toumanoff 1963: 380 and n.111 seriously overestimates the Persian grip on Persarmenia. During this period the leaders of the Armenian Church at Constantinople were pressured into communing with the Chalcedonians, thus causing divisions within Armenia. See Cowe 1991: 265–76 (on the evidence of the *Narratio*), Garsoïan 1999: 250–9, Joh. Eph. *HE* II.23.

84 On the region of P'aytakaran see Hewsen 1992: 253–5: it lay on the western side of the Caspian Sea, south of Albania and north of the Araxes (see map 21, p.67A). On Siwnik' and its often uneasy relationship with the rest of Armenia, see Garsoïan 1989: 490–1, Garsoïan 1999: 302–3 and n.19 above.

85 See Stein 1919: 38, Thomson and Howard-Johnston 1999: 162–4.

86 Turtledove 1977: 189 sees John's report as his inference from the victory of Vardan at Khałamakh (on which see above, n.82).

87 The text of Sebeos preserves two accounts of the Persian counter-attack here, the second of which is generally regarded as the more credible: see Stein 1919: 39, Thomson and Howard-Johnston 1999: 163, 166. See n.90 on the identity of the Persian commander. Some Iberians seem to have been pushed westwards by the conflict and were to be found near Amasea in 576: see below, Chapter 11 n.25.

88 The manuscript has Mzldrhmn. Adarmahan is the subject of the next few clauses.

89 Not mentioned by other sources, cf. Stein 1919: 45.

90 Thomson and Howard-Johnston 1999: 166 equate Gołon Mihran and Mihran Mihrewandak, whose campaigns in Sebeos are generally identified (n.87 above). They

also identify Theoph.'s Miranes with this general. Stein 1919: 39, 49 n.2 argued that this commander is in fact with Bahram Gushnasp (above n.57), the father of Bahram Chobin.

91 Theophanes' Saroes is Menander's Sarosius, cf. *PLRE* III, Saroes.
92 On the Dilimnites, see Chapter 8 n.24. On the Daganes see Gamzatov 1993: 568; they lived in the eastern Caucasus area (modern Dagestan).
93 Only Theophanes makes this assertion, which seems implausible. Cf. Schreiner 1985: 280 n.388.
94 This Justinian is unknown, cf. *PLRE* III, Iustinianus 1.
95 The ambassadors (said to have been forty philosophers, Mohl 1868: 521) are reported to have each brought 30,000 dinars with them – an interesting correlation with the 30,000 *solidi* agreed for the truce of 575–8.

CHAPTER 11

1 Cf. Whitby 1988: 258–9 and 268, connecting the recruitment drive with Theoph. A.M. 6074 (251.24–8). But Theoph. is more likely to be referring to a second round of recruiting in 577, cf. Stein 1919: 71–2, since he reports it in the same year as the elevation of Maurice (rather than Justinian) to the post of *magister militum per Orientem*. Joh. Bicl. a.575? (below) confirms that some forces were recruited in 574/5, however.
2 I.e. after news of the fall of Dara reached him.
3 The rest of the sentence is missing several words. Hertzsch 1884: 36 provides a restored text, the sense of which, is obscure.
4 Mich. Syr. X.9 (349a/312) offers a figure of 650 *litrē* of gold, i.e. 650 lbs, the equivalent of 46,800 *solidi (nomismata)*. Cf. Schreiner 1985: 281 n.391.
5 Stein 1919: 55 n.14, followed by Szádeczky-Kardoss 1976: 113, puts the start of the truce in mid-February 574, noting that Mich. Syr. (X.9, 349a/312) refers to a fifteen-month truce and supposing that the extra three months covered the time which had elapsed since the fall of Dara. Whitby 1988: 259 suggests that the extra three months, if Mich. Syr.'s account is to be believed, may fall at the end of the one-year truce, and argues that the truce was probably concluded in late March. This truce is also recorded by Th. Sim. III.11.3.
6 Cf. Menander frg.18.6.5–8 on the relationship between major and minor embassies.
7 Eusebius had replaced Theodore Tzirus as commander, perhaps after the fall of Dara, cf. *PLRE* III, Eusebius 7.
8 Blockley 1985b: 272–3 n.197 argues (*contra*, e.g., Stein 1919: 60) that this embassy was not that promised in frg.18.2 (since it only aimed at obtaining a further truce, rather than seeking to draw the war to a close), and that it took place in 574. His first point must be correct, since Justin had not recovered. The dating of the embassy is less clear. The following sequence of events may be proposed. First, given the brevity of the truce period, it is highly unlikely that no further diplomatic activity was initiated. Zachariah and Trajan were therefore more probably despatched late in 574 rather than in the following year. Then, in the spring, they were joined by further ambassadors, including Theodore (mentioned by Joh. Epiph. 5, below; this is also the embassy noted by Th. Sim. III.12.3). Cf. *PLRE* III, Traianus 3 and n.12 below.
9 This is based on the translation of Whitby 1988: 261 n.18. Although he correctly notes that Menander frg.18.1.1–4 implies that Menander saw Tiberius as having gained power in winter 573/4, this opening phrase may well still refer to his proclamation as Caesar in December 574. Since Zachariah and Trajan are already at the frontier by this point (and hence writing to the emperor), it is clear that they must have left Constantinople earlier in 574 (cf. Stein 1919: 60, *contra* Whitby 1988: 260–1).
10 Despite Whitby 1988: 260, following Stein 1919: 81 n.5, it is far from certain that this

raid of Tamkhusro's is to be identified with that attributed to Adarmahan by Joh. Eph. *HE* VI.13, which took place in the same area. See also n.51 below.

11   After July 575, cf. Whitby 1988: 260–2 and Stein 1919: 82 n.6. Szádeczky-Kardoss 1976: 112–13 argues for late June 575, working back from events in 578 (but his argument is completely flawed, since it relies on Brooks' mistranslation of 'three' days as 'thirty' days, on which see below, n.54).

12   Whitby 1988: 260 n.15 suggests that Theodore may have been part of the embassy of Trajan and Zachariah, while Blockley 1985b: 273–4 n.205 proposes that John may have confused his embassy with that of the other two envoys. For a simpler solution, see n.8 above. Theodore should not be identified with the ambassador sent later in 575, Theodore, son of Bacchus. *PLRE* III, Theodorus 33 identifies the two, but relies on Stein's dating of the campaign of Melitene to 575 (on which see below).

13   As is clear from *NovJ*.163 (April 575), Tiberius also bore in mind the interests of provincials, lightening tax payments by 25% for four years; he ensured, however, that military needs continued to be met. Cf. Whitby 1988: 259.

14   Menander frg.23.1.1–16 also concerns these negotiations and the raid undertaken by Tamkhusro to back up Persian demands, cf. Blockley 1985b: 281 n.269. Constantina is Menander's rendering of Constantia.

15   Joh. Bicl., a.575?.3, reports that Mundhir visited Constantinople in 575; this is accepted by Shahîd 1995: 384–9, but doubted by *PLRE* III, Alamundarus.

16   See n.12 above (and Whitby 1988: 263) on Theodore, referred to by Joh. Eph. *HE* VI.8 as a *silentiarius*. This campaign is now generally agreed to have taken place in 576, cf. Whitby 1988: 263 and Turtledove 1977: 498–9 n.92 (against Stein 1919 and *PLRE* III, who place it in 575).

17   Cf. Whitby 1988: 264. Menander also notes that the pay for the soldiers had failed to arrive on time.

18   On Khusro's route, see Blockley 1985b: 274 nn.206, 210, Honigmann 1935: 21, and Stein 1919: 82 n.7. On the (remarkably little) time allowed to Theodore, see Whitby 1988: 261.

19   The united Roman armies (of Armenia and Mesopotamia), which Joh. Eph. claims amounted to 120,000 men.

20   Stein 1919: 65 suggests that this city is Amasea, although he notes that Khusro was probably making for Caesarea rather than Helenopontus. Stein, *loc. cit.*, proposes that Khusro's line of advance was Theodosiopolis–Satala–Nicopolis–Sebastea but it is odd that no sources mention the important Roman base at Satala, where the Persians had been defeated in 530. See also Whitby 1988: 26–5.

21   Evagrius *HE* V.14 (210.4) also refers to Caesarea as the object of Khusro's attack. Stein 1919: 65 argues that it was between Sebastea and Caesarea that the Roman forces of Justinian, Curs and Vardan Mamikonian converged.

22   As is attested by the *life* of Eutychius (below).

23   The text is problematic here, cf. Brooks' translation, p.227 n.1. He suggests reading 'to the east', which makes better sense, instead of 'to a city'.

24   Although grammatically unlikely, 'They' must refer to 'The Persians'.

25   Eustratius goes on to relate how the exiled patriarch miraculously ensured that there were sufficient quantities of food for the refugees (the passage is translated in Turtledove 1977: 243–4). Stein 1919: 65 infers from this passage that the Persians launched a secondary attack on Iberia, perhaps in order to counter Curs' campaigning in the region. See also Trombley 1985: 73 on Amasea's defences.

26   Having been confronted by the more numerous and powerful army of Justinian than he had expected.

27   Stein 1919: 83 n.9 argues that Evagrius is mistakenly inserting material on Curs relating

to a victory reported by Joh. Eph. *HE* VI.28 (dated by Whitby 1988: 272 to 579). Cf. *PLRE* III, Cours.

28 Artaz lies south of Dvin; Karin is Theodosiopolis, and Bagrevand is situated between the two. See Thomson and Howard-Johnston 1999: maps 2–3.

29 The chief priest of the Zoroastrian religion.

30 Stein 1919: 83 n.9 is justly sceptical of some of Sebeos' details in this last section.

31 For a detailed account, see Stein 1919: 66–8, who considers it to have been one of the greatest Roman victories of the century. Cf. Whitby 1988: 265–6 (with Stein 1919: 83 n.9) on the various accounts of it, preferring that of Joh. Eph. to the more propagandistic and cliché-ridden versions of Evagrius (*HE* V.14 above) and Theophylact (III.14.1–11). The victory described by Joh. Eph. in *HE* VI.8 (above) is that outside Melitene, although its location is not clarified. On the decree issued by Khusro see Whitby 1994: 227–31.

32 This region was possibly called 'campus' like the Campus Martius. Cf. Honigmann 1935: 21 and n.13 (placing it on the Euphrates, outside Melitene).

33 On such interpreters see Lee 1993a: 51.

34 Literally, 'camps': cf. the use of *castra* in Latin.

35 Honigmann 1935: 22 n.3 places these mountains to the east of Bezabde, just south of Corduene (see Karte 1). Markwart 1930: 302 puts them as far north as Manzikert. As Jan van Ginkel has pointed out to us, however, Qurha must refer rather to the mountainous area to the south-east of Melitene, near Claudias, mentioned again by Joh. Eph. in *Lives of the Eastern Saints*, PO 17.229, cf. Honigmann 1935: 88–9 and idem 1939: 623. See also Whitby 1988: 266, who puts Khusro's line of retreat through Arzanene and the Hakkari mountains.

36 I.e. (Persian) Mesopotamia.

37 On this term see Schroeder 1891: 172–4, connecting it to the Lombardic Arammani (i.e. 'army men', on whom see Christie 1995: 118).

38 Campos 1960: 122 identifies this victory with the battle of Melitene. John's placing of the battle in Mesopotamia, remains a puzzle.

39 Cf. Joh. Eph. *HE* VI.10 on the many elephants captured in the wake of the Roman victory by Melitene.

40 The Greek word here, *aphraktos*, would usually imply that the city was unfortified. Yet it is clear from Proc. *de Aed.* III.4.19–20 that its fortifications were strengthened by the Emperor Justinian.

41 Theophylact's account of the battle is largely his own creation, cf. Olajos 1988: 33. His source for this section is probably Joh. Epiph. (who was in turn using Menander).

42 Cf. Joh. Eph. *HE* VI.10. Stein 1919: 68 notes the problems this invasion caused for Khusro, requiring him to maintain forces on home territory, something to which the Persians were not accustomed (cf. e.g. Greatrex 1998a: 59).

43 See Stein 1919: 69 on this event, which followed the Roman victory at Melitene. *PLRE* III, Romanus 4, puts this event in late 575/early 576, relying, however, on Stein's placing of the battle of Melitene in 575. Following Whitby's chronology, Romanus' success must have occurred in late 576 or early 577.

44 The extent of the difficulties experienced by the Persians at this time may be gauged firstly from the mutiny among Khusro's soldiers (Th. Sim. III.15.3–4) and secondly from the report of a certain Asterius, a Roman captive in Persia, who advised his compatriots to exploit the Persian weakness (Menander frg.20.1.19–23). See also Rubin 1995: 292–3 on the general problems affecting the Sasanian state in this period.

45 Joh. Eph. *HE* VI.12 (cf. II.24) says that the negotiations went on for over a year; hence it is likely that this stage of negotiations was not reached until early 577. The closeness of the versions of Joh. Eph. and Menander here might be attributed to use of a common source, probably the account of one of the ambassadors; cf. Lee 1993a: 38–9.

46 Cf. Joh. Eph. *HE* VI.12 (307) for the same line of argument.

47 Basean is the region east of Theodosiopolis. On Bagrevand, see above n.28. The precise location of the two places is uncertain, but cf. Thompson and Howard-Johnston 1999: 166 (with map 3, where Bolorapahak is located just south-east of Theodosiopolis).

48 Cf. Turtledove 1977: 265 connecting Sebeos' account here with the account of Roman defeats in Th. Sim. (below) and Joh. Eph. *HE* VI.10.

49 Cf. Menander frg.20.2.79–149 (reporting that secret discussions concerning the return of Dara continued nevertheless, in which Mahbodh sought to outwit Zachariah, and the future Maurice played a role), Joh. Eph. *HE* VI.10 with Whitby 1988: 267.

50 According to Joh. Eph., Khusro undertook to treat the Armenians well. Stein 1919: 63 notes that already in 576 Khusro's invasion had received the support of some Armenians (Menander frg.18.6.48–52).

51 This episode is problematic. Its context in Joh. Eph. is clear: the raid is undertaken in response to the breakdown of negotiations in 577 (for the date see above n.45). The three-year truce in Mesopotamia should still have been in effect, but the Persians had had recourse to a similar raid during negotiations (and perhaps a period of truce) in 575 (cf. Menander frg. 18.4, above). Menander's reference at frg.23.1.26 to the breaking of the truce 40 days early in 578 does not tell against such a raid in 577, which was a different matter from the much larger invasion of the following year. Whitby 1988: 260 and n.16 (cf. Stein 1919: 61, 81 n.5), however, believes that John is referring to events of 575, although there is no mention of a raid by Adarmahan in other sources at this point; *contra* Whitby, *loc. cit.*, the mention of Justinian as general in Joh. Eph. does not settle the issue, since he was *magister militum* from 574/5 to (late) 577, and at the time of the raid will probably have been returning from his campaigns further north (on which see p.160 above). *PLRE* III, Adarmaanes, dates this raid to 577/8, cf. Turtledove 1977: 273–4 (577).

52 Whitby 1988: 268, accepts the statement of Joh. Eph. *HE* VI.27 (where the manuscript actually refers to Constantine, son of Germanus, rather than Justinian) that Justinian had died not long before, a claim doubted by *PLRE* III, Iustinianus 3. Cf. also Whitby 1995: 89 and n.121. Maurice was *comes excubitorum* and perhaps also *comes foederatorum*, as well as *magister militum*, cf. *PLRE* III, Mauricius 4.

53 Maurice also received some reinforcements from the Balkans, Theoph. A.M. 6074 (251.24–8), with Stein 1919: 71–2. Theoph. gives a figure of 15,000 *Tiberiani*, a more credible total than Evagrius' 150,000 (cf. Stein 1919: 85 n.15). Stein, *loc. cit.*, puts Maurice's stay in Citharizon in April–June (578).

54 Brooks wrongly translates the Syriac word *talata* (310.27 and 331.12 in the Syriac text) as thirty rather than three (referring to the length of time Tamkhusro besieged Amida). The operation of Tamkhusro is identified by many with the attack of Adarmahan noted above (see n.51); certainly both raids struck the same area (which was hit also in 575 [by Tamkhusro] and 581 [by Adarmahan]). There is no reason to conflate the raids of 577 and 578 because they affected the same region.

55 Cf. Whitby 1988: 269–70, noting also that the bishop of Chlomaron may well have been Isho-Yab, the future *catholicos* of the Persian Church, and a faithful servant of Persian interests. The captives from Arzanene were settled on Cyprus, ibid.: 269 and n.38. For possible evidence of these deportees there see Olson 1976. Aphumon is rightly placed by Whitby 1983: 208 on the west bank of the river Redwan, opposite Chlomaron. See also Honigmann 1935: 23 on the geography of this campaign.

56 Agathias is referring to the time of his death. Szádeczky-Kardoss 1976: 111–12 puts Khusro's flight in mid-July.

57 I.e. Thamnon/Thamanon in Corduene. On its location see Honigmann 1935: 23 and Karte 1, Talbert 2000: 89 E3.

58 Khusro was therefore obliged to flee precipitately to Ctesiphon, according to Agathias. The Zirma is the Bohtan Su (Talbert 2000: 89 D3).

59   As Whitby and Whitby 1986: 97 n.73 note, this refers to Beth Arabaye. Shahîd 1995: 396–7 argues that the Jafnids were involved in this attack. Menander frg. 23.5 (the evacuation of Thannuris by the Persians) probably concerns part of the Persian reaction to this incursion.

60   I.e. late 578. The attack of Curs and Romanus was directed against Adiabene, as Stein 1919: 75 notes.

61   *PLRE* III, Theodorus 36, Stein 1919: 87–8.

62   Justin II died on 4 or 5 October, cf. *PLRE* III, Iustinus 5.

63   Arzanene had been Persian territory since 363, and the fact that Tiberius was now proposing to hand it over to the Persians, in addition to Persarmenia and Iberia, indicates just how the frontiers of the Roman empire were expanding north of Mesopotamia.

64   Cf. Blockley 1992: 152–3 on the distinction between major and minor embassies between Rome and Persia.

65   This entry comes just after the death of Justin II (in October 578).

66   Prentice 1922: 60–1 (no.947) records an inscription from Stabl 'Anbar, north-east of Epiphaneia, dated 578/9, which Whitby 1988: 267–8 and n.33 connects with Tiberius' wider efforts to bolster the Roman position in the East.

67   As Whitby 1988: 271 notes, the year 579 was thus taken up with the time spent by the ambassadors at Hormizd's court and in their difficult journey back to Constantinople, cf. Stein 1919: 91 and Turtledove 1977: 288. The Roman acceptance of an impostor claiming to be a son of Khusro, reported by Joh. Eph. *HE* VI.29, may have helped to determine Hormizd's reaction to the embassy. See Mosig-Walburg 2000: 71–2 on the episode. According to Menander, the Persians needed time to raise more troops; Beth Arabaye in particular was suffering as a result both of the Roman invasion and of a plague of locusts. Blockley 1985b: 283 n.291 argues that Menander frg.23.10 refers to campaigning in 579, but the passage is too brief to allow certainty.

68   Whitby 1988: 272 places the construction of Shemkhart in Sophanene in this year, but Joh. Eph. *HE* VI.35 clearly dates it to after Maurice had been in Persia, most probably in 582 (cf. Stein 1919: 97 and van Ginkel 1995: 77 n.46). The year was probably spent (perhaps like 529) in restoring discipline among the troops (Menander frg. 23.3); Menander (frg.23.9.124–5) also notes how the morale of the Roman forces was boosted by the arrival of their pay.

69   Turtledove 1977: 303–4 and Whitby 1988: 272 date both Sebeos' reference to Varaz Vzur (accorded both a defeat and a victory) and Joh. Eph.'s to 579. Cf. Thomson and Howard-Johnston 1999: 166. Stein 1919: 97–8, however, puts Varaz Vzur's defeat in 578 and Curs' victory in 579. *Contra* Stein 1919: 83 n.9 there seems no need to connect Evagr. *HE* V.14 (on Curs' exploits at Melitene) with this battle. Joh. Eph. *HE* VI.28 notes discontent in the Roman army in Armenia at this time over the non-payment of wages, cf. Whitby 1995: 90–1 and n.129; according to Joh. Eph., Tiberius rectified the problem by the prompt despatch of Domentziolus to the front with funds. This may be connected with Menander's reference to the arrival of pay (n.68 above).

70   Another (Iranian) tradition was more hostile, as is clear from Tabari, I, 990/297–8 (Nöldeke 265) and Th. Sim. III.16.7–13, cf. Frendo 1989: 78–80.

71   Tabari is here reporting a written reply of Hormizd to the Zoroastrian priests, who had urged him to persecute the Christians.

72   Although Joh. Bicl. ?a.580, 216.1–2, may well also refer to these events (especially since Maurice's accession is correctly dated to 582). According to him Maurice wintered in Persian territory after his successes.

73   Cf. Whitby 1988: 272–3. As he notes, Maurice's aim was probably to capture Ctesiphon; he may also have wished to link up with the Romans living nearby at Khusro's Antioch (see Chapter 7, p.107 above), cf. Joh. Eph. *HE* VI.19. Shahîd 1995: 418–21 argues that Mundhir did return to Roman territory with Maurice, cf. ibid. 439–55 for a critique of

the Roman sources' accounts of Mundhir's treachery. Goubert 1950: 107–8, on the other hand, believes the accusations against Mundhir to have substance.

74 At III.40 John is more forthright, asserting that Maurice certainly did bring accusations against Mundhir, which led Tiberius to plot against him.

75 Whitby 1988: 272–3 is highly sceptical of John's account, rightly seeing in it an attempt to defend Mundhir's reputation. He also doubts (273 n.49) whether the mention of Mundhir's camp (*hirtha*) should be interpreted as a reference to Hira rather than just to a temporary camp, cf. Shahîd 1995: 420–5.

76 Mich. Syr. X.20 (376b/353–4) offers a few more details on this incursion.

77 Stein 1919: 93 believes that there was indeed a battle, but Joh. Eph.'s account (above) implies otherwise, cf. Turtledove 1977: 313 and Shahîd 1995: 416.

78 On the Qartmin monastery see Palmer 1990. It lies 40 km north-east of Nisibis, Talbert 2000: 89 D3.

79 As Whitby 1988: 273 n.48 notes, this entry is one year out. The *Chr. 1234* entry clearly shows that this passage refers to the events of 581.

80 Cf. *PLRE* III, Theodericus 2, suggesting that Theoderic was *comes foederatorum*. Shahîd 1995: 415 believes that Theoderic's rout was the result of Lakhmid attacks during the Roman retreat. Evagrius' passage is too unclear to allow certainty.

81 Cf. Whitby 1988: 273, following Stein 1919: 98, who tentatively identifies Menander's fragment with Sebeos (71/11–12), reporting a victory by the 'great Parthian and Pahlaw *aspet*' (tr. Thomson) at Shirak. See also Blockley 1985b: 283 n.292.

82 Mundhir and Nu'man stood trial in Constantinople; the former was exiled to Sicily, the latter sentenced to death but spared. See Shahîd 1995: 529–49, Goubert 1950: 109–16 and below.

83 Among the participants in the negotiations were the bishops of Nisibis and Resaina, according to Joh. Eph. Whitby 1988: 274 dates the discussions to winter 581/2.

84 See Whitby 1988: 272 (with *PLRE* III, Cours) on Shemkhart, in western Arzanene (Joh. Eph. *HE* VI.35), with Whitby 1983a: 208–9 (against Honigmann's placing of the fort in eastern Sophanene, followed by Talbert 2000: 89 D2). See also n.68 above on the dating of this episode.

85 Evagr. *HE* V.20 mentions the presence of Adarmahan in Tamkhusro's army, cf. *PLRE* III, Adarmaanes (putting the battle in 581, however). Maurice had been improving the defences of Monocarton too, cf. Stein 1919: 97 (dating the work to 582). The location of Monocarton is not entirely clear, but it evidently lay not far to the east of Constantia, cf. Whitby 1988: 270 n.40. Talbert 2000: 89 C3 places it 75 km east of Constantia. Tamkhusro must have bypassed the fortress in his drive westwards towards Constantia.

86 The Persians remained encamped on the river Beth Washe, cf. Honigmann 1935: 24, *idem* 1939: 624 and Dillemann 1962: 290, 292. As Whitby notes, Maurice may no longer have been in the East by this point: on 5 August he was proclaimed Caesar in Constantinople. Honigmann 1935: 24 claims that Monocarton was renamed Tiberiopolis following this defeat, but there is no evidence as to when the name was changed.

CHAPTER 12

1 Th. Sim. was in turn used by Theophanes as his source for these events, and his relevant entries are therefore omitted from consideration here.

2 John's former fellow commander Curs may have held aloof from the battle from jealousy at John's promotion. Olajos 1988: 36 regards Joh. Epiph. as Theophylact's source here. Kardarigan is in fact a Persian title, rather than a name, as Th. Sim. I.9.6 notes; cf. Schreiner 1985: 251 n.128.

3 For the location of Aphumon, see Chapter 11 n.55. For Akbas see Dillemann 1963: 232,

Talbert 2000: 89 D2. Schreiner 1985: 256 nn.163–4 places the attack on Akbas in late 582 (but see Whitby 1988: 285). He also identifies the initial failure to take Akbas with a reference made in Maurice's *Stratēgikon* (X.1, 337) to the surprising of a Roman force left in charge of a siege in Arzanene. Mich. Syr. X.21 (379b/360–1) relates that the Persians subsequently forced some defeated Romans into rebuilding the fort; Whitby 1988: 278 n.3 argues that this took place in 588/9. On this section of Mich. Syr. and its relationship to Joh. Eph., see Marquart 1903: 480–6; see also van Ginkel 1998 on the dangers of trying to reconstruct Joh. Eph.'s work from Michael's.

4 The opening few sentences of Joh. Eph. *HE* VI.37 place the sending of a Persian ambassador to Maurice at the same time as the Roman capture of Akbas, i.e. late summer 583 (AG 894). The Roman embassy which responded may be that reported in the Georgian account of the *Life of Golinduch,* cf. Garitte 1956: 430 (translation) and 409–10. The *Life* names Aristobulus as the Roman ambassador, and claims that he visited Golinduch in the Prison of Oblivion.

5 Cf. Whitby 1988: 278–9. As he notes, Theophylact has probably given two accounts of the same attack by Philippicus (drawn from different sources). The geography of this campaign is problematic, cf. Whitby and Whitby 1986: 39 n.72. Carcharoman should not necessarily be situated where Talbert 2000: 89 C3 places it. On Evagrius' account see Allen 1981: 248.

6 Whitby 1988: 289 associates this chapter with Roman successes in 588. But although Joh. Eph. was certainly still alive then (cf. van Ginkel 1995: 71–2), he can only have been adding to his chronicle year by year; since subsequent chapters refer to events earlier in the 580s, it is preferable to date this episode to the context which fits chronologically. See also van Ginkel 1995: 77, 84.

7 See Shahîd 1995: 541–9 (noting other sources on this episode), dating (542, 548) this division to 584; cf. Sartre 1982a: 191–2. Although some Jafnids still served with the Romans, there was no longer any chief phylarch, and hence the term 'dissolution' is not inappropriate (*contra* Shahîd 1995: 549, who also puts Joh. Eph.'s death too early).

8 Whitby ascribes the inactivity of the Romans to the need to deal with attacks by rebellious Jafnids, but a failure of Philippicus' deputies to co-ordinate their attacks is more likely (cf. operations in the same area in 503, Greatrex 1998a: 96–101).

9 For this chronology see Whitby 1988: 285.

10 Cf. Whitby 1988: 280–1 and n.7. For Mambrathon see Talbert 2000: 89 C3; Bibas lies south of Mardin on the Arzamon river, cf. Whitby and Whitby 1986: 242.

11 See Dillemann 1962: 65–6 and fig.9, p.73, on the aridity of this area. The Roman camp, as Whitby 1988: 281 states, was probably east of the river Arzamon and just south of the Tur Abdin. A likely place (see the map in Dillemann 1962: 293) might be Apadna.

12 Cf. Olajos 1988: 39–40, who argues that Th. Sim. used the campaign journal indirectly, through the account of Joh. Epiph. Whitby and Whitby 1986: 46 n.7 on the Heraclius source, cf. Whitby 1988: 230–3 (doubted by Olajos 1988: 43 n.135 and 149 n.668). See also Shahîd 1995: 550–2 on the two phylarchs involved in the capture of the Persians; one he identifies as a Jafnid or Kindite, the other as a Salihid.

13 The word used by Joh. Eph. *HE* for 'third' is the Syriac *tryt* (Greek *tritos*), which has been identified with an indiction year (year 3, which would be 584/5). If this, like other dates in Joh. Eph., is one year too early, it could well be a reference to the battle of Solachon (which also fits with the stress on God's involvement). See Whitby 1988: 247, 285 (preferring a later date) and n.6 above.

14 Evagr. *HE* I.13 tells us also that Philippicus sent for the head of Symeon the Stylite (the Elder) from Antioch to help his troops.

15 Whitby and Whitby 1986: 54 n.20 rightly stress that Th. Sim. probably exaggerates Philippicus' difficulties here, cf. Whitby 1988: 282. We intend to discuss elsewhere the location of Phathacon and Alaleisus, the forts strengthened by Philippicus.

16 Whitby 1988: 284 plausibly reconstructs Heraclius' movements. See Chapter 11 n.57 above on the location of Thamnon/Thamanon. Schreiner 1985: 263 n.237 needlessly doubts this reference and thinks Theophylact must be referring to a place in Roman territory near Cephas.

17 Cf. *PLRE* III, Theodorus 32 and Andreas 11 on the the two last commanders named. Andrew is described as an interpreter for the Arab tribes allied with Rome (cf. Shahîd 1995: 552–4, who rightly prefers to translate Th. Sim.'s *hermēneus* as 'interpreter' rather than 'intermediary').

18 Cf. Whitby 1988: 284. He correctly rejects Dillemann's identification of the fort captured by Heraclius with Cephas (Dillemann 1962: 228–9). On the location of Matzaron and Beiuades, see Dillemann 1962: 227 fig.31 with 230–1 and now Talbert 2000: 89 C–D3. Olajos 1988: 45 considers that Th. Sim. (following Joh. Epiph.) derived his material for this year largely from reports by participants (rather than an official campaign account). It may have been in this (otherwise fairly inactive) year that Domitian, the bishop of Melitene and a relative of Maurice, was sent on an embassy to Persia to negotiate a truce, if the Georgian account of the martyrdom of Golinduch is credited (ch.17 in Garitte 1956: 438, cf. 415). According to the *Life* of Golinduch, Domitian was dissuaded from continuing on his mission after meeting Golinduch at Hierapolis, who informed him that Hormizd would shortly be overthrown in any case. Sako 1986: 103–7 places an embassy of the *catholicos* Isho-Yab to Maurice in this year too.

19 See Allen 1981: 248 and Whitby 1988: 286–7 on Maurice's measures. Note that Hormizd too reduced soldiers' pay, cf. Whitby and Whitby 1986: 102 n.91 (on Th. Sim. III.16.13). On the accounts of the mutiny see Krivouchine 1993.

20 *PLRE* III, Germanus 6 for a good discussion of the identity of this Germanus. Th. Sim. appears to regard him as the bishop of Damascus, but there is probably a lacuna in the text. See also Whitby and Whitby 1986: 72 n.3, Mango and Scott 1997: 384 n.28.

21 It must be assumed that most of the Roman forces which had been assembled at Monocarton had therefore gone with Germanus towards Edessa, leaving the frontier region almost devoid of troops. Philippicus would have had to take a round-about route to reach Monocarton without passing through Edessa.

22 Th. Sim. indicates that 3000 Persians were captured and 1000 escaped; presumably about another 1000 will have been killed; Evagrius states that not a single Persian survived. It would appear that these were small-scale operations (cf. Th. Sim. III.3.10, where Germanus sends a force to invade Persian territory which is only 4000 strong). Whitby 1988: 289 associates Joh. Eph. *HE* VI.43 with this victory.

23 On the prison see Whitby and Whitby 1986: 77 n.16 and Kettenhoffen 1988 (placing the prison near Gundeshapur in Khuzistan, rather than Media). Cf. also Mundell 1974: 226. Whitby 1983b: 329–30 suggests that Th. Sim. and Theoph. derive their material here from a common chronicle source. Schreiner 1985: 273 n.326 rightly places this event in 588 (cf. Th. Sim. III.5.8). It is also mentioned in the *Life of Golinduch* by Eustratius (composed in 602), §9 (p.156); cf. Peeters 1944: 82.

24 Note Evagr. *HE* VI.10 for the link between the ongoing war in the East and the absence of sufficient Roman troops in the Balkans (with Allen 1981: 254).

25 Cf. Higgins 1939: 33 for the chronology. Worthy of note is Evagrius' mention that Gregory had provided the equipment for some of the Roman forces (and hence was well placed to mediate), on which see Whitby 1995: 82. Evagr. *HE* VI.10 mentions a further unsuccessful attempt to effect a reconciliation before Gregory's, led by Andrew, Maurice's chief bodyguard; cf. Allen 1981: 252–3, *PLRE* III, Andreas 12, Whitby 1988: 289.

26 As Higgins 1939: 34 notes, Evagrius extends the siege of Martyropolis for far too long; ibid. 46–7 for a plausible explanation of Evagr.'s error, placing the battle in July. Higgins

1939: 34 also suggests that this battle is that reported by Sebeos 71/12 (at Nisibis), although it is placed by Sebeos before the engagement at Tsalkajur (p.170 above).

27 Cf. Whitby and Whitby 1986: 79 n.24, Whitby 1988: 289–90 and Higgins 1939: 39–40 (placing the battle after August). See also Olajos 1988: 50 on the differing accounts of this battle (suggesting that Th. Sim. here consciously departs from his main source, Joh. Epiph.). A (late) Georgian chronicle translated by van Esbroeck 1976: 90, §41, attributes the victory to Comentiolus and states that the Persians fled to Nisibis.

28 Toumanoff believes that Maurice's offensive of 582 restored some Roman control to 'Armenia', but it is clear that by now Persarmenia at least had reverted to Persian control. Otherwise Khusro II would not have been able to offer these territories to Maurice in 590 (see below).

29 Principalities in western Iberia, on which see Hewsen 1992: 134 nn.22, 27 and map 22, p.68.

30 On the ancestry of Guaram, see Toumanoff 1963: 379 n.105; ibid. 383 and n.5 on the chronology. See also Whitby 1988: 290–1. Guaram's son Stephen I sided with the Persians, however: see p.179 below.

31 As Whitby notes, Romanus must have been appointed to his command before Bahram turned against Suania. Olajos 1988: 46 n.150 makes the interesting suggestion that Bahram invaded Siunia (Siwnik') rather than Suania. See Schreiner 1985: 276 n.351 on the location of the Roman victory (the plains by the Araxes). On Bahram's revolt see also Schippmann 1990: 61–2, Frendo 1989: 80–2 (using *Chr. Seert* 43, *PO* 13.443), Shahbazi 1989.

32 Frendo 1989: 81–4 considers these events in detail and suggests that Khusro may have fled to Azerbaijan in late 589 before returning to Ctesiphon in early 590 to replace his father; see also Winter 1989: 79–91. Worthy of note is Khusro's use of a certain Jafna, a Christian Arab general who was subject to the Romans, as an intermediary (*Chr. 1234*, 80 [215–16/115], Agap. *PO* 8.442); Jafna was probably a Jafnid ruler, and thus it appears that despite Maurice's dissolution of the Jafnid federation, some members of the tribe remained loyal. See Shahîd 1995: 556–60, *PLRE* III, Jafnah.

33 Theophylact adds, however, that Khusro sent a subsequent message, urging the defenders not to surrender. As Olajos 1988: 56 and n.203 (cf. 62) notes, this must be his own addition, since Joh. Epiph. is not likely to have recorded such duplicity. Joh. Epiph. is the prime source of Th. Sim. for all these events, but Th. Sim. occasionally slants the account against Khusro (Olajos 1988: 54–5, 58–60).

34 Th. Sim. IV.13.3 puts the despatch of the embassy in spring, but Whitby 1988: 298 rightly thinks summer more probable (cf. Higgins 1939: 43–5).

35 I.e. Beth Arabaye, cf. Honigmann 1935: 29.

36 I.e. Persarmenia. See Adontz 1970: 180–2.

37 The lake of Bzunik' is Lake Van. Arestawan is a district at the north-west tip of Lake Van. See Hewsen 1992: 166, 186 and map 18, p.66.

38 See n.54 below on the new frontier agreed.

39 On the Armenian role in Khusro's restoration, see Garitte 1952: 234–5, Grousset 1947: 250–1 and below n.88.

40 Cf. Honigmann 1935: 29 on this passage, with n.54 below.

41 E.g. from the patriarch of Constantinople, John the Faster, cf. Joh. Nik. 96.10–13 and Sebeos 76/19 with Whitby 1988: 299, Peeters 1947: 12 and Paret 1957: 46–7.

42 *Chr. 1234* 80–1 (216/115), 87 (221–3/122–4), has Khusro visit Edessa before Hierapolis (albeit in a somewhat anecdotal account). Peeters 1947: 16 n.1 is sceptical on this tradition, but it is accepted by Segal 1970: 114 n.1. The story of Maurice giving one of his daughters, named Maria, to Khusro in marriage, reported in Tabari (994/305, cf. 999/312, Nöldeke 283) and *Chr. 1234*, 81 (217/117) (cf. Mich. Syr. X.23 [387a/372]), is extremely doubtful and most probably an elaboration of the fact that Khusro had a

Christian wife, Shirin (see below). See Goubert 1951: 179–82, Flusin 1992: II, 103 n.43, *PLRE* III, Maria 6 and Bosworth 1999: 312 n.729.

43 He also offered significant concessions to the Armenians in order to win their support, according to Sebeos 77–8/20–1, cf. Frendo 1989: 84–5. Thomson and Howard-Johnston 1999: 173 note that Sebeos places this offer after Khusro's invasion of Persia.

44 See Higgins 1939: 42–5, putting the final decision to offer full support to Khusro only in November or December 590.

45 According to Mich. Syr. X.23 (387a/117 n.267) Resaina too was restored to the Romans, although in 589 the city was still in Roman hands (cf. Theoph. Sim. III.6.1 with Whitby 1988: 290) and it is difficult to see how the Persians could have captured it since then.

46 Mango 1985: 101 suggests that Khusro refers to Martyropolis as Nekra (cf. Sinclair 1994–5: 231 n.64, deriving Nekra from the Syriac Maipherqat).

47 Cf. Mango 1985: 100 n.36 (noting parallels).

48 Cf. Whitby 1988: 297. As he notes, it was doubtless for this reason that Khusro had wanted to be accompanied by the patriarch Isho-Yab in his flight to Roman territory (*Chr. Khuz.*, 16).

49 *Chr. 1234* refers to 20,000 men under John (Mystacon), described anachronistically as 'the general of the Thracian division' and to 20,000 under Anastasius (an error for Narses, cf. *PLRE* III, Narses 10). It also refers to the sum of 40 *centenaria* (= 4000 Roman lbs). Zatsparham is Theophylact's Zadesprates, Zadespras in *PLRE* III.

50 Th. Sim. V.3.11, cf. Evagr. *HE* VI.17 (234.11) and Th. Sim. IV.11.11 (Khusro's first missive to Maurice, in which he calls himself the emperor's son); also *Chr. 1234*, 81 (217/117). See Garsoïan 1983: 578–9 and note the uncertainty such a step had occasioned in the 520s: see Chapter 5 n.53 above. In Dara, Khusro took up residence in the (Great) Church, a move which caused great offence (Th. Sim. V.3.4–7), and therefore soon moved out. See Key Fowden 1999: 165–7 for an attempt to explain Khusro's actions, arguing that it 'was a ritual gesture of power' familiar in Iran, but unacceptable to Christians.

51 See also *Chr. 1234*, 81 (216–17/116–17). Riedlberger 1998: 161–73 offers a detailed reconstruction of the campaign, placing the final victory in Azerbaijan (p.172) in early August 591 (p.165); cf. also Minorsky 1943–6: 243–8, Thomson and Howard-Johnston 1999: 173. Frendo 1995: 209–11 compares Th. Sim.'s account to the romanticised version of events in Firdausi. Despite Th. Sim. V.11.7–8, other sources, such as *Chr. 1234, loc. cit.*, Tabari 999–1000 (Nöldeke 287), and Sebeos (80/24), report that Khusro's Roman allies did receive payment from the king; cf. Whitby 1988: 303 and Garitte 1952: 238.

52 Cf. Whitby and Whitby 1986: 153 n.77 for the continuing rebellion. Bahram fled to the Turks, but Khusro succeeded in engineering his murder at the Turkish court; see Tabari 1001/315–16 (Nöldeke 289).

53 As Whitby 1988: 304 notes, Theophylact is a little misleading here, since the Romans gained a considerable amount of territory by the peace (see above). No money, however, changed hands, and thus he refers to 'equal terms' (cf. Menander, frg. 20.2.33, 79, *ex isotimias*; Th. Sim. has *en isē moira* here). Tabari too (999/313, Nöldeke 284) notes the cessation of Roman payments.

54 Cf. Sebeos 76/18–19, p.172 above, for some comments. On this passage see the notes of Thomson and Howard-Johnston 1999: 28 (with map 3) and Garsoïan 1999: 264–7. The reference to the river Hurazdan is incorrect: the frontier lay rather on the Azat (cf. the *Narratio* with Garitte 1952: 236–7 and van Esbroeck 1983: 185–6). Cf. Yovhannes Katʻołikos 16 (67–8/94) on the frontier change (independent of Sebeos but less accurate). See also Goubert 1951: 290–5 and Honigmann 1935: 29–30, who argues that much of the territory acquired by the Romans was not integrated fully into the empire.

55 See Hewsen 1992: 18–25 for a thorough treatment of the new provinces (with excellent

maps). Honigmann 1935: 30–7 argued that Arzanene remained Persian and that the border did not change from that of 363, but Hewsen, *loc. cit.* rightly argues for Arzanene's inclusion among Roman territories. See also Schreiner 1985: 302 n.590. The extension of Armenia IV southwards, to include Amida, clearly will have had an impact on the command structure of the frontier, presumably reducing the area under the control of the *magister militum per Orientem.*

56 Olajos 1988: 69 and n.273 and Peeters 1944: 91 on the date of composition of Eustratius' work. It is derived from, but less complete than, the Georgian account of Golinduch's life, cf. Garitte 1956: 420–3. Eustratius was from Melitene and his work tends to highlight the role of Domitian, bishop of Melitene, cf. Peeters 1944: 81 and Garitte 1956: 414, 416.

57 Or, translating the seventeenth-century manuscript noted by Papadopoulos-Kerameus in 1898, 'Thus these things were in this condition'.

58 We here translate *basileus* as king (rather than emperor) in order to fit in with the biblical allusions. The king is Maurice, the priest is Domitian, cf. Peeters 1944: 90.

59 The reference is (again) to Maurice and Domitian. Cf. Th. Sim. VIII.11 for a somewhat hagiographical account of Maurice, with Whitby and Whitby 1986: 227 n.64 (noting the existence of a Syriac hagiography of the emperor) and Olajos 1988: 149 n.668.

60 Golinduch was actually martyred under king Hormizd but (it was said) restored to life by an angel, cf. Garitte 1956: 411–12.

61 Golinduch refused the offer and died soon afterwards (13 July 591), cf. Peeters 1944: 91. The reference to the peace is thus a little premature.

62 Bindoes and Bestam were uncles of Khusro; they had helped unseat Hormizd, and had backed Khusro against Bahram. See *PLRE* III, Bindoes, Bistam (dating the start of the latter's rebellion to 594), Nöldeke 1879: 479–87, dating it to 591/2. Goubert 1951: 283–7 argues for a ten-year uprising, from 591 to 601, cf. H-iggins 1947: 225–30. Thomson and Howard-Johnston 1999: 179–81 place the rising in 594/5, while Bosworth 1999: 316 n.740 prefers 590–6 for the duration of the rebellion.

63 Higgins 1955: 90 for the chronology (although Allen 1981: 264 suggests October 591 for the dedication). Higgins (92–8) convincingly explains the minor divergences between the two sources by arguing that Evagius was using the text of the inscriptions, while Theophylact was using that of the letters on which the inscriptions were based. Cf. Olajos 1988: 83–9, Allen 1981: 261, 265–6; *contra*, Peeters 1947.

64 Some manuscripts have 'son of Hormizd', which is correct. But it is clear (cf. below) that Khusro wishes to claim to be the son of Khusro I. Cf. Peeters 1947: 19 and Schreiner 1985: 317 n.757.

65 Khusro's text consists almost entirely of two extremely long sentences, the first of which begins 'when' and does not end until the phrase 'a jewelled golden cross to his home'. We have therefore broken up the sentences somewhat for clarity.

66 The Greek here is 'Romania', an increasingly common term for the Roman empire in late antiquity.

67 Peeters 1947: 21–2 draws attention to the Greek word, *kaballarioi*, used here, arguing that it implies use of heavy cavalry. Cf. Flusin 1992: II, 224 n.17.

68 Peeters 1944: 121 (cf. *idem* 1947: 25) suggests that Khusro met Golinduch at Circesium, and that it was she who told him of St Sergius. See also Garitte 1956: 415–16 and the Georgian *Life of Golinduch*, ch.17.8–11, p.438.

69 Higgins 1955: 97 suggests that Khusro may have written 'second year', which would be correct by Sasanian usage, but was corrected by our sources.

70 Theophylact just refers to 'the cross', 213.14; cf. Higgins 1955: 93, 95 for an explanation.

71 Cf. p.134 above on Ahudemmeh and p.162 on Hormizd.

72 Dated to 591 by Allen 1981: 261, cf. Higgins 1955: 91–2 (placing it after Khusro's first offerings to Sergius).
73 Cf. *PLRE* III, Domitianus. Maurice had been intransigent towards the opponents of Chalcedon from the outset, cf. Frend 1972: 332; on Domitian's persecutions, ibid. 334 and Paret 1957: 51–2. But, as van Ginkel 1998: 356 warns, Mich. Syr. has a tendency to play up persecution of Monophysites and his account must be treated with caution.
74 See p.186 below.
75 Higgins 1955: 90 for the chronology, putting the donation earlier, in mid-593; we follow Allen 1981: 264. See n.62 above on the differences between the two sources. Khusro reports in the inscription that Sergius had informed him of his wife's conception.
76 Flusin 1992: II, 99–101 suggests that Khusro II was merely acting in accordance with the treaty of 562 in tolerating Christians (as Tabari says). Goubert 1951: 173–5 and Allen 1981: 265 n.100 on the legends of Khusro's conversion.
77 Whitby and Whitby 1986: 209 n.1 place this mission 'towards the end of Maurice's reign', cf. Olajos 1988: 172 and *PLRE* III, Georgius 14. But Goubert 1951: 287–9 argues in detail for a date before 595, probably 592, which should be preferred. Olajos 1988: 126, 144, 151, attributes Th. Sim.'s information here either to an oral report or the ambassador's account itself. Joh. Epiph.'s introduction (tr. below) also probably alludes to this embassy (and he died in 594), cf. Schreiner 1985: 353 n.1055 and Higgins 1947: 220–2. Higgins 1947: 222–3 identifies this mission of George with a mission of George and Narses referred to in the *V. Sabrisho*, 303–4 (summary in Braun 1900: 278). Rothstein 1899: 112, cf. Nöldeke 1887: 39 notes a reference in a later Arabic source to a raid of the Jafnids on Lakhmid territory during the reign of Nu'man, which they connect with Th. Sim.'s passage.
78 Referring to Bestam's continuing revolt, cf. n.61 above with Schreiner 1985: 353 n.1058.
79 Or perhaps 'gaining the alliance of the moment', if de Boor's suggestion of *symmakhian* for *symmakhon* (which reads oddly with the feminine article) is accepted.
80 *Iliad* IV.43.
81 Hertzsch 1884: 36, like Müller in his edition, supposed that the name George was an error for Gregory. But since a mission of George is securely attested (above), there is no need to change the text.
82 See Sako 1986: 108–13, Tamcke 1988: 30 and Whitby and Whitby 1986: 154 nn.82–3 on these events. Frendo 1992: 66 n.39 prefers to date Probus' mission to 593 and to dissociate it from that reported in the eastern sources.
83 The date for the letter must be between Sabrisho's election (596) and Maurice's fall (602).
84 Sako 1986: 114 places the uprising in 599 (but without argument for the date), while Whitby and Whitby 1986: 234 n.91 assign it to 602 (offering no grounds); see Labourt 1904: 214–17 on the disputes involved. The revolt must have taken place between 596 and 602 at any rate, and *Chr. Seert* puts it in the month of May, precisely one year after Gregory left. Tamcke 1988: 38 argues for a date of (May) 599 at the earliest. On the prominence of Christians in Khusro's service see Flusin 1992: II, 104.
85 For a good assessment of this period, see Howard-Johnston and Thomson 1999: xx–xxii.
86 On Mushel see Goubert 1951: 191–7 with *PLRE* III, Mushegh Mamikonian; he died fighting in the Balkans, perhaps in 594 (so *PLRE*). On the Armenian role in Khusro's restoration, see Thomson and Howard-Johnston 1999: 173.
87 Whether this implies that Corduene was now part of Roman territory is uncertain, cf. Honigmann 1935: 30–1 (doubtful) and Grousset 1947: 252.
88 Cf. Grousset 1947: 261–4, Thomson and Howard-Johnston 1999: 181.
89 The Roman violation of the frontier is important, as Goubert notes.
90 Maurice's attempt to win over the Armenians to allegiance to Chalcedon was similarly

unsuccessful, cf. Garitte 1952: 225–31 (analysing all the sources in detail), Garsoïan 1999: 267–8.

91   On the date of the work, see Whitby 1988: 242 and n.3 above.

92   We refrain from noting instances of all the various tactics and points described. See (e.g.) Greatrex 1998a: 169–85, 195–207, on the battles of Dara and Callinicum, where the use of tactics mentioned in the *Stratēgikon* is noted. For more detail see Wiita 1977: 53–111.

CHAPTER 13

1   Speck 1993: 233–9 discusses the episode at length, suggesting that there was no such embassy at this point, and that Theophylact's account is based on what happened to the mission of 615, but see nn.53 and 92 below.

2   I.e. April 603.

3   Phocas' agent in executing Maurice, cf. *PLRE* III, Lillis.

4   Another possible translation would be 'when Khusro had incurred the hatred of Narses'.

5   Narses 10 in *PLRE* III, the commander who had led the Roman forces of Mesopotamia to help restore Khusro to his throne. Schreiner 1985: 269 n.290 is needlessly sceptical of this identification. Speck 1993: 240 is sensibly suspicious of Theophylact's account here, arguing that it was Phocas rather than Maurice who ousted Narses.

6   The chronicle was used extensively in the ninth century by Dionysius of Tel-Mahre, and his chronicle was used (independently) by Michael the Syrian and (through an intermediary) by the *Chronicle of 1234*. Agapius appears to have used Theophilus directly, while Theophanes is thought to have had access to a Greek translation undertaken in northern Syria c.780. On Theophanes and this source, see now the comments of Brandes 1998: 554–8. The chronicles of Theophilus and Dionysius are both lost. See Conrad 1992: 322–38, Hoyland 1997: 400–9 (and his excursus C, a reconstruction of the 'Syriac common source', i.e. Theophilus), Flusin 1992: II, 68–70 and Mango and Scott 1997: lxxxii–iv. Palmer 1993: 95–102 argues that Dionysius did not use Theophilus alone, but incorporated other sources too.

7   So Hoyland 1997: 401 and n.52 and Flusin 1992: II, 69 and n.12. The date (and authorship) of the *Chronicle of Seert* are disputed: see Hoyland 1997: 443–6.

8   Dionysius of Tel-Mahre and Agapius may have used a common source (not necessarily Theophilus) from as early as 589. Hoyland 1997: 402 and 632 argues that Theophanes does not appear to start using the common source (Theophilus) until 610, but cf. Olster 1993b: 222–5 for parallels between Mich. Syr. and Theoph. concerning events in Phocas' reign. Theophanes' chronicle nevertheless does have value as an independent source up to 610.

9   Cf. Hoyland 1997: 402 and n.53, 407-8 on Theophilus' work, which appears to have contained few dates. As Hoyland notes, Theophanes' dates can therefore be accorded little credence, since he was forced to insert items where he thought best. The same seems true of most of his entries concerning the reign of Phocas too (even where they are derived from the common source), cf. Flusin 1992: II, 76–7.

10   Cf. *Chr. 1234*, 86 (220–1/121) and *Chr. Seert* 70, 79, *PO* 13.499, 519–20 for Khusro's vehement (reported) reaction to news of Maurice's death.

11   Cf. *PLRE* III, Theodosius 13 for the sources. *Chr. Khuz.* 20 reports that Khusro had him crowned as Roman emperor, cf. *Chr. Seert* 79, *PO* 8.519–20 with Olster 1993a: 92 (although there is no evidence that the coronation took place at Nisibis). Speck 1993: 226–8 argues that doubts on the genuineness of Theodosius began to be expressed only late in the reign of Heraclius.

12   Olster 1993a: 87 argues the date is two years too early; *Chr. 846* dates the event to AG 914 in any case. Narses appears to have sought popularity in the city by executing its Chalcedonian bishop. *Chr. 1234*, 85 (220/120–1 with parallel sources) offers a more

extensive account, asserting that Narses had Severus killed on the grounds that he was a supporter of Phocas.

13 Flusin 1992: II, 71–4 for a full consideration of the date; he puts its fall in July, cf. Thomson and Howard-Johnston 1999: 197–8. Olster 1993a: 95 prefers summer 605, which is also possible.

14 We must suppose that Theoph. is abbreviating his source here, since the location of the battle is not specified. It is possible that Theoph.'s order of events here is confused, and that he is referring to the battle at Arzamon mentioned below; Constanti(n)a lies almost due west of Arzamon, and would be the natural place of refuge after a defeat. *Chron. Khuz.*, 20, mentions an initial Roman victory (over Theodosius) at Bebasa, and Olster 1993a: 95 therefore seeks to argue that Theoph. is here referring to this Roman victory. Given the explicit reference to a Roman defeat (and the different locations), one cannot, however, identify the two events.

15 *PLRE* III, Leontius 29.

16 To be identified with the place Arzamon, cf. Dillemann 1962: 315. As Mango and Scott 1997: 420 n.5 note, the Greek here is ambiguous and could be translated 'Khusro, together with the Romans, came to Arxamoun'.

17 Here in lines 19–20 the phrase used, *tou polemou apērxato*, is identical to that in lines 8–9. *Polemos* could be translated as 'battle' rather than 'war', although this is not the word's usual meaning. If the victory over Germanus and the battle at Arzamon are not identified, the two references to Khusro assembling forces might alternatively be construed as an instance where Theoph. has run together the entries of two years from his source.

18 Not otherwise known.

19 Domnitziolus 2 in *PLRE* III.

20 A partial English translation of the *Life* in Dawes and Baynes 1948 (but omitting sections discovered more recently, for which see Festugière 1970). The work was composed by his disciple George not long after his death. For a recent discussion of the *Life* and its evidence for life in Asia Minor see Mitchell 1993b: 122–50.

21 Just west of Sykeon. See the map in Michell 1993b: 135.

22 Neither Sergius' conspiracy nor the Lazic raid are otherwise attested. The extension of Roman power in the Transcaucasus may have led to the sort of abuse of power in Lazica that had occurred in the 540s; cf. Chapter 8 above.

23 See Flusin 1992: II, 74 n.32 on the names of this man (also Farrukhan, his patronymic), cf. *PLRE* III, Shahrbaraz.

24 No more reference to Theophanes will be made for Phocas' reign because his chronology is so unreliable (see n.9 above); Sebeos' references to campaigns outside Mesopotamia are also too vague to be of use. The *Chronicle of 724*, the most contemporary source, together with the Syriac common source, forms the basis of any attempt to construct an account of these years.

25 Cf. Pernice 1905: 20–1 and Olster 1993a: 94–5 on the two Persian forces. *Contra* Olster 1993a: 96, however, there seem to be no grounds for supposing that any Roman force was active in Mesopotamia or Osrhoene after the defeats of 604/5: Sebeos 111/63 notes how Edessa surrendered when it became clear that there was no hope of relief.

26 The entry in *Chr. 724* reports that the Persians found many immigrants in Emesa (in 610/11).

27 But see Palmer 1993: 122 n.278, arguing for emending this to 918.

28 According to Flusin 1992: II, 74 n.34, Jacob reports only the fall of Cephas and places it in year 5 of Phocas (606–7), while he puts the capture of Amida, Constantia and Resaina in years 7–8 of Phocas (608/10); however, it is hard to arrive at such precise figures from Jacob's tables. *Chr. 819*, 10/76, AG 916, dates the fall of Rhabdion to 604/5, but, as

Olster 1993b: 225 argues, the date here is two years too early, and so the fortress must rather have fallen in 606/7. (Jacob also mentions Rhabdion.)

29 According to Mich. Syr. (*loc. cit.*) Khusro had initially favoured the Nestorians as his agents, but soon abandoned his backing for them when it became clear that they commanded no support among the populace. See Frend 1972: 336–7, Hoyland 1997: 177, Morony 1987: 93–4, Flusin 1992: II, 112–14 (noting tensions between the bishops installed by Khusro and those consecrated earlier by the patriarch of the region, Athanasius of Antioch). Ibid. 114–18 on the council held in Persia between 605 and 609 which sealed Khusro's support for the Monophysites. According to Mich. Syr. (X.25, 390–1a/122 n.279) the Persians attacked 'the Romans' in particular; the sense is not altogether clear, but might be taken as part of an attempt to kill soldiers rather than civilians, and thus to win the favour of the inhabitants. So Frend 1972: 336. Sebeos 110/ 62–3, reports that Khusro ordered Shahrvaraz to accept submissions and crush resistance, which also implies a programme of annexation. See further Butler 1978: 70, 90–1 on Persian toleration once initial opposition had been overcome.

30 Hence we reject the interpretation of Olster 1993a: 95–6, who, attempting to exculpate Phocas, sees the war as no different from earlier conflicts until the Persian successes of 609.

31 Jac. Ede. *Chron.* 325/38 puts the fall of Edessa in 611, after Heraclius' accession, but, as Flusin 1992: II, 74 n.34 notes, this is clearly too late. See (e.g.) Segal 1970: 74–8 on the legends surrounding the impregnability of Edessa. Sebeos, 110–11/63, asserts that Edessa, Amida, Constantia and Resaina (and later Antioch) all capitulated voluntarily to the Persians, but the Syriac clearly implies a violent capture.

32 A large number of skeletons were found in one of the funeral towers (no.13) outside Zenobia, prompting Lauffray 1991: 213 n.12 to suggest that they were massacred in their place of refuge. Cf. Fortin 1999: 209 no.197.

33 Nicephorus Callistus' account is generally overlooked, but since he refers to the Persians overrunning Syria, Palestine, Phoenicia, Armenia, Cappadocia, Galatia and Paphlagonia, some of which are not mentioned by Theophanes, he must have had access to an earlier source (perhaps that used by Theoph.?). Cf. Hoyland 1997: 632–3 for this entry in the common source. For a rejection of any Persian advance into Asia Minor during the reign of Phocas see Olster 1993a: 90–1, 96, cf. Flusin 1992: II, 75–7.

34 Sebeos, where he offers dates, does so by the regnal year of Khusro II. As Higgins 1939: 47–9 established, he dates Khusro's accession from June 589 (and not 590, as some Syriac sources do). Grousset's conversions of Sebeos' dates are therefore one year too late. Sebeos seems to prolong the siege of Dara unduly, setting its length at 18 months and synchronising it with events in Armenia up to 605/6; for events outside Armenia we have preferred to follow the Syriac sources. Flusin 1992: II, 79–80, argues for an early date for the first three Persian campaigns in Armenia (setting more store by Sebeos' synchronisms).

35 Cf. Grousset 1947: 270 (misdating the battle), Stratos 1968: 62–3 and *PLRE* III, D̄uan Veh. On the location of the battle see Thomson and Howard-Johnston 1999: 198–9. A rebellion in Persian-controlled Albania in 603 is reported (only) in Movsēs II.14 (150/93), cf. Dowsett 1961: 93 n.1.

36 Cf. Grousset 1947: 270, *PLRE* III, Datoyean and Thomson and Howard-Johnston 1999: 199. See Hewsen 1992: 69 map 24 for a map of the province of Ayrarat. Getik may be found in Thomson and Howard-Johnston 1999: map 3, just north of Lake Sevan.

37 Not to be confused with Roman Ingilene, this Angł (Proc.'s Anglon) is in the province of Ayrarat. Cf. Toumanoff 1963: 310 and n.30 and Hewsen 1992: 211 (with 69 map 24).

38 Cf. *PLRE* III, Theodosius 38 Khorkhoruni, Senitam Chosroes, Stratos 1968: 63 and Thomson and Howard-Johnston 1999: 199–201. Garitte 1952: 257 notes that all these three first Persian campaigns focus on the Armenian province of Ayrarat, which now

comprised the Roman province of Armenia Inferior (Lower Armenia), cf. Hewsen 1992: 212. On Basean cf. ibid. 213 n.268 and 69 map 24.

39 Grousset 1947: 271 and *PLRE* III, Ashtat Yeztayer put this campaign in 607/8; but Khusro's year 18 for Sebeos is 606/7. See Thomson and Howard-Johnston 1999: 201–2.

40 Literally, 'when'. Abraham was installed as *catholicos* in 607, cf. Garitte 1952: 257–9.

41 Abraham was an opponent of the Council of Chalcedon and is therefore labelled a heretic by the *Narratio*.

42 The chronological indicators are problematic. 'After three years' implies 3 years after 607, i.e. 610. The fifth year of Phocas is 606/7, while the twentieth of Khusro is either 608/9 or 609/10 (probably the latter for the *Narratio*, cf. Garitte 1952: 236, 258–9). See Flusin 1992: II, 80–1. It is likely that the *Narratio* has confused the capture of Theodosiopolis (in 606/7) with the deportation of its inhabitants (in year 21 of Khusro, i.e. 609/10, see below). Garitte 1952: 261 prefers to accept the *Narratio*'s chronology, however.

43 John was the *catholicos* appointed by the Romans, who supported Chalcedon; the opponents of the council had their own *catholicos*, Moses, at Dvin, the predecessor of Abraham. John was captured by the Persians when Theodosiopolis fell and deported with its inhabitants to Hamadan (see below). Cf. Grousset 1947: 265–6, Garitte 1952: 263–5.

44 On Shahin see *PLRE* III, Shahin and Flusin 1992: II, 84–5. On these successes in Armenia see Thomson and Howard-Johnston 1999: 202.

45 As Whitby 1988: 201–2 notes, the Armenian highlands are also more suitable for those resisting large-scale invasions.

46 Garsoïan 1999: 364 dates the fall of Theodosiopolis to 610/11.

47 But the Iberian Church, unlike the Armenian, remained in communion with the Church of Constantinople. See Garsoïan and Mahé 1997: 61, Martin-Hisard 1998b: 1229–33.

48 See Olster 1993a: 101–15, arguing for a strong link between Heraclius' revolt and the Levantine riots (and playing down the Jewish involvement). Cf. Sharf 1955: 106–8, who likewise sees the Jews as taking part in the disturbances only as faction members; also A. Cameron 1976: 282–4. The death of the patriarch Anastasius is ascribed by some sources (Theophanes, Michael the Syrian) to the Jews, but by the *Chronicon Paschale* (p.699) to 'soldiers'. See Whitby and Whitby 1986: 150 n.420. Olster 1993a: 103–6, who dates Anastasius' death to 610, argues that it was due to strife between supporters and opponents of Chalcedon.

49 Olster 1993a: 106–8 puts Bonosus' appointment and suppression of the disturbances at Antioch in 608, after which he went first to Caesarea in Palestine, and then to Jerusalem (where, Olster notes, 113, he set up a mint for the use of his army); see also Schick 1995: 14–15, Speck 1997: 25–35. Hendy 1985: 413–14 notes that the mint continued to operate until c.615, becoming in effect Heraclius' replacement for the mint at Antioch. On the disturbances in Jerusalem under Phocas, see Flusin 1992: II, 142–5. From Caesarea, according to Olster's chronology, Bonosus proceeded to Egypt in spring or summer 609. *PLRE* III, Bonosus 2, puts all these events, it seems, in 609. See Butler 1978: 14–27 (for an account of Nicetas' takeover of Egypt), 31 (for the chronology, placing Bonosus' defeat in late November 609), Stratos 1968: 85–6 and Baynes 1913: 659–66.

50 Kaegi 1973: 311–19 assembles the evidence on the revolt (from *V. Theod. Syk*, ch.152 [122–3/128–9]); see also Kaegi 1979: 221–4 and Foss 1977: 68–9. Cf. *PLRE III*, Comentiolus 2; he may have been *magister militum per Orientem* or *per Armeniam*.

51 At Jerusalem, however, the partisans appear to have taken a hard line in resisting the invaders (as at Antioch in 540).

52 This point is well brought out by Olster 1993a: 112; cf. Kaegi 1973: 323. As Flusin 1992: II, 151 notes, it is also something brought out at the start of Ant. Strateg.'s work.

53 Stratos 1968: 103 doubts that an attempt was made in 610–11, cf. Mango and Scott

1997: 430 n.1, who argue that *Chron. Pasch.* 708 (the text of a letter sent by Roman officials to Khusro in 615, translated below), in referring to Heraclius' failure to inform the king of his accession hitherto, rules out any previous mission. But since two independent sources (the Common Source, although Hoyland 1997 does not note this episode, and Sebeos) record it, it is possible that the Roman officials simply thought it prudent to pass over such a disastrous earlier embassy. Theophanes reports an unsuccessful peace mission in A.M. 6015 (612/13), 300, which is probably to be equated with this one. Cf. also Speck 1988: 65 n.120.

54 We are told explicitly that Zenobia fell in August 610, see p.186 above. No source records the capture of Sergiopolis, but it had defied the Persians successfully in 542 (see Chapter 7 above).

55 See Kaegi 1973: 324–6 on the chronology with *PLRE* III, Priscus 6 and Thomson and Howard-Johnston 1999: 203. On the removal of Priscus from his command see Speck 1988: 234–9. Sebeos seems to place the attack on Caesarea too early, in the twentieth year of Khusro (608/9), and is followed in this (e.g.) by Stratos 1968: 105. *Chr. 1234* names the Persian commander as Bahram rather than Shahin.

56 Theodore died on 22 April 613 cf. Kaegi 1973: 330.

57 On the dating of this episode (to 612), see Kaegi 1973: 322–8.

58 As Flusin 1992: II, 78 and n.49 notes, the chronology here is problematic. We follow *Chr. 724* here, which dates these cities' fall to AG 922 (610/11), while *Chr. 1234* has 923 (implicitly). The latter and Agap. both place the fall of the cities in October, while Theoph. dates their capture to May. The cities clearly fell between October 610 and October 611 at any rate (although Trombley 1997: 196 and n.156 argues for 613). Balty 1970: 4 n.3 accepts the date of May 611, but argues against the usual emendation of Theophanes' Edessa to Emesa. Other sources report the capture of other cities: Mich. Syr. (X.25, 390a/378) gives Hierapolis, Chalcis, Beroea and Antioch.

59 Already in the 520s Kavadh had been attracted by the wealth of the region, reported to him by dissident Samaritans, 18.54 (455), cf. Proc. *Wars* II.20.18 (translated above, Chapter 7, p.109), on Khusro I.

60 Sebeos claims that the two commanders met in Pisidia, but there is no other evidence that the Persians had penetrated so deep into Asia Minor at this stage. Grousset 1947: 272 dates this campaign to 612, but *PLRE* III, Shahin, rightly prefers 613, cf. Stratos 1968: 106. Thomson and Howard-Johnston 1999: 203–4 date the campaign in Pisidia to 617.

61 Cf. Stratos 1968: 106 and Flusin 1992: II, 89–90, on these manoeuvres, with *PLRE* III, Philippicus 3. *PLRE* III, 350 for Heraclius Constantine's elevation.

62 Agapius actually refers to a victory of Nicetas over Kesrou'an (? Khoream, i.e. Shahrvaraz) in a battle in which 20,000 on each side died. The placing of the entry certainly favours identifying the battle with that in Sebeos although the outcome must be incorrect. See also *PLRE* III, Nicetas 7 (since he was in Constantinople in late 612, he probably came from there rather than Egypt) and Theodorus 163. Flusin 1992: II, 78 and n.50 connects Agapius' entry with events in 610/611, however, while Schick 1995: 17 puts the battle in 612.

63 Literally, 'with it' – i.e. Theodore's holiness.

64 A slightly different account is given by Tabari, I, 1005/324 (Nöldeke, 297) from a different source.

65 This Qatma is otherwise unknown, although Götz 1968: 118–19 identifies him with Nicetas (Nicetas 7 in *PLRE* III), dating Heraclius' counter-offensive to 614 (114–15).

66 Cf. Schick 1995: 20 n.2 on this battle between Adraa (Der'a) and Bostra in the Hawran. Sartre 1982a: 194 considers that the Romans involved were probably just the local garrisons. Sartre 1985: 131 notes other Arabic sources on the battle. Two Safaitic graffiti might refer to this battle, on which see Schick 1992: 109.

67 An allusion to the verses of the Qu'ran quoted below. The letters ALM are mystical in nature. Cf. Shahîd 1995: 639 and Götz 1968 on the verses below.

68 See Flusin 1992: II, 153–4. Schick 1995: 21–6 offers a very full consideration of the Persians' route and the impact their advance had on the region. As he notes, their progress was swift and consequently spared many places from destruction. Ant. Strateg. 3 (503) reports a Persian setback at Caesarea, with which (following *PLRE* III, Nicetas 7 and Flusin 1992: 78 n.50) we might connect *Anth. Pal.* XVI.46, reporting Nicetas' 'great Persian-slaying deeds' and *Cont. Isid. Byz. Arabica* ?7, *MGH* XI.335 (tr. in Hoyland 1997: 613). Baynes 1914: 37 associates these passages instead with the close-fought battle in 613 (n.62 above), which he dates to 611. Whether traces of destruction at Caesarea can be attributed to the Sasanians is doubted by Holum 1992.

69 Sebeos 115/68–9, implies that an arrangement was initially made by the city, and that Persian officers were then stationed inside it. After a few months, however, 'youths' (presumably partisans) killed the Persians and attacked the Jews in the city; and so the Persians started their siege. Antiochus' reference to Zachariah's willingness to negotiate does not altogether rule out such an initial phase of cooperation, although Sophronius' evidence is against it (cf. Couret 1897: 132–3). Cf. Schick 1995: 33–4 and Flusin 1992: II, 145–7. On the attempt to call in Roman troops, undertaken by Modestus, who was soon to replace Zachariah as patriarch, see Flusin 1992: II, 158–9.

70 For the date of the city's fall see Flusin 1992: II, 154–8, arguing for either 5 May or between 17 and 20 of the same month, cf. Thomson and Howard-Johnston 1999: 207 (favouring 18 or 19 May). For a full assessment of all the various sources on the fall of Jerusalem and its impact on Roman morale see Flusin 1992: II, ch.5–6. For possible traces of damage to the Damascus gate (and the walls near it) at Jerusalem during this siege see Wightman 1989: 30 with Magness 1992b: 96.

71 Baynes 1914: 198 notes that the Greek term here, *mangana*, occurs also in the Arabic version of Ant. Strateg. Clermont-Ganneau 1898: 37 argues that the fires beneath the wall indicate mining operations for which he finds confirmation in Thom. Arts.

72 For a detailed consideration of Jewish collaboration with the Sasanians see Schick 1995: 26–31, who concludes that little damage was done to the region except at Ptolemais and Tyre; cf. also Flusin 1992: II, 152 n.3, Vailhé 1909: 15–17 and Morony 1987: 92–3. The souces no doubt exaggerate the extent of Jewish involvement. The Jews had little reason for enthusiasm for the Persian cause: Khusro's general Mahbodh had persecuted the Jews in 591 (Th. Sim. V.9.10), and the king later (see below) expelled them from Jerusalem. See Herrin 1987: 206 for a sober assessment. On the deportation of the people of Jerusalem, see Flusin 1992: II, 164–70. Sebeos 116/69 puts the number of deportees at 35,000, while Ant. Strateg. offers a figure of only 3000 (18 [511]); he also asserts that the Persians sought out only those most useful to them, especially architects and craftsmen (9 [507–8]). Cf. Morony 1984: 267.

73 Maeir 2000: 178–9 associates some Sasanian objects discovered in the Jordan valley, the Transjordan and Damascus, with this march.

74 Mich. Syr. XI.1 (403b/128 n.289) and Theoph. A.M. 6104 (300) report a Saracen incursion into Syria in the first year of Heraclius' reign; Michael attributes it to a drought. Hoyland 1997: 633 n.13 attributes this entry to the Common Source, but suggests that it belongs rather to 617, the year of an eclipse mentioned by Michael and of an Arab incursion mentioned by two other sources. Even if the entry is misplaced, the *V. Georg Khozeb.* (30–1, 34, [127–30, 134]) and the *Life* by Leontius of John the Almsgiver (7), as well as a letter of Antiochus, the *hegoumenos* of the monastery of St Sabas (*PG* 89.1422–8, tr. in Flusin 1992: II, 177–9), clearly show that raids took place at this time, cf. Schick 1995: 31–3 and Flusin 1992: II, 153 and n.4, 177–80.

75 For a full assessment of the damage inflicted on Jerusalem, see Schick 1995: 33–9; it was clearly extensive (but note Magness 1992a: 71 arguing against widespread destruction, at

least in one part of Jerusalem and cf. Schick 1992: 109–10). Cf. Flusin 1992: II, 159–64, Stratos 1968: 109. Maeir 2000: 175–83 discusses traces of Sasanian objects found in the region and argues that not all of them can be connected to this invasion. On Nicetas' removal of the relics, see *Chr. Pasch.* 705 (with Whitby and Whitby 1989: 157 n.438), Stratos 1968: 110. On the Persians' seizure of the Cross see *Chr. Khuz.* 25 and Ant. Strateg. 18 [510–11] with Flusin 1992: II, 170–2. On the importance attached by later accounts to the capture of the Cross, see Frolow 1953: 88–91. See also B. Wheeler 1991 and Wilken 1990–1.

76 On the site of George's monastery at Khozeba see Di Segni 1991: 48–56 and Talbert 2000: 70 G2.

77 The Indians represent the Persians, cf. Di Segni 1991: 144 n.53.

78 It is odd that these young men are not referred to as soldiers. Given the involvement of the partisans in the resistance at Jerusalem, one might therefore wonder whether they are referred to here (which would also explain why their equipment is rather patchy). On the other hand, we know from Antiochus Strategius (below) that there were Roman forces stationed at Jericho.

79 Indicating that Bostra too would fall to the Persians, cf. Di Segni 1991: 144 n.54.

80 Cf. Butler 1978: 67–8, Stratos 1968: 111. But Leontius' work must be handled with caution, cf. Mango 1984b: 35–41. Sebeos 116–18/70–2, gives the text of a letter from Modestus, the Persian-appointed replacement for Zachariah, to the Armenians, seeking help in the rebuilding.

81 Note also the letter of patriarch Zachariah, sent from exile, *PG* 86.2.3228–33, the tone of which clearly implies that the city had revived considerably in the time since the sack. Mango 1984a: 5 notes that the precise date of the restrictions on the Jews is unclear (although 617 is often put forward). Elsewhere too church-building continued under the Persian occupation, cf. e.g. Foss 1997: 262 (in Arabia).

82 Cf. Stratos 1968: 112. Negotiations were also held between the anti-Chalcedonian patriarch of Antioch, Athanasius, who was among those who had fled to Egypt (with other high-ranking Monophysite clergy), and his counterpart in Alexandria, Anastasius. The two entered into communion in late 616, but Anastasius died soon afterwards. See Butler 1978: 50–2 and Frend 1972: 339–43.

83 On the monastery of Ennaton see Butler 1978: 51 and n.2. It lay nine miles west of Alexandria.

84 Galling 1966 notes evidence (in the form of Graeco-Coptic ostraca found at Jerusalem) for the sending of supplies from Egypt to Palestine in 620 (i.e. after the fall of Alexandria). He infers that the Sasanians continued John's efforts, at any rate until 622 (after which time no more ostraca are found).

85 Dawes and Baynes 1948: 265, cf. Shahîd 1995: 640 n.21, take this as an allusion to the biblical Midians. Others (e.g. Festugière 1974: 335) see in it a reference to the Maʿadd tribe, on which see (e.g.) Shahîd 1995: 160–6.

86 The text has Rhinocoroura, cf. Butler 1978: 67 and n.3.

87 Cf. Leontius, *V. Ioh. Eleem.* 6, 18 (7, 20 in Dawes and Baynes 1948) for a similar account of John's generosity after the fall of Jerusalem; also Eutych. *PG* 111.1082–4 with Butler 1978: 67–8 (although his chronology is incorrect). A later synaxarion preserves the detail that the *hegoumenos* of the monastery of St Sabas spent 1200 gold pieces (presumably *solidi*) in ransoming twenty men and women, cf. Festugière 1974: 317 and Lappa-Zizicas 1970: 270, 276.

88 The fullest discussion of Shahin's advance is in Flusin 1992: II, 83–93; see also Whitby and Whitby 1989: 159 n.442 and Stratos 1968: 115. The Persian army did not set off until after the fall of Jerusalem and can hardly therefore have arrived at Chalcedon much before the end of 614. On the destruction of Ephesus see Foss 1975a: 738–9 and *idem*

1979: 77 and n.56 (uncertain whether an earthquake or the Persians were responsible for the destruction).

89 Cf. Flusin 1992: II, 84. As Flusin notes, ibid. 88–90, Philippicus' diversions in 613 and 615 seem very similar, and some have sought to identify the one reported by Sebeos with that in the *Acts of St Anastasius*.

90 Both Howard-Johnston (*loc. cit.*) and Mango 1990: 176–7 are inclined to take Sebeos' account seriously here although he confuses this episode with the siege of 626. From both Sebeos and *Chr. Pasch.* it is clear that Heraclius was prepared to make concessions to Khusro.

91 Literally, 'to so great a reduction'. As has been seen, Phocas had in fact sent an embassy to Khusro in April 603: see p.182 above.

92 Cf. Kaegi 1979: 221–4, connecting the 'civil strife' with the revolt of Comentiolus (on which see above).

93 We have suggested above (n.53) that, despite the implication of *Chr. Pasch.* here, that there may have been an earlier (unsuccessful) embassy to Khusro.

94 The Persian title *Wohu-mananh*, i.e. personification of the Good Spirit, as noted by Whitby and Whitby 1989: 162 n.444 (citing Justi 1895: 374–5). Cf. Nöldeke 1879: 291 n.2.

95 The Persian military title *spahbadh*, on which see Christensen 1944: 131.

96 *PLRE* III, Olympius 6, Leontius 31, Anastasius 36.

97 In the same way that Khusro himself had been received by Maurice as his child; see Chapter 12 above.

98 Cf. Flusin 1992: II, 90–1, Stratos 1968: 116–17 (perhaps overestimating the strength of the Roman position). Foss 1975a: 743 also puts the capture of Chalcedon in 616. Whitby and Whitby 1989: 159 n.442 argue, however, that there was only one advance to Chalcedon in this phase of the war; cf. Speck 1988: 276–8. Nicephorus' report of the execution of Shahin at 7.15–20 is inaccurate, cf. Mango 1990: 177.

99 Cf. Foss 1976: 53–4 and Morrisson 1986: 155. Russell 1986: 140 (cf. Trombley 1985: 78) expresses doubt about the date of the sack, but cf. Foss 1975b: 18–21 refuting such scepticism (with *idem* 1987: 36). Foss stresses in particular the lack of any coins after 615/16 and the widespread nature of the destruction at the site; but see now Russell 2001: 62–8, an important reconsideration of what can be ascertained by archaeological evidence and the case of Sardis in particular, noting the discovery of a *follis* of 617/18, and pointing out that many other sites also lack coins from this period. See Grierson 1965: 216–18 on two hoards from Aydin (near Tralles) probably also from this period.

100 Cf. Hendy 1985: 416, Grierson 1968: 37–9, 219, 231. Soldiers were usually paid in gold, and so these mints, which produced only copper coins, might have been producing smaller denominations for change; alternatively, they may rather show how short of gold (and silver) the Roman government was. See Hendy 1985: 416, 643 and Haldon 1990: 224 and n.61; also Foss 1975a: 729–46 (on the mints generally), Grierson 1951, Mango 1994: 120–2 (with a useful map). Hendy 1985: 416 notes that a *follis* of 618/19 from Isaura has been found. Russell 2001 argues that Roman resistance continued probably even after the closure of the mints, pointing to traces of destruction at the city of Anemurium in Isauria. Foss 1996b: 45–6 notes that the large number of coins found at Side from Heraclius' reign indicates that it too played an important role in the Roman defence. Trombley 1985: 75–9 rightly challenges the extent to which the Sasanians controlled Asia Minor in this period, cf. Howard-Johnston 1999: 15 and n.117 below.

101 Foss 1975a: 724 and n.2 confidently places these events in 617 and argues that the commander sent against Constantia was a Persian (see below). But see Mango 1984b: 38–9 on the difficulties presented by the episode.

102 As Dawes and Baynes 1948: 265–6 note, this incident is puzzling. It is unclear whether Aspagourius is a Persian or a Roman commander. Foss 1975a: 724 and n.2 confidently makes Aspagourius a Persian, pointing to his Persian name – hardly a decisive point,

given (e.g.) Theophylact's record of the courage of a Roman soldier called Sapeir (II.18.15-24), also clearly a Persian name. *PLRE* III, Aspagourius, believes him to have been a Roman, cf. Festugière 1974: 336. Grierson 1950: 82–3 argues that the incident is misplaced, that Aspagourius was an officer of Nicetas, and that the episode took place in 609/10.

103 Cf. Foss 1975a: 724, 732. We follow Foss here in supposing Aspagourius to be a Persian commander.

104 See Butler 1978: 70–1 (with Altheim-Stiehl 1991: 15) on Pelusium and on the identity of the Persian commander. The latter question has not been definitively resolved: see *PLRE* III, Shahin, Shahrbaraz. Whitby and Whitby 1989: 164 n.449 put the start of the Persian invasion in 616; certainty is impossible, but since the siege of Alexandria did not last very long, it seems unlikely that the Persians would have occupied only a small portion of the country for so long before either moving southwards or attacking Alexandria. That the Persians did not move southwards in Egypt until after Alexandria is clear from papyrus evidence (see below).

105 The story is doubted by Mango 1990: 177.

106 Howard-Johnston 1999: 14–15 prefers to place the siege in 622, however. Cf. Metcalf 1962 for the evidence of coin hoards in the Aegean in this period (indicating widespread insecurity).

107 It was worth one twelfth of a *solidus*. The legend *Deus adiuta Romanis* was accompanied on the obverse by a 'cross potent on base above globe and three steps' (Grierson 1968: 270). On the reduction in pay implemented see Treadgold 1995: 47–9 and Haldon 1990: 224. Clearly the dire situation of the empire enabled Heraclius to introduce measures which Maurice had not been able to implement. Such coins have been found in large quantities in Armenia and the regions where Heraclius campaigned, cf. Thierry 1997: 171.

108 Cf. Grierson 1968: 6, 24 on the decline of copper coinage, with Hendy 1985: 498. See also Whitby and Whitby 1989: 158 n.441 and Herrin 1987: 197.

109 Military reforms may also have been begun at this time: some scholars (Herrin 1987: 196, following Haldon 1984: 144–5, 174–82) have argued that already by 615 the palace guards had been formed into a new force known as the Opsikion (cf. *Chr. Pasch.* 715), which was to become the core of Heraclius' new army. Howard-Johnston 1999: 38–9 suggests that the Opsikion was formed from the allies recruited by Heraclius in the Transcaucasus, on the other hand. See also Haldon 1990: 213–14 (more cautious) and Lemerle 1960: 355–60.

110 See Altheim-Stiehl 1992b: 89–90 on the route of the invaders to Alexandria and the capture of Nikiu and Babylon.

111 *Orac. Sib.* XIV.296–307 as edited and clarified by Scott 1915: 162–3 also concerns the fall of Alexandria and the Persian takeover of the country. Severus' work reports a massacre in Alexandria after the capture, on which see Altheim-Stiehl 1992b: 91.

112 Butler 1978: 73–81 for an assessment of the sources. His chronology there and at 498–507 has been largely superseded. See (most recently) Altheim-Stiehl 1991: 3–16, who systematically compares the papyrological and literary evidence. The capture of Alexandria is noted briefly by Theoph. A.M. 6107 (614/15), 301, *Chr. 1234*, 93 (227/128) and Mich. Syr. XI.1 (404a/128 n.289). Both Mich. Syr. and Theoph., no doubt following the Common Source (cf. Hoyland 1997: 634 for this entry), assert that the Persians penetrated as far as Libya and Ethiopia; see Speck 1988: 75–7 on this mistake. Anon., *V. Ioh. Eleem.* 15 claims that the city was betrayed by a Roman commander Isaac (*PLRE* III, Isaacius 7), who then escaped to Cyprus; he may have been the commander who surrendered the city after Peter's treachery. See also Mango 1984b: 39.

113 Cf. Butler 1978: 91–2. A few references to the invaders can be found in the papyrological

evidence, cf. MacCoull 1987, Crum 1926: 100–2, Hardy 1929, Altheim-Stiehl 1992b: 92–6.

114 Cf. Whittow 1996: 76–7, Haldon 1990: 45. *Chr. 724* 147/17 (AG 934 = 622/3) reports that the Slavs even penetrated as far as Crete. See also Stratos 1968: 118–21.

115 Cf. Hoyland 1997: 634 for this entry in the Common Source (which he dates to 622, since *Chr. 1234* and Agapius place the fall of Ancyra in the same year as Mohammed's arrival at Medina). Archaeology corroborates the dating of Ancyra's fall, cf. Foss 1975a: 735–6, 1977: 70–1. Trombley 1985: 78 argues that the Slavs, rather than the Persians, were responsible for raiding the coast of Asia Minor.

116 Cf. Oikonomides 1976: 8 with Foss 1975a: 741 and Haldon 1984: 436–8. In general see also Trombley 1985: 75–9, a stimulating attack on Foss' arguments.

117 There is no evidence to suppose that Persian policy in Asia Minor changed after 615. Mich. Syr. XI.1 (404a/401) ascribes a generally plunderous attitude to the Persians throughout the East, noting in particular their removal of building materials (and other wealth), cf. Khusro I's actions at Antioch in 540 (Chapter 7, above). Tchalenko 1953: 433–6 argues that Syria suffered under the Sasanians through being cut off from its export markets to the west.

CHAPTER 14

1 We shall continue to refer to Theoph. and Nic. when we note Speck's views, although he prefers to talk of a 'compiler'.

2 Speck 1988: 101–7, 124 doubts the existence of a separate 622 campaign altogether, arguing that it is a creation of George Syncellus, having been conflated with Heraclius' 623 campaign (which we have dated to 624).

3 Cf. Stratos 1968: 127, Haldon 1984: 169.

4 On such exactions see Hendy 1985: 231 cf. 495.

5 A large bronze ox which stood at one time in the Forum Bovis (Forum of the Ox). Cf. Janin 1964: 69–71.

6 The date of this measure is unknown, but Herrin et al. 1984: 229 associate it with the melting down of church vessels just mentioned. Evidence from the *Parastaseis* must always be handled with caution, and Janin 1964: 70 notes that it is possible that the Ox was not melted down by Heraclius. On the emperor's recruitment in Pontus (after 622) see Herrin et al. 1984: 229–30. On the terms used for treasury and guardpost (or 'Watch') see Kaegi 1982: 90–8 (dating the measure to 622) and Haldon 1984: 436, 439. Speck 1997b: 460 and n.25 doubts the whole episode, cf. Speck 1989; but see Whitby 1995: 111. Nic. 9 notes the baptism in Constantinople of a Hunnic chief around this time, which Beševliev 1978: 234–5 associates with the Huns north of the Caucasus, Heraclius' future allies.

7 Oikonomides (cf. Stratos 1968: 137–8, but mistakenly using Sebeos) and Haldon 1984: 438–9 argue that Heraclius conducted his exercises in Cappadocia; Howard-Johnston prefers the closer and more plausible Bithynia. Theoph. refers to the *themata* (themes), which has led to much scholarly debate but no greater geographical precision, cf. Mango and Scott 1997: 438 n.5. Speck 1988: 107–26 argues that neither Geo. Pis. nor Theoph. can here be trusted: Geo. Pis. composed a stock poem on the emperor's successes, and the historical details added by Theoph. are merely inventions.

8 For a consideration of the size of Roman armies in this period see Howard-Johnston 1999: 30–2. Sebeos 124/81 puts Heraclius' army at 120,000, a figure taken seriously by Stratos 1968: 130, but clearly an exaggeration. Baynes 1904: 697 translates Theoph.'s phrase as 'he collected the garrisons and added to their number his young army' but Haldon (1979: 36–9) prefers 'he imposed a new obligation on them', arguing that Heraclius now insisted on hereditary recruitment.

9   For earlier use of the Camuliana image see Chapter 7 n.56 above. Cf. M. Whitby 1998: 253 and n.33 for its use on this occasion.

10   On the religious dimension of the war, increasingly stressed by George of Pisidia and Heraclius see Howard-Johnston 1994: 85, *idem* 1999: 39–40, M. Whitby 1998: 253–4, Haldon 1999: 19–21. Lemerle 1960: 351–3 notes that this aspect of the war is played up by later sources.

11   Oikonomides 1976: 4–6 interprets George's reference to a lunar eclipse literally (see n.14 below), a view doubted by Howard-Johnston 1999: 3 n.11, who nonetheless accepts a date of July/August. After Maurice's reorganisation of Armenia (Chapter 12 above), the province extended almost to Dara; hence the presence of Arabs in Armenia should not occasion surprise.

12   Cf. Oikonomides 1976: 3–4, rightly rejecting Theoph.'s garbling of George here. Howard-Johnston 1999: 4 argues for an advance by Shahrvaraz westwards towards Bithynia, ignoring the confrontation which had already taken place in Armenia. One of the passes will probably have been the Bitlis pass; cf. Whitby 1988: 201 on the geography of this region. Speck 1988: 110 and n.212 doubts whether Theoph.'s reference to Shahrvaraz (*barbaros* in Geo. Pis.) can be trusted.

13   Cf. Oikonomides 1976: 4. Scepticism in Speck 1988: 110–11.

14   Cf. Oikonomides 1976: 4–5, accepting the reference to a lunar eclipse in Geo. Pis. Zuckerman 1988: 209–10 doubts whether Geo. Pis. can be taken so literally, but cf. Oeconomides and Drossoyianni 1989: 173 n.55.

15   Howard-Johnston 1999: 14–15 argues that it was the Avar and Slav attack on Thessalonica (often dated instead to 618) which forced Heraclius back west. Speck 1988: 123 argues that the reference to Armenia is merely Theoph.'s conjecture. Vasiliev 1935: 32 suggests that Heraclius withdrew through Trebizond, but this is doubted by Brown et al. 1978: 24.

16   Cf. Howard-Johnston 1999: 11, 14–15, Mango 1990: 178–9, and Whitby and Whitby 1989: 165 n.421, 203–4. Consensus certainly now favours placing this incident in 623 rather than 619 (the year in which Theophanes places it), although Speck 1988: 265–6 prefers Baynes' dating of the episode to 617. Baynes 1914: 401 argues that the 200,000 *solidi* were not an annual payment.

17   Cf. Hoyland 1997: 634 and n.18 for this entry from the Common Source. Palmer 1993: 18 n.115 proposes emending *Chr. 724*'s date to AG 937 (625/6); Agap., *PO* 8.451 (not noted by Palmer) placing the capture of Rhodes in year 15 of Heraclius, would corroborate such a revision, but we follow Howard-Johnston 1999: 15 in assigning these events to 623. See also p.197 and n.114 above.

18   Cf. Hoyland 1997: 634 and n.19 (another entry from the Common Source), but omitting the second Theoph. passage. The sources vary in their precise dating of this development; see also Speck 1988: 80–1. Further confiscations of church treasure and deportations took place at Edessa in 625/6, cf. Hoyland 1997: 634 and n.22, assembling the sources. It is doubtful whether even then there was a general persecution, cf. Flusin 1992: II, 118–27. On the wealth accumulated by Khusro from his conquests see Tabari, I, 1041–2/375–8 (Nöldeke 351–6) with Morony 1984: 31 and n.19.

19   Cf. Howard-Johnston 1999: 16. Sebeos, 123/79–80, gives the text of an arrogant letter sent to the emperor by Khusro, deriding him, which Howard-Johnston plausibly suggests represents Roman propaganda. Frendo 1985 argues in favour of its historicity. Theoph. 306.23–6 reports that Heraclius wrote to Khusro, on the other hand, threatening to invade Persia if he did not agree to peace (doubted by Speck 1988: 127–8). Speck 1988: 101–7 prefers to date this campaign to 623 (the year in which Theoph. places it according to the indiction date), but see Zuckerman 1997: 477 for a refutation.

20   Cf. Thomson and Howard-Johnston 1999: 214–15. Heraclius' route is considered in detail by Manandjan 1950: 134–9 (with maps), but cf. the criticisms of Stratos 1968:

154–5 and 365–6 n.16. From Nakhchawan Heraclius passed east of Lake Urmia to Ganzak (see below). See also Gerland 1894: 353 n.2 on the impact of the sack of Dvin.

21 Cf. *PLRE* III: 1143 (wrongly dated). There is no evidence that Shahrvaraz reached Chalcedon in this year, *contra* Mango 1985: 106.

22 In Azerbaijan (Atropatene), modern Leylan, south-east of Lake Urmia, cf. Minorsky 1943–6: 248–52 and Stratos 1968: 366 n.17.

23 Identified by many with Darartasis in Geo. Pis. *Her.* II.167–230, cf. Thomson and Howard-Johnston 1999: 215, Minorsky 1943–6: 254–8 and Frendo 1976: 226–30. See also Honigmann 1944–5: 391–2, Schippmann 1971: 347–9. Here, at modern-day Takht-i Suleiman (ancient Adhur Gushnasp, cf. Boyce 1985), lay one of the sacred fires of the Persians, cf. Howard-Johnston 1999: 17.

24 Cf. Minorsky 1943–6: 255: the fire supposedly burned without leaving any ashes. Speck 1988: 129 n.238 suggests that the reference to Croesus is a misunderstanding by Theoph. of the name Khusro in Geo. Pis.

25 On this favourite palace of Khusro, north-east of Ctesiphon, see Sarre and Herzfeld 1920: II, 76–8 (with an excellent map on p.81), Christensen 1944: 454–5, Flusin 1992: II, 244 n.123, Bosworth 1999: 322 n.756. Cedrenus, 721–2, describes a remarkable throne of Khusro at this point, for which there are parallels in the Persian tradition. See Herzfeld 1920, Christensen 1944: 466–9, Lehmann 1945: 24–5.

26 The pursuit of Khusro led south-eastwards. Thom. Art. 92–3/159 refers to a Roman advance as far as Hamadan and May, cf. Manandjan 1950: 138 and Stratos 1968: 156.

27 Hoffmann 1880: 253 n.1998 identifies where Heraclius halted with Movsēs' Gayshavan (below).

28 Cf. Howard-Johnston 1999: 17 and Stratos 1968: 157–8 on Heraclius' decision to winter in Albania.

29 As Dowsett 1961: 79 n.3 notes, Movsēs appears to be conflating two campaigns here. Heraclius' move to Egeria (Lazica) did not occur until 626.

30 Continued from the passage cited just above.

31 As Tim Greenwood points out to us, this report is significant: Khusro himself ordered that Partaw be evacuated (according to Movsēs). This of course made it easier for Heraclius to winter on the plains nearby.

32 Kałankatuk lies not far to the southwest of Partaw, cf. Dowsett 1961: 80 n.2. On the province of Uti see Hewsen 1992: 60 map 10, 260. The immense multitude refers to the Roman and allied forces.

33 The Trtu is a tributary of the Kur river which flows past Partaw. Diwtakan lies about 50 km west of Partaw, cf. Manandjan 1950: 139.

34 On whom see *PLRE* III, Shahraplakan.

35 Referring to Shahrvaraz.

36 On Heraclius' manoeuvres here see Gerland 1894: 358, Thomson and Howard-Johnston 1999: 215–16. Zuckerman 2002 (with map) analyses Heraclius' manoeuvres in detail.

37 But he appears not to have died, cf. *PLRE* III and Dowsett 1961: 85 n.2. This victory took place at Tigranakert in the district of Gardman, cf. Thomson and Howard-Johnston 1999: 82 n.509.

38 Emended by Manandjan 1950: 141 to Siunia (Siwnik'), accepted by Stratos 1968: 161. The emendation puts Sebeos (125/82) and Theoph. in agreement: Heraclius was now moving southwestwards from Albania.

39 Stratos 1968: 162 notes that peasants comprised a large portion of the Persian army (cf. Shahbazi 1986: 497) and that it was probably these who dispersed in winter.

40 North of Lake Van, perhaps to be identified with Sebeos' Ali (125/82–3), cf. Manandjan 1950: 143–4, Mango and Scott 1997: 444 n.4, Thomson and Howard-Johnston 1999: 216.

41 Stratos 1968: 162–3 places this defeat in November or December 625. See n.42 below for an alternative dating.

42 In fact, as is clear from Theoph., Heraclius remained north of Lake Van, cf. Howard-Johnston 1999: 19. Zuckerman 2002 dates this whole sequence of manoeuvres to January–February 625, on the basis of Sebeos' reference to winter (125/82). If his scheme is followed, then the next section of Theophanes (translated below) may refer to 1 March 625.

43 According to Geo. Pis. *Bell. Avar.* 341 and *Chr. Pasch.* 721, the Persians promised the Avars a force of 1000 or 3000 men, cf. Howard-Johnston 1995b: 139–40, but there is no evidence that they materialised. Aside from burning Chalcedon, the Persians were of no practical assistance to the Avars, cf. Howard-Johnston 1995b: 133, Barišić 1954: 390–1.

44 Cf. Chr. Seert., *PO* 13.540–1 with Hoyland 1997: 635 and n.23: this is another entry from the Common Source. Nic. 12.49–64 has a similar account.

45 In favour of Mango's line is Shahrvaraz's subsequent inactivity during the war, cf. *PLRE* III, 1143. In 629 he was in Alexandria, cf. Sebeos 129/88 with Mango 1985: 109. Tabari, I, 1007–8/327–9 contains a similar story, cf. Bosworth 1999: 328 n.775. Theod. Sync. *Hom.* 37 (p.313), in describing Shahrvaraz's withdrawal, makes no mention of the agreement.

46 Heraclius was setting out from north of Lake Van, cf. n.42. Taranton (modern Darende) lay 70 km north-west of Melitene. The route to Taranton, along the river Arsanias, was almost due west; that to Syria would have taken the emperor through the Bitlis pass into Arzanene and thence into Roman Mesopotamia. Cf. Stratos 1968: 166–7 and 367 n.21 (against Manandjan 1950: 144), Howard-Johnston 1999: 19.

47 Heraclius would not have reached the Tigris until he arrived at Amida. Theoph.'s geography here is very confused, cf. Stratos 1968: 168, suggesting that the emperor reached Amida in mid-March.

48 Pernice 1905: 133 n.3 suggests that Theoph.'s Greek *pros anatolēn* refers not to the East but to Asia Minor, well to the west of Heraclius, but cf. Brooks 1906: 142, Baynes 1914: 410–11. In any case, the account is confused, as Baynes notes. See n.49 below.

49 Again, Theoph.'s geography is unclear, cf. Stratos 1968: 367–8 n.22. The Nymphius (Batman Su) lies east of Amida and is not on the way from there to Samosata. Stratos 1968: 168 argues that Shahrvaraz only caught up with Heraclius at the Euphrates, where he moved the bridge; certainly it is hard to see how Shahrvaraz could have met Heraclius east of Amida and then beaten him to the Euphrates.

50 Some scholars prefer to emend Adana to Adata, a place just north of Germaniceia, arguing that Heraclius pushed northwest from Germaniceia, directly towards Sebastea. So Stratos 1968: 169 (with the map in *idem* 1965: 441), cf. Anderson 1897: 33–4. Alternatively Heraclius may have continued west and slightly south, into Cilicia, through Mopsuestia, to Adana on the Sarus. So Howard-Johnston 1999: 19 and Baynes 1914: 411.

51 See Stratos 1968: 170–1, Howard-Johnston 1999: 19–20. Theoph. is mistaken in supposing that the Romans, arriving in Sebastea in April 626, spent the rest of the year there. Brown et al. 1978: 16–22, accepting that Heraclius wintered near Sebastea in 625, suggest that his camp lay at Bathys Rhyax nearby. As Speck 1988: 130 n.242 notes, Theoph. was using Geo. Pis. for some of the details concerning the battle of the bridge.

52 Cf. Speck 1980: 45–7 on this division. The first group reached Constantinople probably before the siege, cf. Howard-Johnston 1995b: 134 and n.10. Theodore may have arrived in Constantinople as the Avar siege came to an end, cf. *PLRE* III, 1278 and Howard-Johnston 1995b: 141 and n.39 (sceptical).

53 The description of these (western) Turks as Khazars is generally seen as anachronistic, cf. Howard-Johnston 1999: 23 n.72 with Bombaci 1970: 12–13, but cf. e.g. Noonan 1992:

111 for uncertainty. Golden in Sinor 1990: 263 asserts that 'there may have been no distinction' between Khazars and Turks.

54 Howard-Johnston 1995b: 134 describes this victory as 'one of the decisive battles of the war, since it allowed Heraclius to regain the strategic initiative once Constantinople had weathered the Avar storm.' He prefers to ascribe the victory to Heraclius himself rather than Theodore, arguing that the mention of Theodore has come about because of a connection with St Theodore the Recruit of Euchaita, ibid. 134 n.11. The army was divided only after this victory, he proposes.

55 Miracle two concerns the same Persian invasion and their entry into Theodore's shrine.

56 The geography of this episode is discussed in detail by Trombley 1985: 72–4 and Zuckerman 1988: 207–8.

57 I.e. the Derbend pass.

58 *PLRE* III, Andreas 23.

59 Bombaci 1970: 15–16 argues persuasively that 'the king of the north' and yabghu khagan are one and the same. They appear to be different because of alterations to Movsēs' text.

60 Apparently implying a visit to Constantinople, which cannot be correct. The precise location of Heraclius in summer/autumn 626 is unclear, however, cf. Howard-Johnston 1999: 20. Brown et al. 1978: 22–30 suggest that Heraclius was based at Hyssou limen (on which cf. Zuckerman 1991: 530), just east of Trebizond. Eger is the Roman Lazica.

61 I.e. spring 626, cf. Stratos 1968: 200.

62 A reference to the marriage of Khusro I to the daughter of the western Turk leader Ishtemi, cf. Bombaci 1970: 13 with Christensen 1944: 380 and Tabari 899/160 (Nöldeke 167). Hormizd IV was their son and Khusro II therefore their grandson.

63 Armenian *ktrichn*, 'the valiant one'. In the ninth century, this word came to be used as a personal name. According to Acharyan 1972: II, 681, it may have had a Turkic origin.

64 Another entry from the Common Source, cf. Hoyland 1997: 635 and n.24. The figure of 40,000 men is found in every source.

65 I.e. Atropatene.

66 I.e. Tʻung yebghu khagan, cf. *PLRE* III, J̌ebu Xakʻan and Bombaci 1970: 22–4.

67 Speck 1988: 134–5, 288–91 is more sceptical, detecting a Heraclius romance behind some of the details presented here; cf. *idem* 1997: 464–5.

68 Cf. *PLRE* III, Stephanus 55. As Toumanoff notes, Stephen had broken with the pro-Roman policy of his father, Guaram I, in the 590s.

69 I.e. the Caspian Sea. See Kettenhoffen 1996a: 16 on the Persian fortifications here.

70 South-west of Partaw, bordering on Siwnikʻ. See Baynes 1914: 667 on these developments.

71 See n.32 above on its location.

72 Perhaps referring to Iberians who had been under Roman control (in Maurice's reign).

73 On the Armenians see *Chr. 1234*, 99, 233/137: they joined the emperor in Armenia. On coin finds in Armenia and the Transcaucasus (linked to Heraclius' campaigns) see now Mousheghian et al. 2000: 34–5.

74 Stratos 1968: 206–8 argues that their departure must have taken place in March 628 rather than September 627, as Theoph. implies, noting (for instance) that winter had hardly started already in September.

75 Theophylact's Chnaitha, the region north/north-east of Arbela, cf. Minorsky 1943–6: 244 and map 13 in Whitby 1988: 301. The date here is incorrect: the 15th indiction is 626/7, and so this would be October 626, cf. Speck 1988: 154–5. Stratos 1968: 210 suggests that Theoph.'s 9 October be emended to 9 November in order to avoid such a long interval before the next date (1 December), when we find Heraclius not far from here. It must also have taken some time to get from the Transcaucasus to Chnaitha.

76 *PLRE* III, Baanes, suggesting that he was an Armenian.

77 The order of march here seems obscure.

78 I.e. with the Persian.
79 These events take place before the two armies clashed: hence, if Theoph. is believed, Heraclius seems to be engaging in single combat. Cf. Proc. I.13.29–38 for a similar episode in 530 and Mal. 14.23 (364) on the Roman general Areobindus fighting in the war of 421–2. Speck 1988: 138–9 ascribes this section to a Heraclius romance.
80 An important detail: despite his victory, Heraclius still had to contend with a battleworthy Persian force, cf. Flusin 1992: II, 272. Other sources (e.g. *Chr. 1234*, 99, 234/137–8, Agap. *PO* 8.464) make the victory more emphatic.
81 Cf. *PLRE* III, Barsamouses with Toumanoff 1961: 101.
82 Sebeos 126/84 supplements Theoph.'s account, although he implies that the 3000 reinforcements joined Rahzadh in time for the battle at Nineveh. See further Pernice 1905: 161 n.3 (arguing that Rahzadh had received some reinforcements earlier) and Thomson and Howard-Johnston 1999: 219–20.
83 But Shahrvaraz was not near Constantinople at this point, cf. Mango and Scott 1997: 455 n.8. Heraclius is now moving south-eastwards parallel to the Tigris.
84 *PLRE* III, Georgius 49. On the term turmarch see *ODB* III.2100.
85 Or the phrase could mean that the bridges were seized by night, cf. Mango and Scott 1997: 455 n.9 and Flusin 1992: II, 272 n.36.
86 I.e. in Karkha de Beth Selok (where Yazdin was born), cf. Fiey 1968a: 23–30 and Hoffmann 1880: 264-5. But already in 484 or 485 we hear of a synod being held in a house of Yazdin at Karkha de Beth Selok, cf. Flusin 1992: II, 246.
87 On Dezeridan see Sarre and Herzfeld 1920: 88 and Klima 1961: 16–19; its precise location is uncertain. The Tornas is generally identified with the Diyala river, although Flusin 1992: II, 271 implicitly distinguishes them. Pernice 1905: 162 n.2 suggests that the Torna could be the third major river flowing into the Tigris here, the modern Adhem, cf. Stratos 1968: 377 n.34. Pernice and Stratos call this the modern Adhem, i.e. Shatt al-Adhaim (al-'Uzaim on the useful map of Fiey 1968a: pl.1). On Khusro's palaces in general see Christensen 1944: 454–60.
88 Sarre and Hertzfeld 1920: II, 88 identify the place with Zengābād, north of the Diyala river. Devos 1946: 104 (following Sarre and Herzfeld) suggests identifying the palace with Rhesonchosron, on the north bank of the Diyala (Th. Sim. V.14.7), cf. Whitby and Whitby 1986: 247. See also Fiey 1995: 334–6.
89 Sarre and Herzfeld 1920: 88 connect Beklal with the later Beth Jalula. Baynes 1914: 672, following Rawlinson, identifies it with Beth Garmai (the region between the Lesser Zab and the Diyala).
90 This is the meaning of the text as it stands. Flusin 1992: II, 273 n.47 notes problems with the manuscript reading of 'hippodrome' and suggests that Khusro should be the subject of 'built'.
91 On Dastagerd see n.25 above. Minorsky 1943-6: 247 identifies Barasroth with the modern Beled-rūz, cf. Flusin 1992: II, 273 n.48. An adequate map of this region is Nebenkarte II on *TAVO* B VI 3.
92 As Flusin 1992: II, 278–9 notes, Theoph. is manifestly inconsistent here, having earlier (p.321) reported that Heraclius crossed the Lesser Zab (not the Tornas) on 23 December; see also Stratos 1968: 377–8 n.35. We accept the suggestion of Stratos, cf. Flusin 1992: II, 278 n.87, that 23 December is an error, to be modified to 28 December, which fits both with the chronology of Heraclius' advance reported earlier and the report of the Persian stewards to Heraclius below. Flusin 1992: II, 281 prefers to reject Theoph.'s account altogether, and to accept the dates offered in the *Acta S. Anast.*, which puts the saint's execution on 22 January 628 (ch.40) and the meeting of the monk with Heraclius at Dastagerd on 1 February (ch.43). We follow Stratos 1968: 378 n.36 and Howard-Johnston 1999: 5 n.15 in setting more store by Theoph.'s chronology.
93 Location unidentified.

94 On these products see Sarre and Herzfeld 1920: II, 89 n.1.
95 Cf. *Chr. 1234* 96, 230–1/133–4 on the deportation of people from Edessa, mitigated by the governor; also Agap. *PO* 8.460–1, Mich. Syr. XI.3 (408b/411) with Hoyland 1997: 634 n.22.
96 On 6 January 628.
97 Sarre and Herzfeld 1920: II, 89–93 emphasise the great strength of the walls defending Dastagerd, probably built by Khusro II. His abandonment of such a strong site was indeed remarkable and doubtless undermined his credibility, cf. Nöldeke 1879: 296 n.1.
98 Heraclius arrived at Dastagerd on 6 January. Nine days before this would therefore be 28 December.
99 Veh-Ardashir, cf. Fiey 1967: 11.
100 As Pernice 1905: 165 suggests, the offer of Heraclius may have been deliberately aimed at undermining Khusro's position.
101 The Nahrawan canal.
102 Shahrazur, north-east of Ctesiphon, cf. Hoffmann 1880: 264–5, Minorsky 1943–6: 250 (near modern Marivan). Theoph.'s chronology here is faulty: as Howard-Johnston 1999: 5 n.15 argues (*contra* Flusin 1992: II, 265–81), Heraclius will have spent January (not February) ravaging the lands north of Ctesiphon. On 22 January St Anastasius (the former Persian cavalryman Magundat) and 70 other prisoners were executed at Bethsaloe, just outside Ctesiphon, cf. *Acta S. Anast.* 38 with Flusin 1992: II, 259–60 and Tabari 1043/378.
103 The modern Saqqiz, cf. Minorsky 1943–6: 250–4. Minorsky's map, opposite p.250, gives a good view of Heraclius' probable route (across the Zagros mountains, back towards Ganzak); cf. also Stratos 1966: 595 (a good route map).
104 *PLRE* III, Mezezius, the Armenian Mžež Gnuni.
105 Ctesiphon itself was well fortified and had held out against Julian, cf. Dodgeon and Lieu 1991: 235. Cf. Simpson 2000: 61 on the city in the seventh century, whose population, according to one source, was 100,000.
106 Movsēs refers to the battle at Nineveh. Tabari, I, 1004/322–3 recounts communication between Rahzadh and Khusro of a similar nature.
107 This unnamed figure, highly praised by Movsēs, is reasonably identified by Dowsett 1961: 90 n.2 with Gusdanaspes (Aspad-Gushnasp, cf. *PLRE* III, 578). His prominent role emerges also from Tabari, I, 1046/382, where he is referred to as Asfādh Jushnas and described as 'head of the cavalry of the military host' (we prefer not to correct the text, as Bosworth does, cf. Nöldeke 1879: 362 n.3). But it is also possible that Shamta is meant, to whom the lead in overthrowing Khusro is attributed in *Chr. Khuz.*, 28-9, *Chr. Seert* 92, *PO* 13.551–2 and Thomas of Marga, *Book of Governors* I.35 (63/113–15).
108 Again presumably referring to Gusdanaspes, cf. n.107.
109 A significant point in explaining Heraclius' decision not to press on to Ctesiphon.
110 On this prison see p.170 above.
111 The account given by Thomas of Marga, *Book of Governors*, I.35 (63/114) is remarkably similar, although in it the lead role is played by Yazdin's son Shamta. According to Thomas, Shamta elevated Kavadh Shiroe to the throne and opened up the prisons at Ctesiphon, arming the prisoners released and equipping them with horses.
112 Various divisions of Khusro's guards are here referred to.
113 This was the house of the *mobadhan mobadh*, the chief priest of the Zoroastrian clergy, according to Pernice 1905: 166. It is also mentioned by Tabari, I, 1046/382, cf. Nöldeke 1879: 362 n.1. We might connect this reference to the 'House of the Indians' with a speech attributed to Khusro by Tabari, I, 1052–3/389, in which mention is made of gifts to Kavadh from an Indian king and a message prophesying the date of his accession.
114 Sebeos 127/85 recounts Khusro's hiding in the garden and the slaughter of his forty sons in similar fashion, cf. *Chron. Khuz.* 28 with Thomson and Howard-Johnston 1999: 222.

115 Cf. Whitby 1992: 253–4 on the loss of support for Khusro among the military.

116 Cf. Ps. 99 (100).

117 We follow the translation of Pernice 1905: 168 in believing that Khusro is said to have written blasphemies against Christ (against Whitby and Whitby 1989: 183, who have Christ apparently writing). The translation offered by Frendo 1985: 35 is also inaccurate, but he rightly draws attention to the letter of Khusro to Heraclius reported by Sebeos 123/80, which does indeed insult Christ.

118 Mark 14.21.

119 Theoph.'s Siazouros, cf. n.102.

120 Kalkhas may be Karka de Beth Selok, cf. Whitby and Whitby 1989: 185 n.487 (also on the two roads); also Fiey 1968a: 30 n.2. On the mansions of Yazdin, see n.86 above. Stratos 1968: 220–1 suggests that Heraclius sent his scouts westwards because he was apprehensive about the possible arrival of Shahrvaraz's army.

121 Sebeos 128/85–6 mentions 'a certain prince Rashnan' (in fact it is a rank, cf. *PLRE* III, 1015) sent to Heraclius to confirm peace terms by Kavadh. Cf. Thomson and Howard-Johnston 1999: 222.

122 Hoffmann 1880: 252 n.1997 identifies Arman with Beth Aramaye (but his identification of this with Thebarmais is mistaken). Baynes 1914: 677 prefers to identify it with Mount Auroman, 'which rises above the plain of Shehrizur' (modern Kuh-e Avrománn).

123 The Narbas is the Nahrawan canal, see n.101 above.

124 *PLRE* III, Elias qui et Barsoca 10, Theodotus 7.

125 On Phaiak, see *PLRE* III, 1015; above n.121 on the office Rasnan. Baynes 1914: 677 identifies Phaiak with Khosdaes, which is possible, cf. *Chr. Pasch.*, p.737 below.

126 Cf. *PLRE* III, Eustathius 12 on this official and his position, also mentioned by Sebeos 128/86.

127 Reading *kharin* rather than *kharan* ('joy'), following the suggestion of Oikonomides 1971: 272. On the elaborate opening formulae, ibid. 274–5.

128 Henceforth only fragments remain: the last surviving page of the sole manuscript is torn, cf. Oikonomides 1971: 270–1. We here present a translation of Oikonomides' restored text, which aims 'to clarify the essence of the text' rather than to offer what it necessarily originally read. We have also provided page references to his text from this point (1971: 271–4).

129 Cf. Oikonomides 1971: 275–7 on his restoration of the opening of Heraclius' reply.

130 Oikonomides restores 'your sonship' here, based on Nic. 15 (see below). But Mango 1990: 183 doubts whether Nic. used *Chr. Pasch.* as a source (*contra* Oikonomides 1971: 278); hence Nic. remains the only source for Heraclius' addressing of Kavadh as his son.

131 Speck 1988: 141–4 argues that Theoph.'s account here is somewhat novelistic (stemming from a Heraclius romance) and inferior to that of *Chr. Pasch.*

132 As Howard-Johnston 1999: 6 n.16 notes, Theoph. seems to conflate two people – the envoy who came to Heraclius, called Gusdanaspes Razei, and the architect of Khusro's downfall; cf. Stratos 1968: 379–80 n.39.

133 Taken by Speck 1988: 335 n.713 to indicate that part of Shahrvaraz's forces at least were now back in Persia (and not all in Roman territory).

134 Theoph. gives Kavadh's name as Siroes, but he is generally referred to as Kavadh Shiroe, cf. *PLRE* III, Cavades II *qui et* Siroes.

135 An error for February, cf. Howard-Johnston 1999: 6 n.16.

136 Theoph. is in error about the cross, which was not found until Shahrvaraz came to the throne; see below. Speck 1988: 336, on the other hand, thinks Theoph. is correct here and that Kavadh Shiroe did return the cross. The attribution of this step to Shahrvaraz is part of the Shahrvaraz legend, he argues.

137 Cf. Sebeos 128/86 with Thomson and Howard-Johnston 1999: 222, arguing that the

terms were to return to the Roman–Persian frontier of 387 (not 591), but cf. Flusin 1992: II, 284. There is no evidence to support Howard-Johnston's view, although it is not implausible.

138   Cf. Flusin 1992: II, 285. *PLRE* III, Narses 11 held the rank of *praepositus sacri cubiculi* around this time, but fails to note this passage of Ant. Strat. The identification is uncertain.

139   Clearly from the Common Source, cf. Hoyland 1997: 635 and nn.26–7 and Flusin 1992: II, 286.

140   On the earlier pact see n.45 above. Heraclius' movements after April 628 are very hard to trace: Agap. *PO* 8.465 states that he visited Thamanin (no doubt Thamanon in Corduene) and then spent the winter at Amida. Ps.-Yov. 279/156 mentions a visit to Eveznavan, Armenia, and Caesarea in Cappadocia, cf. Baynes 1912b: 290.

141   Presumably from the Common Source, although not in Theoph. and not noted by Hoyland. See Flusin 1992: II, 286–8.

142   Movsēs Daskhurants'i II.13 (149/92) offers a very favourable account of Kavadh's reign, noting that peace was established and taxes remitted, cf. Sebeos 129/87.

143   Cf. Flusin 1992: II, 288–9. Jerusalem, as he notes, presumably also still remained in Persian hands.

144   Heraclius will presumably have called upon the Turks to invade in 628 before negotiations with Shahrvaraz were underway, as Zuckerman notes. We find his redating of the Turkish invasion (usually placed in winter 629/30, cf. Howard-Johnston 1999: 28) convincing. On the Turks' power at this time see Sinor 1990: 309. Speck 1988: 329 is doubtful whether Shahrvaraz's army indeed remained in Roman territory. His insistence, 356–7, 371, that Heraclius remained in Constantinople throughout 629 is unconvincing, however.

145   In fact, Ardashir, the grandson of Hormizd IV, was killed by Shahrvaraz (later). See Speck 1988: 331–2.

146   See Mango 1985: 105, 112 on these marriage arrangements; also Zuckerman 1995: 121–3. As Mango notes, these arrangements followed the meeting at Arabissus, but took place before Shahrvaraz was crowned king (27 April 630); and Nicetas, Shahrvaraz's son and heir, must have been a Christian. Heraclius no doubt hoped to convert the kingdom upon his accession. Speck 1988: 341–7 argues that the marriages took place much later, after the fall of Shahrvaraz; he is also, 327–35, not unreasonably suspicious of the story of Shahrvaraz restoring the Cross.

147   Thom. Arts. (96/162) is more specific than Sebeos concerning the regions and cities returned to the Romans: he names Jerusalem, Caesarea (Palestine), Tarsus and most of Armenia.

148   Howard-Johnston argues that Shahrvaraz exploited his stronger bargaining position and thus secured the lands east of the Euphrates. But given the attention lavished by the Common Source on events at Edessa, the silence of *Chr. 1234* and the other sources derived from it concerning such a swift return of the city to the Persians is decisive.

149   Cf. Flusin 1992: II, 290–1 and Mahé 1984: 225–6. *Hist. Her.* describes how Shahrvaraz knelt before Heraclius, imploring his aid; the emperor therefore gave him troops under the generals George, David, Vahan and Smbat.

150   A proposed emendation for 'cross'.

151   Cf. Sebeos 130/88 without, however, mentioning David.

152   Cf. *Chr. Khuz.* p.29.

153   We pass over other commemorations of Heraclius' victory, such as the David Plates, probably produced in 629 or 630, on which see (e.g.) Alexander 1977: 232–7 and Mango 1994: 122–31 (with earlier bibliography and illustrations). For a specific rejection of Speck's dating see Flusin 1990: 323.

154   Important negotiations between the Nestorian patriarch and the emperor also took

place, on which see Flusin 1992: II, 319–27. As Flusin, *loc. cit.*, notes, Heraclius, according to *Translat. Anast.*, visited Constantia again at some point in 630 – perhaps to exert pressure on Boran's government.

CHAPTER 15

1 On the nature of this source see the brief description in the Notes on sources and p.183 above.
2 In fact the work covers a rather longer period, and the title itself was probably appended to the work by a compiler. See Nöldeke 1893: 5 n.1 and Robinson forthcoming (*ad init.*).
3 Literally 'the Gate of the Kingdom', cf. Nöldeke 1893: 5 n.4.
4 *Sic.* Peeters 1947: 50–1 wished to emend the text here (cf. Guidi and Nöldeke 1893: 6 n.1; also Goubert 1951: 133–4), but, as Whitby 1988: 296 n.30 argues, the 'south road' can quite easily refer to the route taken by Khusro on the south side of the Euphrates.
5 Isho-Yab had been a loyal servant of Persian interests, as has been noted during his tenure as bishop of Arzanene (571–82), see above, Chapter 11 n.55. See also Flusin 1992: II, 102 on Khusro's relations with the *catholicos.*
6 On Isho-Yab, see n.5 above and Whitby 1988: 295, 297.
7 Nöldeke 1893: 7 n.1 is sceptical of Isho-Yab's argument. But given that the Jews had supported Bahram (Th. Sim. V.7.5) and that the hated Hormizd had favoured the Christians (see p.162 above), it was not unreasonable to suppose that the usurper would be hostile to the Christians. Cf. *Chr. Seert, PO* 13.441 for Isho-Yab's reasons with Labourt 1904: 205–6.
8 Mahoza = Kokhe = Veh-Ardashir, across the Tigris from Ctesiphon, cf. Fiey 1967: 14.
9 On the location of the final defeat of Bahram, see p.174, above.
10 *Chr. Seert* 65, *PO* 13.481–2 recounts the same episode at greater length, but in the context of a campaign by Khusro against Bestam in the fifth year of his reign (593/4).
11 Cf. *PLRE* III, Bindoes, Bistam. They were the sons of Aspebedes, who is identified in *PLRE* II as the general who negotiated peace with the Romans in 506; *PLRE* III, Aspebedes, is rightly more sceptical as to whether this Aspebedes (the uncle of Khusro I) should be identified with the father of Bindoes and Bestam.
12 On Bestam's revolt, see p.175 above and Nöldeke 1879: 478–87.
13 The Persian Gundeshapur, in Khuzistan, cf. Nöldeke 1893: 8 n.8.
14 Cf. *Chr. Seert* 42, *PO* 13.440–2 on Khusro's anger against Isho-Yab.
15 Otherwise unknown.
16 Cf. *PLRE* III, Naamanes 4 with Evagr. *HE* VI.22 and *Chr. Seert* 60 in *PO* 13.468-9 (which adds that he ruled over all the Arabs, both Roman and Persian). See also Allen 1981: 261, Nöldeke 1879: 347 n.1, Labourt 1904: 206 and Rothstein 1899: 142-3. Trimingham 1979: 198–9 notes that other sources place his conversion somewhat earlier.
17 On this Hind see Labourt 1904: 206 n.4. She is not to be confused with the elder Hind, the wife of Mundhir the Lakhmid. Cf. also Trimingham 1979: 198 and *PLRE* III, Hind.
18 On this convent, just to the north of Hira, see Fiey 1968a: 215–16.
19 Isho-Yab died in 595, but an interval of one year passed before his successor was elected on 19 April 596, Easter day, cf. Labourt 1904: 209–10 with Flusin 1992: II, 102–5 on Sabrisho's election. But Tamcke 1988: 30 puts Isho-Yab's death in 596, while Higgins 1947: puts Sabrisho's election in 595.
20 As Nöldeke 1893: 10 n.3 notes, the *Chron. Khuz.* appears to be the best-informed source on this individual.
21 On Maria, see Chapter 12 n.41, *PLRE* III, Maria 6 and Bosworth 1999: 312 n.729. The later oriental tradition transformed Maria into a daughter of Maurice.

22 On these quarrels between 'hard-line' Nestorians (advocating two natures and two hypostases), led by such men as Babai the Great, and more moderate Nestorians (advocating two natures but only one hypostasis and closer to Chalcedonian and even Monophysite doctrines), such as Henana, see Labourt 1904: 214–16, Reinink 1999: 178–83, Brock 1996: 77 and Flusin 1992: II, 108–9. Cf. also *Chr. Seert* 74, *PO* 13.507–13 on Gregory the Kashgarite, with Tamcke 1988: 36–7.

23 Cf. Labourt 1904: 215, dating Gabriel's deposition to 596.

24 The root *nçb* meaning 'to plant'. Nöldeke 1893: 11 n.5 instead connects the reference to Mygdonia, *mgda* meaning fruit. Wallis Budge 1893: II, 40 n.2 notes that Yaqut mentions that there were 40,000 gardens at Nisibis.

25 Cf. Reinink 1995: 77–89, esp. 88 on the controversies at Nisibis at this time; also Tamcke 1988: 31–4.

26 A reference to Theodore of Mopsuestia, cf. Nöldeke 1893: 11 n.7.

27 On the disputes between the hard-line and moderate Nestorians, see n.22 above.

28 On the Messalians at this time see Labourt 1904: 213, Tamcke 1988: 23–4. According to Fiey 1964: 220–3 they were at the height of their fortunes.

29 Cf. *Chr. Seert* 74, *PO* 13.510, on Gregory's departure.

30 *Chr. Seert* 74, *PO* 13.509 notes Khusro's admiration for Gregory. Cf. Tamcke 1988: 37–8 on Gregory's fall.

31 I.e. Bizz al-Anhār, on which see Fiey 1968a: 252–3 (with the map opposite p.152). Cf. *Chr. Seert* 75, *PO* 13.512–13.

32 Cf. *Chr. Seert* 75, *PO* 13.513–15. On the date of this uprising, see above, Chapter 12 n.83.

33 This is a Persian title, meaning a doctor. So Nöldeke 1893: 13 n.2.

34 Cf. the second dedication made by Khusro to St Sergius, reported by Th. Sim. V.14 and Evagr. *HE* VI.21, on which see above, Chapter 12. As Labourt 1904: 219–20 suggests, Gabriel may well have ascribed his success to the saint already revered by the king.

35 I.e. a Monophysite, cf. Nöldeke 1893: 13 n.4.

36 I.e. the Nestorians, cf. Nöldeke 1893: 13 n.4.

37 On Gabriel's influence and changes of allegiance see Flusin 1992: II, 110–11.

38 On this episode see Trimingham 1979: 199-200, Whitby 1988: 296 and Potts 1990: II, 252–3. Nu'man was deposed c.602, cf. Bosworth 1983: 607 and *PLRE* III, Naamanes 4.

39 Nöldeke 1893: 14 n.3 takes this as a general reference to Arabs rather than a specific allusion to the tribe of the Ma'add.

40 Northern Mesopotamia, the region around Dara and Nisibis.

41 One of the islands of Bahrain, cf. Nöldeke 1893: 14 n.5. The interpreter was for communication between Arabic and Persian: see Potts 1990: II, 245.

42 Khusro also now took the opportunity of removing the Lakhmids from their role as the principal Arab allies of the Persians. In their place a new Arab ruler was appointed, Iyas ibn Qabisa, alongside a Persian governor, Nakhoragan (the *nakhveragan*). Cf. Tabari, 1038/371-2 (Nöldeke 347) with Trimingham 1979: 200 and Bosworth 1999: 372 n.911 (dating Iyas' reign to 602–11). For a detailed consideration of the various sources concerning Nu'man's death see Rothstein 1899: 114–19. The new arrangement was not a success, and the Persians suffered a significant defeat at the hands of other Arabs between 604 and 611 at Dhu Qar, cf. Bosworth 1983: 607–8, Rothstein 1899: 120–3. See also Donner 1980: 27–9 and Bosworth 1999: 337 n.794 on Dhu Qar.

43 Cf. Tamcke 1988: 59. On such coronation rituals see MacCormack 1981: 242–4.

44 This is Ammianus' Bebase, also mentioned in connection with the Solachon campaign (cf. Chapter 12 n.10). It is 'beyond' Dara from a Persian perspective, i.e. west of it.

45 Tamcke 1988: 59 notes that Sabrisho was by this time eighty years old. According to Amr 51 (29–30), Sabrisho was asked to accompany Khusro against Dara, but chose to remain in Nisibis, where he died in AG 917 (605/6).

46 Cf. Mal. 14.23 (364) for the use of a lasso in war (reporting a duel between Areobindus

and a Persian champion in the reign of Theodosius II). Mal. associates the lasso with the Goths.

47 This battle, clearly not far from Dara, might well be identical with that reported by Theophanes at Arxamoun (Arzamon), on which see p.184 above. Both sources also refer to Khusro as involved in this engagement.

48 This must be an artery, as Nöldeke 1893: 17 n.1 notes.

49 603/4 according to Nöldeke 1893: 17 n.2, but, following the chronology of Higgins (1939: 49), 602/3. For a discussion of the date of Dara's fall see Chapter 13 n.13 above.

50 A Persian official, on which see Peeters 1951a: II, 139 and Gignoux 1980: 200–2.

51 Shahrazur, south-east of Karkha de Beth Selok, cf. Fiey 1968a: 67 and above p.312 n.102.

52 See Fiey 1968a: 69 and Labourt 1904: 224 on this episode, which they date to 605; cf. also Flusin 1992: II, 120–1. Despite the words of the chronicler, Khusro only persecuted Christians intermittently until the very end of his reign, ibid. 118–27.

53 Cf. Labourt 1904: 221, Fiey 1968a: 73, 75 on the location of the monastery (in Beth Garmai).

54 Perath de Maishan, near modern Basra, cf. Wallis Budge 1893: II, 181 n.5.

55 This Gregory was *catholicos* between 605 and 609. See Fiey 1968a: 162, Labourt 1904: 222, cf. *Chr. Seert* 80, *PO* 13.521–4 on Gregory (noting that Khusro compelled the *catholicos* to buy many books from him which he had captured at Dara). Cf. also Thomas of Marga, *Book of Governors*, I.25 (50/87–8). On the intrigues surrounding Gregory's election see Flusin 1992: II, 107–8.

56 From 609 to 628. Cf. Labourt 1904: 223 n.6.

57 Both these monasteries lie near Hulwan, north-east of Ctesiphon. On that built by Khusro for Shirin see Wallis Budge 1893: II, 80 n.5, Fiey 1967: 33 and Flusin 1992: II, 103 n.42. On the decline of Nestorian fortunes in this period, see Flusin 1992: II, 110–14, who rightly links it to the support given by Khusro to the Monophysites in his newly conquered territories.

58 The editor suggests that the text may have been transposed here, and that Ionadab enjoyed familiarity with the king and love of God.

59 On which see Fiey 1968a: 20, Labourt 1904: 224 and Nöldeke 1893: 20 n.3.

60 On whom see Labourt 1904: 223. He may have been a disciple of Sabrisho.

61 On these individuals see Labourt 1904: 223–6. On Aphrahat (the form of the name is textually uncertain), Nöldeke 1893: 20 n.7. A similar list in *Chr. Seert* 83, *PO* 13.529.

62 This debate took place in 612. See Labourt 1904: 225–8 and (in greater detail) Reinink 1999: 178–9. Fiey 1968a: 163 (citing *Chr. Seert*) notes that Sergius was not bishop of Kashgar, but rather a doctor there.

63 This church lies near Ctesiphon, cf. Nöldeke 1893: 22 n.1 and Fiey 1967: 32–3. More details on the martyrdom of Gregory, a Persian convert whose original name was Mihr-Mah-Gushnasp, are to be found in his *Life*, composed by Babai the Great, partially tr. by Hoffmann (with an excursus) 1880: 91–121. See now Reinink 1999.

64 I.e. Karkha de Beth Selok.

65 On Yazdin, whose influence remained great until his death, see Fiey 1968a: 23–5, Labourt 1904: 230–1 and Flusin 1992: II, 246–52; cf. *Chr. Seert* 81, *PO* 13.524–5.

66 On the monastery of Mar Abraham see (e.g.) Fiey 1968a: 26 and (for its location) Palmer 1990: xx–xxi (in the join between the pages, in the southern Tur Abdin).

67 On which see Nöldeke 1893: 22 n.7, Fiey 1968a: 56 n.8, Wallis Budge 1893: I, xli–lxix; also Thomas of Marga, *Book of Governors*, I.28–30 (54–7/95–101). The monastery was founded in 595/6, cf. Wallis Budge 1893: I, xlvii, lxx–lxxii.

68 That is, the Hebrew fortress, near ancient Nineveh, cf. Budge 1893: II, 337 n.2.

69 This is Babai 'the Lesser': see Nöldeke 1893: 23 n.1, Labourt 1904: 229–30. We follow here the translation of Budge 1893: I, xlvi.

70 Cf. *Chr. Seert* 84, *PO* 13.530–2 on Babai.

71 Cf. Fiey 1968a: 26. Clearly this event must have postdated the fall of Jerusalem (614).

72 I.e. the two Babais'.

73 We take this as critical/ironic: the followers of Mar Babai the Great were behaving badly.

74 *Chr. Seert* 84, *PO* 13.532–4, offers a list of Babai the Great's works, cf. Ortiz de Urbina 1965: no.81 (139–41).

75 *CSCO* translates as a singular, referring to God, but the verb is in the plural, and presumably refers to certain Romans.

76 Tabari, I, 1002/318 (Nöldeke 291) has a very similar account, cf. Bosworth 1999: 318 n.747.

77 It was probably in this new treasury that Khusro was himself later imprisoned, cf. Nöldeke 1893: 25 n.1 and below. On the Persian capture of the cross, see Labourt 1904: 232–3, Flusin 1992: II, 170–2 and Schick 1995: 37–9.

78 Literally, 'The water of the Nile surrounds it'.

79 *PLRE* III, Petrus 59.

80 This word *syna* is tricky, as the editor notes; it literally means 'mud'.

81 This is the most detailed account of the city's capture. Cf. Butler 1978: 76–7, explaining how the canal connecting the city with the sea was poorly guarded. As has been noted above (Chapter 13 n.11), some senior officials did escape from the city.

82 Probably in 617, cf. Chapter 13 n.80 above. See also Fiey 1968a: 27 and Labourt 1904: 233.

83 See Chapter 13 nn.79–80 on the rebuilding work at Jerusalem.

84 This is the famous St George, who was said to have been martyred at Lydda (Diospolis) in Palestine, cf. *ODB* II.834–5. The city boasted an important *martyrium* of St George, which was visited by the martyr Anastasius in 627 (cf. *Acta Anast.* 15 with Flusin 1992: II, 210). This episode must have taken place during Shahrvaraz's advance on Jerusalem from Caesarea, cf. Flusin 1992: II, 153–4.

85 On this place (Dastagerd) see Chapter 14 n.25.

86 Presumably a reflection of the emphasis placed by the emperor on the religious nature of the war. Cf. M. Whitby 1994: 213–16 and eadem 1998: 252–5 on religious imagery applied by George of Pisidia to Heraclius; also Chapter 14 n.10. On the wooden bells used by the Persian Christians see Christensen 1944: 453 and n.2.

87 In line with other accounts, cf. p.213–19 above.

88 No mention is made in this account of Gusdanaspes (Aspad-Gushnasp).

89 See p.219 above for other sources on Khusro's seeking refuge in a garden, such as Movsēs, 148/91–2 and Sebeos 127/85.

90 Cf. the accounts of Movsēs 148/91–2 (p.219 above) and Tabari, I, 1046/382 (Nöldeke 362).

91 The date of Yazdin's death is uncertain, cf. Flusin 1992: II, 252. The persecution of his family after his death is confirmed by Thomas of Marga, *Book of Governors*, I.35 (62–3/ 112–13) and *Chr. Seert* 92 (*PO* 13.551); but as Flusin 1992: II, 252 notes, evidence from the *Acta Anast.* implies that both Shamta and his brother Kortak may have continued to have a role at court.

92 More details in Tabari, I, 1058–60/395–7. According to Tabari's account, it had been predicted to Khusro that Nehormizd (Nimruz in Tabari, Hormizd in *Chr. Seert* 92, *PO* 13.551) would kill him. Khusro therefore had his father Mardanshah mutilated and then executed; Tabari also relates that Nehormizd's initial axe-blows were unsuccessful because of an amulet-shaped gem which protected his neck. Cf. Stratos 1968: 226–8 on the differing accounts of Khusro's death and p.219 above.

93 Cf. Tabari, I, 1060-1/398 (Nöldeke 382–3), *Chr. Seert* 92, *PO* 13.552. See Nöldeke 1879: 383 n.1 and Flusin 1992: II, 253.

94 Cf. *Chr. Seert* 92, *PO* 13.552, according to which Shamta was in league with the Magi and was accused to the king by an (unnamed) general. See Flusin 1992: II, 253.

95   Cf. Thomas of Marga, *Book of Governors*, I.35 (63/115). Gedhala lies near the later Mosul, cf. Wallis Budge *ad loc.*

96   Tabari, I, 1061/399 (Nöldeke 383–5) ascribes his death to illness but places it at Dastagerd. See *PLRE* III, 276–7, for a full list of sources recording Kavadh's death (and the causes given).

97   Same figure in Tabari 1061/399 (Nöldeke 385), cf. Nöldeke 1879: 383 n.5.

98   Nothing further is known of this woman, although *Chr. Seert* 92, *PO* 13.552, calls her a Roman named Bore and claims that she conceived after the intervention of Babai of Nisibis.

99   Tabari, I, 1061/400 (Nöldeke 386) puts him at seven years old. Cf. *PLRE* III, Ardashir III.

100 Shahrvaraz was in fact the honorary name of Farrukhan, bestowed by Khusro, cf. *PLRE* III, 1141.

101 Not in the Zab region, as Nöldeke 1893: 31 n.5 supposes, but near Seleucia, cf. Labourt 1904: 240 and n.1.

102 Cf. *Chr. Seert* 93, *PO* 13.556 on the death of Shamta.

103 On the Roman troops which assisted Shahrvaraz to take the Persian throne see p.227 above.

104 For a discussion of the chronology here see p.227–8 above.

105 Tabari, I, 1062–3/401–3 (Nöldeke 388–90) offers the same figures for the length of reigns. Ardashir reigned from September 628 to 27 April 630; Shahrvaraz reigned from April to 9 June 630, cf. e.g. Bosworth 1999: 403 n.995.

106 Cf. Sebeos 130/89, recounting how Shahrvaraz was struck from behind.

107 And his sister, cf. *PLRE* III, Boran.

108 Cf. Fiey 1968a: 31 on this mission and the individuals involved; as he notes, all were from dioceses recently occupied by the Romans. A slightly different list in Thomas of Marga, *Book of Governors*, II.4 (70/126–7).

109 Cf. *Chr. Seert* 93, *PO* 13.557 with Flusin 1992: II, 321 and see p.228 above.

110 *Chr. Seert* 94, *PO* 13.579 states that Boran was strangled by Peroz, a general. On her reign see Tabari, I, 1064/403–5 (Nöldeke 390–1); it lasted (according to Tabari) 16 months, to autumn 631. Tabari incorrectly ascribes to this mission the return of the Cross.

CHAPTER 16

1   We shall not consider evidence for the provinces of Palestine and Arabia for the most part, however, since only briefly in the seventh century did they come under attack from the Persians. On these two provinces see now Di Segni 1995, 1999. We have translated the ranks of the people mentioned in the chapter into English (e.g. 'most glorious', 'illustrious') rather than into their Latin equivalents; readers wishing for clarification on precise ranks may turn to the *PLRE*.

2   Mouterde and Poidebard 1945: 238 with ibid. 188 inscription 15 (from Burj Za'rour in the Jebel Hass) on the abandonment of forts, but cf. Liebeschuetz 1977: 490. Cf. Jerome, *Vita Malchi* 4 with Shahîd 1984: 284–7 (on the capture of Malchus by Saracens, apparently in the 350s).

3   Not to be confused with Han el-Abyad (Khirbet el-Beida in Kennedy and Riley 1990: 228), cf. Gregory 1997: II, 199.

4   The inscription probably dates to the late fourth century, cf. *PLRE* I, Silvinus and Trombley and Watt 2000: xliv–xlv (where another tr. is offered). The mention of 'emperors' might suggest the reign of Arcadius and Honorius.

5   The lintel comes from a tower, cf. Mango 1984: 296. Burj el-Qai lies north-west of Emesa.

6 We pass over *IGLS* 2246 from Emesa, dated 488/9, which may attest to the restoration of the city wall by a certain Leontius. See Trombley and Watt 2000: xlvii.

7 According to the editors, the inscription (a white marble plaque, only part of which survives) was probably found on the border of the steppe and inhabited regions. It concerns rights of asylum, cf. *IGLS* V.212–16 for comments with Trombley 1997: 172, who suggests that it comes from 'an estate forming the endowment of a Christian shrine that enjoyed the right of asylum'.

8 Cf. Mal. 18.63 (467) on the former praetorian prefect Demosthenes being sent to the east in 530 'to prepare granaries'.

9 The word for granary is the Greek *hōrion*, i.e. *horreum*. On the term and the restitution of 'public', see *IGLS* V.56; ibid. on the date (there is a slight discrepancy between the Seleucid era year and the indiction year). Cf. Capizzi 1969: 227–8. Note also the church's involvement in the construction of a refuge-place at Bouz el-Khanzir on the western side of Lake Gabboul, *IGLS* 270 (AD 506/7), on which see Trombley 1997: 187, Capizzi 1969: 226, Liebeschuetz 1977: 491. The inscription is now translated in Trombley and Watt 2000: xlix.

10 Individuals might also help their city financially, cf. Di Segni 1995: 331; they might alternatively assist it by appealing to the emperor to release funds, ibid. 329–30 (on Scythopolis).

11 Cf. Capizzi 1969: 228, Lassus 1935: no.11, 26–7. Capitolinus – if the name has been restored correctly – held very high rank, but is otherwise unattested.

12 See Tate 1992, esp. 343–50, cf. *idem* 1996: 331–4 (assembling the epigraphic data) and now Feissel 2000. Foss 1997, esp. 232–7, considers fortifications in northern Syria, where most of the inscriptions have been found. See too Foss 1995: 218–23 (a review of Tate) and Gregory 1997: I, 210–11 (with a map of datable building work from the sixth century).

13 Cf. Mango 1984: 31–2 *contra* the views of Mouterde and Poidebard 1945: 237–40 and Liebeschuetz 1977: 491–2. It is true, however, as Liebeschuetz notes, that Procopius does not refer to many smaller forts in Syria, as he does in Mesopotamia. On Procopius' evidence see Whitby 1986a and 1987 (reacting to Croke and Crow 1983). Fourdrin 1994: 299–304, taking into account architectural similarities between defensive works at several cities in the East, plays up imperial involvement; note the inscriptions from Chalcis below.

14 The date of the *Buildings* itself is controversial, some scholars advocating c.554 (so Greatrex 1994a: 107–13), others preferring c.559 (so Whitby 1985: 141–7).

15 Kfellousin (Kaper Lusin in Mango 1984: 281–2) lies in the Jebel Halaqa, north-west of Beroea. For a description of the tower see *PUAES* II B 225. Butler, ibid., dated it to the fifth, rather than the sixth, century, but the editors of *IGLS* prefer the later date.

16 Other *metata* (staging-posts for troops, cf. Isaac 1992: 177–8) have been found in the region, e.g. *IGLS* 1610 (from el-Burj, south-west of Taroutia Emporōn, AD 526) and *IGLS* 1397 (Raphanea, undated). Sergius and Bacchus, who had been martyred in Euphratesia in the early fourth century, were special protectors of troops in Syria, cf. *IGLS* V.91. See now Key Fowden 1999: 3–4, 113–14 on the importance of Sergius and *metata*.

17 There is a slight discrepancy between the indiction and Seleucid years.

18 Seyrig 1950: 239–42 dated this inscription to the reign of Justinian, connecting it with Justinian's rebuilding work there in 527 (on which see Mal. 18.2 [425–6] with Greatrex 1998a: 151 and Zanini 1995: 75–9). If the Justinianic date is accepted, 527 should be preferred to the dating of Mango 1984: 323 (to c.540). *PLRE* I, Fl. Platanius Serenianus 3, however, prefers a mid-fourth century date.

19 This is Lassus 1935: 120 no.65; cf. Mango 1984: 309.

20 Liebeschuetz 1977: 492–3 argues against a coherent building programme, believing the

work to be undertaken mainly by individuals for local needs. Foss 1997: 234–5 notes an increase in fortification-building between 556 and 577; Pentz 1992: 25–7 puts the increase between 550 and 600 and attributes it to anxiety about Arab raids. The data for Palestine and Arabia compiled by Di Segni 1999: 164 imply a downturn in building in the 540s, which she associates with the impact of the plague. See also Howard-Johnston 1989: 223 on work carried out at fortifications in Armenia at this period.

21 The literature on this point is considerable. See Liebeschuetz 1977 (491 for the quotation), Greatrex 1998a: 40–2, Casey 1996, Key Fowden 1999: 141–9, Kaegi 1992: 50–1 (a useful summary), Isaac 1992: 211–13, Isaac 1995: 149 (on evidence from Palestine), Sartre 1982a: 172, Gregory 1997: I, ch.4, esp. 85–7.

22 Mango and Mango 1991: 465 tentatively assign the inscription to 541/2, but the fifth indiction could also refer to 556/7 during Justinian's reign; and since the reading is uncertain, and could also be the fifteenth, the years 536/7 and 551/2 are also possible. The provenance of the inscription is uncertain, but it may have come from the area around Derik, between Constantia and Dara; Mango and Mango also suggest that it comes from a work of fortification, ibid. 466. A Thomas, *dux* of Mesopotamia, is known c.542 from Mich. Syr. and Ps.-Dion., cf. *PLRE* III, Thomas 11. See also now Feissel 2000: 97.

23 Trombley 1997: 176 n.85 notes this construction work, connecting it with the penetration of Roman defences further north.

24 See n.9 above on the term used for a granary, *hōrion*; cf. also Mouterde and Poidebard 1945: 199.

25 See Trombley 1997: 163 for an analysis of this inscription, which combines Old Testament citations with Homeric language. According to Trombley, *loc. cit.*, 'the inscription most likely reflects raids by the Lakhmid Arabs in the War of 540–544.'

26 Cf. *PLRE* III, Ioannes 43 and Theodorus 16. *PLRE* suggests that John may have been 'a wealthy inhabitant rather than an imperial official', judging by the word *philoktistēs* ('who takes delight in building'), which implies that he undertook a lot of building in the region. The editors of *IGLS* V.283, on the other hand, take John's high rank as indicative of imperial involvement, cf. Mango 1984: 303 and Mouterde and Poidebard 1945: 238, and this view seems more consonant with the acclamation of Justinian in the inscription. See also Trombley 1997: 173, Whitby 1986a: 723.

27 For a detailed commentary see Feissel in Fourdrin 1994: 305–7. *IGLS* 349 = *AAES* 306 has an almost identical text.

28 Qasr el-Mharram (*sic*) is to be found on fig.3 in Mouterde and Poidebard 1945: 47. Several other inscriptions have been found here (*IGLS* 1812–18), cf. Lassus 1935: nos.81–6. Lassus (p.150) has plausibly suggested a concerted programme to build up the village's defences between 540 and 550; his attribution of the initiative in this to Justinian, however, is uncertain. In 569/70 (*IGLS* 1812) another tower was erected. See also Foss 1997: 234.

29 See Trombley 1997: 170–1 on this inscription. While Chalcis clearly benefited from imperial intervention, it appears that Androna had to rely on local assistance.

30 Cf. Di Segni 1999: 164, noting a downturn (in Palestine and Arabia) under Justin II and Tiberius, but a revival under both Maurice and Phocas.

31 We have been advised that the identification of the buildings is not entirely secure, however. De Maffei 1995: 112–20 goes on to argue that in the 550s and 560s there was a concerted imperial building effort at Qasr ibn Wardan and forts nearby (Il-Habbat, Androna, Stabl' Antar). She suggests that Qasr ibn Wardan was constructed as a new headquarters for the *magister militum per Orientem* in the wake of the peace of 561.

32 This is Lassus 1935: 29 no.12. A *periodeutes* was a priest responsible for tending to Christians in the countryside, cf. Greatrex 1998a: 273. This Thomas, as the editors of

IGLS IV note (p.249) may well be identical with the Thomas referred to in inscriptions at Ruweyda and Androna.

33 The editors of *IGLS* IV.258 suggest that Macedonius was a *comes*, rather than an ecclesiastical official, since he was served by a *notarius*. See also Lassus 1935: 50 no.26 for the inscription. Worthy of note, since not in *IGLS*, is a nearly contemporary Syriac inscription from the Jebel Bil'as (north-west of Palmyra and south-east of Occaraba), which records the construction of some sort of fortification (a *koditha*, a mule or mound) carried out by a monastery in AG 886 (574/5). See Mouterde 1942–3: 83–6.

34 On this inscription see Shahîd 1995: 495–501, Sartre 1982a: 182, Waddington 1870: 585. It dates from between 566 and 580.

35 Trombley 1997: 176–82 argues for a massive depopulation of the Limestone Massif in northern Syria, caused by the invasions of 540 and 573; and he points to the reduction in the number of inscriptions as an indicator of this. See, however, the data and the conclusions presented by Tate 1992: 173–88, esp. 187–8; the vast majority of inscriptions after 550 comes from churches, cf. ibid. 335–7. Cf. also Di Segni 1999: 164.

36 The date is uncertain. Taking into account the indiction date, the year could also be 504 or 579, cf. Prentice 1908: 254. The commander's name may be Gregory Abimenus, mentioned in *IGLS* 281 and 292 (cf. *IGLS* II.165). Prentice also suggests that the inscription itself comes from the town's walls. Cf. Trombley 1997: 188, preferring to date it to 594/5, following the editors of *IGLS*; according to him, 'the wording of the inscription suggests at least one Sasanid or Lakhmid siege of Anasartha between c.573–591 and betrays a certain anxiety about the situation on the eastern frontier in the immediate aftermath of the war ...'

37 *IGLS* 2123, a lintel from a tower at Gagar al-Amiri, is dated AG 892 (AD 580/1). See Mango 1984: 90, ascribing the decision to build the *peribolos* (below) to Tiberius and Maurice, although noting that Sergius may have provided the funds.

38 The editors of *IGLS* assume that the *peribolos* was that of a church, although this does not necessarily follow from the mention of the patriarch Gregory of Antioch.

39 Phocas' name has been erased because his memory was condemned by the Romans after his fall from power in 610.

40 On this inscription see Trombley 1997: 190. Note also *IGLS* 291–2 (*AAES* 324–5), the second of which mentions the involvement of an Abimenus Gregorius. *IGLS* 298 from 606 shows that the city was still in Roman hands at that point.

41 As Trombley 1997: 193–4 notes, the inscription testifies to continuing resistance to the Persians and to probable imperial investment in fortifications, given the senatorial rank of the person involved.

BIBLIOGRAPHY

PRIMARY SOURCES

In the case of works indicated by an asterisk below, the translation noted in the text (usually the second page number given) is that of Palmer 1993 for the period covered by that work (582 onwards); where it is not available, the translation referred to is noted under the work in question.

Acta S. Anast. Les actes de Saint Anastase, ed. and tr. B. Flusin in Flusin 1992: I, 40–91.

Agap. Agapius, *Kitab al-'Unvan*, part 2.2, ed. and tr. A. A. Vasiliev, *PO* 8 (1912).

Agath. Agathias, *Historiae*, CFHB, ed. R. Keydell. Berlin 1967; tr. J.D. Frendo. Berlin–New York 1975.

Ammianus Marcellinus, *Res Gestae*, ed. W. Seyfarth. Leipzig 1978; also ed. and tr. J. Fontaine (books 23–25, Paris 1977, 2 vols.), M.-A. Marié (books 26–28, Paris 1984); tr. C.D. Yonge. London 1902.

Amr. *Amri et Slibae de patriarchis Nestorianorum commentaria*, 2 vols. ed. and tr. H. Gismondi. Rome 1897–9.

Anon., *V. Ioh. Eleem.* 'Une vie inédite de saint Jean l'aumonier', ed. H. Delehaye, *AnBoll* 45 (1927): 5–74. (Partial) tr. in Dawes and Baynes 1948: 199–206.

Anth. Gr. Anthologia Graeca, 4 vols., ed. H. Beckby. Munich 1957–8.

Ant. Strateg. Antiochus Strategius, *La prise de Jérusalem par les Perses en 614*, ed. and tr. G. Garitte (Georgian and Arabic versions). Louvain 1960. English tr. by F.C. Coneybeare, 'Antiochus Strategos' Account of the Sack of Jerusalem in AD 614', *EHR* 25 (1910): 502–17. In the text the first number is the chapter in Garitte's editions, the second is the page in Coneybeare's translation.

Antoninus of Placentia, *Itinerarium*, in *Itinera Hierosolymitana, saeculi IV–VIII*, ed. P. Geyer. Leipzig–Vienna–Prague 1898, repr. New York–London 1964: 159–91; also in *PL* 72: 897–918.

Augustine, *De civitate Dei*, 2 vols., edd. B. Dombart and A. Kalb. Turnhout 1955.

Bal'ami. *Chronique de Tabari traduite sur la version persane*, 2 vols, tr. M.H. Zotenberg. Paris 1869.

Barhadbeshabba, *Histoire Ecclésiastique*, part 2, ed. and tr. F. Nau. *PO* 9 (1911).

Barhebraeus. Gregory bar Hebraeus, *The Chronography of Gregory Abu'l Faraj (Bar Hebraeus)*, 2 vols., ed. and tr. E. A. W. Budge. London 1932.

Barhebraeus. *Gregorii Barhebraei Chronicon Ecclesiasticum*, 2 vols., ed. and tr. J.B. Abbeloos and T.J. Lamy. Louvain 1872–7.

Bar 'Idta. *The Histories of Rabban Hormizd the Persian and Rabban Bar-'Idtā*, ed. and tr. E.A. Wallis Budge, 2 vols. London 1893.

Cedrenus, *Compendium Historiarum*, CSHB, ed. I. Bekker, 2 vols. Bonn 1838–9.

Chr. 724. Chronicon Miscellaneum ad AD 724 pertinens, *CSCO* Scr. Syr. 3–4, ed. and tr. J.-B. Chabot (Paris, 1903); partial translation in Palmer 1993: 14–23.

Chr. 819. Chronicon anonymum ad a.d. 819, ed. J.-B. Chabot along with *Chr. 1234*, vol.1. Partial tr. in Palmer 1993: 75–82.

Chr. 846. Chronicon ad AD 846 pertinens, *CSCO* Scr. Syr. 3–4, ed. and tr. J.-B. Chabot. Louvain 1904. Partial tr. in Palmer 1993: 75–82.

Chr. 1234. Chronicon anonymum ad a.c. 1234 pertinens, *CSCO* Scr. Syr. 55–6, ed. and tr. J.-B. Chabot. Louvain 1937. Partial translation in Palmer 1993: 111–221.

Chron. Arbela. Die Chronik von Arbela – Ein Beitrag zur Kenntnis des ältesten Christentums im Orient, ed. and tr. P. Kawerau, *CSCO* Scr. Syr. 199–200. Louvain 1985.

Chr. Ede. Chronicon Edessenicum, *CSCO* Scr. Syr. 1–2, ed. I. Guidi. Paris 1903; also in *Untersuchungen über die Edessenische Chronik*, ed. and tr. L. Hallier. Leipzig 1892.

Chr. Khuz. Chronicon Anonymum, ed. and tr. I. Guidi, *CSCO* Scr. Syr. 1–2. Leipzig 1903.

Chr. Pasch. Chronicon Paschale, ed. L. Dindorf. Bonn 1832. Partial tr. by M. and M. Whitby, *Chronicon Paschale 284–628 AD*. Liverpool 1989.

Chr. Seert. Chronicle of Seert (= *Histoire nestorienne inédite*), ed. A. Scher, tr. l'abbé Pierre, *PO* 4 (1908), 5 (1910), 7 (1911) and 13 (1919).

C.J. Codex Justinianus, ed. P. Krueger, eleventh edition. Berlin 1954.

C.Th. Codex Theodosianus, ed. T. Mommsen, third edition. Berlin 1962. Tr. C. Pharr. Princeton 1952.

Claudian. *Claudii Claudiani Carmina*, ed. J.B. Hall. Leipzig 1985.

Conf. Peroz, Confession of the renowned Peroz in Bedjan 1894: 253–62.

Cons. CP. Consularia Constantinopolitana, ed. R.W. Burgess in *The Chronicle of Hydatius and the Consularia Constantinopolitana*. Oxford 1993.

Cont. Isid. Byz. Arabica. Continuatio Byzantia Arabica a. DCCXLI in *MGH* XI (1894), 334–68, tr. in Hoyland 1997: 612–27.

Corippus, *In laudem Iustini Augusti minoris Libri IV*, ed., tr. and comm. Averil Cameron. London 1976.

Corippus, *Ioh. Flavii Cresconii Corippi Iohannidos libri VIII*, edd. J. Diggle and F.R.D. Goodyear. Cambridge 1970.

Cyr. Scyth. Cyril of Scythopolis, ed. E. Schwartz, *Kyrillos von Skythopolis*, TU 49.2. Leipzig 1939; tr. and comm. A.J. Festugière, *Les moines d'Orient: Les moines de Palestine*, III.1–3. Paris 1962–3; and R. M. Price with J. Binns, *The Lives of the Monks of Palestine*. Kalamazoo, Mich., 1991.

Cyrillonas. 'Die Gedichte des Cyrillonas', ed. G. Bickell, *ZDMG* 27 (1873) 566–625; tr. P.S. Landersdorfer, *Ausgewählte Schriften der syrischen Dichter*. Munich 1913.

De Cer. Constantine Porphyrogenitus, *De Cerimoniis*, ed. J.J. Reiske, CSHB. Bonn 1829.

Denha, *Vie de Marouta*, ed. and tr. F. Nau, *PO* 3 (1905): 52–96.

Elias Nis. Elias of Nisibis, *Eliae Metropolitae Nisibeni Opus Chronologicum*, pars prior, *CSCO* Scr. Syr. 21–2, ed. and tr. E. W. Brooks. Rome–Paris–Leipzig 1910.

Ełishe. *Ełishe vasn Vardanay ev Hayots' Paterazmin*, ed. E. Tēr Minasean. Erevan 1958; tr. R.W. Thomson, *Ełishē: History of Vardan and the Armenian War*. Cambridge, Mass., 1982.

Ephrem Syrus, *Hymni contra Iul.* E. Beck, ed. and tr., *Des hl. Ephraim Hymnen de paradiso und Contra Julianum*, *CSCO* Scr. Syr. 174–5. Louvain 1957.

Epic Histories. Patmut'iwn Hayots', ed. K'. Patkanean. St Petersburg 1883, repr. Delmar, NY,

1984; tr. and comm. N.G. Garsoïan, *The Epic Histories attributed to P'awstos Buzand* (*Buzandaran Patmut'iwnk'*). Cambridge, Mass., 1989.

Epitome de Caesaribus, ed. F. Pichlmayr, rev. R. Gruendel. Leipzig 1970.

Eunapius, in *FCH* II: 1–127.

Euphemia. *Euphemia and the Goth with the acts of Martyrdom of the confessors of Edessa*, ed. and tr. F.C. Burkitt (Syriac). London 1913. *Die Akten der Edessenische Bekenner Gurjas, Samonas und Abibos*, ed. E. von Dobschütz, TU 37.2, Leipzig 1911 (Greek).

Eustath. Eustathius of Epiphaneia, fragments, ed. C. Müller, *FHG* IV: 138–42.

Eustratius, *Vita martyris Golindouch*. Εὐστρατίου πρεσβυτέρου Βίος καὶ πολιτεία ἤγουν ἄθλησις καὶ δια Χριστον ἀγώνες τῆς ἁγίας ὁσιομάρτυρος Γολινδούχ, τῆς ἐν τῳ ἁγίῳ Βαπτίσματι μετονομασθείσης Μαρίας in Ἀνάλεκτα ὠΙεροσολυμιτικῆς Σταχυολογίας 4: 149–74, 5: 392–5, ed. A. Papadopoulos-Kerameus. St Petersburg 1897–8.

Eustratius. *V.Eutychii*. See *V.Eutychii* below.

Eutropius. *Breviarium*, ed. and tr. J. Hellegouarc'h. Paris 1999.

Eutychius. Eutychius, *Annales*, ed. and tr. M. Breydy, *Das Annalenwerk des Eutychios von Alexandrien*, *CSCO* Scr. Arab. 44–5. Louvain, 1985; tr. Pocock, *PG* 111.

Evagr. *HE*. Evagrius, *Ecclesiastical History*, edd. J. Bidez and L. Parmentier. London, 1898. Anonmyous translation *A History of the Church in six books from AD 431 to AD 594 by Evagrius*. London 1846. New tr. by M. Whitby, *The Ecclesiastical History of Evagrius Scholasticus*. Liverpool 2000.

Exc. de Virt. Constantine Porphyrogenitus, *Excerpta de virtutibus et vitiis*, ed. T. Büttner-Wobst and A. Roos, 2 vols. Berlin 1906–10.

Festus. *Breviarium*, ed. and tr. M.-P. Arnaud-Lindet. Paris 1994.

Firdausi. *Le livre des rois par Abou'lkasim Firdousi*, tr. J. Mohl, vols.5–6. Paris 1866–8.

Georg. Cypr. *Le Synecdèmos d'Hieroclès et l'opuscule géographique de Georges de Chypre*, ed. and comm. E. Honigmann. Brussels 1939.

Geo. Pis. *Giorgio di Pisidia, Poemi I: Panegirici epici*, ed. and tr. A. Pertusi. Ettal 1959.

Geo. Pis. *Bell. Avar.* George of Pisidia, *Bellum Avaricum* in Pertusi (above): 176–200.

Geo. Pis. *Exp. Pers.* George of Pisidia, *Expeditio Persica* in Pertusi (above): 84–136.

Geo. Pis. *Her.* George of Pisidia, *Heraclias* in Pertusi (above): 240–307.

Geo. Pis. *In Restitutionem S. Crucis* George of Pisidia, *In Restitutionem S. Crucis* in Pertusi (above): 225–30.

Geo. Pis. *Hexaemeron*. George of Pisidia, *Hexaemeron* in *PG* 92: 1425–1578.

Greg. Naz. Gregory Nazianzenus, *Discours 4–5. Contre Julien*, ed. and tr. J. Bernardi. Paris 1983.

Greg. Tur. Gregory of Tours, *Historia Francorum*, ed. W. Arndt and B. Krusch, *MGH Scr. rer. Mer.* I, Hannover 1884.

Hist. Rabban bar 'Idta, *The Histories of Rabban Hormizd the Persian and Rabban Bar-'Idta*, ed. and tr. E.A.W. Budge, 2 vols. London 1902.

Hist. Her. Sebeos, (fragments of) *The History of Heraclius*, ed. G. Abgarian, *Patmut'iwn Sebeosi*: 429–33. Erevan 1979; tr. Mahé 1984: 227–32.

HVG, Juansher, *The History of Vaxt'ang Gorgasali*, ed. Qauxč 'išvili 1955–9: II, 139–244 (see K'art'lis C'xovreba below); tr. Thomson 1996: 153–250.

Hyd. Hydatius, *Chronicle*, ed. and tr. R.W. Burgess: see *Cons CP.* above.

Isaac of Antioch. *S. Isaaci Antiocheni Opera Omnia*, ed. and tr. G. Bickell, vol.1. Giessen 1873.

Jac. Ede. *Chron.* *Chronicon Iacobi Edesseni*, *CSCO* Scr. Syr. 5–6, ed. and tr. E.W. Brooks. Paris 1903. Translations by E.W. Brooks, 'The Chronological Canon of James of Edessa,' *ZDMG* 53 (1899): 261–327, partial tr. in Palmer 1993: 36–40.

Jac. Serug. *Iacobi Sarugensis epistulae quotquot supersunt*, ed. G. Olinder, *CSCO* Scr. Syr. 57. Louvain 1952.

Jerome, *Die Chronik des Hieronymus*, 3rd ed., ed. R. Helm. Berlin 1984.

Jerome, *Epistulae*, 2nd ed., ed. I. Hilbert, 3 vols., CSEL 54–6. Vienna 1996.

Jerome, *Vita Malchi. Sancti Eusebii Hieronymi Vita Malchi Monachi Captivi*, ed. and tr. C.C. Mierow in *Classical Essays presented to James A. Kleist, S.J.* Saint Louis 1946: 31–60. Also in *PL* 23: 55–62.

Joh. Ant. John of Antioch, fragments, ed. C. Müller, *FHG* IV: 535–622, V: 27–38.

Joh. Bicl. John of Biclar, *Chronicle*, ed. T. Mommsen, *MGH AA* XI.211–20; tr. K. Wolf, *Conquerors and Chroniclers of Early Medieval Spain.* Liverpool 1990.

Joh. Chrys., *De sancto Babyla.* John Chrysostom, *De sancto Babyla contra Iulianum et Gentiles*, ed. and tr. M.A. Schatkin et al., SC 362, Paris 1990; tr. M.A. Schatkin, *St John Chrysostom. Apologist*, The Fathers of the Church 73, Washington D.C. 1985.

Joh. Diakrin. Johannes Diakrinomenos, fragments, ed. G.C. Hansen with Theod. Lect. (as below).

Joh. Eph. *HE. Historiae Ecclesiasticae Pars Tertia*, *CSCO* Scr. Syr. 54–5, ed. and tr. E.W. Brooks. Louvain 1952. Translated also by R. Payne Smith, *The Third Part of the Ecclesiastical History of John of Ephesus.* Oxford 1860.

Joh. Eph., *Lives.* John of Ephesus, *Lives of the Eastern Saints*, ed. and tr. E.W. Brooks, *PO* 17 (1923), 18 (1924) and 19 (1925).

Joh. Lyd. *De Mag.* John Lydus, *De Magistratibus Populi Romani*, ed. and tr. A. C. Bandy. Philadelphia, Penn., 1983.

Joh. Nik. *Chronicle of John, bishop of Nikiu*, tr. R.H. Charles London 1916.

Jord. *Rom.* Jordanes, *Romana*, *MGH AA* V.1, ed. Th. Mommsen. Berlin 1882.

Joshua the Stylite in J.B. Chabot, *Incerti Auctoris Chronicon Pseudo-Dionysianum vulgo dictum*, vol.1, *CSCO* Scr. Syr. 43: 235–316. Louvain 1927; also ed. and tr. W. Wright, *The Chronicle of Joshua the Stylite.* Cambridge 1882 and tr. J. Watt and F. Trombley. Liverpool 2000.

Julian Romance, ed. J.G.E. Hoffmann, *Iulianos der Abtrünnige. Syrische Erzählungen.* Leiden 1880; tr. Sir H. Gollancz, *Julian the Apostate, now translated for the first time from the Syriac original.* London 1928.

Kʿartʿlis Cʿxovreba, ed. S. Qauxčʿišvili, 2 vols. Tbilisi 1955–9.

Koriun, *V. Mesrop*, tr. and comm. S. Winkler, *Koriwns Biographie des Mesrop Maštocʿ.* Rome 1994.

Łazar. *Patmutʿiwn Hayotsʿ*, ed. G. Tēr-Mkrtchʿean and S. Malkhasean. Tiflis 1904, repr. Delmar, NY, 1985; tr. R.W. Thomson, *The History of Łazar Pʿarpecʿi.* Atlanta, GA, 1991.

Leonti Mroveli, *The Conversion of Kʿartʿli by Nino*, ed. Qauxčʿišvili 1955–9: II, 72–138; tr. Thomson 1996: 84–153.

Leontius, *V. Ioh. Eleem.* (*Life of John the Almsgiver*), ed. and tr. A.J. Festugière and L. Rydén, *Léontios de Néapolis, Vie de Syméon le fou et Vie de Jean de Chypre.* Paris 1974; tr. Dawes and Baynes 1948: 207–62.

Libanius, *Orationes*, ed. R. Foerster, 7 vols. Leipzig 1903–13; tr. A.F. Norman, *Selected Works*, 2 vols., Cambridge, Mass., 1987 and *Autobiography and Selected Letters*, 2 vols., Cambridge, Mass., 1992.

Life of: see under *V.* or *Vita*.

Malalas, *Chronographia*, ed. J. Thurn, CFHB. Berlin 2000, also ed. L. Dindorf, CSHB. Bonn 1831; tr. E. and M. Jeffreys and R. Scott. Melbourne 1986.

Malchus. Malchus of Philadelphia, *FCH* II: 402–54.

Marc. com. *The Chronicle of Marcellinus*, ed. Th. Mommsen, tr. B. Croke. Sydney 1995. Mommsen's original text in *MGH AA* XI (Berlin 1894): 60–104.

Marc. com. addit. *Additamentum* to *The Chronicle of Marcellinus* in Croke (above) and Mommsen (above): 104–8.

Mari. *Maris Amri et Slibae de patriarchis Nestorianorum commentaria*, vol.1, ed. H. Gismondi. Rome 1899.

Mart. Grig. *Martyrdom of Grigor*, ed. Bedjan 1895: 347–94, abbreviated tr. in Hoffmann 1880: 78–86.

Mart. Shir. *Martyrdom of Shirin*, ed. P. Devos, 'Sainte Shirin, Martyre sous Khosrau Ier Anosarvan', *AnBoll* 64 (1946): 87–131, tr. P. Devos, 'La jeune martyre perse sainte Shirin († 559)', *AnBoll* 112 (1994): 4–31.

Mas'udi, *Les prairies d'or*, ed. C.B. de Meynard and P. de Courteille, 9 vols. Paris 1861–77; tr. C.B. de Meynard, P. de Courteille, C. Pellat, 5 vols. Paris 1962–97.

Maurice, *Stratēgikon*, ed. G.T. Dennis. Vienna 1981; tr. G.T. Dennis. Philadelphia, Penn., 1984.

Menander. *The History of Menander the Guardsman*, ed. and tr. R.C. Blockley. Liverpool 1985.

*Michael the Syrian, ed. and tr. J.-B. Chabot, *Chronique de Michel le Syrien, patriarche jacobite d'Antioche (1166–1199)*, 4 vols. Paris 1899–1924. The references to a, b and c refer to columns in the Syriac: from left to right these are arranged in the order c, a, b. In Chabot's French translation, a is usually translated first, followed by two columns: c (ecclesiastical affairs) is placed on the right, b (secular affairs) on the left.

Mos. Khor. Moses Khorenats'i. *Patmut'iwn Hayots'*, ed. M. Abełean and S. Yarut'iwnean. Tiflis 1913, repr. Delmar, NY, 1981; tr. R.W. Thomson, *Moses Khorenats'i, History of the Armenians*. Cambridge, Mass., 1978; also A. and J.-P. Mahé. Paris 1993.

Movsēs Daskhurants'i. Movsēs Kałankatuats'i, *Patmuti'iwn Ałuanits' Ashkhanarhi*, ed. V. Arak'elyan. Erevan 1983; tr. C.J.F. Dowsett *The History of the Caucasian Albanians by Mives Dasxuranc'i*. London 1961.

Narratio. Narratio de rebus Armeniae, ed. G. Garitte. Louvain 1952. French tr. by J.-P. Mahé in *REArm* 25 (1994–5): 429–38.

Narrationes Variae, ed. and tr. E. W. Brooks and I. Guidi, *CSCO* Scr. Syr. 3–4. Paris 1903.

Nic. Call. Nicephorus Callistus Xanthopulus, *Ecclesiasticae Historiae*, ed. J.-P. Migne, *PG* 145–7.

Nic. *Nikephoros. Short History*, ed. and tr. C. Mango. Washington, D.C., 1990.

NovJ. Justinian, *Novellae* in *Corpus Juris Civilis* vol.3, edd. R. Schoell and W. Kroll, sixth edition. Berlin 1954.

NTh. Theodosii II Leges Novellae in *C.Th.* (above).

Oracle of Baalbek, see Alexander 1967 below.

Orac. Sib. Die Oracula Sibyllina, ed. J. Geffcken. Leipzig 1902. See also W. Scott (below).

Orosius, *Hist. Pauli Orosii Historiarum adversum paganos libri VII*, ed. and tr. M.-P. Arnaud-Lindet. Paris 1990–1.

Pacatus, see *Pan. Lat.* below.

Pan. Lat. Panegyrici Latini, ed. R.B. Mynors. Oxford 1964; tr. C.E.V. Nixon and B. Rodgers, *In Praise of Later Roman Emperors*. Berkeley 1994.

Parastaseis Syntomoi Chronikai. A. Cameron and J. Herrin, *Constantinople in the Early Eighth Century. The* Parastaseis Syntomoi Chronikai. Leiden 1984.

Passio S. Isbozetae, ed. and tr. P. Peeters in *AASS* Nov. IV (1925): 204–16.

P'awstos. See *Epic Histories*.

Peri Strategias. Anon. (? Magister Syrianus) *Peri Strategias*, ed. and tr. G.T. Dennis in *Three Byzantine Military Treatises*, CFHB. Washington, D.C., 1985.

Petr. Patr. Peter the Patrician, fragments, in *FHG* IV: 180–91.

Philostorgius, *Kirchengeschichte*, ed. J. Bidez, rev. G. Winkelmann. Berlin 1981.

Philoxenus, *Letter to the monks of Senun*, ed. and tr. A. de Halleux, *Lettre aux moines de Senoun CSIO*. Scr. Syr. 231–2. Louvain 1963.

Priscus. Priscus of Panium, in *FCH* II: 222–376.

Proc. *Aed*. Procopius, *De Aedificiis*, ed. J. Haury, rev. G. Wirth. Leipzig 1964; ed. and tr. H. B. Dewing. Cambridge, Mass., 1940.

Proc. *Anecd*. Procopius, *Anecdota*, ed. J. Haury, rev. G. Wirth. Leipzig, 1963; ed. and tr. H. B. Dewing. Cambridge, Mass., 1935.

Proc. *Wars*. Procopius, *Bella*, ed. J. Haury, rev. G. Wirth, 2 vols. Leipzig 1963; ed. and tr. H. B. Dewing, 5 vols. Cambridge, Mass., 1914–28. References to just Proc. refer to the *Wars*.

Ps. Dion. II. *Chronicon pseudo-dionysianum vulgo dictum*, vol.2, ed. J.-B. Chabot, *CSCO* Scr. Syr. 104. Paris 1933. Tr. R. Hespel, *CSCO* Scr. Syr. 213. Louvain 1989. Partial tr. in W. Witakowski, *Pseudo-Dionysius of Tel-Mahre, Chronicle, known also as the Chronicle of Zuqnin. Part III*. Liverpool 1996.

Quodvultdeus, *Opera Quodvultdeo Cathaginiensi episcopo tributa*, CCSL 60, ed. R. Braun. Turnhout 1976; also tr. and ed. R. Braun, 2 vols., Paris 1964.

Rufinus, *Kirchengeschichte*, ed. T. Mommsen in Eusebius, *Werke* II.2, *Die Kirchengeschichte*. Leipzig 1908. Tr. P.R. Amidon, *The* Church History *of Rufinus of Aquileia, Books 10 and 11*. Oxford 1997.

Sebeos, *Patmut'iwn Sebeosi*, ed. G.V. Abgaryan. Erevan 1979. Tr. R.W. Thomson, comm. J.D. Howard-Johnston, with T. Greenwood. Liverpool 1999.

Sidonius Apollinaris, *Carmina*, ed. and tr. A.G. Loyen, vol.1. Paris 1960.

Socr. *HE*. Socrates, *Kirchengeschichte*, ed. G.C. Hansen. Berlin 1995.

Sophronius, *Anacr*. Sophronius, *Anacreontica*, ed. M. Gigante. Rome 1957.

Soz. *HE*. Sozomen, *Kirchengeschichte*, 2nd ed., ed. J. Bidez, rev. G.C. Hansen. Berlin 1995.

Spurious Life of Jacob Baradaeus, ed. and tr. E.W. Brooks, *PO* 19 (1925): 228–68.

Stephen of Taron, ed. K. Šahnazareants', *Tiezerakan patmuti'iwn Step'annos vardapeti Taronets'isoy*. Paris, 1859; tr. H. Gelzer and A. Burckhardt, *Stephanos von Taron. Armenische Geschichte*. Leipzig 1907; also tr. E. Dulaurier, *Etienne Açoghig de Daron. Histoire universelle*. Paris 1883.

Suda. Suidas, *Lexicon*, ed. A. Adler, 4 vols. Leipzig 1928–38.

Synodicon Orientale, ed. and tr. J.-B. Chabot. Paris 1902.

Tabari, ed. M.J. de Goeje, vol.1. Leiden 1879. Tr. T. Nöldeke, *Geschichte der Perser und Araber zur Zeit der Sassaniden*. Leiden 1879; tr. C.E. Bosworth, *The Sāsānids, the Byzantines, the Lakhmids, and Yemen*. Albany, NY, 1999. References give the page in de Goeje and then that in Bosworth.

Themistius. *Themistii Orationes quae supersunt*, ed. H. Schenkl and G. Downey, vol.1. Leipzig 1965.

Thdrt. *ep. Théodoret de Cyr. Correspondance*, ed. and tr. Y. Azéma, 3 vols. Paris 1955–65.

Thdrt. *Graec. affect.* Theodoret of Cyrrhus, *Graecarum affectionum curatio*, ed. and tr. P. Canivet, *Thérapeutique des maladies helléniques*, 2 vols. Paris 1958.

Thdrt. *HE*. Theodoret of Cyrrhus, *Historia Ecclesiastica*, ed. L. Parmentier, rev. G. Hansen, GCS. Berlin 1998.

Theod. Lect. *HE*. Theodore Anagnostes (= Theodore Lector), *Kirchengeschichte*, ed. G. C. Hansen, GCS. Berlin 1971.

Theod. Sync. *Hom.* Theodore Syncellus, *Sermon on the siege of Constantinople in 626* in *Analecta Avarica, Rozprawy Akademii Umiejetnosci, Wydzial Filologiczny*, series 2, vol.15, ed. L. Sternbach: 298–320. Krakow 1900. A reprint of Sternbach's edition and a French translation and brief commentary in F. Makk, *Traduction et commentaire de l'homélie écrite probablement par Théodore le syncelle sur le siège de Constantinople en 626, Acta Universitatis de Atilla József Nominatae, Acta Antiqua et Archaeologica 19 (Opuscula Byzantina 3)*. Szeged 1975.

Theoph. Theophanes, *Chronographia*, ed. C. de Boor. Leipzig 1883. Tr. C. Mango and R. Scott, *The Chronicle of Theophanes Confessor*. Oxford 1997.

Theoph. Byz. Theophanes Byzantinus, fragments, ed. C. Müller, *FHG* IV: 270–1; tr. in Wilson 1994.

Th. Sim. Theophylact Simocatta, *Historiae*, ed. C. de Boor, rev. P. Wirth. Stuttgart 1962. Tr. and annot. M. and M. Whitby. Oxford 1986; also tr. and annot. P. Schreiner. Stuttgart 1985.

Thom. Arts. Thomas Artsruni, *Patmut'iwn Tann Artsruneats'*, ed. K. Patkanean. St Petersburg 1887; tr. R.W. Thomson, *Thomas Artsruni: History of the House of the Artsrunik'*. Detroit 1985.

Thomas of Marga, *The Book of Governors*, 2 vols, ed. and tr. E.A. Wallis Budge. London 1893.

Translat. Anast. Retour des reliques du saint martyr Anastase le Perse à son monastère, ed. and tr. B. Flusin in Flusin 1992: I, 98–107.

V. Alex. Akoim. Vie d'Alexandre l'acémète, ed. and tr. E. de Stoop, *PO* 6 (1911): 605–704.

V. Dan. Styl. Vita Sancti Danielis Stylitae, ed. H. Delehaye in *Les Saints stylites*. Paris-Brussels 1923; tr. Dawes and Baynes 1948: 7–71.

V. Eutychii. Eustratii presbyteri Vita Eutychii patriarchi Constantinopolitani, ed. C. Laga, CC ser. gr. 25. Louvain 1992.

V. Georg. Khozeb. 'Sancti Georgii Chozebitae confessoris et monachi vita auctore Antonio ejus discipulo', ed. and tr. C. Houze, *AnBoll 7* (1887): 95–144 with notes and corrections in *AnBoll* 8 (1888): 209–10. Tr. Di Segni 1991.

V. Ioh. ep. Tell. Elias of Nisibis, *Vitae Iohannis episcopi Tellae* in *Vitae Virorum apud Monophysitas celeberrimorum*, ed. and tr. E.W. Brooks, *CSCO* Scr. Syr. 7–8. Paris 1907.

V. Mar Aba in Bedjan 1895: 206–74.

V. Nerses, 'Généalogie de la famille de saint Grégoire et vie de saint Nersès patriarche des Arméniens', tr. J.-R. Emine in *Collection des historiens anciens et modernes de l'Arménie*, ed. V. Langlois, vol.2: 21–41. Paris 1869.

V. Sabrisho. Peter, *Life of Sabrisho*, in Bedjan 1895: 288–331; summary in Braun 1900: 278–82.

V. Sym. Styl. Vita Mar Symeon Stylites in Bedjan 1894: 507–644.

V. Sym. Styl. Iun. La vie ancienne de Syméon stylite le jeune, ed. and tr. P. van den Ven, Subsidia Hagiographica 32, 2 vols. Brussels, 1962–70.

V. S. Theodori. Vita, educatio et miracula S. Theodori, ed. H. Delehaye, *AASS* Nov. IV (1925): 49–55.

V. Theod. Syk. Vie de Théodore de Sykéon, ed. and tr. A.J. Festugière, 2 vols. Brussels 1970.

Yovhannēs Kat'oŀikos, *Patmut'iwn Hayots'*, ed. M. Emin. Moscow 1853, repr. Delmar, NY, 1980; tr. K. Maksoudian, *Yovhannēs Drasxanakertc'i: History of Armenia*. Atlanta, GA, 1987.

Ps.-Yov. Pseudo-Yovhannes Mamikonean, *The History of Taron*, tr. L. Avdoyan. Atlanta, GA, 1993.

Zach. *HE. Historia Ecclesiastica Zachariae Rhetori vulgo adscripta*, vol.2, *CSCO* Scr. Syr. 39, 42, ed. and tr. E. W. Brooks. Paris 1924. Translations also by J.F. Hamilton and E.W. Brooks,

The Syriac Chronicle known as that of Zachariah of Mitylene. London 1899; and K. Ahrens and G. Krüger, *Die sogennante Kirchengeschichte des Zacharias Rhetor.* Leipzig 1899.

Zon. Zonaras, *Epitome Historiarum,* ed. L. Dindorf, vol.3. Leipzig 1870.

Zos. Zosime, *Histoire Nouvelle,* ed. and tr. F. Paschoud, 6 vols. Paris 1979 (II, 1–2), 1986 (III, 1), 1989 (III, 2).

SECONDARY SOURCES

Acharyan, H. 1972. *Hayots' Andznanunneri Baaran (Dictionary of Armenian Personal Names).* Beirut.

Adontz, N. 1970. *Armenia in the period of Justinian: The political conditions based on the 'Naxarar' system,* tr. and rev. N. G. Garsoïan. Lisbon.

Akinean, H.N. 1913. 'Apstambut'iwne ev jajord tasnameay shrjane', *Handes Amsorya* 26: 61–80.

Alexander, P.J. 1967. *The Oracle of Baalbek. The Tiburtine Sibyl in Greek Dress,* Washington, D.C.

Alexander, S.S. 1977. 'Heraclius, Byzantine imperial ideology and the David plates', *Speculum* 52: 217–37.

Allen, P. 1979. 'The 'Justinianic' Plague', *Byzantion* 49: 5–20.

Allen, P. 1981. *Evagrius Scholasticus the Church Historian.* Louvain.

Altheim-Stiehl, R. 1991. 'Wurde Alexandreia im Juni 619 n. Chr. durch die Perser erobert?', *Tyche* 6: 3–16.

Altheim-Stiehl, R. 1992a. 'Zur zeitlichen Bestimmung der Sāsānidischen Eroberung Ägyptens' in O. Brehm and S. Klie, eds, *Mousikos anēr. Festschrift für Max Wegner.* 5–8. Bonn.

Altheim-Stiehl, R. 1992b. 'The Sasanians in Egypt – some evidence of historical interest', *Bulletin de la société d'archéologie copte* 31: 87–96.

Altheim-Stiehl, R. 1998. 'Egypt. iv. Relations with Persia in the Sasanian period', *EIr* VIII: 252–4.

Anderson, J.G.C. 1897. 'The road-system of eastern Asia Minor', *JHS* 17: 22–44.

Angeli Bertinelli, M.G. 1989. 'Al confine tra l'impero romano e la Persia in età tardoantica: la questione della Lazica', *Quaderni catanesi di studi classici e medievali* 1: 117–46.

Antonopoulos, P. 1990. *Peter the Patrician. The Byzantine diplomat, official and author* (in Greek). Athens.

Asmussen, J.P. 1983. 'Christians in Iran' in *CHI* III: 924–48.

Azarpay, G. 1981–2. 'Bishapur VI. An artistic record of an Armeno-Persian alliance in the fourth century', *Artibus Asiae* 43: 171–89.

Azarpay, G. 1982. 'The role of Mithra in the investiture and triumph of Šāpūr II', *Iranica Antiqua* 17: 181–7.

Baker, D. 1976. 'Theodore of Sykeon and the historians' in D. Baker, ed., *The Orthodox Churches and the West,* Studies in Church History 13: 83–96.

Bakhit, M.A. 1987. *Proceedings of the Second Symposium on the History of Bilad al-Sham during the Early Islamic Period up to 40 AH/640 AD,* vol.1. Amman.

Baldwin, B. 1988. 'Nicholas Mysticus on Roman History', *Byzantion* 58: 174–8.

Ball. W. 1989. 'Soundings at Seh Qubba, a Roman frontier station on the Tigris in Iraq', *EFRE:* 7–18.

Balty, J.C. and Napoleone-Lemaire, J. 1969. *Fouilles d'Apamée de Syrie. I.1. L'église à atrium de la grande colonnade.* Brussels.

Balty, J.C. 1970. 'Un follis d'Antioche daté de 623/624 et les campagnes syriennes d'Héraclius'. *Schweizer Münzblätter* 20: 4–12.

Bardill, J. 1999. 'The Great Palace of the Byzantine emperors and the Walker Trust excavations', *JRA* 12: 216–30.

Bardill, J. and Greatrex, G. 1996. 'Antiochus the *Praepositus*, A Persian Eunuch at the Court of Theodosius II', *DOP* 50: 171–97.

Barišić , F. 1954. 'Le siège de Constantinople par les Avares et les Slaves en 626', *Byz* 24: 371–95.

Bauzou, T. 1993. 'Épigraphie et toponymie: le cas de la Palmyrène'. *Syria* 70: 27–50.

Barnes, T.D. 1998. *Ammianus Marcellinus and the Representation of Historical Reality.* Ithaca and London.

Baynes, N. 1904. 'The first campaign of Heraclius against Persia', *EHR* 19: 694–702.

Baynes, N. 1912a. Review of E. Merten, *Zum Perserkriege der byzantinischen Kaiser Justinos II und Tiberios II (571–579 n. Chr.* (Weimar, 1911), *BZ* 21: 527–8.

Baynes, N. 1912b. 'The restoration of the Cross at Jerusalem', *EHR* 27: 287–99.

Baynes, N. 1913, 1914. 'The Military Operations of Emperor Heraclius', *United Services Magazine* 46: 526–33, 659–66, 47: 30–8, 195–201, 318–24, 401–12, 532–41, 665–79.

Baynes, N. 1955. 'Rome and Armenia in the Fourth Century' in *Byzantine Studies and Other Essays*: 186–208. London.

Bedjan, P. 1894. *Acta Martyrum et Sanctorum Syriace*, vol.4. Leipzig.

Bedjan, P. 1895. *Histoire de Mar-Jabalaha, de trois autre patriarches, d'un prêtre et de deux laïques, nestoriens*, 2nd ed. Leipzig.

Beševliev, V. 1978. 'Zur Chronik des Johannes von Nikiu CXX.46–49', *Byzantinobulgarica* 5: 229–36.

Bird, H.W. 1986. 'Eutropius and Festus: some reflections on the empire and imperial policy in AD 369/370', *Florilegium* 8: 11–22.

Bíró, M. 1997. 'On the presence of the Huns in the Caucasus', *Acta Orientalia Academiae Scientiarum Hungaricae* 50: 53–60.

Bishop, M.C., and Coulston, J.N.C. 1993. *Roman Military Equipment.* London.

Blockley, R.C. 1981, 1983. See p.xv, *FCH*.

Blockley, R.C. 1984. 'The Romano–Persian Peace Treaties of AD 299 and 363', *Florilegium* 6: 28–49.

Blockley, R.C. 1985a. 'Subsidies and Diplomacy: Rome and Persia in Late Antiquity', *Phoenix* 39: 62–74.

Blockley, R.C. 1985b. See Menander (above).

Blockley, R.C. 1987. 'The Division of Armenia between the Romans and the Persians at the end of the fourth century AD', *Historia* 36: 222–34.

Blockley, R.C. 1992. *East Roman Foreign Policy*, Leeds.

Blockley, R.C. 1998. 'The dynasty of Theodosius', in Cameron and Garnsey 1998: 111–37.

De Blois, F. 1990. 'The date of the martyrs of Nagrān', *Arabian Archaeology and Epigraphy* 1: 110–28.

Bombaci, A. 1970. 'Qui était Jebu Xak'an?', *Turcica* 2: 7–24.

Bosworth, C.E. 1983. 'Iran and the Arabs before Islam' in *CHI* III: 593–612.

Bosworth, C.E. 1999. See Tabari, above.

Bowersock, G.W. 1980. 'Mavia, Queen of the Saracens', in W. Eck. H. Galsterer, H. Wolff (eds.), *Studien zur antiken Sozialgeschichte. Festschrift Friedrich Vittinghoff*, 477–95. Köln.

Boyce, M. 1985. 'Adur Gushnasp', *EIr* I: 475–6.

Brakmann, H. 1992. 'Axomis', *RAC, Supplement Band I*: 718–810.

Brandes, W. 1998. Review of Mango and Scott 1997, *BZ* 91: 249–61.

Braun, O. 1900. *Das Buch der Synhados oder Synodicon Orientale*. Vienna.

Braun, O. 1915. *Ausgewählte Akten persischer Märtyrer*. Kempten and Munich.

Braun, R. 1964. See Quodvultdeus.

Braund, D. 1991. 'Procopius on the economy of Lazica', *CQ* 41: 221–5.

Braund, D. 1992. 'Priscus on the Suani', *Phoenix* 37: 62–5.

Braund, D. 1994. *Georgia in Antiquity*. Oxford.

Bréhier, L. and Aigrain, R. 1947. *L'histoire de l'église. V. Grégoire le Grand, les Etats barbares et la conquête arabe (590–737)*. Paris.

Brock, S.P. 1985. 'The Christology of the Church of the East in the Synods of the fifth to early seventh centuries' in G. Dragas, ed, *Aksum-Thyateira: a Festschrift for Archbishop Methodios*: 125–42 (= Brock 1992, XII). London.

Brock, S.P. 1992. *Studies in Syriac Christianity*. London.

Brock, S.P. 1994. 'The Church of the East in the Sasanian empire up to the sixth century and its absence from the councils in the Roman empire' in *Syriac Dialogue. First non-official consultation on dialogue within the Syriac tradition*: 69–85. Vienna.

Brock, S.P. 1996. 'The 'Nestorian' church: a lamentable misnomer'. *BJRL* 78.3: 23–35.

Brock, S.P. and Harvey, S.A. 1987. *Holy Women of the Syrian Orient*. Berkeley.

Brooks, E.W. 1893. 'The Emperor Zenon and the Isaurians', *EHR* 8: 209–38.

Brooks, E.W. 1906. Review of Pernice 1905 in *EHR* 21: 141–3.

Brown, T.S., Bryer, A., and Winfield, D. 1978. 'Cities of Heraclius', *BMGS* 4: 15–38.

de Bruijn, E. and Dudley, D. 1995. 'The Humeima Hoard: Byzantine and Sasanian Coins and Jewelry from Southern Jordan', *AJA* 99: 683–97.

Bryer, A. and Winfield, D. 1985. *The Byzantine Monuments and Topography of the Pontos*, 2 vols. Washington D.C.

Bundy, D.D. 1978. 'Jacob Baradaeus. The State of Research, a Review of Sources, and a New approach', *Muséon* 91: 45–86.

Bury, J.B. 1907. 'The Ceremonial Book of Constantine Porphyrogennetos', *EHR* 22: 209–27, 417–39.

Bury, J.B. 1923. *History of the Later Roman Empire*, 2 vols. London.

Butler, A.J. 1978, rev. Fraser, P.M. *The Arab Conquest of Egypt*. Oxford.

Cameron, A.D.E. 1968. 'Notes on Claudian's invectives', *CQ* 18: 387–411.

Cameron, A.D.E. 1970. *Claudian. Poetry and Propaganda at the Court of Honorius*, Oxford.

Cameron, A.D.E. 1976. *Circus Factions. Blues and Greens at Rome and Constantinople*. Oxford.

Cameron, Averil. 1970. *Agathias*. Oxford.

Cameron, Averil. 1966. '*Anth. Plan.* 72: a Propaganda Poem from the Reign of Justin II', with Alan Cameron. *BICS* 13: 101–4 (= 1981: VII).

Cameron, Averil. 1969–70. 'Agathias on the Sassanians', *DOP* 23–44: 69–183.

Cameron, Averil. 1975. 'The Byzantine sources of Gregory of Tours', *JTS* 26: 421–6 (= 1981: XV).

Cameron, Averil. 1976. 'The early religious policies of Justin II', *Studies in Church History* 13, ed. D. Baker: 51–67 (= 1981: X).

Cameron, Averil. 1981. *Continuity and Change in Sixth-century Byzantium*. London.

Cameron, Averil. 1983. 'The History of the Image of Edessa: The Telling of a Story', *Okeanos. Harvard Ukrainian Studies* 7: 80–94.

Cameron, Averil. 1985. *Procopius and the Sixth Century*. London.

Cameron, Averil and Conrad, L.I., eds. 1992. *The Byzantine and Early Islamic Near East. I. Problems in the Literary Source Material*. Princeton.

Cameron, Averil and Garnsey, P., eds. 1998. *The Cambridge Ancient History*, vol.13, *The Late Empire, AD 337–425*. Cambridge.

Campos, J. 1960. *Juan de Biclaro, obispo de Gerona. Su vida y su obra*. Madrid.

Canivet, P. 1958. See Thrdt. *Graec. affect.*, above.

Capizzi, C. 1969. *L'imperatore Anastasio I*. Rome.

Casey, P.J. 1996. 'Justinian, the *limitanei*, and Arab–Byzantine relations in the sixth century', *JRA* 9: 214–22.

Chabot, J.-B. 1902. See *Synodicon Orientale*.

Charanis, P. 1974. *Church and State in the Later Roman Empire. The religious policy of Anastasius I (491–518)*. Thessalonika.

Chaumont, M.-L. 1974. 'A propos d'un édit de paix religieuse d'époque sassanide' in *Mélanges d'histoire des religions offerts à Henri-Charles Puech*: 71–80. Paris.

Chaumont, M.-L. 1976. 'L'Arménie entre Rome et l'Iran', *ANRW* II.9.1: 71–194.

Chaumont, M.-L. 1987. 'Armenia and Iran II', *EIr* II: 418–38.

Chauvot, A. 1998. *Opinions romaines face aux barbares au IVe siècle ap. J.-C*. Paris.

Christensen, A. 1944. *L'Iran sous les Sassanides*, second edition. Copenhagen.

Christie, N. 1995. *The Lombards*. Oxford.

Chrysos, E.K. 1976. 'Some Aspects of Roman–Persian Legal Relations', *Kleronomia* 8: 1–48.

Chrysos, E.K. 1993. 'Räumung und Aufgabe von Reichsterritorien. Der Vertrag von 363', *BJb* 193: 165–202.

Clauss, M. 1980. *Der* magister officiorum *in der Spätantike (4.–6. Jahrhunert)*. Munich.

Clermont-Ganneau, C. 1898. 'The taking of Jerusalem by the Persians, AD 614', *Palestine Exploration Fund. Quarterly Statement*: 36–54.

Colvin, I. 2003. *Procopius and Agathias on Roman and Sasanian intervention in Lazika in the sixth century*. D. Phil. thesis, Oxford.

Conrad, L.I. 1990. 'Theophanes and the Arabic historical tradition: some indications of intercultural transmission', *ByzF* 15: 1–44.

Conrad, L.I. 1992. 'The Conquest of Arwād: a source-critical study in the historiography of the early medieval Near East' in Cameron and Lawrence 1992: 317–401.

Couret, M. 1897. 'La prise de Jérusalem par les Perses en 614', *ROC* 2: 125–64.

Cowe, S.P. 1991. 'The significance of the Persian War (572–91) in the *Narratio de rebus Armeniae*', *Muséon* 104: 265–76.

Croke, B. 1984a. 'Dating Theodoret's Church History and Commentary on the Psalms', *Byzantion* 54: 59–74.

Croke, B. 1984b. 'Marcellinus and Dara: a fragment of his lost *de temporum qualitatibus et positionibus locorum*', *Phoenix* 38: 77–88.

Croke, B. 1995. *The Chronicle of Marcellinus*. Sydney.

Croke, B. and Crow, J. 1983. 'Procopius and Dara', *JRS* 73: 143–59 (= XI in B. Croke, *Christian Chronicles and Byzantine History – Fifth–Sixth Centuries*. Aldershot. 1992).

Crum, W.E. 1926. *The Monastery of Epiphanius at Thebes. Part II. The Literary material*. New York.

Curiel, R. and Gignoux, P. 1975. 'Sur une intaille sasanide du cabinet des médailles de Paris', *Studia Iranica* 4: 41–9.

Curran, J. 'From Jovian to Theodosius' in Cameron and Garnsey 1998: 78–110.

Dabrowa, E., ed. 1994. *The Roman and Byzantine Army in the East*. 1994.

Dabrowa, E., ed. 1998. *Electrum*, vol.2. *Ancient Iran and the Mediterranean World*. Cracow.

Dagron, G. 1987. "Ceux d'en face": les peuples étrangers dans les traités militaires byzantins', *TM* 10: 207–32.

Davis, A. 1999. *Jacob of Serug, Letter 20. Translation and Commentary*, M.A. thesis. Cardiff.

Dawes, E. and Baynes, N.H. 1948, repr. 1996. *Three Byzantine Saints*. Crestwood, NY.

Decret, F. 1979. 'Les conséquences sur le christianisme en Perse de l'affrontement des empires romain et sassanide', *Recherches augustiniennes* 14: 91–152.

Demandt, P. 1989. *Die Spätantike – Römische Geschichte von Diocletian bis Justinian*. Munich.

Devos, P. 1946 and 1994. *Mart. Shir.*, see above.

Devos, P. 1966. 'Les martyrs persans à travers leurs actes syriaques' in *La Persia e il mondo greco-romano*, Accademia Nazionale dei Lincei, Problemi attuali di scienza e di cultura, Quaderno no.76: 213–25.

Dewar, M. 1996. *Claudian. Panegyricus de sexto consulatu Honorii Augusti*, Oxford.

Dillemann, L. 1962. *Haute Mésopotamie et pays adjacents*. Paris.

Dodgeon, M. and Lieu, S. 1991. *The Eastern Roman Frontier and the Persian Wars AD 226–363*. London.

Donner, F.M. 1980. 'The Bakr b. Wā''il tribes and politics in northeastern Arabia on the eve of Islam', *Studia Islamica* 51: 5–38.

Downey, G. 1938. 'Ephraemius, patriarch of Antioch', *Church History* 7: 364–70.

Downey, G. 1939. 'Procopius on Antioch: a study of method in the *De Aedificiis*', *Byz* 14: 361–78.

Downey, G. 1941. 'The wall of Theodosius at Antioch', *AJP* 62: 207–13.

Downey, G. 1953. 'The Persian Campaign in Syria in AD 540', *Speculum* 28: 340–8.

Downey, G. 1961. *A History of Antioch in Syria*. Princeton.

Dowsett, C.J. 1961. See Movsēs Daskhurants'i, above.

Drijvers, H.J.W. 1994. 'The Syriac Romance of Julian. Its function, place of origin and original language', *VI Symposium Syriacum (1992)*, ed. R. Lavenant: 201–14. Rome.

Durliat, J. 1989. 'La peste du VIe siècle' in *Hommes et Richesses dans l'empire byzantin*, I: 107–19. Paris.

Dussaud, R. 1927. *Topographie historique de la Syrie antique et médiévale*. Paris.

Ehling, K. 1996. 'Der Ausgang des Perserfeldzuges in der Münzpropaganda des Jovian', *Klio* 78: 186–91.

Elton, H. 2000. 'The nature of the sixth-century Isaurians' in Mitchell and Greatrex 2000: 293–307.

van Esbroek, M. 1976. 'Une chronique de Maurice à Héraclius dans un récit des sièges de Constantinople', *Bedi Kartlisa* 34: 74–96.

van Esbroeck, M. 1983. 'La naissance du culte de Saint Barthélémy en Arménie', *REArm* 17: 171–95.

van Esbroeck, M. 1996a. 'Lazique, Mingrélie, Svanéthie et Aphkhazie du IVe au IXe siècle', *Settimane di Studio del centro Italiano di studi sull' alto medioevo* 43: 195–218.

van Esbroeck, M. 1996b. 'L'invention de la croix sous l'empereur Héraclius', *PdO* 21: 21–46.

van Esbroeck, M. 1997. 'La postérité littéraire des villes fortifiées de Théodose' in Mahé and Thomson 1997: 361–78.

Eupsychia. 1998. *Eupsychia. Mélanges offerts à Hélène Ahrweiler*, 2 vols. Paris.

Evans, J.A.S. 1996a. *The Age of Justinian: The Circumstances of Imperial Power*. London.

Evans, J.A.S. 1996b. 'The Dates of Procopius' Works: A Recapitulation of the Evidence', *GRBS* 37: 301–13.

Fahd, T., ed. 1989. *L'Arabie préislamique et son environnement historique et culturel*. Leiden.

Felix, W. 1996. 'Deylamites', *EIr* VII: 342–3.

Feissel, D. 2000. 'Les édifices de Justinien au témoignage de Procope et de l'épigraphie', *AnTard* 8: 81–104.

Ferber, J. 1981. 'Theophanes' account of the reign of Heraclius' in E. and M. Jeffreys, eds., *Byzantine Papers: Proceedings of the First Australian Byzantine Studies Conference, Canberra 1978*: 32–42.

Festugière, A.J. 1959. *Antioche païenne et chrétienne*. Paris.

Festugière, A.J. 1970. See *V. Theod. Syk.*, above.

Festugière, A.J. 1974. See Leontius, *V. Ioh. Eleem.* above.

Festugière, A.J. 1979. 'Notabilia dans Malalas II', *RPhil* 53: 227–37.

Fiey, J.M. 1964. 'Encore Adulmasīh de Singār', *Muséon* 77: 205–23.

Fiey, J.M. 1966. 'Autour de la biographie de Rabban Bar 'Ēta', *L'orient syrien* 11: 1–16.

Fiey, J.M. 1967. 'Topography of Al-Madai'n', *Sumer* 23: 3–38.

Fiey, J.M. 1968a. *Assyrie chrétienne. Bét Garmaï, Bét Aramayé et Maišan nestoriens*, vol.3. Beirut.

Fiey, J.M. 1968b. 'Ahoudemmeh. Notule de littérature syriaque', *Muséon* 81: 155–9.

Fiey, J.M. 1976. 'Mārūtā de Martyropolis d'après Ibn Al-Azraq († 1181), *AnBoll* 94: 35–45.

Fiey, J.M. 1977. *Jalons pour une histoire de l'église en Iraq*. Louvain.

Fiey, J.M. 1987. 'The last Byzantine Campaign into Persia and Its Influence on the Attitude of the Local Populations Towards the Muslim Conquerors 7–16 H./628–636 AD' in Bakhit 1987: 96–103.

Fiey, J.M. 1995. 'Les résidences d'été des rois perses d'après les actes syriaques des martyrs', *PdO* 20: 325–36.

Flemming, J. 1917. *Akten der ephesinischen Synode von Jahre 449, Abhandlungen der königlichen Gesellschaft der Wissenschaften zu Göttingen, Ph.-Hist. Kl.* 15.1.

Flusin, B. 1990. Review of Speck 1988 in *REB* 48: 321–3.

Flusin, B. 1992. *Saint Anastase le Perse et l'histoire de la Palestine au début du VII siècle*. 2 vols. Paris.

Fontaine, J. 1977. See Ammianus Marcellinus (above).

Fortin, M. 1999. *Syria. Land of Civilizations*, tr. J. Macaulay. Quebec.

Foss, C. 1975a. 'The Persians in Asia Minor and the end of Antiquity', *EHR* 90: 721–47, repr. in Foss 1990: I.

Foss, C. 1975b. 'The Fall of Sardis in 616 and the Value of Evidence', *JÖBG* 24: 11–22.

Foss, C. 1976. *Byzantine and Turkish Sardis*. Cambridge, MA.

Foss, C. 1977. 'Late Antique and Byzantine Ankara', *DOP* 31: 29–87, repr. in Foss 1990: VI.

Foss, C. 1979. *Ephesus after Antiquity: A late antique, Byzantine and Turkish City*. Cambridge.

Foss, C. 1987. 'Coin Archaeology and the Decline of Classical cities in Asia Minor' in P.L. Gupta and A.K. Jha, *Numismatics and Archaeology*: 32–44. Maharashtra.

Foss, C. 1990. *History and Archaeology of Byzantine Asia Minor*. Aldershot.

Foss, C. 1994. 'The Lycian Coast in the Byzantine Age'. *DOP* 48: 1–52, repr. in Foss 1996a: II.

Foss, C. 1995. 'The Near Eastern countryside in late antiquity: a review article' in *RBNE* I: 213–34.

Foss, C. 1996a. *Cities, Fortresses and Villages of Byzantine Asia Minor*. Aldershot.

Foss, C. 1996b. 'The Cities of Pamphylia in the Byzantine Age' in Foss 1996a: IV.

Foss, C. 1997. 'Syria in Transition, AD 550–750: An Archaeological Approach', *DOP* 51: 189–269.

Fourdrin, J.-P. 1994. 'Une porte urbaine construite à Chalcis de Syrie par Isidore de Milet le Jeune (550/551)', *TM* 12: 299–307.

Fowden, G. 1993. *Empire to Commonwealth. Consequences of monotheism in late antiquity*. Princeton.

Frend, W.H.C. 1972. *The Rise of the Monophysite Movement*. Cambridge.

Frendo, J.D. 1976. 'New evidence concerning the birth date of one of the last kings of

Sassanian Persia and the foundation date of the fire-temple of Shiz', *Siculorum Gymnasium. Rassegna semestrale della facoltà di lettere e filosofia dell' università di Catania* 29: 221–31.

Frendo, J.D. 1985. 'The Territorial Ambitions of Chosroes II: an Armenian View?', *Florilegium* 7: 30–6.

Frendo, J.D. 1989. 'Theophylact Simocatta on the Revolt of Bahram Chobin and the Early Career of Khusrau II', *Bulletin of the Asia Institute* 3: 77–88.

Frendo, J.D. 1992. 'Sasanian Irredentism and the Foundation of Constantinople: Historical Truth and Historical Reality', *Bulletin of the Asia Institute* 6: 59–68.

Frendo, J.D. 1995. 'The Early Exploits and Final Overthrow of Khusrau II (591–628): Panegyric and Vilification in the Last Byzantine–Iranian Conflict', *Bulletin of the Asia Institute* 9: 209–14.

Frézouls, E. 1969. 'L'exploration archéologique de Cyrrhus', *Apamée de Syrie*, ed. J. Balty: 81–91. Brussels.

Frolow, A. 1953. 'La vraie croix et les expéditions d'Héraclius en Perse', *REB* 11: 88–105.

Frye, R.N. 1977. 'The Sasanian system of walls for defense' in M. Rosen-Ayalon, ed., *Studies in Memory of Gaston Wiet*: 7–15. Jerusalem.

Frye, R.N. 1983. 'The political history of Iran under the Sasanians' in *CHI*: 116–80.

Gabriel, A. 1940. *Voyages archéologiques dans la Turquie orientale*. Paris.

von Gall, H. 1990. *Das Reiterkampfbild parthischer und sasanidischer Zeit*. Berlin.

Galling, K. 1966. 'Datum und Sinn der graeco-koptischen Mühlen-ostraka im Lichte neuer Belege aus Jerusalem', *ZDPV* 82: 46–56.

Gamzatov, G. 1993. 'Dagestan, i', *EIr* VI: 568–75.

Garitte, G. 1952. See *Narratio de rebus Armeniae*, above.

Garitte, G. 1956. 'La passion géorgienne de sainte Golindouch', *AnBoll* 74: 405–40.

Garsoïan, N.G. 1967. 'Politique ou orthodoxie? L'Arménie au quatrième siècle', *RÉArm* 4: 297–320, repr. in eadem, *Armenia between Byzantium and the Sasanians* (London, 1985), IV.

Garsoïan, N.G. 1983. 'Byantium and the Sasanians' in *CHI*: 568–92.

Garsoïan, N.G. 1989. See P'awstos above.

Garsoïan, N.G. and Mahé, J.-P. 1997. *Des Parthes au califat. Quatres leçons sur la formation de l'identité arménienne*. Paris.

Garsoïan, N.G. 1998a. 'Armenia Megale kai eparkhia Mesopotamias' in *Eupsychia*: 239–64.

Garsoïan, N.G. 1998b. 'La Perse: l'église d'orient' in Pietri 1998: 1103–24.

Garsoïan, N.G. 1998c. 'L'Arménie' in Pietri 1998: 1125–68.

Garsoïan, N.G. 1999. *L'église arménienne et le grand schisme d'orient*. Louvain.

Gatier, P.-L. 1995. 'Un moine sur la frontière, Alexandre l'Acémète en Syrie' in A. Rousselle, ed., *Frontières terrestres, frontières célestes dans l'antiquité*: 435–57. Perpignan.

Gerland. E. 1894. 'Die persischen Feldzüge des Kaisers Heraklios', *BZ* 3: 330–73.

Gero, S. 1981. *Barsauma of Nisibis and Persian Christianity in the Fifth Century*. Louvain.

Gignoux, P. 1980. 'Titres et fonctions religieuses sasanides d'après les sources syriaques hagiographiques'. *AAASH* 28: 191–203.

van Ginkel, J. 1995. *John of Ephesus. A Monophysite Historian in sixth-century Byzantium*. Groningen.

van Ginkel, J. 1998. 'Making History: Michael the Syrian and His Sixth-Century Sources' in R. Lavenant, ed., *Symposium Syriacum VII*: 351–8. Rome.

Göbl, R. 1983. 'Sasanian Coins' in *CHI*: 322–39.

Goodyear, F.R.D. 1968. 'Six notes on the *Iohannis* of Corippus'. *BICS* 15: 70–1.

Goossens, G. 1943. *Hiérapolis de Syrie*. Louvain.

Götz, M. 1968. 'Zum historischen Hintergrund von Sure 30, 1–5' in E. Graf, ed., *Festschrift Werner Caskel* 111–20. Leiden.

Goubert, P. 1950. 'Le problème ghassanide à la veille de l'Islam', *Actes du VIe congrès international d'études byzantines* 103–18. Paris.

Goubert, P. 1951. *Byzance avant l'Islam. I. Byzance et l'Orient sous les successeurs de Justinien. L'empereur Maurice.* Paris.

Graf, D. 1989. 'Rome and the Saracens: Reassessing the nomadic menace' in Fahd 1989: 341–400.

Grancsay, S.V. 1963. 'A Sasanian chieftain's helmet', *Bulletin of the Metropolitan Museum of Art* 21: 253–62.

Greatrex, G. 1993. 'The two fifth-century Wars between Rome and Persia', *Florilegium* 12: 1–14.

Greatrex, G. 1994a. 'The dates of Procopius' works', *BGMS* 18: L101–14.

Greatrex, G. 1994b. *Procopius and the Persian Wars*, D. Phil. thesis. Oxford.

Greatrex, G. 1998a. *Rome and Persia at War: 502–532.* Leeds.

Greatrex, G. 1998b. 'Isaac of Antioch and the sack of Beth Hur', *Muséon* 111: 287–91.

Greatrex, G. 2000a. 'The background and aftermath of the partition of Armenia in AD 387', *AHB* 14: 35–48.

Greatrex, G. 2000b. 'Roman identity in the sixth century' in Mitchell and Greatrex 2000: 267–92.

Greatrex, G. and Greatrex, M. 1999. 'The Hunnic invasion of the East of 395 and the fortress of Ziatha', *Byzantion* 69: 65–75.

Gregory, S.E. 1997. *Roman Military Architecture on the Eastern Frontier*, 3 vols. Amsterdam.

Grierson, P. 1950. 'The consular coinage of "Heraclius" and the revolt against Phocas of 608–610', *NumChr* 10: 71–93.

Grierson, P. 1951. 'The Isaurian Coins of Heraclius', *NumChr* 11: 56–67.

Grierson, P. 1965. 'Two Byzantine coin hoards of the seventh and eighth centuries at Dumbarton Oaks', *DOP* 19: 209–28.

Grierson, P. 1968. *Catalogue of the Byzantine Coins in the Dumbarton Oaks Colection and in the Whittemore Collection*, P. Grierson and A.R. Bellinger, eds, vol.2. Washington D.C.

Grierson, P. and Mays, M. 1992. *Catalogue of late Roman coins in the Dumbarton Oaks Collection and in the Whittemore Collection: from Arcadius and Honorius to the accession of Anastasius.* Washington, D.C.

Grignaschi, M. 1966. 'Quelques spécimens de la littérature sassanide conservés dans les bibliothèques d'Istanbul', *JA* 254: 1–142.

Grignaschi, M. 1980. 'La chute de l'empire hephthalite dans les sources byzantines et perses et le problème des Avars', *AAASH* 28: 219–48.

Grousset, R. 1947. *Histoire de l'Arménie.* Paris.

Grumel, V. 1966. 'La réposition de la vraie croix à Jerusalem par Héraclius', *ByzF* 1: 139–49.

Guillaumont, A. 1969–70. 'Justinien et l'église de Perse', *DOP* 23–4: 41–66.

Güterbock, K. 1906. *Byzanz und Persien in ihren diplomatisch-völkerrechtlichen Beziehungen im Zeitalter Iustinians.* Berlin.

Gutmann, B. 1991. *Studien zur römischen Aussenpolitik in der Spätantike (364–395 n. Chr.).* Bonn.

Haase, C.-P. 1983. 'Ein archäologischer Survey im Ǧabal šbēt und im Ǧabal al-Ahass', *Damaszener Mitteilungen* 1: 69–76.

Haldon, J.F. 1979. *Recruitment and Conscription in the Byzantine Army, c.550–950.* Vienna.

Haldon, J.F. 1984. *Byzantine Praetorians: An Administrative, Institutional and Social Survey of the Opsikion and Tagmata, c.580–900.* Bonn.

Haldon, J.F. 1990. *Byzantium in the Seventh Century.* Cambridge.

Haldon, J.F. 1999. *Warfare, State and Society in the Byzantine World, 565–1204.* London.

Hamilton, J.F. and Brooks, E.W. 1899. See Zach. *HE* (above).

Hanfmann, G. (with Mierse, W.G.). 1983. *Sardis from Prehistoric to Roman times.* Cambridge, MA.

Hannestad, K. 1955–7. 'Les relations de Byzance avec la Transcaucasie et l'Asie centrale aux 5ème et 6ème siècles', *Byzantion* 25–7: 421–56.

Hansen, G.C. 1995. See Socrates.

Hardy, E.R. 1929. 'New light on the Persian occupation of Egypt', *Journal of the Society of Oriental Research* 13: 185–9.

Harmatta, J. 1996. 'The Wall of Alexander the Great and the *limes Sasanicus*'. *Bulletin of the Asia Institute* 10: 79–84.

Harper, P.O. and Meyers, P. 1981. *Silver Vessels of the Sasanian Period. I. Royal Imagery.* New York.

Harvey, S.A. 1980. 'Asceticism in Adversity: An Early Byzantine Experience', *BMGS* 6: 1–11.

Harvey, S.A. 1990. *Asceticism and Society in Crisis. John of Ephesus and* The Lives of the Eastern Saints. Berkeley–Los Angeles.

Heather, P.J. 1991. *Goths and Romans, 332–489.* Oxford.

Heather, P.J. 1998. 'Goths and Huns, c.320–425' in Cameron and Garnsey: 487–515.

Heather, P. and Matthews, J.F. 1991. *The Goths in the Fourth Century.* Liverpool.

Helm, R. 1932. 'Untersuchungen über den auswärtigen diplomatischen Verkehr des römischen Reiches im Zeitalter der Spätantike', *Archiv für Urkundenforschung* 12: 375–436.

Hendy, M.F. 1970. 'On the administrative basis of the Byzantine coinage c.400–900 and the reforms of Heraclius', *University of Birmingham Historical Journal* 12.2: 129–54.

Hendy, M.F. 1985. *Studies in the Byzantine Monetary Economy, c.300–1450.* Cambridge.

Herrin, J. et al. 1984. See *Parastaseis Syntomoi Chronikai* above.

Herrin, J. 1987. *The Formation of Christendom.* Princeton.

Hertzsch, G. 1884. 'De scriptoribus rerum imperatoris Tiberii Constantini', *Commentationes philologae Ienenses* 3: 1–48.

Herzfeld, E. 1920. 'Der Thron des Khosro', *Jahrbuch der preussichen Kunstsammlungen* 41: 1–24, 103–47.

Hewsen, R.H. 1978–9. 'The successors of Tiridates the Great: A contribution to the history of Armenia in the fourth century', *REArm* 13: 99–126.

Hewsen, R.H. 1992. *The Geography of Ananias of Širak (AŠXARHACʻOYCʻ). The Long and Short Recensions.* Wiesbaden.

Higgins, M.J. 1939. *The Persian War of the Emperor Maurice (582–602). Part I. The Chronology with a brief history of the Persian calendar.* Washington, D.C.

Higgins, M.J. 1941. 'International relations at the close of the sixth century', *Catholic Historical Review* 27: 279–315.

Higgins, M.J. 1947. 'Chronology of Theophyl. Sim. 8.1.1–8', *OCP* 13: 219–32.

Higgins, M.J. 1955. 'Chosroes II's votive offerings at Sergiopolis', *BZ* 48: 89–101.

Hitti, P.K. 1970. *History of the Arabs from earliest times to the present,* tenth edition. Princeton.

Hoffmann, G. 1880. *Auszüge aus syrischen Akten persischer Märtyrer.* Leipzig.

Holum, K.G. 1977. 'Pulcheria's Crusade and the Ideology of Imperial Victory', *GRBS* 18: 153–72.

Holum, K.G. 1982. *Theodosian Empresses: Women and Imperial Dominion in Late Antiquity*. Berkeley–Los Angeles–London.

Holum, K.G. 1992. 'Archaeological evidence for the fall of Byzantine Caesarea', *BASOR* 286: 73–85.

Hommes et Richesses dans l'Empire byzantin, IVe–VIIe siècle. 1989. Paris.

Honigmann, E. 1923. *Historische Topographie von Nordsyrien im Altertum*. Leipzig.

Honigmann, E. 1935. *Die Ostgrenze des Byzantinisches Reiches*. Brussels. (= part III of A. A. Vasiliev, *Byzance et les Arabes*).

Honigmann, E. 1939. 'Comptes rendus', *Byz* 14: 615–37.

Honigmann, E. 1944–5. Review of Minorsky 1943–6, *Byz* 17: 389–93.

Howard-Johnston, J.D. 1989. 'Procopius, Roman defences north of the Taurus and the new fortress of Citharizon,' *EFRE*: 203–28.

Howard-Johnston, J.D. 1994. 'The Official History of Heraclius' Persian Campaigns' in Dabrowa 1994: 57–87.

Howard-Johnston, J.D. 1995a. 'The Great Powers in Late Antiquity: A comparison,' *SRA*: 157–226.

Howard-Johnston, J.D. 1995b. 'The siege of Constantinople in 626' in C. Mango and G. Dagron, eds, *Constantinople and its hinterland*: 131–42. Aldershot.

Howard-Johnston, J.D. 1999. 'Heraclius' Persian campaigns and the revival of the East Roman empire, 622–630', *War in History* 6: 1–44.

Hoyland, R. 1997. *Seeing Islam as others saw it. A survey and evaluation of Christian, Jewish and Zoroastrian writings on early Islam*. Princeton.

Hübschmann, H. 1904. *Die Altarmenischen Ortsnamen*. Strasbourg, repr. Amsterdam, 1969.

Humann, K. and Puchstein, O. 1890. *Reisen in Kleinasien und Nordsyrien*. Berlin.

Iacobini, A., and Zanini, E., eds. 1995. *Arte Profana e arte sacra a Bisanzio*. Rome.

Isaac, B. 1992. *The Limits of Empire*, revised edition. Oxford.

Isaac, B. 1998a. 'The Eastern Frontier', in Cameron and Garnsey 1998: 437–60.

Isaac, B. 1998b. *The Near East under Roman Rule. Select Papers*. Leiden.

Janin, R. 1964. *Constantinople byzantine*, 2nd ed. Paris.

Jantzen, U., Felsch, R., Kienast, H. 1972. 'Samos 1972', *Archäologischer Anzeiger* 88: 401–14.

Jeffreys, E. and Scott, R. 1986. See Malalas above.

Jones, A.H.M. 1964. A.H.M. Jones, *The Later Roman Empire, 284–602*, 3 vols. Oxford.

Justi, F. 1895. *Iranisches Namenbuch*. Marburg.

Kaegi, W.E. 1973. 'New evidence on the early reign of Heraclius'. *BZ* 66: 308–30.

Kaegi, W.E. 1979. 'Two notes on Heraclius'. *REB* 37: 221–7.

Kaegi, W.E. 1982. 'Two studies in the continuity of late Roman and Byzantine military institutions', *ByzF* 8: 87–113.

Kaegi, W.E. 1992. *Byantium and the Early Islamic Conquests*. Cambridge.

Kawar, I. See Shahîd, I.

Kelly, J.N.D. 1975. *Jerome. His Life, Writings and Controversies*. London.

Kennedy, D. and Riley, D. 1990. *Rome's Desert Frontier from the air*. London.

Kent, J.P.C. 1981. *The Roman Imperial Coinage*, vol.8. London.

Kent, J.P.C. 1994. *The Roman Imperial Coinage*, vol.10. London.

Kettenhoffen, E. 1982. *Die römisch-persischen Kriege des 3. Jahrhunderts n. Chr.*, Beihefte zum TAVO, Reihe B, Nr.55. Wiesbaden.

Kettenhoffen, E. 1988. 'Das Staatsgefängnis der Sāsāniden', *Die Welt des Orients* 19: 96–101.

Kettenhoffen, E. 1996a. 'Darband', *EIr* VII: 13–17.

Kettenhoffen, E. 1996b. 'Deportations II. In the Parthian and Sasanian period', *EIr* VII: 297–308.

Kettenhoffen, E. 1998. Review of Luther 1997, *BZ* 91: 159–66.

Key Fowden, E. 1999. *The Barbarian Plain. St Sergius between Rome and Iran*. Princeton.

Kislinger, E. and Stathakopoulos, D. 1999. 'Pest und Perserkriege bei Prokop. Chronologische Überlegungen zum Geschehen 540–545', *Byzantion* 69: 76–98.

Klima, O. 1961. 'Der Ortsname Dezeridan bei Anastasius Bibliothecarius', *BSl* 22: 16–19.

Klugkist, A.C. 1987. 'Die beiden Homilien des Isaak von Antiocheia über die Eroberung von Bet Hur durch die Araber', *IV Symposium Syriacum 1984*: 237–56. Rome.

Kraeling, C.H. 1938. *Gerasa, City of the Decapolis*. New Haven, Conn.

Kramers, J.H. 1935–7. 'The Military Colonisation of the Caucasus and Armenia under the Sassanids', *BSOS* 8: 613–18.

Krivouchine, I.V. 1993. 'La révolte près de Monocarton vue par Evagre, Théophylacte Simocatta et Théophane', *Byzantion* 63: 154–72.

Labourt, J. 1904. *Le christianisme dans l'empire perse sous la dynastie sassanide*. Paris.

Lane Fox, R. 1997. 'The *Life of Daniel*' in S. Swain and M.J. Edwards, eds, *Portraits. Biographical Representation in the Greek and Latin Literature of the Roman Empire*: 175–225. Oxford.

Lang, D.M. 1983. 'Iran, Armenia and Georgia' in *CHI*: 505–36.

Lappa-Zizicas, E. 1970. 'Un épitomé inédit de la vie de S. Jean l'aumonier par Jean et Sophronios', *AnBoll* 88: 265–78.

Lassus, J. 1935. *Inventaire archéologique de la région au Nord-Est de Hama*, 2 vols. Damascus.

Lauffray, J. 1983–91. *Halabiyya–Zenobia, place forte du limes oriental et la haute-Mésopotamie au VIe siècle*, 2 vols. Paris.

Lee, A.D. 1986. 'Embassies as evidence for the movement of military intelligence between the Roman and Sasanian Empires', *DRBE*: 455–61.

Lee, A.D. 1987. 'Dating a Fifth-Century War in Theodoret', *Byzantion* 57: 188–91.

Lee, A.D. 1993a. *Information and Frontiers*. Cambridge.

Lee, A.D. 1993b. 'Evagrius, Paul of Nisibis and the Problem of Loyalties in the Mid-Sixth Century', *JEH* 44: 569–85.

Lee, A.D. and Shepard, J. 1991. 'A double life: placing the *peri presbeon*', *BSl* 52: 15–39.

Lehmann, K. 1945. 'The Dome of Heaven', *The Art Bulletin* 27: 1–27.

Lemerle, P. 1960. 'Quelques remarques sur le règne d'Héraclius', *Studie Medievali* 1: 347–61.

Letsios, D.G. 1988. Βυζάντιο και Ερυθρά Θάλασσα. Σχέσεις με τη Νουβία, Αιθιοπία και Νότια Αραβία ως την Αραβική κατάκτηση. Athens.

Letsios, D.G. 1989. 'The case of Amorkesos and the question of Roman *foederati* in Arabia in the Vth century' in Fahd 1989: 525–38.

Levy, H.L. 1948. 'Claudian's *In Rufinum* and an Epistle of St Jerome', *AJP* 69: 62–8.

Levy, H.L. 1971. *Claudian's In Rufinun: An exegetical commentary*. Case Western Reserve.

Liebeschuetz, W. 1977. 'The defences of Syria in the sixth century', *Studien zu den Militärgrenzen Roms II*, ed. C.B. Rüger. Köln: 487–99.

Liebeschuetz, W. 1997. 'The Rise of the bishop in the Christian Roman Empire and the Successor Kingdoms', *Electrum 1. Donum Amicitiae*: 113–25.

Lieu, S.N.C. 1986. 'Captives, Refugees and Exiles: A study of cross-frontier civilian movements and contacts between Rome and Persia from Valerian to Jovian', *DRBE*: 475–505.

Lieu, S.N.C. 1996. Review of Lee 1993a, *BSOAS* 59: 133–5.

Loewe, M. 1971. 'Spices and Silk. Aspects of world trade in the first seven centuries of the Christian era', *JRAS*: 166–79.

Lordkipanidse, O. and Brakmann, H. 1994. 'Iberia II', *RAC* 129: 12–106.

Luther, A. 1997. *Die syrische Chronik des Josua Stylites.* Berlin.

MacCormack, S. 1981. *Art and Ceremony in Late Antiquity.* Berkeley.

MacCoull, L. 1987. 'Coptic Egypt during the Persian occupation', *Studi Classici e Orientali* 36: 307–13.

Maeir, A.M. 2000. 'Sassanica Varia Palaestiniensia: a Sassanian seal from Tolstaba, Israel, and other Sassanian objects from the southern Levant', *Iranica Antiqua* 35: 159–83.

Maenchen-Helfen, O.J. 1973. *The World of the Huns,* Berkeley, CA.

De Maffei, F. 1995. 'Il palazzo di Qasr ibn-Wardan dopo gli scavi e i restauri' in Iacobini and Zanini 1995: 105–87. Rome.

Magness, J. 1992a. 'A reexamination of the archaeological evidence for the Sasanian Persian destruction of the Tyropoeon Valley'. *BASOR* 287: 63–74.

Magness, J. 1992b. Review of Wightman 1989, *BASOR* 287: 96.

Magoulias, H. 1990–3. 'The lives of the saints in the sixth and seventh centuries as sources for the internal and external enemies of the Byzantine order', *EEBS* 48: 281–316.

Mahé, J.-P. 1984. 'Critical Remarks on the Newly Edited Excerpts from Sebeos' in T.J. Samuelian and M.E. Stone, eds, *Medieval Armenian Culture*: 218–39. Chico, CA.

Mahé, J.-P. and Thomson, R.W., eds. 1997. *From Byzantium to Iran. Armenian Studies in Honour of Nina G. Garsoïan.* Atlanta, GA.

Malek, H.M. 1993. 'A survey of Sasanian Numismatics', *NumChr* 153 (1993): 227–69.

Manandian, H.A. 1965. *The Trade and Cities of Armenia in relation to ancient world trade,* tr. N.G. Garsoïan. Lisbon.

Manandjan, J.A. 1950. 'Marshruty persidskikh pokhodov imperatora Iraklia', *VizVrem* 3:133–53.

Mango, C. 1959. *The Brazen House: a study of the vestibule of the Imperial Palace of Constantinople.* Copenhagen.

Mango, C. 1976. *Byzantine Architecture.* New York.

Mango, C. 1984a. 'The Temple Mount, AD 614–638' in J. Johns and J. Raby, eds, *Bayt al-Maqdis. 'Abd al-Malik's Jerusalem,* part 1: 1–16. Oxford.

Mango, C. 1984b. 'A Byzantine Hagiographer at Work: Leontios of Neapolis' in I. Hutter, ed., *Byzanz und der Westen:* 25–42. Vienna.

Mango, C. 1985. 'Deux études sur Byzance et la Perse sassanide'. *TM* 9: 91–118.

Mango, C. 1990. See Nic. above.

Mango, C. and Mango M. 1991. 'Inscriptions de la Mésopotamie du nord', *TM* 11: 465-71.

Mango, C. and Scott, R. 1997. See Theophanes above.

Mango, M.M. 1984. *Artistic Patronage in the Roman Diocese of Orions.* D. Phil. thesis. Oxford.

Mango, M.M. 1994. 'Imperial art in the seventh century' in P. Magdalino, ed, *New Constantines:* 109–38. Aldershot.

Maraval, P. 1995. 'Les nouvelles frontières' in Pietri 1995: 937–51.

Marcus, R. 1932. 'The Armenian Life of Marutha of Maipherkat', *HThR* 25: 47–73.

Marié, M.-A. 1984. See Ammianus Marcellinus (above).

Marquart, J. 1901. 'Ērānšāhr nach der Geographie des Ps. Moses Xorenac'i' *Abhandlungen der königlichen Gesellschaft der Wissenschaften zu Göttingen, Phil.-Hist. Klasse, N.F.,* Band III, no.2. Berlin.

Marquart, J. 1903. *Osteuropäische und ostasiatische Streifzüge.* Leipzig.

Markwart, J. 1930. *Südarmenien und die Tigrisquellen nach griechischen und arabischen Geographen.* Vienna.

Martin-Hisard. 1998a. 'Le "Martyre d'Eustathe de Mcxeta": Aspects de la vie politique et religieuse en Ibérie à l'époque de Justinien' in *Eupsychia:* 493–520.

Martin-Hisard. 1998b. 'Le christianisme et l'église dans le monde géorgien' in Pietri 1998: 1169–1233.

Matthews, J.F. 1989. *The Roman Empire of Ammianus*. London.

Mayerson, P. 1980. 'Mauia, Queen of the Saracens. A Cautionary Note', *IEJ* 30: 123–31 (repr. in Mayerson 1994: 164–72).

Mayerson, P. 1988. 'A note on the Roman *Limes*: 'Inner' versus 'Outer'', *IEJ* 38: 181–3 (repr. in Mayerson 1994: 301–3).

Mayerson, P. 1989. 'Saracens and Romans: Micro-macro relationships', *BASOR* 274: 71–9.

Mayerson, P. 1994. *Monks, Martyrs, Soldiers and Saracens*. Jerusalem.

McCormick, M. 1986. *Eternal Victory*, Cambridge.

Metcalf, D.M. 1962. 'The Aegean coastlands under threat: some coins and coin hoards from the reign of Heraclius'. *ABSA* 57: 14–23.

Millar, F.G.B. 1993. *The Roman Near East, 31 BC – AD 337*, Cambridge, Mass.

Millar, F.G.B. 1998. 'Il ruolo delle lingue semitiche nel vicino oriente tardo-romano (V–VI secolo)', *Mediterraneo Antico* 1: 71–94.

Minorsky, V. 1943–6. 'Roman and Byzantine Campaigns in Atropatene', *BSOAS* 11: 243–65.

Mitchell, S. 1993a. *Anatolia. I. The Celts and the Impact of Roman Rule*. Oxford.

Mitchell, S. 1993b. *Anatolia. II. Land, Men and Gods in Asia Minor*. Oxford.

Mitchell, S., and Greatrex, G., eds. 2000. *Ethnicity and Culture in Late Antiquity*. London.

Mohl, J. 1866–8. See Firdausi (above).

Moorhead, J. 1994. *Justinian*. London.

Morony, M.G. 1984. *Iraq after the Muslim Conquest*. Princeton.

Morony, M.G. 1987. 'Syria under the Persians, 610–629' in Bakhit 1987: 87–95.

Morony, M. 1995. 'Sasanids', EI2 IX: 70–83.

Morrisson, C. 1986. 'Byzance au VIIe siècle: le témoignage de la numismatique' in *Byzantium. Tribute to Andreas Stratos*: 149–63. Athens.

Morrisson, C. 1989. 'Monnaie et prix à Byzance du Ve au VIIe siècle', in *Hommes et Richesses* I: 239–60.

Mosig-Walburg. K. 2000. 'Die Flucht des persischen Prinzen Hormizd und sein Exil im römischen Reich – eine Untersuchung der Quellen', *Iranica Antiqua* 35: 69–110.

Mousheghian, M., Mousheghian, A., Bresc, C., Depeyrot, G., Gurnet, F. 2000. *History and Coin Finds in Armenia*. Wetteren.

Mouterde, P. 1942–3. 'Inscription syriaque du Gebel Bil'ās', *MUSJ* 25: 83–6.

Mouterde, R. and Poidebard, A. 1945. *Le Limes de Chalcis. Organisation de la Steppe en Haute-Syrie Romaine*. Beirut-Paris.

Mouterde, P. and Poidebard, A. 1945. *Le limes de Chalcis*. Paris.

Mundell (Mango), M.C. 1974. 'A sixth-century funerary relief at Dara in Mesopotamia', *JÖBG* 24: 209–27.

Nicholson, O. 1983. 'Taq-i Bostan, Mithras and Julian the Apostate: an irony', *Iranica Antiqua* 18: 177–8.

Nicholson, O. 1985. 'Two notes on Dara', *AJA* 89: 663–71.

Nigosian, S. 1978. 'Zoroastrianism in fifth-century Armenia', *Studies in Religion* 7: 425–34.

Nixon, C.E.V. and Rodgers, B.S. 1994. *In Praise of Later Roman Emperors*. Berkeley.

Nöldeke, T. 1874. 'Über den syrischen Roman von Kaiser Julian', *ZDMG* 28: 263–92.

Nöldeke, T. 1879. *Geschichte der Perser und Araber zur Zeit der Sasaniden*. Leiden.

Nöldeke, T. 1887. *Die Ghassānischen Fürsten aus dem Hause Gafna's*. Berlin.

Nöldeke, T. 1893. 'Die von Guidi herausgegebene syrische Chronik übersetzt und commentiert', *Sitzungsberichte der kaiserlichen Akademie der Wissenschaften*, Phil.-Hist. Classe, 128: 1–48.

Noonan, T.S. 1992. 'Byzantium and the Khazars' in Shepherd and Franklin 1992: 109–32.

Noret, J. 1973. 'La vie grecque ancienne de S. Marūtā de Mayferqat', *AnBoll* 91: 77–103.

Oates, D. 1968. *Studies in the Ancient History of Northern Iraq.* London.

Oeconomides, M. and Drossoyianni, P. 1989. 'A Hoard of gold Byzantine coins from Samos', *RevNum* 31: 145–82.

Oikonomides, N. 1971. 'Correspondence between Heraclius and Kavadh-Široe in the Paschal Chronicle (628)', *Byzantion* 41: 269–81.

Oikonomides, N. 1976. 'A chronological note on the first Persian campaign of Heraclius (622)', *BMGS* 2: 1–9.

Olajos, T. 1981. 'Le monument de triomphe de Trajan en Parthie', *AAASH* 29: 379–83.

Olajos, T. 1988. *Les sources de Théophylacte Simocatta, Historien.* Leiden.

Oleson, J.P. 1976. 'An unpublished Sassanian seal, with a comment on the deportation of Armenians to Cyprus in AD 578', *Levant* 8: 161–4.

Olinder, G. 1927. *The Kings of Kinda of the family of Akil Al-Murār.* Lund.

Olster, D. 1993a. *The Politics of Usurpation.* Amsterdam.

Olster, D. 1993b. 'Syriac sources, Greek sources, and Theophanes's lost year', *ByzF* 19: 215–28.

von Oppenheim, M., Lucas, H. 1905. 'Griechische und lateinische Inschriften aus Syrien, Mesopotamien und Kleinasien', *BZ* 14: 1–72.

Ortiz de Urbina, I. 1965. *Patrologia Syriaca*, 2nd ed. Rome.

Palmer, A. 1990. *Monk and Mason on the Tigris Frontier.* Cambridge.

Palmer, A. 1993 (with Brock, S. and Hoyland, R.). *The Seventh Century in the West-Syrian Chronicles.* Liverpool. (See also above, under primary sources).

Paret, R. 1957. 'Dometianos de Mélitène et la politique religieuse de l'empereur Maurice', *REB* 15: 42–72.

Paschoud, F. See also Zosimus (above).

Paschoud, F. 1975. *Cinq études sur Zosime.* Paris.

Peeters, P. 1925. 'De Sancto Isbozeta', *AASS* Nov. IV: 191–203.

Peeters, P. 1934. Review of Poidebard 1934 in *AnBoll* 52: 370–4.

Peeters, P. 1943. 'S. Syméon Stylite et ses premiers biographes', *AnBoll* 61: 29–71.

Peeters, P. 1944. 'Sainte Golindouch, martyre perse', *AnBoll* 62: 76–124.

Peeters, P. 1947. 'Les ex-voto de Khosrau Aparwez à Sergiopolis', *AnBoll* 65: 5–56.

Peeters, P. 1951a. 'Observations sur la vie syriaque de Mar Aba, Catholicos de l'église perse', in Peeters 1951b: II, 117–63.

Peeters, P. 1951b. *Recherches d'histoire et de philologie orientales*, 2 vols. Brussels.

Pentz, P. 1992. *The Invisible Conquest. The ontogenesis of sixth and seventh century Syria.* Copenhagen.

Pernice, A. 1905. *L'imperatore Eraclio: saggio di storia Bizantina.* Florence.

Peters, F. 1977–8. 'Byzantium and the Arabs of Syria', *AnnArchSyr* 27–8: 97–113.

Pharr, C. 1952. See *Codex Theodosianus*, above.

Pieler, P.E. 1972. 'L'aspect politique et juridique de l'adoption de Chosroès proposée par les Perses à Justin', *Revue international des droits de l'antiquité*, ser.3, 19: 399–433.

Pietri, L. 1995. *Histoire du Christianisme des origines à nos jours*, vol.2, *Naissance d'une chrétienté (250–430).* Paris.

Pietri, L. 1998. *Histoire du Christianisme des origines à nos jours*, vol.3. *Les églises d'orient et d'occident.* Paris.

Pigulewskaja, N. 1963. *Les villes de l'état iranien aux époques parthe et sassanide.* Paris.

Pigulewskaja, N. 1969. *Byzanz auf den Wegen nach Indien.* Berlin.

Poidebard, A. 1934. *La Trace de Rome dans le désert de Syrie. Le Limes de Trajan à la Conquête arabe. Recherches aériennes*, 2 vols. Paris.

Potter, D. 1990. *Prophecy and history in the crisis of the Roman Empire: A historical commentary on the thirteenth Sibylline Oracle.* Oxford.

Potts, D.S. 1990. *The Arabian Gulf in Antiquity II. From Alexander the Great to the Coming of Islam.* Oxford.

Prentice, W.K. 1908. *Greek and Latin Inscriptions* (part III of *AAES*).

Prentice, W.K. 1922. *Greek and Latin Inscriptions. Section B. Northern Syria* (part III, section B of *PUAES*).

Qauxč'išvili, S. 1955–9. See *K'art'lis C'xovreba* above.

Rabello, A.M. 1987. *Giustiniano, Ebrei e Samaritani.* 2 vols. Milan.

Redgate, A.E. 1998. *The Armenians.* Oxford.

Reich, R. 1996. '"God knows their names". Mass Christian grave revealed in Jerusalem', *Biblical Archaeology Review* 22.2: 26–33, 60.

Reinink, G.J. 1995. 'Edessa grew dim and Nisibis shone forth': The School of Nisibis at the transition of the sixth–seventh century' in J.W. Drijvers and A.A. MacDonald, eds., *Centres of Learning and Location in Pre-Modern Europe and the Near East*: 77–89. Leiden.

Reinink, G.J. 1999. 'Babai the Great's *Life of George* and the propagation of doctrine in the late Sasanian empire' in J. Watt and H. Drijvers, eds., *Portraits of Spiritual Authority*: 171–93. Leiden.

Riedlberger, P. 1998. 'Die Restauration von Chosroes II' in Dabrowa 1998: 161–75.

Rist, J. 1996. 'Die Verfolgung der Christen in spätantiken Sasanidenreich: Ursachen, Verlauf und Folgen', *Oriens Christianus* 80: 17–42.

Robin, C. 1996. 'Le royaume Hujride, dit "royaume de Kinda" entre Himyar et Byzance', *CRAI*: 665–714.

Robinson, C. forthcoming. 'The Conquest of Khūzistān: a Historiographical Reassessment' in L. Conrad, ed., *History and Historiography in Early Islamic Times: Studies and Perspectives.* Princeton.

van Rompay, L. 1995. 'Impetuous Martyrs? The situation of the Persian Christians in the last years of Yazdgard I (419–20)', in M. Lamboigts and P. van Deun, eds., *Martyrium in multidisciplinary Perspective. Memorial Louis Reekmans*: 363–75. Louvain.

Rothstein, G. 1899. *Die Dynastie der Lahmiden in al-Hîra – Ein Versuch zur arabisch–persischen Geschichte zur Zeit der Sasaniden.* Berlin.

Roueché, C. 1984. 'Acclamations in the Later Roman Empire', *JRS* 84: 181–99.

Roussel, P. 1939. 'Un monument d'Hiérapolis-Bambykè relatif à la paix <<perpétuelle>> de 532 ap. J.-C.' in *Mélanges syriens offerts a M. René Dussaud*, vol.1: 367–72. Paris.

Rubin, B. 1960. *Das Zeitalter Iustinians*, Band I. Berlin.

Rubin, Z. 1986a. 'The Mediterranean and the Dilemma of the Roman Empire in Late Antiquity', *Mediterranean Historical Review* 1.1, 13–62.

Rubin, Z. 1986b. 'Diplomacy and War in the relations between Byzantium and the Sassanids in the fifth century AD', *DRBE*: 677–95.

Rubin, Z. 1989. 'Byzantium and Southern Arabia', *EFRE*: 383–420.

Rubin, Z. 1995. 'The Reforms of Khusro Anūshirwān', *SRA*: 227–97.

Russell, J. 1986. 'Transformations in Early Byzantine Urban Life: The Contributions and Limitations of Archaeological evidence' in *Seventeenth International Byzantine Congress. Major Papers*: 137–54. New York.

Russell, J. 2001. 'The Persian Invasions of Syria/Palestine and Asia Minor in the Reign of Heraclius: Archaeological and Numismatic Evidence' in E. Kontoura-Galake, ed. *The Dark Centuries of Byzantium (7th–9thc.)*: 41–71. Athens.

Sako, L. 1986. *Le rôle de la hierarchie syriaque orientale dans les rapports diplomatiques entre la Perse et Byzance aux Ve–VIIe siècles.* Paris.

Sanspeur, C. 1975–6. 'L'Arménie au temps de Peroz', *REArm* 11: 83–172.

Sarre, F. and Herzfeld, E. 1920. *Archäologische Reise im Euprat – und Tigris – Gebiet,* vol.2. Berlin.

Sartre, M. 1982a. *Trois études sur l'Arabie romaine et byzantine.* Brussels.

Sartre, M. 1982b. *IGLS XIII.* Paris.

Sartre, M. 1985. *Bostra. Des origines à l'Islam.* Paris.

Sauvaget, J. 1939. 'Les Ghassanides et Sergiopolis', *Byzantion* 14: 115–30.

Schick, R. 1992. 'Jordan on the Eve of the Muslim Conquest, AD 602–634' in P. Canivet and J.P. Rey-Coquais, eds., *La Syrie de Byzance à l'Islam*: 107–19. Damascus.

Schick, R. 1995. *The Christian Communities of Palestine from Byzantine to Islamic Rule.* Princeton.

Schippmann, K. 1971. *Die iranischen Feuerheiligtümer.* Berlin and New York.

Schippmann, K. 1990. *Grundzüge der Geschichte des sasanidische Reiches.* Darmstadt.

Schreiner, P. 1985. *Theophylaktos Simokates. Geschichte.* Stuttgart.

Schrier, O.J. 1992. 'Syriac evidence for the Romano-Persian War of 421–2'. *GRBS* 33: 75–86.

Schroeder, E. 1891. 'Heriman', *Zeitschrift für deutsches Altertum und deutsche Litteratur* 35: 172–4.

Scott, R. 1992. 'Diplomacy in the sixth century: the evidence of John Malalas', in Shepard and Franklin 1992: 159–65.

Scott, W. 1915–16. 'The last Sibylline oracle of Alexandria', *CQ* 9: 144–66, 207–28, 10: 7–16.

Scourfield, J.H.D. 1993. *Consoling Heliodorus. A commentary on Jerome, Letter 60.* Oxford.

Seager, R. 1996. 'Ammianus and the Status of Armenia in the Peace of 363', *Chiron* 26: 275–84.

Seager, R. 1997. 'Perceptions of eastern frontier policy in Ammianus, Libanius and Julian (337–363)', *CQ* 47: 253–68.

Seeck, O. 1919. *Regesten der Kaiser und Päpste.* Stuttgart.

Seeck, O. 1920. *Geschichte des Untergangs der antiken Welt,* 2nd ed., vol.5. Berlin.

Segal, J.B. 1955. 'Mesopotamian communities from Julian to the rise of Islam', *ProcBrAc* 41: 109–39.

Segal, J.B. 1970. *Edessa, 'The blessed city'.* Oxford.

Di Segni, L. 1991. *Nel deserto accanto ai fratelli.* Magnano.

Di Segni, L. 1995. 'The involvement of local, municipal and provincial authorities in urban building in late antique Palestine and Syria', in *RBNE* I: 312–32.

Di Segni, L. 1999. 'Epigraphic documentation on building in the provinces of *Palaestina* and *Arabia,* 4th–7th c.' in *RBNE* II: 149–78.

Seyfarth, W. 1971. *Ammianus Marcellinus. Römische Geschichte,* vol.4. Berlin.

Seyrig, H. 1950. 'Antiquités syriennes', *Syria* 27: 229–52.

Shahbazi, S. 1986. 'Army. 5. The Sasanian Period', *EIr* II: 496–9.

Shahbazi, S. 1989. 'Bahrām VI Čōbīn', *EIr* III: 519–22.

Shahîd, I. 1956. 'The Arabs in the Peace Treaty of AD 561', *Arabica* 3: 181–213 (= Shahîd 1988: VII).

Shahîd, I. 1958. 'The last days of Salih', *Arabica* 5: 145–58.

Shahîd, I. 1964. 'Byzantino-Arabica: the conference of Ramla, A.D. 524', *JNES* 23: 115–31.

Shahîd, I. 1971. *The Martyrs of Najran. New Documents.* Brussels.

Shahîd, I. 1984. *Byzantium and the Arabs in the Fourth Century.* Washington D.C.

Shahîd, I. 1988. *Byzantium and the Semitic Orient before the Rise of Islam.* London.

Shahîd, I. 1989. *Byzantium and the Arabs in the fifth century.* Washington D.C.

Shahîd, I. 1995. *Byzantium and the Arabs in the sixth century,* I. Washington D.C.

Shahîd, I. 2000. 'Byzantium and the Arabs in the sixth century: à propos of a recent review'. *ByzF* 26: 125–60.

Sharf, A. 1955. 'Byzantine Jewry in the seventh century'. *BZ* 48: 103–15.

Shepard, J. and Franklin, S. eds. 1992. *Byzantine Diplomacy.* Aldershot.

Sherk, R.K. 1988. *The Roman Empire: Augustus to Hadrian.* Cambridge.

Simpson, St J. 2000. 'Mesopotamia in the Sasanian Period: Settlement Patterns, Arts and Crafts' in J. Curtis, ed., *Mesopotamia and Iran in the Parthian and Sasanian Periods*: 57–66. London.

Sinclair, T. 1994–5. 'The Site of Tigranocerta I', *REArm* 25: 183–254.

Sinor, D., ed. 1990. *The Cambridge History of Early Inner Asia.* Cambridge.

Smith, S. 1954. 'Events in Arabia in the sixth century AD', *BSOAS* 16: 425–68.

Solari, A. 1933. 'Il non Intervento nel Conflitto tra la Persia e Valente'. *Klio* 26: 114–20.

Speck, P. 1980. *Zufälliges zum Bellum Avaricum des Georgios Pisides.* Munich.

Speck, P. 1988. *Das geteilte Dossier.* Poikila Byzantina 9. Bonn.

Speck, P. 1989. 'War Bronze ein knappes Metall? Die Legende von dem Stier auf dem Bus in den *Parastaseis* 42', *Hellenika* 39: 3–17.

Speck, P. 1993. 'Eine Gedächtnisfeier am Grabe des Maurikius' in *Varia IV*: 175–254. Berlin.

Speck, P. 1997a. *Varia VI. Beiträge zum Thema byzantinische Feindseligkeit gegen die Juden im frühen siebten Jahrhundert.* Bonn.

Speck, P. 1997b. 'Épiphania et Martine sur les monnaies d'Héraclius', *RevNum* 152: 457–65.

Speck. P. 1999. Review of Howard-Johnston 1999, *BZ* 92: 639.

Stein, E. 1919. *Studien zur Geschichte des byzantinischen Reiches, vornehmlich unter den Kaisern Justinus II und Tiberius Constantinus.* Stuttgart.

Stein, E. 1949. *Histoire du Bas-Empire,* vol.2, ed. J.-R. Palanque. Paris-Brussels-Amsterdam.

Stock, K. 1978. 'Yazdān-Friy-Šāpūr, ein Grossgesandter Šāpūrs III. Ein Beitrag zur persisch–römischen Diplomatie und Diplomatik,' *Studia Iranica* 7: 165–82.

Stratos, A.N. 1965. *Byzantio ston hebdomon aiona,* vol.1. Athens.

Stratos, A.N. 1966. *Byzantio ston hebdomon aiona,* vol.2. Athens.

Stratos, A.N. 1968. *Byzantium in the Seventh century,* vol.1. Amsterdam.

Synelli, K. 1986. *Οἱ διπλωματικες σχέσεις Βυζαντίου και Περσίας ἕως τὸν στ′ αἰῶνα.* Athens.

Szádeczky-Kardoss. 1976. 'Bemerkungen zur Geschichte (Chronologie und Topographie) der sassanidisch-byzantinischen Kriege', *AAASH* 24: 109–14.

Szaivert, W. 1987. 'Die Münzprägung des sāsāniden-Königs Peroz', *Litterae Numismaticae Vindobonenses* 3: 157–68.

Talbert, R.J., ed. 2000. *The Barrington Atlas of the Greek and Roman World.* Princeton.

Tamcke, M. 1988. *Der Katholikos-Patriarch Sabrišoʿ I. (596–604) und das Mönchtum.* Frankfurt.

Tate, G. 1992. *Les campagnes de la Syrie du nord du IIe au VIIe siècle,* vol.1. Paris.

Tate, G. 1996. 'Le problème de la défense et du peuplement de la steppe et du désert, dans le nord de la Syrie, entre la chute de Palmyre et le règne de Justinien', *AnnArchSyr* 42: 331–6.

Tate, G. 1999. 'La route de la soie au VIe siècle', *AnnArchSyr* 43: 195–201.

Tchalenko, G. 1953–8. *Villages antiques de la Syrie du nord,* 3 vols. Paris.

Teixidor, J. 1995. 'Conséquences politiques et culturelles de la victoire sassanide à Nisibe' in E. Frézouls and A. Jacquemin, eds., *Les Relations Internationales. Actes du Colloques de Strasbourg, 15–17 juin 1993*: 499–510. Paris.

Thierry, N. 1981. 'Le culte de la croix dans l'empire byzantin du VIIe siècle au Xe dans ses rapports avec la guerre contre l'infidèle. Nouveaux témoignages archéologiques', *Rivista di Studi Bizantini e Slavi* 1: 205–28.

Thierry, N. 1997. 'Héraclius et la vraie croix en Arménie', in Mahé and Thomson: 165–86.

Thomson, R.W. 1991. See Łazar (above).

Thomson, R.W. 1998. *Rewriting Caucasian history. The Medieval Armenian Adaptation of the Georgian Chronicles*. Oxford.

Thomson, R.W. and Howard-Johnston, J.D. 1999. See Sebeos (above).

Thompson, E.A. 1996. *The Huns* (rev. Heather, P.J.). Oxford.

Thurn, J. 2000. See Malalas (above).

Tinnefeld, F. 1993. 'Ceremonies for foreign ambassadors at the court of Byzantium and their political background', *ByzF* 19: 193–213.

Tisserant. E. 1928. 'Marouta de Mayperqat', *DTC* 10: 142–9.

Tisserant, E. 1933. 'Philoxène de Mabboug', *DTC* 12: 109–32.

Toumanoff, C. 1952. 'Iberia on the Eve of Bagratid Rule', *Muséon* 65: 17–49.

Toumanoff, C. 1961. 'Introduction to Christian Caucasian History, II: States and Dynasties of the Formative Period', *Traditio* 17: 1–106.

Toumanoff, C. 1963. *Studies in Christian Caucasian History*. Georgetown.

Treadgold, W. 1995. *Byzantium and Its Army, 284–1081*. Stanford.

Tricca, A. 1915. 'Evagrio e la sua fonte più importante Procopio', *Roma e l'Oriente* 9: 102–11, 283–302, 10: 51–62, 129–45.

Trimingham, J.S. 1979. *Christianity among the Arabs in Pre-Islamic Times*. London and New York.

Trombley, F. 1985. 'The Decline of the Seventh-Century Town: The Exception of Euchaita', *Byzantine Studies in honor of M. Anastos*: 65–90. Malibu.

Trombley, F. 1997. 'War and society in rural Syria c.502–613 AD: some observations on the epigraphy', *BMGS* 21: 154–209.

Trombley, F., and Watt, J. 2000. See Joshua the Stylite (above).

Trümpelmann, L. 1975. *Jahrbuch für Numismatik und Geldgeschichte* 25: 107–11.

Turcan, R. 1966. 'L'abandon de Nisibe et l'opinion publique (363 ap. J.-C.)', in R. Chevallier (ed.) *Mélanges d'archéologie et d'histoire offerts à André Piganiol*: 875–90. Paris.

Turtledove, H. 1977. *The Immediate Successors of Justinian*, Ph.D. thesis. Los Angeles.

Turtledove, H. 1983. 'Justin II's observance of Justinian's Persian Treaty of 562', *BZ* 76: 292–301.

Vailhé, S. 1901. 'La prise de Jérusalem par les perses en 614', *ROC* 6: 643–9.

Vailhé, S. 1909. 'Les Juifs et la prise de Jérusalem', *EO* 12: 15–17.

Van den Ven, P. 1970. See *Vit. Sym. Styl. Iun.*, above.

Vanderspoel, J. 1995. *Themistius and the Imperial Court*. Ann Arbor.

Vasiliev, A.A. 1935. 'Notes on the history of Trebizond in the seventh century' in *Eis mnēmēn Spyridonos Lamprou*: 29–34. Athens.

Vasiliev, A.A. 1950. *Justin I: An introduction to the Epoch of Justinian the Great*. Cambridge, MA.

Verosta, S. 1965. 'Die oströmisch-persischen Verträge von 562 n. Chr. und ihre Bedeutung für das Völkerrecht', *Anzeiger der österreichischen Akademie der Wissenschaften*, phil.–hist. Kl. 102: 153–6.

Verosta, S. 1966. 'International Law in Europe and Western Asia between 100 and 650 AD', *Recueil des cours de l'académie de droit international 1964*, 113: 485–630.

Vööbus, A. 1962. *The Statutes of the School of Nisibis*. Stockholm.

Vööbus, A. 1965. *History of the School of Nisibis*. Louvain.

Voronov, Y. 1998. *Drevnjaja Asilija.* Sukhum.

Waddington, W.H. 1847–73. *Voyage archéologique en Grèce et en Asie Mineure … par P. Le Bas,* 8 vols. Paris.

Wallis Budge, E.A. 1893. See Thomas of Marga, above.

Ward-Perkins, B. 1984. *From Classical Antiquity to the Middle Ages. Urban public building in northern and central Italy, AD 300–800.* Oxford.

Wheeler, B.M. 1991. 'Imagining the Sasanian Capture of Jerusalem', *OCP* 57: 69–85.

Wheeler, E. 1999. Review of Greatrex 1998a in *Journal of Military History* 63: 435–6.

Whitby, L.M. 1983a. 'Arzanene in the late sixth century' in S. Mitchell, ed., *Armies and Frontiers in Roman and Byzantine Anatolia*: 205–17. Oxford.

Whitby, L.M. 1983b. 'Theophanes' Chronicle source for the reigns of Justin II, Tiberius and Maurice', *Byz* 53: 312–45.

Whitby, L.M. 1985. 'The Sangarius bridge and Procopius', *JHS* 105: 129–48.

Whitby, L.M. 1986a. 'Procopius and the development of defences in Upper Mesopotamia', *DRBE*: 717–35.

Whitby, L.M. 1986b. 'Procopius' description of Dara (*Buildings* II.1–3), *DRBE*: 737–83.

Whitby, L.M. 1987. 'Notes on some Justinianic constructions', *BNJ* 23: 89–112.

Whitby, L.M. 1988. *The Emperor Maurice and his historian.* Oxford.

Whitby, L.M. 1989. 'Procopius and Antioch', *EFRE*: 537–53.

Whitby, L.M. 1994. 'The Persian king at war' in Dabrowa 1994: 227–63.

Whitby, L.M. 1995. 'Recruitment in Roman armies from Justinian to Heraclius (*ca.* 565–615), *SRA*: 61–124.

Whitby, L.M. 1998. '*Deus nobiscum*: Christianity, warfare and morale in late antiquity' in M. Austin, J. Harries and C. Smith, eds, *Modus Operandi*: 191–208. London.

Whitby, L.M. and Whitby, M. 1986. *The History of Theophylact Simocatta.* Oxford.

Whitby, L.M. and Whitby, M. 1989. See *Chronicon Paschale* above.

Whitby, M. 1994. 'A New Image for a New Age. George of Pisidia on the Emperor Heraclius' in Dabrowa 1994: 197–225.

Whitby, M., ed. 1998a. *Propaganda and Power. The Role of Panegyric in Late Antiquity.* Leiden.

Whitby, M. 1998b. 'Defender of the Cross: Georgia of Pisidia on the Emperor Heraclius and his deputees' in M. Whitby 1998a: 247–73.

Whittaker, C.R. 1994. *Frontiers of the Roman Empire.* London.

Whittow, M. 1996. *The Making of Orthodox Byzantium, 600–1025.* London.

Whittow, M. 1999. 'Rome and the Jafnids: Writing the History of a Sixth-Century Tribal Dynasty' in *RBNE* II: 207–24.

Widengren, G. 1952. 'Xosrau Anōšurvān, les Hephthalites et les peuples turcs', *Orientalia Suecana* 1: 69–94.

Wiesehöfer, J. 1996. *Ancient Persia.* London.

Wightman, G.J. 1989. *The Damascus Gate, Jerusalem. Excavations by C.-M. Bennett and J.B. Hennessy at the Damascus Gate, Jerusalem, 1964–66,* BAR International Series 519.

Wiita, J.E. 1977. *The Ethnika in Byzantine Military Treatises,* Ph.D. thesis. Minneapolis.

Wilken, R.L. 1990–1. 'The Expugnatio Hierosolymae AD 614', *PdO* 16: 73–81.

Williams, A.V. 1996. 'Zoroastrians and Christians in Sasanian Iran'. *BJRL* 78.3: 37–53.

Wilson, N.G., 1994. *The* Bibliotheca *of Photius.* London.

Winkler, S. 1994. See Koriun above.

Winter, E. 1989. 'Legitimt als Herrschaftsprinzip: Kaiser und "Knig der Knige" im wechselseitigen Verkehr', in H.-J. Drexhage and J Sünskes, eds, *Migratio et Commutatio. Studien zur alten Geschichte und deren Nachleben. Festschrift Thomas Pekry.* St Katharinen: 72–92.

Winter, E., and Dignas, B. 2001. *Rom und das Perserreich. Zwei Weltmächte zwischen Konfrontation und Koexistenz.* Berlin.

Witakowski, W. 1984–6. 'Chronicles of Edessa', *Orientalia Suecana* 33–5: 487–98.

Witakowski, W. 1991. 'Source of Pseudo-Dionysius for the Third part of his *Chronicle*', *Orientalia Suecana* 40: 252–75.

Witakwoski, W. 1996. See Ps. Dion. II, above.

Woods, D. 1996. 'The Saracen defenders of Constantinople', *GRBS* 37: 259–79.

Woods, D. 1998. 'Maurus, Mavia and Ammianus', *Mnemosyne* 51: 325–36.

Woods, forthcoming. *Magistri Militum in the Fourth Century.*

Yannopoulos, P. 1978. *L'hexagramme. Un monnayage byzantin en argent du VIIe siècle.* Louvain.

Yarshater, E. 1983. 'Mazdakism' in *CHI* III: 991–1024.

Yuzbashyan, K.N. 1986. 'The Chronology of the Armeno-Georgian insurrection against the Sassanides at the end of the V Century', *Palestinskij Sbornik* 28: 51–5 (Russian with English summary).

Yuzbashian, K.N. 1999. 'L'Arménie et les Arméniens vus par Byzance', *ByzF* 25: 189–202.

Zanini, E. 1995. 'Il restauro giustinianeo delle mura di Palmira' in Iacobini and Zanini 1995: 65–104.

Zuckerman, C. 1988. 'The reign of Constantine V in the miracles of St Theodore the Recruit (*BHG* 1764)', *REB* 46: 191–210.

Zuckerman, C. 1991. 'The early Byzantine strongholds in eastern Pontus', *TM* 11: 527–53.

Zuckerman, C. 1994. 'L'empire d'orient et les Huns. Notes sur Priscus', *TM* 12: 159–82.

Zuckerman, C. 1995. 'La petite Augusta et le Turc. Epiphania–Eudocie sur les monnaies d'Héraclius', *RevNum* 150: 113–26.

Zuckerman, C. 1997. 'Au sujet de la petite Augusta sur les monnaies d'Héraclius', *RevNum* 152: 473–8.

Zuckerman, C. 1998. 'Sur le dispositif frontalier en Arménie'. *Historia* 47: 107–28.

Zuckerman, C. 2002. 'Heraclius in 625', *REB* 60 (forthcoming).

INDEX OF SOURCES

GENERAL INDEX